D0365559

MUSCULOSKELETAL DISORDERS AND THE WORKPLACE
Low Back and Upper Extremities

Panel on Musculoskeletal Disorders and the Workplace

Commission on Behavioral and Social Sciences and Education

National Research Council
and
Institute of Medicine

NATIONAL ACADEMY PRESS
Washington, D.C.

NATIONAL ACADEMY PRESS   2101 Constitution Avenue, N.W.   Washington, D.C. 20418

NOTICE: The project that is the subject of this report was approved by the Governing Board of the National Research Council, whose members are drawn from the councils of the National Academy of Sciences, the National Academy of Engineering, and the Institute of Medicine. The members of the committee responsible for the report were chosen for their special competences and with regard for appropriate balance.

The study was supported by Contract No. HHS-100-99-0001 between the National Academy of Sciences and the U.S. Department of Health and Human Services. Any opinions, findings, conclusions, or recommendations expressed in this publication are those of the author(s) and do not necessarily reflect the view of the organizations or agencies that provided support for this project.

Suggested citation: National Research Council and the Institute of Medicine (2001) *Musculoskeletal Disorders and the Workplace: Low Back and Upper Extremities*. Panel on Musculoskeletal Disorders and the Workplace. Commission on Behavioral and Social Sciences and Education. Washington, DC: National Academy Press.

Library of Congress Cataloging-in-Publication Data

Musculoskeletal disorders and the workplace : low back and upper
    extremities / Panel on Musculoskeletal Disorders and the Workplace,
    Commission on Behavioral and Social Sciences and Education, National
    Research Council and Institute of Medicine.
        p. ; cm.
    Includes bibliographical references and index.
      ISBN 0-309-07284-0 (hardcover)
     1. Backache. 2. Industrial accidents. 3. Arm--Wounds and injuries.
4. Back--Wounds and injuries. I. National Research Council (U.S.).
Panel on Musculoskeletal Disorders and the Workplace. II. Institute of
Medicine (U.S.)
   [DNLM: 1. Musculoskeletal Diseases--epidemiology. 2. Arm Injuries
--epidemiology. 3. Back Injuries--epidemiology. 4. Low Back Pain
--epidemiology. 5. Occupational Diseases--epidemiology. WE 140
M98515 2001]
RD771.B217 M875 2001
617.4'7044--dc21
                                2001000906

Additional copies of this report are available from National Academy Press, 2101 Constitution Avenue, N.W., Washington, D.C. 20418

Call (800) 624-6242 or (202) 334-3313 (in the Washington metropolitan area)

This report is also available online at **http://www.nap.edu**

Printed in the United States of America

Cover photographs: Background figure: © Charles Gupton/Stock, Boston/PictureQuest. Inset: © PhotoDisc.

THE NATIONAL ACADEMIES

National Academy of Sciences
National Academy of Engineering
Institute of Medicine
National Research Council

The **National Academy of Sciences** is a private, nonprofit, self-perpetuating society of distinguished scholars engaged in scientific and engineering research, dedicated to the furtherance of science and technology and to their use for the general welfare. Upon the authority of the charter granted to it by the Congress in 1863, the Academy has a mandate that requires it to advise the federal government on scientific and technical matters. Dr. Bruce M. Alberts is president of the National Academy of Sciences.

The **National Academy of Engineering** was established in 1964, under the charter of the National Academy of Sciences, as a parallel organization of outstanding engineers. It is autonomous in its administration and in the selection of its members, sharing with the National Academy of Sciences the responsibility for advising the federal government. The National Academy of Engineering also sponsors engineering programs aimed at meeting national needs, encourages education and research, and recognizes the superior achievements of engineers. Dr. William A. Wulf is president of the National Academy of Engineering.

The **Institute of Medicine** was established in 1970 by the National Academy of Sciences to secure the services of eminent members of appropriate professions in the examination of policy matters pertaining to the health of the public. The Institute acts under the responsibility given to the National Academy of Sciences by its congressional charter to be an adviser to the federal government and, upon its own initiative, to identify issues of medical care, research, and education. Dr. Kenneth I. Shine is president of the Institute of Medicine.

The **National Research Council** was organized by the National Academy of Sciences in 1916 to associate the broad community of science and technology with the Academy's purposes of furthering knowledge and advising the federal government. Functioning in accordance with general policies determined by the Academy, the Council has become the principal operating agency of both the National Academy of Sciences and the National Academy of Engineering in providing services to the government, the public, and the scientific and engineering communities. The Council is administered jointly by both Academies and the Institute of Medicine. Dr. Bruce M. Alberts and Dr. William A. Wulf are chairman and vice chairman, respectively, of the National Research Council.

DAVID VLAHOV, Center for Urban Epidemiologic Studies, New York Academy of Medicine, and Johns Hopkins University School of Public Health

DAVID H. WEGMAN, Department of Work Environment, University of Massachusetts, Lowell

ANNE S. MAVOR, *Study Director*

JAMES P. McGEE, *Senior Research Associate*

SUSAN R. McCUTCHEN, *Senior Project Assistant*

ALEXANDRA K. WIGDOR, *Deputy Director, Commission on Behavioral and Social Sciences and Education*

ANDREW M. POPE, *Director, Division of Health Sciences Policy, Institute of Medicine*

FREDERICK J. MANNING, *Senior Program Officer, Division of Health Sciences Policy, Institute of Medicine*

Contents

APPENDIXES

Preface

This report is the output of two years of dedicated labor on the part of a diverse, talented, and energetic panel of experts supported by an experienced, dedicated, and equally energetic staff. The effort was organized by the National Research Council (NRC) and the Institute of Medicine (IOM), in response to a charge from the National Institute for Occupational Safety and Health and the National Institutes of Health to conduct a comprehensive review of the scientific literature on the relationship of work and the workplace to musculoskeletal disorders of the low back and upper extremities. The impetus for the study was a set of questions posed by Congress. These questions and the panel's responses, are presented in Appendix A.

The current effort was focused on the science base supporting current concepts of musculoskeletal disorders as they relate to the workplace, ranging from consideration at the level of tissue biology, through the variety of mechanical, organizational, and psychosocial factors operating in the complex environment that is the workplace. It also extended to the array of clinical expressions of such disorders, as acted on and modified by the interaction of the individual with the range of influences and responses that characterize his or her milieu. In addition, the literature on interventions, as appropriate to low back and upper extremity disorders and the workplace, was reviewed with regard to its scientific quality; the literature on best practices interventions was also reviewed to provide information on approaches thought by industry to be worthy of incorporation into industrial practice. Both types of evidence were weighed and considered by the panel as it formulated its conclusions and recommendations.

The panel, in seeking to be responsive to its task, confined itself in this fashion to the science base and the conclusions that the science could bear.

Policy considerations were not part of the panel's mandate and were not addressed in its deliberations.

The panel members worked hard and in a collegial fashion throughout the study. We talked, listened, and argued, and the process resulted in an almost unanimous outcome. One panel member found, at the end, that he was unable to agree with all the conclusions and recommendations endorsed by the rest of the panel and wrote a dissent (see Appendix B). We believe that dissent misstates part of this report, and we have responded to it (see Appendix C).

In addition to its own study and deliberations, the panel sought and received information from many sources. We commissioned 19 outside scholars to examine the scientific literature in a variety of areas germane to its work. We had the benefit of briefings by a number of individuals from industry, the Bureau of Labor Statistics, the Livermore National Laboratories, the United Auto Workers, and researchers active in the field. Presentations by representatives of a number of clinical societies, corporations, and public service groups were heard, at the panel's invitation, in an open forum. Finally, the panel had the advantage of a visit to two auto assembly plants to which the Ford Motor Company kindly provided access. A list of those who provided commissioned papers, those who briefed the panel, and others who presented their views in various formats is presented in Appendix D.

This report has been reviewed in draft form by individuals chosen for their diverse perspectives and technical expertise, in accordance with procedures approved by the Report Review Committee of the National Research Council (NRC). The purpose of this independent review is to provide candid and critical comments that will assist the institution in making the published report as sound as possible and to ensure that the report meets institutional standards for objectivity, evidence, and responsiveness to the study charge. The review comments and draft manuscript remain confidential to protect the integrity of the deliberative process.

We thank the following individuals for their participation in the review of this report: Jacqueline Agnew, Johns Hopkins Education and Research Center in Occupational Health and Safety, Johns Hopkins School of Hygiene and Public Health; Peter Amadio, Department of Orthopedic Surgery, Mayo Clinic, Rochester, Minnesota; Gunnar Andersson, Department of Orthopedic Surgery, Rush Presbyterian St. Lukes Medical Center, Chicago, Illinois; Thomas Armstrong, Department of Industrial and Operations Engineering, Center for Ergonomics, University of Michigan; Peter Buckle, Robens Centre for Health Ergonomics, European Institute of Health and Medical Science, University of Surrey, England; Fredric Gerr, Department of Environmental and Occupational Health, Rollins School of Public Health, Emory University; Ronald K. Leonard, Deere and

Company (retired); Michael D. Lockshin, Barbara Volcker Center, Hospital for Special Surgery; J. Steven Moore, Department of Nuclear Engineering, Texas A&M University; Neal A. Vanselow, School of Medicine and Chancellor (emeritus), Tulane University Health Sciences Center; Eira Viikari-Juntura, Musculoskeletal Research Unit, Finnish Institute of Occupational Health, Helskinki.

Although the reviewers listed above have provided many constructive comments and suggestions, they were not asked to endorse the conclusions or recommendations nor did they see the final draft of the report before its release. The review of this report was overseen by Enriqueta C. Bond, Burroughs Wellcome Fund, Durham, North Carolina, and Dorothy P. Rice, Institute for Health & Aging, School of Nursing, University of California, San Francisco. Appointed by the National Research Council, they were responsible for making certain that an independent examination of this report was carried out in accordance with institutional procedures and that all review comments were carefully considered. Responsibility for the final content of this report rests entirely with the authoring panel and the institution.

I would like to thank our sponsor representatives, Lawrence J. Fine, National Institute for Occupational Safety and Health, and James S. Panagis, National Institute of Arthritis, Musculoskeletal, and Skin Diseases for their interest in this important project. My personal gratitude goes to our talented staff, Anne Mavor, James McGee, Susan McCutchen, and Alexandra Wigdor for the efficiency and good cheer with which they shepherded the group through its task. My appreciation to the members of the panel, for the intelligence and sense of public purpose with which they approached our task, is unbounded. I regret that as a panel we were unable to reach complete consensus; however, I appreciate the diligent efforts made throughout the process in this regard.

Jeremiah A. Barondess
Chair, Panel on Musculoskeletal
Disorders and the Workplace

MUSCULOSKELETAL DISORDERS AND THE WORKPLACE

Executive Summary

There is no doubt that musculoskeletal disorders of the low back and upper extremities are an important and costly national health problem. Musculoskeletal disorders account for nearly 70 million physician office visits in the United States annually and an estimated 130 million total health care encounters including outpatient, hospital, and emergency room visits. In 1999, nearly 1 million people took time away from work to treat and recover from work-related musculoskeletal pain or impairment of function in the low back or upper extremities. Conservative estimates of the economic burden imposed, as measured by compensation costs, lost wages, and lost productivity, are between $45 and $54 billion annually. There is some variation in estimates of occurrence and cost as a result of inconsistencies within and across existing databases. The ability to better characterize the magnitude of the problem and formulate targeted prevention strategies rests on improved surveillance and more rigorous data collection.

There is also debate concerning sources of risk, mechanisms of injury, and the potential for intervention strategies to reduce these risks. The debate focuses on the causes, nature, severity, and degrees of work-relatedness of musculoskeletal disorders as well as the effectiveness and cost-related benefits of various interventions. None of the common musculoskeletal disorders is uniquely caused by work exposures. They are what the World Health Organization calls "work-related conditions" because they can be caused by work exposures as well as non-work factors. There are a number of factors to be considered: (1) physical, organizational, and social aspects of work and the workplace, (2) physical and social aspects of life outside the workplace, including physical activities (e.g., household work, sports, exercise programs), economic incentives,

1

and cultural values, and (3) the physical and psychological characteristics of the individual. The most important of the latter include age, gender, body mass index, personal habits including smoking, comorbidities, and probably some aspects of genetically determined predispositions. In addition, physical activities away from the workplace may also cause musculoskeletal syndromes; the interaction of such factors with physical and psychosocial stresses in the workplace is a further consideration. The task herein is to evaluate the significance of the risk factors that result from work exposure while taking into account the different types of individual and non-work factors. The complexity of the problem is further increased because all of these factors interact and vary over time and from one situation to another. Research is needed to clarify such relationships, but research is complicated by the fact that estimates of incidence in the general population, as contrasted with the working population, are unreliable because the two overlap: more than 80 percent of the adult population is in the workforce.

The panel approached the complex of factors bearing on the risk of musculoskeletal injury in the work setting from a whole-person perspective, that is, from a point of view that does not isolate disorders of the low back and upper extremities from physical and psychosocial factors in the workplace, from the context of the overall texture of the worker's life, including social support systems and physical and psychosocial stresses outside the workplace, or from personal responses to pain and individual coping mechanisms (see Figure ES.1).

The size and complexity of the problem and the diversity of interests and perspectives—including those of medical and public policy professionals, behavioral researchers, ergonomists, large and small businesses, labor, and government agencies—have led to differing interpretations of the evidence regarding the work-relatedness of musculoskeletal disorders of the low back and upper extremities and the impact of interventions. As a result, Congress requested a study by the National Research Council and the Institute of Medicine covering the scientific literature on the causation and prevention of these disorders. The congressional request was presented in the form of seven questions, which are addressed in Appendix A of this report. The funding for the study was provided by the National Institute for Occupational Safety and Health (NIOSH) and by the National Institutes of Health (NIH).

PANEL CHARGE, COMPOSITION, AND APPROACH

The charge to the panel from NIOSH and NIH was to undertake a series of tasks that would lead to a detailed analysis of the complex set of factors contributing to the occurrence in the workplace of musculoskeletal

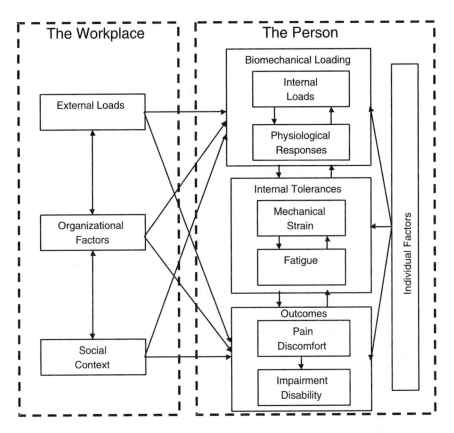

FIGURE ES.1 A conceptual model of the possible roles and influences that various factors may play in the development of musculoskeletal disorders. The dotted box outline on the right indicates the possible pathways and processes that could occur within the person, including the biomechanical load-tolerance relationship and the factors that may mediate the load-tolerance relationship, such as individual factors and adaptation. Outcomes may be a result of this relationship and may be influenced by individual factors, such as conditioning or psychological state. The dotted box on the left indicates the possible influences of the workplace on the sequence of events that can lead to musculoskeletal disorders in the person. Arrows between "the workplace" factors and "the person" box indicate the various research disciplines (epidemiology, biomechanics, physiology, etc.) that have attempted to explain the relationship. For example, epidemiology typically searches for associations between external loading characteristics and reported outcomes, whereas the relationship between external loads and biomechanical loading is usually explored via biomechanical studies (adapted from National Research Council, 1999b).

BOX ES.1 The Charge

1. Assess the state of the medical and biomechanical literature describing the models and mechanisms characterizing the load-response relationships and the consequences (adaptation, impairment, disability) for musculoskeletal structures of the neck, the upper extremities, and the low back.

2. Evaluate the state of the medical and behavioral science literature on the character of jobs and job tasks, the conditions surrounding task performance, and the interactions of person, job, and organizational factors and, in addition, examine the research literature on the individual and nonwork-related activities that can contribute to or help prevent or remediate musculoskeletal disorders.

3. Assess the strengths and weaknesses of core datasets that form the basis for examining the incidence and epidemiology of musculoskeletal disorders reported in the workplace.

4. Examine knowledge concerning programs and practices associated with primary, secondary, and tertiary prevention of musculoskeletal injuries, ranging from organization-wide promotion of a safety culture to modified work and a variety of clinical treatment programs.

5. Characterize the future of work, how the workforce and jobs are changing and the potential impact of these changes on the incidence of musculoskeletal disorders.

6. Identify most important gaps in the science base and recommend needed research.

---

disorders of the low back and upper extremities and that would provide the information necessary to address the questions posed by Congress. The charge appears in Box ES.1. The panel viewed this charge as an opportunity to conduct a comprehensive review and interpretation of the scientific literature, with the goal of clarifying the state of existing knowledge concerning the roles of various risk factors and the basis for various efforts bearing on prevention. The focus of the study was on work-related factors. In this context, individual risk factors, such as age, body mass index, gender, smoking, and activities outside the workplace, were considered as sources of confounding and were accounted for in the research reviews.

The panel was composed of 19 experts representing the fields of biomechanics, epidemiology, hand surgery, human factors engineering, internal medicine, nursing, occupational medicine, orthopedics, physical medicine and rehabilitation, physiology, psychology, quantitative analysis, and rheumatology. The panel's work was guided by two underlying principles. The first, noted above, was to approach musculoskeletal disorders in the context of the whole person rather than focusing on body regions in isolation. The second was to draw appropriate scientific inferences from basic tissue biology, biomechanics, epidemiology, and intervention strategies in order to develop patterns of evidence concerning the strength of the relationship between musculoskeletal disorders and the multiplicity of work and individual factors.

The panel applied a set of rigorous scientific criteria in selecting the research studies for its review. Because the literature includes both empirical and theoretical approaches and covers a wide variety of research designs, measurement instruments, and methods of analysis, the quality selection criteria varied somewhat among disciplines (see Chapter 1 for details). At one level, there are highly controlled studies of soft tissue responses to specific exposures using cadavers, animal models, and human subjects. At another level, there are surveys and other observational epidemiologic studies that examine the association among musculoskeletal disorders and work, organizational, social, and individual factors. At yet another level, there are experimental and quasi-experimental studies of human populations designed to examine the effects of workplace interventions. Each level provides a different perspective; together they provide a complementary picture of how various workplace exposures may contribute to the occurrence of musculoskeletal disorders. Although each level has its attendant strengths and limitations when considered alone, together they provide a rich understanding of the causes and prevention of musculoskeletal disorders.

The wide and diverse body of literature addressing the work-relatedness of musculoskeletal disorders suggests various pathways to injury. Figure ES.1 summarizes the analytic framework used by the panel to organize and interpret these various strands of research. This framework is central to the panel's assessment, and it is used to orient and structure the panel's report. The factors are organized into two broad categories: workplace factors and characteristics of the person that may affect the development of musculoskeletal disorders. Workplace factors include the external physical loads associated with job performance, as well as organizational factors and social context variables. A person is the central biological entity, subject to biomechanical loading with various physical, psychological, and social features that may influence the biological, clinical, and disability responses. The rationale underlying the figure is that there may be many pathways to injury, and the presence of one pathway does not negate nor suggest that another pathway does not play an important role. The various pathways simply represent different aspects of the workplace-person system.

PATTERNS OF EVIDENCE

The panel's review of the research literature in epidemiology, biomechanics, tissue mechanobiology, and workplace intervention strategies has identified a rich and consistent pattern of evidence that supports a relationship between the workplace and the occurrence of musculoskeletal disorders of the low back and upper extremities. This evidence suggests a strong role for both the physical and psychosocial aspects of work. There is also evidence that individual factors, such as age, gender, and physical condition, are important in mediating the individual's response to work factors associated with biomechanical loading.

Back Disorders and the Workplace

Low back disorder risk has been established through epidemiologic studies of work that involves heavy lifting, frequent bending and twisting, and whole body vibration, as well as other risk factors. The relative risks have been derived from a rigorous evaluation of the literature and have been found to be strong and consistent. Strong points in this research include control for confounding, temporal association, and characterization of dose-response relationships; the principal limitation is that a number of the studies are based on self-reports of injury. The epidemiologic literature that specifically quantifies heavy lifting shows the greatest risk for injury when loads are lifted from low heights, when the distance of the load from the body (moment) is great, and when the torso assumes a flexed, asymmetric posture. Biomechanical studies reinforce the epidemiologic findings. Studies in basic biology also describe the mechanisms involved in the translation of spinal loading to tissue injury within the intervertebral disc. In addition, the basic science literature has described pathways for the perception of pain when specific structures in the spine are stressed. Intervention studies have shown how lift tables and lifting hoists are effective in mediating the risk of low back pain in industrial settings. Since risk is lowered when the load is changed from a heavy lift to a light lift, this finding is also consistent with the rigorous epidemiologic findings.

In epidemiologic studies, psychosocial factors in the workplace have also been found to play a role. Specifically, there is evidence for a relationship between low back disorders and job satisfaction, monotonous work, work pace, interpersonal relationships in the workplace, work demand stress, and the worker's perceived ability to work. In addition, recent evidence from biomechanics studies points to a mechanism whereby psychosocial stress contributes to increases in spine loading. There is also evidence that exposure to psychosocial stressors may result in greater trunk muscle activity independent of biomechanical load. Some part of the variance in response described in the biological and biomechanical literature appears to be explained by individual host factors, such as age, gender, and body mass index. For example, age and gender appear to play a role in determining the magnitude of load to which a person's spine may be exposed before damage would be expected.

Upper Extremity Disorders and the Workplace

The pattern of evidence for upper extremity disorders, as for the low back, also supports an important role for physical factors, particularly repetition, force, and vibration. The most dramatic physical exposures occur in manufacturing, food processing, lumber, transportation, and other heavy industries, and these industries have the highest rates of upper extremity disorders reported as work related. Psychosocial factors were found to play a role in upper extremity disorders as well, particularly high job stress and high job demands. In addition, several epidemiologic studies of physical exposures (force, repetition) and psychosocial exposure (perceived stress, job demands) have documented an elevated risk of upper extremity disorders among computer users. Nonwork-related anxiety, tension, and psychological distress are also associated with upper extremity symptoms. Biomechanical studies have shown that extraneural pressure in the carpal tunnel is increased with hand loading and nonneutral wrist postures. Basic science studies demonstrate that extraneural pressures may lead to intraneural edema and fibrosis, demyelination, and axon degeneration. These changes in nerve structure may cause impairment of nerve function. The findings in the intervention literature are congruent with those in the basic biology and epidemiology literatures. There is strong support across these bodies of work that high force and repetition are associated with musculoskeletal disorders of the upper extremities; basic biology data provide evidence of alteration in tissue structure. The intervention literature supports the efficacy of tool and workstation design changes, job rotation, and other interventions that directly address these risk factors with regard to upper extremity symptomology.

Although the upper extremity literature is less well developed than the literature on low back pain, an analogous set of themes emerges, lending further support to the conclusion that external loads and psychosocial factors associated with work influence outcomes. These exposure-response associations persist when adjusted for individual factors that may increase vulnerability, such as age, gender, and body mass index. The basic biology and biomechanics studies provide a plausible basis for the exposure-response relationships. The evidence related to the efficacy of ergonomic interventions further supports these relationships.

Interventions

Data from scientific studies of primary and secondary interventions indicate that low back pain can be reduced under certain conditions by engineering controls (e.g., ergonomic workplace redesign), administrative controls (specifically, adjusting organizational culture), programs designed to modify individual factors (specifically, employee exercise), and combinations of these approaches. Multiple interventions that actively involve workers in medical management, physical training, and work technique education can also be effective in controlling risk. Similarly, with respect to interventions for musculoskeletal disorders of the upper extremities, some studies of engineering controls for computer-related work (reducing static postural loads, sustained posture extremes, and rapid motions, and changing the designs of workstations and tools) have resulted in a decrease in upper extremity pain reports. Studies of administrative controls (modifying organizational culture by an emphasis on participatory team involvement) have also reported success. For such interventions, the commitment of management and the involvement of employees have been important to success.

These findings are based on a research and development process that tailors interventions to specific work and worker conditions and evaluates, on a continuing basis, the effectiveness of these interventions in the face of changing workplace and worker factors. It is therefore neither feasible nor desirable to propose a generic solution. The development and application of effective interventions requires an infrastructure that supports (1) gathering data, through surveillance and research, about the engineering, administrative, and worker factors that affect the effectiveness of interventions; (2) using these data to refine, implement, and assess alternative interventions; and (3) translating knowledge from research to practice. These efforts will benefit from cooperation and information exchange among researchers, practitioners, and workers and managers in industry and labor, government, and academia. These practices should be encouraged and extended.

CONCLUSIONS

Based on a comprehensive review and analysis of the evidence, as described above, the panel has reached the following conclusions:

1. Musculoskeletal disorders of the low back and upper extremities are an important national health problem, resulting in approximately 1 million people losing time from work each year. These disorders impose a substantial economic burden in compensation costs, lost wages, and

productivity. Conservative cost estimates vary, but a reasonable figure is about $50 billion annually in work-related costs.

2. Estimates of incidence in the general population, as contrasted with the working population, are unreliable because more than 80 percent of the adult population in the United States is in the workforce.

3. Because workplace disorders and individual risk and outcomes are inextricably bound, musculoskeletal disorders should be approached in the context of the whole person rather than focusing on body regions in isolation.

4. The weight of the evidence justifies the identification of certain work-related risk factors for the occurrence of musculoskeletal disorders of the low back and upper extremities.

- The panel concludes that there is a clear relationship between back disorders and physical load; that is, manual material handling, load moment, frequent bending and twisting, heavy physical work, and whole-body vibration. For disorders of the upper extremities, repetition, force, and vibration are particularly important work-related factors.
- Work-related psychosocial factors recognized by the panel to be associated with low back disorders include rapid work pace, monotonous work, low job satisfaction, low decision latitude, and job stress. High job demands and high job stress are work-related psychosocial factors that are associated with the occurrence of upper extremity disorders.

5. A number of characteristics of the individual appear to affect vulnerability to work-related musculoskeletal disorders, including increasing age, gender, body mass index, and a number of individual psychosocial factors. These factors are important as contributing and modifying influences in the development of pain and disability and in the transition from acute to chronic pain.

6. Modification of the various physical factors and psychosocial factors could reduce substantially the risk of symptoms for low back and upper extremity disorders.

7. The basic biology and biomechanics literatures provide evidence of plausible mechanisms for the association between musculoskeletal disorders and workplace physical exposures.

8. The weight of the evidence justifies the introduction of appropriate and selected interventions to reduce the risk of musculoskeletal disorders of the low back and upper extremities. These include, but are not confined to, the application of ergonomic principles to reduce physical as well as psychosocial stressors. To be effective, intervention programs should

include employee involvement, employer commitment, and the development of integrated programs that address equipment design, work procedures, and organizational characteristics.

9. As the nature of work changes in the future, the central thematic alterations will revolve around the diversity of jobs and of workers. Although automation and the introduction of a wide variety of technologies will characterize work in the future, manual labor will remain important. As the workforce ages and as more women enter the workforce, particularly in material handling and computer jobs, evaluation of work tasks, especially lifting, lowering, carrying, prolonged static posture, and repetitive motion, will be required to guide the further design of appropriate interventions.

RECOMMENDATIONS

1. The consequences of musculoskeletal disorders to individuals and society and the evidence that these disorders are to some degree preventable justify a broad, coherent effort to encourage the institution or extension of ergonomic and other preventive strategies. Such strategies should be science based and evaluated in an ongoing manner.

2. To extend the current knowledge base relating both to risk and effective interventions, the Bureau of Labor Statistics should continue to revise its current data collection and reporting system to provide more comprehensive surveillance of work-related musculoskeletal disorders.

- The injury or illness coding system designed by the Bureau of Labor Statistics should be revised to make comparisons possible with health survey data that are based on the widely accepted ICD-9 and ICD-10 coding systems.
- The characterization of exposures associated with musculoskeletal disorders should be refined, including enhanced quantification of risk factors. Currently, exposure is based only on characterization of sources of injury (e.g., tools, instruments, equipment) and type of event (e.g., repetitive use of tools) derived from injury narratives.
- Information collected from each employer should contribute to specificity in denominators for jobs including job-specific demographic features in the workplace, such as age, gender, race, time on the job, and occupation.
- Injury and illness information should include, in addition to the foregoing demographic variables, other critical variables, such as event, source, nature, body part involved, time on the job, and rotation schedule. Combining these with the foregoing variables would, with appropriate denominator information, allow calcula-

tion of rates rather than merely counts or proportions, as is now the case for all lost-workday events.

- Resources should be allocated to include details on non-lost-workday injuries or illnesses (as currently provided on lost-workday injuries) to permit tracking of these events in terms of the variables now collected only for lost-workday injuries (age, gender, race, occupation, event, source, nature, body part, time on the job).

3. The National Center for Health Statistics and the National Institute for Occupational Safety and Health should include measures of work exposures and musculoskeletal disorder outcomes in ongoing federal surveys (e.g., the National Health Interview Surveys, the National Health and Nutritional Examinations), and NIOSH should repeat, at least decennially, the National Occupational Exposure Survey.

- To upgrade and improve passive industry surveillance of musculoskeletal disorders and workplace exposures, the National Institute for Occupational Safety and Health should develop adaptable surveillance packages with associated training and disseminate these to interested industries.
- To provide more active surveillance opportunity, the National Institute for Occupational Safety and Health should develop a model surveillance program that provides ongoing and advanced technical assistance with timely, confidential feedback to participating industries.

4. The National Institute for Occupational Safety and Health should take the lead in developing uniform definitions of musculoskeletal disorders for use in clinical diagnosis, epidemiologic research, and data collection for surveillance systems. These definitions should (1) include clear and consistent endpoint measures, (2) agree with consensus codification of clinically relevant classification systems, and (3) have a biological and clinical basis.

5. In addition to these recommendations, the panel recommends a research agenda that includes developing (1) improved tools for exposure assessment, (2) improved measures of outcomes and case definitions for use in epidemiologic and intervention studies, and (3) further quantification of the relationship between exposures and outcomes. Also included are suggestions for studies in each topic area: tissue mechanobiology, biomechanics, psychosocial stressors, epidemiology, and workplace interventions. The research agenda is presented in Chapter 12.

ADDITIONAL CONSIDERATIONS

Because of the importance of continued data collection and research to further elucidate the causes and prevention of musculoskeletal disorders of the low back and upper extremities, the panel believes it would be useful for relevant government agencies, including the National Institute for Occupational Safety and Health, the Occupational Safety and Health Administration, and the National Institute of Arthritis and Musculoskeletal and Skin Diseases to consider the following program initiatives.

1. Expanding research support and mechanisms to study musculoskeletal disorders in terms of risk factors at work, early detection, and effective methods of prevention and their cost effectiveness. Some examples include:

- Developing new mechanisms and linkages among funding agencies (e.g., the National Institute for Occupational Safety and Health, the National Institute of Arthritis and Musculoskeletal and Skin Diseases) to expand ongoing basic research on relevant tissues (e.g., skeletal muscle, tendon, peripheral nerve) to promote study of those parameters that are directly relevant to work-related musculoskeletal disorders.
- Creating mechanisms to stimulate collaboration and cross-training of researchers in the basic and applied sciences directly relevant to work-related musculoskeletal disorders.
- Developing mechanisms to promote research jointly conducted by industry and the relevant academic disciplines on work-related musculoskeletal disorders.

2. Expanding considerably research training relevant to musculoskeletal disorders, particularly with relation to graduate programs in epidemiology, occupational health, occupational psychology, and ergonomics, to produce additional individuals with research training.

3. Expanding education and training programs to assist workers and employers (particularly small employers) in understanding and utilizing the range of possible workplace interventions designed to reduce musculoskeletal disorders. In addition, consideration should be given to expanding continuing education (e.g., NIOSH Education and Research and Training Projects) for a broad range of professionals concerning risk factors that contribute to musculoskeletal disorders inside and outside the workplace.

4. Developing mechanisms for cooperative studies among industry, labor unions, and academia, including:

- Establishing a database of and mechanism for communicating "best practices."
- Providing incentives for industry and union cooperation with due regard for proprietary considerations and administrative barriers.
- Encouraging funding for such studies from industry, labor, academia, and government sources.

5. Revising administrative procedures to promote joint research funding among agencies.

6. Encouraging the exchange of scientific information among researchers interested in intervention research through a variety of mechanisms. Areas that could benefit include the development of (1) research methodologies, especially improved measurement of outcomes and exposures, covariates, and costs and (2) uniform approaches, allowing findings to be compared across studies. In addition, periodic meetings should be considered to bring together individuals with scientific and "best practices" experience.

In order to implement these suggestions, the scope of research and training activities of the National Institute for Occupational Safety and Health would have to be expanded and funding significantly increased. In addition, other federal agencies (e.g., the National Institute of Arthritis and Musculoskeletal and Skin Diseases, the National Institute of Mental Health) would have to broaden their support of research programs examining musculoskeletal disorders and the workplace. In the panel's view these steps deserve serious consideration.

Part 1
Introduction

1

Introduction

Nearly 1 million people each year report taking time away from work to treat and recover from musculoskeletal pain or loss of function due to overexertion or repetitive motion either in the low back or upper extremities (Bureau of Labor Statistics, 1999a).[1] Although there is a risk of long-term disability in both types of disorder, the majority of individuals return to work within 31 days. Estimated workers' compensation costs associated with these lost workdays range from $13 to $20 billion annually. However, in order to determine the total economic burden, indirect costs related to such factors as lost wages, lost productivity, and lost tax revenues must be added to the cost of compensation claims, leading to estimates as high as $45 to $54 billion annually for musculoskeletal disorders reported as work-related. These figures are conservative and represent only reported cases. Several studies suggest that many disorders that could be attributed to work are not reported and therefore are not counted in any of the existing databases. According to Praemer, Furner, and Rice (1999), data collected in 1995 show that when nonoccupationally related disorders are included, the economic burden is as high as $215 billion.

Given the national dimensions of the problem and the diverse positions of interested parties—including medical and public health professionals, behavioral researchers, ergonomists, large and small businesses, labor, and government agencies—on the strength of the evidence regarding causation, Congress requested a study of the scientific literature on the causation, diagnosis, and prevention of musculoskeletal disorders.

---

[1]The median number of days away from work for overexertion is 7; for repetitive motion, it is 18.

CHARGE TO THE PANEL

The Panel on Musculoskeletal Disorders and the Workplace was established by the National Research Council (NRC) and the Institute of Medicine (IOM) in January 1999, to conduct a two-year study of the contribution of workplace physical and psychosocial factors to the occurrence of musculoskeletal disorders of the low back and upper extremities and to examine the effectiveness of various prevention strategies. The panel is composed of 19 experts representing the fields of biomechanics, epidemiology, hand surgery, human factors engineering, internal medicine, nursing, occupational medicine, orthopedics, physical medicine and rehabilitation, physiology, psychology, quantitative analysis, and rheumatology. The impetus for the study was a request from Congress to examine the causation, diagnosis, and prevention of musculoskeletal disorders (House Report 105-635). The congressional request was presented in the form of seven questions (see Box 1.1). The charge to the panel, prepared by the NRC and the IOM, was designed to provide a comprehensive review of the science base and to address the issues outlined in the congressional questions. The tasks specified in the charge are:

- Assess the state of the medical and biomechanical literature

---

**BOX 1.1 Seven Questions Posed by Congress
House Report 105-635**

1. What are the conditions affecting humans that are considered to be work-related musculoskeletal disorders?
2. What is the status of medical science with respect to the diagnosis and classification of such conditions?
3. What is the state of scientific knowledge, characterized by the degree of certainty or lack thereof, with regard to occupational and non-occupational activities causing such conditions?
4. What is the relative contribution of any causal factors identified in the literature to the development of such conditions in (a) the general population; (b) specific industries; and (c) specific occupational groups?
5. What is the incidence of such conditions in (a) the general population; (b) specific industries; and (c) specific occupational groups?
6. Does the literature reveal any specific guidance to prevent the development of such conditions in (a) the general population; (b) specific industries; and (c) specific occupational groups?
7. What scientific questions remain unanswered, and may require further research, to determine which occupational activities in which specific industries cause or contribute to work-related musculoskeletal disorders?

describing the models and mechanisms characterizing the load-response relationships and the consequences (adaptation, impairment, disability) for musculoskeletal structures of the neck, the upper extremities, and the low back.

• Evaluate the state of the medical and behavioral science literature on the character of jobs and job tasks, the conditions surrounding task performance, and the interactions of person, job, and organizational factors and, in addition, examine the research literature on the individual and nonwork-related activities that can contribute to or help prevent or remediate musculoskeletal disorders.

• Assess the strengths and weaknesses of core datasets that form the basis for examining the incidence and epidemiology of musculoskeletal disorders reported in the workplace.

• Examine knowledge concerning programs and practices associated with primary, secondary, and tertiary prevention of musculoskeletal injuries, ranging from organization-wide promotion of a safety culture to modified work and a variety of clinical treatment programs.

• Characterize the future of work, how the workforce and jobs are changing and the potential impact of these changes on the incidence of musculoskeletal disorders.

• Identify the most important gaps in the science base and recommend needed research.

The disorders of particular interest to the panel, in light of its charge, focus on the low back and the upper extremities. Some of these are clinically clear-cut, others less so. With regard to the upper extremities, these include rotator cuff injuries (lateral and medial), epicondylitis, carpal tunnel syndrome, tendinitis, tenosynovitis of the hand and wrist (including DeQuervain's stenosing tenosynovitis, trigger finger, and others), and a variety of nonspecific wrist complaints, syndromes, and regional discomforts lacking clinical specificity. With regard to the low back, there are many disabling syndromes that occur in the absence of defined radiographic abnormalities, or commonly occur in the presence of unrelated radiographic abnormalities. Thus, the most common syndrome is nonspecific backache. Other disorders of interest include back pain and sciatica due to displacement and degeneration of lumbar intervertebral discs with radiculopathy, spondylolysis, spondylolisthesis, and spinal stenosis[2]—

---

[2]Radiculopathy is a disease of the roots of the spinal nerves. Spondylosis is a defect in the spinal arch—the part of the vertebrae that lies behind the nerves and the spinal cord. Spondylolisthesis is the slippage of a vertebra on the vertebra below. Spinal stenosis is a narrowing of the spinal canal, usually due to osteoarthritis and sometimes with pressure on the nerve root.

International Classification of Disease (ICD-9) categories 353-357, 722-724, and 726-729.

Estimates of the frequency of these disorders may be gleaned from the fact that Americans make some 70 million physician office visits annually for musculoskeletal disorders. Of these, nearly 20 million are for back complaints and 2.7 million are for complaints related to the wrist. Comparative estimates of the incidence of these disorders in the non-working general population are not available, since more than 80 percent of American adults are in the workforce. In addition, low back pain is a common complaint and mechanical stressors are not confined to the workplace. Defining the proportion of musculoskeletal disorders due to workplace injuries is therefore a complex undertaking.

BACKGROUND

In the workplace, the multiplicity of factors that may affect reported cases—including work procedures, equipment, and environment; organizational and social factors; physical and psychological characteristics of the individual; and workplace reporting practices—has led to an ongoing debate about causes, nature, severity, and degrees of work-relatedness.[3] In response, the National Institute for Occupational Safety and Health published an extensive review of the literature describing the epidemiology of musculoskeletal disorders of the back and upper extremities (Bernard, 1997b). This review focused on the results of research projects designed to examine the causal link between physical activities in the workplace and musculoskeletal disorders; in addition, one section was devoted to the assessment of the research on psychosocial factors, such as workload, social support, job control, and activities outside the workplace. The authors reported strong evidence for the combined effects of repetitive motion, force, and posture on elbow and hand/wrist disorders as causative factors, although the evidence was weaker for each factor individually.

---

[3]Work-related illnesses or diseases may be caused by, aggravated, accelerated, or exacerbated by workplace exposures, and they may impair working capacity. Personal characteristics and other environmental and sociocultural factors usually play a role as risk factors in work-related illnesses and diseases. These are more common than occupational diseases, which are at one end of the work-relatedness spectrum, whereby the relationship to specific causal factors at work has been fully established and the factors concerned can be identified, measured, and eventually controlled. At the other end of the spectrum are diseases with a weak, inconsistent, unclear relationship to working conditions, although the strength and magnitude of the relationship may vary. This definition also includes conditions that are not caused by work but are aggravated by it (World Health Organization, 1985).

In summer 1998, the National Academy of Sciences/National Research Council convened a workshop to review the scientific literature regarding the effects of a wide range of potential contributing factors and their interactions. The report of the workshop's organizing committee found that although the strength of the evidence varied, some broad conclusions could be drawn (National Research Council, 1999b:27):

• "There is a higher incidence of reported pain, injury, loss of work, and disability among individuals who are employed in occupations where there is a high level of exposure to physical loading than for those employed in occupations with lower levels of exposure.
• There is a strong biological plausibility to the relationship between the incidence of musculoskeletal disorders and the causative exposure factors in high-exposure occupational settings.
• Research clearly demonstrates that specific interventions can reduce the rate of reported musculoskeletal disorders for workers who perform high-risk tasks. No known single intervention is universally effective. Successful interventions require attention to individual, organizational, and job characteristics, tailoring the corrective actions to those characteristics."

Other researchers have developed different interpretations of the available data. These researchers contend that there is insufficient evidence to establish a causal relationship between workplace activities and the occurrence of musculoskeletal disorders (see, for example, Hadler, in press; Nathan et al., 1992). Their argument hinges on the proposition that the methodology for most studies is inadequate and thus uncertain results are obtained. The panel shares the view that sound conclusions must be based on valid data, and accordingly developed rigorous criteria for the inclusion of studies in the present effort. These criteria are detailed later in this chapter.

APPROACH TO THE PROBLEM

In responding to its charge, the panel conducted a comprehensive review of the scientific literature describing the biological responses to load on tissue; biomechanical models of static, dynamic, and repetitive motion and the effects of various forces and loads on the body; the relationships among the occurrence of musculoskeletal disorders and physical work, social and organizational factors, activities outside the workplace, and individual differences; changes in the workplace or the addition of workplace programs designed to reduce the risks for the occurrence of musculoskeletal disorders; and trends in workplace characteristics and their implications for musculoskeletal disorders in the future.

Several screening criteria were used by the panel in selecting the research literature for review. Criteria that applied to all areas included:

1. Focused on low back and upper extremity musculoskeletal disorders
2. Conducted within the last 20 years
3. Published in peer-reviewed publications
4. Published in English

Because the scientific literature has various purposes; includes both empirical and theoretical approaches; and covers a wide variety of research designs, measurement instruments, and methods of analysis, the selection criteria necessarily varied among disciplines. Reviews in tissue mechanobiology and biomechanics were further limited to controlled studies measuring physical and physiological responses using cadavers, animal models, and human subjects. The review of the biomechanical literature focused on studies that assessed the basic load-tolerance construct, had quantifiable exposure metrics, had outcome measures that were quantifiable on a continuous measurement scale, did not rely solely on self-reports, and were designed as prospective, case-controlled, or randomized controlled trial studies. The criteria used in screening literature for the epidemiology review were: a participation rate of 70 percent or more, well-defined exposure and referent populations, and well-defined criteria for measuring health outcomes determined before the study. Finally, the review of the intervention literature was restricted to studies with control groups that examined the effects of primary and secondary interventions in the workplace. The intervention review was supplemented by an evaluation of reports from industry describing best practices in the workplace.

As part of its information gathering activities, the panel commissioned 12 literature reviews including: (1) five on biological responses to load on nerves, tendons, ligaments, muscle, and bone; (2) two on the biomechanics of the back and upper extremities; (3) four on epidemiologic research on the contribution of physical and psychosocial factors to musculoskeletal disorders of the back and upper extremities; and (4) one on economic and cultural context factors that influence the reporting and duration of these disorders. In addition, the panel was given the opportunity to observe work performed at two Ford Motor Company automobile plants and to hold discussions with union representatives, plant managers, and members of ergonomics teams. The panel also heard a presentation describing the Bureau of Labor Statistics database on musculoskeletal disorders and others outlining the experiences of various industries with these disorders, including trends in reported cases and the effectiveness of various intervention strategies. Finally, the panel held an open forum in which representatives from orthopedics, occupational medicine, industry, and labor offered their views on the weight of the scientific evidence. The information gathered in the site visit to Ford Motor Company and in the presentations enriched the panel's discussions of workplace activities and the effectiveness of various intervention strategies in selected work environments.

THE WHOLE PERSON: INJURY, ILLNESS, AND DISEASE

We begin the discussion with some basic concepts that guided the panel's analysis of the scientific literature. These include the concept of physical injury, including the response of the whole person and the challenges of diagnosis based on symptoms (e.g., pain), objective, measurable biological change, or both.

In the most immediate sense, injury is a biological event representing the impact of an environmental alteration on the individual. Such alterations are of numerous types and intensities and may range from invasion by biological agents, such as viruses or bacteria, through exposure to toxic substances or various forms of radiant energy, to physical forces, including those capable of damaging musculoskeletal structures. The extent of physical injury after such exposure varies widely depending on the intensity of the adverse event, the duration of exposure to it, and the characteristics of the injured individual.

Just as there is wide variability in the nature of the inciting event, there is wide variability among individuals in response to pain and functional limitation, including a variety of individual coping mechanisms, the effectiveness, extent, and adequacy of personal support systems at home and at work, and the individual's broader adjustment to the work context. These factors mean that injury is a psychosocial event as well as a biological or physical one. In addition, physical activities outside the workplace, including, for example, those deriving from domestic responsibilities in the home, physical fitness programs, and others are also capable on one hand of inducing musculoskeletal injury and on the other of affecting the course of such injuries incurred at the workplace. Because injury and its impact on the individual are inextricably bound, the panel approached its charge by considering the context of the whole person as the injured and reacting entity, rather than focusing on the low back or upper extremities in isolation.

Among individuals who have the same level of physiological impairment, there is wide variation with regard to symptom intensity, associated interference with activity, and contributing and comorbid factors in the individual's health status and in the wider social context of his or her life. Important diagnostic issues are involved in workplace injuries, just as they are in most situations in which individuals look to physicians or others in the health care system for diagnosis and management of symptoms. Furthermore, in the case of many clinical disorders, it is common for complete and unambiguous objective support of the diagnostic formulation to be lacking. Thus, clinicians are accustomed to the concept of diagnostic thresholds; that is, acceptable levels of evidence on the basis of which treatment and other management decisions are made. Such evidence may include the extent to which the patient's symptoms are characteristic of the disorder under consideration, the degree to which the findings on physical examination are consonant with it, the presence of predisposing factors and precipitating events sufficient to lend support to the diagnosis, and the level of confirmation available from objective studies, such as laboratory tests, electrocardiograms, and X-rays. Assessments lacking such objective medical evidence can sometimes achieve high degrees of diagnostic reliability, as is the case in some pain syndromes in other areas, for example, classic migraine headache, angina pectoris, and premenstrual syndrome, although in may instances presenting syndromes are less specific.

Several studies of varying design (chart review, clinic questionnaire, community surveys) have examined how often patients with common physical complaints have symptoms only, in the absence of correlated measurable change (Kroenke and Mangelsdorff, 1989; Kroenke and Price, 1993; Kroenke et al., 1994; Marple et al., 1997; Kahn, Kahn, and Kroenke, 2000). It appears that at least one of every three patients who present with physical complaints in the primary care setting fall into this category, regardless of the specific symptoms or complaints. In these studies, the proportion of individuals with back pain who had symptoms only ranged from 16 to 90 percent. The widely ranging estimates arise from substantial differences in study methodology. Those studies relying on retrospective review of medical records (Kroenke and Mangelsdorff, 1989; Khan et al., 2000) for back pain diagnosis only yielded higher estimates (70 to 90 percent), while those using directed inquiry of physicians (Kroenke et al., 1994; Marple et al., 1997) provided lower estimates (16 to 30 percent). These data do not mean that such symptoms are trivial, but rather that patients presenting for care frequently experience symptomatic illness in the absence of abnormalities on physical examination and available diagnostic tests. The predominance of a symptom-only diagnosis is not restricted to musculoskeletal disorders but has been demonstrated also for other symptoms, including chest pain and abdominal pain (Wasson, Sox, and Sox, 1981; Martina et al., 1997).

These factors point to an important distinction that obtains widely throughout clinical medicine: the distinction between illness and disease or, framed in an alternative manner, the distinction between the experience of being ill or sick (symptoms, other discomforts, dysfunctionality, fear, and social impacts) on the one hand, and disease, a biological event characterized usually but not invariably by definable and objective change (for example, abnormalities in X-rays, blood tests, or on examination of the heart) on the other. Disease and illness are usually present together and in related fashion, but this is not inevitably the case. Thus, it is possible to be ill in the absence of objective change (migraine headache is a good example), and it is possible to have objective disease without being ill (for example, a small lung tumor evident on a chest X-ray that has not yet produced any symptoms). The important derivative of these considerations for the purposes of the deliberations of the panel is that symptomatic injury of the low back or upper extremity may or may not be accompanied by definitive objective change, for example, on X-ray examinations, and, conversely, abnormalities of a variety of types may be found on X-rays or other studies that do not bear on and have no relation to the symptoms with which the patient may be presenting to the care system. Clinical judgment, that is, the weighing of all of the evidence by the physician, is thus an important factor in arriving at a diagnostic conclusion.

Not infrequently, pain syndromes related to the low back or upper extremities do not satisfy rigorous diagnostic criteria for well-defined clinical entities. Thus, most instances of acute or chronic low back pain are not accompanied by classical radiation of the pain in the distribution of the sciatic nerve, a syndrome that usually indicates herniation of a lumbar intervertebral disc with impingement on nerve roots. In such instances, the poor fit of the symptom pattern in the particular patient with diagnostic criteria for well-defined disorders is not an indication that the patient's symptoms are trivial or unrelated to identifiable risk factors. Indeed, the lack of such a fit with clearly defined disorders is more often the case than not.

Pain is the most common symptom for which patients see physicians, and chronic pain is a particularly difficult problem in clinical management. Pain can have no precise definition because only the suffering individual perceives it. Pain receptors are widely distributed in the tissues of the body and appear to be stimulated either by strong mechanical deformation, by extremes of hot or cold, or by various chemical substances liberated by inflammation or other processes. Pain is transmitted through peripheral nerves to the spinal cord and to the brain. Various responses are elicited, through a variety of neural connections involving the spinal cord as well as descending pathways from the brain. Some of these are reflex in nature and others involve complex reactions that vary widely from individual to individual, based on pain intensity, the implications of the pain to the individual, the extent to which the pain interferes with physical or social function, and many other factors. (Chapter 5 contains a more detailed discussion.)

Somatization is a clinical phenomenon that requires consideration in the context of understanding the perception of pain. It is generally defined as the experiencing and reporting of bodily symptoms lacking a plausible physical explanation and the attribution by the symptomatic individual of such symptoms to disease. Medical attention is frequently sought for such symptoms. Somatization must be distinguished from malingering. Malingering is the *intentional* production of false or grossly exaggerated physical or psychological symptoms prompted by a conscious desire to obtain tangible external rewards. Somatization, which is both unintentional and involuntary, shares neither of these characteristics (Sadock and Sadock, 1999).

Medically explained symptoms that occur in somatizing patients can sometimes persist for long periods of time. Cognitive processes (e.g., increased attention to normal bodily sensations or excessive worry about a serious cause) as well as psychological factors both contribute to somatization. Among the psychological factors, depression and anxiety are particularly important influences in the experience of pain related to somatization. These factors are present in 30 to 60 percent of somatized patients (Kroenke et al., 1994, 1997; Simon et al., 1996). Both pharmacological and nonpharmacological treatments may lead to symptom reduction in somatizing patients (O'Malley et al., 1999; Kroenke and Swindle, 2000). A small subset of somatizing individuals have a history of chronic multiple, unexplained symptoms and are classified as having a somatoform disorder. Early recognition of the role somatization may play in some patients with musculoskeletal disorders or other persistent symptoms is essential to avoid excessive diagnostic testing as well as inappropriate medical and surgical interventions. The evaluation and management of somatization are reviewed by Barsky and Borus (1995, 1999).

A particular challenge in the treatment of musculoskeletal disorders in the worker in whom somatization is a causative or aggravating factor is the potential stigma related to experiencing or reporting a concomitant psychological problem, such as depression or anxiety. Such stigmatization may preclude access to appropriate management of the psychological distress that accompanies these problems. Although denial of requests for behavioral health evaluations may be based on claims adjusters' fears of adding a secondary "mental claim" to a primary "physical claim," related to a belief among claims adjusters that such an addition drives up the cost of the claim significantly, an analysis of detailed medical costs for back pain by private workers' compensation carriers indicates that psychiatric or psychological care accounts for a very small percentage of health care costs, despite the high prevalence of idiopathic low back pain and co-occurrence of anxiety and depression in this diagnostic group. Only 0.4 percent of the cost of the care delivered for low back pain was allocated to psychiatric or psychological evaluation and treatment in one study (Williams et al., 1998). A similarly low percentage of health care costs was allocated to behavioral health services in a large group of federal workers diagnosed with carpal tunnel syndrome or tendinitis of the elbow managed within the federal workers' compensation system (Feuerstein et al., 1998).

Workplace and individual psychosocial factors can interact with ergonomic factors to affect clinical and functional outcomes even in those workers not receiving workers' compensation and actively working with pain. The practical implication is the importance of early evaluation of injured workers to determine if there are psychosocial issues that might influence the outcome. If such problems are detected, intervention should be aggressively targeted at these areas early.

LEVELS OF ANALYSIS: INDIVIDUALS AND POPULATIONS

Analysis of musculoskeletal disorders and the workplace must take place on two levels. The first of these addresses the individual, and the second addresses populations at risk in the aggregate. Individual considerations in workplace injury include elements of individual exposure to risk, the characteristics of the injuring event, the responses of the individual to the injury, diagnostic issues, and case management, including both clinical and nonclinical aspects. Aggregate or population approaches to workplace injury allow the accumulation of epidemiologic information, which in turn permits the analysis of patterns of injury, patterns of responses, and the design of potential preventive measures. There is a broad scientific literature in each of these areas—that is, at the level of both the individual and the population at risk—and the panel has analyzed both in the process of its examination of the evidence bearing on workplace injury.

Analysis at the aggregate level provides a useful structure for considering a wide range of strategies for reducing the risk factors for the occurrence of musculoskeletal disorders. One intervention strategy, for example, might be redesigning elements of the physical workplace; others might be creating a more supportive organizational culture or introducing an exercise program for strengthening workers both physically and psychologically. In introducing any intervention strategy, it is important to take into account the whole person and his or her interactions with the environment. Hence, many of those working in this area have used multifactorial approaches based on programs that include, for example, changes in workplace design, exercise regimens, training in pain control techniques, and efforts to affect other aspects of the workplace environment, such as equipment design.

Modifications of workplace infrastructure are intended to be enduring and appropriate for a population of workers. Although the potential effects of workplace activities on the body occur in workers as individuals, employer remedies and preventive strategies are more logically and economically directed toward a workplace system in which the aggregation of workers is characterized by a range of human physical and psychological features. The goal is to create workplace conditions that are robust to changes in the workforce over time and adaptable to changes in the nature of the work being performed.

CONTEXTUAL FACTORS

Figure 1.1 provides an overview of the risk factors for injury, impairment, and disability attributed to musculoskeletal disorders in the individual. It shows that the association between physical exposure and the development of a musculoskeletal disorder occurs in a broad context of economic and cultural factors and reflects the interaction of elements intrinsic to, as well as extrinsic to, the individual. Most research on musculoskeletal disorders in the workplace has focused on physical exposures and psychosocial factors, and indeed these factors are treated in greatest detail in this report. Here we briefly discuss the potential impact of economic incentives, workplace organizational policies, and research, because in our view these are important to any interpretation of the basic scientific data on the relationship between exposure and rates of worker disability. In this regard, there is convincing evidence to support the hypothesis that compensation wage replacement rates, local unemployment rates, and cultural differences can influence the reporting of musculoskeletal pain or disability—even though assessment of the direction and magnitude of these factors is quite complex.

Disability Benefits

Virtually every study that addresses workers' compensation disability benefits shows that the nature of these benefits has a significant effect on the timing of return to work after a work-related injury. The probability of return to work decreases and duration of work absence increases as benefit levels increase (Loeser, Henderlite, and Conrad, 1995). The causal direction of the reimbursement effect, however, may not always be clear. While higher reimbursement rates may indeed prompt some workers

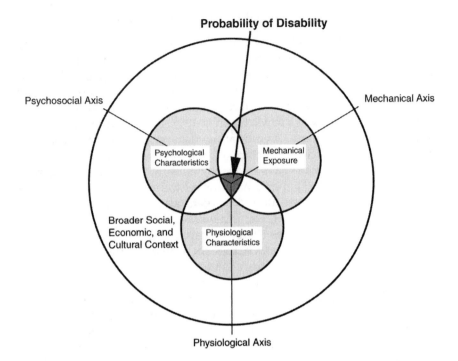

FIGURE 1.1 Risk factors for the injury, impairment, and disability attributed to musculoskeletal disorders in the individual.

who would otherwise return to work to remain absent longer, lower rates may prompt others to return to work too early, while still symptomatic, and with significant functional limitations. Separate from benefits, an association between attorney representation and the frequency and duration of claims has been documented. This linkage has prompted policy recommendations to remove disincentives to return to work (Johnson, Baldwin, and Butler, 1998). The direction of this "attorney effect," however, is difficult to establish. It is not obvious that representation by an attorney is the cause of a claim's being filed or prolonged. For example, patients with the most severe functional limitations are most likely to seek assistance from attorneys. It may also be that the legal proceedings prolong the period until a claim is settled and the worker returns to work.

Organizational Policies and Practices

The rise of direct and indirect costs of work-associated injuries during the 1980s prompted employers and researchers to examine the ways in which workplace policies and practices may influence work disability. Hunt and Habeck (1993) studied the role of organizational policies and practices on the frequency and duration of worker disability among employees of 220 companies in Michigan in 1991. Firms that reported maintaining safe equipment, investigating risks and accidents promptly, enforcing safety policies, and emphasizing safety in all aspects of operations had fewer lost workdays. Firms that reported active involvement of the injured worker and supervisor in the return-to-work process, creative strategies to accommodate injured workers, and cooperation and coordination of workers also had fewer lost workdays and fewer claims.

Shannon and colleagues (1996) surveyed employers and workers at 435 manufacturing workplaces across six industries in Ontario. Several factors were associated with lower rates of lost-time injuries, including greater experience (seniority) of the workforce, greater involvement of the workers in decision making, and greater commitment of the company to workers' career development. Profitability and unionization were not associated with lost-time frequency rates in this study, nor were the structure or functioning of the joint health and safety committees. Union membership has been shown to delay return to work in the United States but not in Canada, perhaps because in the United States unions often provide workers with attorneys and legal representation, which may prolong work absence (Johnson, Baldwin, and Butler, 1998; Baldwin, 2000).

There is consistent evidence that providing injured employees with modified work (typically modified tasks and schedules) increases the rate of successful return to work twofold and reduces the length of work absence following injury by half (Krause, Dasinger, and Neuhauser, 1998). Furthermore, the employer's attitude toward injured workers may have important effects on return to work (Strunin and Boden, 2000).

These findings indicate that organizational policies and practices in the workplace influence rates of worker disability. In particular, companies that make a greater commitment to worker health, safety, involvement in decision making, and availability of modified work appear to have lower rates of lost-time injuries. Of note is the observation that structural elements such as health and safety committees appear not to lead to lower lost-time rates unless they are coupled with a commitment to worker well-being.

Culture

There is also some evidence that cultural factors influence reporting. Although this literature is difficult to interpret due to the elusive definition of such factors, there is work on low back pain and whiplash injury suggesting that cultural differences may affect musculoskeletal epidemiology. Specifically, Westernization, industrialization, and social security systems may be associated with a greater willingness of workers to report low back pain (Volinn, 1997). With regard to whiplash injury, investigators have speculated that insurance for personal injury drives rates upward in some countries and the lack of insurance depresses rates in others (Obelieniene et al., 1999; Partheni et al., 1999). The conversion in Saskatchewan from tort-based compensation, including payments for pain and suffering, to a no-fault system that did not provide such payments was accompanied by substantial decreases in the incidence of claims (Cassidy et al., 2000). The effect of the change in compensation system on whiplash symptoms was not evaluated in this study.

MECHANICAL, PHYSIOLOGICAL, AND PSYCHOLOGICAL FACTORS

Every clinical disorder represents a complex interaction between the affected individual and a variety of determinants of the response of the particular individual to injury. Thus, the "dose" of the injuring agent or circumstance may vary widely from person to person, interacting with relevant characteristics of the individual that determine vulnerability or resistance. In addition, symptoms, disease, injury, and disability have varying meaning among individuals, reflecting a wide array of psychological and social responses. The spheres in Figure 1.1 represent individual risk factors for musculoskeletal disorders and their potential interaction with mechanical stressors—one sphere contains the mix of the individual's psychological characteristics, such as coping strategies, and his or her social context; the second includes physiological characteristics of the individual, including tissue response to load, age, and the presence of medical comorbidities; and the third includes mechanical exposures, such as physical job demands resulting in external loading. The importance of each sphere, and hence its contribution to the risk of disorder, varies among individuals and work environments. At the center, the three spheres overlap to define a region of risk for disorder, emphasizing the principle that the risk is multifactorial and reflects the varying contribution of each set of factors. In addition to their specific contributions, the extent to which the spheres interact is influenced by social, medical, organizational, and other factors, and the probability of disorder varies accordingly.

The psychological characteristics sphere represents the nature of the individual's psychological response to extrinsic stressors, largely reflecting social context and its implications for the individual. The relative importance of this sphere is determined by such psychological characteristics as attitudes, values, and a variety of coping mechanisms. The psychosocial axis represents the psychosocial factors to which the individual is exposed.

The physiological characteristics sphere represents the individual's biology/physiology: the structure and function of the body. This sphere reflects how individual physical factors contribute to risk of disability. These factors include age, body mass index, gender, and general physical condition, including the presence of comorbidities. Medical interventions, such as clinical treatments and surgery, can influence the individual's physical state and thus the position of the physiological sphere along the physiological axis.

The mechanical exposure sphere represents factors associated with physical load arising in the environment—physical work procedures and equipment as well as physical activity outside the workplace. Physical work procedures include activities such as lifting, reaching, bending, twisting, and repetitive motion, all of which affect the physical load experienced by body tissues. Examples of relevant physical activities outside the workplace include exercise regimens, sports, and lifting and bending in the course of household or other daily activities. Many of these activities of daily living may involve physical stresses similar to those present in the workplace. The mechanical axis implies variation of work and organizational factors that may contribute to risk. For example, putting time pressure on the worker may result in poor execution of prescribed procedures and lack of attention to safety considerations.

Interaction among physiological, psychological, and mechanical load levels is reflected in the figure by sphere overlap. The interplay of psychological characteristics and mechanical exposure represents the intersection between imposed physical load and the individual's psychological response to the workload. The overlap between psychological and physiological characteristics represents the interaction among tissue vulnerability to load, the experience of pain, and the effect of pain on the individual. Finally, the overlap between the physiological and mechanical spheres symbolizes the relationship between physical stressors and the response of body tissue. Figure 1.1 is intended to describe variation from person to person and in the individual over time, as well as the capacity of any of its subelements to diminish or expand. There is also a capacity implied for adaptation on the part of the individual, as well as for alteration in mechanical factors, social and cultural context, etc.

Figure 1.2 provides an elaboration of these factors and their interrelationships as a basis for the panel's review and analysis of the scientific literature. This figure is central to the panel's assessment, and provides a framework for organizing and structuring the research reviewed in this volume. Here the factors are organized into two broad categories: workplace factors and characteristics of the person that may affect the development of musculoskeletal disorders. Workplace factors include the external physical loads associated with job performance, as well as organizational factors, and social context variables. The person is identified as the central biological entity subject to biomechanical loading with the various physical, psychological, and social features associated with the individual that may influence the biological, clinical, and disability response. These individual factors are represented in the physiological and psychological spheres shown in Figure 1.1 and include age, gender, smoking habits, comorbidities, and perhaps genetically determined predispositions, as well as participation in physical activities away from the workplace (e.g., physical exercise, household work, etc.).

External loads resulting from work are transmitted through biomechanical forces of the limbs and trunk to create internal loads on the tissues and anatomical structures. Relevant biomechanical factors include body position, exertions, and motions. Biomechanical loading is also affected by individual factors such as anthropometry, strength, agility, dexterity, and other factors mediating the transmission of external loads to internal loads on anatomical structures. When the load exceeds mechanical tolerance or the ability of the structure to withstand the load, tissue damage occurs. The outcomes of pain, discomfort, impairment, and disability are the result of the interaction of the three categories of workplace factors portrayed and the physical and psychological characteristics of the individual.

Organizational and social context factors may affect the external demands of work and the individual's response to these demands. Organizational factors influence external loads in terms of the organization of tasks, work pace, characteristics of interpersonal interactions, and the utilization of ergonomic principles to modify tasks so as not to exceed the physical capacity of the worker. Social context factors may influence both organizational procedures and worker expectations and motivations. The impacts of the organizational and social factors on the individual are mediated through cognitive and perceptual mechanisms (represented by individual factors in Figure 1.2). These mechanisms vary from one individual to another; thus, the threshold at which external stimuli evoke psychological stress and mobilize coping mechanisms varies due to indi-

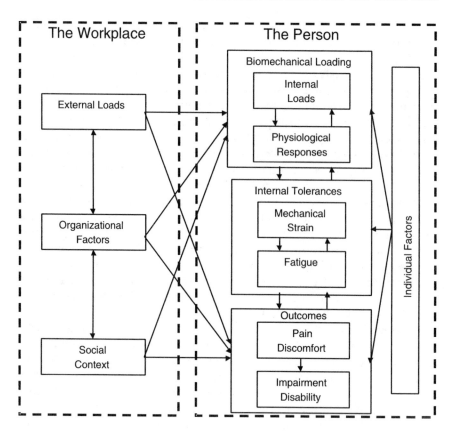

FIGURE 1.2 A conceptual model of the possible roles and influences that various factors may play in the development of musculoskeletal disorders. The dotted box outline on the right indicates the possible pathways and processes that could occur within the person, including the biomechanical load-tolerance relationship and the factors that may mediate the load-tolerance relationship, such as individual factors and adaptation. Outcomes may be a result of this relationship and may be influenced by individual factors, such as conditioning or psychological state. The dotted box on the left indicates the possible influences of the workplace on the sequence of events that can lead to musculoskeletal disorders in the person. Arrows between "the workplace" factors and "the person" box indicate the various research disciplines (epidemiology, biomechanics, physiology, etc.) that have attempted to explain the relationship. For example, epidemiology typically searches for associations between external loading characteristics and reported outcomes, whereas the relationship between external loads and biomechanical loading is usually explored via biomechanical studies (adapted from National Research Council, 1999b).

vidual factors. Furthermore, responses to stress may affect the manifestations of musculoskeletal disorders by influencing pain perception and tolerance, altering cognitive function and behavior, and altering the physical and/or psychological state of readiness for the performance of physical tasks. The arrows between workplace factors, the individual factors and the biomechanical loading mechanism provide a roadmap for the panel's analysis of the relationships that have been examined in the scientific literature. This framework is used throughout the book to structure the presentation and assessment of the evidence. In addition, there are a number of key terms used throughout this volume that may be interpreted variously depending on the reader's orientation. Definitions of these terms as used in this report appear in Box 1.2.

GUIDE TO THE REPORT

Part I provides general introductory and contextual material. It includes the introduction (Chapter 1) and a chapter on the prevalence, incidence, and costs associated with musculoskeletal disorders and the economic and social factors that influence their reporting (Chapter 2). An overview of the methodological issues and approaches used in the research on musculoskeletal disorders is provided (Chapter 3).

Part II contains a review of the evidence. Presented are detailed descriptions of the evidence from epidemiologic studies of physical and psychosocial variables (Chapter 4), tissue mechanobiology (Chapter 5), biomechanics (Chapter 6), physical and behavioral responses to stress (Chapter 7), workplace interventions (Chapter 8), and general characteristics of the workplace now and in the future.

Part III presents an integration of the evidence and the panel's conclusions and recommendations, including suggestions for future research directions.

There are five appendixes. Appendix A presents the panel's response to congressional questions. Appendix B is the dissent statement by Robert Szabo. Appendix C is the panel's response to the dissent signed by the other 18 panel members. Appendix D lists the contributors to the report, and Appendix E contains the biographical sketches of panel members and staff.

BOX 1.2 Definitions

Compensability: Qualifying under the law for payment for medical expenses and/ or loss of earning capacity because of partial or total loss of function or capacity (impairment) as the result of an injury or illness.

Disability: A social definition indicating inability or limitation in performing socially defined activities and roles expected of individuals within a social and physical environment. Examples are inability to perform a job or inability to swim recreationally (Institute of Medicine, 1997:6).

Disease: An objective pathologic condition, involving interruption or interference with normal body structures or function (adapted from the definition of "pathology" in Institute of Medicine, 1997:5).

Disorder: Is variously defined as an alteration in an individual's usual sense of wellness or ability to function. A disorder may or may not interfere with usual activities of daily living or work activities. A disorder may or may not be associated with well-recognized anatomic, physiologic, or psychiatric pathology.

Exposure: Proximity or contact with a putative risk factor in such a manner that an injury, disease, or illness may occur (from Last, 1988). The concept carries with it the dose of the causative risk factor.

Illness: A clinical definition indicating the subjective state of the person who feels aware of not being well (from M.W. Susser, cited in Last, 1988). This subjective experience may or may not be associated with objective signs of disease.

Impairment: A functional definition indicating a loss and/or abnormality of mental, emotional, physiological, biomechanical, or anatomical structure or function. This includes, for example, losses or abnormalities due to pain and/or gait abnormality or at the extreme, invalidism, and may refer to organs and organ systems function or to the intact individual. (derived from Institute of Medicine, 1997:6).

Injury: Any damage to the individual (anatomic, physiologic, or psychiatric) resulting from exposure to thermal, mechanical, electrical, or chemical energy or other stessors or from absence of such essentials as heat or oxygen (adapted from National Committee for Injury Prevention and Control, 1989).

Outcome: All the possible results that may stem from exposure to a causal factor or from preventive or therapeutic interventions: all identified changes in health status arising as a consequence of the management of a health problem. (from Last, 1988).

Work: The act of expending human labor or effort, usually for financial remuneration, to create a product or to produce goods or services. The expenditure of effort to create, transform, or process goods, services, or intellectual models.

continues

Workplace: The physical structure and location where work is undertaken and organized. A physical location specifically designed and dedicated to organizing human labor for the creation of goods and services, such as a factory, office, or construction site.

Work-Related Illness or Disease: Work-related illnesses and diseases may be caused by, aggravated, accelerated, or exacerbated by workplace exposures, and they may impair working capacity. Personal characteristics and other environmental and sociocultural factors usually play a role as risk factors in work-related illnesses and diseases, which are more common than occupational diseases. [*Occupational diseases are at one end of the work relatedness spectrum, where the relationship to specific causal factors at work has been fully established and the factors concerned can be identified, measured, and eventually controlled. At the other end of the spectrum are diseases with a weak, inconsistent, unclear relationship to working conditions; and in the middle of the spectrum there is a possible causal relationship, but the strength and magnitude of it may vary.*] (from World Health Organization, 1985). This definition also includes conditions that are not caused by work, but which are aggravated at work.

2

Dimensions of the Problem

This chapter provides a review of the major databases covering the musculoskeletal disorders in the general population and in the work place. An analytic approach is used to extract relevant information as well as to identify key limitations. The discussion covers both the occurrence of musculoskeletal disorders and the annual costs to society.

MUSCULOSKELETAL DISORDERS IN
THE GENERAL POPULATION

Six data sources are available for estimating the extent of the musculo-skeletal disorder burden in the general U.S. population—the National Health Interview Surveys (1988 and 1995), the National Health and Nutrition Examination Survey (1976-1988), the Health and Retirement Survey (1992-1994), the Social Security Supplemental Security Income system (1998), the National Ambulatory Medical Care Survey (1989), and two regional surveys. The limitations of these datasets are considerable and are discussed in detail later in the chapter.

It is essential here to note that: (1) there are no comprehensive national data sources capturing medically determined musculoskeletal disorders; (2) almost all of the data regarding musculoskeletal disorders are based on individual self-report in surveys; and (3) the survey data do not and cannot distinguish musculoskeletal disorders that may be associated with work from those likely not associated with work in the study populations, which are comprised primarily of working American adults. From these facts two inferences may be drawn:

1. Explicitly, these data include work as well as nonwork-related musculoskeletal disorders without distinction. Rates derived from these

general population sources cannot be considered in any sense equivalent to rates for background, reference, or unexposed groups nor, conversely, as rates for musculoskeletal disorders associated with any specific work or activity.

2. There are no comprehensive data available on occupationally unexposed groups. Given the proportion of adults now in the active workforce in the United States, any such nonemployed group would, by definition, be unrepresentative of the adult population.

Table 2.1 summarizes all available information regarding the rates in the general population from the six sources, organized by category: (1) all musculoskeletal disorders, (2) upper extremity disorders (including carpal tunnel syndrome), and (3) disorders of the back. Because there are relatively more data available in the latter category, Tables 2.2 and 2.3 are included to provide the detailed findings in each of the relevant study groups. The overwhelming thrust of the data reveals that musculoskeletal disorders are very prevalent among adults in the United States, especially after the age of 50, and are a source of an extraordinary burden of disability.

According to the 1997 report from the National Arthritis Data Workgroup (Lawrence et al., 1998), a working group of the National Institute of Arthritis and Musculoskeletal and Skin Diseases, 37.9 million people, or 15 percent of the entire U.S. population, suffered from one or more chronic musculoskeletal disorders in 1990. Moreover, given the increase in disease rates and the projected demographic shifts, they estimate a rate of 18.4 percent or 59.4 million people with these disorders by the year 2020. Results of the National Health Interview Survey for 1995 showed a 13.9 percent prevalence of impairment from musculoskeletal disorders (Praemer, Furner, and Rice, 1999).

Other estimates were generated from the Health and Retirement Survey (1992-1994), which found a rate of 62.4 percent among men and women between ages 51 and 61 reporting one or more musculoskeletal disorders; 41 percent of these reported work disability as a consequence. Among all disabled workers in that age group, almost 90 percent reported one or more musculoskeletal disorders, making musculoskeletal disorders overwhelmingly the largest reason for disability. According to data from Supplemental Security Income, a program that covers chronically ill as well as previously employed persons, 7.7 percent of people under the age of 65 receiving assistance attribute it to musculoskeletal disorders. This proportion rises to 16.9 percent among adults in their 50s, and to 23.9 percent among adults 60 to 64 years old.

Data regarding upper extremity disorders and low back pain are consistent and show that both are important national concerns. Data regarding the former, available from the National Health Interview Survey, show

TABLE 2.1 General Population Data Sources

Disorder	Data Source	Year	Observation	Reference
All musculoskeletal disorders	National Health Interview Survey	1988	37.9 million prevalence (15 percent U.S. population)[a]	Lawrence et al., 1998
		1995	13.9 percent impairment, U.S. population	Praemer, Furner, and Rice, 1999
All musculoskeletal disorders	Health and Retirement Survey (1992-1994)	1992-1994	62.4 percent prevalence in 51 to 61-year-olds; 41 percent of these disabled; 90 percent all disabled had musculoskeletal disorders	Health and Retirement Survey Yelin, Trupin, and Sebesta, 1999
All musculoskeletal disorders	Social Security Insurance Disability	1998	7.7 percent of all disabled Americans on Social Security Insurance (N=4.53 million, with 16.9 percent of all 50 to 59, 23.9 percent of all 60 to 64)	Social Security Bulletin Annual Statistics Summary, 1999:360
Upper extremities (all musculoskeletal disorders) (Hand or wrist)	National Health Interview Survey	1988	9.4 percent overall prevalence of musculoskeletal disorders; 1.55 percent prevalence carpal tunnel syndrome; 0.4 percent prevalence tendinitis	Tanaka et al., 1994, in press

Upper extremities or shoulder impairment	National Health Interview Survey	1995	1.74 percent prevalence	Praemer, Furner, and Rice, 1999
Upper extremities (carpal tunnel syndrome)	Atroshi	1998	14.4 percent prevalent carpal tunnel syndrome (symptoms); 2.7 percent prevalent carpal tunnel syndrome (diagnosis)	Atroshi et al., 1999
	Marshfield Clinic		Approximately 1 incident case per 100 adults/3 years	Nordstrom et al., 1997
Back or spine impairment	National Health Interview Survey	1995	7.0 percent prevalence	Praemer, Furner, and Rice, 1999
Low back pain	National Health and Nutrition Examination Survey II – National Health Interview Survey (1976, 1988) Sternbach, 1986	1976-1993	19 to 59 percent prevalence for any	See Table 2.2 and Table 2.3 (from Lawrence et al., 1998)
	Frymoyer et al., 1983 Quality of Employment Survey (1992-1993)		10 to 18 percent frequent	Leigh and Sheetz, 1989

[a]Projected to rise to 59.4 by 2020 or 18.4 percent population.

TABLE 2.2 Annual and Lifetime "Prevalence" of Various Categories of Low Back Pain

Category of Back Pain	Source and Survey Size	Sample	Description of Back Pain	Prevalence (%)	
				Annual	Lifetime
Any low back pain	Taylor and Curran, 1985 (148) (n = 1,254)	Both sexes, age ≥18; national sample (Sternbach, 1986)	Any backache in past year	56	
	Frymoyer et al., 1983 (142) (n = 1,221)	Men, age 18 to 55; family practice clinic			70
	Olsen et al., 1992 (143) (n = 1,242)	Both sexes, ages 11 to 17; urban school district			30
Frequent or persistent low back pain	Nagi, Riley, and Newby, 1973 (144) (n = 1,135)	Both sexes, ages 18 to 64; citywide population	Frequent pain	18	14
	Deyo and Tsui-Wu, 1987 (7) (n = 10,404)	Both sexes, age >25; national sample (National Health and Nutrition Examination Survey II)	Ever had pain >2 weeks	10	
	Taylor and Curran, 1985 (148) (n = 1,254)	Both sexes, age ≥18; citywide sample (Louis Harris Survey Group [Sternbach, 1986])	Pain >30 days in past year	15	
	Reisbord and Greenland, 1985 (145) (n = 2,792)	Both sexes, age >25; national sample (National Health and Nutrition Examination Survey II)	Frequent back pain	18	
Low back pain with features of sciatica	Deyo and Tsui-Wu, 1987 (7) (n = 10,404)	Both sexes, age >25; national sample (National Health and Nutrition Examination Survey II, 1976)	Pain ≥2 weeks, radiating to leg, increased with cough, sneeze, and deep breathing		1.6
Herniated disc diagnosed by a physician	Kelsey, Golden, and Mundt, 1990 (146)	Both sexes, ages 7 to 64; national sample (National Health Interview Survey, 1976)	Prolapsed disc diagnosed by physician	1.0	
	Deyo and Tsui-Wu, 1987 (7) (n = 10,404)	Both sexes, adults; national sample (National Health and Nutrition Examination Survey II)	Ever told by physician they had ruptured disc	2.1	

TABLE 2.3 Prevalence of Various Categories of Low Back Pain, by Race, Age, and Sex (percentage)

	Any in Past Year[a]	Frequent in Past Year[b]	Lifetime Occurrence Lasting ≥2 Weeks[c]	On Most Days for 1 Month or More[d]	
Race					
White	59	19	14	25	
Black	46	19	11	20	
Other	48		9	21	
Age, years					
18 to 34	61	14	10	18 to 44	20
35 to 49	53	21	12		
50 to 64	56	21	17	45 to 64	30
≥65	49	18	16	≥65	29
Sex					
Male	53	15	14	24	
Female	57	20	13	24	

[a]Data from Louis Harris Survey Group, 1985 (from Sternbach, 1986).

[b]Data from a citywide population survey; see Reisbord and Greenland, 1985.

[c]Data from the National Health and Nutrition Examination Survey II, as reported by Deyo and Tsui-Wu (1987). The percentages are estimates because the reported age categories differed slightly from the ranges presented here. Although the decline in lifetime occurrence of low back pain in the highest age category may be surprising, it has been noted in several surveys. Possible explanations are patients' limited recall for distant past events, selective mortality (persons with low back pain have shorter survival, perhaps due to associated health habits or socioeconomic circumstances), or a "cohort" effect, in which persons over age 65, for unexplained reasons, had a lower likelihood of low back pain throughout their lives.

[d]Data from the National Center for Health Statistics, National Health Interview Survey, 1995, as reported by Praemer, Furner, and Rice (1999).

slightly over 9.4 percent of the entire projected U.S. population reporting hand or wrist conditions in 1988; 1.55 percent (1.62 million people) of these are self-reports of carpal tunnel syndrome. Results of the National Health Interview Survey for 1995 showed a 1.74 percent prevalence of impairment from upper extremity or shoulder musculoskeletal disorders (Praemer, Furner, and Rice, 1999). Atroshi et al. (1999) have documented a rate of 14.4 percent for working-age adults with symptoms referable to the wrist, and a physiological and clinical diagnosis could be made for about 3 percent. Nordstrom et al. (1998), studying the catchment area of the Marshfield Clinic, documented 378 new cases of carpal tunnel syndrome among a total population of 55,000 over three years, equaling a new diagnosis for about 1 percent of all adults in the region. Multiple data sources confirm the high prevalence of low back pain (see Tables 2.2 and 2.3). Depending on how survey questions are posed, between 19 and 56 percent report having some back pain within a given year, while between 10 and 18 percent report frequent pain or pain lasting more than 2 weeks. Notably, as has been stressed in the low back pain literature, the proportion of these for whom either sciatica is present (suggesting focal anatomic defect) or a herniated disc is diagnosed by a physician is relatively small by comparison.

Furthermore, the National Ambulatory Medical Care Survey of 1989, on the basis of a probability sample of all outpatient health care facilities in the United States, ranks musculoskeletal disorders second after respiratory conditions as the most common reason for seeking health care. For 1989, it was estimated that there were 19.9 million visits for low back pain, 8.1 million for neck pain, and 5.2 and 2.7 million for hand and wrist pain, respectively.

In summary, data on the general population suggest the following: (1) musculoskeletal disorders, especially low back pain, are very prevalent and a major reason for seeking health care, (2) musculoskeletal disorders represent the most common cause for disability among workers in their 50s and 60s, and (3) projections suggest that these figures are rising, largely because of changes in the demographics of U.S. society and the workforce.

WORK-RELATED MUSCULOSKELETAL DISORDERS

Information about the distribution of musculoskeletal disorders by type of work across the U.S. workforce is needed in order to estimate the burden of work-related musculoskeletal disorders. However, there is no single, comprehensive surveillance data system that provides the necessary data to link musculoskeletal disorders and work. Without such a system, it is necessary to examine elements of the association, as represented in several incomplete, somewhat overlapping data sources. Several national systems and some systems from smaller or more targeted jurisdictions may contribute to developing a reasonably robust estimate of burden. Elements to be considered are discussed below and shown in Table 2.4.

The Annual Survey of Occupational Injuries and Illnesses, which is the responsibility of the U.S. Department of Labor's Bureau of Labor Statistics (BLS), reports annually on the number and incidence of workplace injuries and illnesses in private industry. The private industry workforce covered includes approximately 75 percent of the total workforce, which is estimated to be 135 million (Bureau of Labor Statistics, 2000b). Beginning with the 1992 survey, BLS has collected additional information on more seriously injured or ill workers in the form of worker and case characteristics. Excluded are the self-employed, farms with fewer than 11 employees, private households, and federal, state, and local government agencies.

Comparable occupational injury and illness data for railroad activities are provided by the U.S. Department of Transportation's Federal Railroad Administration, and for coal, metal, and nonmetal mining are provided by the U.S. Department of Labor's Mine Safety and Health Administration.

The National Center for Health Statistics conducts numerous surveys designed to provide national estimates of the disease burden and health status of the nation. Only the National Health Interview Survey contributes to estimating prevalence by type of work and musculoskeletal disorder. In 1988, these data were collected by a supplemental survey on work and selected musculoskeletal conditions, with self-report of work-relatedness for those conditions. The objective of this survey is to monitor the health of the U.S. population by self-reported health conditions. The survey covers the civilian noninstitutionalized population of the United States. It was used to gather information annually on a sample of approximately 100,000 individuals.

The state of Washington provides workers' compensation for two-thirds of the state's workforce, while the other third are covered by employer programs of self-insurance. Through the Washington State Fund, the state maintains data from accepted compensation claims that permit examination of conditions by standard diagnostic codes and by industry.

The Federal Employees' Compensation program provides workers' compensation benefits to federal employees, numbering 2.9 million in 1994. Data from the U.S. Department of Labor Office of Workers' Compensation Programs provide detailed coding by the International Classification of Disease (ICD-9) along with other demographic features.

There are at least two other potential resources that could contribute to building a proper estimate of the total burden of work-related musculoskeletal disorders. These are medical care utilization data (with proper protection of medical confidentiality) and the National Occupational Exposure Survey undertaken by the National Institute for Occupational Safety and Health.

A combination of these national and regional databases could be used to provide improved and more informative estimates of the burden of work-related musculoskeletal disorders. Some combination of them could also serve to provide an improved mechanism for tracking trends at the level at which the role of risk factors themselves could also be closely followed. Tracking systems would inform employers, employees, and relevant government agencies about important trends in both the devel-

TABLE 2.4 Comparison of Data Elements in Major Systems Reporting on Musculoskeletal Disorders at Work

Database	Population	Denominator	Exclusions	Case Definition
BLS Part I	165,000 establishments	Hours worked by SIC	Small farms, self-employed, private household, government workers	OSHA recordable
BLS Part I	165,000 establishments	Hours worked by SIC	Small farms, self-employed, private household, government workers	OSHA recordable with at least one missed day
NHIS	43,000 households 106,000 persons	U.S. population	None (sample chosen to represent U.S. population)	Self-reported conditions (1988 supplement on musculo-skeletal disorders)
Washington State Fund	2/3 employers	Hours worked	Self-insured, self-employed	Accepted cases, gender/race
Medical claims data	Insured populations	Difficult to characterize	None	Algorithms need to be created

NOTE: BLS = Bureau of Labor Statistics; ICD = International Classification of Disease; NHIS = National Health Interview Survey; OSHA = Office of Safety and Health Administration; SIC = Standard Industrial Classification; SOC = Standard Occupational Classification.

opment and the amelioration of risk factors related to musculoskeletal disorders.

Annual Survey of Occupational Injury and Illnesses

Survey Structure and Sampling Strategy

As interest in the importance of work and musculoskeletal disorders has grown over the past two decades, the most common data reference has been the Annual Report on Injuries and Illnesses provided by the

Case Coding	Exposure Factors	Timing	Demographic Data	Severity Measures
BLS coding	Hours worked in SIC	Year	None	None
BLS coding body part, Nature	SIC, SOC, event, source	Year	Age, gender, race, years worked	Lost days, restricted workdays,
None	Occupation: longest, last 12 months, last 2 weeks	Within last 12 months	Age, gender, race	Disability, time away from work
ICD9	Occupation	NA	None	Lost time >4 days, costs
ICD9	Job-specific information must be matched	Algorithm needs to be created for onset	Age, gender, race	Algorithm needs to be created

Bureau of Labor Statistics. Since 1982, the source for these data has been a national sample of private industry reports of injury and illness according to the requirements of the Occupational Safety and Health Administration (OSHA Form 200). This source is therefore limited to employment in the private sector and includes only cases that have been determined to be work-related by the employer, using definitions provided by OSHA. Annually, a stratified random sample of establishments is selected to provide data. (For the mining workforce, the Mine Safety and Health Administration requires that full details of all work-related injuries and illnesses be reported to BLS. Currently, the sample of nonmining establishments is approximately 165,000, significantly reduced from the sample size of 250,000 establishments selected for the annual survey a decade ago).

When an employer is selected to be part of an annual sample, two-part forms are provided for recording and submitting the necessary summary information about occupational injuries and illnesses. In Part I (Summary of Occupational Injury and Illnesses), the employer is instructed to provide information from personnel records and from the Log and Summary of Occupational Injury and Illnesses (OSHA 200) that reports: (a) the size of the establishment, (b) the number of hours worked during the year, (c) the total number of injuries separated into those with and without lost workdays, (d) the total types of illnesses (using OSHA's classification of skin diseases or disorders, dust diseases of the lungs, respiratory conditions due to toxic agents, poisoning, disorders due to physical agents, disorders associated with repeated trauma, and all other occupational illnesses), and (e) the number of illnesses separated into those with and without lost workdays. At the level of this survey, BLS is able to estimate total employment by industry or by occupation, thus permitting the calculation of injury and illness incidence rates. On the basis of reports in Part I, musculoskeletal disorders are identified only by category of illness or "disorders associated with repeated trauma." For the guidance of those completing the OSHA log and summary, this category is described with the following examples: noise-induced hearing loss; synovitis, tenosynovitis, and bursitis; Raynaud's phenomena; and other conditions due to repeated motion, vibration, or pressure. Thus, while the category includes a case of hearing loss, it is unlikely to include a case of back strain or pain from overexertion.

In Part II (Reporting of Cases with Days Away from Work), each establishment covered by OSHA is required to maintain detailed information about each injury and illness on the form entitled Supplemental Record of Occupational Injury and Illnesses (OSHA 101). Since 1992, BLS has requested that each establishment included in the annual sample provide information from this supplemental record for cases reported to result in at least one day away from work. The Mine Safety and Health Administration requires all mines to report the full details of all cases. Information extracted from this supplemental form provides the following details about the lost-time cases: date of event, days away from work, days of restricted work activity, length of service, race, age, gender, and occupation. Three additional details are provided in a descriptive or narrative form: event (what the employee was doing and how the injury occurred); nature (what the injury or illness was), and source (what object or substance directly harmed the employee). These details are then coded according to a BLS-developed system that allows better focus on musculoskeletal disorders, although it is not based on the standard ICD categories. Participating establishments take information from workers' compensation reports, insurance forms, or other supplementary records to complete this second survey.

While all establishments are required to maintain the details used to complete Part II of the BLS survey—with the exception of requirements of the Mine Safety and Health Administration for mine operators to report the added details on all injuries and illnesses—BLS requests the additional details only on events that are associated with lost time. Therefore, events that result only in restricted work activity or no restrictions are not sampled for the available greater detail.

Lost-workday events included in the Part II sample account for approximately 25 percent of the reported conditions. The added detail available from these reports allows more refined specification of illnesses and injuries. For example, *event* includes information that allows classification into categories relevant to musculoskeletal disorders, such as overexertion or repetitive trauma, and *nature* includes relevant categories such as sprain/strain/tears, carpal tunnel syndrome, tendinitis, back pain, and other pain. If the data OSHA requires for all injuries and illnesses were reported to BLS, the data system would be much more robust and would allow a better understanding of these conditions.

Survey Results

BLS injury and illness data from Part I of the annual summary show an increase in all reported illnesses between 1982 and 1994, rising from an estimated 105,600 reports in 1982 to 514,700 in 1992. This trend was followed by a small decline over the past four years, with the total reports in 1998 estimated to be 392,000. No appropriate denominator for these numbers is available to calculate rates based on the current reporting scheme. The subset of conditions described as "disorders associated with repeated trauma" showed a similar but much more striking trend, with an estimated 22,600 reports in 1982 rising to 332,100 in 1992; the most recent estimate is 253,300. Events attributed to repeated trauma have therefore risen from 21 to 65 percent of all reported illnesses in the portion of the private sector sampled by BLS.

BLS examined the recent decline in overall occupational injury and illness rates in an effort to understand these trends (Conway and Svenson, 1998). Although the examination did not address musculoskeletal disorders specifically, the general observations probably apply to these disorders as well. The BLS study speculated that the downward trend was not due to a shift in employment from high- to low-hazard industries, nor an increase in underreporting, but rather from better recognition of the causes of occupational injuries and illnesses by all parties involved. This led to a nationwide adoption and implementation of safety and health programs that contain accident-related costs.

BLS injury and illness data from Part II are available only since 1992. During this period there has been a gradual decline in the total number of lost-time injuries and illnesses. Using the information on the nature of the injury associated with the different body parts allows a more refined way to examine trends in musculoskeletal disorders than is possible from Part I data. The relevant nature of injury designations that may be related to musculoskeletal disorders are sprains and strains, carpal tunnel syndrome, tendinitis, and soreness/pain.

In 1997, Part I data were used to estimate the total number of illnesses related to repeated trauma as 276,600. In the same year, the added information provided in the Part II dataset for conditions related to musculoskeletal disorders provided an estimate of 846,000 lost-workday cases. The large majority of these conditions occur in the neck, shoulder, upper extremity, and back. Note that this number counts only the events that occurred in 25 percent of the cases—those reporting lost work time. In 1997, only 1.8 million of the 7.1 million total injuries and illnesses were reported as lost-workday cases in Part II.

Some differences exist by industry when the results of Part I and Part II are compared. For the Part I subcategory of illnesses that are identified as due to repeated trauma, the largest proportion of reports come from manufacturing (72 percent), with service (10 percent) and retail trade (6 percent) the two next largest. When the same data are examined by incidence rates, manufacturing has three times the total industry rate (106/10,000 full-time workers versus 32/10,000). It is difficult to compare these results with those available from the Part II data because the categories are different. However, among the categories of conditions that could be related to musculoskeletal disorders, the proportional distribution of events changes substantially. Manufacturing is responsible for only 22 percent of sprains/strains, carpal tunnel syndrome, or tendinitis, while the service industry accounts for 26 percent. When the incidence rates for carpal tunnel syndrome alone are examined (the only specific musculoskeletal disorder), manufacturing still leads the other sectors showing a twofold excess over all private industry (6.5/10,000 versus 3.4/1,000), but both the transportation and finance sectors also exceed the overall average rates. Among the musculoskeletal disorder-related categories, the most common, but less specific, sprains and strains have the highest overall incidence rates (92.5/1,000); but now the transportation sector has the highest sector-specific rate (191/1,000) with construction, mining, agriculture, and wholesale trade all showing rates higher than overall industry. These data suggest that there is no single industrial sector in which musculoskeletal disorders are a unique problem and, furthermore, that the problem is not limited to the traditional environments of heavy labor represented by agriculture, mining, and manufacturing.

The Part II detailed information on each lost-time case is particularly important, as it permits much better examination of trends and the association of specific risk factors with occupation. Some examples of the possible use of the detailed data are provided to illustrate the potential of the added detail.

1. Three conditions—carpal tunnel syndrome, tendinitis of the upper extremity, and hurt back/back pain—show age-specific time trends that deserve attention. For example, in 1996, median days away from work for female typists is 50 percent longer for younger (ages 35 to 44) than for older typists (ages 55 to 64). The same direction in age difference was seen for receptionists (median 5 times longer for younger versus older workers), but billing clerks showed the opposite trend. Median days away from work were 10 times longer for the older age group compared with the younger.

2. Details about type of condition in 1997 provide further insights. Injuries or illnesses attributed to repetitive motion were examined. The proportion of repetitive motion events attributed to typing or key entry was determined for three conditions: carpal tunnel syndrome, tendinitis, and sprains or strains (the only conditions common enough not to be suppressed). According to BLS, repetitive motion accounts for 98 percent of all carpal tunnel syndrome, 63 percent of tendinitis, and only 2 percent of sprains and strains. Among the subset of these three conditions attributed to repetitive motion, almost one-quarter of all carpal tunnel syndrome cases were associated with typing or key entry, compared with only 13 percent of tendinitis and 5 percent of sprains and strains.

3. Trends between 1992 and 1997 deserve further investigation. During this period, when all injury and illness reports decreased, sprains, strains, and tears of the wrist decreased by 30 percent, while carpal tunnel reports decreased by only 13 percent. When examined by industrial sector, carpal tunnel rates in the manufacturing sector decreased from 9.7 to 6.5 per 10,000 full-time employed workers, while rates in transportation and public utilities increased from 3.1 to 3.6. Differing trends were also observed for sprains, strains, and tears between 1992 and 1997. In the agriculture sector, incidence rates were significantly reduced (from 183.2 to 97.6 per 10,000 full-time employed workers), while the rates for transportation and public utilities remained fairly stable (from 211.2 to 190.8 per 10,000 full-time employed workers). Explanations for these different trends should be undertaken.

An example of a less obvious value derived from these data is provided in a BLS study examining the changing composition of lost-workday cases (Ruser, 1999). The Part I injury and illness reports between 1976 and 1997 show the annual incidence of lost-workday cases has not changed substantially. However, there is a trend toward decreasing days off the job and an increasing use of restricted work activity assignments. Even though the Part II data have been collected by BLS only since 1992, the 1992 to 1996 data provide important insights not available from the Part I data. The Part II data show a slight reduction in the number of days away from work coupled with a growing use of restricted activity days and a substantial increase in the proportion of cases with lost workdays accompanied by restricted workdays. Furthermore, the Part II data allow examination of the trends by the nature of the injury. They show the highest percentage increase in restricted work activity days among those with carpal tunnel syndrome. The increased fraction was from 31 to 47 percent of lost-workday cases between 1992 and 1996. Considerable value would come from being able to examine all injuries and illnesses using the added detail available from the Part II survey data already routinely collected by employers but not reported to the BLS.

National Health Interview Survey

Survey Structure and Sampling

In 1988, the National Institute for Occupational Safety and Health (NIOSH) provided support to the National Center for Health Statistics (NCHS) to undertake a supplement to its annual survey that collected detailed information on interviewees' work histories and on self-reported health conditions of the back and hand. The data available from this source have been examined in order to estimate the work-relatedness of selected musculoskeletal disorders of the back and hand (specifically, carpal tunnel syndrome). The National Health Interview Survey (NHIS) is a continuous personal interview survey conducted by NCHS on a probability sample of the households of noninstitutionalized civilians. In 1988, interviews were completed on 44,000 individuals, 30,000 of whom were working. The detail available from this survey provides a much richer resource than BLS data to understand the relationship of work to health conditions, but, at the same time, the sampled workforce is much smaller than that represented by the BLS data. As a result, the level of detail about industry or job-specific risk is not as great.

NIOSH scientists have taken primary responsibility for the analysis and publication of results from this special survey related to musculoskeletal disorders, primarily back pain and carpal tunnel syndrome.

Recently, tendinitis and related conditions as well as arthritis have been examined for their relationship to work.

In order to examine the reports of back pain that are likely to reflect musculoskeletal disorders of the back, analysts examined responses of interviewees who reported back pain occurring for at least a week in the past 12 months. These analyses were carried out for all back pain as well as for a subset defined as work-related back pain (back pain brought on by repeated activities or resulting from a single accident or injury at work). For those with report of hand discomfort, subjects could volunteer their sense of the cause of discomfort.

Survey Results for Back Pain

The NHIS survey data for those who reported to have worked in the past 12 months were used to estimate that 22.4 million people (prevalence of 17.6 percent) suffered from back pain, without regard to whether it was related to work. A small majority of those with back pain (56 percent) were males (Guo et al., 1995). When cause of back pain was sought, 78 percent reported that the pain was associated with repeated activity, a single accident or injury, or both, and two-thirds of those reported the activity or event occurred while at work. Risk of back pain by occupation was examined by comparing specific occupations to all workers. Among males, the highest-risk occupations—prevalence ratio >2.0—were construction laborers, carpenters, and industrial truck and tractor equipment operators. Among females, the highest-risk occupations with a prevalence ratio of >2.0 were nursing aides/orderlies/attendants, licensed practical nurses, maids, and janitor/cleaners. A literature review indicated that many of the highest-risk occupations were under study, but it was noted that several that had relative risks among the top 15 for gender were previously unrecognized occupations, including: carpenters, hairdressers, automobile mechanics, janitors, and maids, often employed in small businesses or self-employed.

In a separate study utilizing the same data set, NIOSH examined the subset of reports of back pain that were specifically attributed by the respondent to work. Severity was measured by recording the number of days away from work (Guo et al., 1999). With this more stringent definition, 5.6 million work-related back pain cases were estimated. In this analysis, NIOSH reported cases by industry rather than by occupation. Among males, the industries with a prevalence ratio of >2.0 were lumber and building material retailing, crude petroleum and natural gas extraction, and sawmills/planing mills/millwork. Among females, industries with a prevalence ratio of >2.0 were nursing and personal care facilities, beauty shops, and motor vehicle equipment manufacturing.

The estimated overall prevalence of cases of work-related back pain with at least one lost workday was 4.6 percent of the working population. Furthermore, the proportion of back pain cases reporting lost workdays was 50 percent higher among those who attributed their pain to work than among those who did not. The investigators grouped industries according to the most workdays lost (overall average of 9.2 days for work-related cases) and according to the highest number of workdays lost per lost-workday case. Nationally, back pain of any type was estimated to account for 149 million lost workdays, the majority of which (68 percent) were associated with work-related back pain. The industry with the most lost workdays was construction for men (1.76 million days) and elementary and secondary schools for women (760,000 days). Examining severity of the back pain cases among those with work-related pain, the industry with the highest average lost workdays was the electronic computing equipment industry (29 days/case) for men and the U.S. Postal Service (61 days/case) for women. Both sexes were ranked high for grocery stores, hospitals, banking, and eating and drinking establishments. However, there is substantial variation by gender. For example, in the U.S. Postal Service, men reported average lost workdays of only 1.9 days per case, one-thirtieth of that found among women.

Survey Results for Hand Discomfort

The survey questions about hand discomfort elicited information about carpal tunnel syndrome, tendinitis and related syndromes, and arthritis. Analyses of these self-reports indicate that annually among working adults:

1. 1.87 million report having carpal tunnel syndrome, of which over one-third report that their health care provider diagnosed their condition as carpal tunnel syndrome and half of these were believed to be work-related (Tanaka et al., 1995, 1997).

2. 588,000 report having tendinitis or related syndromes, of which 28 percent were labeled as work-related by a health care provider (Tanaka, Petersen, and Cameron, in press; Tanaka et al., 1997).

3. Almost 2 million active or recent workers were estimated to have hand-wrist arthritis that caused a major change in work activities, jobs, or missed workdays among almost 20 percent (Dillon, Petersen, and Tanaka, in press, Tanaka et al., 1997).

The cases in which one or more of these three disorders confirmed by a health care practitioner were evaluated for associations with a number of risk factors, including age, race, gender, and work requiring repetitive bending and twisting. All three conditions were significantly more common among those whose work required bending and twisting of the hands and wrists (Dillon, Petersen, and Tanaka, in press; Tanaka, Petersen, and Cameron, in press; Tanaka et al., 1995, 1997).

Washington State Workers' Compensation Reports

The Washington State Fund provides workers' compensation for two-thirds of the state's workforce, with the other third offered through employer programs of self-insurance. As a result, the state has an unusually complete and uniform data resource for analyzing workers' compensation cases. Particularly important is the fund's access to medical information that permits identifying conditions by ICD code. This facilitates comparisons with similarly coded general medical information. Recently, these data have been used to examine the work experience of those whose conditions of the back and upper extremity qualify for compensation after a determination of work-relatedness (Silverstein and Kalat, 1999).

Claims data for 1990 to 1997 concerning back injury claims showed a total of 228,500 cases, for an annual incidence rate of 2.3/100 full-time workers. Gradual-onset back injuries represented two-thirds of the awarded claims, and 60 percent of the lost workdays attributed to back injuries. Claims data for the same period involving upper extremities revealed a total of 254,600 cases for an annual incidence rate of 2.6/100 full-time workers. Gradual-onset upper extremity injuries represented over one-third of the awarded claims and almost half of the lost workdays attributed to upper extremity injuries. Similar incidence rates were found in the review of data from self-insured workers. When age and gender characteristics of the occupational carpal tunnel syndrome cases from this dataset were compared with those reported in population-based studies of carpal tunnel syndrome the results were:

- Women and men had almost equivalent incidence rates (1.2:1) and onset was at 37 years of age.
- For the general population, the gender ratio was 3:1 and average age of onset for carpal tunnel syndrome was 51 years (Franklin et al., 1991).

Analyses of the Washington State Fund data also provide information about the leading industries in which workers' compensation claims are awarded for back or upper extremity disorders. For gradual-onset back disorders, these are nursing homes, roofing, wood frame building construction, landscaping, and wallboard installation. For upper extremity disorders, these are wood products manufacturing, wholesale meat dealers, nursing homes, and temporary help in assembly work and saw-mills. The self-insured companies—the 400 largest in the state—represent a different industrial mix. For gradual-onset conditions, the additional industries of concern were package delivery, bus companies, warehouses, supermarkets, and municipal workers, including schools.

U.S. Department of Labor Office of Workers' Compensation Programs

The U.S. Department of Labor Office of Workers' Compensation Programs data have been used to examine characteristics of compensated claims for upper extremity disorders. Since this dataset also provides ICD specific diagnostic information, carpal tunnel syndrome can be identified with confidence. Similar to the Washington State Fund report, the range of almost all cases was between ages 31 and 50, but women were a higher proportion of all cases of carpal tunnel syndrome (2.3:1). Data were not available on job or industry equivalents, so gender differences in other likely exposures could not be evaluated (Feuerstein et al., 1998).

Medical Claims Data

Until recently, it has been uncommon to access general medical claims data to determine the patterns of musculoskeletal disorders among working adults. A collaboration between the United Auto Workers and Chrysler Corporation permitted the development of a successful methodology for examining these data without breaching medical confidentiality. The study reported on employees from five plants chosen to represent a diversity of automotive manufacturing activity (Park et al., 1992). The medical claims data over three years were linked with job histories, permitting examination of rate differences by job or department. These data do not include medical treatment information for any workers' compensation claim. The target conditions for the initial analyses were selected musculoskeletal disorders (carpal tunnel disorder, other musculoskeletal disorders of the upper extremity, rotator cuff syndrome, musculoskeletal disorders of the neck, and musculoskeletal disorders of the back). The findings revealed wide differences when crude incidence rates were examined across departments, especially when departments with suspect biomechanical risks were compared with departments considered as having low or no occupational risk factors for these conditions.

Although the current limitations in the use of these data are substantial, the striking finding was the apparent frequent occurrence of musculoskeletal disorders that might prove to be work-related but were not identified as such with respect to workers' compensation claims. There are two implications. The first is that workers' compensation records are likely to be very incomplete for estimating the relative importance and distribution of musculoskeletal disorders related to work. Second, study of the incidence or prevalence of work-related musculoskeletal disorders in the general population is likely to include a large number of conditions that are not recognized as work-related.

National Occupational Exposure Survey

The National Occupational Exposure Survey was designed by NIOSH to provide data descriptive of health and safety conditions in the work environment in the United States. Almost 4,500 facilities were visited to evaluate working conditions and potential exposures to workplace risks in most types of work settings in the country. Among the factors identified were (1) potential exposure to whole body and segmental vibration and (2) work conditions associated with passive or awkward postures, lifting, arm or shoulder transport movements, hand-wrist manipulation, finger manipulations, and machine-paced work. Although the survey was carried out in the early 1980s and may be outdated in some regards, it offers data to better characterize work factors related to musculoskeletal disorders in specific jobs in a wide variety of workplaces. One analysis of these data indicated that hand-wrist manipulations were observed almost as frequently as continuous noise exposure. Using these data, an estimated 2.2 million workers were exposed to continuous noise and 2.0 million workers to hand-wrist manipulations (Wegman and Fine, 1990).

DATA ON ECONOMIC COSTS

Data are available on the cost of musculoskeletal disorders in the general population. A 1999 report from the American Academy of Orthopaedic Surgeons (Praemer, Furner, and Rice, 1999) estimates the total cost of all musculoskeletal conditions in the United States at $215 billion in 1995. Included are the direct treatment cost that accounted for 41 percent of the 1995 total; morbidity costs, the value of reduced or lost productivity, 52 percent; and mortality costs, 7 percent, based on a 4 percent discount rate of the value of productivity forgone in future years as a result of premature mortality in 1995. These figures include occupationally as well as nonoccupationally related disorders.

There is a wealth of information on the direct cost to workers' compensation insurers for claims filed in the 50 states as well as in the federal compensation system. Data from two states, Washington and Wisconsin, have been extensively analyzed in relation to musculoskeletal disorders

(Silverstein and Kalat, 1999; Boden and Galizzi, 1999). Moreover, Liberty Mutual has undertaken a series of studies looking at the costs per musculoskeletal disorder by type, as well as in the aggregate. Using the figure derived above from BLS for reported musculoskeletal disorder-like illnesses or injuries involving lost work time of about 1 million cases, and the average direct cost in workers' compensation per case estimate of over $8,000, one may estimate a minimal direct cost for compensation of $8 billion. However, using the proportion of all workers' compensation expenditures related to musculoskeletal disorders (about one-third) and the total workers' compensation cost in the United States of $55 billion (National Academy of Social Insurance, 2000), the estimate for direct workers' compensation costs would be closer to $20 billion.

Economic assessment of the actual cost for these compensated claims is higher, of course, since there are many indirect costs to employers, the affected individuals, and society. These include lost productivity, uncompensated lost wages, personal losses, such as household services, administration of the programs, lost tax revenues, social security replacement benefits, and so forth (Morse et al., 1998; Boden and Galizzi, 1999). Estimating the additional costs associated with these uncompensated components yields estimates of total costs associated with reported musculoskeletal disorders as high as $45 to $54 billion, a figure around 0.8 percent of the nation's gross domestic product.

As noted above, there is substantial reason to think that a significant proportion of musculoskeletal disorders that might be attributable to work are never reported as such. Morse and his colleagues (1998) in Connecticut, using a population-based phone survey, estimated that about 1 in 10 working-age adults suffers from a condition that would meet qualification for work-related musculoskeletal disorders of the neck, arm, wrist, or hand, and that in over 20 percent of these a physician had made such a diagnosis by report. However, only 10 percent of these workers had accepted workers' compensation claims, which would suggest a very high rate of underreporting. Moreover, these investigators found additional hidden costs associated with work-related musculoskeletal disorders in their survey, including losses of homes and cars, divorces, and job dislocations.

The Health and Retirement Survey, which is a population-based survey of adults ages 51 to 61 (Yelin, 1997; Yelin, Trupin, and Sebesta, 1999), approached the question differently, comparing direct markers of economic function in workers with and without musculoskeletal disorders in their population. On average, workers with musculoskeletal disorders earned approximately $3,000 less per person than those without, after adjusting for all other health and social differences. Given the high prevalence of musculoskeletal disorders in adults ages 51 to 61 (62 percent in their study), this would translate into an income loss nationally for men and women in that age group of over $41 billion. Of course, there is no evidence on the fraction of these individuals that would qualify for a diagnosis of work-related musculoskeletal disorders. Nonetheless, the economic impact of musculoskeletal disorders, when expanded to younger adults, would certainly exceed 1 percent of the nation's gross domestic product.

LIMITATIONS OF THE DATA

Musculoskeletal Disorders in the General Population

It has already been highlighted that the data derived from the general population estimates are intrinsically limited by the absence of any linkage to data that would allow discrimination or apportionment among work and nonwork-related factors. Nor are there any data available that provide musculoskeletal disorder rates in an "unexposed" population, since the exposures of interest are so widespread. Nor are such data capable of being easily developed.

There are other intrinsic limitations to the general population data worthy of note. First, as has been mentioned, most available data have been derived from self-report. In other words, these data are not summaries of medical diagnoses but responses of individuals regarding symptoms or their knowledge of a physician's diagnoses. This problem stems in part from the difficulty associated with diagnosis of many of the conditions of concern, such as low back or wrist pain, which are, even in physicians' evaluation, judged largely on patient complaints. While other conditions, such as carpal tunnel syndrome and herniated disc, may be more amenable to specific testing approaches (albeit each with substantial controversy within the medical community), such conditions represent only a small minority of cases of musculoskeletal disorders. This problem is intrinsic to the nature of the musculoskeletal disorders themselves and not amenable to simple scientific or biomedical solution.

The paucity of data due to the small number of surveys and the infrequency of their conduct is a limitation that is potentially amenable to solution. Strategies for linking physician diagnoses with other demographic data, as has been done in a very limited way for low back pain (see, e.g., Frymoyer et al., 1983), could provide more reliable indices for estimating the burden of musculoskeletal disorders within different strata of the population. Equally important, linkages between these diagnoses and metrics of exposure to the major risk factors that may be associated with musculoskeletal disorders would theoretically allow direct estimation of the proportion of cases associated with the varying factors, the degree to which these factors covary in relation to the disorders, and the potential proportion that could be prevented by interventions aimed at these specific factors. Currently, none of the existing databases available for the general population offers such a possibility.

Finally, it must be reiterated that no databases provide rates of musculoskeletal disorders in representative populations without exposure to the risk factors of concern. Identification of such "unexposed" populations could meaningfully be achieved only within the context of linkage among demographic, health, and work data that is not currently foreseeable.

Work-Related Musculoskeletal Disorders

Annual Survey of Occupational Injuries and Illnesses

The Annual Survey of Occupational Injuries and Illnesses survey is the only resource that currently provides ongoing, consistent reporting of injuries and illnesses that permits examination of trends over time. Therefore, it is the only national resource that can be used for the surveillance goal of tracking trends in injury and illness rates. Trend analysis is useful both to identify new risks and to evaluate efforts to reduce known risks. The survey has limitations that are well recognized.

Limitations of Part I

1. The survey represents only private industry, excluding approximately 25 percent of the workforce, primarily government workers, those who are self-employed, those who work on small farms, and those employed in places with fewer than 10 individuals.

2. In order to gain cooperation from the reporting establishments, BLS protects the confidentiality of results by not making them publicly available if (a) the estimates for the industry are based on too few reporting units, (b) average employment in the industry is too small (generally < 10,000), (c) statistical estimates do not meet minimum reliability criteria, or (d) there is any other way that publication might disclose confidential information.

3. The sample size of 165,000 is too small to permit estimates at any level below the national level except for large aggregated industry groupings. This is not the case for the subcategory of mining, since the Mine Safety and Health Administration requires reporting of all injuries and illnesses, not just a sample of these events.

4. The illness coding system is not ICD-based. Rather, it utilizes very crude collapsing of unlike conditions and is determined by a person with no specific training for the task.

5. The demographic characteristics of individuals are not reported, and only industry, not occupation or task, is collected, limiting the description of the injuries and illnesses with adequate specificity.

Limitations of Part II

In addition to the first three limitations listed for Part I:

1. The greater detail on each injury or illness that is provided in Part II is collected exclusively for lost-time injury or illness cases. OSHA, however, requires this level of detail to be recorded on all injuries and illnesses. BLS has neither the mandate nor the resources to collect and analyze the additional data, although such data would greatly enhance the usability of the database available for surveillance purposes.

2. The more detailed nature and body part coding system is not ICD-based and the narrative is provided by an individual with no specific training for the task. Although the coding is done by trained BLS staff, the inputs are still not adequately standardized.

3. While there are proper demographic characteristics associated with all reports as well as the occupation or task being performed, no comparable denominator data are collected. This prevents the calculation of rates for these better-specified conditions. A recent analysis of workplace fatality rates indicates that it is possible to address this problem (Ruser, 1998.)

4. Data items are suppressed at a national level if the number of cases is fewer than five.

National Center for Health Statistics Surveys

These surveys provide a number of ways to characterize the health of the U.S. population. The different survey elements allow for the development of a comprehensive measurement of health as self-reported and as diagnosed by health care providers. When these reports are combined, the result is an excellent resource for use to describe the health of the workforce. There are some important limitations that could be corrected, however, as is seen in the NIOSH-funded 1988 supplement to the National Health Interview Survey:

Limitations

1. For the interview surveys (National Health Interview Survey and the National Health and Nutrition Examination Survey), only the job title or industry is collected and then only for the preceding week, month, or 12 months. For the health care records (e.g., the National Ambulatory Medical Care Survey), no data are collected on job or industry.

2. Despite the importance of musculoskeletal disorders in the population (both work-related and nonwork-related), the currently designed surveys collect little detail about these disorders. The added detail in the 1988 NHIS supplement presents a good example of how informative survey data can be when these disorders are better characterized.

Workers' Compensation Records and the Washington State Fund

The data available from the Washington State Fund are valuable because they have a well-defined population base to which they refer. However, while the Washington State Fund data are among the best, the occupation and industry distribution in one state does not provide an adequate national representation of either those occupations and industries and cannot provide information about occupations and industries not prevalent in Washington.

Data based on workers' compensation vary across states as each state applies differing definitions and criteria in determining the conditions that are compensable. The between-state differences are substantial, placing further limits on efforts to derive national estimates of burden from workers' compensation claims. There is evidence that such claims are an underestimate of work-related musculoskeletal disorders, suggesting some limitations of workers' compensation reporting for surveillance and for estimating the national burden of work-related musculoskeletal disorders (Biddle et al., 1998; Morse et al., 1998).

While some limitations of the system are administrative, other limitations should be noted. The decision to file a workers' compensation claim is determined by knowledge that the option exists (Sum, 1996). This varies by state and by the education or training of each worker and employer. A decision to file a claim also depends on how likely the claim is to be contested (Herbert, Janeway, and Schecter, 1999), workers' concerns about employer retribution if they file (Speiler, 1994; Pransky et al., 1999; Ochsner et al., 1998), and the alternatives available for payment of medical costs (medical insurance).

National Occupational Exposure Survey

The National Occupational Exposure Survey is an important national resource for hazard surveillance providing the data to describe the distribution of ergonomic risk factors by industry and occupation. The survey, however, was last carried out almost 20 years ago and is not likely to represent well the distribution of current exposures. It also does not provide exposure characterization of the risk factors present in emerging industrial sectors.

Medical Care Utilization Data

Data from medical care records could be particularly valuable in providing much greater detail about the nature, distribution, time course, and disability associated with musculoskeletal disorders. Such data, however, have important limitations:

1. Medical confidentiality mechanisms need to be developed to allow use of these data for surveillance purposes and to protect the individual identity of those whose records are in the system.
2. Although specific diagnostic information is recorded by ICD-9 coding, algorithms will need to be developed to ensure consistency in diagnostic practice across providers and determine reliability.
3. Systems to match information on occupation or employer will need to be developed so that patterns of musculoskeletal disorders among different working groups can be examined.

Data on the Economic Costs

Since the estimates of cost are contingent on estimates of incidence, severity, and prevalence rates for musculoskeletal disorders and differentiation of work from nonwork-related cases, all of the above limitations apply to these estimates. In addition, there are issues unique to the economic estimates: (1) other than the direct costs of health services and wage offsets, there is no uniformly agreed-on formula for estimating the additional costs of each case, such as domestic productivity, reduced future occupational productivity, reduced educational opportunities for children, etc.; (2) it appears likely that additional costs, over and above health services and wage replacement, accrue not only to victims of musculoskeletal disorders, but also to their employers and to society. These include administrative costs, training of replacement workers, lost tax revenues, utilization of public replacement benefits or assistance, etc.

Strategies for assessing these additional costs remain understudied and controversial and are one basis for the wide range of estimates cited above.

SUMMARY

There are sufficient data regarding the occurrence of musculoskeletal disorders in the general U.S. population, including workers and non-workers, to conclude that the musculoskeletal disorder problem is a major source of short- and long-term disability, with economic losses in the range of 1 percent of the gross domestic product. However, these sources suffer from severe limitations: (1) they use nonstandard criteria for designation of musculoskeletal disorders, making comparison among them impossible; (2) data points are infrequently collected, making analysis of trends or changes impossible; and (3) none is currently structured in such a way as to allow distinctions between musculoskeletal disorders that may be related to work activities and those that are not.

BLS and workers' compensation data are sufficient to (1) confirm that the magnitude of the work-related musculoskeletal disorder problem is very large; (2) demonstrate that rates differ substantially between industries and occupations consistent with the assumption that work-related risks are important predictors of musculoskeletal disorders; and (3) document that the rapid growth in the problem or its recognition that occurred in the 1980s has shown a slight decline in the 1990s. These data provide substantial information regarding those musculoskeletal disorders that are considered work related. Moreover, they have been obtained regularly and provide some insight into the relationship between certain kinds of industries and occupations and the rates of musculoskeletal disorders. In these databases, cases have been selected in variable, nonuniform ways that are likely to underrepresent the spectrum of work-related musculoskeletal disorders that occur; musculoskeletal disorders are coded in nonstandard ways, further limiting comparability between data sources; and information available in terms of demographic and occupational risks is very limited.

Taken collectively, review of all available data sources underscores the need for more complete, more frequent, and better standardized databases that include, at a minimum, uniform coding of musculoskeletal disorders and sufficient information about industry, occupation, and tasks to allow accurate quantification of the musculoskeletal disorder problem, separation into those aspects that are and those that are not related to work factors, and tracking to determine the effects of interventions as they are undertaken.

3

Methodological Issues and Approaches

The scientific literature relevant to the problem of work-related musculoskeletal disorders represents a wide variety of research designs, assessment instruments, and methods of analysis. Therefore, the panel's representation of the science base covers a wide range of theoretical and empirical approaches. For example, there are highly controlled studies of soft tissue responses to specific exposures that are based on work with cadavers, animal models, and human biomechanics. There are also surveys and other observational epidemiologic studies that examine the associations between musculoskeletal disorders and physical work and organizational, social, and individual factors. In addition, there are experimental and quasi-experimental studies of human populations that are designed to examine the effects of various interventions.

Each of these approaches contributes a different perspective to the overall topic of musculoskeletal disorders in the workplace; together they provide a more complete, cross-validated understanding of how different workplace exposures may contribute to the occurrence of musculoskeletal disorders. Each approach has important strengths and limitations when viewed alone. When information from the three approaches is viewed together, as in this report, however, the perspective on musculoskeletal disorders in the workplace is enriched. Illustrations of these approaches are provided below, using the example of the examination of the relationship between repetitive lifting and back disorders. Similar illustrations could be provided for upper extremity disorders.

In other reports, such as the recent National Institute for Occupational Safety and Health report on musculoskeletal disorders in the workplace (Bernard, 1997b), the emphasis has been on the preponderance of evidence within one area of literature (e.g., the report focused on observational epidemiology). Here, however, we review all three approaches: basic science, observational epidemiology, and intervention studies. Rather than review each approach with the aim of examining a preponderance of evidence, this report considers the *pattern of evidence* across the different areas of scientific study. The pattern of evidence analysis, described in detail by Cordray (1986) and discussed below, has been used in an earlier National Research Council report (1995); it is particularly useful when considering causal inferences across different fields of study.

RESEARCH PERSPECTIVES

Basic Sciences

From the perspective of basic sciences, studies are designed and performed to isolate discrete events that are carefully engineered to deliver a set of exposures characterized by replicable frequency, dose, and duration. These exposures are applied to isolated anatomical and physiological systems (e.g., muscles, nerves) that are then measured for anatomical damage or adverse biochemical changes. For example, the question of the extent to which repetitive lifting is related to back disorder can be examined with the assistance of an apparatus that applies a repeatable frequency, dose, and duration of a load to a cadaver or relevant animal models; then biological measures, such as tissue biopsy for measurement of biochemical changes consistent with damage, can be obtained. The results from this type of study provide data on basic mechanisms to show, for example, whether repetitive compression similar to that involved during lifting is associated with tissue damage, and the extent to which damage can be identified as following these discrete events. In the laboratory context, the goal is to isolate events of exposure and outcome to the greatest degree possible, by precise and refined measurement and by controlling extraneous environmental conditions (e.g., temperature, humidity).

The results provide confidence in drawing inferences on whether tissue damage follows application of exposure, but these inferences are tempered by several factors. First, isolation of human tissue for study (such as a particular muscle or group of muscles) may demonstrate damage, but it may remain unclear whether the load applied in the experiment is similar to that experienced by humans. There are studies that report precise physiological abnormalities but no correlation with symptoms or function of the person being studied. These fine measurements may be trivial, or they may represent an early disease process that will become manifest only later. Second, the complexity of the human biological system includes compensatory mechanisms that are excluded in studies that focus on the isolation of mechanisms. For example, some combination of muscle groups and positioning of the whole person could provide a pattern of motion that may partially offset the insulting exposure in the real work environment. Therefore, the degree to which the results from these more focused studies can be generalized to workers in the context of their ongoing tasks must be carefully interpreted. Third, the degree to which an animal model is analogous to the human must be considered. How experiments that involve loading of mouse tails are relevant to human musculoskeletal disorders is a meaningful question that scientists need to clarify for others. While seemingly distant from human experience, this animal model is relevant from the perspective of comparative anatomy and provides a quantifiable aspect to measurement of the impact of physical stresses. Ultimately, the basic science studies contribute important information about the mechanisms by which injury can occur following a prescribed set of exposures, but the application of the findings to the whole human depends on the extent to which the results are congruent with data from human studies.

Observational Epidemiology

From the perspective of observational epidemiology, studies of human populations are designed that measure both exposures (e.g., repetitive motion) and outcomes (e.g., back disorders). A key feature of measurement in observational epidemiologic studies is that the results are generated from populations of humans. There are limits to the measurements that persons (as opposed to cells or tissues) will allow or tolerate. Because the comparisons involve groups, there are levels of detail that remain desirable but are not feasible to measure (e.g., the cost may be prohibitive). However, surveys provide information, such as symptoms, that cannot be obtained in the same way from certain types of laboratory study; for example, back pain may be disabling even in the absence of objective diagnostic test findings, and the frequency of this condition is important to ascertain.

The presence of symptoms in the absence of objective findings needs careful attention. Symptoms are often the first presentation of an illness and may represent changes that are due to physical damage (due, in this case, to repetitive lifting) that has not progressed enough to be measured by physiological tests or physical exam. Self-reports of symptoms may also reflect other factors, such as psychological stress. These trade-offs (e.g., in detail versus feasibility of measurement) are inherent in observational epidemiologic studies.

The basic strategy in an epidemiologic study is to identify the extent to which the outcome (e.g., back disorder) occurs more frequently in the exposed group than the unexposed group. The strength of this type of study over basic science investigations is that the results are generated in a real-world context. The assumption is that the persons being compared are similar in all respects (e.g., age, weight for height) other than the exposure (e.g., repetitive lifting) being considered in the investigation. In fact, observational epidemiologic studies use techniques from biostatistics to evaluate the degree of differences in the extraneous variables between the two groups and to perform statistical adjustment that makes these other factors similar. The goal of these statistical techniques is to control for confounding. It also allows precise estimation through statistical adjustment for a variety of factors, including whether the "appropriate" variables are collected and entered into the calculations and whether the number of people enrolled in the study is sufficient to permit the level of comparisons after accounting for other extraneous variables. No amount of application of statistical procedures can redeem a study if important variables are missing from the data collection or the study size is too small.

Another aspect of observational epidemiologic studies is the variety of designs that can be used to build inferences about causal associations. To illustrate this, we consider one of the most common types of studies, the cross-sectional survey. This survey involves collection of data from a sample of people of whom measures of exposure are made usually by interview. It can involve observation of work tasks and measurement of the environment (e.g., average load weight, frequency, duration of lifting). The outcomes can also be measured by interview (e.g., incidence and duration of back pain), physical examinations, or application of standardized diagnostic tests. Applied to the example given here, a population surveyed to examine the relationship between repetitive lifting and back disorder, the design involves collecting information from the individuals about their current and past lifting experience (exposure) and their current and past episodes of back pain or diagnoses of back disorder (outcome).

This survey design is efficient in that the scientists conducting the study can collect a group of people, ask questions (and check medical records, etc.), and tabulate the results all within a reasonable time frame. However, this survey approach has limitations. Because data on the exposures and outcomes are collected simultaneously, it is possible that persons who had back disorders left job categories involving repetitive lifting. Therefore, in this case, the survey may show, for those who remained to be questioned, that back disorders were not related to repetitive lifting; the result, however, may be affected by the fact that the injured persons were no longer at these work tasks, or even the possibility that lifting is "protective" against back disorders. Because there are a variety of such considerations that complicate interpretation of a survey, a number of other study designs have been developed that permit the ability to establish a relationship with greater confidence. However, these study designs, described later in the chapter, are more time- and resource-intensive.

Interventions

From the perspective of intervention studies, investigations of human populations are designed on the basis of data from basic sciences and observational epidemiologic studies, to formally test whether reduction (or enhancement) of an exposure results in a lower incidence of a disorder (and an elevation of a state of well-being). Intervention studies in basic sciences and epidemiology are rooted partly in the fact that the effort to undertake rigorous study is resource intensive, and scientists need a basis of understanding before embarking on a program that could have unintended and untoward consequences. The ideal of the intervention study is to achieve, to the extent possible, the features of laboratory studies that involve control of the ambient environment.

After a discrete intervention is identified (for example, introducing job redesign to address the relationship between repetitive lifting and back disorders), a population of workers who are exposed (e.g., engage in repetitive lifting) is randomly assigned to receive either the intervention (i.e., job redesign) or the usual activity (if considered an ethical alternative). Random assignment of intervention treatments is done in an attempt to equalize the effect of extraneous variables across those who receive the intervention and those who do not. The design is prospective, in that people undergo the intervention or comparison conditions (modified exposure) and are then followed over time to examine the incidence of the outcome (rates of back disorders in this case). The rate of incidence in the outcome in the two groups is compared, and if a difference is observed, it is attributed to the intervention. The key to this inference is the recognition that if the two groups are comparable on all factors measured, except the intervention itself, an assumption can be made that the groups are probably comparable on unmeasured factors. Therefore, the factor that most likely explains the difference in rates of disease or other outcomes is the intervention.

This feature of randomized allocation distinguishes intervention from observational epidemiologic studies. In prospective epidemiologic studies, the variable of the intervention (such as exercise) is measured on those who self-select to perform the intervention (or it is intentionally selected based on some preconceived preferences of those responsible for the selection process) rather than on those who are selected on a random basis (e.g., to undergo exercise activities in the trial). While the techniques for comparison are similar in the two study designs, self-selection in the epidemiologic study means that there may be other, unmeasured, factors that contribute to the selection of who performs the activity under study. These other factors may be critical for contributing to and explaining the outcome of interest (e.g., back disorder).

While the randomized controlled design is powerful for testing the effectiveness of interventions, it is not appropriate for all situations. For example, if the data from basic and epidemiologic studies and clinical experience suggest that the proposed intervention is highly likely to be effective, then questions can arise about how ethical it would be to withhold an intervention from a group for the sake of a formal comparison. The converse question to consider is whether absence of a study would be ethical. Probably more important for workplace studies is the consideration that there is constant change at work, independent of any planned intervention, that makes the laborious process of planning and implementing a randomized controlled trial challenging, if not impractical.

In these situations, another design, variously termed "historical control study," "before/after design" study, and "time-series analysis," has been used. For this design, an intervention is prescribed (or simply happens) in a population that has been followed and for whom the preintervention disease or outcome incidence is already known; after the intervention is introduced to all in the population, incidence of disease or outcome is ascertained over time. The basis of comparison is the incidence of the outcome, since an effective intervention should result in a lower rate of disease or other outcome in the population "after" compared with the "before" interval being studied. While ethically less complicated to institute than randomized trials, this design is limited by the possibility that any number of other unmeasured factors may have occurred during the course of the study, and these other factors may have contributed to the outcomes observed. For example, while instituting job redesign in factories, new medications for low back pain could be introduced. The extent to which this other factor accounts for the results that are attributed to the intervention would need to be considered. However, the before/after study is an efficient design that takes advantage of natural changes that occur in the workplace and are applied uniformly to all people (so selection issues are minimized). Therefore, findings from these studies can be accumulated more quickly to suggest directions for program implementation and, if appropriate and necessary, additional studies using randomized controlled trials.

Randomized trials can be limited in other ways besides costs and ethical concerns about withholding interventions. Concerns include whether the intervention was applied as designed (fidelity to the plan), contamination of effect (whereby persons randomized to the control condition have contact with persons who received the intervention and adopt some elements of the intervention indirectly), and inadequate randomization procedures. Randomized trials are difficult to conduct in the workplace because work practices change frequently, workers are reassigned frequently, and it is difficult to mask participants in this setting. Scientists involved with randomized controlled trials plan carefully to minimize the concerns whenever possible.

Prevention represents the ultimate goal of pubic health science, the objectives of which are to build on the basic sciences and observational epidemiology and to test practices designed to reduce the incidence of disease and facilitate the well-being of the population. Prevention is best tested through intervention studies. Intervention studies serve not only as formal tests to demonstrate practices that should be implemented in different settings, such as the workplace, but also provide another layer in developing confident inferences on which health factors are related. For example, basic science and epidemiologic studies may provide information about the association of repetitive lifting and back disorder. This information provides the basis for developing interventions, including job redesign, that are aimed at reducing the frequency or some other characteristic of repetitive lifting. The successful intervention studies with job redesign that show a reduction in repetitive job lifting and a resultant reduction in the incidence of back disorders provide evidence for instituting activities in practice and for confirming that the repetitive lifting and back disorder were truly related.

In summary, the three types of scientific inquiry described briefly here—basic science, observational epidemiology, and intervention studies—provide different perspectives, but they contribute to each other in generating support, as well as checks and balances, in building scientific certainty. This chapter reviews some of the methodological approaches used by the various fields that address the questions on musculoskeletal disorders in the workplace. While the methods are in many ways powerful, it is the variety of observations from different perspectives that continues to provide an evolving picture of the causes of and interventions for preventing musculoskeletal disorders in the workplace. To develop prediction, a view is needed on how causal inferences are made.

DETERMINING CAUSALITY WITHIN STUDIES

Making sense of the diverse literature requires approaches to show how causality is established. How is it that a claim can be made that repetitive lifting "causes" back disorder? How is it that repetitive motion contributes to upper extremity disorders? Before extensive resources are committed to modify the workplace or the ways workers approach their jobs, one should examine the certainty of the statement that repetitive lifting is responsible for back disorder. The basis for understanding, whether it is from a laboratory study, a field study, or an intervention trial, rests on key concepts. The first is that there is an exposure and the second is that there is an outcome of interest. The exposure can be one of any number of events of a biological, physical, chemical, or psychological nature. In the example used in this chapter, the exposure has been repetitive lifting, but one could study trunk bending, trunk twisting, temperature, and so on. In public health literature, the outcome is usually a disease condition for which risk factors are being sought in order to find strategies to prevent the disease. In this chapter, we are using the example of back disorder. In more recent public health literature, there has been a greater emphasis on health and well-being, and certainly this can be operationalized into an outcome for study. Here we use the terms "exposure" and "outcome," while in other settings, the analogous terms would be "stimulus" and "response" or "cause" and "effect," respectively.

The third concept is the association between the exposure and the outcome. While the association of the exposure and outcome can be made based on an individual at a single point in time, such an inference will be more speculative than causal, because it is based on limited information (e.g., a nurse reports back pain and her job involves repetitive lifting). Clinicians do this all the time, but the single observation for the clinician is actually cumulative, because the findings from one patient are placed in the context of medical knowledge learned and catalogued to date. The circumstances in science are different; the focus is not on categorizing patients into established categories, but on establishing a novel association. A hallmark for scientific inference is that there are repeated observations. This is in part to ensure replication (and why scientific activity is called "re-search"). Also, given the biological diversity of the human species, the observations of many studies help to ensure that associations between outcomes and exposures are found across different layers of human characteristics, showing that they are not simply a by-product of some other characteristic that is coincidental in the population.

For associations to be causal, they must be based on multiple observations; there are also necessary characteristics of the association between exposure and outcome. Some refer to these characteristics as "criteria"; and others would use the term "conditions" or "conventions" for causation. The five characteristics listed by Campbell and Stanley (1966) and updated by Cook and Campbell (1979) and Cordray (1986) include: (1) temporal ordering, (2) that exposure and outcome vary together ("covary"), (3) the absence of other plausible explanations, (4) temporal contiguity, and (5) congruity between exposure and outcome. These characteristics serve as criteria when reviewing individual studies for their likelihood of generating causal inferences. Later in this chapter, characteristics that are considered across studies are presented.

Temporal ordering refers to the importance of having the exposure precede the outcome in time; for example, repetitive lifting is more likely to be considered a cause of back disorder if it precedes it in time. In laboratory studies, temporal ordering can be established by the type of control that an investigator has over the timing and delivery of an exposure. In epidemiologic studies, this involves a recording of events in the real world. Prospective studies involve measuring exposures and then following people for the development of an outcome. Temporal ordering may be difficult to establish in cross-sectional surveys because information about exposure and outcome are obtained during the same interview. The survey approach, though operationally efficient, is less powerful for generating causal inferences than a prospective study (e.g., that follows individuals who vary in terms of performing repetitive lifting and who are then followed systematically for development of back disorder).

The second characteristic, *exposure and outcome covary*, refers to the observation that if the exposure is present, an outcome will occur; a reduction of exposure will also result in a reduction of outcome. For example, when no compressive force is applied to a spinal disk, it becomes thickened, but when loaded, it thins. While this suggests a one-to-one correspondence, it represents more of an ideal in human population studies, in which a number of factors may be contributing and offsetting each other in establishing the outcome. Therefore, the epidemiologic equivalent is that if the exposure is present, it is *more likely* that an outcome will occur.

The third characteristic is the *absence of other plausible explanations*. This includes the concept of *confounding*. Confounding is the circumstance in which the basic association of interest is in fact due (at least in part) to another factor. The definition of a confounding variable is that it is associated with both the exposure and the outcome, and that after accounting for this third variable, the relationship between the exposure and outcome is reduced, sometimes to the point at which an association can be said to be no longer meaningful. Suppose, for example, that studies find a strong association of repetitive lifting and back disorder, and an inference is evolving that the former is causing the latter. Then suppose that another set of studies is performed that includes a measure of recreational activities outside the workplace. From these studies, suppose it is found that these activities are associated with repetitive lifting (presumably because people in these jobs are likely to engage in similar levels of activities outside the workplace compared with other workers) and back disorder. The question can then be raised as to whether repetitive lifting itself is the culprit for back disorders at work, or whether the back disorders are in fact due to recreational activities that are characteristic of workers who happen to select (or be selected for) jobs involving repetitive lifting. In this case, recreational activity serves as a potential confounder and represents a possible alternative explanation for the association between repetitive lifting and back disorder.

Fortunately, in field studies of workers, there are biostatistical methods to assist with disentangling the effects of putative confounders. The techniques include stratification (i.e., examine whether the association of repetitive lifting and back disorder persists across groups of persons stratified by levels of recreational activity) and adjustment (i.e., statistical procedures to examine and average associations between exposure and outcome in the presence of other variables). The selection of variables for examination as confounders is based on those found to be plausible from the literature as well as those identified empirically in the population being studied.

Exposures that remain associated with the outcome of interest are then termed "risk factors." Because of the variability in biological diversity, it is infrequent that the association of an outcome is limited to a single risk factor. Instead, there may be a combination of risk factors that are implicated for an outcome of interest; this is referred to as the multifactorial nature of causation. Thus, it is often observed that examination of a third (putatively confounding) variable does not eliminate the fundamental association of the exposure and outcome; rather it reduces the primary association, leaving it intact. In this circumstance, the investigation could then identify a combination of risk factors that contribute to the outcome, each of which is important both alone and additively. Recognizing that the etiologic nature of many diseases, including musculoskeletal disorders, is likely to be multifactorial, scientists search for a "web of causation" (Susser, 1973).

The fourth consideration for establishing causality is *temporal contiguity*. This addresses the time interval between exposure and outcome. It may be more compelling if the exposure immediately precedes the outcome (as is the case with an acute injury) than if the exposure preceded the outcome in the remote past. The assumption is that the more temporally remote an exposure is, the more likely it is that some other (possibly unmeasured) factor may be the true explanation for the etiology of the outcome. This could mean that the observed association is, in fact, spurious. However, there may also be a "chain of causation" within a multifactorial model, whereby a series of different conditions must be met in order for the outcome to be observed. In this reasoning, there are factors that are proximal to (immediately preceding) the outcome, and factors that are more distal from (further removed in time preceding) the outcome. In occupational epidemiologic studies, there is frequently a consideration of cumulative proximal and distal exposures, so that the distinction made here is at times less relevant to generating causal inferences than for some other fields. Therefore, temporal contiguity is satisfactory as a condition to isolate only in analyses for the proximal risk factors. Slavish reliance on a requirement for temporal contiguity can be limiting in developing a full understanding of the relationships (such as cumulative exposures) that lead to an outcome of interest.

Congruity of exposure and outcome involves the finding that if the exposure is increased, then the outcome is expressed more frequently. This could be expressed as a *dose-response* effect, whereby an increase in exposure should lead invariably to an increase in outcome (or an increase in stimulus leads to an increase in response). This assumes a continuous and linear relationship of the stimulus and response. However, there are circumstances in which the relationship may be expressed more as a threshold (no response is observed until the stimulus rises to a minimum level, after which there is an increase until some maximum threshold is achieved and response no longer increases or, with fatigue, actually decreases). When the dose-response relationship is not linear, investigators search for the circumstances that can account for these findings. This deviation from a linear relationship could be due to operational characteristics of a study (e.g., delays in implementation of job redesign). There may also be factors other than the exposure and outcome that modify the basic exposure-outcome association; an interaction occurs when the joint effect of two exposures exceeds (or offsets) the independent effect of each variable alone.

Put another way, the scientist looks for interaction. This refers to the relationship of exposure and outcome in the presence of a third variable, whereby the primary association differs significantly across different levels of the third variable. While the association of the exposure and outcome may be impressive when viewed alone or when summarized across the levels of the third variable, closer examination reveals that the primary association is vastly larger at the first than at the second level of the third variable. This definition distinguishes confounding from interaction, in that confounding represents the effect of a third variable that is related to both primary variables (exposure and outcome) that accounts for the primary relationship. By contrast, interaction represents the effect of the third variable in synergizing (or offsetting) the exposure's effect on the outcome. A classic example is the relationship between alcohol consumption and esophageal cancer. While this relationship is strong, it is also true that cigarette smoking is associated with both alcohol use and cancer. Therefore, cigarette smoking could be a confounder in this association. However, when examined more closely, the association of alcohol and esophageal cancer is many times greater among smokers than non-smokers, showing that there is combination or a joint effect of alcohol and cigarettes that is greater than the significant effects of each factor alone. The potency of identifying interactions is important for targeting public health interventions, and the extent to which these interactions can be deciphered for musculoskeletal disorders in the workplace is discussed in later chapters.

Thus far, the discussion has covered basic characteristics of an association between a putative exposure and outcome in a study in order to consider it a causal relationship. There are other important methodological issues as well. In generating causal inferences, there must be considerable attention to errors in measurement. Random error can occur through imprecise measurement that allows a broader array of responses than would be necessary, whether through questionnaires or with an apparatus that captures information within a range of the true values. An example is the measurement of blood pressure, which depends on the skill and experience of the reader as well as the setting of the sphygmomanometer and other circumstances. If important variables are not measured, this contributes to random error. Random error results in attenuation of an observed association (when one existed in reality) and does not undermine confidence in a study that yields positive findings. In fact, random error can increase confidence in a positive study, since the strength of the effect was sufficient to permit its observation despite the null basis created by random error. Efforts can be made to consider research questions comprehensively and to sharpen measurements for greater precision, but while random error can be reduced, it can never be eliminated. Despite residual random error, studies can still contribute well to assessment of causality.

Another general area of concern is error that is systematic. Systematic error is also called bias, which can relate to the sampling of people for a study, the collection of information that is used to generate associations, and analyses. An example involves case-control studies in which cases are selected from clinical practice and controls are selected from the general population. If cases identified in the hospital do not represent all cases in the community, this could lead to a bias (especially if the cases in the hospital are more severe). The bias can be exaggerated further if the controls are selected not from the community, but from hospital services that systematically exclude musculoskeletal diseases or happen to exclude the possibility of work (e.g., a chronic care psychiatric ward). The result would provide an artificial association of work-related activities and musculoskeletal disorder. Another example of bias involves the type of information collected. For example, in a case control study, musculoskeletal cases, especially those identified in a hospital, might be questioned more thoroughly about their exposures and ruminate about possible risk factors more than controls (free of disorders) who are questioned in a community setting. Clearly, it is important to design studies in which the same information is obtained in the same way from individuals who are comparable. Rather than review here the extensive array of potential biases that are possible, the reader is referred to a more detailed discussion elsewhere (Sackett, 1979).

CRITERIA FOR CAUSALITY ACROSS STUDIES

Thus far the discussion has considered characteristics of causal inference that can be examined within studies. These serve as a means to sort through individual studies and identify those that can contribute to generating causal inferences. The emphasis in this discussion has not been on study design, but rather generic considerations that could apply to basic science, observational epidemiologic, and intervention studies. There is, however, an approach for considering a body of literature to generate causal inferences across a variety of studies. The approach used in epidemiology has been attributed to Sir A.B. Hill (Lilienfeld and Lilienfeld, 1980). The Bradford Hill criteria for causality address strength, temporality, consistency, and specificity of association; dose-response association; and biological plausibility.

The *strength of association* refers to the magnitude of the measure of the association; the larger the summary measure, the more confident one can be that the putative association may be causal. The type of measure used includes the relative risk or odds ratio. In our example, the ratio could be higher rates of back disorders in persons engaged in repetitive lifting than in those not engaged in this activity. The larger the ratio of incidence rates (especially across studies), the greater confidence one can have that the observed association is meaningful. There are no hard and fast rules for the minimum size of the association, although Lilienfeld and Lilienfeld (1980) have suggested that associations (e.g., relative risks) greater than 3 were probably less likely to be due to selection bias.

Temporality of association refers to the need, in establishing causality, that the exposure must precede the outcome in time. This point has been addressed earlier.

Consistency of association refers to similarity of findings within subgroups of a study or similarity of findings in other populations studied at different times, even by different study designs (e.g., retrospective versus prospective studies). The greater the degree of consistency across subgroups or across studies, the more confidence the reviewer can have that the association under study is likely to be considered causal. Failure to find consistency of association across studies is not necessarily evidence for the lack of association; rather, it is possible that factors associated with the outcome of interest could respond differently in the presence of other factors. This circumstance is referred to as "interaction" and should be considered before discarding associations as inconsistent.

Specificity of association refers to the concept that if a factor is associated with one outcome but not others, then a causal inference is more likely to be entertained. Many epidemiologists who note that some exposures can in fact be related to numerous disease outcomes (e.g., tobacco exposure) have concluded that specificity of association, as a criterion for causality, needs to be considered with caution.

The *dose-response relationship* is a direct association between levels of the exposure and levels of the outcome, for example, when reduction in levels of exposure, through intervention, is associated with reduction in levels of the outcome (e.g., rates of disease within subgroups). In epidemiologic studies in which exposure levels are difficult to measure at the individual level, studies can classify individuals by ambient exposures; in other settings, special population groups characterized as having extremes of the putative exposure (i.e., none, considerable) might be used to assist in contributing to the understanding of the response to the dose.

Biological plausibility refers to the likelihood that an association is compatible with existing knowledge of biological mechanisms. This point is an explicit statement of the concordance of the basic science and the epidemiologic literature. However, failure to have an established mechanism does not necessarily negate the observed association; rather, if other criteria of causality are observed for the association, we might consider the observed association for hypothesis generation. Indeed, there are numerous examples in the history of epidemiology in which associations observed in the field led to important public health practice and policy change, even though the association initially preceded biological theory development, which was established later. Historically, Snow's (1936) work in London on the cholera epidemic and Goldberger and colleagues' (Goldberger, Waring, and Tanner, 1923) work on pellagra are classic examples in which epidemiologists made important observations and interventions based on epidemiologic observations prior to the development of basic science observations or understanding.

These criteria have been used in numerous other reports for the past 40 years and have represented important guidance for drawing etiologic causal inferences in studies of human disease that were characterized by the use of observational epidemiologic studies.

STUDY DESIGNS

As noted above, the Bradford Hill criteria have been used primarily with observational epidemiologic studies. The principal designs used in such studies include surveillance, the cross-sectional survey, the case-control design, the prospective study, the randomized controlled trial, and the community trial. *Surveillance* involves a systematic collection of data on cases of disease (or exposures of interest, such as the National Occupational Exposure Survey project of the National Institute for Occupational Safety and Health). The data collection is usually passive, as when doctors complete forms to report diseases or conditions to the government or to insurance companies, or it can be active, with trained surveillance technicians conducting systematic surveys in selected settings using established protocols. In either case, the purpose of surveillance is to monitor a population for departures in the typical number of cases observed over time or across jurisdictions. Surveillance data can be analyzed for trends, and it has been used for analyses to generate and to test hypotheses. However, the level of information obtained in surveillance projects is typically limited, as is the sampling scheme, in order to provide a cost-efficient means of monitoring a population to identify periods when more focused studies are warranted.

The *cross-sectional study* is typically a single survey in which ascertainment of the exposures and the outcome of interest are conducted at the same time. The survey is done with an interest in determining whether the outcome is present at the time of the survey and whether the exposure has been present at some point. Although the cross-sectional study is more efficient than designs described below, its general limitation is that such surveys obtain information on prevalence of conditions (and exposures), so the temporal association between exposure and outcome may be more difficult to document. However, often the temporal association in cross-sectional studies is sufficiently clear that such an association can be inferred (e.g., to address such questions as whether workers with carpal tunnel syndrome have jobs that require forceful and repetitive use of the hand more often than those without carpal tunnel syndrome).

To address the difficulty of establishing temporal ordering, some cross-sectional studies can provide proper temporal information by using a careful history of exposure and onset of disease or historical data. However, depending on the accrual of the sample (and departures of those disabled before the study begins), the association determined from a cross-sectional study might reflect information on those who have survived up to that point. As was noted earlier in this chapter, the effect of selective survival on the observed association between exposure and outcome is an important limitation of cross-sectional studies. Estimates of risk may be erroneously low as a result of such sample distortion. The cohort study is not prone to this effect. Thus, the cross-sectional survey needs to be reviewed to determine whether the correlates identified represent suggestions for risk factors for the disease outcome, or represent correlates for survival in the population up to the point at which the study is done.

The prospective study is a longitudinal design that starts with measuring exposure and then follows individuals over time to identify incidence of disease (or other outcome). This design can be concurrent (starting with exposure currently and then following individuals over time) or nonconcurrent (have a record of exposures that were recorded in the past and then identify incidence of outcomes subsequent to those measurements). One of the greatest strengths of the prospective study is the ability to have information on temporal association. These studies can be used to examine the incidence of disease given exposure, the spectrum of disease, the incubation period (given a discrete date of exposure and onset of outcome), prognostic indicators for disease given exposure, and survival. These studies are also used for nested case-control studies and evaluation of interventions in practice settings. However, evaluation of interventions is limited by the fact that exposure for individuals is based on some selection process that is usually nonrandom; therefore, differences attributed to intervention could be also due to factors related to selection. As noted earlier, although prospective studies are difficult to carry out, it is important to emphasize their value.

The *randomized controlled trial* is the design used to formally test an intervention. Essentially, the randomized controlled trial is a prospective study that has the added feature of random allocation of the exposure of interest. The advantages of the randomized controlled study and the prospective study are similar; both are able to demonstrate temporal ordering between exposure and outcome. The trial has the key feature of having random allocation of treatment, whereby the investigator controls assignment of an intervention to a portion of the participants. Selection of participants is not controlled by the investigator, so bias in assignment is less likely. Similarly, because the process of assignment is random, on average the groups assigned to treatment and control conditions are, in theory, similar. This similarity does not always occur in fact, because the random procedure for assignment by chance can produce unequal groups as well. If the groups are unequal, the investigators make statistical adjustments. If the groups are equivalent (based on characteristics the investigators had available to measure), then the investigators can extrapolate that the groups being compared are likely to be comparable on unmeasured factors. This assumption may or may not be true. However, this equivalence of groups is the unique feature of randomized controlled trials that can make them potentially so powerful in generating inferences. As noted earlier, the strengths of the randomized controlled trial are contrasted by a number of considerations (feasibility, practicality, ethics), so this design involves a number of decisions that frequently limit its use.

PATTERN OF EVIDENCE COMPARISONS

Results across the variety of datasets are also summarized in this report using the "pattern of evidence" approach. This is an alternative approach to analyzing a collection of datasets, contrasted with the traditional approach of "preponderance of evidence," which by strict definition is reserved for summarizing a larger body of studies with more uniform research designs. Rather than summarizing the results of studies to determine whether the direction and magnitude of association is similar across studies to develop a preponderance of evidence, the pattern of evidence approach looks at *the extent to which results from one class of studies help to compensate for the limitations from another class of studies*. The goal is to establish a pattern of evidence that can be discerned from multiple data sources that are based on different sampling frames and methods.

This approach considers interrelated conditions, such as intermediate outcomes (e.g., if there is a reduction in back disorders after the implementation of job redesign), and can be used to decide whether there are other pieces of evidence available to *rule in* its plausibility (Cordray, 1986). For example, such evidence could include: epidemiologic evidence that shows an association of repetitive lifting and back disorder among different occupational groups, independent of organizational, psychological, and recreational factors; biomechanical literature showing precise load location, load moment, spinal load, three-dimensional trunk position, frequency, and kinematics that points to a well-defined pathway for exposure and risk of spine structure loading; and basic biological studies showing that a greater magnitude of spinal loading can explain deterioration of spinal tissue and can cause damage. Thus, the more supportive the pattern of evidence, the more plausible the perceived effect. The strength of this method is that, alone, self-reports of work practices in epidemiologic studies might be important but could be questioned as being subject to socially desirable responding; having data from other sources helps to strengthen inferences that this behavior occurred. Similarly, having a reduction in back disorders after implementing job redesign could be due to any number of factors, but having data to show that there was a decrease in specified biomechanical actions at the level of the individual bolsters confidence that the observed results might be due to the intervention. Of course, there can be inconsistencies, such as no change in the frequency of back disorder in a workplace where a program was implemented. However, further investigation might show that the program, while well intended, had elements that did not target behaviors properly. This pattern of evidence, with the contribution of different studies with different forms of measurement, may suggest that while the program was utilized, the intended effect was not observed. Ideally, these results can be obtained early enough to focus data collection toward the factors that might be related to such a finding.

In other words, if certain conditions are met, then it is possible to probe the plausibility that the intervention was responsible, at least in part, for the observed outcomes. As empirical evidence or assessments are repeated, the plausibility increases. Through multiple assessments, involving a logical network of evidence, it may be possible to derive a portrait of the plausibility. While there is a pool of studies of varying quality, the *pattern of evidence* approach requires at least some higher-quality studies (i.e., prospectively collected data) within the total pool of studies to be available to assess whether the evidence from the lower-quality studies is meaningful. This approach is particularly appropriate as an inferential strategy in the situation in which the number of any single type of studies (e.g., behavioral surveys, incidence data, surveillance data) is limited, precluding a preponderance of evidence approach. This pattern of evidence approach is not novel; it was described and used in a recent report that investigated the role of sterile syringes and bleach disinfection in HIV prevention (National Research Council, 1995).

This report reviews the literature on musculoskeletal disorders in the workplace, drawing on studies from basic sciences, epidemiology, and intervention research. Each of these types of research is reviewed separately in different chapters. However, there is also cross-referencing between chapters, and an integration chapter, to assemble inferences that are based on patterns of evidence about the associations that lead to the conclusions and recommendations in this report.

Part II
Review of the Evidence

4

Epidemiologic Evidence

The panel's effort to evaluate the scientific basis for a relationship between work factors and musculoskeletal disorders of the back and upper extremities required comprehensive reviews of the epidemiologic literature. For each of the two anatomical regions, reviews of the physical and the psychosocial factors were undertaken. Referring back to Figure 1.2, the review of the epidemiologic evidence addresses several components. The workplace factors considered include all three main elements and their relationship to the person. The person is considered in terms of the several outcomes reported in these studies, while adjusting or stratifying for the individual factors that are relevant.

METHODS

Criteria for Selection and Review of Articles

In planning for this process, the panel set a number of criteria specific to the task of selecting articles for the epidemiology review:

• Both the exposed and the nonexposed (or comparison) populations are clearly defined with explicit inclusion and exclusion criteria. It is evident why subjects who were studied were eligible and why those not studied were ineligible.
• The participation rate was 70 percent or more.
• Health outcomes relate to musculoskeletal disorders of the low back, neck, and upper extremities and were measured by well-defined criteria determined before the study. The health outcomes studied are carefully defined so that it is evident how an independent investigator

could identify the same outcome in a different study population. Outcomes are measured either by objective means or by self-report. For self-reported outcomes, however, there are explicit criteria for how the data were collected and evidence that the collection method would permit another investigator to repeat the study in another population.

• The exposure measures are well defined. Self-report of exposure is acceptable so long as the method of collecting self-reports was well specified and there was evidence that the self-reports were reliable reflections of exposures. Job titles as surrogates for exposure were acceptable when the exposure of interest was inherent in the job (e.g., vibration exposure for those operating pneumatic chipping hammers).

• The article was published in English.

• The article was peer reviewed.

• The study was done within the last 20 years (preferably).

No specific limitations were placed on study designs acceptable for consideration. The advantages of prospective studies, however, were recognized. For example, there were sufficient prospective studies of low back pain to examine these separately among the studies of physical factors and exclusively among the studies of psychosocial factors.

Literature Search Methods

The literature reviews were conducted using computer-based bibliographic databases, with MEDLINE (National Library of Medicine, United States of America) a component of all searches. Additional databases included: NIOSHTIC (National Institute for Occupational Safety and Health, United States of America), HSELINE (Health and Safety Executive, United Kingdom), CISDOC (International Labour Organization, Switzerland), Ergoweb (Internet site of the University of Utah), Psychinfo, Oshrom, Ergonomics Abstracts, and ArbLine (National Institute for Working Life, Sweden).

The bibliographies of articles (particularly review articles) and the NIOSH comprehensive review (Bernard, 1997b) were examined to identify additional relevant articles.

Using these sources, a candidate list of articles was established and then systematically screened to determine which ones met the strict criteria, described above, for inclusion in the review. Each process reduced the list substantially. For physical work factors studied in association with back disorders, 255 studies were initially identified as relevant and 41 met the selection criteria and were reviewed. For psychophysical factors and back disorders, the search resulted in 975 references, which were then reduced to 21 work-related risk factor studies and 29 individual risk factor studies. For work-related physical factors and upper extremity disorders, the initial list of 265 references was reduced to 13 that provided direct and 29 that provided indirect measures of exposure. For psycho-physical factors and upper extremity disorders, the initial 120 references were reduced to 28.

Analysis of Study Results

Definition of Measures: Relative Risks

In epidemiology, the *relative risk* is a measure of the strength of an association, here meaning the relationship between the frequency of an exposure and the occurrence of an outcome (e.g., amount of vibration and incidence of back pain). Because human populations typically have a variety of exposures occurring in near proximity, relative risk is typically measured as the incidence of disease in the exposed (e.g., helicopter pilots who experience vibration) and the incidence of disease in the unexposed (similar people, like ground crews, who are considered to share nearly the same other exposures as the exposed, such as recreational activities, diet, and living conditions). The ratio of incidence provides a measure of association, and the higher this ratio of incidences (the relative risk), the stronger the association, the more confidence we can place in a conclusion that the association is meaningful.

Because incidence is a rate calculated by following people over time, and many studies are cross-sectional or retrospective (case-control), other measures, such as the *prevalence ratio* and the *odds ratio*, have been developed to summarize the association between exposure and outcomes for these other study designs. Our analysis focused on associations expressed by such risk estimates as the odds ratio and the relative risk. These estimates were retrieved from the original article or calculated when sufficient raw data were presented.

Definition of Measure: Attributable Risk

The *attributable risk* is another measure used to help generate inferences. In its simplest form, it is the difference between the incidence in those exposed and those unexposed—a risk difference. This risk difference is thought of as the attributable risk in that, in theory, removing this exposure entirely would reduce the frequency of the outcome to the level of those who are unexposed. Rotham and Greenland (1998a, 1998b) discuss some of the limitations of this simple assumption. Attributable risk is often calculated as a ratio rather than a difference: risk in the exposed is divided by risk in the unexposed, producing an attributable fraction. The attributable fraction is the proportion by which the rate of the outcome among the exposed would be reduced if the exposure were eliminated. This fraction is calculated as the ratio of $(RR - 1)/RR$, where RR is the relative risk or the prevalence ratio of risk in the exposed compared with the unexposed:

$$AF_e = (RR - 1)/RR$$

The attributable fraction helps scientists and policy makers recognize that in many cases a variety of factors contribute to the total incidence of a disease or other outcome, so that removal of an exposure typically does not reduce the outcome rate to zero. However, in its simplest form, the attributable risk is a measure that suggests that if the offending exposure were removed (by intervention or regulation), then the amount of disease outcomes would be estimated to be reduced by the calculated amount. As is noted below, this simple summary is enmeshed in caveats.

It is important to recognize in this calculation that the result depends on what is included. That is, if one considers a calculation of one factor as it relates to an outcome and then performs a separate calculation for another factor for the same outcome, there is overlapping (correlation) between factors that could make the sum of the two separate factors sum to more than 100 percent. Attributable fraction, then, represents a crude but important estimation of the impact of control of risk factors. An estimate of the attributable fraction for a multifactorial disease such as a musculoskeletal disorder provides only an estimate of the relative importance of the various factors studied. It is not, and cannot be, considered a direct estimate of the proportion of the disease in the population that would be eliminated if only this single factor were removed (Rotham and Greenland, 1998a). Rather it provides guidance to the relative importance of exposure reduction in those settings in which the exposure under study is prevalent. Consequently, we have not attempted to rank or further interpret the findings for attributable fractions and have chosen only to report them as a rough guide to the relative importance of the factors in the study settings in which they have been examined.

In this review, the relative risk in longitudinal studies and the prevalence or odds ratio in cross-sectional surveys were used to calculate the attributable fraction for the risk factors studied. For example, if workers exposed to frequent bending and twisting have a prevalence of low back pain that is 3 times that of those not exposed, then among the exposed the attributable fraction will be:

$$AF_e = (3 - 1)/3 = 0.67$$

By this hypothetical calculation, 67 percent of low back pain in the exposed group could be prevented by eliminating work that requires bending and twisting.

Confounding

None of the musculoskeletal disorders examined in this report is uniquely caused by work exposures. They are what the World Health Organization calls work-related conditions. "Work-related diseases may be partially caused by adverse working conditions. They may be aggravated, accelerated, or exacerbated by workplace exposures, and they may impair working capacity. Personal characteristics and other environmental and socio-cultural factors usually play a role as risk factors in work-related diseases, which are often more common than occupational diseases" (World Health Organization, 1985).

In Chapter 3 we note that the epidemiologic study of causes related to health outcomes such as musculoskeletal disorders requires careful attention to the several factors associated with the outcome. The objective of a study will determine which factor or factors are the focus and which factors might "confound" the association. In the case of musculoskeletal disorders, a study may have as its objective the investigation of individual risk factors. Such a study, however, cannot evaluate individual risk factors effectively if it does not also consider relevant work exposures; the work exposures are potential confounders of the association with individual risk factors. Conversely, a study that evaluates work exposures cannot effectively evaluate these factors if it does not also consider relevant individual risk factors; the individual risk factors are potential confounders of the association with work exposures.

Therefore, when studying the relationship of musculoskeletal disorders to work, it is necessary to consider the other known factors that cause or modify the likelihood that the disorder will occur, such as individual factors and nonwork exposures. For example, the frequency of many musculoskeletal disorders is a function of age, so age has to be taken into account before attributing a musculoskeletal disorder to a work exposure. Another common concern is whether a recreational exposure accounts for an outcome that otherwise might be attributed to work.

In every epidemiologic study, confounders need to be measured and, when relevant, included in the data analysis. The confounders selected for consideration in the analysis of data from a specific study depend on the types of exposures studied, the types of outcomes measured, and the detail on potential confounders that can be accurately collected on a sufficient number of the study subjects. As a consequence, our approach to reviewing epidemiologic studies of work and musculoskeletal disorders documented the attention given to a wide range of potential confounders (see the panel's abstract form in Box 4.1). No study can measure every possible confounder; however, the papers included by the panel were judged to have given adequate attention to the primary individual factors

**BOX 4.1 Individual Factors Considered in Analyses
Form Used in Describing Studies Included in the Review**

	Described	Used in Analysis	Does Not Vary
❏ Age	❏	❏	❏
❏ Gender	❏	❏	❏
❏ Body mass index	❏	❏	❏
❏ Weight	❏	❏	❏
❏ Height	❏	❏	❏
❏ Smoking	❏	❏	❏
❏ Marital status	❏	❏	❏
❏ Income	❏	❏	❏
❏ Educational status	❏	❏	❏
❏ Comorbid states	❏	❏	❏
❏ Hormone-related conditions (e.g., pregnancy)	❏	❏	❏
❏ Strength or capacity	❏	❏	❏
❏ Race	❏	❏	❏
❏ Workers' compensation policies	❏	❏	❏
❏ Nonoccupational exposure factors	❏	❏	❏

Methods used to control confounding:
    ❏ Matching
    ❏ Stratification
    ❏ Standardization
    ❏ None
    ❏ Regression
    ❏ Other: ———

Consideration of interactions:
    ❏ Interaction between different types of work exposures
    ❏ Interaction between work exposures and nonwork exposures/cofactors

that might have confounded the work exposures under study. These include in particular age and gender, as well as, when necessary and possible, such factors as obesity, cigarette smoking, and comorbid states.

The role of potential confounders in epidemiologic studies and their proper management is often confusing to the nonepidemiologist. The difficulty stems from the fact that the potential confounder is often known to be associated with the disease, in this case musculoskeletal disorders. The association of a risk factor such as age with the disease, however, does not make it a true confounder of the study's examination of a separate risk factor such as work exposures. True confounding occurs only when, for example, both the risk factors being studied (age and work exposures) are associated with the outcome (musculoskeletal disorders) *and* the two risk factors are also correlated (for example, those with more work exposure are also older). Fortunately, as noted in Chapter 3, there are statistical methods available to manage confounding that provide a way to "separate," in this example, the effects of the work exposure from the effects of age.

The panel recognizes that a number of nonwork factors are associated with or also cause the musculoskeletal disorders under study. These were not separately studied, but they were considered, as necessary, to evaluate the significance of the work factors that were studied. In our judgment, it is evident that confounding alone is highly unlikely to explain the associations of musculoskeletal disorders with work that are noted. More detailed consideration of confounding in future studies, however, should further improve the precision and accuracy of risk estimates.

Measures of Workplace Exposures

Physical Exposures

The measures of physical exposures investigated include force, repetition, posture, vibration, and temperature. Available approaches to estimating exposure to these physical stressors include worker self-report, bioinstrumentation, and direct observation. The optimal choice among methods depends on characteristics of the methods as well as of the jobs under study. Job exposure can be considered a weighted sum of the different task-specific exposures that make up the job, with weights coming from task distributions (Winkel and Mathiassen, 1994). Each of two components—exposures in each task and the relative frequency of each task—must be estimated. Workers with the same job title may have different exposure levels because of between-worker variability in either the duration and distribution of tasks within jobs or the exposures within tasks. Furthermore, job title may indicate homogenous exposure groups for some stressors, such as repetitiveness and force demands, while other features such as posture may vary widely among workers in the same job (e.g., Punnett and Keyserling, 1987; Silverstein, Fine, and Armstrong, 1987). In highly routinized or cyclical work, such as that at a machine-paced assembly line, without job rotation there is only one task, the short duration and regularity of which make the exposure determination a relatively simple problem. In contrast, in nonroutinized work, such as construction and maintenance, determination of task distributions over an extended period of time may be a more difficult undertaking. As jobs become less routinized, i.e., less predictably structured, valid estimation of both task distributions and task-specific exposures becomes increasingly challenging.

Typically, both observational and direct measurement techniques generate highly detailed, accurate exposure analyses for a relatively short period of elapsed time in each job. Most protocols for these methods assume that the work is cyclical, with little variability over time, so that it is reasonable to measure exposures for a short period and extrapolate them to the long term. But many jobs do not fit this model: they are not comprised of work cycles, or the cycles are highly variable in their total duration or content (the number or sequence of steps that comprise each cycle) and do not account for all of the work performed by an individual with any given job title. For these jobs, it would be infeasible to undertake continuous measurements for entire cycles as an exposure assessment strategy, because either there are no cycles, or a very large number of (long) cycles would have to be recorded in order to quantify accurately the total and average duration of exposures. With short measuring times, the data collected are of uncertain representativeness because these time periods do not match the duration of exposures that are thought to be relevant to musculoskeletal disorder development.

A versatile alternative for estimating physical exposures is the use of data collected directly from workers. Such reports may address both task-specific exposures within jobs and the distributions of tasks performed by each worker. In addition to being time-efficient, self-reports permit assessment of exposures in the past as well as the present and may be structured with task-specific questions or organized to cover the job as a whole. Some researchers have explicitly recommended a composite approach to the analysis of nonroutine jobs, in which task-specific exposures are measured directly and the temporal distribution (frequency and duration) of each task is obtained from self-report. Self-reported data can take various forms, including duration, frequency, and intensity of exposure. In some studies, absolute ratings have agreed well with observations or direct measurements of the corresponding exposures, while others have diverged significantly, especially with use of continuous estimates or responses that required choices among a large number of categories (e.g., Burdorf and Laan, 1991; Faucett and Rempel, 1996; Lindström, Öhlund, and Nachemson, 1994; Rossignol and Baetz, 1987; Torgén et al., 1999; Viikari-Juntura, 1996; Wiktorin et al., 1993).

Retrospective recall of occupational exposures has been frequently employed in studies of musculoskeletal disorders, but there are few data on the reproducibility of such information. Three studies have examined the potential for differential error (i.e., information bias) in self-reported exposure with respect to musculoskeletal disorders with mixed results;

some risk estimates were biased away from the null value, some toward it, and others not at all (Torgén et al., 1999; Viikari-Juntura, 1996; Wiktorin et al., 1993). In the REBUS[1] study follow-up population, Toomingas et al. (1997a) found no evidence that individual subjects systematically over-rated or underrated either exposures or symptoms in the same direction. Self-reported exposures have promise, but their validity depends on the specific design of the questions and response categories.

A variety of instrumentation methods exist for direct measurement of such dimensions as muscle force exertion (electromyography), joint angles and motion frequency (e.g., electrogoniometry), and vibration (acceler-ometers). For example, the goniometer has been used in a variety of stud-ies of wrist posture, including field assessments of ergonomic risk factors (Moore, Wells, and Ranney, 1991; Wells et al., 1994), comparisons of key-board designs (Smutz, Serina, and Rempel, 1994), and clinical trials (Ojima et al., 1991). Hansson et al. (1996) evaluated the goniometer for use in epidemiologic studies, and Marras developed a device for measuring the complex motion of the spine (Marras, 1992). While many consider these methods to represent collectively the standard for specific exposures, each instrument measures only one exposure, and usually only at one body part. When multiple exposures are present simultaneously and must be assessed at multiple body parts, the time required to perform instru-mented analyses on each subject may limit their applicability to epide-miologic research (Kilbom, 1994). Another practical concern is the potential invasiveness that may interfere with job performance, alter work practices, or reduce worker cooperation. Thus, there is a trade-off be-tween the precision of bioinstrumentation and the time efficiency and flexibility of visual observation and worker self-report. As discussed in Chapter 6, gross categorical exposure measures (e.g., >10 kg versus < 10 kg) used in epidemiologic studies may limit the possibility of observing an exposure-risk relationship; a continuous measure based on bioinstru-mentation might make such a relationship more apparent. Thus, their high accuracy (for the period of measurement) gives these methods utility for validating other methods on population subsets and added value when they can be applied in epidemiologic studies.

A large number of observational methods for ergonomic job analysis have been proposed in the last two decades (see Kilbom, 1994). These

---

[1]In the original REBUS study conducted in 1969, participants were asked to complete a questionnaire regarding health status—all selected were given a medical examination. A diagnosis of musculoskeletal disorder required signs and symptoms. The follow-up study, conducted in 1993, asked the younger participants in the original REBUS study to partici-pate in a reexamination.

include checklists and similar qualitative approaches to identify peak stressors (e.g., Keyserling et al., 1993; Stetson et al., 1991). The limitation with checklists is that they provide little information beyond the presence or absence of an exposure, with a possibly crude estimate of the exposure duration. The qualitative approaches are not likely to provide sufficient detail to effectively assess exposure for epidemiologic studies.

The most common observational techniques used to characterize ergonomic exposures are based on either time study or work sampling. Both of these techniques require a trained observer to characterize the ergonomic stressors. Methods based on time study (e.g., Armstrong et al., 1982; Keyserling, 1986) are usually used to create a continuous or semicontinuous description of posture and, occasionally, force level. Therefore, changes in the exposure level, as well as the proportion of time a worker is at a given level, may be estimated. Because methods based on time study tend to be very time intensive, they are better suited to work with fairly short and easily definable work cycles. A different approach, work sampling, involves observation of worker(s) at either random or fixed, usually infrequent, time intervals and is more appropriate for nonrepetitive work (e.g., Karhu, Hansi, and Kuorinka, 1977; Buchholz et al., 1996). Observations during work sampling provide estimates of the proportion of time that workers are exposed to various stressors, although the sequence of events is lost. Though less time intensive than time study, work sampling still requires too much time for use in an epidemiologic study, especially one that employs individual measures of exposure.

There are also a few highly detailed, easily used observational analyses for use as an exposure assessment tool in an epidemiologic study. These methods employ subjective ratings made by expert observers. For example, Rodgers (1988, 1992) has developed methods based on physiological limits of exposure that rate effort level, duration, and frequency. The method developed by Moore and Garg (1995) employs ratings similar to those of Rodgers and adds posture and speed of work ratings. Moore and Garg's strain index is designed to estimate strain for the distal upper extremity. It is the weighted product of six factors placed on a common five-point scale (subjective ratings of force, hand/wrist posture, and speed of work and measurement of duration of exertion, frequency of exertion, and duration of task per day). The strain index is a single priority score designed to represent risk for upper extremity musculoskeletal disorders and is conceptually similar to the lift index for low back disorders. The lift index was developed as part of the revised NIOSH lifting equation (Waters et al., 1993) and is the ratio of the load lifted and the recommended weight limit.

Recently, Latko et al. (1997) developed a method employing visual analog scales for expert rating of hand activity level (called HAL). The method has also been generalized to assessment of other physical stressors, including force, posture, and contact stress (Latko et al., 1997, 1999). The HAL employs five verbal anchors, so that observers can rate the stressors reliably. In an evaluation, a team of expert observers comes to a consensus on ratings for individual jobs. These ratings correlated well with two quantitative measures, recovery time/cycle and exertions/second, and are found to be reliable when compared with ratings of the same jobs 1.5 to 2 years later (Latko et al., 1997).

In sum, there are many methods for assessment of ergonomic exposures. The challenge for ergonomists and epidemiologists is to determine a method of characterizing level of exposure that is efficient enough to permit analysis of intersubject and intrasubject variability across hundreds of subjects and that can also produce exposure data at the level of detail needed to examine etiologic relationships with musculoskeletal disease. The HAL, as developed by Latko, is easy to apply and has proven to be predictive of the prevalence of upper extremity musculoskeletal disorders in cross-sectional studies.

Psychosocial Exposures

Measures of psychosocial exposures reported in the literature are obtained through the use of various self-report surveys. These surveys are typically presented to subjects in a paper format in which the subject is requested to complete a series of questions. These survey tools typically comprise multiple scales used to assess psychosocial risk factors. Many of these measures assess the construct of interest using a continuous scale of measurement, by which it is possible to provide a measure of exposure in terms of degree, and not simply whether it was present or absent. Response items vary depending on the scale and typically range from 0-5, 0-7, or 0-10, with options anchored so that the respondent has a frame of reference for various responses.

Some measures are standardized, well-developed, self-report tools whose psychometric properties (reliability and validity) have been established based on past research, while other items or scales were developed for the purposes of a single study. Currently, all scales used are self-report. Depending on the length of the survey, the time to completion can range from 10 minutes to several hours. It is rare that the perceptions reported by the respondent are corroborated by an independent assessment tool or process (e.g., supervisor or coworker evaluations or direct observation of a workplace). Although it can be helpful to assess such independently collected information to support workers' reports of their sense or opinions of their environments, perceptions are, by their nature, best collected through self-report.

The most common work-related psychosocial constructs measured in the epidemiologic literature include: job satisfaction, mentally demanding work, monotony, relationships at work that include coworker and supervisor support, daily problems at work, job pressure, hours under deadline per week, limited control over work, job insecurity, and psychological workload (a composite of a number of subitems that include stress at work, workload, extent of feeling tired, feeling exhausted after work, rest break opportunities, and mental strain).

The Job Content Questionnaire (JCQ) is an example of a workplace psychosocial measure whose measurement properties are well defined; it has been used frequently in the psychosocial epidemiology literature. The JCQ comprises three key measures of job characteristics: mental workload (psychological job demands), decision latitude, and social support (Karasek, 1985). Decision latitude is based on the worker's decision authority and the worker's discretion over skill use—that is, the worker's ability to control the work process and to decide which skills to utilize to accomplish the job. Psychological job demands reflect both physical pace of work and time pressure in processing or responding to information. In the Karasek and Theorell model (1990), high psychological job demands in combination with low decision latitude result in residual job strain and, over time, chronic adverse health effects. The JCQ, as an instrument for measuring such strain, has been shown to be highly reliable and has been validated as a predictor, in numerous countries and industrial sectors, of increased risk of cardiovascular morbidity (Karasek and Theorell, 1990; Karasek et al., 1998; Kawakami et al., 1995; Kawakami and Fujigaki, 1996; Kristensen, 1996; Schwartz, Pickering, and Landsbergis, 1996; Theorell, 1996).

Measures of Musculoskeletal Disorder Outcomes

The epidemiologic literature on the relationship between exposure to physical and psychosocial risk factors and the development of musculoskeletal disorders in the workplace focuses on four major types of outcome. Two outcomes rely on patient self-report (symptoms and work status), and two rely on sources independent of the patient (evaluation by a clinician and review of workplace or insurance records). Table 4.1 summarizes the outcomes assessed in 132 epidemiologic studies. These do not include the 29 upper extremity studies that provided indirect measures of exposure.

Self-report symptom measures were the most common outcome, with 61 studies assessing presence of symptoms (usually nonstandardized questionnaires asking about prevalence or incidence), 19 studies assessing symptom severity (often with standardized pain and symptom ques-

TABLE 4.1 Outcome Measures in Epidemiologic Studies of Work and Back and Upper Extremity Musculoskeletal Disorders

Risk Factor and Body Region	Number of Studies	Self-Report Symptoms			Self-Report Work Status		Clinical Evaluation[a]			Records		
		Present	Severity[b]	Disability	Sick Days	Return to Work	Visit Only	Physical Exam	Tests	Claim	Sick Days	Return to Work
Psychosocial—back												
• Work-related factors (longitudinal)	21	6	5	2	2	4		2		3	4	1
• Individual factors (longitudinal; not including studies above)	29	9	8	6	2	6	1	1				1
Psychosocial—upper extremities												
• All factors (cross-sectional)	25	13	6	1				8				
• All factors (longitudinal)	3	1						2				
Physical—back												
• Workers only (cross-sectional)	21	21										
• Community (cross-sectional)	9	7					1	1		4		
• Workers (longitudinal)	7	2								2	1	
• Workers (case-control)	4						1	1				
Physical—upper extremities												
• Workers (cross-sectional)	13	2						7	4			
Total[c]	132	61	19	9	4	10	3	22	4	9	5	2

[a]Studies are counted only once regarding clinical evaluation; some studies simply noted that a clinical visit occurred; some further specified that a physical examination was performed; and some also noted that diagnostic tests were done.

[b]Severity usually measured with standardized pain or symptom severity measure.

[c]The total number of specific outcomes exceeds the number of studies (i.e., 132), since some studies assessed multiple outcomes.

tionnaires), and 9 studies assessing symptom-related disability. A total of 14 studies assessed the self-reported effect of the musculoskeletal disorder on work status, either as number of sick days ($n = 4$) or return (or nonreturn) to work ($n = 14$). Formal clinical evaluation constituted an outcome in 29 studies, most of which relied on a physical examination by a physician or other health care professional (e.g., physical therapist). Diagnostic tests such as X-rays or nerve conduction studies were a standard outcome in only a few studies. Information obtained from records constituted an outcome in 16 studies, including claims data, sick days, or return to work. The predominance of symptoms as an outcome is inherent in the nature of musculoskeletal disorders, which are primarily defined by pain or other symptoms. Indeed, the results of physical examination and diagnostic tests may be normal in a large proportion of individuals with musculoskeletal disorders.

There were a greater number of high-quality studies related to back pain than to upper extremity musculoskeletal disorders. More of the back pain studies were longitudinal rather than cross-sectional, providing stronger evidence for a potentially causal relationship between particular risk factors and back disorders. A greater proportion of upper extremity musculoskeletal disorder studies used clinical evaluation as an outcome.

RESULTS

Work-Related Physical Factors

Back Disorders

The scientific literature on work-related back disorders was reviewed to identify those risk factors of physical load that are consistently shown to be associated with back disorders and to determine the strength of their associations. A total of 43 publications were selected that provided quantitative information on associations between physical load at work and the occurrence of back disorders. These risk factors were found significant in almost all of the studies: lifting and/or carrying of loads in 24 of the 28 in which it was studied, whole-body vibration in 16 of the 17, frequent bending and twisting in 15 of the 17, and heavy physical work in all 8 in which this factor was studied. The following significant findings are summarized from these studies: for lifting and/or carrying of loads, risk estimates varied from 1.1 to 3.5, and attributable fractions were between 11 and 66 percent; for whole-body vibration, risk estimates varied from 1.3 to 9.0, with attributable fractions between 18 and 80 percent; for frequent bending and twisting, risk estimates ranged from 1.3 to 8.1, with attributable fractions between 19 and 57 percent; and for heavy physical work, risk estimates varied from 1.5 to 3.7, with attributable fractions between 31 and 58 percent. Appendix Tables 4.1 to 4.4 provide the detailed findings in the 43 publications selected in this review. Three publications are not included in these tables because they did not present any significant association (Hansen, 1982; Lau et al., 1995; Riihimäki et al., 1994).

The evidence on static work postures and repetitive movements is not consistent. The characteristics of the studies have some impact on the magnitude of the risk estimate, but these characteristics do not explain the presence or absence of an association. Table 4.2 provides a compilation of results from all studies in terms of the importance of each general type of exposure.

Study designs affect these findings. Studies with small samples tend to have higher risk estimates, which may be an indication of publication bias. Due to power considerations, in smaller studies the effect of a risk factor needs to be larger in order to reach the level of statistical significance. Hence, the evaluation of the magnitude of a particular risk factor should take into account the sample size.

Case-control studies (Appendix Table 4.4) reported higher risk estimates than cross-sectional studies (Appendix Tables 4.1 and 4.2) for manual material handling and frequent bending and twisting. An expla-

TABLE 4.2 Summary of Epidemiologic Studies with Risk Estimates of Null and Positive Associations of Work-Related Risk Factors and the Occurrence of Back Disorders

	Risk Estimate				Attributable Fraction (%)	
	Null Association[a]		Positive Association			
Work-Related Risk Factor	n	Range	n	Range	n	Range
Manual material handling	4	0.90-1.45	24	1.12-3.54	17	11-66
Frequent bending and twisting	2	1.08-1.30	15	1.29-8.09	8	19-57
Heavy physical load	0		8	1.54-3.71	5	31-58
Static work posture	3	0.80-0.97	3	1.30-3.29	3	14-32
Repetitive movements	2	0.98-1.20	1	1.97	1	41
Whole-body vibration	1	1.10	16	1.26-9.00	11	18-80

[a]Confidence intervals of the risk estimates included the null estimate (1.0). In only 12 of 16 null associations was the magnitude of the risk estimate presented.

NOTES: n = number of associations presented in epidemiologic studies. Details on studies are presented in Appendix Tables 4.1 through 4.4.

nation may be that in case-control study design, recall bias (by subjects of exposure) is stronger than in cross-sectional studies, since there was usually a long period between exposure and recall. However, the case-control study with the highest risk estimate was based on observations at the workplace.

In general, risk estimates in community-based surveys (Appendix Table 4.2) were smaller than those in cross-sectional studies in occupational populations (Appendix Table 4.1). A reasonable explanation is that contrast in exposure is less in community-based studies that survey a large variety of jobs. In various cross-sectional studies, contrast in exposure has played a role in the selection of subjects.

Multivariate analyses with more than two confounders showed smaller risk estimates (see, for example, the longitudinal study by Smedley et al., 1997) than statistical analyses with just one or two confounders (see, for example, the longitudinal studies by Gardner, Landsittel, and Nelson, 1999; Kraus et al., 1997; Strobbe et al., 1988; and Venning, Walter, and Stitt, 1987). For lifting as a risk factor, this difference was statistically significant, with average risks of 1.42 and 2.14. Most studies have adjusted only for a limited number of potential confounders.

In addition to study design issues, some of the differences in findings appear related to the different ways exposure was measured. For manual material handling, the 7 studies with observations and direct measurements showed a significantly higher risk estimate than the 21 studies based on questionnaires, with average risk estimates of 2.42 and 1.86, respectively. This finding may be explained by larger misclassification of exposure in questionnaire studies, or by larger contrast in exposure in studies that used actual workplace surveys to determine exposure levels. In general, questionnaire studies showed associations between physical load and back disorders similar to those shown in studies that represented much more detailed exposure characterization. Therefore, the information from these questionnaire studies provides useful corroborating evidence.

The magnitude of the risk estimate could not be evaluated in relation to the contrast in exposure, since exposure parameters were not very comparable. Some studies have used reference groups (low exposure) that may nonetheless have had measurable exposures to physical load in other studies.

This review concludes that there is a clear relationship between back disorders and physical load imposed by manual material handling, frequent bending and twisting, physically heavy work, and whole-body vibration. Although much remains to be learned about exposure-outcome relationships (see Chapter 3), the epidemiologic evidence presented suggests that preventive measures may reduce the exposure to these risk factors and decrease the occurrence of back disorders (see Chapter 6). However, the epidemiologic evidence itself is not specific enough to provide detailed, quantitative guidelines for design of the workplace, job, or task. This lack of specificity results from the absence of exposure measurements on a continuous scale, as opposed to the more commonly used dichotomous (yes/no) approach. Without continuous measures, it is not possible to state the "levels" of exposure associated with increased risk of low back pain.

Upper Extremity Disorders

A variety of disorders of the upper extremity were studied in the selected literature. Primary among these was carpal tunnel syndrome, identified by symptoms and physical examination alone or in combination with nerve conduction testing. A second important outcome was hand-arm vibration syndrome (Raynaud's disease or other vibration-related conditions of the hand). There were also a number of operationally defined but less well-specified outcomes (defined for epidemiologic, not clinical, purposes) such as musculoskeletal disorders of the wrist, tendinitis, and bone- or joint-related abnormalities. Studies that met the most stringent criteria were not based on self-report alone. The anatomical areas with the greatest number of studies were the hand and the wrist, although a number of studies focused more generally on the upper extremities. Although a number of studies of the neck/shoulder region were considered, only two were included. The neck, shoulders, and upper arms operate as a functional unit, which makes it difficult to estimate specific exposure factors for the neck/shoulder region at a level beyond that of job or job tasks. Further complicating study of the region is the fact that most of the reported musculoskeletal problems of this region are nonspecific, without well-defined clinical diagnoses.

Table 4.3 provides a compilation of point estimates of risk from all studies across the major types of work-related physical exposure that were studied. Appendix Table 4.5 presents the risk ratios for various exposures; these ratios cover a very wide range (2 to 84), depending on how specifically the exposure and the outcome were defined. With the exception of the few studies of bone- and joint-related abnormalities, most of the results demonstrate a significant positive association between upper extremity musculoskeletal disorders and exposure to repetitive tasks, forceful tasks, the combination of repetition and force, and the combination of repetition and cold. A number of good studies demonstrated that there is also an important role for vibration.

There were 9 studies in which carpal tunnel syndrome was defined

TABLE 4.3 Summary of Epidemiologic Studies with Risk Estimates of Null and Positive Associations of Specific Work-Related Physical Exposures and the Occurrence of Upper Extremity Disorders

| | Risk Estimate | | | | | |
| | Null Association[a] | | Positive Association | | Attributable Fraction (%) | |
Work-Related Risk Factor	n	Range	n	Range	n	Range
Manual material handling	4	0.90-1.45	24	1.12-3.54	17	11-66
Repetition	4	2.7-3.3	4	2.3-8.8	3	53-71
Force	1	1.8	2	5.2-9.0	1	78
Repetition and force	0	-	2	15.5-29.1	2	88-93
Repetition and cold	0	-	1	9.4	1	89
Vibration	6	0.4-2.7	26	2.6-84.5	15	44-95

[a]Confidence intervals of the risk estimates included the null estimate (1.0).

NOTES: n = number of associations presented in epidemiologic studies. Details on studies are presented in Appendix Table 4.5.

by a combination of a history of symptoms and physical examination or nerve conduction testing (Appendix Tables 4.5 and 4.6). In these studies, there were 18 estimates of risk based on various specificities of carpal tunnel syndrome diagnosis and varying degrees of work exposure. Of these, 12 showed significant odds ratios greater than 2.0 (range 2.3 to 39.8), 4 showed non-significant odds ratios of greater than 2.0 and 2 showed non-significant odds ratios between 1.7 and 2.0. These findings were supported when less specific outcomes were examined. In most instances (8 out of 10), conditions classified as "wrist cumulative trauma disorders" or "nonspecific upper extremity musculoskeletal disorders" were found to be significantly associated with work-related physical risk factors with a similar range of elevated risk. Hand-arm vibration syndrome and other vibration disorders were significantly associated with vibration exposures in 12 of 13 studies, with risk elevated 2.6 to 84.5 times that of nonexposed or low-exposed comparison workers.

It should be noted that the majority of studies were cross-sectional. Therefore, it is important to consider the temporal direction of the findings. It is likely that the occurrence of upper extremity symptoms or disorders contributes to increased work-related and nonwork-related stress. If this is the case and a reciprocal relationship exists, it does not preclude the need to reduce the impact of stress (as either cause or consequence) on these disorders, given the potential health effects of repeated or prolonged stress. A second limitation in cross-sectional studies is the healthy-worker effect. This effect refers to the observation that healthy workers tend to stay in the workforce, and unhealthy workers tend to leave it. Those who may have left the workforce due to the health condition being studied will be absent from the study group, resulting in an underestimation of an effect if one is present.

The findings from the studies reviewed indicate that repetition, force, and vibration are particularly important work-related factors associated with the occurrence of symptoms and disorders in the upper extremities. Although these findings are limited by the cross-sectional nature of the research designs, the role of these physical factors is well supported by a number of other studies in which exposure assessment was less specific (Appendix Table 4.6). Despite indirect objective exposure information, the jobs studied appeared to represent conspicuously contrasting ergonomic exposures. These articles were not used to estimate exposure-response relationships for specific physical hazards (e.g., repetition, force, and posture), but they do provide a foundation for demonstrating a hazard (Appendix Table 4.6). Only three studies included in the review examined the effects of computer keyboard work (Bernard et al., 1994; Murata et al., 1996; Sauter, Schleiffer, and Knutson, 1991). In two, significant associations were found with pain or discomfort in the upper extremity, and the third found association with slowed median nerve velocity in subclinical carpal tunnel syndrome.

The attributable fractions related to the physical risk factors that were found to be important provide additional useful information. They suggest that, when present, each of the physical factors listed in Table 4.3 is an important contributor to upper extremity disorders. The studies for which attributable fractions are reported explored associations primarily with hand/wrist disorders such as carpal tunnel syndrome and hand-arm vibration syndrome. Study of these physical factors in each of the other upper extremity disorders is indicated to further explore how strong an influence these same factors might have specifically on the other disorders. Even given the limitations on generalizing from specific studies, the estimates suggest that substantial benefit could result from reducing the most severe of these physical risk factors (Table 4.3 and Appendix Table 4.5).

As with other epidemiology study reviews, there are limitations in the available literature. Characterization of exposure with sufficient specification to segregate and adequately describe exposure to the different physical factors for such regions as the neck/shoulder area provides an important example. Literature reviews by Anderson (1984), Hagberg and Wegman (1987), Sommerich, McGlothlin, and Marras (1993), Bernard

(1997a), and Ariens et al. (2000) provide support for the view that physical work factors are associated with neck and shoulder musculoskeletal disorders. Had the review of the literature presented in this chapter been less restrictive regarding study specifications of exposure, it is likely that much stronger conclusions would have been drawn for each of the upper extremity musculoskeletal disorders. Our review, along with the substantial literature that has used less well-specified exposures, demonstrates the high priority to be placed on developing better exposure measures for study of the neck/shoulder as well as the other upper extremity disorders.

An equally important need is for more prospective studies to address individual physical risk factors and their combination as these relate to each of the upper extremity musculoskeletal disorders. The cross-sectional findings demonstrating a strong interaction between repetition and force and between repetition and cold indicate combinations that should be priorities for future study. Given the findings on work-related psychosocial risk factors and upper extremity disorders (see below), it will be particularly important to carry out studies that examine the combined effects of physical and psychosocial factors.

Psychosocial Factors

Psychosocial risk factors for work-related musculoskeletal disorders can be separated into two major categories: those that are truly specific to the workplace (job satisfaction, poor social support at work, work pace, etc.) and those that are individual psychosocial factors (such as depression). Both types of factors are important to review for several reasons. First, there is an abundance of literature regarding the relationship between both types, particularly for back pain. Second, individual psychosocial factors such as depression are typically present both at work and outside it, making it nearly impossible to distinguish which aspects of depression are work-related and which nonwork-related. As a result, we summarize the literature on both types of risk factors, describing each separately. For research on back pain, separate tables are provided. For upper extremity disorders, fewer studies examining individual psychosocial factors were identified. Therefore, the two types of risk factors are distinguished but included in the same table.

Back Disorders

Work-Related Psychosocial Factors

A relatively large number of work-related psychosocial factors have been suggested as related to back pain and the resultant disability. These range from general conceptualizations, such as "job satisfaction," to more specific variables, such as "decision latitude" or "work pace." A great many measurement techniques and research designs have been employed, making direct comparison among studies difficult.

The robustness of the association between work-related psychosocial factors and back pain is suggested by two facts. First, the findings are relatively consistent in this literature despite vastly different methodologies. Second, the relationship remains and sometimes becomes stronger when possible biasing factors are controlled.

When discrepancies are found, it may be necessary to call on several factors to help explain them. These include the sample composition and size, severity of the injury/disease, measures of predictors, time of outcome, outcome criteria, study design, and possible treatment received between initial assessment and outcome. It is difficult to calculate the exact size of the effects observed, even though many of the psychosocial variables prove to be better predictors than biomedical or biomechanical factors.

Taken as a whole, the body of research provides solid evidence that work-related psychosocial factors are important determinants of subsequent back pain problems (Table 4.4 and Appendix Table 4.7). The studies produced strong evidence (i.e., at least three studies showing a positive association) for six factors, including low job satisfaction, monotonous work, poor social support at work, high perceived stress, high perceived job demands (work pace), and perceived ability to return to work. In

TABLE 4.4 Summary of Work-Related Psychosocial Factors and Back Pain: 21 Prospective Studies

Work-Related Psychosocial Factor	Null Association	Positive Association	Attributable Fraction (%)	
	n	n	n	Range
High job demands	1	5	2	21-48
Low decision latitude/control	0	2		
Low stimulus from work (monotony)	2	4	1	23
Low social support at work	0	7	3	28-48
Low job satisfaction	1	13	6	17-69
High perceived stress	0	3	1	17
High perceived emotional effort	0	3		
Perceived ability to return to work	0	3		
Perceived work dangerous to back	0	2		

NOTE: Details on studies are presented in Appendix Table 4.7.

addition, moderate evidence was found for linking low back pain to low job control, an emotionally demanding job, and the perception that the work could be dangerous for the back. General measures, such as job satisfaction and stress, showed a very distinct relationship. However, such general measures may reflect other aspects of the psychological work environment, such as relationships at work or job demands. Therefore, the studies provide relatively little information about the mechanisms or processes involved. Despite huge differences in study design and some problems outlined below, the general methodological quality of these studies is relatively high, and participation rates are good. Few studies employed a theoretical framework, and a consequence has been difficulty in specifying which predictor variables should be measured.

The relationships examined involve a large number of parameters that may influence the strength of the association. A given risk factor may, for instance, interact with the outcome variable employed. The belief that work is dangerous would seem to be relevant for the outcome variable of return to work, but possibly not for the onset of back pain. Similarly, some risk factors may be relevant only for certain types of work. As an illustration, for assembly line employment, work pace may be strongly related to future back pain complaints, but for professionals, such as nurses, it may have a weaker relationship.

The general quality of the studies was high. By selecting prospective investigations, a minimum standard was set. Nevertheless, there is great diversity in the methodology and this causes several prominent problems. One concern is that the same concept has been measured in many different ways. Since reliability and validity are generally not specified, it is possible that two studies claiming to measure the same entity may in fact be measuring quite different ones. There was also substantial variation from study to study in the definition and measurement of the outcome variable, and this may have had considerable consequences on the results obtained. There is, for example, a difference between a simple report of having had back pain during the past year with dysfunction, with health care visits, or with sick leave.

Individual Psychosocial Factors

The results demonstrate that individual psychosocial factors are related to back pain from its inception to the chronic stage (Table 4.5 and Appendix Table 4.8). Indeed, these variables were shown to be important in the development of pain and disability. Nonetheless, since psychosocial factors account for only a portion of the variance, and since other factors are known to be of importance, the present findings may underscore the necessity of a multidimensional view in which psychological

TABLE 4.5 Summary of Individual Psychosocial Factors and Back Pain: 38 Prospective Studies

Individual Psychosocial Factor	Null Association n	Positive Association n	Attributable Fraction (%) n	Range
Depression or anxiety[a]	5	17	6	14-53
Psychological distress[b]	0	11	4	23-63
Personality factors	3	4	4	33-49
Fear-avoidance-coping	1	8	1	35
Pain behavior/function[c]	1	6	1	38

[a]17 studies assessed depression only, 2 studies anxiety only, and 3 studies both depression and anxiety.
[b]9 studies assessed psychological distress, and 2 assessed stress.
[c]4 studies assessed pain behavior, and 3 assessed pain-related functioning.

NOTE: Details on studies are presented in Appendix Table 4.8.

factors interact with other variables. Although psychological factors are considered to be of particular importance in chronic pain, the data reviewed show distinctly that psychosocial factors are also pivotal in the transition from acute to chronic pain as well as being influential at onset. Moreover, the results suggest that psychosocial factors are not simply an overlay, but rather an integral part of a developmental process that includes emotional, cognitive, and behavioral aspects.

Considerable research has examined the relationship between psychosocial variables and back pain, but few have penetrated the reasons why these variables may be important. A challenge for future research is therefore to devise studies that include a theoretical perspective. Too often, studies have simply employed a convenience measure of a "psychological" variable, without considering why or how the variable might work. With a theoretical model, stronger designs could be used that would provide answers to specific questions.

Few investigations have amply treated the temporal aspects of the problem. The data reviewed suggest that certain factors are important very early, while others may be important at first consultation or a recurrence. Moreover, the reciprocal nature of pain and psychological variables was almost always treated as unidirectional, such as depression causing pain rather than pain affecting depression.

Even though all studies were prospective, methodological shortcomings ranged from selection bias and inappropriate use of statistical tests to failure to account for the intercorrelation of measures. The use of self-ratings as both the dependent and independent variable is a particular problem that may inflate risk estimates. It is difficult to summarize some results, because different terminology and measurement methods have been used to assess similar concepts (e.g., reluctance to participate in activities being "fear-avoidance," "disability," or "somatic anxiety"). There is a need to improve the quality of prospective studies in this area and to foster the use of a more structured terminology.

Some prominent psychological factors do emerge, however. First, a cognitive component represented by attitudes, beliefs, and thoughts concerning pain, disability, and perceived health seems to be a central theme. A second theme is an emotional dimension in which distress, anxiety, and depression are central. Third, a social aspect appears, in which family and work issues seem to be relevant, even if the data are less convincing. Finally, a behavioral domain emerges, in which coping, pain behaviors, and activity patterns are consequential elements.

It is tempting to conclude that since the studies included in Appendix Tables 4.7 and 4.8 have prospective designs, the observed relationships are causal; however, this may be incorrect. Although the relationships may be temporal, they need not be causal in nature. Caution in drawing conclusions concerning causality does not lessen the value of the reviewed findings, but points to the need for experimental or other designs to advance understanding.

An important implication is how this knowledge may be incorporated into clinical practice. First, considerable psychosocial information that could be of the utmost importance in conjunction with medical examinations may be overlooked if proper assessment of these variables is not conducted. Second, if psychosocial elements play a central role in back pain, then better interventions could be designed to deal with these factors to provide better care and prevention.

Summary of Work-Related and Individual Psychosocial Factors

Based on the studies reviewed here, there is ample evidence that both work-related and individual psychosocial factors are related to subsequent episodes of back pain (Tables 4.4 and 4.5; Appendix Tables 4.7 and 4.8). *Strong* evidence for a risk factor was defined as at least 3 studies demonstrating a positive association and a distinct majority (i.e., at least 75 percent) of the studies examining that risk factor showing a positive association. *Moderate* evidence for a risk factor was defined as two studies showing a positive association and none showing a negative association. *Inconclusive* evidence for a risk factor meant neither strong nor moderate evidence was demonstrated. Of the nine types of work-related psychosocial risk factors, six had strong evidence for an association with back pain (low job satisfaction, monotonous work, poor social support at work, high perceived stress, high perceived job demands, and perceived ability to return to work), and 3 had moderate evidence (low job control, emotionally demanding job, and perception that work could be dangerous). Of the 5 types of individual psychosocial risk factors, 4 had strong evidence, while 1 was inconclusive. Conclusions regarding psychosocial risk factors are further strengthened by the fact that a main criterion for selection of back pain studies for review was a prospective design, thus ensuring that the psychosocial factor was measured before the outcome. Nonetheless, the studies do not elucidate the mechanisms or the developmental process whereby "normal" acute back pain becomes chronic.

The attributable fractions related to work-related psychosocial risk factors suggest that improvement in job satisfaction may reduce risk for back disorders by 17 to 69 percent, while improved social support at work might reduce risk by 28 to 48 percent. Acknowledging the limitations associated with the interpretation of attributable fractions (as discussed earlier in the chapter) we conclude that these results point to the potential for structural changes in job supervision, teamwork structures, and the ways in which work may be organized to reduce risk. The most consistent evidence related to individual psychosocial risk factors suggests that reduction in depression and anxiety symptoms could reduce the risk for back disorders by 14 to 53 percent, and reduction in psychological distress could reduce risk by 23 to 63 percent. This is important because a number of effective treatments are available for depression, anxiety, and psychological distress. In a number of studies, the attributable risk associated with a particular psychosocial factor could not be estimated, because although the factor was significantly associated with back disorders in multivariate models, the exact data sufficient to calculate relative risk were not provided.

Upper Extremity Disorders

Exposure measures investigated among the 28 reviewed studies of the impact of psychosocial factors on upper extremity disorders included specific work demands (e.g., number of hours on deadline), perceptions of the degree of support from supervisors and coworkers; perceived control over high work demands; and reports of symptoms that may be stress-related (e.g., stress-related abdominal distress), which is a measure of response to stressors rather than a stressor itself. Such a measure is used as a proxy to stress exposure (assuming the response is indicative of exposure to stress) and is not therefore a direct measure of exposure to a stressor. This type of measure was found only in studies of nonwork-related psychosocial exposures. Table 4.6 provides a compilation of results from all studies across all anatomic areas, as well as for each specific anatomic location. Detailed summaries can be found in Appendix Tables 4.9 and 4.10.

The most frequently studied outcome was the report of symptoms (pain, numbness, tingling, aching, stiffness, or burning) in a specific anatomical area over the past week, month, or year, measured by self-report survey. Of 28 studies, 7 included confirmation of symptoms by physical examination. The anatomical areas with the greatest number of studies were the shoulder and the neck, although a number of studies focused on the hand and the elbow.

The tables indicate that the risk ratios for work-related exposures ranged from 1.4 to 4.4. The majority of the findings were below 2.0. Considering all upper extremity sites, this table indicates that the number of studies reporting a positive association for high job demands, high perceived stress, and nonwork-related worry and distress was greater than those reporting no significant effect for these exposures. This table also indicates that a number of potential psychosocial risk factors were not shown to be associated with the onset of work-related upper extremity symptoms or disorders. Specifically, the majority of studies that met the methodological criteria for inclusion did not report a significant effect for low decision latitude, work-related and nonwork-related (friends and family) social support, or few rest break opportunities. A similar pattern of results was observed for each of the specific anatomical locations. It should be noted that the majority of studies were cross-sectional; therefore, it is difficult to determine the direction of the findings.

The findings from the review of psychosocial work factors indicate that high job stress and high job demands are work-related factors that are consistently associated with the occurrence of symptoms and disorders in the upper extremities. The review also indicated that nonwork-related worry, tension, and psychological distress were consistently associated with work-related upper extremity symptoms and disorders. Although these findings are limited by the cross-sectional nature of the research designs, the role of job stress as a risk for upper extremity disorders was also supported by one large-scale prospective study (Bergqvist, 1995). These findings are also consistent with a prospective study in a community sample of recently diagnosed workers with a number of work-related upper extremity diagnoses (Feuerstein et al., 2000). This study indicated that level of perceived job stress predicted a composite index of outcomes (symptoms, function, lost time from work, mental health) at 3 months after diagnosis.

TABLE 4.6 Summary of Epidemiologic Studies: Psychosocial Risk Factors and Work-Related Upper Extremity Disorders

| | Risk Estimate | | | | | |
| | Null Association[a] | | Positive Association | | Attributable Fraction (%) | |
Work-Related Risk Factor	n	Range	n	Range	n	Range
A. Wrist/Forearm						
High job demands	4	1.2-1.4	5	1.6-2.3	4	37-56
Low decision latitude; low control and low stimulus from work	8	1.0-1.7	3	1.6-6.3	3	37-84
Low social support	4	-	3	1.4-2.1	3	28-52
Low job satisfaction	4	1.4	0	-	-	-
High perceived stress	1	1.5	3	-	-	-
Few rest break opportunities	5	2.7	2	1.5	1	33
Low support nonwork-related	4	-	0	-	-	-
Worry, tension, psychological distress, nonwork-related	0	-	2	2.3-3.4	2	56-71
B. Shoulder/Upper Arm						
High job demands	6	1.1	6	1.5-1.9	3	33-47
Low decision latitude; low control and low stimulus from work	8	1.1	6	1.6-1.9	3	37-47
Low social support	7	1.2	5	-	-	-
Low job satisfaction	2	-	0	-	-	-
High perceived job stress	3	1.5	3	-	-	-
Few rest break opportunities	3	-	1	3.3	1	70
Low support nonwork-related	3	-	0	-	-	-
Worry, tension, psychological distress, nonwork-related	1	-	1	4.8	-	79
C. Elbow/Arm						
High job demands	3	1.1	6	2.0-2.4	2	50-58
Low decision latitude; low control and low stimulus from work	5	1.0-3.0	1	2.8	1	64
Low social support	5	1.2-1.7	0	-	-	-
Low job satisfaction	2	-	0	-	-	-
High perceived job stress	1	1.4	2	2.0	1	50
Few rest break opportunities	1	-	1	3.1	1	67
Low support nonwork-related	1	-	0	-	-	-
Worry, tension, psychological distress, nonwork-related	0	-	1	1.4-1.8	1	28-44

continues

TABLE 4.6 Continued

Work-Related Risk Factor	Risk Estimate				Attributable Fraction (%)	
	Null Association[a]		Positive Association			
	n	Range	n	Range	n	Range
D. All Upper Extremity						
High job demands	6	1.1-1.4	10	1.5-2.4	6	33-58
Low decision latitude; low control and low stimulus from work	10	1.1-1.7	6	1.6-2.8	4	37-64
Low social support	7	1.2	7	1.4-2.1	3	28-52
Low job satisfaction	4	1.1-1.4	0	-	-	-
High perceived job stress	2	1.4	5	2.0	1	50
Few rest break opportunities	3	1.4-1.5	3	1.5-3.3	2	33-70
Low support nonwork-related	3	-	0	-	-	-
Worry, tension, psychological distress, nonwork-related	1	-	3	1.4-4.8	3	28-79

[a]Confidence intervals of the risk estimates included the null estimate (1.0). The magnitude of the risk estimate often was not presented.

NOTES: n = number of associations presented in epidemiologic studies. Details on studies are found in Appendix Table 4.9.

The attributable fractions related to these risk factors suggest that modification of the high job demands could potentially reduce the risk for upper extremity disorders and symptoms by 33 to 58 percent. Reduction in perceived levels of job stress could reduce the risk for upper extremity disorders and symptoms by 50 percent, and reduction in nonwork-related worry, tension, and distress has the potential to reduce risk by 28 to 79 percent. These findings highlight the potential impact of modifying both work-related and nonwork-related sources of stress; however, they must be considered within the limitations presented earlier in this chapter on the interpretation of attributable fractions. The observation that no study that considered both psychosocial and physical risk factors met review inclusion criteria is important, since many models assume a complex interaction among medical, physical/ergonomic, and workplace and individual psychosocial factors (e.g., Armstrong et al., 1994).

There is a need for more prospective studies. Unlike the area of back pain, there are very few prospective studies of psychosocial risk factors in work-related upper extremity disorders. There is also a need for more consistent use of measures that assess specific psychosocial exposures.

These measures should have sound psychometric properties (e.g., reliability and validity) that justify their use. The inclusion of various measures should also be based on well-conceived hypotheses based on working models of how these factors may affect the occurrence of these symptoms and disorders (Chapter 7 discusses such models). The case definitions used in studies should be carefully delineated, and a more consistent use of outcome measures of symptoms, disorders, and/or functional limitations should be implemented. The criteria used to select studies for review may have been too restrictive, given the relative level of sophistication of the psychosocial literature in this area. Nevertheless, despite this rigor, an association among perceived job stress, high job demands, nonwork-related distress, and upper extremity disorders was noted. These findings highlight the importance of conducting additional studies to identify specific factors that contribute to the identified risk factors and to explain how these interact to influence the development, exacerbation, or maintenance of work-related upper extremity disorders. It is also important to determine how these psychosocial factors interact with medical and ergonomic risk factors to modify risk. It is possible that the psychosocial factors that were not found to be consistently associated with the occurrence of work-related upper extremity symptoms and disorders may influence the recovery process following onset. It is also possible that these factors may impact other outcomes, such as functional limitation or the ability to sustain a full day's work. The role of psychosocial factors in the exacerbation and maintenance of these disorders requires further investigation.

This review highlights the potential utility of increased efforts directed at understanding the mechanisms by which job stress may impact work-related upper extremity disorders and the biological basis for such an association. The review also supports the need to investigate approaches that eliminate or reduce work- and nonwork-related sources of stress in prevention efforts.

CONCLUSION

A number of general and specific reviews were identified in which physical and psychosocial factors were examined in relation to musculoskeletal disorders of the upper extremities and back [see review references]. These reviews served as a resource to supplement the panel's efforts to identify relevant epidemiologic studies. They also were examined to determine whether conclusions drawn from the panel's review were consistent with previous review efforts. The objectives of the reviews differed; some focused on specific industries, jobs, or exposures, but others were more general. As a whole, the findings from these other reviews are consistent with those arrived at in the panel's review and provide additional support for the conclusions.

The approach for considering causal inferences described in Chapter 3 is useful for summarizing our review of the data from epidemiologic studies. As the tables in this chapter show, a number of studies were judged to be of sufficient quality for inclusion in this review, and these vary in terms of the types of designs and measurement approaches. While this variety complicates the generalization of causal inferences, the summary tables indicate meaningful associations between work-related physical and psychosocial exposures and musculoskeletal disorders. The tables show not only a preponderance of evidence for some exposures (e.g., 26 of 32 studies found a significant association between vibration and upper extremity musculoskeletal disorders), but also a consistency of association for many of the exposures and outcomes. Although the literature contains mostly cross-sectional surveys, some work to establish temporality; combined with the available prospective studies, evidence for temporal association has been included in this chapter.

Most studies reviewed here also show a meaningful strength of association measured by both estimates of the relative risk and calculation of attributable risk. The attributable risk provides an estimate of the proportion of musculoskeletal disorders that might be prevented if effective interventions were implemented; the calculations are appreciable for most for the exposures summarized here.

While the measure of attributable risk is meaningful for conceptualizing public health impact, the calculations are presented for one factor at a time and do not account for other factors. As noted in this chapter, many studies did account for potential confounders that could provide alternative explanations for the observed findings, but the number of confounders examined in each study tends to be limited. While this is due to multiple factors (including expense associated with satisfying sample size requirements), the fact that the associations persist after accounting for the confounders measured to date supports the fundamental association, but it also justifies more detailed investigation.

The joint effect of exposures is another element of the risk estimation suggested in Chapter 3 and illustrated in this chapter. The attributable fraction summarizes the impact of a single exposure. However, scant attention has been paid to the joint effect, or interaction, of two (or more) exposures, increasing risk beyond the level of either alone. As noted in Chapter 3, some combinations of exposures might work jointly, although their individual actions may or may not be significant. The studies by Silverstein (e.g., Silverstein, Fine, and Armstrong, 1987) showed an interaction between high force and high repetition for upper extremity disorders among industrial workers. Further investigation for joint effects of exposures is indicated from the current review. The effect of joint exposures can be investigated within physical (vibration, force, load, etc.), and psychosocial (job strain, job demand, etc.) domains. This review indicated the utter lack of studies that were found to be of sufficient quality and that examine both physical and psychosocial factors together. Because evaluation of each has shown important effects on the development of musculoskeletal disorders, and some of the current evidence (although modest) suggests that one does not explain the other, it is unlikely that more detailed investigation will demonstrate that the association of either with musculoskeletal disorders is due to confounding with the other. However, additional studies are needed to understand the degree to which each contributes to the overall incidence of musculoskeletal disorders, and the extent to which both work synergistically in selected work settings.

While the results presented in this chapter are consistent with one another, it is important to examine the degree to which they are consistent with the results from the basic science and the biomechanics studies (Chapters 5 and 6). Some of these studies have been mentioned in this chapter; their results are generally consistent, providing here some suggestion of biological plausibility for the association between physical forces and musculoskeletal disorders. The degree of consistency across different levels of study will be discussed in more detail in the integration chapter.

Most epidemiologic studies have been summarized as having exposure and/or outcome measures dichotomized. The ability to make inferences about dose-response relationship is limited in this context. While there are step-wise differences in dichotomous measures across studies (e.g., see Boshuizen, Bongers, and Hulshof, 1992, and Bovenzi and Zadini, 1992) that make cross-comparisons tantalizing, the differences in comparison groups and other design features hinder the combining of results for generating inferences on dose-response relationships. Future studies can help generate strong inferences by paying greater attention to more refined levels of measurement. While this is a challenge, the strength of the current studies justifies this effort.

In conclusion, the epidemiologic evidence provides support for associations between workplace physical and psychosocial exposures and both back and upper extremity musculoskeletal disorders.

Appendix

APPENDIX TABLE 4.1 Significant Associations Between Work-Related Risk Factors and the Occurrence of Back Disorders, Expressed as Odds Ratio, in Cross-Sectional Epidemiologic Studies Among Occupational Populations

Author	Study Population	Outcomes	Work-Related Risk Factor	Risk	95% Confidence Interval	Attributable Fraction Exposed
Alcouffe et al., 1999	7,010 workers (M&F)	LBP in past 12 months (56%)	Lifting (every day > 10kg)	1.4	1.2-1.6	NA
			Whole-body vibration (> 4 h/day vs. never)	1.3	1.0-1.6	NA
			Awkward postures (yes/no)	2.0	1.7-2.2	NA
Arad and Ryan, 1986	831 nurses (F)	LBP in past month (42%)	Lifts per shift (> 6 vs. less)	2.5	1.8-3.4	41%
Bongers et al., 1990	133 helicopter pilots and 228 non-flying officers (M)	Regularly experienced LBP (55% and 11%)	WBV ($a_z > 0.5$ m/s^2)	9.0	4.9-16.4	80%
Boshuizen, Bongers, and Hulshof, 1990	450 tractor drivers and 110 agriculture workers (M)	Regularly experienced LBP (31% and 19%)	WBV ($a_z > 0.3$ m/s^2)	1.9	1.1-3.4	39%
Boshuizen, Bongers, and Hulshof, 1992	242 drivers and 210 operators (M)	LBP in past 12 months (51% and 42%)	WBV ($a_z > 0.5$ m/s^2)	1.7	1.1-2.8	18%
Bovenzi and Zadini, 1992	234 bus drivers and 125 maintenance workers (M)	LBP in past 12 months (83% and 66%)	WBV ($a_z > 0.6$ m/s^2)	3.6	1.6-8.2	NA
			Awkward posture (frequent)	2.3	1.2-4.3	NA

Reference	Sample	Outcome	Exposure			
Bovenzi and Betta, 1994	1,155 tractor drivers and 220 office workers (M)	LBP in past 12 months (67% and 35%)	WBV ($a_z > 0.5$ m/s^2) Awkward posture (hard)	2.4 2.2	1.5-3.8 1.3-3.8	NA NA
Burdorf, Govaert, and Elders, 1991	114 concrete workers and 52 maintenance workers (M)	LBP in past 12 months (59% and 31%)	Bends and twists (37% and 27%) WBV (yes/no)	2.8 3.1	1.3-6.0 1.3-7.5	30% NA
Burdorf, Naaktgeboren, and de Groot, 1993	94 crane operators and 86 office workers (M)	LBP in past 12 months (50% and 34%)	Static sedentary posture (yes/no)	3.3	1.5-7.1	32%
Burdorf et al., 1997	161 tank terminal workers	LBP in past 12 months (35%)	Lack of social support (yes/no)	3.8	1.6-9.1	47%
Estryn-Behar et al., 1990	1,505 nurses (F)	LBP in past 12 months MMH (high vs. low)	Postural load (high vs. low) MMH	2.1 2.0	NA NA	19% 21%
Gilad and Kirschenbaum, 1986	250 production workers (M)	BP in past 12 months (59%)	Lifting (frequent vs. never)	3.1	1.1-8.7	35%
Holmström, Lindell, and Moritz, 1992a, 1992b	1,772 construction workers (M)	LBP in past 12 months (54%)	MMH (every 5 min vs. less) Daily stooping (> 4 h vs. <1h)	1.1 1.3	1.0-1.3 1.1-1.5	11% 22%
Magnusson et al., 1996	228 drivers and 137 sedentary workers (M)	LBP in past 12 months (58% and 42%)	WBV (yes/no) Lifting (frequent vs. none) Lifting > 10 kg (frequent vs. none)	1.8 1.6 1.9	1.2-2.8 1.0-2.4 1.2-2.8	27% NA NA

continues

APPENDIX TABLE 4.1 Continued

Author	Study Population	Outcomes	Work-Related Risk Factor	Risk	95% Confidence Interval	Attributable Fraction Exposed
Ory et al., 1997	418 tannery workers (M)	LBP in past 12 months (61%)	Lifting (regular over 20 kg vs. seldom)	3.5	1.4-8.8	NA
Pietri et al., 1992	1,709 commercial travellers (M & F)	LBP in past 12 months (27%)	WBV (> 20 h vs. < 10 h)	2.0	1.3-3.1	39%
			Frequent load carrying	1.3	1.0-1.7	22%
			Prolonged standing (yes/no)	1.3	1.0-1.6	14%
Riihimäki et al., 1989a	852 machine operators, 696 carpenters, 674 office clerks	Sciatica in past 12 months (34%, 29% and 19%)	Bending and twisting (rather much vs. rather little)	1.5	1.2-1.9	NA
Smedley et al., 1995	1,616 nurses (F)	LBP in past 12 months (45%)	Lifting (> 1 patient/day)	1.3	1.1-1.6	13%
Suadicani et al., 1994	469 steel workers (M&F)	LBP in past 12 months (50%)	Lifting (> 1 year heavy objects vs. 0)	2.4	1.5-3.6	28%
			Awkward posture (> 1 year vs. 0)	2.4	1.6-3.7	28%
Waters et al., 1999	284 industrial workers (M)	LBP in past 12 months (30%)	Lifting (lifting index > 1)	2.1	1.1-4.0	43%
Wells et al., 1983	196 letter carriers, 76 meter readers, 127 clerks (M)	Significant BP (28%, 21% and 11%)	Carrying weight (yes/no)	2.2	1.3-3.7	46%

NOTE: M = male; F = female; BP = back pain; LBP = low-back pain; WBV = whole-body vibration; MMH = manual material handling; NA = not available.

APPENDIX TABLE 4.2 Significant Associations Between Work-Related Risk Factors and the Occurrence of Back Disorders, Expressed as Odds Ratio, in Cross-Sectional Community, Based on Epidemiologic Studies

Author	Study Population	Outcomes	Work-Related Risk Factor	Risk	95% Confidence Interval	Attributable Fraction Exposed
Heliovaara et al., 1991	2,946 Finnish women and 2,727 Finnish men	Medically diagnosed LBP (12% and 12%)	Physical load (yes/no)	2.6	2.1-3.2	56%
		Medically diagnosed sciatica (5% and 6%)	Physical load (yes/no)	2.5	1.8-3.4	58%
Houtman et al., 1994	5,865 Dutch workers (M&F)	Back complaints (25%)	Heavy physical load (yes/no)	1.6	1.4-1.9	NA
Leigh and Sheetz, 1989	1,414 U.S.A workers (M&F)	BP in past 12 months (20%)	Heavy physical load (yes/no)	1.7	1.1-2.9	37%
Liira et al., 1996	8,020 Canadian blue-collar workers (M&F)	Long-term back problems (8.4%)	Bends & lifts (> 50x/day)	1.7	1.3-2.2	39%
			Frequent lifts < 50 lb	1.5	1.1-1.9	32%
			WBV (yes/no)	1.8	1.3-2.7	46%
			Awkward back posture	2.3	1.7-3.2	57%
Linton, 1990	22,180 Swedish workers (M&F)	LBP in past 12 months with medical consultation (16%)	Lifting heavy loads (yes/no)	1.8	1.5-2.1	NA
			Awkward postures (yes/no)	2.2	1.8-2.6	NA
			Vibration (yes/no)	1.8	1.5-2.2	NA
Saraste and Hultman, 1987	2,872 Swedish women and men	LBP (36%)	Bends & twists (always/no)	2.6	2.1-3.3	56%
			Daily heavy lifting (yes/no)	1.9	1.6-2.3	40%
			WBV (yes/no)	2.1	1.3-3.5	52%
			Repetitive work (always/no)	2.0	1.6-2.4	41%

continues

APPENDIX TABLE 4.2 Continued

Author	Study Population	Outcomes	Work-Related Risk Factor	Risk	95% Confidence Interval	Attributable Fraction Exposed
Svensson and Andersson, 1983	940 Swedish men ages 40-47	LBP in past month (31%)	Frequent lifting (yes/no)	1.7	1.1-2.6	36%
			Heavy physical load (yes/no)	1.5	1.0-2.4	31%
Svensson and Andersson, 1989	1,410 Swedish women	LBP in past month (35%)	Regularly bending (yes/no)	1.4	1.1-1.8	21%
Xu, Bach, and Orhede, 1997	5,940 workers (M&F)	LBP in past 12 months (43%)	Bending and (all the time vs. seldom) twisting	2.0	1.7-2.4	32%
			Heavy physical load (all the time vs. seldom)	2.5	1.6-3.9	35%
			Whole-body vibration (all the time vs. seldom)	1.8	1.2-2.7	23%
			Standing (all the time vs. seldom)	1.6	1.3-1.8	22%

NOTE: M = male; F = female; BP = back pain; LBP = low-back pain; WBV = whole-body vibration; NA = not available.

APPENDIX TABLE 4.3 Significant Associations Between Work-Related Risk Factors and the Occurrence of Back Disorders, Expressed as Relative Risk, in Longitudinal Epidemiologic Studies Among Occupational Populations

Author	Study Population	Outcomes	Work-Related Risk Factor	Risk	95% Confidence Interval	Attributable Fraction Exposed
Boshuizen, Bongers, and Hulshof, 1990	789 tractor drivers (M)	Sickness absence > 28 days due to back disorders	WBV ($a_z > 0.4$ m/s^2)	1.5	1.0-2.1	32%
		Due to intervertebral disc	WBV ($a_z > 0.4$ m/s^2)	73.1	1.2-8.3	68%
Gardner, Landsittel, and Nelson, 1999	31,076 material handlers in retail merchandise stores	BP claim due to material handling (2.8%/year)	Material handling (lifting jobs versus light lifting jobs)	1.6	1.2-1.9	38%
Kraus et al., 1997	31,000 employees (M&F) in retail stores	BP claim (± 3.4%/year)	Lifting (frequently lifting or carrying loads > 11.35 kg)	2.9	2.6-3.3	66%
Pietri, 1992	601 commercial travellers	LBP incidence (13%/year)	WBV (> 20 h vs. < 10 h)	3.3	1.0-10.5	70%
Smedley et al., 1997	838 female nurses (no LBP in past month)	LBP incidence (47% cumulative incidence / 2 year)	Lifting (≥ 1 patient vs. 0)	1.4	1.0-1.9	19%
			Transfer (≥ 5 patients vs. less)	1.6	1.1-2.3	18%
Stobbe et al., 1988	415 nurses (F)	BP claim (5.2%/year)	Lifting (> 5 patients vs. < 2)	2.2	1.1-4.2	54%
Venning, Walter, and Stitt, 1987	4,306 nurses (M&F)	BP claim (2.8%/year)	Lifting (≥ 1 patient vs. 0)	2.2	NA	54%

NOTE: M = male; F = female; BP = back pain; LBP = low-back pain; WBV = whole-body vibration; NA = not available.

APPENDIX TABLE 4.4 Significant Associations Between Work-Related Risk Factors and the Occurrence of Back Disorders, Expressed as Odds Ratio, in Case-Control Epidemiologic Studies Among Occupational Populations

Author	Study Population	Outcomes	Work-Related Risk Factor	Risk	95% Confidence Interval	Attributable Fraction Exposed
Josephson and Vingard, 1998	81 female nurses (referents: 188 female nurses)	LBP medical care	Severe trunk flexion (at least 1 hour/day)	4.3	1.6-12	NA
			High perceived exertion (PPE - Borg ≥ 14)	2.3	1.2-4.5	NA
Kelsey et al., 1984	325 medical patients (referents: 241 care seekers in same clinics)	Acute prolapsed lumbar intervertebral disc	Lifting loads > 11.3 kg (25lb)(> 25 times/day)	3.5	1.5-8.5	NA
			Carrying loads > 11.3 kg (25lb)(> 25 times/day)	2.7	1.2-5.8	NA
Nuwayhid, Stewart, and Johnson, 1993	115 fire fighters (referents: 109 fire fighters)	LBP claim	Physical exertion on job	3.7	1.9-7.1	NA
			Lifting (> 18 kg vs. less)	3.1	1.3-7.9	NA
			Climbing (> 100 steps/ day vs. less)	2.3	1.2-4.4	NA
Punnett et al., 1991	95 assembly workers (referents: 124 assembly workers)	LBP claim	Bends & twists (100% vs. 0%)	8.1	1.5-44.0	NA
			Lifting (> 44.5 N/minute)	2.2	1.0-4.7	NA

NOTE: LBP = low-back pain; PPE = perceived physical exertion; NA = not available.

APPENDIX TABLE 4.5 Associations Between Work-Related Risk Factors and the Occurrence of Upper Extremity Disorders, Expressed as Odds Ratio, in Epidemiologic Studies Among Occupational Populations

Author	Study Population	Outcomes	Work-Related Risk Factor	Risk[a]	95% Confidence Interval	Attributable Fraction Exposed[b]
Silverstein, Fine, and Armstrong, 1986	574 industrial workers	Hand/wrist CTDs (Sx & PE)	High force/low repetition	OR=5.2	1.1-25.0	78%
		Hand/wrist CTDs (Sx & PE)	Low force/high repetition	OR=3.3	0.7-15.9	78%
		Hand/wrist CTDs (Sx & PE)	High force/high repetition	OR=29.1	5.9-142.7	93%
Bovenzi, Fiorito, and Volpe, 1987	67 foundry workers and 46 manual laborers	Olecranon spurs (X-ray)	Hand-held vibrating tools: frequency-weighted energy-equivalent acceleration for 4 hours	OR=2.6	1.2-5.8	44%
		Osteoarthritis in elbow (X-ray)	Hand-held vibrating tools: frequency-weighted energy-equivalent acceleration for 4 hours	OR=2.1	0.6-6.9	47%
		Calcification in elbows (X-ray)	Hand-held vibrating tools: frequency-weighted energy-equivalent acceleration for 4 hours	OR=1.7	0.4-6.8	38%

continues

APPENDIX TABLE 4.5 Continued

Author	Study Population	Outcomes	Work-Related Risk Factor	Risk[a]	95% Confidence Interval	Attributable Fraction Exposed[b]
		Bone cysts in wrist (X-ray)	Hand-held vibrating tools: frequency-weighted energy-equivalent acceleration for 4 hours	OR=1.0	0.4-2.3	0
		Osteoarthritis in wrist (X-ray)	Hand-held vibrating tools: frequency-weighted energy-equivalent acceleration for 4 hours	OR=5.3	1.1-24.7	78%
		Osteoarthritis in shoulder (X-ray)	Hand-held vibrating tools: frequency-weighted energy-equivalent acceleration for 4 hours	OR=0.4	0.1-1.6	NA
Silverstein, Fine, and Armstrong, 1987	652 industrial workers	CTS (Sx & PE)	High force/low repetition	OR=1.8	0.2-20.6	38%
		CTS (Sx & PE)	Low force/high repetition	OR=2.7	0.3-28.4	70%
		CTS (Sx & PE)	High force/high repetition	OR=15.5	1.7-141.5	88%

Study	Population	Outcome	Exposure	OR	CI	%
Bovenzi, Franzinelli, and Strambi, 1988	76 stonedrillers and stonecutters and 60 controls	Raynaud's/VWF	Hand-held vibrating tools: frequency-weighted energy-equivalent acceleration for 4 hours	OR=6.1	2.2-17.0	77%
Nilsson, Burstrom, and Hagberg, 1989	89 platers (n=89) and 61 office workers	Raynaud's/VWF	Hand-held vibrating tools	OR=13.9	5.1-38.0	NA
	105 any vibration exposure and 45 no vibration exposure	Raynaud's/VWF	Hand-held vibrating tools	OR=56.0	11.6-269	NA
	71 current vibration exposure and 45 no vibration exposure	Raynaud's/VWF	Hand-held vibrating tools	OR=84.5	14.7-486	NA
Chiang et al., 1990	207 frozen food factory workers	CTS (Sx, PE, & NCV)	repetition and/or cold exposure	OR=7.4	2.0-27.5	89%
	86 frozen food factory workers	CTS (Sx, PE, & NCV)	repetition, but no cold exposure	OR=2.2	0.2-21.2	90%
	170 frozen food factory workers	CTS (Sx, PE, & NCV)	repetition and cold exposure	OR=9.4	2.4-37.2	89%
Bovenzi et al., 1991	34 forestry workers and 31 hospital maintenance workers	Persistent pain in any upper extremity site	<7.5 m/s^2 (vibration exposure expressed in energy-equivalent frequency-weighted acceleration)	OR=2.7	Not significant	NA

continues

APPENDIX TABLE 4.5 Continued

Author	Study Population	Outcomes	Work-Related Risk Factor	Risk[a]	95% Confidence Interval	Attributable Fraction Exposed[b]
	31 forestry workers and 31 hospital maintenance workers	Persistent pain in any upper extremity site	>7.5 m/s^2 (vibration exposure expressed in energy-equivalent frequency-weighted acceleration)	OR=14.1	P<0.005	NA
	34 forestry workers and 31 hospital maintenance workers	At least one muscle-tendon syndrome (Sx & PE)	<7.5 m/s^2 (vibration exposure expressed in energy-equivalent frequency-weighted acceleration)	OR=6.0	P<0.005	NA
	31 forestry workers and 31 hospital maintenance workers	At least one muscle-tendon syndrome (Sx & PE)	>7.5 m/s^2 (vibration exposure expressed in energy-equivalent frequency-weighted acceleration)	OR=11.9	P<0.0001	NA
	34 forestry workers and 31 hospital maintenance workers	Carpal tunnel syndrome (Sx & PE)	<7.5 m/s^2 (vibration exposure expressed in energy-equivalent frequency-weighted acceleration)	OR=13.6	P<0.03	NA

continues

			OR=39.8	P<0.0001	NA
31 forestry workers and 31 hospital maintenance workers	Carpal tunnel syndrome (Sx & PE)	>7.5 m/s^2 (vibration exposure expressed in energy-equivalent frequency-weighted acceleration)			
Bovenzi, 1994					
137 vibration-exposed stone workers and 258 unexposed controls	HAV—sensorineural disturbances (Sx)	Hand-held vibrating tools: ln (lifetime vibration dose) > 24 m^2·h^3/s^4	OR=4.69	2.81-7.82	73%
137 vibration-exposed stone workers and 258 unexposed controls	Symptoms of VWF	Hand-held vibrating tools: ln (lifetime vibration dose) > 24 m^2·h^3/s^4	OR=27.3	13.1-56.6	93%
137 vibration-exposed stone workers and 258 unexposed controls	CTS (Sx & PE)	Hand-held vibrating tools: ln (lifetime vibration dose) > 24 m^2·h^3/s^4	OR=3.24	1.21-8.69	83%
137 vibration-exposed stone workers and 258 unexposed controls	Dupuytren's contracture	Hand-held vibrating tools: ln (lifetime vibration dose) > 24 m^2·h^3/s^4	OR=3.20	1.39-7.37	82%
137 vibration-exposed stone workers and 258 unexposed controls	Muscular weakness	Hand-held vibrating tools: ln (lifetime vibration dose) > 24 m^2·h^3/s^4	OR=14.7	3.25-66.6	95%
137 vibration-exposed stone workers and 258 unexposed controls	Pain in the upper limbs	Hand-held vibrating tools: ln (lifetime vibration dose) > 24 m^2·h^3/s^4	OR=3.15	1.91-5.20	69%

APPENDIX TABLE 4.5 Continued

Author	Study Population	Outcomes	Work-Related Risk Factor	Risk[a]	95% Confidence Interval	Attributable Fraction Exposed[b]
Moore and Garg, 1994	Pork processing workers	Total UEMSDs	"Hazardous" vs. "safe" (dichotomized on Strain Index)	RR=11.7	P<0.001	NA
	Pork processing workers	Total UEMSDs excluding CTS	"Hazardous" vs. "safe" (dichotomized on Strain Index)	RR=38.9	P<0.001	NA
	Pork processing workers	Total "specific disorders"	"Hazardous" vs. "safe" (dichotomized on Strain Index)	RR=6.9	P≤0.02	NA
	Pork processing workers	Specific disorders excluding CTS	"Hazardous" vs. "safe" (dichotomized on Strain Index)	RR=19.4	P≤0.02	NA
	Pork processing workers	CTS (Sx and NCV)	"Hazardous" vs. "safe" (dichotomized on Strain Index)	RR=2.8	P=0.44	NA
Bovenzi et al., 1995	56 forestry workers and 194 controls	VWF (Sx and abnormal digital artery response to cold provocation)	Hand-held vibrating tools: In (lifetime vibration dose) < 19 m²s⁻⁴hd	OR=4.06	1.06-16.4	65%

Study	Population	Outcome	Exposure	OR	CI	%
	56 forestry workers and 194 controls	VWF (Sx and abnormal digital artery response to cold provocation)	Hand-held vibrating tools: ln (lifetime vibration dose) = 19-20 m^2s^{-4}hd	OR=4.65	1.34-16.1	76%
	56 forestry workers and 194 controls	VWF (Sx and abnormal digital artery response to cold provocation)	Hand-held vibrating tools: ln (lifetime vibration dose) = 20-21 m^2s^{-4}hd	OR=9.37	3.10-28.4	88%
	56 forestry workers and 194 controls	VWF (Sx and abnormal digital artery response to cold provocation)	Hand-held vibrating tools: ln (lifetime vibration dose) > 21 m^2s^{-4}hd	OR=34.3	11.9-99.2	95%
Roquelaure et al., 1997	65 factory workers and 65 case controls	CTS (Sx, PE, NCV, and/or surgery for CTS)	Force greater than 1 kg	OR=9.0	2.4-33.4	NA
	65 factory workers and 65 case controls	CTS (Sx, PE, NCV, and/or surgery for CTS)	Elementary operation (cycle time) ≤ 10 sec	OR=8.8	1.8-44.4	NA
Latko et al., 1999	352 manufacturing workers	Nonspecific upper extremity discomfort	Hand repetition ("low" vs. "high")	OR=2.45	1.42-4.24	53%
	352 manufacturing workers	Tendinitis	Hand repetition ("low" vs. "high")	OR=3.23	1.27-8.26	71%
	352 manufacturing workers	CTS (hand diagram)	Hand repetition ("low" vs. "high")	OR=2.32	1.07-4.99	61%
	352 manufacturing workers	CTS (hand diagram & NCV)	Hand repetition ("low" vs. "high")	OR=3.11	0.89-10.87	66%
Lundström et al., 1999	125 vibration-exposed and 45 nonexposed	Impaired multifrequency vibrotactile sensation (both hands)	Cumulative vibration exposure (nonexposed vs. CVE up to 24,000 meters-hours/sec^2)	OR=1.3	0.25-7.03	NA

APPENDIX TABLE 4.5 Continued

Author	Study Population	Outcomes	Work-Related Risk Factor	Risk[a]	95% Confidence Interval	Attributable Fraction Exposed[b]
	125 vibration-exposed and 45 nonexposed	Impaired multifrequency vibrotactile sensation (both hands)	Cumulative vibration exposure (nonexposed vs. CVE greater than 24,000 meters-hours/sec²)	OR=3.3	1.41-7.57	NA
	125 vibration-exposed and 45 nonexposed	Impaired multifrequency vibrotactile sensation (both hands)	Cumulative vibration exposure (CVE greater than 24,000 meters-hours/sec² vs. CVE up to 24,000 meters-hours/sec²)	OR=2.6	1.32-4.98	NA

[a]Odds ratios adjusted for age and other factors, if available.
[b]Attributable fractions were not presented by the article authors and, therefore, were calculated using results available from the data presented in the published studies.

NOTE: CTD = cumulative trauma disorder; CTS = carpal tunnel syndrome; CVE = cumulative vibration exposure ; HAV = hand-arm vibration; NA = not available; NCV = nerve conduction velocity; OR = odds ratio; PE = physical examination; Sx = symptoms; RR = relative risk; UEMSD = upper extremity musculoskeletal disorder; VWF = vibration white finger.

APPENDIX TABLE 4.6 Epidemiologic Studies Providing Supportive Evidence on Associations of Physical Factors with Upper Extremity Musculoskeletal Disorders

Author	Study Population	Outcomes	Work-Related Risk Factor	Risk	95% Confidence Interval	Comments
Load or Force						
Gorsche et al., 1998	665 meat packing workers	Incidence of trigger finger ~1-yr follow-up	Hand tool use (yes/no)	OR = 4.7		Knife use Digits 3 & 4 most frequently affected
Kurppa et al., 1991	Meat packing plant employees— 377 strenuous and 338 nonstrenuous	Tenosynovitis, peritendinitis, epicondylitis (clinical diagnosis)	Level of physical work (cutters, sausage makers, packers)	Tenosynovitis (OR = 18) Epicondylitis (OR = 7.8)		Physical work not measured —repetition and force; Incidence per 100 hour reported
Luoparjärvi et al., 1979	152 assembly line packers and 133 shop assistants	Muscle-tendon syndrome (clinical diagnosis)	Repetition and/or static load by job group (yes/no)	OR = 4 crude ratio		Grasping and forceful movements in addition

continues

APPENDIX TABLE 4.6 Continued

Author	Study Population	Outcomes	Work-Related Risk Factor	Risk	95% Confidence Interval	Comments
Ohlsson et al., 1995	82 female industrial workers and 64 controls	Neck, shoulder, hand-wrist, elbow pain, tendinitis, neck tension, etc. (Sx, physical exam, blood and urine)	Repetition (yes/no) pressing and assembling fuses	POR = 4.6	1.9-12	Job category used as index of exposure; workers taped, controls not taped
Roto and Kivi, 1984	90 meatcutters and 77 construction foremen	Epicondylitis, tenosynovitis (PE and Sx)	Meatcutting (yes/no)	Epicondylitis Tenosynovitis	-6.4	0.99-40.9
Stetson et al., 1993	Industrial workers in high exposure jobs—103 with hand/wrist symptoms, 137 asymptomatic, and 105 controls	Median and ulnar nerve dysfunction (Sx-questionnaire, electrophysiological measures)	Repetition, force, hand grip, posture, etc. (low, medium, high)	Distal conduction significantly lower for those with symptoms		Gripping and carrying loads associated with reduced NCV
Vibration						
Bovenzi, Petronio, and Di Marino, 1980	169 caulkers, 50 welders, and 10 electricians	Raynaud's (Sx), temperature differences	Vibration (yes/no)	OR = 4.7		All caulkers exposed regularly, others rarely if ever

Study	Population	Outcome measure	Exposure	Risk estimate	Comments
Brubaker et al., 1983	147 tree fellers and 142 controls	VWF, Raynaud's (Sx, delayed finger rewarming)	Vibration (yes/no); over 11 years	OR = 53.0	70% occurrence with 11-15 years exposure; 75% with 20 years
Burdorf and Monster, 1991	101 riveters and bucketers and 76 controls	VWF (Sx) self reports, questionnaire	Vibration (yes/no); work samples, self reports	OR = 3.0	Analysis based on job titles—no quantitative data used
Härkönen et al., 1984	279 lumberjacks and 279 peat bog workers	VWF (Sx) self reports, questionnaire	Vibration (yes/no)	OR = 6 crude ratio	Mean 10 yrs exposure-dose response demonstrated
Iwata, Makimo, and Miyashita, 1987	Student nurses and examinees at health care center —635 males and 835 females	Raynaud's, stiffness, numbness (self report)	No exposure to vibration— females with higher incidence	OR = 1.69	
Kaji et al., 1993	384 carpentry, forestry, and mining	Bracial arteriography (hyopthenar hammer syndrome)	Vibration	7.2% occurrence (HHS)	No control
Kiveka et al., 1994	213 lumberjacks and 140 controls (camp workers)	VWF (Sx, clinical exam, radiographs)	Vibration	Risk Ratio = 8.9; 2.5-28.9	Risk ratio for lumberjacks (25 years exposure)

continues

APPENDIX TABLE 4.6 Continued

Author	Study Population	Outcomes	Work-Related Risk Factor	Risk	95% Confidence Interval	Comments
Koskimies et al., 1992	Forest workers (1972-1990; n varies between 118 and 205)	VWF numbness (Sx, self report, clinical exam)	Vibration (1,500 hours of chainsaw operation); chainsaw redesign over time	Prevalence rate reduced from 40% to 5%		
Letz et al., 1992	271 shipyard workers—53 no vibration, 115 part-time vibration, and 103 full-time vibration	HAV (questionnaire responses, vascular scale, VWF, numbness)	Vibration (3 levels)	Prevalence—Numbness: High = 84%; Med = 50% None = 17% White finger: High = 71% Med = 33% None = 6%		OR=2.9 when vascular stage was polychotomous outcome variable (CI = 1.7-5.0) for each log unit increase in total hours of vibration tool use; OR = 1.8 (CI = 1.2-2.9) when sensorineural stage was the outcome
McKenna et al., 1993	Riveters (46 matched with 46 controls	Systolic blood pressure (after cold	Vibration (riveter —non riveter);	OR = 7.7 Incidence C		

Study	Population	Outcome measure	Exposure measure	Results	CI / p-value	Comments
	on age and smoking status)	immersion, after work; 3 circulating markers of vascular activity)	Counter pressure group, gun holder group, both	pressure = 45% Gun holder = 10% Both = 27%		
Nagata et al., 1993	179 forestry workers and chainsaw operators, and 205 controls	Raynaud's, sclerodactyly hand edema (clinical exam, interviews)	Vibration (yes/no)	Raynaud's: OR = 7.06 Sclerodactyly: OR = 6.54 (long term) OR = 7.05 (short term)	2.51-19.87 3.30-13.36 3.41-14.60	
Taylor et al., 1984	30 stone cutters	VWF (PE)	Vibration (yes)	80% VFW		No controls
Virokannas, 1995	31 railway workers and 32 lumberjacks	Sensory disturbances in peripheral nerves (VPT, clinical exam, ENMG)	Vibration (hand held tamping machines vs. chainsaws)	Exposure duration & VPT (log scale) Rail workers: r = .55-.47 Lumberjacks: r = .77-.59	p=.017-.001 p=.003-.0001	

Posture and Vibration

Study	Population	Outcome measure	Exposure measure	Results
Dimberg et al., 1989	2,814 industrial workers in aircraft engine division	Cervobracial (Sx, self report, quest, clinical exam)	Physical work (low, medium, high based on amount of body rotation); vibration (yes/no)	Vibration (OR = 2.0) Prevalence significantly higher for shoulder, neck, and hand symptoms in high work condition

continues

APPENDIX TABLE 4.6 Continued

Author	Study Population	Outcomes	Work-Related Risk Factor	Risk	95% Confidence Interval	Comments
Posture and Motion						
Bernard et al., 1994	973 newspaper workers	Neck, shoulder, hand-wrist pain (Sx) self report	Hours of keyboard use (work sample, self-report)	Hand-wrist OR = 2.5	1.6 - 3.9	
Murata et al., 1996	23 VDT workers and 19 students	NCV median nerve	VDT use > 6 hrs/day	Mean differences wrist-finger, wrist-palm	p<0.001	Students: very minor VDT use
Sauter, Schleiffer, and Knutson, 1991	539 VDT workers in two state agencies —detailed analysis for 40	Upper extremity discomfort (self report by body region)	Workstation layout (e.g., keyboard height)	Significant r² for upper arm angle, relative keyboard height, relative document distance, right hand extended; Overall adjusted r² modest		No epidemiologic measures, no psychosocial measures
All Exposures (and Load)						
Franklin et al., 1991	Workers in Washington State reporting CTS	CTS based on workers' compensation claims	Analysis by industry	Rate ratio: 13.8 (meat packing); 1.1 (Clerical NOC)	Meat packing (11.6-16.4) Cler NOC (0.1-0.1)	

Schierhout, Meyers, and Bridger, 1995	401 workers from 7 sectors of manufacturing industry (11 factories, 46 jobs with ergonomic stressors)	Musculoskeletal pain (self-report body diagnosis)	Posture, repetition, force, vibration, and other workplace environment factors	Neck/shoulder (repetition) OR = 5.38	1.16-25	
				Forearm, wrist, hand (wrist posture) OR = 10.2	1.39-75.6	
Stenlund, 1993	Construction workers—54 bricklayers, 55 rock blasters, and 98 foremen	Shoulder tendinitis (PE, medical history)	Load, vibration, hours of exposure	Rockblasters vs. foremen: OR = 3.3 left shoulder	1.21-9.15	
				OR = 1.71 right shoulder	0.71-4.17	
				Vibration: OR = 1.84 left shoulder	1.10-3.07	
				OR = 1.66 right shoulder	1.06-2.61	
Stenlund et al., 1992	Construction workers—54 bricklayers, 55 rock blasters, and 98 foremen	Osteoarthrosis acromioclavicular joints (radiograph)	Load, years of lifting, vibration	Right side: Load: OR = 3.18	1.09-0.24	Exposure based on job title (all subjective)
				Vibration: OR = 2.18	1.04-4.56	
				Left side: Load: OR = 10.34	3.10-34.46	
				Vibration: OR = 3.13	1.40-6.99	

continues

APPENDIX TABLE 4.6 Continued

Author	Study Population	Outcomes	Work-Related Risk Factor	Risk	95% Confidence Interval	Comments
Wells et al., 1983	Letter carriers—104 with weight increase and 92 without weight increase; 76 meter readers; and 127 postal clerks	Significant joint problems (questionnaire and point scale)	Carrying weight (increased, standard, none), walking (yes/no)	Increased weight: 23% shoulder, 31% back; Standard weight: 13% shoulder, 24% back; Meter readers: 7% shoulder, 21% back; Postal clerks: 5% shoulder, 11% back		25-35 lbs vs. none
Wieslander et al., 1989	38 men who underwent surgery for CTS, 69 hospital controls, and 74 general population controls	CTS (hospital records, telephone interviews)	Repetition, load, vibration, etc. (obtained by interview)	Number of risk factors: 1: OR = 1.7; 2: OR = 3.3; >2: OR = 7.1	0.6-4.4; 1.2-9.1; 2.2-5.2	

NOTE: CTD = cumulative trauma disorder; CTS = carpal tunnel syndrome; CVE = cumulative vibration exposure; ENMG = electoneuromyography; HAV = hand-arm vibration; HHS = hypothenar hammer syndrome; NA = not available; NOC = not otherwise classified; NCV = nerve conduction velocity; OR = odds ratio; PE = physical examination; POR = prevalence odds ratio; Sx = symptoms; VPT = vibration perception threshold; VDT = video display terminal; VWF = vibration white finger.

APPENDIX TABLE 4.7 Prospective Studies of Work-Related Psychosocial Factors and Back Pain

Author	Study Population	Outcomes	Psychosocial Risk Factors	Significance[a]	Attributable Fraction[b]	Design Comments	Other Comments
Bergenuud and Nilsson, 1988	1,542 general population, 55-year-olds (575 at follow-up)	Back pain report (yes/no)	Job satisfaction (self-report, nonstandardized item) Mentally demanding work (self-report, nonstandardized)	S S	NA	Prospective 45 years	69% participation
Biering-Sörensen, Thomsen, and Hilden, 1989	928 general population	LBP report past 12 months (yes/no)	Work speed Monotony Job satisfaction (measures were self-reports, nonstandardized)	NS NS S	NA	Prospective 12 months	99% participation
Bigos et al., 1991	1,223 ages 21-67 in aircraft industry, 22% female	Reported injury (injury claim or treatment at occupational health service)	Enjoy work Work relations (both measured by Modified Work APGAR)	S S	41% (satisfaction)	Longitudinal, 12-month follow-up	Study controlled for other factors. MMPI also significant predictor
Cats-Baril and Frymoyer, 1991	252 patients with new episode of LBP, % female not stated	Reported return to work (not employed and attributed to LBP)	Job satisfaction (self-report)	S	NA	Prognostic 3 and 6 months	Psychosocial factors correctly classify 89%

continues

APPENDIX TABLE 4.7 Continued

Author	Study Population	Outcomes	Psychosocial Risk Factors	Significance[a]	Attributable Fraction[b]	Design Comments	Other Comments
Coste et al., 1994	103 primary care patients, pain <72 hours	Recovery and return to work (no reported pain, VAS, or disability, not on sick leave, Roland & Morris Disability Questionnaire)	Job satisfaction (self-report, not stated how measured)	S	NA	Prospective 5 assessments during 3 months	Low job satisfaction one of significant factors (others = pain, previous disability, compensation, male)
Fishbain et al., 1997	128 patients with back pain > 6 months, 57% female	Work status (insurance and medical records = normal employment)	Intent to work Job stress Belief work is dangerous (self-reports, nonstandardized items)	S S S	NA	Prospective 30 months	54% participation rate 75% correctly classified
Hasenbring et al., 1994	111 acute disc prolapse, 38% female	Pain intensity (self-rated, numerical scale) Recurrence (surgeon's rating yes/no) Early retirement (application made)	Daily hassles at work (self-reports, standardized)	S	NA	Prognostic 6 months	Hassles was one of two best predictors (other = depression) for early retirement

Study	Sample	Outcome	Predictor		Design	Comments
Hazard et al., 1996	166 LBP injury report, % female not stated	Return to work (self-report, not working due to LBP)	Perceived job demands S Relations at work S Perceived chance to work S Perceived blame S (Vermont Disability Prediction Questionnaire)	NA	Prospective 3 months follow-up	11 items were good predictors producing 94% sensitivity, 84% specificity. Poor participation rate (37%)
Hellsing, Linton, and Kälvemark, 1994	121 acute back pain, 48% female	Sick leave (number of sick days, National Insurance Authority)	Monotonous work S (self-report, nonstandardized)	NA	Prospective 12 months	Found function and pain intensity not to be related
Hemingway et al., 1997	6,894 male and 3,414 female office workers	Sick leave <= 7 days Sick leave > 7 days (workplace records)	Work control S Job satisfaction S Pace (self-report, nonstandardized) S	<7 days sick: control: 55%m/32%f Satisfaction: 49%m/25%f Pace: 52%m/44%f Support: 31%m/7%f Conflict: 1%m/38%f >7 days sick: Control: 38%m/48%f	Prospective	Controlled for other variables. All psychosocial factors significant before adjustment. Job satisfaction significant only in age-adjusted models

continues

APPENDIX TABLE 4.7 Continued

Author	Study Population	Outcomes	Psychosocial Risk Factors	Significance[a]	Attributable Fraction[b]	Design Comments	Other Comments
					Satisfaction: 33%m/20%f Pace: 32%m/0%f Support: 33%m/17%f Conflict: 28%m/31%f		
Hurri, 1989	188 female patients with back pain < 1 year	Return to work (self-report) Spontaneous recovery (Oswestry LBP Questionnaire)	Job satisfaction (self-report, standardized)	S	NA	Prospective not clear, 6 months	92% participation. Included guidance, influence, learning new, feedback, communication, etc.
Lancourt and Kettelhut, 1992	134 patients on workers' compensation	Return to work (not stated how measured)	Stress Job satisfaction Perceived load (self-reports, nonstandardized)	S NS S	NA	Prospective 6 months	
Leino and Hänninen, 1995	902 workers, 32% female	LBP (rated frequency, examination)	Work content Work control Social relations (self-report, standardized)	S S S	NA	Prospective 10-year follow-up	men = all women = S For white collar, blue collar only work control S

Reference	Sample	Outcome	Predictors		Percentage	Design	Comments
Linton and Halldén, 1998	142 acute spinal pain, 65% female	Sick leave (reported number of days)	Monotonous work Perceived work function Job satisfaction Belief should not work with pain (self-report, standardized)	S S S S	NA	Prospective 6 months	Adjusted for confounders. Five best predictors were fear-avoidance beliefs, perceived future pain, perceived work function, stress, and previous sick leave.
Papageorgiou et al., 1997	4,501 general population, 55% female	New episode of back pain (LBP>1 day, yes/no)	Job satisfaction Social relations Sufficient money (self-report, nonstandardized)	S S S	Satisfaction: 41% Social relations: 29%	Prospective 12 months	Dissatisfied twice as likely to experience a new episode
Ready et al., 1993	131 nurses	Back injury (claims at work)	Job satisfaction (RR=2.29, 1.08 - 4.85) (self-report, nonstandardized)	S	56%	Prospective 18 months	91% participation rate
Riihimäki et al., 1989b	167 concrete workers and 161 house painters	Sciatic pain (self-report, pain radiating to a leg)	Job stress (self-report, nonstandardized)	S	17%	Longitudinal 5 years	The effect was relatively small

continues

APPENDIX TABLE 4.7 Continued

Author	Study Population	Outcomes	Psychosocial Risk Factors	Significance[a]	Attributable Fraction[b]	Design Comments	Other Comments
Riihimäki et al., 1994	From 2,222 male longshoremen, construction, carpenters, and office workers selected 1,149 without pain	Cumulative incidence (3 yrs) of sciatic pain (self-report, pain radiating to a leg)	Work pace Monotonous work Problems in relations with workmates/supervisors (self-report, nonstandardized)	S S S	48% (relations with work mates)	Prospective 36 months	
Rossignol, Lortie, and Ledoux, 1993	269 aircraft assembly workers	Compensation past year (workers' compensation) Absenteeism past year (company records) Work limitation past wk. (rating) Back symptom past wk. (duration, quality, frequency)	Boredom Job satisfaction: Compensation Other outcomes (OR>=3.0) (self-report, nonstandardized)	NS NS S	66%	Longitudinal 12 months	76% participation

Reference	Sample	Outcome measures		Attributable fractions[b]	Study design	Comments
van der Weide et al., 1999	142 workers on sickleave >10 days for LBP; Participation = 85%	Functional disability (Roland & Morris Disability Questionnaire) Time to return to work (computerized records, days to return)	12 months for function: Lack of work variation — S; Emotional (work) effort — S; Lack of energy at work — S; Social isolation at work — S; Job satisfaction — S; For time to work: Relations with colleagues — S; Work tempo — S; Work quantity (self-report, nonstandardized) — S	Lack of variation: 23% per 10 units (0-100 scale) Satisfaction: 69% Social isolation: 88%	Prospective 3 and 12 months	The main factors found were radiating pain, functional disability at pretest, relations with colleagues, and high work tempo/quantity
van Poppel et al., 1998	238 males with heavy work	New episode LBP (self-report, yes/no) Sick leave, LBP (self-report, number of days)	Job satisfaction (self-report, standardized) — S	New episode: 17% Sick leave: 17%	Longitudinal	Controlled for earlier back pain, age, etc.

[a]Results of the relationship are denoted as S for a significant finding and NS for not significant.
[b]Attributable fractions were not presented by the article authors and, therefore, were calculated using results available from the data presented in the published studies.

NOTE: m = male; f = female; LBP = low back pain; NA = not available; NCV = nerve conduction velocity; PE = physical examination; Sx = symptoms; VAS = visual analog scale; VWF = vibration white finger.

APPENDIX TABLE 4.8 Prospective/Longitudinal Studies of Individual Psychological Risk Factors

Author	Study Population	Outcomes	Psychosocial Risk Factors[a]	Attributable Fraction[b]	Design Comments	Other Comments
Adams, Mannion, and Dolan, 1999	403 health care workers with no serious back pain, 92% female	"Serious" back pain (medical attention or time off work)	Distress: + Depression: + Health locus of control: 0 (3 standardized questionnaires)	Distress and depression: 23%	Prospective 3 years	90% participation rate. Included medical factors. Lateral bending, long back, lumbar lordosis, and previous back pain also predictors.
Bigos et al., 1991	3,020 (1,223 participated) aircraft workers, 22% female	Reported injury (injury claim or treatment at occupational health service)	Enjoy work: - MMPI (hysteria): + Work relation: - (enjoy work, MMPI best predictors) (Standardized: Work APGAR)	Enjoy work: 41%	Prospective 3 years	Study controlled for other factors
Burton et al., 1995	252 LBP, primary care, 48% female	Disability (Roland & Morris questionnaire)	Distress: + Catastrophize: + Pain intensity: + Pray/hoping: + Dysfunction: + (5 standardized questionnaires)	NA	Prospective 1 year	Strong design. 76% correctly classified, psychosocial factors better predictors than standard medical/history variables

Cats-Baril and Frymoyer, 1991	250 patients, new episode LBP, % female not stated	Reported return to work (not employed and attributed to LBP)	Work satisfaction, Status: - Perceived injury as compensatable: - Education level: - (self-reports, nonstandardized)	NA	Prognostic 3 and 6 months	Predictive model with psychosocial factors correctly predicts 89%
Croft et al., 1996	4,501 general population, % female not stated	New episodes of pain (either a consultation or self-reported symptoms in postal survey)	Distress: - (standardized; General Health Questionnaire)	44%	Prospective 12 months	1.8 increase even when bias factors controlled
Cherkin et al., 1996a	219 primary care patients LBP, 47% female	Symptom satisfaction (self-report, standardized)	Depression: + (standardized, Symptom Checklist-90 Depression Scale)	52%	Prospective 12 months	Depression (OR=2.3), Pain below knee (OR=2.2)
Dionne et al., 1997	1,213 primary care, acute LBP, 53% female	Disability	Somatization: + Depression: +	NA	Prospective 24 months	85% correctly classified with depression and somatization

continues

APPENDIX TABLE 4.8 Continued

Author	Study Population	Outcomes	Psychosocial Risk Factors[a]	Attributable Fraction[b]	Design Comments	Other Comments
Engel, von Korff, and Katon, 1996	1,059 primary care, LBP, 53% female	Costs (computerized records, back pain, and total)	Depression: + (Standardized; Symptom Checklist 90-Depression Scale) Pain: + (1. standardized; Graded Chronic Pain Scale; 2.0 number of days/6 months)	Depression: 38% Pain: 70%	Prospective 12 months	Pain status and disc disorders strong predictors, depression also predicted high costs.
Estlander, Takala, and Viikari-Juntura, 1998	452 forestry-industry workers with neck, shoulder or back pain	Change in pain status (standardized ratings)	Distress: 0 Depression: 0 Self-efficacy: 0 Work Prognosis: 0 Disability: + Work characteristics: 0 (3 standardized, 3 nonstandardized questionnaires)	NA	Prospective 24 months	Distress, self-efficacy, depression, and work prognosis were significant in univariate analyses. All had pain at baseline.

Feyer et al., 2000	694 nursing students (61% participation at 1 year), 85% female	New episode(s) of back pain (self-report, yes/no)	During training: Distress: +; Life events: +; Job satisfaction: + At 1 year: Distress: +; Life events: 0; Job satisfaction: 0 (3 standardized questionnaires)	During training; Distress: 30%; Life events: 5%; Satisfaction: 2% At 1 year: Distress: 63%; Life events: NA; Satisfaction: NA	Prospective Every 6 months up to 3 years	Relatively low participation rate (61%). Controlled for previous back pain and other confounders.
Fishbain et al., 1997	128 patients with back pain > 6 months, 57% female	Work status (insurance and medical records = normal employment)	Gender: +; Intent to work: +; Job stress: +; Age: +; Education: +; Belief work dangerous: + (nonstandardized questionnaire)	NA	Prospective 30 months (work assessed retrospectively)	75% correctly classified at 30 months
Gatchel et al., 1994	152 chronic LBP, 36% female	Return to work (self-report; yes/no)	Psychopathology: 0 (standardized; SCID)	NA	Prospective Prognosis 12 months	If psychopathology is addressed, it does not affect outcome

continues

APPENDIX TABLE 4.8 Continued

Author	Study Population	Outcomes	Psychosocial Risk Factors[a]	Attributable Fraction[b]	Design Comments	Other Comments
Gatchel, Polatin, and Kinney, 1995	324 acute LBP, 36% female	Return to work (self-report; yes/no)	Pain and disability score: + Axis I depression, anxiety, substance abuse disorders: 0 Axis II personality disorder: + MMPI Hysteria: + (Standardized questionnaires and interview)	Pain and disability: 38% Axis II personality: 49%	Prospective 6 months	Pain and disability are important predictors even when injury severity and work controlled for. 87% correctly classified.
Gatchel, Polatin, and Mayer, 1995	421 patients with acute back pain, 38% female	Job status (self-report and insurance data)	Pain and disability: - Psychopathology: 0 MMPI: - (Standardized; MMPI, SCID)	Pain and disability: 38% MMPI: 33%	Prospective 3, 6, 9, 12 months	91% correctly classified robust psychological factor; psychopathology does not predispose
Hansen, Biering-Sörensen, and Schroll, 1995	673 general population, 43% female	Back pain (10 prevalence; yes/no)	MMPI: 0 (standardized; MMPI)	NA	Prospective 10 and 20 years	MMPI not related to a new episode

Hasenbring et al., 1994	111 acute disc prolapse, 38% female	Pain intensity (numerical scale) Recurrence (surgeon's rating) Early retirement (application made)	Depression: + Avoidance: + Nonverbal pain behavior: + Search social support: + (4 standardized questionnaires)	NA	Prognostic 6 months	Psychosocial variables correctly classified 70%, while all variables classified= 86% Psychosocial variables are most important
Hazard et al., 1996	166 LBP injury report, % female not stated	Working (not working = self-report not working due to LBP)	Pain intensity: + Job demands: + Perceived future problem: + Relations at work: + Perceived chance to work/6 months: + Blame: + (Standardized; Vermont Disability Prediction Questionnaire)	NA	Prospective measure within 15 days, 3 months outcome	11 questions were good predictors. 94% sensitivity, 84% specificity
Hellsing, Linton, and Kälvemark, 1994	121 acute neck/back pain, 48% female	Sick leave (Insurance Authority, number of days)	ADL function: 0 Pain intensity: 0 Monotonous work: + (ADL and pain = standardized; monotonous = nonstandardized)	NA	Prospective 1 year	

continues

APPENDIX TABLE 4.8 Continued

Author	Study Population	Outcomes	Psychosocial Risk Factors[a]	Attributable Fraction[b]	Design Comments	Other Comments
Junge, Dvorak, and Ahern, 1995	164 secondary care, chronic LBP, 40% female	Response to surgery (Good = pain <6 VAS; sick leave <6 months; no regular visits to doctor or hospitalization during past year)	Depression + (Standardized; Beck's Depression Inventory)	NA	Prospective 6-12 months	Outcome correctly classified by pain (73%), psychological variables (63%), and overall score (80%)
Klenerman et al., 1995	300 acute LBP, 50% female	Pain and disability (rated pain, Roland & Morris Disability Questionnaire) Sick leave (self-report)	Fear avoidance beliefs: + Psychosocial variables (distress, experienced disability, depression, pain intensity): + (7 standardized questionnaires)	NA	Prospective measures at 1 and 8 weeks to predict 12 months	66% correctly classified with only fear-avoidance variables, 88% with all variables.

Reference	Sample	Outcome	Predictors		Design	Comments
Lancourt and Kettelhut, 1992	134 patients receiving workers' compensation, acute to chronic, % female not stated	Return to work (not stated how measured)	Stress: + Family factors: + Coping: + Job satisfaction: 0 Nonorganic signs: + (self-reports, nonstandardized)	NA	Prospective 6 months	Combination of physical and psychological factors showed good predictive ability
Lehmann, Spratt, and Lehmann, 1993	55 acute LBP, 33% female	Time to return to work (self-report; <1 month to not returned)	Pain: 0 Job satisfaction/ work: 0 History: 0 Function: 0 (Standardized and some nonstandardized)	NA	Prospective 6 months	Small n provides limited power
Leino and Magni, 1993	607 employees, 36% female	Musculoskeletal pain (self-report, rated frequency)	Depressive symptoms: + Distress: + (nonstandardized questionnaire)	NA	Prospective 3-, 5-year periods	Effects of depression were general as they predicted pain at various sites
Linton et al., 1999	449 pain free general population, 49% female	New episode spinal pain (self-report, yes/no) Activity hindered (standardized exam)	Fear-avoidance: + (modified Fear-Avoidance Behavior Questionnaire) Catastrophizing: + (Pain and Catastrophizing Scale)	Fear-avoidance: 51% pain 41% activity Catastrophizing: 35% pain 33% activity	Prospective 1 year	Fear-avoidance produced an OR=2.04 for pain, while catastrophizing was 1.5.

continues

APPENDIX TABLE 4.8 Continued

Author	Study Population	Outcomes	Psychosocial Risk Factors[a]	Attributable Fraction[b]	Design Comments	Other Comments
Linton and Halldén, 1998	142 acute spinal pain, 65% female	Pain (rated) Function (ADL) Sick leave (days) (self-report on standardized items)	Work: - Pain: + Fear-avoidance: + ADL: - Coping: 0 Job satisfaction: - Perceived future: - Stress/anxiety: + Mood: - (standardized)	NA	Prospective 6 months	The best predictors for sick leave were fear-avoidance, perceived future pain, perceived work function, stress, and earlier sick leave.
Magni et al., 1993	2,341 general population (representative 25- to 74-year-olds) 57% female	Chronic pain (pain > 1 month during past year)	Depression: + (Center for Epidemiologic Studies Depression Scale)	NA	Prospective 8 years	Depression increased the risk for MSP by 2- to 3-fold.
Magni et al., 1994	2,324, 57% female	Chronic pain (pain > 1 month during past year)	Depression: + (Center for Epidemiologic Studies Depression Scale)	53%	Prospective 8 years	Depression related to pain (OR=2.14) and pain related to depression (OR=2.85)

Main et al., 1992	567 patients LBP referred to orthopedic clinic (107 included in follow-up), 51% female	Disability (Roland and Morris Disability Questionnaire)	Depression (Zung): + Distress (MSPQ): + DRAM (distress and depression): +	Mild depression: 48% DRAM: 81%	Prognosis 1 to 4 years	Scores on DRAM highly related to future disability
Mannion, Dolan, and Adams, 1996	403 volunteers, no pain, 92% female	Back pain (yes/no) Pain-absenteeism (yes/no) Consultation (yes/no)	Distress: + (MSPQ) Depression: + (Zung) Health locus of control: 0 (Multidimensional Health Locus of Control)	NA	Prospective 6,12,18 months	Distress and depression were good predictors, but present at beginning so not causal
Papageorgiou et al., 1997	4,501 general population, 55% females	New episode of back pain (LBP >1 day, yes/no)	3 questions: 1. job satisfaction: - 2. relations at work: 0 3. sufficient money: - (nonstandardized)	Satisfaction: 41% Social relations: 29%	Prospective 12 months	Dissatisfied were twice as likely to experience a new episode

continues

APPENDIX TABLE 4.8 Continued

Author	Study Population	Outcomes	Psychosocial Risk Factors[a]	Attributable Fraction[b]	Design Comments	Other Comments
Philips and Grant, 1991	117 acute back, 57% female	Pain status (pain/no pain)	Pain intensity: + Pain quality: + Negative cognitions: + Anxiety: + Impact (SIP): + (6 standardized questionnaires)	NA	Measures at pre-3 and -6 months	80% were correctly classified
Pietri-Taleb et al., 1994	1,015 men < 7 day neck pain	Severe neck pain (> 30 days neck pain preceding year)	Hysteria: + Neuroticism: + Depression: + (Middlesex Hospital Questionnaire, Maudsley Personality Inventory)	Hysteria: 44% Neuroticism: 21% Depression: 14%	3 years	Complex interaction between occupation and results. Other parts of Maudsley and Middlesex not significant
Potter and Jones, 1992	45 patient at 4 weeks pain, % female not stated	Pain (persistent pain for 26 weeks)	Pain intensity: + Depression: + Passive coping: + (Standardized)	NA	Prospective followed 26 weeks	
Radanov et al., 1994	117 whiplash	Symptoms (self-reported symptoms, yes/no)	Personality: 0 Cognitive failure: 0 (Standardized)	NA	Longitudinal 3, 6, 12 months	Neither personality nor psychoneurological variables predicted

Study	Sample	Outcome	Measure		Design	Results
Werneke, Harris, and Lichter, 1993	183 LBP patients off work, 33% female	Return to work (self-report, yes/no)	Behavioral signs test: - (standardized)	NA	Prognostic 3 months	All 8 behavioral signs significantly higher for the "failed" group at discharge
Viikari-Juntura et al., 1991	154 general population, 47% female	Neck or back pain as adult (> 7 days sick leave, high disability rating = severe)	Intelligence: 0 Alexithymia: 0 Social confidence: 0 (mostly standardized)	NA	Prospective measures taken in adolescence	Personality. etc... in childhood did not predict future problem
Von Korff, Le Resche, and Dworkin, 1993	803 HMO enrollees, 59% female	Back pain onset (self-report)	Depression: 0 (Symptom Checklist 90-Depression) Number of pain conditions: + (self-report, yes/no)	Depression: NA Number of pain: 52%	Prospective 3 years	Depression related to chest and headache pain, but not directly to back pain onset. Number of pain sites was predictive
Öhlund et al., 1996	103 patients LBP, subacute	Return to work (working >50%)	Pain drawing: + (standardized)	NA	Prospective prognosis	

[a]A positive relationship is denoted with a plus (+), a negative relationship with a minus (-) and no relationship with a zero (0).
[b]Attributable fractions were not presented by the article authors and, therefore, were calculated using results available from the data presented in the published studies.

NOTE: ADL = activities of daily living; LBP = low back pain; MMPI = Minnesota Multiphasic Personality Inventory; NA = not available; OR = odds ratio; SCID = Structured Clinical Interview for DSM Disorders; SIP = Sickness Impact Profile.

APPENDIX TABLE 4.9 Summary Tables of Psychosocial Factors and Work-Related Upper Extremity Disorders: Cross-Sectional Studies

Author	Study Population	Outcomes	Psychosocial Risk Factors	Risk	95% Confidence Interval	Attributable Fraction[a]
Ahlberg Hultén, Theorell, and Sigala, 1995	90 female health care personnel	Symptoms of the shoulder: Pain during the last month (self reported questionnaire alternatives from no to almost daily) Prevalence total population: 26 % Prevalence unexposed not presented	Poor support—Low positive factors index: 5-item factor on relationships at work, which was the result of a factor analysis of a 16-item index of relationships at work; Items: calm and pleasant atmosphere, good sense of fellowship, support of workmates, bad days accepted by workmates	Positive association, ordinal logistic regression estimate (0.18)	-	-
			High job strain (JCQ)—sum score for skill utilization (4 items) and authority over decisions (2 items) (combined often called control) divided by job demands scale (5 items)	No association —ordinal logistic regression estimate (0.94)	-	-
Bergqvist et al., 1995b	260 VDU workers, Prevalence unexposed not presented	Shoulder/neck discomfort during the last 12 months (self reported Nordic Questionnaire) Prevalence total population: 61.5%	Limited rest break opportunities High perceived stress: Stomach related stress reaction	2.7 3.5	1.2-5.9 1.5-8.2	63% 71%

continues

Worry/distress; negative affectivity: sum score containing items on anger, disgust, scorn, guilt, fearfulness, depression	2.0	1.0-4.2	50%
Shoulder/neck symptoms during the last 7 days that interfered with work activities (self report questionnaire) Prevalence total population: 7.3%			
High perceived stress: Stomach related stress reaction	5.4	1.6-7.6	81%
Any diagnosis in the shoulder region established in a physiotherapy examination based on tests and anamneses over the previous 12 months Prevalence total population: 11.9%			
Limited work task flexibility	3.2	1.2-8.5	69%
Limited rest break opportunities	3.3	1.4-7.9	70%
High perceived stress: Stomach related stress reaction	4.8	2.1-10.7	79%
Arm/hand discomfort during the last 12 months (self reported Nordic Questionnaire) Prevalence total population: 29.9%			
Poor social support: Limited or excessive peer contacts	2.1	1.1-4.1	52%
High demands: Frequent overtime	2.2	1.2-4.1	55%
High perceived stress: Stomach related stress reaction	3.8	2.0-7.3	74%

APPENDIX TABLE 4.9 Continued

Author	Study Population	Outcomes	Psychosocial Risk Factors	Risk	95% Confidence Interval	Attributable Fraction[a]
		Any diagnosis in the arm/hand region established in a physiotherapy examination; examination based on tests and anamneses over the previous 12 months Prevalence total population: 8.7%	Poor support: Limited or excessive peer contacts	4.5	1.3-15.5	78%
			Limited rest break opportunities	2.7	0.8-9.1	63%
			High perceived stress Stress reaction	3.4	1.3-8.4	70%
Bernard et al., 1994	973 newspaper workers	NIOSH case-definition (self-reported questionnaire): Pain, numbness, tingling, aching, stiffness, or burning in the shoulder area within the preceding year and no previous non-work-related accident/injury Symptoms began after current job Lasted > 1 week or at least once a week Intensity > moderate (midpoint 5-point scale) Prevalence total population: 17%	Poor control: Perceived lack of participation in job-decision making (very little versus moderate: upper quartile versus lower quartile); NIOSH general job stress instrument (multi-item scale with adequate internal consistency)	1.6	1.2-2.1	37%
			High demands: Perceived increased job pressure (moderately disagree versus moderately agree, upper quartile versus lower quartile); NIOSH general job stress instrument (multi-item scale with adequate internal consistency)	1.5	1.0-2.2	33%

continues

Study	Population	Case-definition	Risk factor	Measure	OR	CI	Prevalence
		Same case-definition in the elbow-region; prevalence total population: 10% Same case-definition in hand or wrist region Prevalence total population: 22%		-	-	-	-
			High demands: Number of hours spent under a deadline per week (30-39 hours versus 0-10 hours)	1.6		1.2-2.3	37%
			Poor support: Perceived lack of support from an immediate supervisor (very much vs. a little, upper quartile versus lower quartile)	1.4		1.2-2.5	28%
Bru and Mykletun, 1996	492 female hospital staff No prevalence presented (only average symptoms scores)	Pain in the shoulder in the last 12 months; self reported, Nordic Questionnaire with adjusted answering categories on a 5-point scale developed by Westgaard Janssen, 1992a, combined with intensity score (mild to severe, 3-point scale of the Ursin Health Inventory). Final scale reflects maximal intensity of pain during the last 12 months as well as the level of pain during the more recent days.	Poor support: Social relations; multi-item factor based on Cooper stress check (relations with colleagues, relations with subordinates, relations with boss)	Positive association (multiple linear regression)	Change in T score	-	
			Low skill discretion/ monotony: Work content multi-item factor based on self-designed questionnaire: Distribution, cooperation, variation, new competence, and challenge in tasks	Positive association (multiple linear regression)	Change in T score	-	

APPENDIX TABLE 4.9 Continued

Author	Study Population	Outcomes	Psychosocial Risk Factors	Risk	95% Confidence Interval	Attributable Fraction[a]
			High demands: Work overload multi-item factor based on Cooper stress check (mistakes, time pressure, overwork, work-home, feeling undervalued, managing people)	Positive association (multiple linear regression)	Change in T score	-
Burdorf, van Riel, and Brand, 1997	144 tank terminal workers; no musculo-skeletal complaints before current job	Self-reported pain that lasted at least a few hours during the past 12 months in the shoulder (adapted Nordic Questionnaire) Prevalence 14%	High demands: Working under pressure (self report, one question yes/no)	NS	-	-
			Poor support: Lack of social support (self report, one question yes/no)	NS	-	-
		Self-reported pain that lasted at least a few hours during the past 12 months in the elbow (adapted Nordic Questionnaire) Prevalence 11%	High demands: Working under pressure (self report, one question yes/no)	NS	-	-
			Poor support: Lack of social support (self report, one question yes/no)	NS	-	-
		Self-reported pain that lasted at least a few hours during the past 12 months in the wrist (adapted Nordic Questionnaire) Prevalence 9%	High demands: Working under pressure (self report, one question yes/no)	NS	-	-
			Poor support: Lack of social support (self report, one question yes/no)	NS	-	-

continues

Dimberg et al., 1989	2,814 industrial workers	Many signs and symptoms established during physical examination	High perceived job stress: Mental stress at the time symptoms started (0 to 10 indication of level)	Correlation with trapeziums myalgia, lateral epicondylitis	-
Engström, Hanse, and Kadefors, 1999	67 assembly operators	Symptoms (ache, pain, discomfort) experienced during the previous 12 months (self-reported Nordic Questionnaire) in the upper extremities (elbow, forearm, wrists, hands, and fingers)	Poor control: Decision latitude (influence and control over work and stimulus from the work itself; both 5-item scales with adequate internal consistency)	Partial correlation 21 (p< 0.10)	-
			Poor support: Social support at work (co-worker and supervisor support, both 5-item scales; with adequate internal consistency)	NS	-
			High perceived job stress: Psychological load (stress at work, work load, extent of feeling tired, exhausted after work, rest break opportunities, mental strain)	NS	-

APPENDIX TABLE 4.9 Continued

Author	Study Population	Outcomes	Psychosocial Risk Factors	Risk	95% Confidence Interval	Attributable Fraction[a]
Hales et al., 1994	518 telecommunication employees (VDU work)	Very well-specified case definition: Self-reported symptoms in shoulder confirmed by physical examination, according to strict criteria Pain, numbness, tingling, aching, stiffness, or burning within the preceding year and No previous nonwork-related accident/injury Symptoms began after current job Lasted > 1 week or at least once a week Positive physical findings in the body region specified Prevalence 22%	Extensive questionnaire (job characteristics inventory and job diagnostic survey included) 21 multi-item scales (i.e. job control, work pressure, work load) Job insecurity: Fear of being replaced by computer (single item)	2.7	1.3-5.8	63%
		Elbow problems according to above definition	Job insecurity: Fear of being replaced by computer (single item)	3.0	1.5-6.1	66%
			Job demands: Surges in work load (multi-item scale)	2.4	1.2-5.0	58%
			Low job control: Routine work lacking decision making opportunities (full-time scale)	2.8	1.4-5.7	64%

Study	Population	Case definition	Exposure measure	Exposure factor	Result	95% CI	%
Hoekstra et al., 1996	108 teleservice representatives with telephone tasks. Prevalence: shoulder: 35% elbow: 20% hand/wrist: 30%	NIOSH case-definition (self reported Q). Pain, numbness, tingling, aching, stiffness, or burning in the neck, shoulder, elbow or hand/wrist area within the preceding year and no previous nonwork-related accident/injury. Symptoms began after current job. Lasted > 1 week or at least once a week. Intensity > moderate (midpoint 5-point scale)	NIOSH general job stress instrument (multi-item scale with adequate internal consistency) Perceived workload variability: (continuing changing workload during the day) Rubenowitz instrument, 5 dimensions all measured with 5-item scales with adequate internal consistency. Poor control: Influence and control over work (influence on rate, method, tasks, technical matters, rules, and regulations)	High qualitative demands: i.e. high information processing demands	2.3	1.4-4.3	56%
				Hand/wrist problems according to above definition	NS in final model (applies to shoulder, elbow, and hand/wrist problems each) NS in final model	-	-
Johansson and Rubenowitz, 1994	167 white- and 241 blue-collar workers of 8 metal companies	Self-reported symptoms (discomfort, aches, pain) in the shoulder region during the last 12 months (Nordic questionnaire); Work-related: and yes to the following question: 'the symptoms are solely related to my present work'	Poor skill discretion: Stimulus from work itself (interesting, varied, use talents and skills, learn new things, general feeling about work)		Blue S	White All work-related S	-

continues

APPENDIX TABLE 4.9 Continued

Author	Study Population	Outcomes	Psychosocial Risk Factors	Risk	95% Confidence Interval	Attributable Fraction[a]
			Poor social support: Supervisor climate (can ask for advice, regards viewpoints, provides information, general communication company)	S	S	-
			Poor social support: Relations with fellow workers (contacts, can talk, cheerful environment, discuss work problems, friends)	NS Work-related: S	S	-
			High perceived job stress: Psychological load (stress at work, work load, extent of feeling tired, exhausted after work, rest break opportunities, mental strain)	S	S	-
Johansson et al., 1993	28 workers of a truck assembly system	Self-reported symptoms (discomfort, aches, pain) in the shoulder region during the last 12 month (Nordic questionnaire)	Rubenowitz instrument 5 dimensions all measured with 5-item scales with adequate internal consistency		-	-

continues

| Kamwendo, Linton, and Moritz, 1991a, 1991b | 420 medical secretaries | Self-reported shoulder pain during the previous year (6-point scale, seldom to often, dichotomized so that the outcome is often shoulder pain). Prevalence 44% Prevalence nonexposed 34% | High perceived job stress: Psychological load (stress at work, work load, extent of feeling tired, exhausted after work, rest break opportunities, mental strain) | 0.39 S (newest workstation layout) | - | - |
| | | | Index of psychosocial work environment based on 10 items (4-point scale, never to usually) and dichotomized in good ≤ 20 or poor > 20. Individual items showing a significant association with shoulder pain: Poor social support: friendly cooperation with co-workers Poor control: Poor influence on working conditions High demands: Given too much to do Work commitment (yes very/yes rather vs. not very/not at all) Poor social support: Support and help from superiors (always/ mostly versus mostly not/never) | 1.87 (prevalence rate ratio of often shoulder pain) | $P < 0.05$ | 46% |

APPENDIX TABLE 4.9 Continued

Author	Study Population	Outcomes	Psychosocial Risk Factors	Risk	95% Confidence Interval	Attributable Fraction[a]
Lagerström et al., 1995	688 female nursing employees	Self-reported symptoms of shoulder pain during the last 12 months (Nordic questionnaire) supplemented with 10-point answering scale (not at all – very much) Symptoms > 0 (prevalence: 53%) Severe symptoms > 5 (prevalence: 18%)	High demands scale JCQ	1.65 (S)	1.05-2.59	39%
			Poor stimulation at work: Skill discretion scale JCQ	-	-	-
			Poor control: authority over decisions scale JCQ	1.73	1.13-2.67	42%
			Work commitment (yes very/yes rather vs. not very/not at all)	-	-	-
		Self-reported symptoms of hand during the last 12 months (Nordic questionnaire) supplemented with 10-point answering scale (not at all – very much) Symptoms > 0 (prevalence: 22%) Severe symptoms > 5 (prevalence: 4%)	Poor social support: Support and help from superiors (always/mostly versus mostly not/never)	-	-	-
			High demands scale JCQ	-	-	-
			Poor stimulation at work: skill discretion scale JCQ	1.62	1.09-2.39	38%
			Poor control: authority over decisions scale JCQ	-	-	-

Leclerc et al., 1998	1,006 workers with industrial repetitive work (assembly, clothing, food, and, packaging)	Diagnosis of CTS based on positive (defined criteria) Tinel's sign or Phalen's test at a medical examination or a diagnosis based on nerve condition velocity was already established Prevalence: 11.8% workers with repetitive work (range from 7.2 in food industry to 16 in packaging) 2.4% nonexposed control group (with comparable education level in jobs such as maintenance, cleaning, or catering)	Poor work satisfaction: Satisfaction with 7 items: work station, workload, variety of work and relations at work dichotomized (high ≥ 5 and low < 5)	1.42	0.95-2.11	29%
			Poor job control: Score 0-5 based on influence on time of break, additional breaks, pace, quantity of work, dichotomized in low and high score	1.43 1.59 (adjusted for organizational factors)	0.92-2.23 1.04-2.34	37%
			Work organization (group level): Autonomy at work station Just in time production External constraints (high competitiveness, subcontractor, seasonal goods, perishable foodstuffs)	- 2.24	- 1.40-3.57	- 55%
			Poor psychological and psychosomatic well being (8-item scale)	2.32	1.40-3.82	57%

continues

APPENDIX TABLE 4.9 Continued

Author	Study Population	Outcomes	Psychosocial Risk Factors	Risk	95% Confidence Interval	Attributable Fraction[a]
Lemasters et al., 1998	522 union carpenters with different types of carpentry work	Telephone interview (data on reliability and validity against physical exam): Within the past 12 months have you experienced any recurring symptoms such as pain, aching, numbness in your shoulder? Plus: Onset after starting as carpenter Symptoms at least once a week or lasting 1 week No history of injury	Poor job control (reliability Q referenced): Control over amount of work, availability of materials, policies and procedures, pace, quality, and scheduled hours	1.9	1.1-3.2	47%
			High demands: Exhausted end of day	1.5	0.9-2.4	33% (NS)
		Same question in elbow	High demands: Exhausted end of day	1.4	0.9-2.2	29% (NS)
			Poor job control (reliability Q referenced): Control over amount of work, availability of materials, policies and procedures, pace, quality, and scheduled hours	1.6	0.9-2.6	37% (NS)
		Same question hand or wrist	High demands: exhausted end of day	1.5	0.9-2.5	33% (NS)

Study	Population	Outcome	Risk factor	Odds ratio	CI	%
			Poor job control (reliability Q referenced): Control over amount of work, availability of materials, policies and procedures, pace, quality, and scheduled hours	1.6	1.0-2.7	37%
Marcus and Gerr, 1996	449 female office workers of 40 years or younger	Pain or soreness of the neck or shoulder at least once per week of at least moderate intensity during the month preceding completion of the questionnaire. Prevalence neck or shoulder symptoms 63%	Low job security (likely to lose job)	2.23	1.3-3.7	54%
			High perceived job stress: High job stress previous 2 weeks	2.47	1.2-5.1	60%
		Pain or soreness in the finger, hands, wrists, forearms or elbows, or numbness or tingling of the fingers of at least moderate intensity during the month preceding completion of the questionnaire Prevalence arm symptoms is 34%	High perceived job stress: High job stress previous 2 weeks	2.04	1.0-4.0	43%

continues

APPENDIX TABLE 4.9 Continued

Author	Study Population	Outcomes	Psychosocial Risk Factors	Risk	95% Confidence Interval	Attributable Fraction[a]
Pickett and Lees, 1991	79 data entry office workers in 5 different offices of the same company	Self-reported work-related symptoms of shoulder, arm or hand/wrist; precise question not presented; shoulder symptoms prevalence 76%	Rest breaks in task Perceived stress: Occupational stress: single item, portion of time at work operators perceived themselves to be under emotional or mental stress (rarely, sometimes, almost, always)	Not presented Not presented	- -	- -
		Hand-wrist symptoms: Prevalence 52%	Occupational stress	Not presented	-	-
		Arm symptoms: Prevalence 53%	Occupational stress	Not presented	-	-

Pocekay et al., 1995	3,175 semiconductor workers from 8 manufacturing companies	Several health outcomes; relationships with risk factors not separately presented: Any distal upper-extremity symptom = physician diagnosed carpal tunnel syndrome within the past year, questionnaire (self-report) diagnosed CTS, hand/wrist pain daily for 1 week within past year; elbow/forearm pain daily for 1 week within the past year	Perceived stress: Job stress index: job is very demanding; job is very tiring; job is very stressful	Range 1.1-1.5	-	9-33%
		Medical diagnosed CTS in past year	Non-work stress: Somatization index (symptoms over the most recent 4 weeks: feeling tired, tingling in fingers or toes, heart palpitations, feeling irritable, light headedness, lack of muscle strength, chest tightness)	Range 1.4-1.8	-	28-44%
		Hand/wrist pain daily for 1 week in past year		1.4	-	28%
		Elbow/forearm pain daily for 1 week within the past year				
		Epidemiologic CTS in past year				
		Daily shoulder pain for 1 week in past year				
		Medical diagnosed tendinitis in past year				

continues

APPENDIX TABLE 4.9 Continued

Author	Study Population	Outcomes	Psychosocial Risk Factors	Risk	95% Confidence Interval	Attributable Fraction[a]
Silverstein, Fine, and Armstrong, 1987	136 workers more than 4 years employed in an investment casting plant	Carefully defined and well described (additional paper) outcome assessment of hand/wrist CTD by interview and physical examination disorders, nerve entrapment, non specific included as clear pattern shown in: Interview: Pain, numbness, tingling Lasting > 1 week or > 20 times last year No acute traumatic onset Onset not before 1983 study job Physical Examination: Characterize signs and endpoints Exclude referred symptoms Prevalence: Low exposed: 5% High exposed (repetition and force): 13%	Poor job satisfaction, assessed by interview: How often do you find your work satisfying? Very often/fairly often/ sometimes/rarely Little variation in job dissatisfaction was presented In general the workers reported to be very or fairly satisfied with their work No stimulus from work, assessed by interview with the following question: How often do you find your work interesting? Very often/ fairly often/sometimes/ rarely	No association

No association | -

- | -

- |

continues

Hoekstra, Hurrell, and Swanson, 1995	108 workers at 2 teleservice centers	Any symptoms (pain, numbness, tingling, aching, stiffness, or burning) within the preceding year and all of the following: No preceding acute and non occupational injury Symptoms began after starting the current job Symptoms lasted > 1 week or occurred at least once a month within the past year Symptoms were reported as moderate (midpoint) or worse on 5-point intensity scale Shoulder: prev 35%	Poor job control: Job control was measured with a multi-item scale. Variability of workload: Perceived workload variability was measured with a multi-item scale; specified as continually changing workload during the day Although not explicitly stated, high-perceived workload variability is presumed to be the risk full exposure and not low	Not presented NS Not presented NS	–
		Elbow prevalence: 20%	Poor job control Variability of workload	Not presented NS Not presented NS	–
		Hand/wrist: prevalence: 30%	Poor job control Variability of workload	Not presented NS Not presented NS	–

APPENDIX TABLE 4.9 Continued

Author	Study Population	Outcomes	Psychosocial Risk Factors	Risk	95% Confidence Interval	Attributable Fraction[a]
Toomingas et al., 1997b	83 male furniture movers, 89 female medical secretaries, 96 men and 90 women from the working population, resulting in 358 men and women in various occupations, but with large groups of males with heavy work and females with office work	Nordic Questionnaire and 24 signs recorded at the physical examination were included concerning neck/shoulder/elbow/hand/wrist. Signs and symptoms were combined in two relevant syndromes for the neck/upper extremities, i.e., tension neck syndrome and tendalgia of the upper extremities. Outcome-variables: Symptoms (Nordic) Signs (24 in total) Syndromes (combined signs and symptoms)	High job demands: Multi-item scale JCQ	-	-	-
			Low control: Multi-item scale: Low decision latitude (low control and little stimulus from work, learning ability, etc.)	NS	NS	-
			Poor social support Multi-item scale	Shoulder 3.2 Hand/wrist 1.8	1.3-7.8 1.1-3.1	68% PR 44% PR
			High job strain: Job demands divided by decision latitude	Shoulder 2.2 Hand/wrist 1.5	1.0-5.1 0.8-2.8	55% PR 33%PR

continues

| Westgaard, Jensen, and Hansen, 1993 | 52 female production workers (chocolate plant) and 34 female office workers | Symptom score for each region based on intensity and frequency of symptoms in the last 12 months and their whole employment period within the present function Ranged from no symptoms to daily occurrence of severe symptoms: Shoulder/neck | Perceived stress Overall psychosocial work-related stress score based on a 14 item questionnaire with items on: Mental stress due to work task, new work tasks Stress due to reorganization Demands because of efficiency, work speed Effect of redundancies Personal development Support by colleagues and supervisor Total score dichotomized, but the way it is dichotomized is unclear | Positive association | – | – |
| | | Arms | Perceived stress | Positive association | – | – |

APPENDIX TABLE 4.9 Continued

Author	Study Population	Outcomes	Psychosocial Risk Factors	Risk	95% Confidence Interval	Attributable Fraction[a]
Westgaard and Jansen, 1992a, 1992b	210 production workers, mainly sewing machine operators in several plants of a garment industry and 35 office workers employed at this industry	Symptoms score based on frequency and intensity Shoulder/neck Arms	Nonwork distress Scoring of psychological problems by the interviewer in low, intermediate, high after a worker interview (based on interviewer's impression) High indicates recurring depression or anxiety Nonwork distress	No association No association	- -	- -
Zetterberg et al., 1997	564 car assembly workers (440 men and 124 women)	Symptoms: Nordic Questionnaire Extensive physical examination; 114 signs established (76 hand/wrist), including: myalgia, impingement, epicondylitis, nerve entrapment, tendinitis, joint signs symptoms/signs shoulder	Perceived stress Work satisfaction 5-item work APGAR but questions taken apart in support, satisfaction, and stress Low social support Poor job satisfaction	Positive association Positive association Positive association	- - -	- - -

		Symptoms/signs wrist hand	Perceived stress	Positive association		
			Low social support	-	-	-
			Poor job-satisfaction	-	-	-
Magnavita et al., 1999	2,041 physician sonographers	Self-reported question with a 21-item symptom list. Divided in syndromes by factor analysis. Hand/wrist concerned 6 items. Three or more of these symptoms of the hand/wrist region is the effect studied. Prevalence: 5.3%	Limited rest break opportunities: Long average time executing sonology activities without intermittent rest break is only a proxy for rest break opportunities. This variable measures more physical load than psychosocial load and additional measures of perceived time pressure or job demands were not included	1.50	1.1-2.1	33%

^aThe attributable fraction is calculated with the OR as estimate for the relative risk. This approximation will be fairly accurate when the prevalence of the health effect at study is below 20-30%. With higher prevalences the OR is an overestimation of the relative risk and thus the attributable fraction is overestimated. Attributable fractions were not presented by the article authors and, therefore, were calculated using results available from the data presented in the published studies.

NOTE: CTS = carpal tunnel syndrome; JCQ = job content questionnaire; NS = not significant; S = significant; VDU = video display unit.

APPENDIX TABLE 4.10 Summary Table of Psychosocial Factors and Work-Related Upper Extremity Disorders: Longitudinal Studies

Author	Study Population	Outcomes	Psychosocial Risk Factors	Risk	95% Confidence Interval	Attributable Fraction
Bergqvist, 1995	341 visual display unit workers	Shoulder-neck discomfort during the last 12 months (Nordic Questionnaire) Prevalence total population at end of follow up: 44%	Increased perceived monotony	-	-	-
	Prevalence unexposed not presented	Elbow-shoulder discomfort during the last 12 months (Nordic Questionnaire) Prevalence total population at end of follow up: 27%	Increased perceived monotony	-	-	-
		Hand/wrist discomfort during the last 12 months (Nordic Questionnaire) Prevalence total population at end of follow up: 16%	Increased perceived monotony	1.7 3.1	0.6-4.4 1.2-7.8	41% 68%

Ferreira, De Souza Conceição, and Hilário Nascimento Salvida, 1997 (retrospective cohort)	106 bank employees (telephone tasks)	History in medical records of one or more periods of upper extremity symptoms with time away from work confirmed by at least two medical specialists (who based the diagnosis on recurrent pain with or without clinical evidence from physical examination of tendon or tendon sheath impairment or nerve entrapment based)	Time pressure increase (i.e., shorter processing time task) Change in management (new administrative procedures) Registered overtime work Rest break opportunities	Limited rest breaks and relatively high time pressure were associated with WRUED	-
Roquelaure et al., 1997	65 (55 women, 10 men) cases with CTS matched with 65 controls (55 women, 10 men) Cases and controls recruited from television manufacturing plant	Case: blue-collar worker, 18-59, with medical history of carpal tunnel syndrome (CTS) between 1/1/1990 and 12/30/1992. Subjects with a history of CTS problems, diabetes, thyroid or musculoskeletal dysfunction, malignancies, rheumatic diseases before 1990 excluded. Referent: blue-collar, same gender, same year of birth, free of CTS or musculoskeletal disorders of the upper limb from 1984 to 1992.	Work organization factors: No job rotation between different work stations No association for: Autonomy: possibility to choose the way the work is done Rest break opportunities: duration and number of breaks	6.3	2.1-19.3 NA

NOTE: CTS = carpal tunnel syndrome; WRUED = work-related upper extremity disorder(s).

5

Tissue Mechanobiology

Basic biology studies, such as those that examine microscopic or biochemical changes in tissues, are a source of our understanding of details of injury mechanisms at the tissue or cellular level. These studies are primarily performed using cadaver samples, animal models, and tissues or cells grown in culture. Direct study of the tissues of concern in live humans (e.g., nerve, tendon, disc, muscle) is limited due to ethical and methodological considerations. The purpose of this chapter is to systematically review basic biology studies in order to determine to what degree they support an association between loading and tissue injury, especially at load levels well below those that cause tissue disruption. Biological plausibility, one of the Bradford Hill criteria for causality (see Chapter 3), refers in this case to the likelihood that associations between loading and tissue damage are compatible with existing knowledge of basic biological mechanisms. These basic biology studies may also address other Bradford Hill criteria, such as specificity, temporality (tissue injury occurs after loading is initiated), and dose-response associations.

In reference to our overall model of the person in the workplace (Figure 1.2), this chapter explores the "Internal Tolerances" box, that is, the tolerance of tissues to loading. The focus is primarily on the mechanical and biological responses of tissues to repeated or continuous loading, not on damage due to a single, sudden load. However, cyclical loads are frequently compared to the single load that causes tissue to rupture or grossly fail. It is well recognized that loading is required to maintain tissue integrity. Lack of loads or disuse leads to tissue atrophy and impaired function (e.g., osteoporosis, muscle atrophy). The implications are that there may be an optimal range of loading below which atrophy occurs and above which tissue injury may occur. This chapter does not focus on the effects of disuse. We do, however, investigate a number of questions: Is there evidence that tissue damage occurs at levels below the strength of the tissue? Is there evidence for microtrauma or damage accumulation? If so, what is the dose-response relationship? What are the mechanisms of injury and repair? How are the responses of tissues to load modified by intrinsic factors (e.g., age, gender)? Do existing studies support or refute an association between repeated loading and injury?

For the purposes of this chapter, several terms are defined. *Elastic materials* are those that regain their original shape after a load is removed. For such materials, the change in shape (e.g., strain) is proportional to the applied load (within certain limits). The constant of proportionality is called the *stiffness*. The force (e.g., stress) necessary to cause rupture or fracture is called the *strength*. In some cases, cyclically applied forces that are below the tissue strength may cause rupture or fracture via damage accumulation. This is called *fatigue*. Tissue fatigue can also lead to changes in other mechanical properties, such as reduced tissue stiffness.

Since pain is a common and important endpoint for humans with musculoskeletal disorders, this chapter begins with a review of the pain pathways from musculoskeletal tissues to the brain. This is followed by reviews of the biological responses of six tissues—vertebral bone, spinal disc, tendon and ligament, muscle, peripheral nerve, and spinal nerve root—to loading. These reviews are based on systematic evaluations of the scientific literature. The chapter summary integrates the findings across all tissues and draws conclusions about current knowledge of injury mechanisms. We conclude with suggestions for future research directions.

PAIN PATHWAYS FROM PERIPHERAL TISSUES

Evolution has provided our bodies with many senses by which to interact with the environment. Each sense (smell, vision, hearing, taste, and somatic sensibilities) has a highly specialized neural pathway. Pain is one of the somatic sensibilities (others are touch, temperature sensation, and proprioception) and itself has its own highly specialized set of neural pathways.

This specialization begins in the peripheral tissues. "Nociceptor" is the term given to the specialized receptors that serve as injury (or noxious stimuli) detectors. Activation of nociceptors evokes pain. Pain arouses us to protect the injured or threatened body part and hence plays a crucial role in survival. Nociceptors innervate a variety of tissues in ways that are appropriate from a teleological perspective. Lightly touching the cornea can injure the eye, and so the nociceptors that serve the cornea are quite sensitive to mechanical stimuli. The skin is a more resilient tissue, and nociceptors that serve the skin are sensitive to higher intensities of stimuli. Not all tissues have nociceptors (e.g., fat tissues are relatively insensitive to noxious stimuli). However, muscle, periosteum, and especially the interface between ligaments or tendons and bone are richly innervated by nociceptors. Correspondingly, surgical manipulation of fat is relatively painless, whereas manipulation of muscle or bone at tendon insertion sites is painful.

Nociceptors can also assist in healing and may even be involved in neuroimmune mechanisms. When nociceptor innervation to the skin is blocked, there is delay in wound healing, and the thickness of the epidermis is reduced. Neurogenic inflammation is another function of nociceptors; activation of nociceptors prompts a release of potent vasoactive peptides that leads to redness and increased permeability of the vessels.

Signals from nociceptors are transmitted by the peripheral nerve to cells in the spinal cord. Damage to the peripheral nerve (e.g., carpal tunnel syndrome, spinal root compression) may lead to unusual sensations, the sensation of pain, or the loss of sensation (e.g., numbness) in the part of the extremity served by the nerve. The spinal cord is an important processing center for noxious information. Nociceptive inputs have connections to motor neurons in the dorsal horn; this accounts for pain-induced muscle contractions (muscle spasms). Specialized cells in the spinal cord also transmit information from nociceptors to higher brain centers. These inputs to higher centers arouse descending pathways back down the spinal column, which in turn regulate the sensitivity of the nociceptive neurons. Other inputs from peripheral pathways (e.g., touch systems) may interact with the nociceptive inputs to regulate the sensitivity of the cells in the spinal cord. Thus, the sensitivity of the pain-signaling pathways is highly plastic.

Nociceptors that serve different deep tissues have convergent inputs to the spinal cord; these lead to the phenomenon of referred pain. Thus, a person with a heart attack may feel pain in the left arm; a person with a herniated cervical disc feels muscle tenderness in the trapezius muscle, and a person with carpal tunnel syndrome may feel pain in the elbow and upper arm.

Injury may induce changes in pain sensibility. Tissues may become hyperalgesic; that is, the same stimulus produces a greater sensation of pain. Lightly touching the skin may be associated with pain (allodynia). Hyperalgesia results from two forms of sensitization: peripheral and central. Nociceptors (peripheral) themselves become more sensitive to heat and mechanical stimuli, and the spinal cord cells (central) become sensitized as well. As part of this central sensitization, the nerve fibers concerned with touch sensation acquire the capacity to activate the spinal cord cells that serve pain. This accounts for the phenomenon of allodynia, in which touch stimuli evoke pain in patients with inflammation of the skin and in patients with nerve injury.

LITERATURE REVIEW

The panel reviewed the scientific literature to evaluate the state of knowledge of the effects of loading on vertebral bone, spinal disc, tendon and ligament, muscle, peripheral nerve, and spinal nerve root. Online databases (e.g., Embase, MEDLINE, Pre-Medline) were searched at least back to 1980 for articles with relevant keywords (e.g., tissue type, damage, pathology, fatigue, tension, compression, repetitive, loading). Appropriate articles were considered for review only if they were published in English-language, peer-reviewed scientific journals. For each tissue type, this process identified between 28 and 190 articles for consideration. The reviews that follow summarize, for each tissue, the function and structure of the tissue; the effects of loads on microstructure, mechanical characteristics, and biological function; and the influence of heterogeneity, aging, and other factors on the response of the tissue to load. The types of load considered, along with the biological and mechanical responses, are appropriate to the tissue.

VERTEBRAL BONE AND SPINAL DISC

Structural and Functional Properties

The intervertebral disc is a complex structure consisting of four distinct tissues: the nucleus pulposus, the annulus fibrosus, the cartilaginous endplates, and the adjacent vertebral bodies (Figure 5.1). The nucleus

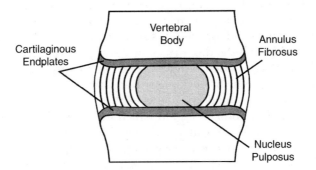

FIGURE 5.1 Schematic representation of the intervertebral disc (from Bass, 1999:2). Reprinted with permission from the author.

pulposus is a viscous, mucoprotein gel that is approximately centrally located within the disc. It consists of abundant sulfated glycosaminogly-cans in a loose network of type II collagen, with a water content that is highest at birth (approximately 80 percent) and decreases with age. The annulus fibrosus is a ligamentous tissue that becomes differentiated from the periphery of the nucleus and forms the outer boundary of the disc. The transition between the nucleus and the annulus is progressively more indefinite with age. The annulus is made up of coarse type I collagen fibers arranged in layers, running obliquely between the adjacent verte-bral bodies. The fibers run in the same direction within a given layer, but opposite to those in an adjacent layer. The cartilaginous endplates cover the end surfaces of the opposed vertebral bodies and serve as the upper and lower surfaces of the intervertebral disc; they are composed predomi-nantly of hyaline cartilage. The vertebral bodies consist of a trabecular (porous) bone core (centrum) surrounded by a thin shell of cortical (dense) bone. The facet joints are part of the posterior vertebral arch and serve as additional points of articulation between adjacent vertebra. They guide vertebral motion by constraining rotation and supporting some axial load.

In the adult, the cells residing within the endplate, nucleus, and inner annulus resemble chondrocytes (cartilage cells), while the cells populat-ing the middle and outer annulus are fibroblastic (fibrous tissue cells). Because the disc is avascular, these cells receive nutrition via diffusion from adjacent vascularized tissues and convective fluid flow (Maroudas, 1988).

Normal Disc Mechanics

The disc derives its structural properties largely through its ability to attract and retain water. The proteoglycans (biochemicals that help resist compressive loading) of the nucleus osmotically pull in water, exerting a "swelling pressure" that enables it to support spinal compressive loads. The pressurized nucleus also creates tensile stress within the collagen fibers of the annulus and ligamentous structures surrounding the disc. In other words, although the disc principally supports compression, the fi-bers of the annulus experience significant tension. This annular and liga-mentous prestress, in turn, functions synergistically with the facet joints to guide normal spinal motion (Adams et al., 1987).

Under long duration loading, in which the spinal stress exceeds the nuclear swelling pressure, water is slowly forced from the disc, princi-pally through the semipermeable cartilaginous endplates, resulting in a creep response (continual change in height from a constant applied force). As a result of this mechanism, a significant disc water loss can occur over the course of hours due to activities of daily living (Tyrell et al., 1985).

Diurnal loss of disc height can approach 2 mm, leading to increased spinal instability via decreased tissue prestress (Adams et al., 1987). Water loss and stability can be recovered during periods of bed rest (LeBlanc et al., 1994).

Effects of Age and Degeneration

After skeletal maturity, the intervertebral disc undergoes numerous alterations with age. These include a progressive loss of cellularity, disorganization of the extracellular matrix, and, as a result, morphological changes and alterations in biomechanical properties (Buckwalter, 1995). These age-related changes represent a form of degeneration, which may be accelerated by a number of factors and have been implicated in increasing the risk of discogenic back pain. Discogenic pain refers to pain originating from the intervertebral disc and is distinguished from back pain of other origins, such as facet joints, spinal ligaments, and muscles.

The most consistent chemical modification observed with aging is loss of proteoglycans and concomitant loss of water (Pearce et al., 1987). Secondary changes in the annulus include fibrocartilage production with disorganization of the annular architecture and increases in type II collagen (Rufai et al., 1995). These alterations precede the morphological reorganization usually attributed to degeneration: loss of disc height, disc bulge, sometimes called protrusion, and disc herniation, sometimes referred to as prolapse (Pearce et al., 1987). Disc bulge can occur when loss of water causes the disc to flatten, bulge beyond its normal margins, and may place pressure on a nerve exiting from or traversing along the spinal column. Disc bulge can also occur when fibrocartilage proliferates within the substance of the annulus fibrosus (Yasuma, 1990). Disc herniation occurs when disc material escapes through a fissure in the annulus fibrosus, which, like a bulge, can place pressure on nerve roots or the spinal cord.

Nociceptive nerve fibers are sparsely present in the outer annulus and vertebral body and extensively present in the facet joint capsule and posterior longitudinal ligament (Cavanaugh et al., 1997; Antonacci et al., 1998; Palmgren et al., 1999). With increasing degeneration, nerves can penetrate to deeper layers within the tissue (Coppes et al., 1997; Freemont et al., 1997), including the vertebral endplate (Brown et al., 1997). Innervation is thought to advance deeper into the disc in concert with vascular granulation tissue (Yoshizawa et al., 1980). These nerves can be stimulated both mechanically and chemically (Yamashita et al., 1993).

There are several mechanisms that purportedly link disc degeneration and low back pain. First, degeneration leads to tissue dehydration (Pearce et al., 1987). Breakdown of the nuclear polymeric structure results in reduction of its osmotic properties— the disc loses its ability to attract and retain water (Urban and McMullin, 1985). Tissue volume loss from dehydration, in turn, leads to a decrease in disc height and an increase in disc bulging (Adams et al., 1987). Both of these geometric changes can adversely affect patients by accelerating facet joint arthritis and by causing mechanical impingement on the adjacent spinal cord or nerve roots. In these cases, alterations in nerve function secondary to chronic compression are thought to be the primary mediators of back pain (Devor, 1995).

Dehydration is also correlated with decreases in disc cellularity, disorganization of the annular layers, and alterations in the density and architecture of adjacent vertebra (Vernon-Roberts, 1988). These changes can begin early in life and have significant consequences for the disc's biomechanical behavior.

Disc degeneration may cause pain indirectly via chemicals secreted by disc cells. These inflammatory factors can diffuse to and sensitize surrounding innervated tissues (McCarron et al., 1987; Kawakami et al., 1996, 1997; Kayama et al., 1998).

As mentioned previously, degenerated discs may be considered a normal consequence of aging. Indeed, a large percentage of the adult population has degenerated discs, with a significant percentage of these being asymptomatic (Wiesel et al., 1984; Powell et al., 1986). For instance, in an MRI study of symptomless adults, greater than 50 percent had disc bulges, protrusions, or vertebral endplate abnormalities (M. C. Jensen et al., 1994). While these data suggest that the presence of a degenerated disc is not diagnostic of back pain, the severity of spinal degeneration (extent and number of levels affected) does correlate with increased risk for symptoms (Luoma et al., 2000).

Influences of Loading on the Disc
Via Mechanical and Biologic Pathways

The disc behaves as a composite structure when loaded: forces exerted on it are distributed among the tissues from which it is constructed (the annulus, nucleus, cartilage endplate, and adjacent vertebra). This tissue stress distribution is dependent on the type of loading (e.g., compression, flexion, lateral bending, or torsion) and duration of loading (creep response).

Tissue stress induced by spinal loading affects the disc through both mechanical and biological pathways. These pathways are usually coupled: that is, the mechanical response influences the biology, and the biological response influences the mechanics. This load-induced response can be either beneficial or detrimental.

An important detrimental mechanical response is overload injury (material failure). This occurs when the tissue stress exceeds the tissue strength. The human tolerance to overload injury has been investigated largely in cadaveric models. These in vitro experiments demonstrate that failure will occur within the tissue that is stressed most severely. The tissue at risk, and therefore the mode of injury, is in part dependent on the type of loading (compression, flexion, lateral bending, or torsion). For instance, under pure compression the disc fails by vertebral body fracture, whereas excessive bending injures the ligaments of the neural arch (Table 5.1). Vertebral body compressive strength is strongly correlated with its cross-sectional size and bone density (Brinckmann, Biggeman, and Hilweg, 1989a, 1989b), making it feasible to predict noninvasively in humans.

Disc tissues can also be injured through a process of fatigue, where subfailure loads are applied repetitively for sufficient cycles to ultimately cause tissue failure via damage accumulation (such as during exposures

TABLE 5.1 Summary of Static Strength for Intact Spinal Segments

Loading Mode	Injury Mode	Average Strength	Notes
Compression	Vertebral endplate fracture	5.2 ($\pm$ 1.8) kN[a] 6.1 ($\pm$ 1.8) kN (male, 20-50 yrs)[a] 10.2 ($\pm$ 1.7) kN* (male, 22-46 yrs)[b]	Dependent on vertebral cross-sectional area and bone density
Shear	Neural arch, facet joint fracture	1.0 kN[c]	Uncertain
Flexion	Posterior ligaments	73 ($\pm$ 18) Nm	measured with 0.5 - 1.0 kN compressive preload
Extension	Neural arch	26 ($\pm$ 9) Nm[d]	Anterior annulus may be damaged
Torsion	Neural arch/facets	25 - 88 Nm[e]	
Compression plus flexion	Posterior annulus, vertebral body	5.4 ($\pm$ 2.4) kN[f]	Disc can prolapse under hyperflexion

[a]Brinckmann, Biggemann, and Hilweg, 1989a, 1989b
[b]Hutton and Adams, 1982
[c]Miller et al., 1986; Adams et al., 1994
[d]Adams et al., 1988
[e]Farfan et al., 1970; Adams and Hutton, 1981
[f]Adams and Hutton, 1982

to extremes of whole-body vibration). Cadaveric experiments demonstrate that cyclic loading in compression, bending, torsion, shear, or combinations thereof damage vertebra (including facet joints) prior to damaging the annulus fibrosus. These studies suggest that vertebral fatigue may result from physiological loading regimens that include between 1,000 and 10,000 compressive cycles (5,000 cycles may easily accumulate in vivo during 2 weeks of industrial exposure). Cyclic compressive stress as low as 50 percent of the vertebral failure strength may result in fracture after 1,000 cycles (Hansson, Keller, and Spengler, 1987). Brinckmann, Biggemann, and Hilweg (1988) developed a probability model to predict the fatigue strength given vertebral size, density, and load magnitude. Based on this model, a "fatigue limit" of 30 percent of ultimate compressive strength has been hypothesized for living vertebrae; in other words, cyclic loading of less than 30 percent of vertebral compressive strength would never cause fatigue failure (Table 5.2). Vertebral microdamage cannot be identified utilizing clinical radiographs, bone scans, or MRIs (Hansson et al., 1980; Mosekilde and Mosekilde, 1986). The clinical significance of these pathological changes remains uncertain. Some evidence suggests that the annulus may also be injured via fatigue and damage accumulation (Gordon et al., 1991; Buckwalter, 1995; Walsh et al., 2000)

Tissue stress developed during spinal loading can influence disc biology. Within vertebra, stress can stimulate cells to produce more bone in areas of high stress or remove bone in areas of low stress. This process,

TABLE 5.2 Cyclic Loading Reduces the Compressive Strength of Lumbar Motion Segments

Relative Load	Number of loading cycles				
%	10	100	500	1000	5000
60-70	10%[a]	55%	80%	95%	100%
50-60	0%	40%	65%	80%	90%
40-50	0%	25%	45%	60%	70%
30-40	0%	0%	10%	20%	25%
20-30	0%	0%	0%	0%	10%

[a]Values indicate the *probability* of compressive failure if a motion segment is loaded for the specified number of cycles at the specified relative load. Relative load is the actual compressive load expressed as a percentage of the load required for compressive failure from single loading cycle. Data from Brinckmann, Biggemann, and Hilweg (1988).

called remodeling, is the body's mechanism to optimize the density and shape of bones for a particular mechanical exposure (e.g., tennis players have denser bone in their dominant arms) (Cowin et al., 1985). These bone cells are also responsible for healing fractures, including microdamage resulting from fatigue (as described above). It is inferred from known bone healing times, amounting to several weeks or months (Martin et al., 1998), that minimal repair of bone microfractures would be expected in a time interval of approximately 2 weeks. This observation suggests that vertebral fatigue damage may accumulate in vivo, not be offset by healing, and lead to fractures. However, while the presence of endplate microfractures appears to increase with age (Roberts et al., 1997), whether these are responsible for patient symptoms is uncertain (Braithwaite et al., 1998).

Within the nucleus and annulus, spinal loading can alter tissue water content (via creep, as discussed above) and tissue shape, leading to altered cell metabolism. In particular, changes in water content, in addition to concomitant modifications of tissue permeability, fixed charge density, oxygen tension, and cell shape, can have adverse biologic consequences (Ohshima et al., 1989; Ohshima and Urban, 1992; Ishihara et al., 1996; Handa et al., 1997; Ishihara and Urban, 1999). For instance, Urban and coworkers utilized an in vitro model to demonstrate that disc cell function is harmed by extremes of water content (either too high or too low) induced by fluctuations of disc compression (Ohshima et al., 1995). The detrimental effect was thought to be due to alterations in the disc cells' pericellular environment. In vivo loading in animals demonstrates that altered disc cell metabolism and death may be related to spinal loading via a quantifiable dose-response relationship (Hutton et al., 1998; Lotz et al., 1998; Lotz and Chin, 2000). These studies and others demonstrate that certain regimens of spinal loading can be harmful to the disc. Implied, though not demonstrated directly, is that other regimens, involving lower compressive loads, may be beneficial.

Summary and Conclusions

The intervertebral disc manifests a complex, time-dependent response to spinal loading. Loading, in turn, alters the joints' biomechanical behavior and the tissues' biological activity. Overload injury and fatigue may cause vertebral body failure, while coupling between tissue stress and cell activity may accelerate annular and nuclear degeneration through more subtle, biological pathways.

Spinal discs degenerate with age. The independent contribution of physical force to degeneration is currently unknown due to inherent physiological variability among individuals, and because aging, by definition, signifies lengthened exposure to cumulative trauma. Furthermore, due to a lack of specificity of disc degeneration for back pain, the patho-physiological mechanisms linking spinal load and pain in humans are still uncertain.

However, significant data exist by which to quantify the failure and fatigue strength of vertebral bodies in humans (related to bone density and bone size). The biological response to spinal stress and its contribution to damage accumulation have been demonstrated in animal and laboratory models, yet the extent by which this pathway affects humans still needs to be established.

TENDONS AND LIGAMENTS

Properties of Tendon and Ligament and Injury Endpoints

Tendon and ligament are composed of dense connective tissue. The collagen fibrils visible with the electron microscope are grouped into fibers and fascicles that are visible with a light microscope. The fibers and fascicles are enclosed in a thin film of loose connective tissue called endotendon or endoligament. The whole tendon is wrapped in a connective tissue called the epitenon, which in turn is surrounded by the paratenon, a loose, areolar connective tissue (Figure 5.2). In some areas of the body, for example at the wrist, the paratenon forms a double layer sheath lined with synovial cells. This tendon sheath or tenosynovium facilitates smooth gliding of the tendon.

Tendons connect muscle to bone, while ligaments connect bone to bone. Tendons and ligaments primarily transmit tension forces but can also experience shear and compressive loads (Luo et al., 1998). Compression occurs when the tendon path is altered, for example around a bony structure or pulley system, or if there is impingement between the bony structures. Cellular remodeling and adaptation of these tissues occurs in response to different types of loading. When a tendon experiences compressive loading in addition to tension, the tendon in this region is gradually transformed from linear bands of collagen fascicles into irregular patterned fibrocartilage. The transformation is accompanied by changes in proteoglycans (Malaviya et al., 2000).

During tendon gliding, the amount of friction against the surrounding sheath and tissue depends on the amount of tension in the tendon, the friction coefficient, and the arc of contact (Uchiyama et al., 1997). Friction force can generate heat and cause thermal effects indirectly and can stimulate cellular reaction directly (Birch, Wilson, and Goodship, 1997). Joint movement determines the amount of tendon excursion; therefore, the specific joint posture, as well as tendon tension, are important determinants of compressive and shear load.

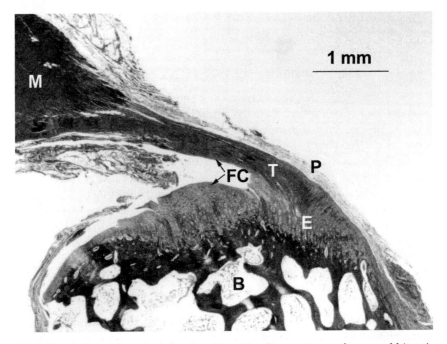

FIGURE 5.2 Control tendon. Tendon (T) with adjacent tissues from a rabbit epicondyle. Peratenon (P), enthesis (E), fibrocartilage (FC), muscle (M), and bone (B). Trichrome stain. (Reproduced with permission from Karen King and David Rempel, 2001.)

Mechanical Properties

Tendon and ligament have characteristic mechanical properties characterized by stiffness, failure strength, and viscoelasticity; these properties have been extensively studied. For example, the strength of human finger flexors is approximately 1,500 N, which corresponds to a strain (length change) of approximately 13 percent (Pring, Amis, and Coombs, 1985). In general, the tension experienced in the tendon during activities of daily living, occupational tasks, and even sport activities is likely to be low compared with the failure strength. For example, a pinch force of 4 kg is likely to require between 70 and 230 N of tensile force in the flexor digitorum superficialis tendon (Dennerlein et al., 1998).

The mechanical fatigue properties of human tendon have been evaluated by subjecting tendon to cyclical loading (Schechtman and Bader, 1997; Hubbard and Chun, 1988). Extensor tendons from the foot, subjected to a cyclic square tension-tension stress waveform at physiological frequencies, failed according to a log-linear model: $S = 101.3 - 14.8 \log (N)$. The number of cycles to failure (N) was inversely related to the stress (S), even at the lowest stress levels (10 percent of failure strength, 70 hours of loading), suggesting the absence of an endurance limit.

Pathology of Human Tendons

The taxonomy for disorders of the tendon and adjacent structures may be confusing. *Tendinitis* is the common term used to describe pain at the site of a tendon and may be accompanied by swelling, warmth, and erythema. However, some tendon disorders, for example, lateral epicondylitis ("tennis elbow"), have no acute inflammatory cells on histologic examination. Instead, at surgery there are tears in the tendon with disorganized collagen, vascular hyperplasia, and fibroblast proliferation near cleavage planes in the tendon (Kraushaar and Nirschl, 1999; Coonrad and Hooper, 1973). It has been proposed that these disorders characterized by degenerative changes be called *tendinosis* (Kraushaar and Nirschl, 1999). Furthermore, tendon disorders can be classified based on the anatomy of the tendon and its surrounding tissues (Viikari-Juntura, 1984; Clancy, 1990):

(a) Tenosynovitis refers to inflammation of the tendon sheath or paratenon. This can occur where the finger flexors pass through the carpal tunnel (e.g., flexor tenosynovitis) or on the back of the wrist (e.g., fourth extensor compartment tenosynovitis). Histologically these are characterized by edema with inflammatory cells and vascularization of the paratenon.

(b) Stenosing tenosynovitis (tenovaginitis) occurs when tendon gliding is restricted due to thickening of the tendon or sheath (e.g., de Quervain's disease or trigger finger). Histologically, the tendon sheath and tendon nodule demonstrate fibrocartilage metaplasia with increased chondrocytes and gylcosaminoglycan matrix (Sampson et al., 1991).

(c) Peritendinitis refers to inflammation of only the paratenon in areas in which there is no tendon sheath. This can occur at the back of the wrist, at the second extensor compartment (e.g., intersection syndrome), where the extensor carpi radialis tendons pass below the muscle bellies of the abductor pollicis longus and the extensor pollicis brevis, which may or may not be lined by the synovium. Histologically, the paratenon areolar tissue is infiltrated with edema, thickening, hypervascularity, and inflammatory cells and the process may extend to the adjacent muscle.

(d) Tendinosis occurs when there are degenerative alterations within the tendon without the evidence of inflammatory cells. Histologic findings are partial ruptures, collagen fiber disorientation, fibroblast hyperplasia, neovascularization, local necrosis, and glycosaminoglycans laid down between tendon fibrils. Tendinosis is observed at the time of surgical treatment of rotator cuff "tendinitis" and lateral epicondylitis (Chard, 1994; Kraushaar, 1999). Whether an early, inflammatory response precedes these changes is unknown. Histologic changes consistent with tendinosis are present in the rotator cuff of 40 percent of cadavers over the age of 50 (Chard, 1994).

Mechanisms of Injury

The mechanism of injury for the various tendon disorders may vary depending on local anatomy and the forces experienced by the tendon and adjacent tissues. A limited number of well-designed animal models have been developed to investigate mechanisms of injury by studying the effects of repetitive motion and loading on the adaptation and pathological changes of soft tissue; Archambault and colleagues (Archambault, Wiley, and Bray, 1995) have recently reviewed these models. The long-term effect of exercise on tendons may be positive, by increasing tendon cross-sectional area and strength, if conditioning duration and repetition rates are controlled (Woo et al., 1980). Remodeling of the tendon can occur with development of fibrocartilaginous tissue along the tendon. At points where the tendon wraps around bone or a pulley and is subjected to transverse compressive loading in addition to tension, tendon remodeling occurs, with the development of fibrocartilaginous tissue with elevated glycosaminoglycan content (Malaviya et al., 2000; Perez-Castro and Vogel, 1999). This tissue diminishes when the compressive loading is removed. These fibrocartilaginous changes are congruent with the pathology observed in the tendon and tendon sheath of humans with stenosing tenosynovitis. The factor that induces the fibrocartilagenous change (e.g., ischemia, compressive force, frictional heat) is unknown.

Repetitive stimulation of the rabbit ankle flexor has been used to investigate the pathogenesis of peritendinitis and tendinosis of the Achilles tendon (Rais, 1961; Backman et al., 1990). In the Backman et al. study (1990), rabbits were exercised in a kicking machine, producing passive flexions and extensions of the ankle joint combined with active contractions of the ankle flexors. The animals were exercised for 5 to 6 weeks, 3 days per week, for 2 hours, at a rate of 150 flexions and extensions per minute. The peak load was estimated at 15 percent of maximal muscle force. Although the rate of loading is high, the number of hours per week is low relative to what might be experienced by humans. Light microscopic examination showed degenerative changes of the tendon and increased number of capillaries, infiltrates of inflammatory cells, edema, and fibrosis in the paratenon. This animal model demonstrates tissue changes due to repetitive loading that are congruent with the pathology of peritendinitis and tendinosis in humans.

Recent studies have suggested that peritendinitis due to repeated loading may be mediated by an early inflammatory response. Using microdialysis techniques, it has been observed that metabolism is accelerated and is accompanied by an elevation of prostaglandin E_2 and thromboxane B_2 in the peritendinous region of the human tendon with dynamic loading (Langberg et al., 1999). In animals trained on a treadmill for 3 to 5 days, the IGF-I immunoreactivity throughout the cytoplasm of the tendon and paratenon fibroblasts was increased (Hansson et al., 1988).

Based on human pathology findings, it has been suggested that tendinosis associated with repeated loading is due to microtears in the tendon, such as side-to-side dehiscence of the fascicles or longitudinal disruption of the fibers (Kraushaar, 1999). Not only are partial tears observed in pathological specimens but repair activity (e.g., fibroblast proliferation, angiogenesis, matrix production) is found near cleavage planes in the tendon. Morphologic changes consistent with microtrauma are elevated in the flexor tendons of horses after galloping exercises (Patterson-Kane et al., 1997, 1998b). Elevated temperature in the core of the tendon associated with repeated strain and compromised blood flow and hypoxia have also been postulated as mechanisms leading ultimately to degenerative changes in the central core of the tendon. However, the evidence supporting either pathway is limited.

An animal model for rotator cuff tendinosis was developed in the rat with treadmill running (Carpenter et al., 1998). Overuse led to an increase in cellularity and collagen disorganization in the tendon compared with controls. This was accompanied by biomechanical changes of an increase in tendon cross-sectional area and a decrease in tissue stiffness. Tendons with a surgical injury plus overuse exhibited a worse histologic grade than those with overuse alone. The study demonstrated that damage to the supraspinatus tendon can be caused by overuse and intrinsic injury, overuse and extrinsic compression, and overuse alone. The changes were congruent with the pathological changes observed in human rotator cuff tendinosis. The differences in anatomy between the rat and human shoulder may be considered a limitation; however, a detailed review of 33 species of animals revealed that the rat was the most appropriate based on acromion anatomy and function.

Effects of Age and Other Factors

In the rat, Achilles tendon strength decreases with age (Simonsen, Klitgaard, and Bojsen-Moller, 1995). Certain kinds of exercise can prevent some of this age-related loss of strength. In the rat, the aging process was not prevented by strength training, but it was compensated to some degree by swim training (Nielsen, Skalicky, and Viidik, 1998). Whether aging increases the risk of injury associated with cyclical loading is unknown.

Summary

Basic science studies support the conclusion that repetitive motion or overuse loading can cause chronic injury to tendon tissues. The external loading exposures are related to the internal stress in the tissue and to interaction between tissues. The resultant physiological and cellular responses can lead to either biological adaptation or chronic pathology. The injury pattern includes inflammatory changes with fibrosis in the paratenon, with evidence of degenerative changes in the tendon, specifically edema, collagen disorganization, and fibrosis. The damage may be initially mediated by inflammatory activity and microtrauma.

Some elements of the pathophysiology pathway are still uncertain. For example, the very early ultrastructural, cellular, and biochemical responses to repetitive tissue loading have not been well explored. The response of tendons at different sites of the body to repeated loading may not be homogeneous. For example, the findings observed in the Achilles tendon may differ from those that might be observed in the extensor carpi radialis tendon insertion into the epicondyle. Stenosing tenosynovitis (e.g., trigger finger) may be associated with repeated loading, but there are no animal models for this condition.

In addition, a better understanding of the specific biomechanical factors that cause injury would be extremely useful for prevention efforts. It is unclear whether the problem with repeated loading has more to do with the rate of loading, the peak loads, cumulative tendon travel, or simply the duration of loading. These issues are complex, and the questions are likely to be resolved only with animal models.

SKELETAL MUSCLE

Skeletal Muscle Body Function Related to Work Performance

Skeletal muscle is unique as the body machine that powers external human work. Skeletal muscle is an elongated, contractile tissue that generates force and shortens when activated to contract by stimuli from alpha (α) motor neurons that originate in the spinal cord. Central nervous system stimuli and spinal reflexes activate the α motor neurons and skeletal muscles to bring about coordinated and efficient movement of limbs, maintenance of posture, and withdrawal from painful stimuli. Because skeletal muscle generates the force for body movement and external work, it also is a source of physical load to other tissues, such as tendons, joints, and nerves.

Although skeletal muscle is a working machine, it has inherent self-repair and adaptation mechanisms that allow it to maintain its structure and remodel over time. In the absence of excessive external forces, muscle does not usually damage itself from overuse because it fatigues, or fails to contract, before the point of irreversible contractile or cellular damage. Skeletal muscle cells, or fibers, recover from fatigue within minutes to hours. Damage or injury to skeletal muscle invariably occurs as a result of external forces that exceed the tolerance limits of the muscle's passive (e.g., connective tissue) and active contractile structures; the nature of the damage is directly related to skeletal muscle structure and the molecular mechanism of force generation.

Skeletal Muscle Structure and Contractile Mechanism

Skeletal muscle has a highly structured architecture. Within each skeletal muscle fiber, or cell, interdigitating thick and thin protein filaments are organized longitudinally into repeating sarcomeres and cross-sectionally into lattices that form myofibrillar bundles (see Figures 5.3a and 5.3b). Thick filaments of the protein myosin form a lattice in the center of each sarcomere, and thin filaments of the protein actin insert into the thick

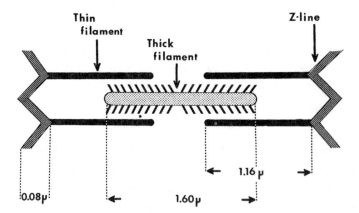

FIGURE 5.3a Schematic of a skeletal muscle sarcomere, showing interdigitating actin protein thin filaments and myosin protein thick filaments. The sarcomere is the smallest structural unit of skeletal muscle. (From Kaldor and DiBattista, 1978:7. Reprinted with permission.)

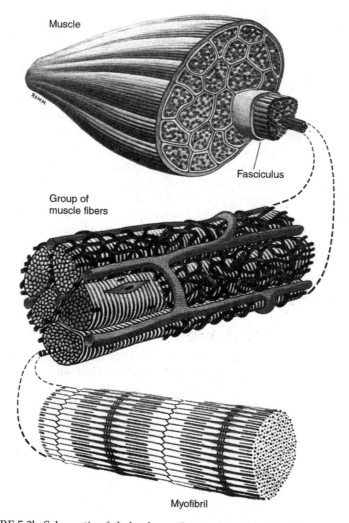

Muscle

Fasciculus

Group of
muscle fibers

Myofibril

FIGURE 5.3b Schematic of skeletal muscle structure showing the muscle, a group of fibers (i.e., muscle cells) surrounded by blood vessels, and a single myofibril of many that constitute the single fiber. (Adapted from Warwick and Williams, 1973:481, Figure 5.8. Reprinted with permission.)

filament lattice from both directions toward the center of each sarcomere. The thick filament myosin heads are the molecular force generators that form cross-bridge attachments to the thin filaments and pull the thin filaments toward the center of the sarcomere, thereby generating force and shortening. The fuel for cross-bridge movement is the energy stored in the chemical adenosine triphosphate (ATP); myosin heads hydrolyze ATP as a part of the cross-bridge cycle and convert the chemical energy released to force generation and heat. Each muscle fiber has a metabolic enzyme system, glycolytic and oxidative for replenishment of cellular ATP.

The smallest intact unit of a skeletal muscle that contracts in response to nerve stimulation is the single cell, or muscle fiber. Each muscle cell, or fiber, is made up of multiple myofibrils, creating the cross-sectional area that determines the fiber's maximal force generation. The skeletal muscle's maximal force generation is determined by the combined cross-sectional area of all of its fibers. The fiber's length is that of the entire muscle, with 2.0-2.2 µm long resting sarcomeres joined end to end at Z protein discs and repeating longitudinally tendon to tendon. The summed shortening of all of the sarcomeres in a fiber determines the total shortening of the fiber, and thus the muscle. Individual muscle fibers are bound together in parallel by connective tissue sheaths to form the muscle. The connective tissue of skeletal muscle serves as passive resistance to stretching of the sarcomeres by external forces and varies in content among skeletal muscles of an individual and among individuals.

Activation of Skeletal Muscle Contraction

The hard wiring of the nervous system determines the pattern of activation, or recruitment, of muscle fibers within a given muscle for either voluntary or reflex contraction. Each muscle fiber is served by only one α motor neuron that drives its contraction; but a single α motor neuron may branch and serve many skeletal muscle fibers. All of the fibers fed by a single α motor neuron are stimulated together and behave as a motor unit. Small motor units have relatively few fibers and are used for fine, delicate movements; large motor units have hundreds to thousands of fibers and are recruited for large forces and gross movement.

Recruitment order of motor units is from small to large for voluntary skeletal muscle contractions. As a consequence, the smaller motor units contract more frequently. Studies of muscle electrical activity have confirmed the preferential activation of small motor units during repetitive, low-intensity, stereotypical movement (Sjøgaard and McComas, 1995; Jensen, Pilegaard, and Sjøgaard, 2000). Because the skeletal muscle fibers of these low-threshold small motor units carry a disproportionate burden, they are referred to as "Cinderella" fibers (Hägg, 1991). Cinderella fibers are the ones at greatest risk of focal injury during low-intensity, repetitive work.

The fibers in a given motor unit are all activated together; therefore, they share the same adaptive, or conditioned, state, and they fatigue and recover as a unit. As a result of variations in use, motor unit fibers are transformed into one of two basic types: fast twitch, fatigable, or slow-twitch, fatigue resistant. Within the fast-twitch category, the primary metabolic enzymes vary from primarily glycolytic to glycolytic/oxidative; the diameter of the glycolytic fibers is larger than that of glycolytic/oxidative fast-twitch fibers. In general, fast-twitch fibers usually have greater diameters than slow-twitch ones. Slow-twitch fibers have primarily oxidative metabolic enzymes, with relatively more mitochondria, and are the fibers with lowest cross-sectional area and maximal force generation. Cinderella fibers are predominantly slow twitch; they are the motor units recruited first, then fast-twitch oxidative/glycolytic, and, finally fast-twitch glycolytic in maximal voluntary contraction (Hennemen and Olson, 1965; Hennemen, Somjen, and Carpenter, 1965a, 1965b; Hennemen et al., 1974).

The average person has a mixture of slow-twitch and fast-twitch motor units in every skeletal muscle. There is little evidence that fibers in a given motor unit convert from one type to the other as a result of exercise or training. This innate fiber type distribution may determine the capacity of an individual for various types of physical work as well as for forms of athletic performance; slow-twitch fibers enhance endurance, and fast-twitch enhance sprint-type performance.

Aside from a motor unit increasing in size through reinnervation of denervated muscle fibers, motor units do not increase in size after birth, because new muscle fibers are not created postnatally. As a consequence of aging, fast-twitch fibers appear vulnerable to dennervation and reinnervation by new branches of α motor neurons of slow-twitch motor units, as shown by Kadhiresan and coworkers (Kadhiresan, Hassert, and Faulkner, 1996) in a study of rats. Thus, aging leads to larger slow-twitch and smaller fast-twitch motor units.

Evidence of Skeletal Muscle Damage and Mechanisms of Injury

Decrements in skeletal muscle force generation in the face of repetitive use without nerve damage is evidence of either fatigue of motor units or skeletal fiber damage. The difference between the two is that force loss from fatigue is recovered within minutes to hours of rest, but fiber damage is repaired more slowly and may be irreversible. Fatigue of skeletal muscle fibers is failure of the fiber to contract in response to continuing α motor neuron stimulation (Bigland-Ritchie, Furbush, and Woods, 1986). While the fatigued fibers are not themselves permanently damaged, they can put other motor units at risk of structural damage due to inappropriate recruitment or excessive strain from external loads. In contrast to fatigue, recovery from fiber structural damage takes weeks to months, depending on rest and reuse, and the damage may result in complete loss of the damaged fibers with persistent reduction of maximal force generation. The only way to increase the maximal force generation capacity of a muscle after fiber loss is through hypertrophy of the remaining skeletal muscle fibers.

Fiber structural damage is also accompanied by products of cell inflammatory and necrotic processes, edema, microscopic evidence of contractile structure disruption, and leaking of intrafiber proteins and enzymes through disrupted cell membranes (Sjøgaard, 1986; Jensen, Jorgensen, and Sjøgaard, 1994; Skjeldal et al., 1993; Hagberg, Michaelson, and Ortelius, 1982). All of these indicators of fiber structural damage should be accompanied by a decrement in force generation if skeletal muscle damage has occurred. However, for repetitive contraction of skeletal muscle fibers under conditions leading to damage, loss of force may be accompanied only by clinical symptoms and pain as precursors to measurable structural damage (Sjøgaard and Jensen, 1997). It is hypothesized that loss of force generation is the result of molecular damage to the myosin heads, or cross-bridges; the methods for testing this hypothesis in intact muscle have not been developed.

Muscle injury may also be mediated by other mechanisms unrelated to contractile structure. When muscle contractions result in an intramuscular pressure exceeding capillary closing pressure (about 30 mmHg) muscle ischemia may result (Sjøgaard and Sjøgaard, 1998; Sadamoto, Bonde-Petersen, and Suzuki, 1983; Jarvholm et al., 1988a, 1988b; Shepherd et al., 1981). Data indicate that intramuscular pressure is inhomogeneous during contractions (Sejersted et al., 1984; Sejersted and Hargens, 1985; Laughlin, Mohrman, and Armstrong, 1984; Frank et al., 1999; Sexton and Poole, 1995) and that damage by this mechanism is most likely to affect small muscles (Sjøgaard and Jensen, 1997) and slow-twitch fibers (Bai et al., 1998) during prolonged static contractions. Intramuscular pressure ≥ 30 mmHg over an 8-hour period can cause muscle fiber atrophy, splitting, necrosis, and other derangements (Hargens et al., 1981; Pedowitz et al., 1990). The interaction between the increased metabolic demand of active muscles and the relative ischemia via increased intramuscular pressure has been hypothesized to contribute to derangements in intracellular pH/lactic acid, calcium, and potassium homeostasis (Sjøgaard, 1990, 1988; Sjøgaard, Savard, and Juel, 1988; Wilkie, 1986; Hermansen, 1981; Saltin et al., 1981; Sjøgaard et al., 1986; Chase and Kushmerick, 1988; Donaldson, Hermansen, and Bolles, 1978; Sjøgaard and Jensen, 1997). However, these mechanisms may relate mainly to the onset of muscle fatigue and not to fiber damage. There is evidence that reperfusion after ischemia leads to microvascular and cellular dysfunction, initiating longer-term symptoms and functional change in skeletal muscle (Seyama, 1993; Skjeldal et al., 1993; Jerome, Kong, and Korthuis, 1994).

In general, skeletal muscle behavior can be viewed from the perspective of the material fatigue model for considering musculoskeletal disorders. Laboratory studies of skeletal muscle show that there is a correlation between the number of contraction cycles and the extent of injury; these data are in agreement with clinical findings of repetitive use of affected muscles (Ranney, Wells, and Moore, 1995; Dennett and Fry, 1988). Stereotypical, repetitive motion is a major risk factor for development of musculoskeletal disorders (Fredriksson et al., 1999; Ohlsson et al., 1995; Ekberg et al., 1995). The muscles of each person have their own endurance limits, creating variations in each person's injury threshold for repetitive motion work. Also, multiple skeletal muscle contractions can be performed at low force before an actual injury, that is, before the person's endurance limit of force times the number of contraction cycles is reached. Working muscles initially tolerate the stress but require rest periods for recovery in order to avert damage.

People do experience symptoms of fatigue, such as discomfort and inability to work as efficiently, as they approach their endurance limit. The small, slow-twitch skeletal muscle fibers are more resistant to physiological fatigue than fast-twitch fibers. Since slow-twitch fibers are also characteristic of the small motor units recruited for low-force, repetitive, endurance work, they are the most vulnerable for being contracted to the point of muscle damage. Small muscles used for low-force, repetitive work are at risk for this type of damage (Lindman et al., 1991; Dennett, 1998; Larsson et al., 1988), as are small, slow-twitch motor units of larger muscles such as the trapezius. Larsson and colleagues (1990) observed a correlation between pain, reduction in muscle blood flow, and mitochondrial changes in slow-twitch fibers of the trapezius muscle for patients with a work history of performance of repetitive, static contractions; the pain and reduced blood flow to the trapezius muscle persisted long after elimination of the work.

The existing measures for damage of muscle appear inadequate for detecting endurance limits and early structural damage at the molecular level. Consequently, the correlation of the symptoms experienced by the worker to beginning structural damage have not been determined in scientific studies.

Types of Contractions and Associated Injury

Muscles always generate force due to cross-bridge cycling and internal sarcomere shortening during contraction, but the type of contraction varies based on what happens to the overall length of the muscle. During an active contraction, the overall length of the muscle may remain constant, yielding an isometric contraction; decrease, yielding a concentric contraction; or increase (i.e., stretch to a longer length), yielding an eccentric contraction. The first two types of active contraction, isometric and concentric, do not normally result in structural damage (McCully and Faulkner, 1985; Armstrong, Ogilvie, and Schwane, 1983; Newham, Jones, and Edwards, 1983; Newham et al., 1983; Balnave, Davey, and Allen, 1997; Lieber and Fridén, 1988; Lieber, Woodburn, and Fridén, 1991; Faulkner, Jones, and Round, 1989). The exception would be repetitive isometric (static) or concentric (kinetic) contractions of small motor units with slow-twitch muscle fibers under conditions in which fatigue does not protect them from overuse, as discussed above (Dennett and Fry, 1988; Larsson et al., 1988; Guidotti, 1992; Ranney, Wells, and Moore, 1995; Larsson, Oberg, and Larsson, 1999).

Due to the cross-bridge mechanism of skeletal muscle force generation and sarcomere structure, there is an optimal length for overlap of thick and thin filaments and cross-bridge formation, reflected as optimal length muscles for maximal force production. Contracting skeletal muscle outside this optimal length range creates a greater risk of structural damage, in addition to reducing force generation. In these less than optimal length ranges, sarcomeres in a fiber may have nonuniformity of force generation, causing hypercontraction of some and overstretching of others along the length of the fiber. Eventually, chronically stretched muscles will lengthen and chronically shortened muscles will shorten, by addition and deletion of sarcomeres at the ends of their fibers, respectively. This remodeling takes days to weeks; in the interim, the muscle is working inefficiently, and the muscles performing at longer lengths are at particular risk of damage to sarcomere structure.

The third type of muscle contraction, eccentric, offers the greatest risk for structural damage to fibers; this risk cannot be reduced by fiber remodeling or exercise training. External loads or work that cause sarcomeres to lengthen during active cross-bridge attachment are very likely to result in structural damage. Evidence of muscle damage may include loss of active force generation capacity, inflammation, necrosis, hemorrhage, and connective tissue tearing. Loss of force generating capacity may precede the other signs of eccentric contraction damage and is hypothesized to be due to shearing of, or damage to, myosin cross-bridges (Jones et al., 1986; Ogilvie et al., 1988; Fridén, Sjøstrom, and Ekblom, 1983; Newham et al., 1983; Newham, Jones, and Edwards, 1986; McCully and Faulkner, 1986; McComas, 1996; Macpherson, Dennis, and Faulkner, 1997; McCully and Faulkner, 1985; Lieber and Fridén, 1993; Brooks, Zerba, and Faulkner, 1995).

Regardless of the etiology, muscle injury results in an inflammatory response (Cannon et al., 1990; Kokot et al., 1988; Smith et al., 1989). Evidence indicates that oxygen free-radical mediated injury, edema, impaired perfusion, and other elements associated with acute inflammation contribute to both the progressive injury noted after injurious eccentric contraction and the so-called reperfusion injury seen after prolonged muscle ischemia (Korthuis et al., 1985; Walker et al., 1987; Granger, 1988; Messmer et al., 1988; Rubin et al., 1990; Seyama, 1993; Skjeldal et al., 1993; Jerome, Kong, and Korthuis, 1994).

Average force, strain, and work done to stretch the muscle (i.e., average force × strain) are the main physical factors in the initiation of muscle fiber injury during eccentric contraction (Brooks and Faulkner, 1996; Brooks, Zerba, and Faulkner, 1995; Hunter and Faulkner, 1997; Lynch and Faulkner, 1998). For repetitive eccentric contractions, available data indicate that an exponential relationship exists between stress and the number of cycles to failure, so that greater stress requires fewer cycles to failure. On the basis of the materials fatigue model, there should exist an endurance limit, or stress threshold, below which any number of contraction cycles could be applied without leading to injury (Armstrong, Warren, and Warren, 1991; Warren et al., 1993). However, the injurious effect of duty cycle and total duration of eccentric contraction have been incompletely characterized; therefore, a damage threshold for human work has not been identified.

Passive Stretch Injury of Skeletal Muscle

Passive stretch is the lengthening of a skeletal muscle while it is relaxed and not actively generating force. Passive stretch has been shown in a variety of studies to be a cause of skeletal muscle damage. The specific conditions requisite for passive stretch injury are not fully elucidated, in part because of different models used to apply passive stretch in scientific studies. However, certain results are common across studies.

The velocity, excursion, duty cycle, and total duration of passive stretch determine the total energy imparted to the muscle (Nikolaou et al., 1987). The combined effect of these variables must exceed a threshold for injury. An amplitude threshold was determined in a study by Noonan and others (1994) of rabbit skeletal leg muscles. Muscle stretch at 20 percent of load to failure showed no decrement in maximal contractile force. In contrast, stretch at 30 percent of load to failure showed significant loss of maximal contractile force and hemorrhage with focal areas of muscle fiber rupture. The relationship of amplitude and duty cycle of passive stretch in injury appears more complex. Cycling of passive stretch has been shown to cause a decrease in maximal force generation without abnormal microscopic or ultrastructural changes (Lieber and Fridén, 1988; Lieber, Woodburn, and Fridén, 1991). A plausible biological explanation for this is that the cycles of passive stretch damage the cross-bridges that attach and detach in relaxed muscle at a rate of 32 s^{-1} at 37° C (Eisenberg, Hill, and Chen, 1980). Such damage to cross-bridges would not be visible using a conventional microscope.

The mechanism of muscle damage during passive stretch has not yet been fully elucidated. Similarly, the effects of cyclical, passive loading and the role of duty cycle and total duration have not been systematically studied.

Vibration Injury of Skeletal Muscle

Working with hand-held vibrating tools has been linked to neurologic, vascular, and musculoskeletal disorders (Pelmear and Taylor, 1992; Armstrong et al., 1987; Stromberg et al., 1997; Färkkilä et al., 1979). In terms of skeletal motor unit function, vibration exposure impairment during intermittent and sustained maximal voluntary contractions has been shown in humans to include reduced electromyogram (EMG) firing rate, decreased motor unit firing rate, and decreased skeletal muscle force generation (Bongiovanni, Hagbarth, and Stjernberg, 1990). The effects on skeletal muscle per se are not so well documented, and the decrease in skeletal muscle maximal force generation is due at least in part to reduced firing of α motor neurons (Färkkilä, 1978; Färkkilä et al., 1980). Relocation of nuclei to the center of muscle fibers, although not structural damage per se, is used as a marker of injury in vibration-exposed muscles because this nuclear change is observed to be a common feature of neuromuscular disorders. In studies, using centralized nuclei as a marker for injury, only the skeletal muscles most directly exposed to the vibration were found to be affected by it (Necking et al., 1992, 1996b; Dubowitz, 1985).

The results of studies of rats by Necking and coworkers (Necking et al., 1996a, 1996b) show that frequency displacement and duration of the vibration interacted as determinants of changes in fiber nuclei location in the contracting skeletal muscle. The most direct indication of skeletal muscle damage from exposure to vibration during active contraction is that plasma levels of intracellular muscle enzymes increase, suggesting disruption of the skeletal muscle fiber cell membrane (Miyashita et al., 1983; Okada, 1986).

Muscular weakness is a common complaint among vibration-exposed workers (Färkkilä, 1978; Färkkilä et al., 1980; Pyykko et al., 1986), and reduced hand grip strength, corrected for aging, may persist for years after exposure (Färkkilä et al., 1986). However, the evidence of skeletal muscle damage per se has not been thoroughly studied for conditions leading to vibration-induced loss of force generation.

Age-Related Skeletal Muscle Injury and Risk

Aging is associated with skeletal muscle decrements in force, power, endurance, and recovery from injury. There are also age-related changes in motor unit innervation and in muscle morphology and metabolism (Kirkendall and Garrett, 1998; Bemben, 1998; Faulkner, Brooks, and Zerba, 1990; Shephard, 1999).

In humans, the decrease in muscle strength begins around age 40 and is more dramatic in humans after age 65; most of this decline is associated with inactivity (Faulkner, Brooks, and Zerba, 1990; Kirkendall and Garrett, 1998; Brooks and Faulkner, 1990, 1994; Shephard, 1999). However, approximately 20 percent of the age-related skeletal muscle weakness cannot be explained by the decrease in muscle mass or cross-sectional area associated with inactivity (Brooks and Faulkner, 1988; Bruce, Newton, and Woledge, 1989; Phillips et al., 1992; Brooks and Faulkner, 1994; Degens, Hoofd, and Binkhorst, 1995; Brown and Hasser, 1996; Jubrias et al., 1997). As evidence for this, training does not completely protect against the changes due to aging (Faulkner and Brooks, 1995).

Aged skeletal muscle is also more vulnerable to injury. In studies of rats subjected to eccentric contractions, researchers have demonstrated that aged skeletal muscle fibers are more easily injured by single and multiple eccentric contractions, muscle fibers regenerate less, and structural and functional recovery is not complete (Zerba, Komorowski, and Faulkner, 1990; Brooks and Faulkner, 1990, 1996; Carlson and Faulkner, 1989). However, extensive studies of the effects of eccentric contraction on aged human muscle have not been published.

Summary

The scientific studies reviewed support the conclusion that repetitive mechanical strain exceeding tolerance limits, imposed in a variety of ways, results in chronic skeletal muscle injury. This conclusion must be tempered by the limitations of the animal studies, which examined only a limited number of independent variables for short time periods that do not match the time frame for chronic work-related exposures. A major void in this area is concrete animal data that links repetitive use to injury after chronic exposure at levels of use that do not cause short-term injury. The conclusions related to repetitive mechanical strain and chronic skeletal muscle injury are dependent on extrapolation of data from short-term animal experiments. However, human studies support the same conclusions, even though the measures of dependent and independent variables are less definitive and the experimental conditions are less controlled. More importantly, the earliest molecular contractile changes in skeletal muscle structural injury have not been identified, and measures to detect them are not available for animals or humans.

Standardizing work will not necessarily guarantee safety or similar risk of injury for all workers. Constant, or standardized, external loads and strains, encountered in the performance of work, will have a different impact on each person, because of individual variations in skeletal muscle (mass, type, condition, structure) and for a given person over time, because of effects of aging and adaptation. For example, younger conditioned persons with the largest contractile mass, or skeletal muscle cross-sectional area, will have the greatest contraction force generation to oppose external load. Similarly, people with longer skeletal muscles have the capacity to withstand the larger length changes, and a person's relative proportion of slow- versus fast-twitch fibers will determine their tolerance for low-intensity endurance versus high-intensity burst-type work. This creates person-based variations in the risk and degree of injury for fixed work and external loads. Better noninvasive measures of skeletal muscle injury threshold are needed, since the match of work to task will be imprecise.

PERIPHERAL NERVE

Structure and Function

Peripheral nerves carry electrical impulses from peripheral tissues (e.g., skin, tendon, muscle) to the spinal columns and from the spinal column to the periphery (e.g., vessels, muscle). A nerve is composed of hundreds or thousands of axons, which are each an extension of a nerve cell body located in the spinal cord. The axon is surrounded by Schwann cells to form myelinated nerve fibers (Figure 5.4). Myelinated and non-myelinated nerve fibers are grouped together in bundles, called fascicles, and surrounded by a perineurial membrane. The amount of connective tissue in and surrounding the nerve varies by level. For example, nerves located superficially in the limb or parts of the peripheral nerve that cross a joint contain an increased quantity of connective tissue, possibly as a response to repeated loading (Sunderland, 1978).

The energy needs of impulse propagation and nutritional transport (axonal transport) are provided by a unique microvascular system. The small vessels supplying the nerve from the surrounding tissue have a coiled appearance that permits the normal gliding of the nerve during movement. When the vessels reach the nerve, they divide into branches running longitudinally in various layers of the nerve. In the endoneurium the environment is protected by a blood-nerve barrier. There are no lymphatic vessels to drain the endoneurial space; therefore, when edema

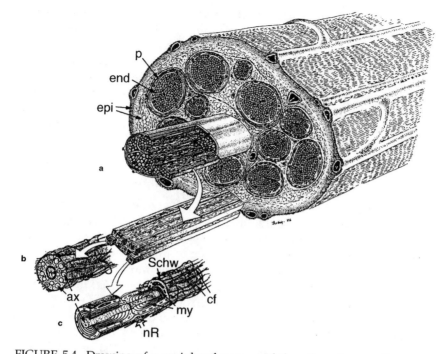

FIGURE 5.4 Drawing of a peripheral nerve with bundles of nerve fibers surrounded by perineurium (p) forming 12 fascicles. The fascicles are embedded in a loose connective tissue called the epineurium (epi). Myelinated (c) and nonmyelinated (b) fibers are shown with Schwann cells (Schw), myelin sheath(my), axons (ax), and nodes of Ranvier (nR). (Reproduced, with modification, from Lundborg, 1988:186. Reprinted with permission.)

forms in this space, the pressure in the fascicle may increase and rapidly interfere with the endoneurial microcirculation (Lundborg and Dahlin, 1996).

Short-Term Effects of Compression

The effects of loading on the peripheral nerve have recently been reviewed (Rempel et al., 1999). The primary mechanism of mechanical injury to the nerve is by regional compression or nerve stretching. Extraneural compression pressures as low as 20 mmHg can decrease intraneural microvascular flow, and pressures of 30 mmHg can impair axonal transport. By increasing vascular permeability, a brief low-pressure (30 mmHg) compression of the nerve can lead to endoneurial edema formation, which persists for at least 24 hours after the compression is removed. In turn, the resultant edema reduces blood flow in the nerve. Both increasing duration of compression and higher pressure lead to greater edema formation.

The effect of fluctuating extraneural pressure on nerve function was investigated in a rat tibial nerve model, wherein a sinusoidal pressure pattern was applied at 1 Hz for 20,000 cycles (Szabo and Sharkey, 1993). The study indicated that when extraneural pressure fluctuates rapidly, the effect on nerve function is associated with the mean value of the pressure waveform, rather than the minimal or peak value.

Long-Term Effects of Nerve Compression

The long-term biological effects of brief, graded nerve compression have been studied in several animal models using small inflatable cuffs (Powell et al., 1986; Dyck et al., 1990). Pressures of 0, 10, 30, and 80 mmHg were applied for 2 hours to a nerve; then at intervals up to 28 days the nerves were examined for evidence of injury. Within 4 hours endoneurial edema formed within all compressed nerves and persisted for the entire time of the study. Inflammation and fibrin deposits occurred within hours of compression, followed by a proliferation of endoneurial fibroblasts and capillary endothelial cells. Within days, vigorous proliferation of fibrous tissue was noted, with marked fibrosis at day 28 and sheets of fibrous tissue extending to adjacent structures. Demyelination and axonal degeneration were first observed a week after compression. The degree of axonal degeneration and demyelination were correlated with the initial pressure.

To model chronic nerve compression, other investigators have placed short silicon tubes of varying internal diameters or loose ligatures around the rat sciatic or sural nerve (Mackinnon et al., 1994; Sommer et al., 1993). These are very effective models for studying pain-related behavior (Mosconi and Kruger, 1996). The biological response of the nerve is similar to that found in the cuff experiments, with early perineural edema followed by a short-term inflammatory response, fibrosis, demyelination, and, finally, nerve fiber degeneration. It is not possible to precisely control the compression level with these chronic models.

Vibration Exposure

Work with handheld vibrating tools can lead to a complex of symptoms known as the hand-arm vibration syndrome, in which sensorineural disturbances are prominent (Strömberg et al., 1996). Biopsies of the posterior interosseus nerve 5 cm proximal to the wrist, from men exposed to hand vibration at work, revealed such pathological changes as breakdown of myelin and the presence of interstitial and perineurial fibrosis in comparison to controls (Strömberg, 1997). The histology results suggest that demyelination may be a primary lesion in the neuropathy, which is followed by fibrosis associated with incomplete regeneration or with organization of an edema. Similar pathological changes are seen in the small nerves at the fingertips from patients exposed to vibrating handheld tools (Takeuchi et al., 1986). Animal models exposing peripheral nerves to vibration demonstrate an initial edema formation followed by demyelination and later a loss of axons (Lundborg et al., 1990, 1987; Ho and Yu, 1989; Chang, Ho, and Yu, 1994).

Summary

Several animal models demonstrate that low magnitude, short- or long-term compression of a peripheral nerve leads to a biological response of endoneurial edema, demyelination, inflammation, axon degeneration, and fibrosis. The degree of axonal degeneration is dependent on the applied pressure in a dose-response pattern. The critical pressure or threshold causing acute changes in nerve function is known, but the critical pressure-duration threshold for chronic nerve compression is unknown.

Exposure to vibrating hand tools at work can lead to permanent peripheral nerve injury. Animal models of vibration exposure confirm a pathophysiological process of edema formation followed by demyelination and axonal degradation. No animal model has been developed to evaluate the effects of repetitive hand-finger loading on nerve structure and function.

SPINAL NERVE ROOTS

Structure and Function of Spinal Nerve Roots

The nerve roots are located along the axis of the spine and serve as routes of communication between the central and peripheral nervous systems. Enclosed by the vertebral bones, the spinal nerve roots are relatively well protected from external trauma. However, spinal canal pathology that compromises the neural space, such as disc herniation or protrusion, spinal stenosis, and degenerative disorders, can create high risk of injury, even under what might be considered moderate physical exposures. Furthermore, nerve roots do not possess so much protective connective tissue as do the peripheral nerves, which makes them particularly sensitive to mechanical and chemical irritation.

Structurally, the axons of the nerve root are located in the endoneural space, which is similar to that of the peripheral nerve but with five times less collagen. The root sheath separates the nerve root from the cerbrospinal fluid, which is surrounded by the spinal dura mater. The vascular supply is complex and may be involved in the pathophysiology of injury. The vessels from the periphery and from the spinal cord meet in the proximal one-third of the nerve root; it has been suggested that this region is particularly vulnerable to injury from ischemia. The blood-nerve barrier in the nerve root is not so well developed as in peripheral nerves; this creates a higher risk of edema.

Acute Nerve Root Compression

The most common mode of nerve root injury is mechanical compression. Recent experiments that precisely control nerve root compression reveal that capillary blood flow can be disrupted by venular occlusion with pressures as low as 5 to 10 mmHg. Such a compression-induced impairment of the vasculature will impede nerve root nutrition and lead to nerve root dysfunction. There is no significant secondary route of nutrition via diffusion from the cerebrospinal fluid.

Low-pressure compression of a nerve root will lead to an increase in the vascular permeability and intraneural edema formation (Olmarker, Rydevik, and Holm, 1989), a response well documented for peripheral nerves (Rydevik and Lundborg, 1977). In peripheral nerves, such edema may increase the endoneurial fluid pressure (Low and Dyck, 1977; Lundborg, Myers, and Powell, 1983; Rydevik, Myers, and Powell, 1989), which in turn may impair the endoneurial capillary blood flow and jeopardize the nerve root nutrition (Myers et al., 1982; Low, Dyck, and Schmelzer, 1982; Low et al., 1985). Edema may negatively affect the nerve root for a longer period than the compression itself, since the edema usually persists for some time after the removal of a compressive agent. The presence of an intraneural edema is also related to subsequent formation of intraneural fibrosis (Rydevik, Lundborg, and Nordborg, 1976), which may delay recovery in some patients with nerve compression disorders. Experimental compression studies have demonstrated that the sensory fibers are more susceptible to compression than the motor fibers (Pedowitz et al., 1992; Rydevik et al., 1991).

Chronic Experimental Nerve Root Compression

Compression that evolves gradually may allow time for the remodeling and adaptation of axons and vasculature. In this case, the clinical consequences of compression may be less severe than if the compression was applied acutely. Despite this, a very gradual increase in compression, over two weeks, still results in structural and functional changes consistent with constriction (Delamarter et al., 1990; Cornefjord et al., 1997).

Following compression of nerve root and dorsal root ganglion, there can be an increase in a chemical factor called substance P, which is a neurotransmitter related to pain transmission (Cornefjord et al., 1995). This finding suggests that compression may lead to pain via both mechanical and chemical pathways.

Mechanical Deformation, Biochemical Factors, and Pain

Mechanical deformation of nerve roots may induce impulses that are perceived by the individual as pain. For instance, mechanical stimulation of nerve roots or peripheral nerves results in nerve impulses of short duration; these impulses are prolonged if the nerve tissue had been exposed to mechanical irritation by a chronic gut ligature (Howe, Loeser, and Calvin, 1977; Cavanaugh, Özaktay, and Vaidyanathan, 1994). Severe mechanical deformation, such as ligation of the nerve root, is generally not painful (Chatani et al., 1995; Kawakami et al., 1994a, 1994b).

An increase in the level of neurotransmitters related to pain transmission has been found in the dorsal root ganglion in response to whole-body vibration of rabbits (Weinstein, 1986; Weinstein et al., 1987). A similar increase has also been seen in the dorsal root ganglion and nerve root after local constriction of the same nerve root (Cornefjord et al., 1995).

Recent data suggest that chemical factors in nucleus pulposus can sensitize a nerve root, making it more susceptible to mechanical perturbations. Applied individually, nucleus pulposus or slight mechanical movement will not produce pain behavior in a rat model, whereas the combination of the two factors produces pain (Olmarker and Myers, 1998; Olmarker et al., 1998). This sensitization is thought to be orchestrated by the cytokine TNF-alpha (Olmarker and Larsson, 1998).

Summary

Although experimental models of low-grade compression have not been so extensively applied to the spinal root as they have to the peripheral nerve, they reveal similar initial damage mechanisms. Compression or direct mechanical stimulation may release cytokines and neurotransmitters (e.g., substance P, TNF-alpha) that stimulate pain transmission. However, due to experimental difficulties associated with chronic pain models, the entire pathway leading to chronic pain remains uncertain. The pathway is likely to involve a combination of compression of the dorsal root combined with the release of biochemical mediators of pain.

SUMMARY

The structural tissues—bone, disc, tendon, and muscle—demonstrate fatigue failure well below their strength. For example, tendons subjected to repeated stretching at 10 percent of strength will ultimately fail. For tissues studied in detail, the relationship between load and number of cycles to failure follows a log-linear dose-response model. The demonstration of this relationship provides evidence for damage accumulation. The ultrastructural correlates to damage accumulation have been observed for some tissues. For example, vertebral bone subjected to cyclical loading develops microfractures. In other tissues, such as the disc, the ultrastructural correlates have yet to be documented.

Although a threshold for fatigue damage below which no damage accumulates has been postulated, such thresholds have yet to be proven. For example, 30 percent compression strength has been postulated as the fatigue threshold for the disc. The duration of fatigue testing at low stress levels (e.g., 10 percent) has been short relative to the time frame for repair and remodeling. Tissue repair and remodeling takes place over weeks and months, but the fatigue tests are conducted for hours or days. The documentation of thresholds for fatigue damage would be a valuable adjunct to the current data.

In vivo animal models are necessary to investigate the whole organism's response to tissue loading. To some degree, the ultrastructural damage due to cyclical loading may be repaired as long as the time frame for the repair and remodeling is not long relative to the rate of damage and as long as the remodeling mechanism is not overwhelmed. With a repair system in place, one would expect a load-duration or a load-repetition threshold below which there is no damage accumulation and a disorder would never manifest. In addition, some injury mechanisms, for example, those mediated by inflammation or ischemia, can only be thoroughly investigated with in vivo models.

In vivo animal models have been developed for the disc, tendon, muscle, and nerve that can support the investigation of the effects of cyclical loading on cellular, biochemical, and mechanical endpoints of tissues in the intact organism. Generally, these studies demonstrate specific damage endpoints, with sustained or repeated loading, that are similar to the pathology observed in humans. For example, the rabbit tendinitis model developed by Backman et al. (1990) demonstrated edema, increased capillary network, and inflammatory cells in the paratenon and degenerative changes in the tendon, findings also observed in histopathology studies of human tenosynovitis and epicondylitis. Most of the in vivo findings have been observed in more than one laboratory. These studies, in addition to demonstrating the specificity of endpoints, also document the temporal relationship between exposure and effect. Due to the different levels of development of these models and the methods used to evaluate tissue damage, the depth of knowledge of the mechanism of injury varies from tissue to tissue.

In vertebral bone, strength diminishes and damage is irreversible with each trabecular fracture. However, the role of the smaller microcracks in the pathophysiology of bone damage is uncertain; they may be a harbinger of fractures, or they may be repaired. In humans, vertebral microfractures are not visible using current imaging methods (e.g., X-ray, CT, MRI), which contributes to the known poor correlation between images of the spine and low back pain. Both disc and vertebra demonstrate fatigue failure, but vertebral endplates fail before the disc in response to repeated loading. Cumulative spinal loading affects disc pressure and water content, and these factors, in turn, influence cell viability and function. In vivo loading of sufficient magnitude can cause altered cell metabolism and cell death following a dose-response relationship.

In vivo animal models that expose tendons to repeated loading demonstrate an inflammatory response with fibrosis in the peritenon. The process may be mediated by an initial release of inflammatory mediators and microtrauma. In the central tendon, degenerative changes are observed with edema, collagen disorganization, and fibrosis. Although the initial steps may include microtrauma, they are not well characterized.

In muscle, prolonged fatigue damage can occur with single or cyclical loads. Eccentric loading is more damaging than concentric loading. Repeated eccentric loading can produce a persistent force decrement with structural damage to the sarcomeres (Z-line streaming, fiber necrosis, and inflammation). A threshold or endurance limit for injury has not been identified. The mechanical fatigue injury mechanism may be complemented by physiological mechanisms (e.g., intramuscular pressure, Cinderella hypothesis).

In the peripheral nerve, compression causes edema accumulation, elevated endoneural pressure, vascular disruption, fibrosis, demyelination, and axon injury. The steps linking the initial effects to demyelination and permanent nerve damage are uncertain. Compression of the nerve for a sufficient duration also leads to chronic pain. Exposure to vibration causes a similar process of edema formation followed by demyelination and axon degradation. Although the relationship between nerve injury and compression follows a dose-response model, the critical pressure and duration relationships for chronic nerve compression have not been determined. For the spinal nerve roots, adjacent tissue compression may release cytokines that stimulate pain transmission.

Age can influence the mechanical and biological properties of bone, disc, muscle, and nerve. Increasing age leads to increased degenerative changes in vertebrae and discs, increased accumulation of extracellular matrix in the peripheral nerve, and reduced muscle strength. However, the independent role of age in modifying the negative effects of cyclical loading on these tissues is not determined. The role of gender as a covariate in the response of tissues to cyclical loading has not been investigated.

6

Biomechanics

This chapter provides a review of the biomechanics literature on the low back and upper extremities. Biomechanics is the study of forces acting on and generated within the body and of the effects of these forces on the tissues, fluids, or materials used for diagnosis, treatment, or research purposes. The discussion begins with an overview of basic concepts and methods. This is followed by the two literature reviews. The study selection criteria are presented at the beginning of each review. The two bodies of literatures differ in maturity; the research on the low back is more substantial. The number of studies reviewed is 196 for the low back and 109 for the upper extremities.

CONCEPTS OF LOAD TOLERANCE

The term "load" describes physical stresses acting on the body or on anatomical structures within the body. These stresses include kinetic (motion), kinematic (force), oscillatory (vibration), and thermal (temperature) energy sources. Loads can originate from the external environment (such as the force generated by a power hand tool) or they may result from voluntary or involuntary actions of the individual (for example, lifting objects). The term "tolerance" is used to describe the capacity of physical and physiological responses of the body to loading.

Acute Trauma Load-Tolerance Injury Model

Acute trauma injuries refer to those arising from a single identifiable event. Examples of acute injuries include fractures, lacerations, and contusions. Disorders resulting from acute trauma may occur when transient external loads, which are transmitted through biomechanical loading of the body, exceed internal tolerances of the affected tissues for mechanical strain, resulting in pain, discomfort, impairment, or disability. These factors may be affected by individual and organizational factors and by the social context in which the individual is operating.

Cumulative Trauma Load-Tolerance Model

Work-related musculoskeletal disorders arise from a complex interaction of events that may accumulate over time. In contrast to the acute trauma model, the cumulative trauma model assumes injury may result from the accumulated effect of transient external loads that may, in isolation, be insufficient to exceed internal tolerances of tissues. It is when this loading accumulates by repeated exposures, or exposures of sufficiently long duration, that the internal tolerances of tissues are eventually exceeded. The cumulative trauma model therefore explains why many musculoskeletal disorders are associated with work, because individuals often repeat actions (often many thousands of times) throughout the workday, or spend long periods of time (as much as eight hours or more daily) performing work activities in many occupations. Internal mechanical tolerance represents the ability of a structure to withstand loading. It is clearly multidimensional and is not considered a threshold but rather the capacity of tissues to prolong mechanical strain or fatigue. Internal tissue tolerances may themselves become lowered through repetitive or sustained loading.

A schematic diagram useful for elaborating the factors that can cause pain, discomfort, impairment, and disability is illustrated in Figure 1.2. External loads are produced in the physical work environment. These loads are transmitted through the biomechanics of the limbs and body to create internal loads on tissues and anatomical structures. Biomechanical factors include body position, exertions, forces, and motions. External loading also includes environmental factors whereby thermal or vibrational energy is transmitted to the body. Biomechanical loading is further affected by individual factors, such as anthropometry, strength, agility, dexterity, and other factors mediating the transmission of external loads to internal loads on anatomical structures of the body.

Measures of External Loads

External loads are physical quantities that can be directly measured using various methodologies. External kinetic measurements, for example, include physical properties of the exertions (forces actually applied or created) that individuals make. These measurements have the most direct correspondence to internal loads because they are physically and biomechanically related to specific anatomical structures of the body. When external measurements cannot be obtained, quantities that describe the physical characteristics of the work are often used as indirect measures. These include (a) the loads handled, (b) the forces that must be overcome in performing a task, (c) the geometric aspects of the workplace that govern posture, (d) the characteristics of the equipment used, and (e) the environmental stressors (e.g., vibration and cold) produced by the workplace conditions or the objects handled. Alternatively, less directly correlated aspects of the work, such as production and time standards, classifications of tasks performed, and incentive systems, are sometimes used as surrogate measures to quantify the relationship between work and physical stress.

The literature contains numerous methodologies for measuring physical stress in manual work. Studies from different disciplines and research groups have concentrated on diverse external factors, workplaces, and jobs. Factors most often cited include forceful exertions, repetitive motions, sustained postures, strong vibration, and cold temperatures. Although the literature reports a great diversity of such factors, it is possible to group these methodologies into a coherent body of scientific inquiry. A conceptual framework is presented below for organizing the physical parameters in manual work.

Physical Stresses

Physical stress can be described in terms of fundamental physical quantities of kinetic, kinematic, oscillatory, and thermal energy. These basic quantities constitute the external and internal loading aspects of work and energy produced by, or acting on, the human in the workplace.

Kinetic (Force) Measurements

Force is the mechanical effort for accomplishing an action. Voluntary motions and exertions are produced when internal forces are generated from active muscle contraction in combination with passive action of the connective tissues. Muscles transmit loads through tendons, ligaments, and bone to the external environment when the body generates forces through voluntary exertions and motions. Internal forces produce torques about the joints and tension, compression, torsion, or shear within the anatomical structures of the body.

External forces act against the human body and can be produced by an external object or in reaction to the voluntary exertion of force against an external object. Force is transmitted back to the body and its internal structures when opposing external forces are applied against the surface of the body. Localized pressure against the body can transmit forces through the skin to underlying structures, such as tendons and nerves. Pressure increases directly with contact force over a given area and decreases when the contact area is proportionally increased.

Contact stress is produced when forces compress the soft tissues between anatomical structures and external objects. This may occur when grasping tools or parts or making contact with the workstation. Contact stress may be quantified by considering contact pressure (force per unit area). An increase in contact force or a decrease in contact area will result in greater contact stress. Pounding with the hands or striking an object will give rise to stress over the portion of body contact. Reaction forces from these stress concentrations are transmitted through the skin to underlying anatomical structures.

Kinematics (Motion) Measurements

Motion describes the displacement of a specific articulation or the position of adjacent body parts. Motion of one body segment relative to another is most commonly quantified by angular displacement, velocity, or acceleration of the included joint. Motion is specific to each joint and therefore motions of the body are fully described when each individual body segment is considered together. Motions create internal stress by imposing loads on the involved muscles and tendons in order to maintain the position, transmitting loads to underlying nerves and blood vessels, or creating pressure between adjacent structures within or around a joint.

Oscillatory (Vibration) Measurements

Vibration occurs when an object undergoes oscillatory or impulsive motion. *Human vibration* occurs when the acceleration of external objects acts against the human body. Vibration is transmitted to the body through physical contact, either from the seat or the feet (whole-body vibration) or when grasping a vibrating object (hand-arm vibration). Whole-body vibration is associated with vibration when riding in a vehicle or standing on a moving platform. Hand-arm vibration, or segmental vibration, is introduced by using power hand tools or when grasping vehicular controls. Physiological reactions to human-transmitted vibration include responses of the endocrine, metabolic, vascular, nervous, and musculoskeletal systems.

External vibration is transmitted from the distal point of contact to proximal locations on the body, which sets into motion the musculoskeletal system, receptor organs, tissues, and other anatomical structures.

Vibration transmission is dependent on vibration magnitude, frequency, and direction. Dynamic mechanical models of the human body describe the transmission characteristics of vibration to various body parts and organs. Such models consider the passive elemental properties of body segments, such as mass, compliance, and viscous damping. Vibration transmission is affected by these passive elements and is modified by the degree of coupling between the vibration source and the body. The force used for gripping a vibrating handle and the posture of the body will directly affect vibration transmission.

Thermal (Temperature) Measurements

Heat loss occurs at the extremities when working outdoors, working in indoor cold environments such as food processing facilities, handling cold materials, or exposing the hands to cold compressed air exhausts. Local peripheral cooling inhibits biomechanical, physiological, and neurological functions of the hand. Exposure to localized cooling has been associated with decrements in manual performance and dexterity, tactility and sensibility, and strength. These effects are attributable to various physiological mechanisms.

Physical Stress Exposure Properties

The physical stresses described above may be present at varying levels. These variations can be characterized by three properties: magnitude, repetition, and duration. The relationship between physical stresses and their exposure properties is illustrated in Figure 6.1. Magnitude is the

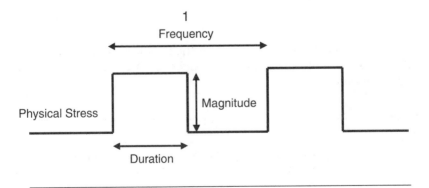

FIGURE 6.1 Representation of magnitude, duration, and repetition for physical stress-time.

extent to which a physical stress factor is involved. Magnitude quantifies the amplitude of the force, motion, vibration, or temperature time-varying record and has the physical units of the corresponding physical measure (e.g., Newtons of force, degrees of rotation, m/s^2 of vibration acceleration, or degrees Celsius of temperature). Repetition is the frequency or rate at which a physical stress factor repeats. Duration corresponds to the time that one is exposed to a physical stress factor and is quantified in physical units of time.

Force is quantified by its magnitude, the repetition rate, and duration of force application at a given location of the human body. Measures of motion include the magnitude of joint angular displacement, velocity, or acceleration; the repetition rate of the motion; and the duration time that the motion is sustained. Vibration is quantified by the magnitude of the acceleration of a body, the repetition rate at which vibration occurs, and the duration time the vibration is sustained. Similarly, temperature level and associated repetition rate and duration quantify cold exposure.

Interactions

The characteristic exposure properties of physical stresses together quantify external loads acting against the body. Combinations of different physical stresses and exposure properties can be used to describe factors that are commonly reported for quantifying exposure. These relationships are summarized in Table 6.1. Physical stresses are correspondingly quantified as described in Table 6.2. This organization is useful because it provides a construct for comparing and combining studies using different measurements and methodologies, as represented in Table 6.1, into a

TABLE 6.1 Theoretical Framework for the Relationship Between External Physical Stress Factors and Properties as Typically Described in the Scientific Literature

Physical Stress	Property		
	Magnitude	Repetition Rate	Duration
Force	Forceful exertions	Repetitive exertions	Sustained exertions
Motion	Extreme postures and motions	Repetitive motions	Sustained postures
Vibration	High vibration level	Repeated vibration exposure	Long vibration exposure
Cold	Cold temperatures	Repeated cold exposure	Long cold exposure

TABLE 6.2 Relationship Between External Physical Stress Factors and
Their Properties as They are Typically Measured

Physical Stress	Property		
	Magnitude	Repetition Rate	Duration
Force	Force generated or applied	Frequency with which force is applied	Time that force is applied
Motion	Joint angle, velocity, acceleration	Frequency of motion	Time to complete motion
Vibration	Acceleration	Frequency with which vibration occurs	Time of vibration exposure
Cold	Temperature	Frequency of cold exposure	Time of cold exposure

common framework. For example, physical stress measurements using a
survey methodology that simply assesses the presence or absence of
highly repetitive wrist motions can therefore be compared with a study
that measures the frequency of motions using an electrogoniometer. This
is possible because both studies have quantified the repetition property of
wrist motion. Similarly, a study that considers the weight of objects lifted
can be compared with a study that assesses muscle force using electromyography because both studies quantify the magnitude of force. A
body of scientific knowledge from diverse investigations thus emerges.

The external physical stress factors described above relate to distinct
internal physical stress factors. This relationship is summarized in Table
6.3. For example, force magnitude is directly related to the loading of
tissues, joints, and adjacent anatomical structures, as are the metabolic
and fatigue processes of contracting muscles. The strength of these relationships depends on the particular measurement and the type of stress.
Biomechanical and physiological mathematical models have been developed to quantitatively describe some of these relationships. Moore, Wells,
and Ranney (1991) and Armstrong et al. (1993) have recognized similar
relationships between external and internal factors.

Internal Loads

The musculoskeletal system is the load bearing structure within ver-
tebrate animals. Bony structures bear gravitational forces and internal
forces of skeletal muscle contraction in maintaining the body posture. As
such, bones are the primary load-bearing tissue within the body. Forces
applied to the body, including gravity, compress or bend the bones. Liga-

TABLE 6.3 Relationships Between External and Internal Physical Stress

Physical Stress	Property		
	Magnitude	Repetition	Duration
Force	• Tissue loads and stress • Muscle tension and contraction • Muscle fiber recruitment • Energy expenditure, fatigue, and metabolite production • Joint loads • Adjacent anatomical structure loads and compartment pressure • Transmission of vibrational energy	• Tissue loading rate and energy storage • Tissue strain recovery • Muscle fiber recruitment and muscle fatigue rate • Energy expenditure, fatigue, and elimination of metabolites • Cartilage or disc rehydration	• Cumulative tissue loads • Muscle fiber recruitment and muscle fatigue rate • Energy expenditure, fatigue, and metabolite production
Motion	• Tissue loads and stress • Adjacent anatomical structure loads and compartment pressure • Transmission of vibrational energy*	• Tissue loading rate and energy storage • Tissue strain recovery	• Cumulative tissue loads
Vibration	• Transmission of vibrational energy to musculoskeletal system • Transmission of vibrational energy to somatic and autonomic sensory receptors and nerves • Transmission of energy to muscle spindles*	• Recovery from vibrational energy exposure	• Cumulative vibrational energy exposure
Cold	• Thermal energy loss from the extremities • Cooling of tissues and bodily fluids • Somatic and autonomic receptor stimulus	• Recovery from thermal energy loss	• Cumulative thermal energy loss

Note: * Indicates internal stress.

ments hold together the bony structure by crossing articulations where bones interconnect. Retinacula share similar structural and biomechanical properties to ligaments that act as pulley systems by guiding tendons around articulations. Tendons are the connective tissues that attach muscle to bone and therefore transmit muscle forces to the skeletal system to produce voluntary movements and exertions. A consequence of force exerted by the body or acting against the body, motions produced by the body, oscillatory energy transmitted to the body, or thermal energy released from the body, is that adjacent tissues are subjected to mechanical and thermal loads. These include ligaments and connective tissue, tendon, muscle, intervertebral discs, and nerves. A detailed examination of how each of these tissues is subjected to internal loading follows.

Ligaments and Connective Tissue

By their nature, as the connective tissues linking bones within the skeletal system, ligaments are primarily exposed to tensile loads. A typical stress-strain curve for ligamentous tissue reveals that the tissue initially offers little resistance to elongation as it is stretched; however, once the resistance to elongation begins to increase, it does so very rapidly. Thus, the ligaments, while loosely linking the skeletal system, begin to resist motion as a joint's full range of motion is approached. By severing ligaments in cadaveric lumbar motion segments, Adams et al. (1980) showed that the supraspinous-interspinous ligaments segments are the first ligamentous tissues to become stressed with forward bending of the lumbar spine. Stability and movement of the spine or any other articulation within the low tensile region of the ligamentous stress-strain curve must be accomplished using muscular contraction. This is not to say that ligaments do not contribute to joint loading. Several authors have shown that with extreme flexion (forward bending) of the torso, there is an electrical silence in the spinal musculature (Floyd and Silver, 1955; Golding, 1952; Kippers and Parker, 1984; Toussaint et al., 1995). This finding suggests that at times ligaments are used to resist the bending moments acting on the spine. The degree of ligamentous contribution to the forces placed on the intervertebral disc during manual material handling tasks has been debated in the scientific literature (Cholewicki and McGill, 1992; Dolan, Earley, and Adams, 1994; Potvin, Norman, and McGill, 1991). Nevertheless, there is consensus that ligaments are subjected to tensile stress with extreme movements and hence can contribute to the mechanical loads placed on the body's articulations, including the intervertebral disc.

When ligaments act as a turning point for tendons (pulleys), they are exposed to shear forces and contact stresses. For example, the transverse carpal ligament, in bridging the carpal bones in the wrist, forms a pulley by which the path of the finger flexor tendons is altered when the wrist is flexed. Similarly, the palmar ligaments maintain the path of the tendons from the finger flexor muscles to the distal phalanges. Goldstein et al. (1987) showed that the tendon strain on the proximal side of the transverse carpal ligament was greater than the strain on the distal side of the ligament. This finding indicates that the friction between the tendon and the ligament results in the ligament being exposed to shear loads in addition to normal loads. Goldstein et al. (1987) also demonstrated that the magnitude of shear was dependent on an interaction between tensile load and posture.

Tendons

Tendons are a collagenous tissue that forms the link between muscle and bone. The orientation of the collagen fibers in tendons is in the form of parallel bundles. This arrangement of fibers minimizes the stretch or creep in these tissues when subjected to tensile loading (Abrahams, 1967). With repeated loading of synovial tissues, surrounding tendons can become inflamed, particularly where the tendons wrap around bony or ligamentous structures. In more severe cases, the collagen fibers of the supraspinatus tendon can become separated and eventually degraded, wherein debris containing calcium salts creates further swelling and pain (Schechtman and Bader, 1997).

Muscles

Skeletal muscles provide locomotion and maintenance of posture through the transfer of tension by their attachment to the skeletal system via tendons. Tension is developed through active contraction and passive stretch of contractile units, or muscle fibers.

The musculoskeletal system uses simple mechanics, such as levers, to produce large angular changes in adjoining body segments. Consequently, the amount of muscular force required to produce a desired exertion or movement depends on the external force characteristics (resistance or load dynamics handled) and the relative distance from the fulcrum to the point of external force application and from the fulcrum to the point of muscular insertion. While the effective distance between the fulcrum and the point of insertion for a specific muscle varies depending on the angle of the joint, the leverage of the muscles is almost always very small relative to the load application point, hence the internal muscle forces are usually several times larger than the external forces. As a result, most of the loads experienced by the joints within the body during exertions result from the internal muscle forces as they work in opposition to the external forces.

Intervertebral Disc

The intervertebral disc serves as a joint since it permits rotation and translation of one vertebra relative to another. It also maintains the space between vertebrae so that spinal nerves remain unimpinged and protects the upper body and head from the large peak forces experienced in the lower extremities. Anatomically, the disc is comprised of two parts: the nucleus pulposus and the annulus fibrosus. The nucleus pulposus is in the central region of the disc and is comprised of a gelatinous mixture of water, collagen, and proteoglycans. The annulus fibrosus is comprised of alternating bands of angled fibers oriented approximately 60 degrees relative to the vertical (White and Panjabi, 1990). In essence, the disc behaves as a pressure vessel and transmits force radially and uniformly. Thus, the disc is capable of withstanding the large compressive forces that result from muscular recruitment. Hutton and Adams (1982) found that cadaver discs from males between the ages of 22 and 46 could, on average, withstand single loads of over 10,000 N before failure occurred. In most cases, the failure was in the thin bony membrane that forms the boundary between the disc and the vertebral body (vertebral endplate) rather than through nuclear prolapse. Since the disc is an avascular structure, the health of the endplate is critical for nutrient exchange, and even small failures may hasten the degenerative process.

Researchers have found that prolapsed discs occurred more frequently when the vertebral segments were wedged to simulate extreme forward bending of the spine (Adams and Hutton, 1982). In this position, the anterior portion of the annulus fibrosis undergoes compression while the posterior portion is under tensile stress. Over 40 percent of the cadaver discs tested by Adams and Hutton (1982) prolapsed when tested in this hyperflex posture, and with an average of only 5,400 N of compression force applied. This finding shows that the disc is particularly susceptible to bending stresses. In a later study in which Adams and Hutton (1985) simulated repetitive loading of the disc, previously healthy discs failed at 3,800 N, again mostly through trabecular fractures of the vertebral bodies. Taken together, these studies show that the disc, especially the vertebral endplate, is susceptible to damage when loading is repetitive or when exposed to large compressive forces while in a severely flexed posture.

Since in vitro studies of lumbar motion segment failure may not fully represent the state of affairs in vivo, additional factors have been considered. It should be clear from earlier discussions of muscle that the internal forces created by the muscles could be quite large in response to even modest external loads. When the muscles that support, move, and stabilize the spine are recruited, forces of significant magnitude are placed on the spine. Several investigators have quantified spine loads during lifting and other material handling activities. The earliest attempts to quantify the spinal loads used static sagittal plane analyses (Morris, Lucas, and Bresler, 1961; Chaffin, 1969). Validation for these modeling efforts came from disc pressure and electromyographic studies (Nachemson and Morris, 1964). More advanced models have been developed to quantify the three-dimensional internal loads placed on the spine. Schultz et al. (1982a) developed and validated an optimization model to determine the three-dimensional internal spine loads that result from asymmetric lifting activities.

Others have quantified spine loads indirectly by examining the reaction forces and moments obtained with linked segment models. McGill and colleagues (McGill, Norman, and Cholewicki, 1996) have shown that there is a very strong predictive relationship ($r^2 = .94$) between the external spine moments and the spine reaction forces generated by their electromyographic-assisted model. This indicates that the changes observed in the more readily quantifiable spine reaction moments, due to changes in the modeled task parameters, are representative of the changes in actual spine loading. Increased lifting speed, lower initial lifting heights, and longer reach distances all significantly increase the spine reaction moments and hence have a significant impact on the compressive and shear forces acting on the disc (de Looze et al., 1993, 1994); Frievalds et al., 1984; Leskinen et al., 1983; McGill and Norman, 1985; Schipplein et al., 1995; Buseck et al., 1988; Dolan, Earley, and Adams, 1994; Tsuang et al., 1992). More recently, three-dimensional dynamic linked segment models have been developed to evaluate the spine loading during asymmetric tasks (Gagnon, Plamondon, and Gravel, 1993; Gagnon and Gagnon, 1992; Kromodihardjo and Mital, 1987; Lavender et al., 1999). These later models have been useful for documenting the spine loads (indirectly) that stem from lifting activities that involve twisting and lateral bending.

Nerves

Nerves, while not contributing either actively or passively to the internal forces generated by the body, are exposed to forces, vibration, and temperature variations that affect their function. Carpal tunnel syndrome is believed to result from a combination of ischemia and mechanical compression of the median nerve within the carpal canal of the wrist. Evidence of compression of the median nerve by adjacent tendons has been reported by direct pressure measurements (Tanzer, 1959; Smith,

Sonstegard, and Anderson, 1977). Electrophysiological and tactile deficits consistent with carpal tunnel syndrome have been observed under experimentally induced compression of the median nerve (Gelberman et al., 1981, 1983). A biomechanical model of the wrist developed by Armstrong and Chaffin (1979) predicts that median nerve compression will increase with increased wrist flexion and extension or finger flexor exertions. Increased intracarpal canal pressure was observed by Armstrong et al. (1991) for wrist and finger extension and flexion and for increased grip exertions. Rempel (1995) reports similar findings for repetitive hand activity and during typing.

Environmental stimuli, for example cold temperatures and vibration, have been shown to affect the response of peripheral nerves. Low temperatures, for example, can affect cutaneous sensory sensitivity and manual dexterity. Vibratory stimuli, with repeated exposure, are believed to cause, via a reflex response, (nerve) contraction of the smooth muscles of the blood vessels associated with Raynaud's syndrome. Less severe nerve damage resulting from vibratory stimuli has been associated with paresthesias and tingling sensations. Hand-arm vibration syndrome includes vascular disorders with the following symptoms: blanching of the digits after the use of vibrating hand tools (Gemne, 1997), and neurological disorders with complaints of persistent paraesthesia, or numbness extending into the hands and upper limbs (Letz et al., 1992). Often these symptoms are suggestive of neurological complaints, such as carpal tunnel syndrome or ulnar nerve entrapment (Palmer, Crane, and Inskip, 1998).

Measurements of Internal Loading

Physical stress imparted to internal tissues, organs, and anatomical structures in manual work is rarely measured directly. Due to the obvious complexities and risks associated with invasive internal physical stress measurements, investigations often employ indirect internal measures or external measurements that are physically related to internal loading of the body. Internal physical stress measures include electrophysiological measurements, such as electromyograms, or external measures of internal compartmental pressures.

Physiological Responses

Muscle Cocontraction

The synergistic activation of the muscles controlling an articulation is often referred to as cocontraction. In many cases, the cocontraction is between muscles working fully or partially in opposition to one another. From a biomechanical perspective, cocontraction is a way in which joints can be stiffened, stabilized, and moved in a well-controlled manner. Cocontraction, however, also has the potential to substantially increase the mechanical loads (compression, shear, or torsion) or change the nature of the loads placed on the body's articulations during an exertion or motion. This is because any cocontraction of fully or partially antagonistic muscles requires increased activation of the agonistic muscles responsible for generating or resisting the desired external load. Thus, the cocontraction increases the joint loading first by the antagonistic force, and second by the additional agonist force required to overcome this antagonistic force. Therefore, work activities in which cocontraction is more common impose greater loads on the tissues of the musculoskeletal system.

Localized Muscle Fatigue

As muscles fatigue, the loadings experienced by the musculoskeletal system change. In some cases, the changes result in alternative muscle recruitment strategies or substitution patterns wherein other secondary muscles, albeit less suited for performing the required exertion, are recruited as replacements for the fatigued tissues. This substitution hypothesis has received experimental support from Parnianpour et al. (1988), who showed considerable out-of-plane motion in a fatiguing trunk flexion-extension exercise. It is believed that the secondary muscles are at greater risk of overexertion injury, in part due to their smaller size or less biomechanically advantageous orientation, and in part due to their poorly coordinated actions. Alternatively, larger adaptations may occur that result in visible changes in behavior. For example, changes in lifting behavior have been shown to occur when either quadriceps or erector spinae muscles have been selectively fatigued (Novak et al., 1993; Trafimow et al., 1993; Marras and Granata, 1997a, 1997b). Fatigue may also result in ballistic motions or exertions in which loads are poorly controlled and rapidly accelerated, which in turn indicates that there are large impulse forces within the muscles and connective tissues.

Localized muscle fatigue can also occur in very low-level contractions, for example those used when supporting the arms in an elevated posture. In this case, the fatigue is further localized to the small, low-force endurance fibers (slow twitch) within the muscle. Because the recruitment sequence of muscle fibers during exertions works from smaller to larger fibers, the same small slow-twitch fibers are repeatedly used and fatigued even during low-level contractions (Sjøgaard, 1996). Murthy et al. (1997), using near-infrared spectroscopy to quantify tissue oxygenation as an index of blood flow, found reduced oxygenation within 10 to 40 seconds of initiating sustained contractions at values as low as 10 percent of the muscle's maximum capacity, thereby indicating an interference with the metabolic processes.

Tonic Vibration Reflex

Vibration can introduce disturbances in muscular control by way of a reflex mediated through the response of muscle spindles to the vibration stimulus (Eklund, Hagbarth, and Torebjork, 1978). This reflex is called the tonic vibration reflex, which results in a corresponding change in muscle tension when vibration is transmitted from a vibrating handle to flexor muscles in the forearm (Radwin, Armstrong, and Chaffin, 1987). Grip force increases observed for sinusoidal vibration at 40 Hz was comparable to grip force when handling a load twice as great. This effect was not observed for 160 Hz vibration.

Vibration direction and the frequency of the vibration stimuli have a strong and significant influence on impedance of the hand (Burstrom, 1997); an increased vibration level resulted in significantly less impedance for frequencies over 100 Hz, while hand and arm flexion and abduction made a significant contribution for frequencies below 30 Hz. The vibration response characteristics of the hand and arm differed, depending on whether the signal was a discrete frequency signal or a signal consisting of several frequencies.

EMG spectral analysis indicates that motor unit harmonic synchronization decreases and subharmonic synchronization increases as vibration frequency increases (Martin and Park, 1997). It has been suggested that the synchronization process influences muscle fatigue, since it forces the driving of motor units, leading to a decrease in contraction efficiency. This phenomenon probably results from an impairment of excitation-contraction coupling. High-frequency vibration (> 150 Hz) tends to induce less motor unit synchronization in a frequency range beyond the known mechanical resonance of biological tissues.

Measures of Internal Tolerances

Physiological Measures

Internal tissue tolerances are often related to external or indirect measures of exposure. These commonly include electrophysiological measures, such as amplitude changes in integrated electromyograms and frequency shifts in electromyogram spectra, and nonspecific physiological measures, such as heart rate, oxygen consumption, substrate consumption, and metabolite production.

Psychophysical Measures

The psychophysical method is an approach used to estimate internal tolerances through the human ability to estimate magnitudes and subjectively express exposure limits to physical stress. The cross-modality matching method asks human subjects to estimate a stimulus magnitude based on a visual-analog scale. A 10-point linear or logarithmic scale is often employed, anchored by verbal conditions at each end of the scale. The general Borg scale (Borg, 1982) is a commonly used visual-analog scale for quantifying perceived exertion levels anchored by the terms "nothing at all" at 0 and "extremely strong" at 10. Intermediate verbal anchors such as "very weak" at 1 and "moderate" at 3, "strong" at 5, and "very strong" at 7 are sometimes included.

Another psychophysical approach is the method of adjustment. This paradigm asks the subject to continually adjust the stimulus to the maximum level that is perceived safe. The method has been pioneered by Snook and used extensively for establishing psychophysical limits for manual lifting and for upper limb exertions and motions. The experimental paradigm for manual lifting requests subjects to perform repetitive lifts at a given rate in a posture and lifting motion dictated by such physical settings as the horizontal distance from the body for the origin and destination of the lift and the distance the object is lifted. The subject repeatedly adjusts the load lifted by adding or subtracting weights to establish the limit.

The Whole-Person Concept

The load tolerance model described in Figure 1.2 illustrates that biomechanical loading does not occur independently of interactions between internal tolerances and adverse outcomes. Biomechanical loading specifically may be altered when internal tolerances are exceeded. This can occur, for example, through substitution muscle recruitment patterns for fatigued muscles, resulting in loads imposed on additional muscles, or by increased compartment pressures, nerve entrapments, or loads acting on anatomical structures caused by swelling and inflammation. Furthermore, adverse outcomes of pain and discomfort may result in individual adaptations or behaviors that alter postures or substitute other aspects of the body for performing a work task. Biomechanical loading is also affected by individual characteristics, such as anthropometry, strength, agility, dexterity, and other factors mediating the transmission of external loads to internal loads on anatomical structures of the body. These interactions are complex and necessitate considering the person as a whole organism.

LOW BACK BIOMECHANICS

The objective of this section is to examine the evidence that there is a biomechanical pathway between physical occupational demands and the risk of suffering a low back disorder. Our assessment is made in relation to the conceptual model adopted in this report and specifically relative to the biomechanical pathways highlighted in Figure 1.2. This figure portrays a biomechanical pathway in terms of a relationship between loads imposed on a structure and the mechanical tolerance of the structure. This model also recognizes that both the loading characteristics and the tolerance levels can be influenced by physiological responses. In terms of the loading, the musculoskeletal system may be influenced by either adaptation to or intensification of the load. The tolerance may be mediated by pain responses or discomfort. Overall, if the loading of the structure exceeds the tolerance, then this situation can result in a disorder. Figure 1.2 accounts for the possibility that various influences may trigger this injury pathway and response.

External loads, such as those associated with work, are expected to influence the biomechanical loading of the spine. This model also allows for the possibility that other factors may influence this load-tolerance-disorder pathway at different points in the pathway. It is important to realize that individual factors as well as organizational factors and social context can influence biomechanical loading and structure tolerance, as well as the risk of suffering a disorder; these issues are covered in other sections of this report. The objective of this section is to explore the evidence, in this context, that external loads can trigger the pathway to low back disorders.

We examine exclusively the evidence that physical loading of the spine and supporting structures may result in low back pain. This contention is assessed via several approaches, including workplace observations of biomechanical factors relative to rates of low back pain reporting, biomechanical logic, pain pathways, and intervention research.

Chapter 2 reviewed trends associated with types of work (job titles) and the reporting of low back disorders. These investigations identified warehousing, patient handling, and general materials handling jobs as associated with back pain at a higher rate than other types of occupations. Laboratory biomechanical analyses have shown that these types of activities can lead to greater loadings on the spine (Leskinen et al., 1983; Schultz et al., 1987; Zetterberg, Andersson, and Schultz, 1987; Cholewicki, McGill, and Norman, 1991; McGill, 1997; Marras and Davis, 1998; Chaffin, Anderson, and Martin, 1999; Granata and Marras, 1999; Marras et al., 1999a, 1999b; and Marras, Granata, et al., 1999), and thus jobs associated with these higher spine loading tasks are consistent with greater reporting of back injuries. This is consistent with the logic described in Figure 1.2.

Biomechanical Risk Factors Measured in the Workplace

The panel reviewed the industrial observation literature for information relating biomechanical loading of the body and reports of low back disorder. For our assessment, the literature was screened with respect to biomechanical relevance. Whereas most epidemiologic studies are primarily concerned with methodological considerations, biomechanical assessments are primarily concerned that the information (exposure metric) assessed has biomechanical meaning. Hence, while many assessments of occupationally related low back disorder risk have occurred in the literature, many of these assessments have not used exposure metrics that would be considered relevant to a biomechanical assessment. Such a situation would mask or obscure any relationship with risk.

For example, numerous studies have found that lifting heavy loads is associated with an increased risk of low back pain (Kelsey et al., 1984; Videman, Nurminen, and Troup, 1984; Bigos et al., 1986; Spengler et al., 1986; Battie et al., 1989; Riihimaki et al., 1989b; Burdorf, Govaert, and Elders, 1991; Bigos et al., 1992; Andersson, 1997; Bernard, 1997b). However, such gross categorical exposure metrics have little meaning in a biomechanical assessment. As discussed in a previous section, from a biomechanical perspective, a given external (to the body) load can impose either large or small loads on the spine (internal forces), depending on the load's mechanical advantage relative to the spine (Chaffin, Andersson, and Martin, 1999). Therefore, in order to understand biomechanical loading, specific quantifiable exposure metrics that are meaningful in a biomechanical context are necessary for the purposes of this review. Only then can one address the issue of how much exposure to a biomechanical variable is too much exposure.

The literature was screened to identify biomechanically relevant, high-quality industrial surveillance studies. High-quality biomechanically related industrial surveillance studies consisted of studies that met the following criteria:

• The assessment addressed an aspect of the basic load-tolerance construct that is the heart of a biomechanical assessment. In other words, specific biomechanical parameters (e.g., load location in space) were of interest as opposed to gross categorical parameters (e.g., load weight alone).

• The exposure metric can provide quantifiable information about loads imposed on the back during work.

• The measurement of risk was not based solely on self-reports, which have been shown to be unreliable (Andrews, Norman, and Wells, 1996).

• Outcome measures are quantifiable on a continuous measurement scale (e.g., studies that relied on self-reports of exposure or simply noted whether the lifted weight was over a given threshold were excluded).

• The experimental design consisted of either a prospective study, case-control study, or a randomized controlled trial.

Study Results

Several industrially based observational studies meeting these criteria have appeared in the literature and offer evidence that low back disorder is related to exposure to physical work parameters on the job. Chaffin and Park (1973) performed one of the first studies exploring this relationship. This study found that "the incidence rate of low back pain (was) correlated (monotonically) with higher lifting strength requirements as determined by assessment of both the location and magnitude of the load lifted" (Chaffin and Park, 1973:513). They concluded that load lifting could be considered potentially hazardous. It is important to note that this study suggested that not only was load magnitude significant in defining risk but also load location was important. This view is consistent with biomechanical logic, discussed later. This evaluation also reported an interesting relationship between frequency of exposure and lifts of different magnitude (relative to worker strength). This study suggested that exposure to moderate lifting frequencies appeared to be protective, whereas high or low rates of lifting were common in jobs with greater reports of back injury.

A prospective study performed by Liles et al. (1984) observed job demands compared with worker's psychophysically defined strength capacity. The job demand definition considered load location relative to the worker, as well as frequency of lift and exposure time. Demands were considered for all tasks associated with a material handling job. This study identified the existence of a job demand relative to a worker strength threshold above which the risk of low back injury increased. This study found that there was a "job severity threshold above which incidence and severity dramatically increased" (Liles et al., 1984:690).

Herrin and associates (1986) observed jobs over three years in five large industrial plants, where they evaluated 2,934 material handling tasks. They evaluated jobs using both a lifting strength ratio as well as estimates of back compression forces. A positive correlation between the lifting strength ratio and low back injury incidence rates was identified. They also found that musculoskeletal injuries were twice as likely for predicted spine compression forces that exceeded 6,800 N. The analyses also suggest that prediction of risk was best associated with the most stressful tasks (as opposed to indices that represent risk aggregation).

Punnett and colleagues (1991) performed a case-control (case-referent) study of automobile assembly workers, in which risk of back pain associated with nonneutral working postures was evaluated. In this study, back pain cases over a 10-month period were studied, referents were randomly selected after review of medical records, interview, and examination, and job analyses were performed by analysts who were blinded to the case-referent status. Risk of low back pain was observed to increase as trunk flexion increased. Risk was also associated with trunk twisting or lateral bending. Finally, this study indicated that risk increased with exposure to multiple postures and increasing exposure time. Specifically, the study indicated that risk increased as the portion of the duty cycle spent in the most severe postures increased.

Marras and colleagues (1993, 1995) biomechanically evaluated over 400 industrial jobs by observing 114 workplace and worker-related variables. Exposure to load moment (load magnitude × distance of load from spine) was found to be the single most powerful predictor of low back disorder reporting. This study has been the only study to examine trunk kinematics along with traditional biomechanical variables in the workplace. This study identified 16 trunk kinematic variables resulting in statistically significant odds ratios associated with risk of low back disorder reporting in the workplace. While none of the single variables was as strong a predictor as load moment, when load moment was combined with three kinematic variables (relating to the three dimensions of trunk motion) along with an exposure frequency measure, a strong multiple logistic regression model resulted that described reporting of back disorder well (O.R. = 10.7). This analysis indicated that risk was multivariate in nature, in that exposure to the combination of the five variables described reporting well. The model recognizes a trade-off between the variables. For example, a work situation that exposes a worker to low magnitude of load moment can still represent a high-risk situation if the other four variables in the model were of sufficient magnitude. This model has been recently validated in a prospective workplace intervention study (Marras et al., 2000a). When the results of this study are considered in conjunction with the Punnett study (1991), it is clear that work associated with activity performed in nonneutral postures increases the risk to the back. Furthermore, as the posture becomes more extreme or the trunk motion becomes more rapid, reporting of back disorder is greater. These results are meaningful from a biomechanical standpoint and suggest that risk of low back disorder is associated primarily with mechanical loading of the spine, as well as that when tasks involve greater three-dimensional loading, the association with risk becomes much stronger. Three-dimensional loading of the spine would be expected to affect the disc, ligaments, muscles, and other structures proximal to the spine.

Norman and associates (1998) recently assessed cumulative biomechanical loading of the spine in automotive assembly workers. This observational study identified four independent factors for low back disorder reporting: integrated load moment (over a work shift), hand forces, peak shear force on the spine, and peak trunk velocity. This study showed that workers in the top 25 percent of loading exposure on all risk factors reported low back pain at a rate about six times greater than those in the bottom 25 percent of loading.

Fathallah and associates (Fathallah, Marras, and Parnianpour, 1998b) evaluated a database of 126 workers and jobs to precisely quantify and assess the complex trunk motions of groups with varying degrees of low back disorder reporting. They found that groups with greater reporting rates exhibited complex trunk motion patterns involving high magnitudes of trunk combined velocities, especially at extreme sagittal flexion, whereas the low-risk groups did not exhibit any such patterns. This study showed that elevated levels of complex simultaneous velocity patterns along with key workplace factors (load moment and frequency) were unique to groups with increased low back disorder risk.

Waters and colleagues (1999) evaluated the usefulness of the revised NIOSH lifting equation in an industrial observation study of 50 industrial jobs. The evaluation considered factors expected to be associated with spine loading, including load location measures. These measures defined an expected worker tolerance (identified by biomechanical, physiological, strength, or psychophysical limits) and were compared with the load lifted. The results of this study indicated that as the tolerance was exceeded, the odds of back pain reporting increased up to a point and then decreased.

The findings from these studies are summarized in Table 6.4. Only two studies have estimated spinal load at work, and both have found a positive association between physical loading at work and low back pain reporting. The other studies are consistent with this finding. Even though these studies have not evaluated spinal loading directly, the exposure measures included were indirect indicators of spinal load. Load location or strength ratings are both indicators of the magnitude of the load imposed on the spine. All but one study found that one of these measures was significantly associated with back pain reporting. Most of the remain-

TABLE 6.4 Summary of High-Quality Field Surveillance Studies for the Back and Spine from a Biomechanical Perspective

		Risk Factors Identified								
Author	# Jobs	Capacity/ Demand Ratio	Load Location	Load Moment	Frequency	Kinematics	Spinal Load	3-D	Multiple Factors	Comments
Chaffin and Park, 1973	103	✓	✓		✓					Prospective
Liles et al., 1984	101	✓	✓		✓				✓	Prospective
Herrin et al., 1986	55	✓	✓		✓		✓			Prospective
Punnett et al., 1991	95 case 124 referent					✓		✓	✓	Case-control
Marras et al., 1993, 1995	403		✓	✓		✓		✓	✓	Case-control
Norman et al., 1998	104 cases 130 referent		✓	✓		✓	✓		✓	Case-control
Fathallah et al., 1998b	126		✓	✓		✓		✓	✓	Case-control
Waters et al., 1999	36	✓	✓	✓	✓	✓		✓	✓	Cross-sectional 1 year prospective
Marras et al., 2000	50		✓	✓	✓	✓		✓	✓	Prospective validation

ing exposure metrics (load location, kinematics, and three-dimensional analyses) are important from a biomechanical standpoint because they mediate the ability of the trunk's internal structures to support the external load. Therefore, as these metrics change, they can change the nature of the loading on the internal structures of the back. This assessment also shows that risk is multifactorial, in that risk is generally much better described when the analysis is three dimensional and more than one risk factor measure is considered. No high-quality biomechanical relevant industrial surveillance studies have been identified that contradict these results.

Implications

Collectively, these studies demonstrated that when meaningful biomechanical assessments are performed at the workplace, strong associations between biomechanical factors and the risk of low back disorder reporting are evident. Several key components of biomechanical risk assessment can be derived from this review. First, all studies that have compared worker task demands with worker capacity have been able to identify thresholds above which reporting of low back disorder increases. Second, increased low back disorder reporting can be identified well when the location of the load relative to the body (load moment or load location) is quantified in some way. Nearly all studies have shown that these factors are closely associated with increased low back pain reports. Third, nearly all studies have shown that frequency of material handling is associated with increased reporting of low back pain. Fourth, many studies have shown that increased reporting of low back pain can be well characterized when the three-dimensional dynamic demands of the work are described, as opposed to static two-dimensional assessments. Finally, nearly all of the high-quality biomechanical assessments have demonstrated that risk is multidimensional, in that a synergy among risk factors appears to intensify increased reporting of low back pain. While many of these relationships are monotonically related to increased low back pain reports, some have identified associations that were nonmonotonic. Specifically, exposure at moderate levels of load and frequency of lifting appears to represent the lowest level of risk, whereas exposure at greater levels represents the greatest level of risk. Whereas many of the high-quality biomechanical studies explored different aspects of risk exposure, none of these studies provides evidence contradicting these key component findings.

Spine Loading Assessments

Biomechanical logic suggests that damage occurs to a structure when the imposed loading exceeds the structure's mechanical tolerance. In support of this, the high-quality biomechanical workplace observation studies demonstrate a positive correlation between increased biomechanical loading and increased risk for low back disorder at work. Currently, it is infeasible to directly monitor the spinal load of a worker performing a task in the workplace. Instead, biomechanical models are typically used to estimate loading. However, an understanding of the differences between methods of spine assessment can help place the findings of these different observational studies in perspective.

Biomechanical models of spinal loading have evolved over the past several decades. The early models of spine loading made assumptions about which trunk muscles supported the external load during a lifting task (Chaffin and Baker, 1970; Chaffin et al., 1977). These models assumed that a single muscle vector could be used to summarize the load supporting (and spine loading) internal force that was required to counteract an external load lifted by a worker. These models assumed that lifts could be represented by a static lifting situation and that no coactivation occurred among the trunk musculature during lifting. All solutions to the model were unique in that workers with the same anthropometric characteristics performing the same task would be expected to yield the exact same spinal loads. The main focus of such models was assessment of spinal compression. These models could be employed in surveillance studies simply by videotaping a lifting task and measuring the weight of the object lifted. Such a model was employed in one of the surveillance studies described earlier (Herrin, Jaraiedi, and Anderson, 1986).

Later models were expanded to the point at which they could account for the contribution of multiple internal muscles' reactions in response to the lifting of an external load. These models predicted compression forces as well as shear forces imposed on the spine. The first functional multiple muscle system model used for task assessment was developed by Schultz and Andersson (1981). This study demonstrated how loads handled outside the body could impose large spinal loads due to the coactivation of trunk muscles necessary to counteract this external load. This model represented a much more realistic situation. However, this modeling approach led to an indeterminant solution (since many muscles were represented in the model, a unique solution became difficult). Therefore, many subsequent modeling efforts attempted to determine which muscles would be active (Schultz et al., 1982b; Bean, Chaffin, and Schultz, 1988; Hughes and Chaffin, 1995). These efforts resulted in models that worked well for static loading situations but did not necessarily represent the more realistic, dynamic lifting situations well (Marras, King, and Joynt, 1984).

Since prediction of muscle recruitment was difficult under realistic (complex) material handling conditions, later efforts attempted to monitor muscle activity directly using muscle activity as an input to multiple muscle models. These biologically assisted models typically employed electromyography (EMG) as the muscle activity monitor. These models were able to realistically model most dynamic three-dimensional lifting activities (McGill and Norman, 1985, 1986; Cholewicki, McGill, and Norman, 1991; Marras and Sommerich, 1991a, 1991b; Cholewicki and McGill, 1992; Cholewicki and McGill, 1994; Granata and Marras, 1993; 1995a; Marras and Granata, 1995, 1997a, 1997b). Available validation measures suggest that these models have good external as well as internal validity (Granata, Marras, and Davis, 1999; Marras, Granata, and Davis, 1999). Granata and Marras (1995a) demonstrated how miscalculations of spinal loading could occur unless realistic assessments of muscle recruitment could be determined. The disadvantage of these biologically assisted models is that they require EMG applications to the worker, which is often unrealistic at the workplace.

The evolution of these models can have an impact on the interpretation of the work relatedness of mechanical loading of the spine. As indicated in the review of quantitative biomechanical surveillance studies, most spine loading estimates performed at the workplace employed two-dimensional, single-equivalent muscle models. Thus, one would expect that in these studies, the spinal compression was underestimated and shear force estimates would not be realistic.

Given that these models are based on different modeling assumptions and vary greatly in their degree of comprehensiveness, it is not unexpected that some variability in reported findings would be apparent. Hence, when reviewing the status of risk-related evaluations, one must be vigilant in considering the analytical assumptions and tools used in reaching their conclusions.

Relationship Between Workplace Observations and Spine Loading

Given these limitations and the impracticality of monitoring EMG at the worksite, many tasks are simulated under laboratory conditions so that a better, more realistic, estimate of spine loading can be derived. A literature exists that has evaluated many work situations under such situations. In this section, we investigate whether the risk factor components identified in Table 6.4 can be associated with greater loading of the spine and back.

It is indeed possible to evaluate several of the risk situations observed in Table 6.4 using quantitative biomechanical models. The assessment by Herrin et al. (Herrin, Jaraiedi, and Anderson, 1986) has applied a single-equivalent muscle model to work situations and found that compressive loads imposed on the spine of more than 6,800 N greatly increased risk.

The assessment by Punnett and colleagues (1991) did include a bio-mechanical analysis of the loads lifted by the worker if the load exceeded 44.5 N. Using a three-dimensional biomechanical static model (Chaffin, Anderson, and Martin, 1999), compressive loads on the spine were evaluated as workers assumed various postures. Even though the risk analysis indicated that risk was associated with extreme flexion, lateral bending, and trunk twisting, the results of the biomechanical analysis indicated that "less than 3% of the analyzed postures resulted in peak compressive forces of 3,430 N (the point at which compressive forces are believed to cause damage)" (Punnett et al., 1991:344). It should be noted that the biomechanical model used for this assessment was a static "single-equivalent" muscle model. As noted earlier, since these types of models are unable to account for muscle coactivation, they often underestimate compression (Granata and Marras, 1995b). In addition, it is not clear from the paper that shear forces were analyzed. Given the nonneutral postures observed, one would expect that spinal shear forces would be more significant from a biomechanical standpoint than compressive loading.

The field observations by Marras and colleagues (Marras et al., 1993, 1995, in press) identified moment, trunk flexion, trunk lateral velocity, trunk twisting velocity, and frequency of lifting as multivariate risk factors. These studies quantified the exposure levels at which each risk factor became safe or risky. Under controlled laboratory conditions, these authors employed biologically assisted models to assess the biomechanical significance of exposure to these "field documented" safe or risky exposure levels for all five risk factors. In a series of studies, they showed that exposure to higher load moments and forward flexion (Marras and Sommerich, 1991a, 1991b; Granata and Marras, 1993, 1995a), exposure to greater lateral trunk velocity (Marras and Granata, 1997b), exposure to greater twisting velocity (Marras and Granata, 1995), and exposure to higher repetitions (Marras and Granata, 1997a) were all similar in that at higher levels of exposure, increased cocontraction of the trunk musculature was observed. This higher level of coactivation was responsible for greater compressive spine loading. In addition, increases in both lateral and anterior-posterior shear were noted especially for the lateral bending and twisting risk factors. These analyses indicated that exposure to greater load moments, nonneutral postures, and trunk motion all resulted in a more complex recruitment of the trunk musculature that logically increased mechanical loading of the spine. Thus, these studies indicated that when more comprehensive, three-dimensional dynamic biomechanical models were employed, field observations of risk correlated well with biomechanical loadings (Granata and Marras, 1999).

These analyses also relate well to the findings of Norman and associates (Norman et al., 1998). They employed a simplified two-dimensional quasi-dynamic model to analyze spinal loading. Even though this model was not three-dimensional and did not assess multiple trunk muscle recruitment, it was calibrated against a biologically assisted three-dimensional fully dynamic model (McGill and Norman, 1986, 1987). Both the field surveillance as well as the biomechanical interpretation of the risk factors in this study agree well with field surveillance and biomechanical interpretation of risk factors described earlier by Marras and colleagues.

Hence, it is clear that unless sufficiently sensitive and robust biomechanical analyses are performed at the worksite, the relationship between factors associated with workplace observations of risk and biomechanical loading may not be apparent or this relationship may be underestimated. Related to this finding is the concept that for ergonomic interventions to be useful, the analysis must be sensitive enough to represent components of risk present in a particular job. For example, a prospective review of ergonomic interventions associated with 36 jobs with a history of back risk demonstrated that only one-third of the interventions sufficiently controlled low back disorder risk (Marras et al., in press). More in-depth analyses of these jobs indicated that workers responsible for ergonomic interventions often did not employ ergonomic assessment tools that were sensitive enough to identify the nature of the risk. This study showed that employment of more sensitive tools would have identified which assessments might have controlled for the biomechanically associated risks. Thus, this study shows that, often when ergonomic interventions are found to be ineffective, it is simply the case that the wrong intervention was selected, not that ergonomic interventions cannot be effective.

Spine Loading During Specific Work Tasks

Certain tasks or jobs have been associated with greater risk of low back disorder. These tasks include patient handling (Videman, Nurminen, and Troup, 1984; Jensen, 1987; Garg and Owen, 1992; Knibbe and Knibbe, 1996), material handling in distribution centers and warehousing operations (Waters, Putz-Anderson, and Baron, 1998), and team lifting (Sharp et al., 1997). Several biomechanical evaluations of these jobs have been performed using some of the more robust models discussed above. A biologically assisted model was used to evaluate patient handling tasks (Marras et al., 1999a). An evaluation of spinal loading indicated that of the one-person and two-person patient handling techniques studied, none resulted in a spinal load that was within acceptable levels. Similar results were found using more traditional biomechanical assessments (Garg and Owen, 1992).

Load handling has been studied from a biomechanical standpoint to a great extent, with numerous studies indicating that excessive loads could be imposed on the spine during lifting (Chaffin, 1979; Schultz and Andersson, 1981; Garg et al., 1983; Freivalds et al., 1984; McGill and Norman, 1985; Anderson, Chaffin, and Herrin, 1986; Chaffin, 1988; Cholewicki and McGill, 1992; Gallagher et al., 1994; Davis, Marras, and Waters, 1998; Fathallah et al., 1998a). Loading pallets in a distribution environment was studied recently (Marras, Granata, and Davis, 1999). This study is significant because it demonstrated that significant loading was not just a function of load magnitude but also a function of position of the load relative to the spine.

Loads handled at low heights and at greater horizontal distances from the spine greatly increase the loading on the spine. This increased loading is due to two features. First, greater distance of the load from the spine increased the load moment, which required greater internal forces to counterbalance the external load. These increased internal forces resulted in greater spine loading in both compression and shear. These findings are consistent with the observations of the importance of load moment noted in Table 6.4. Second, lifting from low positions requires more of the body mass to extend beyond the base of support for the spine. This action also increases the moment imposed about the spine due to the weight of the torso and distance of its center of mass relative to the base of support for the spine. In addition, the supporting muscles must operate in a state of lengthened tension that is known to be one of the weakest positions of a muscle. Thus, risk is associated with greater loading of the spine as well as reduced muscular capacity of the trunk muscles.

Finally, team lifting has been shown to severely alter the lifting kinematics and positions of workers (Marras et al., 1999b). This biomechanical analysis has shown that these constrained postures once again increase coactivation of the trunk musculature and result in increases in both compressive and shear loadings of the spine.

Pathways Between Pain Perception and Tissue Loading in the Spine

If mechanical factors are responsible for low back pain reporting, then logic dictates that there should be evidence that mechanical stimulation of a structure should lead to the perception of low back pain. This section will examine the evidence that such a linkage or pathway exists between mechanical stimulation and low back pain. From a biomechanical standpoint, there are several structures that may lead to pain perception in the back when stimulated. There is evidence in the literature that both cellular and neural mechanisms can lead to pain. Both laboratory and anatomical investigations have shown that neurophysiological and neuroanatomical sources of back pain exist (Bogduk, 1995; Cavanaugh, 1995; Cavanaugh et al., 1997). Typically, these pathways to pain involve pressure on a structure that directly stimulates a pain receptor or triggers the release of pain-stimulating chemicals.

Investigations have identified pain pathways for joint pain, pain of disc origin, longitudinal ligaments, and mechanisms for sciatica. In the case of facet pain, several mechanisms were identified including an extensive distribution of small nerve fibers and endings in the lumbar facet joint, nerves containing substance P, high-threshold mechanoreceptors in the facet joint capsule, and sensitization and excitation of nerves in the facet joint and surrounding muscle when the nerves were exposed to inflammatory or algesic chemicals (Dwyer, Aprill, and Bogduk, 1990; Ozaktay et al., 1995; Yamashita et al., 1996). Evidence for disc pain was also identified via an extensive distribution of small nerve fibers and free nerve endings in the superficial annulus of the disc and small fibers and free nerve endings in the adjacent longitudinal ligaments (Bogduk, 1991, 1995; Cavanaugh, Kallakuri, and Ozaktay, 1995; Kallakuri, Cavanaugh, and Blagoev, 1998).

Several studies have also shown how sciatic pain can be associated with mechanical stimulation of spine structures. Moderate pressure on the dorsal root ganglia resulted in vigorous and long-lasting excitatory discharges that would explain sciatica. In addition, sciatica could be explained by excitation of dorsal root fibers when the ganglia were exposed to the nucleus pulposus. Excitation and loss of nerve function in nerve roots exposed to phospholipase A_2 could also explain sciatica (Cavanaugh et al., 1997; Chen et al., 1997; Ozaktay, Kallakuri, and Cavanaugh, 1998). Finally, the sacroiliac joint has also been shown to be a significant, yet poorly understood source of low back pain (Schwarzer, Aprill, and Bogduk, 1995). Hence, these studies clearly show that there is a logical and well demonstrated rationale to expect that mechanical stimulation of the spinal structures can lead to low back pain perception and reporting. How these relate operationally to clinical syndromes is less certain.

Spine Tissue Tolerance

Biomechanical logic dictates that loads imposed on a structure must exceed a mechanical tolerance limit for damage to occur. In this section we examine the load tolerances associated with different spinal structures that have been shown to be sensitive to pain, in an attempt to determine whether the levels at which the spinal structures are loaded in the workplace can be expected to exceed the tolerances of those structures.

In general, the issue of cumulative trauma is significant for low back pain causality in the workplace. Lotz and colleagues (Lotz et al., 1998) have demonstrated that compressive loading of the disc does indeed lead to degeneration and that the pattern of response is consistent with a dose-response relationship that is central to the idea of cumulative trauma.

Vertebral Endplate

The literature is divided as to the pain pathway associated with trabecular fractures of the vertebral bodies. Some researchers believe that damage to the vertebral endplate can lead to back problems in workers, whereas others have questioned the existence of this pathway. Those supporting this pathway believe that health of the vertebral body endplate is essential for proper mechanical functioning of the spine. Damage to the endplate nutrient supply has been found to result in damage to the disc and disruption of spinal function (Moore, 2000). This event is capable of initiating a cascading series of events that can lead to low back pain (Brinkmann, 1985; Siddall and Cousins, 1997a, 1997b; Kirkaldy-Willis, 1998). The tolerance of the vertebral endplate has been studied in several investigations. Studies have shown that the endplate is the first structure to be injured when the spine is loaded (Brinkmann, Biggemann, and Hilweg, 1988; Calahan and McGill, in press). The tolerance of the endplate has been observed to decrease by 30-50 percent with exposure to repetitive loading (Brinkmann, Biggemann, and Hilweg, 1988). This pattern is consistent with the evidence that the disc is sensitive to cumulative trauma exposure. The endplate is also damaged by anterior-posterior shear loading (Calahan and McGill, in press). Several biomechanical studies have demonstrated that the tolerances of specific spinal structures can be exceeded by work tasks.

Evidence of activity-related damage may also be suggested by the presence of Schmorls nodes. Some research (but not all) suggests that Schmorls nodes are healed trabecular fractures (Vernon-Roberts and Pirie, 1973) and linked to trauma (Vernon-Roberts and Pirie, 1973; Kornberg, 1988).

Significant evidence exists that endplate tolerance is dependent on the position of the spine when the structure is loaded. Fully flexed positions of the spine have been shown to greatly reduce loading tolerance (Adams and Hutton, 1982; Gunning and McGill, in press). Thus, proper biomechanical assessments of low back risk at work can be performed only when the posture of the trunk is considered. The industrial surveillance efforts of Punnett et al. (1991) and Marras et al. (1993, 1995) show that risk of low back disorder increases as trunk postures during work deviate from an upright posture.

Shear forces applied to the spine have also been shown to decrease the tolerance of the disc structure, especially when the spine is in a flexed position (Cripton et al., 1985; Miller et al., 1986; McGill, 1997). These findings are consistent with the field surveillance observations of Norman et al. (1998) as well as spine loading observations (McGill and Norman, 1985, 1986; Granata and Marras, 1993, 1995a).

Finally, age and gender have been identified as individual factors that affect the biomechanical tolerance limits of the endplate. Jagger and colleagues (Jager, Luttman, and Laurig, 1991) have demonstrated through cadaver studies that increasing age as well as gender can affect the strength tolerance of the endplate.

All of the industrial surveillance studies shown in Table 6.4 indicate that load location (known to affect trunk posture), observed trunk posture, or both are associated with an increased risk of low back pain at work. Furthermore, the review of the spine loading literature has also indicated that handling loads with the trunk moving in nonneutral postures increases muscle coactivation and the resultant spine loading (Marras and Sommerich, 1991a, 1991b; Granata and Marras, 1993, 1995a, 1995b; Marras and Granata, 1995, 1997b). Loading the spine in these deviated postures decreases the tolerance of the spine structures. Hence, the pattern or risk in the workplace, spine structure loading, and endplate tolerance reductions are all consistent with a situation that would indicate that certain work conditions are related to an increased biomechanical risk for low back disorder.

Disc

The disc itself is subject to direct damage with sufficient loading. Herniation may occur when under compression and when the spine is positioned in an excessively flexed posture (Adams and Hutton, 1982). Also, repeated flexion under moderate compressive loading has produced repeated disc herniations in laboratory studies (Calahan and McGill, in press). Anterior-posterior shear forces have been shown to produce avulsion of the lateral annulus (Yingling and McGill, in press). Torsion tolerance of the disc is low and occurs at a mere 88 Nm in an intact disc and as low as 54 Nm in the damaged disc (Farfan et al., 1970; Adams and Hutton, 1981). Fatallah and colleagues have shown that such loads are common in jobs associated with greater rates of low back disorder reporting (Fathallah, Marras, and Parnianpour, 1998a, 1998b).

Complex spinal postures including hyperflexion with lateral bending and twisting can also produce disc herniation (Adams and Hutton, 1985;

Gordon et al., 1991). This observation is consistent with industrial surveillance studies indicating increased risk associated with complex working postures, as laboratory investigations of spinal loading while tasks are performed in these complex postures, both by Fathallah, Marras, and Parnianpour (1998a, 1998b). These investigators have also implicated load rate via trunk velocity in complex working postures as playing a significant role in risk.

Evidence exists that biomechanical tolerance to risk factors associated with material handling might also be modulated as a function of the time of day when the lifting is performed. Snook and colleagues (1998) showed that flexion early in the morning is associated with greater risk of pain. Fathallah, Marras, and Wright (1995) showed similar results and concluded that risk of injury was also greater early in the day when disc hydration was at a high level. Hence, the literature suggests a temporal component of risk associated with the time of day of the biomechanical exposure.

Vertebral Body

The cancellous bone of the vertebral body is damaged when exposed to compressive loading (Fyhrie and Schaffler, 1994). This event often occurs along with disc herniation and annular delamination (Gunning and McGill, in press). Damage to the bone appears to be part of the cascading series of events associated with low back pain (Brinckmann, 1985; Siddall and Cousins, 1997a, 1997b; Kirkaldy-Willis, 1998).

Ligaments

Ligament tolerances are affected by the load rate (Noyes, De Lucas, and Torvik, 1994). Thus, this could explain the increased risk associated with bending motions (velocity) that have been observed in surveillance studies (Fathallah et al., 1998a, 1998b). The architecture of the interspinous ligaments can create anterior shear forces on the spine when it is flexed in a forward bending posture (Heylings, 1978). This finding is consistent with the more recent three-dimensional field observations of risk (Punnett et al., 1991; Marras et al. 1993, 1995; Norman et al., 1998). In vitro studies of passive tissue tolerance have identified 60 Nm as the point at which damage begins to occur (Adams and Dolan, 1995). This is consistent with the field observations of Marras et al. (1993, 1995), who found that exposure to external load moments of 73.6 Nm was associated with high risk of occupationally related low back pain reporting. Similarly, Norman and colleagues (1998) reported nearly 30 percent greater load moment exposure in jobs associated with risk of low back pain. The mean moment exposure for the low back pain cases was 182 Nm of *total* load moment (due to the load lifted plus body segment weights).

Spine curvature has also been shown to affect the loading and tolerance of the spinal structures. Recent work has shown that when spinal curvature is maintained during bending, the extensor muscles support the shear forces of the torso. However, if the spine is flexed during bending and posterior ligaments are flexed, then significant shear can be imposed on the ligaments (McGill and Norman, 1987; Potvin, McGill, and Norman, 1991; McGill and Kippers, 1994). Cripton and colleagues (1985) found that the shear tolerance (2000-2800 N) of the spine can be easily exceeded when the spine is in full flexion.

There also appears to be a strong temporal component to ligament status recovery. Ligaments appear to require long periods of time to regain structural integrity, and compensatory muscle activities are recruited (Solomonow et al., 1998; Stubbs et al., 1998; Gedalia et al., 1999; Solomonow et al., 2000; Wang et al., 2000). The time needed for recovery can easily exceed the typical work-rest cycles observed in industry.

Facet Joints

The facet joints can fail in response to shear loading. A tolerance has been estimated at 2,000 N of loading (Cripton et al., 1985). Lateral shear forces have been shown to increase rapidly as lateral trunk velocity increases (Marras and Granata, 1997b), especially at the levels of lateral velocity that have been associated with high-risk jobs (Marras et al., 1993).

Torsion can also cause the facet joints to fail (Adams and Hutton, 1981). More rapid twisting motions have been associated with high-risk jobs and laboratory investigations have explained how increases in twisting motion can lead to increases in spine loading in compression as well as shear (McGill, 1991; Marras and Granata, 1995).

As with most tolerance limits of the spine, the posture of the spine affects the overall loading of the spine significantly (Marras and Granata, 1995). Loading of the specific structure depends greatly on specific posture and curvature of the spine. Load sharing occurs between the apophyseal joints and the disc (Adams and Dolan, 1995). Thus, spinal posture and the nature of the spine loading dictate whether damage will occur to the facet joints or the disc.

Adaptation

It has been well established that tissues adapt and remodel in response to load. Adaptation in response to load has been identified for bone (Carter, 1985), the ligaments (Woo, Gomez, and Akeson, 1985), the disc (Porter, Adams, and Hutton, 1989), and the vertebrae (Brinkmann, Biggeman, and Hilweg, 1989a, 1989b). Adaptation suggests that there is good rationale for the higher risk observed in response to high-risk jobs demanding high spinal loading as well as very low levels of spinal loading (Chaffin and Park, 1973; Videman, Nurminen, and Troup, 1990). The lowest level of risk has been observed at moderate levels of loading. Thus, there appears to be an ideal zone of loading that minimizes risk. Above that level, tolerances are easily exceeded; below that level, adaptation does not occur. This is consistent with epidemiologic findings as well as the adaptation literature.

Psychosocial Pathways

A body of literature exists that attempts to explain how psychosocial factors may be related to the risk of low back disorder. While reviews have implicated psychosocial factors as associated with risk (Bongers et al., 1993; Burton et al., 1995) and some have dismissed the role of biomechanical factors (Bigos et al., 1986), few studies have properly evaluated biomechanical exposure along with psychosocial exposure in these assessments. A recent study by Davis and Heaney (2000) has shown that no studies have been able to adequately assess both dimensions of risk.

A recent biomechanical study (Marras et al., 2000) has shown that psychosocial stress does have the capacity to influence biomechanical loading. This laboratory study has demonstrated how individual factors such as personality can interact with perception of psychosocial stress to increase trunk muscle coactivation and subsequent spine loading. Hence, it appears that psychosocial stress may influence risk through a biomechanical pathway.

Low Back Summary

Collectively, this review has shown that there is a strong biomechanical relationship between risk of low back disorder reports and exposure to physical loading in the workplace. The epidemiologic evidence has shown that risk can be identified when ergonomic evaluations properly consider: (1) worker capacity in relation to job demands, (2) the load location and weight magnitude relative to the worker, (3) temporal aspects of the work, (4) three-dimensional movements while the worker is lifting, and (5) exposure to multiple risk factors simultaneously. The biomechanical literature that has evaluated the loading of the spine structures in response to these field-identified risk factors has shown that there are identifiable changes in the recruitment pattern of the muscles and subsequent increases in spine structure loading associated with greater exposure to these risk factors. The literature has also identified pain pathways associated with increased loading of the structures. Finally, our review of the literature has shown that the loading of these spinal structures can lead to structural damage that can precipitate the pain response pathway.

While there are certainly individual factors that put a person at risk for back pain, overall this body of literature indicates that back pain can be related to levels of excessive mechanical loading of the spine that can be expected in the workplace. The literature also indicates that appropriate reduction of work exposure can decrease the risk of low back disorder. Studies that have not been able to identify this linkage typically have used assessment techniques that were either not appropriate or insufficiently sensitive for proper biomechanical assessment at the workplace. Hence, it is clear, from a biomechanical perspective, that exposure to excessive amounts of physical loading can increase the risk of low back disorder.

UPPER BODY BIOMECHANICS

The following section reviews the literature concerned with the upper limb in the context of the conceptual model presented in Figure 1.2. The focus is the upper body segments or joints (neck, shoulder, elbow, wrist, hand, fingers). Since the upper arms and neck are mechanically linked, it is therefore not practical to consider them in isolation. This is reflected in the literature focusing on these aspects, which usually treats the neck, shoulders, and upper arms as a functional unit. The research reviewed includes primarily laboratory methods (i.e., measuring a tolerance-dependent variable while systematically manipulating selected load variables) but a small number of "in-plant" studies were also considered, in which laboratory methods were followed in the field. While most studies were performed in vivo in a true laboratory setting, we also considered some cadaver studies and biomechanical models in which strain was measured or computed while systematically manipulating external physical stress.

The literature review was limited primarily to articles that were published in English in a refereed journal since 1980. A small number of frequently cited articles published before 1980 are also included. Epidemiologic and clinical studies were excluded, since these studies are considered in Chapter 4. It is important to note, however, that the results from the review of the epidemiologic literature on upper extremities concludes that there is a strong association between physical factors and upper extremity disorders. Specifically, the following factors are implicated—force, vibration, repetition, and temperature as well as combinations of repetition and force or repetition and cold.

The following review discusses the strength of the relationships among (1) physical factors and external loads in the workplace, (2) external physical loads and internal tissue loads, (3) external physical loads and internal tolerances, and (4) external loads and pain, discomfort, functional limitations, and disability.

Physical Stress Factors and External Loading

The cumulative trauma model (Figure 1.2) illustrates how external loads encountered in the workplace act on the person. This section reviews the current literature since 1980 dealing with workplace factors, such as hand tool vibration or weight of objects handled, and their effect on external loading on the human operator. These articles describe how upper extremity exposure to physical stresses (i.e., force, posture, vibration, and temperature) is affected by various attributes of work. A summary of the articles reviewed is contained in Table 6.5. Physical loading as examined in these articles was not necessarily linked to injuries.

Force

Force exerted in occupational tasks can be directly affected by the weight of objects handled, forces for operating equipment and tools, and frictional characteristics between surfaces grasped and the skin (Radwin, Armstrong, and Chaffin, 1987; Radwin et al., 1992; Frederick and Armstrong, 1995). External force exposure is sometimes controlled by altering loads and exertions necessary for accomplishing tasks and the characteristics of objects handled, such as balance and friction. Frederick and Armstrong (1995) suggest that use of friction enhancements for handles and objects handled may help reduce pinch force for objects requiring upward of 50 percent or more of maximum pinch strength.

Numerous articles have considered how keyboard mechanical design characteristics affected finger force magnitude in keyboard use. A common keyboard design uses small plastic domes behind each key to provide resistance. When the finger strikes the key with sufficient force, allowing the switch mechanism to make contact, the dome collapses. These domes can be designed to have different collapsing forces and displacement characteristics.

Several laboratory investigations controlled key switch make- (activation) force. Armstrong et al. (1994) demonstrated that peak forces corresponding to each keystroke were 2.5 to 3.9 times above the required make-force; the lowest forces were associated with the keyboards with the lowest make-forces. Peak forces also decreased as typing speed increased. Rempel et al. (1997b) found that fingertip force increased by 40

TABLE 6.5 Summary Table of Articles Measuring External Loads Due to Physical Work Attributes (Force, Motion, Vibration, and Cold) and Their Properties (Magnitude, Repetition, and Duration)

Reference	External Load	Work Activity	Force			Motion			Vibration			Temperature		
			Mag	Rep	Dur	Mag	Rep	Dur	Mag	Rep	Dur	Mag	Rep	Dur
Hand and Wrist														
Radwin, Armstrong, and Chaffin , 1987	Grip force	Handle vibration and load handled	✓						✓					
Burstrom and Lundstrom, 1988	Energy absorbed by hand-arm	Handle vibration							✓					
Schoenmarklin and Marras, 1989a	Wrist deviation	Angled hammer handles				✓								
Burstrom, 1990	Mechanical impedance of hand-arm	Handle vibration and grip force	✓						✓					
Scheffer and Dupuis, 1989	Finger-tip temperature	Exerting a static load on a vibrating handle in a cold environment	✓						✓			✓		
Martin, Roll, and Hugon, 1990	Energy absorbed by hand-arm	Handle vibration and grip force							✓					
Fritz, 1991	Vibration transmission to hand-arm	Handle vibration							✓					
Radwin and Oh, 1992	Finger force	Load handled	✓			✓								

continues

TABLE 6.5 Continued

Reference	External Load	Work Activity	Force Mag	Force Rep	Force Dur	Motion Mag	Motion Rep	Motion Dur	Vibration Mag	Vibration Rep	Vibration Dur	Temperature Mag	Temperature Rep	Temperature Dur
Schoenmarklin and Marras, 1993	Wrist velocity and acceleration	Wrist flexion/extension and forearm pronation/supination				✓								
Armstrong et al., 1994	Finger force	Keyboard force and typing speed	✓	✓										
Jeng, Radwin, and Rodriquez, 1994	Pinch overexertion	Pinch force required	✓											
Frederick and Armstrong, 1995	Pinch force	Load handled and handle friction for a hand transfer task	✓											
Oh and Radwin, 1997	Hand displacement and velocity	Power hand tool torque, work orientation, and torque buildup time	✓		✓	✓								
Radwin and Jeng, 1997	Keying force	Keyboard force and key travel	✓			✓								
Rempel et al., 1997b	Keying force	Keyboard force	✓											
Oh and Radwin, 1998	Hand displacement	Power hand tool torque and torque buildup time	✓		✓									
Marshall, Mozrall, and Shealy, 1999	Wrist range of motion	Wrist posture				✓								
Radwin and Ruffalo, 1999	Keying force	Keyboard force and key travel	✓			✓								
Gerard et al., 1999	Keying force	Keyboard force and key mechanism	✓											

percent when the key switch make-force was increased from 0.47 N to 1.02 N.

Radwin and Jeng (1997) systematically investigated specific key switch design parameters, including make-force, make-travel, and over-travel during repetitive key tapping. A mechanical apparatus independently controlled key switch parameters and directly measured finger exertions. Peak force exerted decreased 24 percent and key-tapping rate increased 2 percent when the key over-travel (displacement beyond the make-force) was increased from 0.0 to 3.0 mm. These results indicated that a key switch mechanism designed to provide adequate over-travel might enable operators to exert less force during repetitive key tapping without inhibiting performance. Similar results were replicated by Radwin and Rufalo (1999) using the same apparatus. Gerard et al. (1999) evaluated the effects of key switch characteristics on typing force by transcriptionists at an insurance company and concluded that buckling spring keyboards have decreased typing force, possibly due to greater feedback characteristics.

Posture

The availability of electronic equipment for measuring human kinematics has made it possible to quantify dynamic motions of the hand and wrist for different attributes of work. One laboratory study that investigated wrist motion characteristics associated with changing the handle angle of hammers used electrogoniometers for continuously measuring wrist ulnar-radial deviation during each hammer stroke (Schoenmarklin and Marras, 1989a). Hammer handles bent at 20 and 40 degrees resulted in less overall ulnar deviation than straight hammers; however, the reduction in ulnar deviation at hammer impact was possibly offset by increased radial deviation at the beginning of the stroke. Schoenmarklin and Marras (1993) used a similar apparatus for measuring wrist motions in a sample of industrial workers who performed repetitive work on a regular basis. Flexion-extension peak velocity and acceleration were approximately twice that of radial-ulnar and pronation-supination peak velocity, and acceleration was more than twice that of flexion-extension.

Since the upper limbs may be considered biomechanically as a complex series of joined linkages, fixing the position of one joint can greatly affect the limits of motion for other joints. A laboratory study investigated the effects of complex wrist-forearm postures on wrist range of motion in the flexion-extension and radial-ulnar deviation planes (Marshall, Mozrall, and Shealy, 1999). Combinations of wrist-forearm postures had significant effects on wrist range of motion; the largest effects were those of wrist flexion-extension on radial deviation. The study also found that wrist deviation measurements obtained with an electrogoniometer were significantly different from those obtained manually. Gender was also a significant factor.

Vibration

A study by Radwin, Armstrong, and Chaffin (1987) demonstrated that hand-arm vibration exposure, similar to the vibration associated with the operation of power hand tools, directly affects the force exerted when handling tools. Grip force was shown to increase when the hands were exposed to 40 Hz vibration during a one-minute exertion, compared with grip forces in an equivalent task with no vibration or vibration at a frequency of 160 Hz.

Vibration transmission to the body depends on the coupling between the vibrating source and the hands, vibration direction, as well as the frequency characteristics of the vibration. Energy absorbed by the hand-arm system when exposed to sinusoidal vibration exhibited a local maximum for absorption in the range 50-150 Hz with vibration in the x-direction (Burstrom and Lundstrom, 1988). A local maximum was not observed for vibration in the z-direction, and overall differences between postures were not significant. The mechanical impedance of the hand and arm when exposed to sinusoidal vibration was primarily affected by the frequency and direction of vibration (Burstrom, 1990). Impedance also increased with greater levels of vibration and stronger grip force and was greater in males than females, an effect attributed to the larger size and mass of the limbs. A biomechanical model developed by Fritz (1991) computed the forces and torques transmitted between the masses and the energy dissipated for several combinations of vibration frequency and acceleration. The model demonstrated that the hand and palmar tissues dissipated energy for vibration frequencies greater than 100 Hz.

Temperature

One laboratory study systematically investigated the combined effects of exposure to hand-arm vibration and cold air temperature on skin temperature of the fingertips (Scheffer and Dupuis, 1989). Mean skin temperature decreased from 32° F for 25° air temperature to 13° for 5° air temperature. Under the additional stress of vibration and vibration combined with the static load, a further decrease of the mean skin temperature was observed. The individual reaction to the stressors varied considerably across the subjects. The fingertip temperature decrease was more pronounced with concurrent exposure to force and vibration.

Interactions

Several laboratory studies have conducted investigations that consider the specific interactions between multiple physical stress factors. One study examined the interactions between vibration and force when subjects gripped a simulated hand tool (Radwin, Armstrong, and Chaffin, 1987). The magnitude of this increase in hand force was of the same order as for a twofold increase in load weight. The force exerted in power hand tool operation is also affected by the interaction between posture and load. One study demonstrated that the individual finger force contribution was neither equal nor constant over different loads and force requirements (Radwin and Oh, 1992). As exertion levels increased, the contribution of the index and middle fingers increased more than the ring and small finger.

The effects of power hand tool impulsive reaction forces acting on tool operators are dependent on tool-generated forces (torque output and duration), as well as posture (work location and orientation). Oh and Radwin (1997) showed that hand tool and workstation characteristics affect physical stress on operators during right-angle nut runner use. These results showed that involuntary hand motions in reaction to power hand tool torques were minimal when torque was lowest for vertical workstations closest to the operator, or when horizontal workstations were farthest from the operator. Less hand motion was observed for the horizontal workstations than for the vertical workstation. Little correlation was found between static strength of subjects and handle kinematics. Oh and Radwin (1998) observed that the effects of torque buildup time on handle kinematics were not monotonic. Among the five buildup times tested, hand motion was greatest for 150 ms.

External Physical Loading and Internal Loads

The relationship between external loading and biomechanical loading (internal loads and physiological responses) has been investigated in cadaver studies, in situ during surgical procedures, and in vivo by the use of electrophysiological measurements or small transducers attached to catheters. Several studies have identified an increased risk when the magnitude and duration of two or more physical stressors are considered together. A summary of articles dealing with these effects is presented in Table 6.6.

Biomechanical Models of External Forces and Postures on Tendon Loads

Mechanical relationships among external forces, postures, and internal tendon loading were demonstrated by Armstrong and Chaffin (1979)

TABLE 6.6 Summary Table of Articles Measuring Biomechanical Loading (Internal Loads or Physiologic Responses) Due to External Loads (Force, Motion, Vibration, and Cold) and Their Properties (Magnitude, Frequency, and Duration)

Reference	Internal Load	External Load	Force Mag	Rep	Dur	Motion Mag	Rep	Dur	Vibration Mag	Rep	Dur	Temperature Mag	Rep	Dur
Hand and Wrist														
Weiss et al., 1995	In vivo carpal tunnel pressure	Wrist flexion/extension and radial/ulnar directions				✓								
Gerard et al., 1996	EMG muscle activity in finger flexor and extensor muscles	Keyboard force during typing	✓											
Rempel et al., 1997b	EMG muscle activity	Keyboard force during typing	✓											
Grant and Habes, 1997	EMG muscle activity in flexor and extensor digitorum	Simulated meat cutting tasks using different grips and wrist postures				✓								
Rempel et al., 1994	In vivo carpal tunnel pressure	Repetitive load transfer	✓											
Rempel et al., 1997a	In vivo carpal tunnel pressure	Forearm pronation/supination and wrist flexion/extension, finger press force, and wrist posture	✓			✓								
Keir, Bach, and Rempel, 1998	In vivo carpal tunnel pressure	Finger force for press and pinch postures	✓			✓								

continues

Study	Measurement	Loading condition			
Werner et al., 1997	In vivo carpal tunnel pressure	Forearm pronation/supination and wrist flexion/extension		✓	
Seradge et al., 1995	In vivo carpal tunnel pressure	Wrist flexion/extension, finger force, grasping a cylindrical object, and making a fist	✓	✓	
Werner, Bir, and Armstrong, 1994	In vivo carpal tunnel pressure	Reverse Phalen's maneuver (wrist extension with extended fingers)		✓	
Keir et al., 1997	Cadaver carpal tunnel pressure and median nerve contact pressure	Wrist flexion/extension, ulnar/radial deviation, and loaded flexor tendons	✓	✓	
Szabo and Chidgey, 1989	In vivo carpal tunnel pressure	Wrist flexion/extension and 30 cycles per minute passive wrist flexion-extension for one minute		✓ ✓	✓ ✓
Gelberman et al., 1981	In vivo carpal tunnel pressure	Wrist flexion/extension		✓	
Skie et al., 1990	Wrist dimensions and cross-sectional area using MRI	Wrist flexion/extension		✓	
Smith, Sonstegard, and Anderson, 1977	Cadaver median nerve pressure	Load on finger flexor tendons and wrist flexion/extension	✓	✓	
Goldstein et al., 1987	Cadaver wrist tendon creep strain	Wrist flexion/extension and cyclical tendon loading	✓ ✓	✓	
Dennerlein et al., 1998	FDS tendon tension measured in vivo	Finger force	✓	✓	

TABLE 6.6 Continued

Reference	Internal Load	External Load	External Load												
			Force			Motion			Vibration			Temperature			
			Mag	Rep	Dur	Mag	Rep	Dur	Mag	Rep	Dur	Mag	Rep	Dur	
Armstrong and Chaffin, 1979	Finger flexor tendon load	Wrist flexion/extension and grip	✓			✓									
Kim and Fernandez, 1993	EMG muscle activity in finger flexors and extensors, heart rate and systolic blood pressure	Push force and wrist flexion/extension in repetitive drilling task	✓	✓		✓	✓								
Klein and Fernandez, 1997	EMG muscle activity in finger flexors and extensors, and heart rate	Pinch force, wrist flexion/extension, and task duration in a repetitive lateral pinching task	✓	✓	✓	✓	✓	✓							
Dahalan, Jalaluddin, and Fernandez, 1993	EMG muscle activity in finger flexors and extensors, and systolic blood pressure	Grip force and duration in repetitive grip exertions	✓	✓	✓										
Oh and Radwin, 1998	EMG muscle activity in finger flexors, extensors, biceps and triceps	Power hand tool torque and torque buildup time	✓		✓										
Lind et al., 1982	EMG muscle activity	Sustained isometric grip	✓												

Reference	Measure	Task
Marley and Fernandez, 1995	Systolic blood pressure, and EMG muscle activity in finger flexors and deltoids	Wrist flexion/extension for a sustained repetitive drilling task
Radwin, Armstrong, and Chaffin, 1987	EMG muscle activity	Handle vibration and load
Park and Martin, 1993	EMG muscle activity in hand flexor and extensor muscles	Handle vibration and grip level
Martin, Roll, and Hugon, 1990	Energy absorbed by hand-arm	Handle vibration and grip force
Holewijn and Heus, 1992	EMG muscle activity in the FDS	Sustained grip in a cold environment

Neck, Shoulder, and Upper Arm

Reference	Measure	Task
Erdelyi et al., 1988	EMG muscle activity in the upper trapezius	Keyboard tasks using arm supports
Grant and Habes, 1997	EMG muscle activity in the shoulder	Simulated meat cutting tasks in different postures
Hagberg, 1981	EMG muscle activity	Prolonged shoulder flexion and abduction
Hagberg and Sundelin, 1986	EMG muscle activity	Work-rest schedule for a word processing task
Aaras et al., 1997	EMG muscle activity in the upper trapezius	Keyboard and mouse tasks using arm supports

continues

TABLE 6.6 Continued

| | | | External Load | | | | | | | | | | | | |
| | | | Force | | | Motion | | | Vibration | | | Temperature | | | |
Reference	Internal Load	External Load	Mag	Rep	Dur	Mag	Rep	Dur	Mag	Rep	Dur	Mag	Rep	Dur
Feng et al., 1999	EMG muscle activity in the deltoideus anterior, deltoideus latereralis, and trapezius	Manipulative tasks with and without arm balancers	✓											
Cook and Kothiyal, 1998	EMG muscle activity in anterior and middle deltoids and trapezius	Shoulder abduction during mouse operation				✓								
Harvey and Peper, 1997	EMG muscle activity in right posterior deltoid, upper trapezius, and lower trapezius/rhomboid	Using a computer mouse to the right of a keyboard compared to a trackball at the keyboard center				✓								

for the carpal tunnel of the wrist using the analogy of a pulley and a belt. A tendon sliding over a curved articular surface may be considered analogous to a belt wrapped around a pulley. That model reveals that the force per arc length, F_l, exerted on the trochlea is a function of the tendon tension, F_t, the radius of curvature, r, the coefficient of friction between the trochlea and the tendon, μ, and the included angle of pulley-belt contact, θ, such that:

$$F_l = \frac{F_t e^{\mu\theta}}{r}. \tag{1}$$

When the extrinsic finger flexor tendons wrap around the trochlea, the synovial membranes of the radial and ulnar bursas surrounding the tendons are compressed by forces in both flexion and extension. The resulting compressive force is directly proportional to the tension developed in the tendons and the finger flexor muscles, which are related to the external force of exertion by the hand.

Normally the coefficient of friction between the tendon and trochlear surface would be expected to be very small. The model predicts that if the supporting synovia became inflamed and the coefficient of friction μ increased, F_l would increase (Chaffin and Andersson, 1991). This would also result in increased shearing forces F_s as the tendons attempt to slide through their synovial tunnels, since shear forces are generally proportional to F_l and the coefficient of friction:

$$F_s = F_l \mu. \tag{2}$$

This gives rise to the concept that repeated compression could aggravate further synovial inflammation and swelling.

Armstrong and Chaffin (1979) also showed that the total force transmitted from the belt to a pulley, F_R, depends on the wrist angle θ, and the tendon load, F_t, as described by the equation:

$$F_R = 2F_t \sin(\theta / 2). \tag{3}$$

Consequently, the force acting on adjacent anatomical structures, such as ligaments, bones, and the median nerve, depends on the wrist angle. The greater the angle is from a straight wrist, the greater the resultant reaction force on the tendons. The same equation also shows that the resultant force transmitted by a tendon to adjacent wrist structures is a function of tendon load.

The relationship of external to internal loading has been studied using cadaver hands. Armstrong and Chaffin (1978) used sized cadaver hands to statistically evaluate biomechanical models of finger flexor displacements and to develop predictive models of finger flexor tendon displacements that can be used for hands and wrists of various sizes. Tendon excursions during finger and wrist motions were related to hand size. Excursions were consistent with predictions of biomechanical models. An et al. (1983) continuously recorded tendon excursions during rotation of individual index finger joints throughout the joint's ranges of motion using seven cadaver hand specimens from amputated limbs. In this study, excursions and joint-displacement relationships were observed not to be always linear. Moment arms of the tendons with respect to joint centers were derived from excursion data for modeling muscle force in the hand.

Goldstein et al. (1987) investigated the effects of cyclic loading on cumulative strain in tendons and tendon sheaths of human cadaver hands. Viscoelastic properties were measured under simulated physiological loading conditions by attaching strain gauge transducers on tendons just proximal and distal to an undisrupted carpal tunnel. Shear traction forces were significantly greater in the extended and flexed wrist postures compared with the neutral wrist posture and were significantly greater in flexion than in extension. Under conditions of severe loading (long load duration with short recovery time), creep strain increased as a function of load cycle and load magnitude, indicating an accumulation of strain under cyclical loading.

In a laboratory study, Balnave, Davey, and Allen (1997) recorded tension in the tendon, contact force at the fingertip, and finger posture while patients gradually increased the force applied by the fingertip and then monotonically reduced it to 0 N. The average ratio of the tendon tension to the fingertip force ranged from 1.7 to 5.8, which was considerably larger than the ratio predicted by isometric tendon models. Subjects who used a pulp pinch posture had a greater ratio than subjects who flexed the DIP joint in a tip pinch posture.

Studies of External Forces and Postures on Nerve Entrapment

Research has demonstrated and quantified relationships between exertions and posture on internal loading of the median nerve in the wrist. When cadaver wrist median nerves were replaced with a balloon transducer, pressures were significantly greater at 4.54 kg tendon load than at 2.27 kg load (Smith, Sonstegard, and Anderson, 1977). Pressures were also significantly greater with the wrist in flexion, compared with neutral and extended postures. When the profundus tendons were not tensed, pressure in the tunnel remained negligible until wrist flexion approached 60° Keir et al. (1997) similarly observed that hydrostatic pressure in the carpal tunnel was affected by both wrist posture and tendon load. The greatest pressures with no load were seen in wrist extension. Muscle loading elevated carpal tunnel pressure, particularly the loading of profundus longus with the wrist in extension and the digital flexors with the wrist flexed.

Studies of the carpal tunnel serve to elucidate the relationship between external load, posture, and internal pressure. Gelberman et al. (1981) demonstrated that in vivo intracarpal canal pressure was greater in carpal tunnel syndrome patients than in controls. Werner, Bir, and Armstrong (1994) demonstrated that intracarpal canal hydrostatic pressure was significantly greater in the reverse Phalen's posture than in either the Phalen's or modified Phalen's, and the effects on median sensory latency was greater in carpal tunnel syndrome patients than in normal controls.

According to Szabo and Chidgey (1989), patients with early and intermediate carpal tunnel syndrome showed elevated pressures compared with baseline following exercise. Neither controls nor advanced patients showed a significant post-exercise increase. Furthermore, Werner et al. (1997) found that for healthy subjects who underwent a standardized set of maneuvers that systematically varied hand, wrist, and forearm position, intracarpal carpal canal pressure was least when the wrist was in a neutral position, the hand relaxed with fingers flexed and the forearm in a semipronated position. In this study, wrist extension and flexion produced the greatest increase in pressure, followed by forearm pronation and supination. Radial and ulnar deviation also increased the pressure, but to a lesser extent. Weiss et al. (1995) also found that carpal tunnel pressure increased with greater deviation from a neutral position and was greater for patients than for controls.

In a laboratory study, Rempel et al. (1997a) explored the relationship between carpal tunnel pressure and fingertip force during a simple pressing task. This study demonstrated that fingertip loading increased carpal tunnel pressure independent of wrist posture, and that relatively small fingertip loads had a large effect on carpal tunnel pressure. Keir, Bach, and Rempel (1998) found that although the external load on the finger remained constant, the internal loading, as measured by carpal tunnel pressure, experienced a nearly twofold increase by using a pinch grip.

Magnetic resonance images of the wrist in the neutral position, 45-degree flexion, and 45-degree extension have been used to measure the distance between confining structures around the median nerve (Skie et al., 1990). In this study, dimensions in flexion were significantly smaller than dimensions in the neutral and extended positions. Flexion of the wrist produced a palmar rearrangement of the flexor tendons, creating potential compression of the median nerve. The nerve responds to these forces by becoming interposed in various positions between the superficial flexor tendons.

Rempel et al. (1994) investigated the effects of repetitive hand activity on carpal tunnel pressure and whether wearing a flexible wrist splint influences pressure. The task involved healthy subjects loading and unloading 1 lb. cans from a box at a rate of 20 cans/minute for a period of 5 minutes with and without a wrist splint. Carpal tunnel pressure increased from an average of 8 to 13 mm Hg without a splint to 21 mm Hg with the splint. The increase in carpal tunnel pressure while wearing the splint at rest was attributed to increased external pressure.

Electromyographic Studies of Muscle Activity Due to External Loads

Numerous studies have observed how muscle activity increases with increased external loads. Several studies have examined actual or simulated use of hand tools. A simulated drilling task that controlled applied force and wrist flexion found that EMG activity in the finger flexor and extensor muscles increased with force (Kim and Fernandez, 1993). Dahalan and colleagues (1993) observed that EMG activity in the flexors and extensors increased with greater grip force in a similar simulated gripping task. Gerard et al. (1996) investigated the effect of keyboard key stiffness on muscle activity. The peak finger flexor and peak finger extensor EMG increased with increasing keyboard make-force.

Klein et al. (1997) studied pinching using a lateral pinch posture for different combinations of wrist posture and pinch force. EMG activity in the hand flexor and extensor muscles increased with force magnitude and wrist flexion angle. A laboratory study by Grant and Habes (1997) examined upper extremity muscle activity using postures similar to those observed in the meatpacking industry. The results showed that handle position (reach posture) had a significant effect on the EMG/force ratio in all muscles.

Power hand tool reaction force has been shown to affect forearm muscle activity. Oh and Radwin (1998) observed that the effect of torque buildup time in power hand tool use on muscular activity was not monotonic. Greater EMG activity levels were observed for torque buildup times between 150 to 300 ms than for faster or slower buildup times.

EMG has also been a useful measure for studying muscle activity during the use of keyboard and mouse data entry devices. Erdelyi et al. (1988) investigated the influence of forearm angle, as well as the effect of different arm supports, on the electrical activity (EMG) of the upper trapezius muscle during keyboard work in healthy workers and persons with shoulder pain. EMG activity decreased in the patients but not in the controls when the subjects used arm supports. The static load on the shoulders during keyboard use decreased significantly as the forearm was lowered. Aaras et al. (1997) evaluated postural load (muscle activity) during keyboard data entry, using a mouse while seated with forearm support, and using a mouse while seated without forearm support. Muscle activity in the trapezius during keyboard work was significantly reduced when sitting with supported forearms compared with sitting and standing without forearm support. The duration of time when the trapezius load was below 1 percent MVC was also significantly greater with forearm support versus no support. During seated work with a mouse, supporting the forearm significantly reduced the static load on the trapezius. Harvey and Peper (1997) observed that all of their subjects had significantly greater mean surface EMG activity recorded from the right upper trapezius, right posterior deltoid, and right lower trapezius-rhomboid during mouse use compared with using a trackball positioned centrally. Surface EMG levels remained elevated during the entire trial period of right-side mouse use without evidence of micro breaks (< 1 s epochs of low surface EMG activity). The authors attribute the increased EMG activity to shoulder abduction required for mouse use.

Feng et al. (1999) recorded EMG activity and posture angles of the shoulder and arm while subjects performed an upper extremity manipulative task in a seated posture on a horizontal table at elbow height, with and without arm support. The use of an arm balancer reduced EMG activity in the anterior deltoid muscle during a variety of light manipulative tasks. Cook and Kothiyal (1998) examined the influence of mouse position, relative to the keyboard, on shoulder and arm muscular activity and working posture. This study showed that mouse position affects muscle activity levels and upper extremity posture. Moving the mouse closer to the midline of the body reduced shoulder muscle activity.

External Physical Loading and Internal Tolerances

Measures of internal tolerances for mechanical strain and fatigue are often quantified using physiological measurements or psychophysical assessments. A summary of articles measuring internal tolerances due to external loads appears in Table 6.7.

Physiological Measures of Mechanical Strain or Fatigue from External Loads

Electromyography and blood flow have been used to measure the effects of work pauses on localized muscle fatigue in the upper limbs.

TABLE 6.7 Summary Table of Articles Measuring Internal Tolerances (Mechanical Strain or Fatigue) Due to External Loads (Force, Motion, Vibration, and Cold) and Their Properties (Magnitude, Repetition, and Duration)

Reference	Internal Load	External Load	External Load												
			Force			Motion			Vibration			Temperature			
			Mag	Rep	Dur	Mag	Rep	Dur	Mag	Rep	Dur	Mag	Rep	Dur	
Hand and Wrist															
Snook et al., 1997	Maximum acceptable torque	Work duration in repetitive ulnar deviation task	✓	✓		✓	✓	✓							
Kim and Fernandez, 1993	Maximum acceptable frequency, rating of perceived exertion	Push force and wrist flexion/extension in repetitive drilling task	✓			✓	✓								
Klein and Fernandez, 1997	Maximum acceptable frequency, rating of perceived exertion	Pinch force, wrist flexion/extension and task duration in a repetitive lateral pinching task	✓	✓		✓	✓	✓							
Snook, Ciriello, and Webster, 1999	Maximum acceptable torque	Grip posture, wrist ulnar deviation, and exertion frequency in a repetitive wrist extension task	✓	✓		✓	✓	✓							
Ulin et al., 1990	Rating of perceived exertion	Power screwdriver shape and vertical height				✓									

continues

Reference	Measure	Variable						
Harber, Hsu, and Pena, 1994	Rating of perceived exertion	Pull force, wrist flexion/extension, and grip posture	✓					
Dahalan, Jalaluddin, and Fernandez, 1993	Maximum acceptable frequency, rating of perceived exertion	Grip force and duration in repetitive grip exertions	✓	✓	✓			
Davis and Fernandez, 1994	Maximum acceptable frequency	Wrist posture in repetitive drilling task	✓		✓			
Ulin et al., 1992	Subjective preference	Power screwdriver shape, vertical height, work orientation, and reach distance	✓		✓			
Schoenmarklin and Marras, 1989a	EMG mean power frequency	Hammering into vertical and horizontal surfaces using tools with varying handle angles	✓		✓			
Snook et al., 1995	Maximum acceptable torque	Exertion frequency for repetitive wrist flexion-extension using power and pinch grips	✓	✓	✓	✓	✓	
Oh and Radwin, 1998	Rating of perceived exertion	Power hand tool torque and torque buildup time	✓	✓				
Ulin et al., 1993a	Rating of perceived exertion	Reach for a power screwdriver task	✓		✓			
Ulin et al., 1993b	Rating of perceived exertion	Frequency of a power screwdriver task on horizontal and vertical surfaces	✓	✓	✓			

TABLE 6.7 Continued

Reference	Internal Load	External Load	Force Mag	Force Rep	Force Dur	Motion Mag	Motion Rep	Motion Dur	Vibration Mag	Vibration Rep	Vibration Dur	Temperature Mag	Temperature Rep	Temperature Dur
Fleming, Jansen, and Hasson, 1997	EMG mean power frequency	Gripping with and without gloves	✓		✓									
Petrofsky et al., 1982	EMG mean power frequency	Sustained isometric grip	✓		✓									
Baidya and Stevenson, 1988	EMG mean power frequency	Repeated wrist extensions against a load until exhaustion	✓		✓	✓	✓	✓						
Linqvist, 1993	Rating of perceived exertion	Power hand tool torque, torque buildup time, and shutoff time	✓		✓									
Marley and Fernandez, 1995	Maximum acceptable frequency, rating of perceived exertion, and EMG mean power frequency in finger flexors and deltoids	Wrist flexion/extension for a sustained repetitive drilling task	✓	✓		✓	✓	✓						
Armstrong et al., 1989	Subjective rating of comfort	Tool weight, handle circumference, vertical work location, and horizontal reach	✓			✓								
Gerard et al., 1999	Subjective preference	Keyboard key mechanism	✓											

Martin, Roll, and Hugon, 1990	Perceived intensity of an electrical stimulus	Handle vibration	✓
Blackwell, Kornatz, and Heath, 1999	EMG mean power frequency for FDS muscle	Power grip handles with different spans	✓
Murthy et al., 1997	Oxygenation of extensor carpi radialis	Exertion level, duration, and recovery	✓
Bystrom and Kilbom, 1990	Blood flow in forearm and EMG activity in extensor digitorum communis	Intermittent isometric hand grip exertions	✓

Neck, Shoulder, and Upper Arm

Oberg, Sandsjo, and Kadefors, 1994	EMG mean power frequency in the trapezius	Holding loads in the hands for a given shoulder posture	✓
Hagberg and Sundelin, 1986	Perceived exertion	Work-rest schedule for a word processing task	✓

Petrofsky et al. (1982) found that EMG activity level increases and mean power frequency decreases as a function of time during sustained isometric contractions. Hagberg and Sundelin (1986) evaluated the effects of short pauses on EMG activity during word processing tasks and found that static loading was relatively low during the typing tasks, 3.2 percent MVC for the right shoulder, and 3.0 percent MVC for the left shoulder. There was a significant negative correlation between pauses and static load on the right trapezius muscle. In another study, Baidya and Stevenson (1988) observed that the rate of decrease in the center frequency of wrist extensor EMG signals was greater for the larger extension angle than for repetitive wrist movements. In this study, ulnar deviation did not affect the rate of fatigue (center frequency shift).

Bystrom and Kilbom (1990) found that when work-rest duty cycle (contraction/relaxation) and contraction intensity were controlled, forearm blood flow was insufficient even at isometric contractions of low intensity (10 percent MVC), indicating that vasodilating metabolites play an active role for blood flow in low-intensity isometric contractions. This study also showed that maximal blood flow in the forearm during relaxation periods (25-30 ml/min/100 ml) is reached at 25 percent MVC. Only a cycle of intermittent exercise at 10 percent MVC and (10 sec work + 5 sec rest) and (10 sec work + 10 sec rest) at 25 percent MVC was considered acceptable with regard to local fatigue.

Kim and Fernandez (1993) found that heart rate, systolic blood pressure, and flexor and extensor EMG activity increased with force during a simulated drilling task. Heart rate also increased when working with increased wrist flexion angles. Marley and Fernandez (1995) found that when subjects maintained a 5.4 kg simulated drilling force for a total duration of three minutes, systolic blood pressure and deltoid EMG activity increased with trial duration and wrist flexion angle, while deltoid median power frequency decreased with wrist angle and trial duration, indicating localized fatigue.

Dahalan, Jalaluddin, and Fernandez (1993) observed that several physiological measures (systolic blood pressure, EMG activity in the flexors and extensors) increased with increased grip force. Systolic blood pressure increased with exertion duration. Klein and Fernandez (1997) found that mean heart rate increased with increasing pinch force and that EMG activity increased with force magnitude, wrist flexion angle, and task duration. Endurance time was greater without gloves (Fleming, Jansen, and Hasson, 1997). Fatigue of the digitorum superficialis, as inferred from EMG frequency shifts, did not change as a function of grip size; however, there was an optimal grip size for greater absolute forces (Blackwell, Kornatz, and Heath, 1999).

Tissue oxygenation is another measure of muscle fatigue. Murthy et al. (1997) investigated the sensitivity of near-infrared spectroscopy technique to changes in tissue oxygenation at low levels of isometric contraction in the extensor carpi radialis brevis muscle. They found that mean tissue oxygenation decreased from the resting baseline (100 percent tissue oxygenation) to 89, 81, 78, and 47 percent for 5, 10, 15, and 50 percent MVC, respectively. Tissue oxygenation levels at 10, 15, and 50 percent MVC were significantly less than the baseline value.

Holewijn and Heus (1992) evaluated the effects of temperature on muscle function in the upper extremity. The endurance time for the sustained contraction at 15 percent MVC was reduced by 50 percent with warming, compared with the reference condition. RMS EMG was not affected by temperature; however, the mean power frequency shifted to a lower value at the beginning of the sustained grip exertion in the cooled condition.

Psychophysical Measures of Mechanical Strain or Fatigue for External Forces and Postures

Psychophysical measures have been used to study perceptions of comfort and intensity while performing lifting tasks. Automobile assembly workers were asked to use a 10-point scale with verbal anchors to rate the tool mass, grip force, handle size, vertical work location, horizontal work location, and overall satisfaction with a tool (Armstrong, Punnett, and Ketner, 1989). Tools with mass less than 2.0 kg, handle circumferences less than 12 cm, horizontal work locations of 38 cm or less, and vertical work locations between 102 and 152 cm were the most preferred. Harber and colleagues (Harber, Hsu, and Pena, 1994) used the psychophysical approach to demonstrate that grip type, force level, and wrist angle affected perceptions of work intensity and comfort while performing a one-handed lifting task. Subjects preferred wrist extension over wrist flexion and a power grip over a pinch grip.

Oberg and colleagues (Oberg, Sandsjo, and Kadefors, 1994) found that physiological (EMG) and psychophysical measures of fatigue in the trapezius muscle were correlated at high load levels but not at low load levels. This indicates that subject sensations of fatigue may be caused by factors unrelated to changes in recruitment of motor units.

Psychophysical measures have also been applied to the study of perceptions of acceptable torque during repetitive wrist motion. Stover Snook, who pioneered psychophysical methods for lifting, established a procedure to ascertain the maximum acceptable torques for various types and frequencies of repetitive wrist motion (Snook et al., 1995). Four adjustable workstations were built to simulate repetitive wrist flexion with a power grip, wrist flexion with a pinch grip, and wrist extension with a power grip. In general, maximum acceptable torque decreased as the exertion frequency increased for the three types of exertions. Maximum acceptable torque was greatest for power grip flexion and least for power grip extension. Maximum acceptable torque decreased over the seven hours of testing. There were no significant differences in maximum acceptable torque from day to day; however, the average maximum acceptable torque for a 5 days per week exposure was 36.3 percent lower than for the same task performed 2 days per week.

In an experiment similar to the one for wrist flexion-extension, Snook et al. (1997) quantified maximum acceptable torques for ulnar deviation motions of the wrist similar to a knife-cutting task at various repetition rates using the psychophysical method. The subject adjusted the resistance on the handle while the experimenter manipulated or controlled all other variables. The subjects were instructed to work as if they were paid on an incentive basis. Maximum acceptable torque decreased over the 7 hours of testing in both series. Maximum acceptable torque decreased with increasing frequency in both series, but the change was not statistically significant.

Snook, Ciriello, and Webster (1999) employed the same method to determine maximum acceptable torque for extension motions of the wrist performed with a pinch grip. Maximum acceptable torque and extension duration decreased with increasing task frequency. Maximum acceptable torque during wrist extension with a pinch grip was less than wrist flexion with a pinch grip, wrist flexion with a power grip, or ulnar deviation.

Psychophysical measures were used by Kim and Fernandez (1993) to investigate simulated repetitive drilling tasks. Maximum acceptable frequency decreased with greater drilling force and with greater wrist flexion. Ratings of perceived exertion increased with force and with wrist flexion angle. Marley and Fernandez (1995) used the method of adjustment to determine the maximum acceptable frequency for a simulated drilling task. The psychophysically adjusted task frequency was significantly lower when wrist deviation was required, particularly wrist flexion. A similar laboratory study investigated the maximum acceptable frequency for a simulated gripping task (Dahalan, Jalaluddin, and Fernandez, 1993). Maximum acceptable frequency decreased significantly as grip force magnitude and exertion duration increased. Ratings of perceived exertion increased with higher grip force.

Davis and Fernandez (1994) found that the acceptable frequency for a simulated drilling task was maximum with a neutral wrist position and decreased with increased angles of wrist flexion, extension, and radial deviation. Marley and Fernandez (1995) showed that maximum acceptable frequency for a simulated drilling task decreased as a function of wrist flexion angle. Klein and Fernandez (1997) evaluated the effects of wrist posture on maximum acceptable frequency for a simulated drilling task. Wrist flexion (10 and 20 deg), extension (20 and 40 deg), and radial deviation (10 and 20 deg) all produced significant decreases in maximum acceptable frequency compared with the neutral posture.

Another area in which psychophysical measures have been used is to study lifting, positioning, and pinching tasks. Work duration for limiting shoulder-girdle fatigue during lifting-positioning tasks decreased, as with force and with repetition rate (Putz-Anderson and Galinsky, 1993). When repetition and reach height were varied, task duration decreased, as with required working height and with required repetition rate. Males tended to engage in longer work trials than females, despite controlling for upper body strength.

Klein and Fernandez (1997) used the psychophysical approach to determine maximum acceptable frequency for pinching using a lateral pinch posture. Maximum acceptable frequency was reduced as wrist flexion angle, force magnitude, and task duration increased. Perceived exertion increased with force magnitude, wrist flexion angle, and task duration.

A number of experiments performed by Ulin employed psychophysical methods for studying power hand tool orientation, location, and shape. Following each treatment, subjects rated exertion level and discomfort using three psychophysical scales (the Borg 10-point ratio rating scale and two 10-centimeter visual analog scales used to rate comfort and ease of work). Subjects were instructed to imagine that they were assembly line workers performing the task for an 8-hour day. In 1990, Ulin et al. determined the preferred work location for driving screws with a pistol-shaped screwdriver to be 114 to 140 cm for a mixed male-female subject pool. In a 1992 study, Ulin et al. demonstrated how work location, work orientation, and tool selection affected perceived exertion when using pneumatic hand tools. Lowest exertions were observed when working in neutral postures. Ulin and colleagues found (1) that perceived exertion was lowest when the horizontal reach distance was small and when working at mid-thigh or elbow height (1993b) and (2) that perceived exertion increases as a function of work pace (1993a). In addition, perceived exertion is affected by work location, work orientation, and tool type. Both work location and task frequency were significant factors in determining the Borg rating. As work pace increased, so did the Borg rating of perceived exertion for each work location. Driving screws at elbow height on the vertical surface and with the lower arm close to the body on the horizontal surface was the work location that produced the lowest ratings of perceived exertion. Differences in local discomfort were found for the vertical work locations. While driving screws at knee height, the torso was most stressed, at elbow height the wrist-hand were most stressed, and at shoulder height the shoulder and upper arm were the most stressed.

Schoenmarklin and Marras (1989b) demonstrated that hammer handle angle did not significantly affect forearm muscle fatigue based on a shift in EMG mean power frequency, but wall hammering produced marginally greater muscle fatigue than did bench hammering. Linqvist (1993) observed a correlation between power hand tool handle displacement and subjective strain ratings. This laboratory study investigated responses to power tool spindle torque reaction forces during the final stages of tightening threaded fasteners with a right-angled nut runner. A distinctive feature of nut runners during the torque reaction phase is that the handle is rapidly displaced as torque builds up, causing a movement of the upper extremity. Subject ratings of strain increased monotonically as a function of torque level. Ratings of strain were higher for medium-hard joints compared with hard joints, and ratings of strain were higher for slow-shutoff tools compared with high-shutoff tools. Ratings of strain were positively correlated with the handle displacement; correlations were strongest for the slow-shutoff tool used on a hard joint. Oh and Radwin (1998) evaluated the relative effects of power hand tool process parameters (target torque, torque buildup time, and workstation orientation) on subjective ratings of perceived exertion. Increasing the torque reaction force resulted in higher ratings of perceived exertion. Subjective ratings of perceived exertion were lowest when torque buildup time was 35 ms; however, greater peak torque variance was associated with this condition.

Radwin and Ruffalo (1999) investigated the effects of key-switch design parameters on short-term localized muscle fatigue in the forearm and hand. Subject reports of fatigue were reduced with the lower key make-force. Self-reported fatigue occurred in all cases (keying rate decreased over the duration of the test session), but no significant differences were observed based on RMS EMG for low-level exertions in repetitive keying.

A laboratory study evaluated the effects of muscle, tendon, or skin vibration on the early and late components of polyphasic cutaneous responses elicited in the flexor carpi radialis muscle by electrical stimulation of the radial nerve at the wrist (Martin, Roll, and Hugon, 1990). Palm skin vibration depressed both components of the flexor reflex, while skin vibration on the back of the hand induced either a facilitation or an inhibition. In addition, this kind of vibration modified the location of the sensation evoked by the electrical stimulation of the nerve. In all cases, the vibration stimulus attenuated the perceived intensity of the electrical stimulus. These observations suggested to the authors a possible impairment of the protective withdrawal reflex under vibratory environmental conditions at rest and eventually in active muscles.

External Physical Loading and Pain, Discomfort, or Functional Limitations

The following section reviews literature that directly investigated pain, discomfort, or functional limitations due to external loading. The studies that are reviewed report short-term impairments of function observed in the laboratory or in the field, rather than long-term impairments or disabilities. Studies dealing with longer-term effects are reviewed in the epidemiology literature covered in Chapter 4. Rather these studies reveal relationships between workplace exposures and short-term outcomes such as pain, discomfort, and level of function. A summary of these articles is presented in Table 6.8.

Pain and Discomfort Due to External Loading

In some studies, pain and discomfort have been examined in relation to work posture and force. For example, Schoenmarklin and Marras (1989b) found that hammering on a vertical wall resulted in significantly greater discomfort than hammering on a bench. Gerard et al. (1999) found that subjective discomfort increased as a function of key make-force with rubber dome key switches. Lin, Radwin, and Snook (1997) found that force, wrist flexion angle, and repetition are all significant factors in determining discomfort. They developed a subjective model of discomfort on a 10-cm analog scale. The continuous model was compared with and agrees with discrete psychophysical data from other published studies.

Other studies have demonstrated the effects of pace and work schedule on perceived pain, discomfort and exertion. For example, a study by Hagberg and Sundelin (1986) found that pain and discomfort reports increased with longer durations of work time. The increase was smallest when the work-rest cycle included short rest periods. In a laboratory experiment, Snook et al. (1997) found that the rate of pain and discomfort reports increased with longer duration of work in which subjects adjusted the resistance of a handle while grasping it with a power grip and repetitively moving it through 80 deg ulnar deviation wrist motion, similar to a knife-cutting task (Snook et al., 1997). In a study by Ulin et al. (1993b) both work location and task frequency were found to be significant factors—

TABLE 6.8 Summary Table of Articles Measuring Adverse Outcomes (Pain, Discomfort, Impairment, or Disability) Due to External Loads (Force, Motion, Vibration, and Cold) and Their Properties (Magnitude, Frequency, and Duration)

Reference	Adverse Outcome	External Load	External Load												
			Force			Motion			Vibration			Temperature		
			Mag	Rep	Dur	Mag	Rep	Dur	Mag	Rep	Dur	Mag	Rep	Dur
Hand and Wrist														
Imrhan, 1991	Pinch strength	Wrist and pinch posture				✓								
Snook et al., 1997	General discomfort	Work duration in repetitive ulnar deviation task				✓	✓	✓						
Radwin and Jeng, 1997	Keying rate	Keyboard force	✓											
Radwin and Ruffalo, 1999	Keying rate and localized discomfort	Keyboard force	✓											
Ulin et al., 1990	General discomfort	Vertical height in power screwdriver operation				✓								
Schoenmarklin and Marras, 1989b	General discomfort	Orientation for hammering				✓								
Ulin et al., 1993a	General discomfort	Power hand tool shape, work orientation, and work location	✓	✓		✓								
Batra et al., 1994	General discomfort and grip strength	Glove thickness	✓			✓								
Fleming, Jansen, and Hasson, 1997	Endurance time	Gripping with and without gloves	✓	✓										

continues

Reference	Measure	Factor						
Schiefer et al., 1984	Manual performance in block threading, knot tying, peg test, and threading screws	Cold environment						✓
Gerard et al., 1999	Localized discomfort	Keyboard key mechanism	✓					
Gerard and Martin, 1999	Manual performance in visual-manual tracking	Handle vibration and recovery time		✓			✓	
Riley and Cochran, 1984	Manual performance in pegboard, pencil tapping, tweezers manipulation, and assembly	Cold environment		✓				✓
Malchaire, Piette, and Rodriguez-Diaz, 1998	Vibration perception threshold	Handle vibration						
Lin, Radwin, and Snook, 1997	General discomfort	Force and posture repetition frequency	✓	✓	✓	✓		
Lin and Radwin, 1998	General discomfort	Force and posture and repetition frequency	✓	✓	✓	✓	✓	
O'Driscoll et al., 1992	General discomfort	Force and posture and repetition frequency	✓	✓	✓	✓		
Knowlton and Gilbert, 1983	Grip strength	Following hammering tasks using hammers with angled handles						
Mital, Kuo, and Faard, 1994	Torque strength	Use of common hand tools and gloves	✓					

TABLE 6.8 Continued

Reference	Adverse Outcome	External Load	External Load											
			Force			Motion			Vibration			Temperature		
			Mag	Rep	Dur	Mag	Rep	Dur	Mag	Rep	Dur	Mag	Rep	Dur
Holewijn and Heus, 1992	Grip strength, maximum rhythmic frequency and endurance time	Cooling the hands	✓											
Dempsey and Ayoub, 1996	Pinch strength	Wrist flexion/extension, ulnar/radial deviation, and pinch separation				✓								
Pryce, 1980	Grip strength	Wrist flexion/extension and ulnar/radial deviation				✓								
O'Driscoll et al., 1992	Grip strength	Wrist flexion/extension and ulnar/radial deviation and handle size				✓								
Blackwell, Kornatz, and Heath, 1999	Grip strength	Handle size				✓								
Hallbeck and McMullin, 1993	Grip strength	Wearing gloves while varying wrist flexion/extension	✓			✓								
Jeng, Radwin, and Rodriquez, 1994	Maximum pinch rate	Pinch force	✓											

Neck, Shoulder, and Upper Arm

Oberg, Sandsjo, and Kadefors, 1994	Localized discomfort in the trapezius muscle region	Duration of holding a load with the shoulder abducted		✓
Putz-Anderson and Galinsky, 1993	Time for localized discomfort for the shoulder girdle	Load in the hand and repetition rate in repetitive lifting and positioning tasks	✓	✓

that is, as work pace increased, so did the Borg rating of perceived exertion for each work location. Differences in local discomfort were found for the vertical work locations.

Functional Limitations Due to External Loading

Marshall, Mozrall, and Shealy (1999) demonstrated that the combination of wrist-forearm posture had significant effects on wrist range of motion. Pryce (1980) studied the effect of wrist posture (neutral and ulnar deviation, and 15 deg each side of neutral in volar and dorsiflexion) and maximum power grip strength. Strength was affected by ulnar deviation angle, and grip force was greatest in the neutral position and decreased as the deviation angle increased. Strength was also affected by extension-flexion angle. Knowlton and Gilbert (1983) investigated the effects of ulnar deviation on strength decrements when using hammers to drive nails in a standard task. Grip strength was measured before and after performing the hammering task. Peak grip strength was reduced by an average 67 N with a conventional claw hammer compared with 33 N with a curved-handle ripping hammer. Average grip strength was reduced by 84 N with the claw hammer compared with 49 N with the ripping hammer. There was no significant difference between the number of strikes required to complete the task with the two tools.

Imrhan (1991) examined the effects of different wrist positions on maximum pinch force. The results showed that all of the deviated wrist positions reduced the observed pinch strength, with palmar flexion having the greatest effect and radial deviation having the least. O'Driscoll et al. (1992) also investigated the effects of posture on grip strength. Grip strength was reduced in any deviation from a self-selected position. Measured strength and the degree of wrist extension was inversely related to the handle separation distance on the Jamar dynamometer. This was true regardless of hand size, although the effects were more pronounced for small hands. A laboratory study by Hallbeck and McMullin (1993) found that gender, glove type, hand dominance, and wrist position had a significant effect on the magnitude of power grasp. Force was maximized with a bare hand in a neutral wrist posture.

Dempsey and Ayoub (1996) reported that gender, wrist posture (neutral, maximum flexion, maximum extension, maximum radial deviation, and maximum ulnar deviation), pinch type (pulp2, pulp3, chuck, and lateral), and pinch width (1, 3, 5, and 7 cm) all had significant effects on strength. Maximum values were obtained with a neutral wrist, a separation distance of 5 cm, and a lateral grasp. Female strength was on average 62.9 percent of male strength.

Blackwell, Kornatz, and Heath (1999) investigated the effect of grip span on isometric grip force. An optimal grip size allowed for the greatest forces. Batra et al. (1994) demonstrated that reduction in grip strength was positively correlated with glove thickness but not with glove size. In a subsequent analysis, the following selected glove attributes were correlated to reductions in demonstrated strength: (1) tenacity—friction between the glove and a standard piece of plastic, (2) snugness—hand volume versus glove volume, (3) suppleness—a measure of pliability, and (4) thickness. A decrease in grip force was significantly affected by glove type—asbestos and leather gloves reduced grip strength to approximately 82.5 percent of bare-handed levels, while surgical gloves reduced grip strength to 96.3 percent of bare-handed levels.

Mital and colleagues studied the influence of a variety of commercially available gloves on the force-torque exertion capability of workers when using wrenches and screwdrivers in routine maintenance and repair tasks (Mital, Kuo, and Faard, 1994). Subjects exerted a maximum volitional torque during a simulated task. The results indicated that tool type was a predictor of volitional torque. Gloves also affected volitional torque; torque was greater with the use of gloves.

Temperature can be an important moderating variable. Riley and Cochran (1984) studied manual dexterity performance at different ambient temperatures. Subjects wore typical industrial worker apparel without gloves during manual dexterity tests. Results indicated that after 15 minutes of cold exposure, there was no difference between performance at 12.8 and 23.9 degrees Celsius, but there was a difference between performance at 1.7 and 12.8 degrees as well as between performance at 1.7 and 23.9 degrees. Holewijn and Heus (1992) found that isometric grip strength was significantly reduced by cooling. The rate of force buildup was also influenced by temperature, with slower buildup under conditions of cooling. Cooling reduced the maximum grip frequency by 50 percent compared with the reference condition. The endurance time for the sustained contraction at 15 percent MVC was reduced by 50 percent with warming compared with the reference condition.

A psychomotor task was developed by Jeng, Radwin, and Rodriquez (1994) for investigating functional deficits associated with carpal tunnel syndrome. A rapid pinch and release psychomotor task utilizing muscles innervated by the median nerve was administered. Subjects were instructed to pinch the dynamometer above an upper force level and then release below a lower force level as quickly as possible. Average pinch rate decreased from 5.4 pinches/sec to 3.7 pinches/sec as the upper force increased from 5 to 50 percent MVC. Pinch rate was significantly faster and overshoot force was less for the dominant hand. Control subjects performed 25 to 82 percent better than subjects with carpal tunnel syndrome. Age contributed 6 percent of the total variance for pinch rate and 7 percent of the total variance for the time below the lower force level. The results suggest that patients with carpal tunnel syndrome may experience similar functional psychomotor deficits in daily living and manual work activities. Schiefer et al. (1984) demonstrated that finger skin temperature and performance on manual dexterity tests decreased as the ambient air temperature decreases.

Upper Limb Summary

Overall, the literature reveals that there are strong relationships between physical loads in the workplace and biomechanical loading, internal tolerances, and pain, impairment, and disability. Although many of these relationships are complex for the upper limb, the associations are clear. The biomechanical literature has identified relationships between physical work attributes and external loads for force, posture, vibration, and temperature. Research has also demonstrated relationships between external loading and biomechanical loading (i.e., internal loads or physiologic responses). Relationships between external loading and internal tolerances (i.e., mechanical strain or fatigue) have also been demonstrated. Finally, relationships have been shown between external loading and pain, discomfort, impairment, or disability. Although the relationships exist, the picture is far from complete.

Individual studies have for the most part not fully considered the characteristic properties of physical work and external loading (i.e., magnitude, repetition, or duration). Few studies have considered multiple physical stress factors or their interactions. The absence of these relationships, however, does not detract from the basic theoretical construct of the load-tolerance model. In fact, it suggests the need for additional research.

When considered together, a broader picture emerges. The existence of relationships together supports the load-tolerance model presented in this report. Furthermore, biomechanics forms the basis to reduce external loading. The relationships that are established indicate appropriate interventions for reducing exposure to external loads in the work environment through ergonomics and work design. Future research efforts targeting the missing relationships may help provide additional workplace interventions for preventing and reducing the risk of work-related disorders.

7

Occupational Stress

As indicated in the review of the epidemiologic literature in Chapter 4, a number of workplace psychosocial factors can affect work-related back and upper extremity disorders. The literature provides strong evidence for the role, in low back disorders, of job satisfaction, monotonous work, social support at work, high work demands, job stress, and emotional effort at work. The perception of one's ability to return to work was also positively associated with future back pain. While the literature on upper extremity disorders is not so extensive as with back disorders, higher levels of perceived job demands and job stress were the psychosocial factors most consistently linked to upper extremity disorders. The reviews of the epidemiologic literature also indicated that certain psychosocial factors that are not work-specific (e.g., general worry/psychological tension, depression/anxiety, general coping style, and response to pain) were also associated with both back and upper extremity disorders. Nonwork-related variables tend to be more commonly related to back than to upper extremity disorders.

Given that the emphasis of this report is on work-related factors, this chapter reviews various models of occupational stress and discusses how exposure to stresses at work can impact the physiology of musculoskeletal pain in the spine and upper extremities. Nonworkplace psychosocial stressors can exert similar effects, but are not discussed here.

The study of occupational stress is a difficult endeavor because of the many factors that can influence the development, exacerbation, and maintenance of job stress and the highly subjective nature of measures of exposure and outcomes used in this area. In addition, the various biological correlates of stress exposure and, more specifically, the proposed models of how job stress may affect occupational musculoskeletal disorders, are speculative. Also, if biological pathways linking job stress to work-related musculoskeletal disorders exist, it is currently unknown whether they are specific to these disorders or, more likely, represent the final common pathway by which exposure to both work-related and nonwork-related stressors exert an effect on a number of health disorders (e.g., cardiovascular disease). That is, the specificity of these pathways is unknown. It is generally accepted that musculoskeletal pain can be experienced in the absence of evident physiological change or tissue damage (Melzack, 1999) and that such pain is modulated primarily by cognitive processes.

This chapter reviews general models of occupational stress, biological correlates of stress exposure, selected theories related to how occupational stress might impact musculoskeletal disorders, and hypothesized pathways that may account for the relationship.

GENERAL MODELS OF OCCUPATIONAL STRESS

Several general models of occupational stress have emerged that define job stress and explain how certain aspects of work can contribute to the experience of stress. An early model proposed by Levi (1972) includes the components of most models of occupational stress. A simplified version of the major features of this and most models of stress is depicted in Figure 7.1.

The Levi model describes a process by which a worker is in constant interchange with his or her work environment; these interactions require

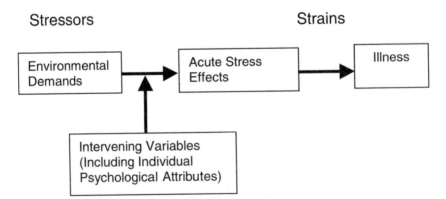

FIGURE 7.1 Generic psychosocial stress model. From Sauter and Swanson (1996:6). Reprinted with permission.

continuous adaptation by the worker. When these transactions are perceived as uncontrollable, the event or situation generates a condition of psychological distress that, if persistent or repeated, can lead to negative health outcomes. The first component of this stress model includes social structures (such as workplace, family) and social processes (events that take place within the social structure). These structures and events are continuously perceived, appraised, and evaluated by the individual. When there is a persistent discrepancy between the worker's abilities, personal needs, expectations, environmental demands, and the opportunities, potential outcomes, social structures, and/or events, or when transactions are perceived as threats, then a complex emotional, cognitive, behavioral, and physiological reaction is evoked.

This response can result in transitory disturbances in mental and physical function (stress response) that, if prolonged, can eventually lead to persistent feelings of distress (frustration, anger, anxiety, dysphoria) and subsequently to physical disorders. Presumably, this response to stress is affected by early environmental influences and genetic factors. It is proposed that this cascade of events can be modified by a number of "interacting variables," including, for example, a worker's coping repertoire and skills, and the availability and use of social support. These models typically propose the existence of a set of stressors, which are generally defined as environmental demands, and responses to these stressors, often referred to as strains. These strains are the acute effects of the exposure to stressors. A set of intervening factors plays a role in modulating the effect of the demands on strain. As indicated earlier, these intervening factors can include coping skills, problem solving abilities, past learning and exposure, and biological predisposition to react to stress. It is important to note that there are other models of occupational stress (e.g., Hurrell, 1987; Karasek and Theorell, 1990) that have not been reviewed in this chapter. The purpose of this section is not to provide an exhaustive review of models but rather to provide a general overview of the components of most models.

BIOLOGICAL RESPONSE

Work can trigger a complex set of behavioral, cognitive, and physiological responses or strains, commonly referred to as the *stress response*. The stress response is typically associated with systemic and localized physiological changes that are intended to reestablish a biological state of homeostasis (Selye, 1956). It is postulated that recurrent or chronic exposure to a wide range of intrinsic or extrinsic stressors or demands repeatedly evokes a stress response, which, in turn, contributes to the etiology, exacerbation, and maintenance of a number of prevalent health problems

(Chrousos and Gold, 1992; Baum and Posluszny, 1999; Kiecolt-Glaser et al., 1995).

Many models of human stress propose that the presence and severity of a stress response are proportional to an individual's appraisal of the extent of threat represented by the specific stressor (Lazarus, 1974). Psychological processes (e.g., emotions, behaviors, memory) involved in stress appraisal or evaluation and subsequent response are assumed to trigger the biological consequences of stress. Pathways linking psychological and biological processes are often referred to as "biobehavioral." In an effort to understand the potential physiological effects of stress on adverse health outcomes, various biobehavioral pathways have been proposed (Kiecolt-Glaser et al., 1995; Glaser and Kiecolt-Glaser, 1998; Baum and Posluszny, 1999).

Two common pathways through which exposure to stressors can affect health are the corticotropin-releasing hormone and the locus ceruleus-norepinephrine/autonomic (sympathetic) systems. These two systems are regulated both centrally (brain) and peripherally; they can exert their effects on target tissues and bodily systems through substances released in response to exposure to stressful conditions. These substances include adrenocorticotropic hormone, glucocorticoids, and catecholamines (epinephrine and norepinephrine). Recent research on neuroimmunomodulation (the bidirectional signaling between both the central and the peripheral nervous systems and the cells and organs of the immune system) has demonstrated that the brain can send neuroendocrine signals to cells within the immune system; the immune system, in turn, through the release of cytokines, can signal neurons in the brain and the peripheral nervous system (Felten and Maida, 2000; Watkins, Maier, and Goehler, 1995; Chrousos and Gold, 1992).

The significance of these findings is that this bidirectional communication system can serve as one pathway by which exposure to stressful events in the environment can translate to profound changes in immune function, thereby affecting a range of health outcomes. Specifically, cytokines or molecules released from various cells throughout the body following injury can interact not only with other cells within the immune system, altering their intracellular capabilities, but can also be directly affected by the brain's processing of the meaning of external events, such as stressors on the job and problems at home. While the complex biological processes involved in the stress response are just beginning to be revealed, current knowledge regarding the biological response to stress provides a foundation for understanding how psychological stressors may modulate activity within the nervous, endocrine, and immune systems, thereby exerting an effect on health.

OCCUPATIONAL STRESS AND
WORK-RELATED MUSCULOSKELETAL DISORDERS:
SOME WORKING HYPOTHESES

A number of nonspecific biobehavioral mechanisms have been hypothesized to delineate how stress may affect the physiological processes involved in common musculoskeletal disorders (Bongers et al., 1993; Smith and Carayon-Sainfort, 1989; Smith and Carayon, 1996; Melin and Lundberg, 1997; Sauter and Swanson, 1996; Feuerstein, 1996; Turk and Flor, 1999; Marras et al., in press; Sjøgaard, Lundberg, and Kadefors, 2000). At present, these efforts have not identified specific pathways linking stress to back or upper extremity pain, but they do provide general information that offers a preliminary framework for identifying such pathways in the future.

The peripheral pain receptors (nociceptors) thought to be responsible for the initiation of back pain have been identified. Nociceptors responsive to mechanical deformations have been identified in facet joint capsules, spinal ligaments, bone, and the outermost fibers of the disc annulus fibrosus, but not in the disc nucleus. The response of spinal nerve roots and dorsal root ganglia to compression, vibration, and chemical stimuli has been analyzed in part. A possible role for the nerve root vascular supply in mediating the nerve root pain associated with spinal stenosis has also been identified. Afferent pathways in the spinal cord have been mapped. In contrast, the role of central mechanisms (i.e., the brain) that are involved in the cognitive interpretation of work as stressful, and in the concomitant emotional response to such an appraisal, remains largely undetermined with respect to the pathophysiology of various back disorders. Similarly, the role of afferent feedback loops (signals back to the brain from the periphery) is largely unknown.

One biobehavioral hypothesis for how exposure to work-related stressors may be associated with physiological processes involved in low back pain is that certain individuals possess a predisposition to respond to a stressor with increased paraspinal muscle activity, which may lead to ischemia, reflex muscle spasm, oxygen depletion, and the release of pain-producing substances (e.g., histamine, substance P) (Flor and Turk, 1989; Turk and Flor, 1999). It has been proposed that this increased reactivity to stress results in a feedback loop that involves subsequent increased pain, triggering further increases in muscle activity, psychological distress, and pain (Flor and Turk, 1989). Attempts to confirm this model in individuals with chronic low back pain have resulted in inconsistent findings (Flor and Turk, 1989). Investigations have typically measured surface paraspinal EMG in a laboratory setting in response to various nonwork-related stressors. These studies have demonstrated that individuals with chronic low back pain have baseline EMG activity similar to normal controls and show no consistent pattern of accentuated activity different from that of controls. This research does indicate that individuals with low back pain demonstrate a delayed muscle recovery to prestress levels, suggesting that the recovery following exposure to stress may be deficient in those with back pain. However, it is difficult to determine whether this delayed recovery predated the onset of the disorder. It is possible that increased muscle reactivity may be observed in addition to the delayed recovery in individuals with less chronic back pain, or that increased reactivity may be observed only during actual work exposure rather than in response to exposure to a simulated laboratory stress (i.e., during stress exposures with greater ecological validity).

Identification of EMG reactivity to stress may require the use of more sophisticated measurement approaches and laboratory protocols. A recent investigation observed that exposure to psychosocial stress while performing a lifting task resulted in greater cocontraction of a number of spinal muscles and significant increases in spine compression and lateral shear (Marras et al., in press). This study also found that how an individual interacts with his or her environment (i.e., personality style) was further predictive of spinal loading. Those who were more internally focused or introverted generated higher spinal loads (greater trunk musculature coactivation and alterations in movement patterns) in response to stress during an identical lifting task than did those with a more extroverted style. These findings suggest a biomechanical pathway in which a worker's response to stress interacts with work demands and individual psychological style to generate increases in spinal loading. This study highlights the utility of testing models of occupational stress and low back pain within the context of the performance of work tasks.

There is a need to develop more sophisticated models of how occupational stress can affect occupational back pain and to identify the physiological processes involved. In the past, most models of low back pain were based on clinical observations with chronic patients. Models and related research on chronic low back pain do not provide information on the more immediate or shorter-term processes by which stress at work can affect the onset of back pain.

Upper Extremity Disorders

Models Linking Occupational Stress to Work-Related Musculoskeletal Disorders

In contrast to the back literature, over the past decade a number of work-specific models have been proposed to help explain how stress at work could affect upper extremity disorders. Four representative models that attempt to link job stress to work-related upper extremity disorders are the balance theory of job design and stress, the biopsychosocial model of job stress, the ecological model of musculoskeletal disorders, and the workstyle model.

The *balance theory of job design and stress* provides a framework for examining the relationships and interactions among work organization, ergonomic exposure, job stress, and work-related upper extremity disorders. Smith and Carayon (1996) identify three general domains of the human stress response: biophysiological, behavioral, and psychological or cognitive. As with the generic models of stress, this model proposes that job stressors produce short-term emotional (e.g., adverse mood states), behavioral (e.g., smoking, excessive use of force in work tasks), and physiological (e.g., increased muscle tension, elevated blood pressure, elevated cortisol and catecholamine levels) reactions. For individuals who are chronically exposed to job stress, these reactions can lead to increased risk for adverse health outcomes, which may include—but are not limited to—work-related upper extremity disorders. This model also incorporates individual characteristics, such as age and personality, which may influence the stress response. In addition, the model emphasizes feedback loops among disease or illness, stress reactions, and stressors, and uniquely considers the experience of symptoms as stressors, in and of themselves, which can increase stress reactivity and lead to further adverse mental and physical health outcomes (Smith and Carayon, 1996).

The *biopsychosocial model* of job stress and musculoskeletal disorders (Melin and Lundberg, 1997) was developed for application to individuals performing light physical work, such as data entry or other types of computer-related work. In this model, job stress (biomechanical or psychological) is defined as any task or situational demand that creates a condition of over- or understimulation (Frankenhaeuser and Gardell, 1976). Both of these conditions can evoke physiological responses, including increased muscle tension and secretion of cortisol and catecholamine. This model also addresses the potential effects of nonwork-related demands (e.g., household work, child care) and their effect on recovery from stress experienced while at work. It is argued that individuals with high levels of total workload (work and home) are at increased risk because they remain at higher levels of physiological arousal or experience a delayed recovery due to prolonged work demands.

The *ecological model* of musculoskeletal disorders (Figure 7.2) (Sauter and Swanson, 1996) addresses the interaction of psychosocial and biomechanical stressors. According to this model, work-related musculoskeletal disorders can be ultimately traced to work technology, which includes tools and work systems. In addition, this model proposes a direct path

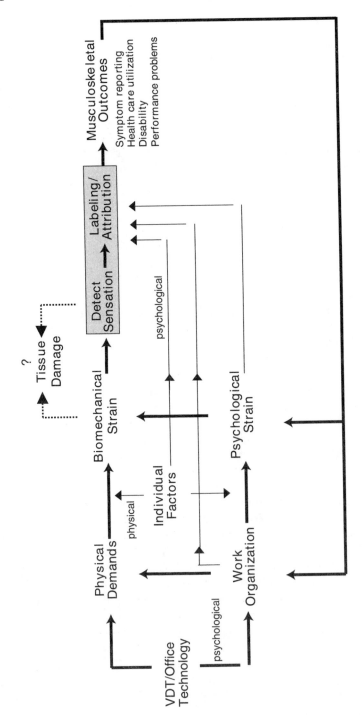

FIGURE 7.2 An ecological model of musculoskeletal disorders. From Sauter and Swanson (1996:8). Reprinted with permission.

among work organization, psychosocial stressors, and musculoskeletal outcomes via two routes. First, psychological strain is hypothesized to produce muscle tension and autonomic effects that, in turn, compound biomechanical strain induced by task-related physical demands. Second, psychological strain is hypothesized to moderate the relationship between biomechanical strain and the appearance of symptoms, by means of perception, attribution, and appraisal of symptoms, without directly affecting physical pathology (i.e., cognitive appraisal or interpretation). For example, in the execution of dull, routine, or repetitive tasks, the need to attend to the details of the work may be reduced, increasing the probability that symptoms, which might have gone unnoticed under more stimulating circumstances, will be detected. As with the appraisal of any internal stimulus, once the symptom is perceived, explanations are then sought (Schacter and Singer, 1962). In a stressful work environment, such symptoms or discomfort may be more likely to be attributed to one's job. In this manner, job stress and the psychosocial work environment may increase the probability of help seeking and injury reporting without exerting a direct influence on the underlying pathology. Finally, the model suggests that the experience of musculoskeletal symptoms themselves can influence stress at work.

The *workstyle model* of job stress and musculoskeletal disorders (Feuerstein, 1996) was proposed to explain the relationship among job stress, ergonomic exposure, and work-related upper extremity disorders (illustrated in Figure 7.3). This model posits the importance of workstyle, that is, how an individual performs work in response to work demands. Workstyle consists of cognitive, behavioral, and physiological components that are consistent with the frequently reported multicomponent stress response. The behavioral component represents the overt manifestations of movement, posture, and activity. These behaviors can interact with workplace exposure to ergonomic risk factors, potentially increasing the risk of musculoskeletal pain (Macfarlane, Hunt, and Silman, 2000). The cognitive component refers to the worker's thoughts, feelings, appraisals, and evaluation of the success or failure of his or her responses to the work demands. The physiological component represents the biological changes that accompany the behavioral and cognitive reactions; these changes include increased muscle tension, tendon force, catecholamine or cortisol release, and stress-induced changes in immune function (Feuerstein, Huang, and Pransky, 1999). In a work environment perceived as stressful or demanding, individuals with a "high-risk" workstyle may continually exert excessive levels of effort to cope with such an environment, thereby exposing themselves to recurrent or chronic physiological, cognitive, and behavioral consequences of stress. This continuous arousal or reactivity can then set the stage for the development of symptoms,

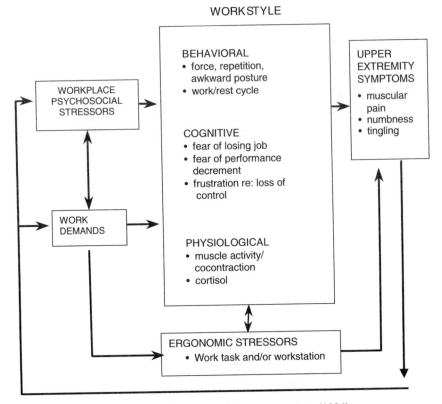

FIGURE 7.3 Workstyle model. Adapted from Feuerstein (1996).

disorders, and, if this process persists, disability. High-risk workstyle has been shown to be associated with symptom severity, functional limitations, and work disability in individuals exposed to hand-intensive work (Feuerstein et al., 1997; Haufler, Feuerstein, and Huang, 2000).

While these models have some components in common, each has a unique contribution, such as a focus on work systems, the integration of work demands and unpaid domestic workload, the labeling of or attributions for symptoms experienced in the process of work, and the potential impact of workstyle. Also, each of these models hypothesizes a psycho-physiological substrate linking occupational stress to various health outcomes, in an effort to explain how job stress may affect work-related upper extremity disorders. The biological plausibility of a link between job stress and work-related upper extremity disorders is a critical element in determining the validity and credibility of such an association.

As with generic stress and health models, the majority of models attempting to describe how exposure to job stress may exert its effects on the physiology of upper extremity disorders focus their attention on musculoskeletal and neuroendocine pathways. These pathways are common to each of the models discussed above.

Potential Biological Pathways

One pathway by which exposure to occupational stress results in pain may be through changes in musculoskeletal activity or reactivity (Melin and Lundberg, 1997; Sjøgaard et al., 2000). Increases in muscular activity have been associated with tasks involving greater psychological demands (Melin and Lundberg, 1997). It has also been observed that muscle activation can be triggered by mental stress independent of physical effort (Melin and Lundberg, 1997). Spectral changes in forearm EMG, increased forearm tremor, and increased musculoskeletal discomfort have been observed in response to stress (Gomer et al., 1987). In the absence of a quantifiable increase in work demands, the perception of an increase in work demands is sufficient to increase forearm muscular tension during task performance (Arndt, 1987). When exposure to psychological stressors cooccurs with physical stressors, levels of EMG, blood pressure, and self-reported stress tend to be greater than in response to either exposure alone (Lundberg et al., 1994). An individual's psychological style, or how he or she characteristically responds to a challenge, has been related to the degree of muscle coactivation during completion of a simple motor task. This finding suggests that muscle activation can vary depending on how one characteristically perceives his or her environment (Glasscock et al., 1999). Taken as a whole, these studies suggest that while a perception of work as demanding is sufficient to increase musculoskeletal activity, the addition of physical exposures and a certain style or personality can further increase this activity. It is possible that such recurrent or chronic forearm muscle tension, secondary to psychosocial stressors, places sustained loads on the tendons in the wrist and elbow.

The fatiguing of low-level motor neurons in the upper trapezius and forearm, secondary to stress-induced muscle contraction, may also lead to musculoskeletal discomfort or injury via the fatiguing of small motor units (Westgaard and Bjorklund, 1987; Waersted, Bjorklund, and Westgaard, 1991; Westgaard and de Luca, 1999). This discomfort or injury may encourage alternative muscle recruitment and exposure to increased biomechanical risks (e.g., compromised postures, increased exertion of less suitable muscles) (Sjøgaard, 1996).

Another potential pathway linking occupational stress to work-related upper extremity disorders may involve the biochemical consequences of the stress response, specifically the release of catecholamines and cortisol. Although serum levels of cortisol, epinephrine, and norepinephrine typically rise and fall throughout the day (Melin et al., 1999; Kirschbaum and Hellhammer, 1989), investigations of psychological and environmental correlates of stress hormone levels have determined that the sympathetic nervous system stimulates the release of these hormones differentially, based on the qualitative interpretation of the exposure to stress. On one hand, in general, it has been reported that the catecholamines appear to be related to the "positive" (i.e., the motivating or challenging) mental and physical demands of a stressor (Lundberg and Johansson, in press). On the other hand, cortisol appears to be generally related to negative aspects of the stress response, including negative emotions, the anticipation of negative consequences, and the perception of events as novel, uncontrollable, or unpredictable (Brantley et al., 1988; Van Eck et al., 1996; Kirschbaum and Hellhammer, 1989; Smyth et al., 1998).

The psychosocial characteristics of the work environment, such as task repetitiveness and rigid work arrangements, also appear to affect circulating catecholamines. Lundberg et al. (1993) reported that "deactivation" (i.e., recovery to baseline) of catecholamines, especially epinephrine, was slower after a repetitive data entry task than after a stimulating, self-learning task. Melin et al. (1999) reported that catecholamine levels in male and female assembly workers who were given the opportunity to work in autonomous groups and to influence their work pace decreased more rapidly after work than did catecholamine levels in individuals who worked in the "traditional" work organization (with fixed workstations and short, repetitive work cycles). In this study, the pattern of heightened reactivity and delayed recovery was observed in female workers in contrast to males and the pattern was even more marked in female workers who had children at home. Luecken et al. (1997) reported that 24-hour cortisol secretion was higher in women with at least one child living at home than in women without children. These cortisol levels were not affected by marital status or social support. These studies suggest a potential interaction among gender, paid and unpaid work demands, and stress reactivity and recovery (Melin et al., 1999; Lundberg and Frankenhaueser, 1999).

Chronic elicitation of the stress response, and the concomitant increases in catecholamine and cortisol release, could also directly affect the structure and function of muscles, tendons, and ligaments (Johnson et al., 1992). In addition to the direct effect these substances can exert on soft tissues, norepinephrine release can, theoretically, affect behavior, resulting in an increased rate at which an individual performs tasks under stress. This, in turn, could result in more rapid and forceful responses during work tasks, thereby potentially increasing exposure to biomechanical risks.

Release of neurotransmitters may also play a role in the exacerbation of muscle pain. It has been observed that serotonin, which is released in response to stress (Stratakis, Gold, and Chrousos, 1995), potentiates the effects of endogenous pain mediators, such as bradykinin (Babenko et al., 1999). The infusion of both serotonin and bradykinin into the tibialis anterior muscle in humans has been associated with elevated pain intensity and prolonged pain in response to mechanical stimulation. This preliminary evidence suggests that exposure to stress could exert a nociceptor sensitization effect on muscle. In addition to the peripheral effect of stress on pain, data exist to support a direct role of the central nervous system (Fields and Basbaum, 1994). This may help explain how psychological processes, such as attention and emotion, influence pain and pain tolerance. In addition, the peripheral vasoconstriction induced by circulating catecholamines could further inhibit blood flow to a potentially compromised nerve in the case of carpal tunnel syndrome.

It has also been shown that exposure to stress exerts an inhibitory effect on inflammatory or immune responses (Chrousos and Gold, 1992). Glucocorticoids (cortisol) decrease the production of cytokines and other mediators of inflammation and inhibit the effects of these agents on target tissues. It is possible that the repeated elicitation of the stress response does not allow for the pain-sensitive tissues to recover following mechanical insult. Although the exact mechanism of injury differs from most work-related upper extremity disorders, it has recently been demonstrated that recovery from an oral puncture wound is significantly delayed following exposure to stress (Marucha, Kiecolt-Glaser, and Favagehi, 1998). Production of interleukin-1ρ, a proinflammatory cytokine important in cell recruitment and activation of fibroblasts, was noted to decrease by 68 percent following exposure to a stressor.

As indicated earlier, the potential pathways described above are speculative and represent a series of hypotheses that require rigorous scientific scrutiny. A critical element in validating these models is the determination of the time course between job stressor exposure, physiological changes, and symptom expression. Given the role that job stress plays in work-related symptoms in both the back and upper extremities, it is critical to identify the biobehavioral pathways underlying this effect, in order to understand how job stress can result in the symptom expressions characteristic of these disorders and in order to develop effective prevention and management strategies. The models reviewed need to be carefully tested using both laboratory and workplace studies.

SUMMARY

Several distinct work-related psychosocial factors have been identified conceptually and can be measured reliably. They are associated with work-related low back pain and, less consistently, with work-related upper extremity disorders. The extent to which these variables interact with physical stressors remains to be determined. Also in terms of intervention, it is currently unclear what impact reducing physical stressors may have on psychological distress. The models of job stress presented in this chapter provide an important conceptual link between work-related psychosocial factors and work-related musculoskeletal disorders. They share many core features, providing additional (face) validity. These features include an association between stressful workplace conditions and a set of physiological responses, which, in turn, are associated with musculoskeletal disorders. These models need to be further validated.

While the precise biological mechanisms through which these physiological responses to stress lead to musculoskeletal disorders have not been fully elucidated, work to date suggests that musculoskeletal, neuroendocrine, and immunological pathways may be prominent. Further work in this area is needed to better define these biologic mechanisms. In addition, the knowledge currently available on psychosocial stress should be incorporated into interventions to ameliorate work-related musculoskeletal disorders.

8

Interventions in the Workplace

This chapter examines the hypothesis that prevention strategies in the workplace can reduce the incidence and impact of musculoskeletal injuries, illnesses, and disorders. Primary prevention occurs when the intervention is undertaken before members of the population at risk have acquired a condition of concern, for example, educational programs to reduce the number of new cases (incidence) of low back pain. Secondary prevention occurs when the intervention is undertaken after individuals have experienced the condition of concern, for example, introduction of job redesign for workers with symptoms of carpal tunnel syndrome. Tertiary prevention strategies are designed for individuals with chronically disabling musculoskeletal disorders; the goal is to achieve maximal functional capacity within the limitations of the individual's impairments.

In this chapter we review the scientific data about interventions in the workplace particularly related to primary and secondary prevention. We have not addressed specific medical interventions, such as drugs, manipulative therapy, and surgery. The scientific bases for medical treatment of musculoskeletal conditions, particularly back pain, have been reviewed in detail by a number of panels of experts, such as the Quebec Task Force and the Agency for Health Care Policy and Research (AHCPR). Although there is significant overlap between secondary and tertiary prevention strategies, we have not addressed the extremely complex issues regarding the medical management of or workplace accommodations for those with chronic musculoskeletal disabilities.

In tertiary prevention the accommodations are usually made on a case by case basis. There often are complex psychosocial issues that may involve a wide array of treatment options, and the medical treatment often involves the management of failed surgical procedures, the utilization of pain clinics, functional restoration programs, and controversial drug regimens and surgical procedures. The panel examined the broader systems approach, dealing with primary and secondary prevention, and thought these more applicable to the interface between job demands and the population of workers.

This chapter is organized as follows: First, we revisit the conceptual model (Figure 1.2) that forms the framework for workplace interventions and discuss the related principles of ergonomics. We then summarize the intervention literature specific to the back and upper extremities. Practical considerations, including assessment of cost-outcome effectiveness, are included, particularly as a framework for future research. Finally, we draw conclusions based on the weight of current evidence and suggest efforts to coordinate the gathering and sharing of further information to assess and prevent musculoskeletal disorders in the workplace.

CONTEXT

The conceptual model described in Figure 1.2 illustrates how the complex relationship among external loads, organizational factors, individual factors, and the social environment of work can lead to adverse outcomes that include pain, impairment, and disability. This conceptual model is also useful to understand how workplace interventions are used to control potentially adverse conditions.

Primary and secondary interventions may prevent adverse outcomes by reducing or eliminating external loads, changing organizational factors, altering the social environment, improving individual stress-coping skills, or matching the physical demands of the job with the employee's physical capacities. The literature suggests that some of these approaches are more successful than others. Some interventions have not yet been adequately assessed.

External loads in the work environment act on the body to create internal loads on tissues and other anatomical structures. Interventions that focus on the reduction or elimination of exposure to external loads must first identify and quantify the motions and forces acting on the individual, including vibration and thermal exposures. Often a systematic study of the work is required to evaluate these physical exposures and their characteristic properties. When specific physical stress factors are identified, the sources of these loads are ascertained. Workplace redesign may include alterations in tools, equipment, workstations, materials handled, tasks, work methods, work processes, and work environment, based on their contributions to the identified stresses. The majority of the intervention literature is based on this approach to injury reduction.

Work organizational factors broadly consist of job content and organization characteristics, as well as temporal and economic aspects of the work and task. Job content is the array of tasks and procedures that make up an employee's workload. These requirements have a direct effect on the exposure to external loads associated with the use of equipment and tools. Other aspects of job content may include specifications to handle certain objects, operate machinery, or work under potentially adverse environmental conditions. Interventions in job content may reduce or eliminate exposure to physical stresses by directly altering the job requirements. Examples include assigning a worker to different tasks or eliminating a specific operation through automation.

Organizational characteristics describe the management structure of the organization and the level of autonomy an employee has when performing a job. These factors may affect employees' attitudes about their work or influence physical stress exposure. Interpersonal relationships among employees and supervisors may also influence physical stress exposure. For example, physical stresses in a cooperative work environment often are reduced when employees informally assist one other. Temporal aspects include job scheduling such as shift work, number of hours on deadline, job rotation, or the frequency and duration of specific tasks. For example, the continuous performance of a monotonous, repetitive task has been associated with physical and psychological stress.

Finally, the economic and compensation policies of a company can affect physical exposures. For example, overtime and extended work can increase the daily duration of exposure to musculoskeletal stressors. Compensation incentives also may affect intensity, frequency, and duration of work and may discourage rest breaks.

PRINCIPLES OF ERGONOMICS

The application of ergonomic principles forms the basis for much of the intervention literature. Ergonomics is the study of work, including workplace interventions to establish compatibility among the worker, the job, and the work environment. Ergonomics professionals, both researchers and practitioners, reflect the variety of factors that affect safety and productivity in the workplace; the disciplines involved include researchers and practitioners in, for example, medicine, epidemiology, psychology, and industrial engineering and other health-related, technical/ engineering, and behavioral disciplines. The process whereby ergonomics is applied to intervention adheres to the scientific method: available data are gathered and analyzed (e.g., through broad or local surveillance and through analysis of jobs); hypotheses are developed (e.g., specific engineering controls are proposed to address specific factors or conditions of the physical workplace and job characteristics; administrative controls are proposed to address characteristics of the organization and management thought to be relevant; and such individual modifiers as age, gender, body mass index, smoking habits, comorbidity, and reaction to the psychosocial environment at home and at work are addressed); the hypotheses are tested (i.e., the effectiveness of the intervention is assessed); and the hypotheses are maintained (for effective interventions) or refined (an intervention is improved or replaced) in response to the outcomes.

Emerging evidence indicates that work-related musculoskeletal disorders and associated disability are the consequence of a complex interplay among medical, social, work organizational, biomechanical, and workplace and individual psychosocial factors. As with most areas of scientific endeavor, the ergonomics of intervention in the workplace is providing an expanding knowledge base and an evolving set of interventions, and continued development of innovative models is needed to allow for the effective management and prevention of these complex disorders. The practice of ergonomics relies on a process that tailors interventions to specific circumstances currently found effective, continues to assess the effectiveness of these interventions in the face of changing workplace and worker factors, and evaluates new interventions. It is therefore neither feasible nor desirable to propose generic interventions expected to apply to every industry, job, and worker, nor "once for all" interventions whose effectiveness need not be regularly assessed. It is, rather, both feasible and desirable to encourage application—with continued assessment—of interventions found useful and promising to date, and to encourage cooperative endeavor and information exchange among researchers, practitioners, and workers/managers in industry/labor, government, and academia. Surveillance and job analysis are critical components of intervention research and practice.

Surveillance

Surveillance is the ongoing, systematic collection, analysis, and interpretation of health and exposure information in the process of describing and monitoring work-related musculoskeletal disorders and evaluating the effectiveness of the program. Surveillance may include the analysis of existing medical records, worker compensation records (passive surveillance), or the surveying of workers with questionnaire and physical examination (active surveillance).

The analysis of existing records is generally less costly, but the reliability of such data is difficult to assess. Standardized questionnaires and physical examinations can be as sensitive as the use of unusually thorough existing occupational medical records; however, it is unclear whether the additional cost of an active surveillance system will deter the routine use of such systems (Fine et al., 1986). Symptoms questionnaires and checklist-based hazard surveillance are feasible within the context of joint labor-management ergonomics programs and are more sensitive indicators of ergonomic problems than preexisting data sources (Silverstein et al., 1997).

Surveillance systems are key methods of collecting information that describes the characteristics of workers (individual factors) that may interact with workplace factors to cause or mitigate musculoskeletal disorders or to affect the success of interventions. Surveillance systems may also be used to evaluate the effectiveness of interventions. In addition, surveillance systems (e.g., employee surveys, absentee and turnover analysis) can be used to gather information that complements that of other analytical procedures (e.g., job analysis, work flow analysis, productivity study) in defining relevant features of tasks, jobs, worker satisfaction, and organizational culture. Surveillance is most important in times of rapid change in the economy and when resources for prevention may be limited (Fine, 1999).

Surveillance data may be collected and analyzed at different levels of task, job, occupation, and industry (see Chapter 2), and they may elucidate features of the physical work environment, work tasks, work organization, psychosocial environment, and worker characteristics relevant to intervention (see Figure 1.2). Intervention can be indicated by case, data, and risk factors identified through surveillance. Case-initiated interventions are triggered by employee reports of symptoms, concerns, or recommendations. An intervention is data-initiated when it is the outcome of an analysis of medical records and injury reports. An intervention is risk-factor initiated when factors known to be significantly related to musculoskeletal disorders are shown to be present.

Surveillance systems at the company level serve as an invaluable resource for evaluating the impact of efforts to reduce risk and to find new risks early, before they cause irreparable harm. For example, in an electronics company in Norway, new cases of sick leave attributed to musculoskeletal disorders were tracked over a number of years. Regular examination of the trends led the company to recognize an increase in the sick leave rates and prompted it to introduce a number of improvements in the work setting. The surveillance of sick leave also served to document the impact of the interventions, showing reductions in the sick leave following the changes. Figure 8.1 (from Westgaard and Aarås, 1985) shows the percentage of lost work days, due to musculoskeletal disorders, of total work force in the electronics company. Record analyses may also reveal trends across jobs, operations, or other common conditions. Inter-

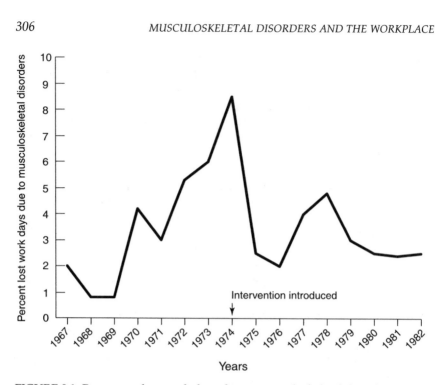

FIGURE 8.1 Percentage lost work days due to musculoskeletal disorders of total work force in an electronics company (based on data from Westgaard and Aarás, 1985).

ventions may be initiated when risk factors are identified from proactive job surveys or other risk factor reviews.

Job Analysis

When it is determined, based on the clinical evaluation and exposure information, that an employee has a work-related disorder, the employer performs an analysis of the employee's job or of a sample of representative jobs. Job analysis is a procedure used to identify potential exposure to risk factors and to evaluate their characteristic properties. When risk factors are identified, job design or redesign, including engineering or administrative controls, is used for eliminating or reducing work-related risk factors or exposure to those factors.

Job analysis consists of a work methods analysis, based on traditional techniques of time-and-motion study to determine the work content of the job, and a systematic analysis of risk factors (Armstrong et al., 1986).

Work methods analysis involves describing the work content of each task as a series of steps or elements and identifying risk factors for each work element. After the major physical stresses have been identified, ergonomic interventions may be applied to minimize exposure to risk factors. Such interventions are often categorized as engineering controls, administrative or production controls, or personal modifiers. Although risk factors are frequently cited in the literature, acceptable exposure levels have not yet been determined for all individual and combined factors. The presence of a risk factor does not necessarily mean that the person doing the job is at excessive risk of an injury or that ergonomic changes are worth their cost. When the presence of risk factors is combined with a history of musculoskeletal disorders among persons doing that job, the risk may be considered excessively high and ergonomic interventions may be worth their cost. In many cases, it is desirable to make changes regardless of the history, because job changes are often inexpensive, and injuries are often very expensive. This is particularly the case when jobs are being initially designed and set up.

Examples of Process-Based Ergonomics Intervention Programs

The Occupational Safety and Health Administration has issued a standard of practice for assessing and addressing musculoskeletal disorders in the workplace. The American National Standards Institute has accredited a national committee (Accredited Standards Committee, 2000) charged with developing a standard process or program for reducing musculoskeletal disorders associated with work. Within industry, Ford Motor Company, for example, uses a team-based approach at each facility, establishing ergonomic committees consisting of labor and management representatives who collect and analyze local data (reviewing surveillance records and medical cases), propose interventions, and assess their effectiveness (Joseph, 2000). Though not targeting specifically the issue of musculoskeletal disorders in the workplace, the Department of Defense has demonstrated for decades that the elements of an effective ergonomics program can be formally defined in broad scope, and that these elements can be successfully tailored to the needs and features of specific workplaces and workers (see U.S. Army Missile Command, no date). We note here that each of these approaches to ergonomics interventions is process-based (i.e., applies a process of analysis, implementation, and assessment of effectiveness), and that any ergonomics program benefits when the scientific method is applied by researchers and practitioners in those programs who collect and analyze data, propose and implement interventions, and assess their effectiveness.

SPECIFIC INTERVENTIONS: BACK

Few high-quality scientific intervention studies related to the primary and secondary prevention of low back pain are available in the literature. The vast majority of the literature consists of retrospective analyses and case reports of intervention effectiveness, better assessed through prospective studies and, if possible, randomized controlled trials.

In order to provide insight as to the effectiveness of interventions in controlling the risk of back pain, the reviewed literature was categorized in three ways. First, high-quality reviews of the literature were evaluated for common indications and trends. Second, since most of these efforts consisted of reviews dating back to the mid-1990s, a review of the literature since that time was performed using similar quality criteria. Finally, a review of reported "best practices" was performed to assess how reported experiences in industry relate to the more rigorous controlled studies of interventions. Collectively, this approach has provided insight into the effectiveness of low back interventions.

Results of High-Quality Reviews Through the Mid-1990s

Six high-quality reviews of the literature were identified that assess the state of knowledge associated with the ability of ergonomic interventions to influence low back disorders. Based on its criteria for quality, this assessment selected reviews that accepted only studies that met rigorous methodological constraints and reviews that comprehensively examined the basic science behind intervention logic. Six reports met these criteria.

The first review, performed by Westgaard and Winkel (1997), assessed 91 studies that met seven inclusion criteria. By these criteria each reviewed study included: (1) field intervention; (2) involvement of a primary or secondary intervention; (3) an exposure-effect analysis; (4) sufficient documentation for repeatability; (5) a unit of analysis that was the entire job (not a task); (6) outcome analyses that included internal exposure, acute responses, and/or health effects; and (7) documentation in English. In addition to these inclusion criteria, this review selected interventions based on seven quality criteria. These quality criteria included: (1) proper statistical analyses, (2) reasonable study group size, (3) variables that were generalizable to other settings, (4) consideration of reliability and sensitivity of variables, (5) inclusion of a control group, (6) an adequate observation period with follow-up measurements, and (7) proper documentation of the intervention process.

The inclusion criteria of the second review (van Poppel et al., 1997) accepted studies that included: (1) a controlled clinical trial that is prospective in nature in which the intervention group is randomly assigned and compared with a randomly assigned control group derived from the same setting as the intervention group; (2) intervention intended to prevent back pain and consisting of education, exercise, or lumbar support; (3) no restrictions on subjects at the start of the study, and (4) intervention occurring in an industrial setting. A total of 14 studies met these inclusion criteria.

The third review (Volinn, 1999) closely examined six studies that based their interventions on various principles. These principles included promotion of back safety, back belt use, introduction of ergonomic devices, and back strengthening exercises. By Volinn's inclusion criteria, these studies contained: (1) use of a primary prevention, (2) a dependent measure consisting of a recordable back injury, (3) only workplace-related injuries, and (4) successful outcomes.

In the fourth review, Kaplansky and colleagues (Kaplansky, Wei, and Reecer, 1998) evaluated 133 studies of occupational low back pain prevention. Their review categorized the interventions by type and collectively assessed the literature within each intervention type. The inclusion criteria considered the state of the body of knowledge associated with each intervention type, focused on the intervention logic, and used selection criteria that varied across the intervention types. The literature reviewed did not consist only of field studies. The assessment was generally of a critical nature.

A fifth review (Scheer, Watanabe, and Radack, 1997) searched 4,000 articles but accepted for review only randomized, controlled trials of interventions: 12 studies met this criterion. The sixth review (Hsiang, Brogmus, and Courtney, 1997) summarized the results of 70 biomechanical and physiological publications. Although the review did not focus on field interventions, it examined the logic behind the advantages and disadvantages of lifting techniques. This represents an alternative assessment of a low back pain intervention approach.

Collectively, the data in these six reviews indicate that certain engineering controls (e.g., ergonomic workplace redesign), administrative controls (specifically, adjusting organizational culture), addressing modifying individual factors (specifically, employee exercise), and the inclusion of a combination of interventions are the only strategies that have been shown to be positively associated with the reduction of work-related low back pain. An important finding in these studies is the observation that multiple interventions that actively involve workers in medical management of workers at risk, physical training, and technique education, in combination, can also be effective in controlling risk. Isolated approaches such as control of the production process, use of back belts, training, relaxation, physiotherapy, health education, and worker selection either have not been proven effective or have proven ineffective.

Results of Recent High-Quality Studies

The high-quality reviews discussed above evaluated the back intervention literature up until the mid-1990s. A search of the back intervention literature published since that time identified seven additional high-quality studies. All but one of these studies involved randomized controlled designs; the remaining study was of a case-control design. These studies are summarized in Table 8.1. Three of the studies were not necessarily related to work. Only two of the studies addressed primary interventions, evaluating the effectiveness of back belts, health education, and back schools: none of these interventions was found to be effective. These findings are consistent with the literature reviews discussed in the previous section.

The findings of the six secondary intervention studies were also in agreement with the literature reviews described above in reporting that engineering controls, exercise (two of three studies), and multiple interventions are effective. The other positive findings for secondary interventions consisted of functional restoration (one study), physiotherapy (one study), cognitive therapy (one study), medical management (two studies), and light duty (one study). Conflicting results were found for back schools (positive findings in two of four studies) and health education (positive results in one of two studies). Back belts and pain management approaches to interventions were found to be ineffective.

Best Practices

Since practical experience with interventions can also be of use in interpreting the effectiveness of ergonomic interventions, we reviewed the literature of best practices interventions to see how it compared with the more rigorous scientific studies. To this end, we reviewed the transcripts from the Effective Workplace Practices and Programs Conference held in Chicago in 1997. A total of 13 interventions relating to the control of low back pain were found; these are reported in Table 8.2. These best practices illustrate the type of intervention approaches that are often applied by industry. As the table shows, many of these approaches are the same as those identified in the high-quality reviews and high-quality studies previously discussed.

Table 8.2 shows that engineering controls are one of the most commonly used interventions in industry. Many of the industries that employ engineering controls as an intervention also report a positive effect on low back pain control. The second most common control is training, which is typically applied along with engineering controls. Many of the industries reported positive control of low back pain through training. These data

TABLE 8.1 Review of High-Quality Studies of Back Interventions Since 1995[a]

Author	N	Intervention Type P=Primary S=Secondary	Engineering Controls	Administrative/ Process Controls	Back Belts	Functional Restoration	Training	Exercise	Relaxation	Physiotherapy	Health Education	Pain Management	Cognitive Therapy	Back School	Facet Injection	Medical Mgmt	Light Duty	Worker Selection	Multiple Intervention	Comments
van Poppel et al., 1998	282	P			0						0									RCT
Loisel et al., 1997	130	S	+					+		+			+	+		+	+		+	RCT
Daltroy et al., 1997	4,000	P/S									+									RCT
Cooper et al., 1996	183	S						0				0		0		+			+	Case/control
Bendix et al., 1997	132	S				+		0				0	0	0						RCT Not necessarily work related
Moffett et al., 1999	187	S						+												RCT Not necessarily work related
Lonn et al., 1999	73	S											+							RCT Confounding present Not necessarily work related

[a]Plus (+) sign indicates positive finding of effectiveness for the given intervention; null (0) sign indicates that the intervention was not found to be effective; empty cell indicates that the intervention was not assessed.

TABLE 8.2 Case Studies of Best Practices—Back Interventions

Environment/Industry	Engineering Controls	Administration/ Production	Personal Modifier
Large Manufacturing			
PPG	✓		
Hay & Forge	✓		
Ford	✓		
Small Manufacturing			
Charleston Ford	✓	✓	
Cross Association	✓		
Perdue, Inc.		✓ rotate/ramp in	
Apparel			
UNITE	✓		
Sequins	✓		
Crest-Caravan	✓		✓
Healthcare			
Mayo Clinic		✓ patient transfer team	
University of Washington	✓		
University of California, Los Angeles	✓ lift assist		
Warehousing			
Murphy Warehousing Co.	✓	✓ light duty	

are consistent with the high-quality reviews, which found no effect of training, in that there was no instance of a positive effect of the program reported when training was the only intervention applied. In many of the cases, engineering controls were also applied; such interventions were often reported as effective in the high-quality analyses.

Review of this table further indicates that administrative controls were also used, often in conjunction with engineering controls, and these cases quite often reported a positive impact on low back pain. The administrative controls reported consisted of worker rotation and ramping in of work, lifting teams for patient transfer in health care, and process control. One industry reported a benefit of light duty or transitional work assignments. Two industries reported the importance of employee involvement, and two reported the importance of employee support, although the associations with impacts are not clearly reported. Medical management and process control were frequently reported interventions. Multiple interventions are often reported as means used to control the risk of low back

Multiple Interventions	Employee Involvement	Management Support	Training	Medical Management	Process Conrol	Positive Impact Reported
✓	✓	✓	✓	✓	✓	
✓	✓		✓	✓	✓	
✓			✓		✓	
					✓	✓
✓						
		✓	✓	✓	✓	✓
✓	✓		✓	✓		✓
			✓		✓	✓
✓						✓
			✓			
						✓
			✓			
			✓			✓

pain in industry. These reports do not clearly stipulate which interventions are considered primary versus secondary.

Consistency of Findings

Overall, the pattern of effectiveness described in the high-quality reviews and studies is consistent with the observations described from the best practices reported by industry.

The classes of interventions described in this review are plausible. Considering the mechanisms by which various interventions influence the sequence of events described in the model illustrated in Figure 1.2, one can identify the consistent logical pathways that correspond to the interventions judged effective by both the high-quality and best practices assessments. For example, on one hand, engineering and administrative controls would be expected to affect the physical exposure to structure loading, thereby reducing risk. Exercise, on the other hand, can have an effect on the individual's tolerance to load. Multiple interventions may affect the system not only by influencing internal mechanical loading, but also through reducing psychological stressors. Collectively, then, the results reported in the high-quality reviews and high-quality studies are consistent with many of the observations noted in the reports of best practices (Table 8.2) as well as with the overall logic influencing musculoskeletal risk described in Figure 1.2.

SPECIFIC INTERVENTIONS: UPPER EXTREMITIES

Evidence from the epidemiologic literature suggests that a number of important risk factors, both physical and psychosocial, are associated with the development of musculoskeletal disorders of the upper extremities. The importance of these risk factors is documented through the study-based estimates of attributable risk already cited (see Chapter 4). The prominent physical risk factors reported include excessive force, repetitive movements, vibration, and cold temperatures, separately and together. The prominent psychosocial factors reported are not so easily characterized, but standardized measures that have been associated with upper extremity musculoskeletal disorders include high job stress; high job demands; nonwork-related worry, tension, and psychological distress; perceptions of the degree of support from supervisors and coworkers; and perceived lack of control over high work demands.

A wide variety of workplace interventions have been implemented in many different industrial settings in order to reduce upper extremity musculoskeletal disorders. Focused interventions can be grouped into two general categories: worker-focused (such as exercises) and workplace-focused (such as redesigning workstations). Broader programs are designed to affect the production system (addressing improved productivity and musculoskeletal health) or the organizational culture (addressing behaviors and attitudes of management, health personnel, and workers, sometimes in participatory group structures organized to address musculoskeletal problems). While there have been formal efforts to study these process or system interventions, reports of these interventions and their effectiveness are provided, for the most part, in the form of case studies. Though not rigorous studies, these case reports provide useful evidence for the potential effectiveness of a number of different approaches (General Accounting Office, 1997; Gjessing et al., 1994).

A recent comprehensive review of studies of intervention to prevent musculoskeletal conditions provided a foundation for considering the value of interventions (Westgaard and Winkel, 1997). The authors acknowledged, however, that their review was narrowly focused and excluded a number of useful studies that were laboratory-based, focused on tool design, limited to task (not job) redesign, aimed at vibration, or focused on the worker rather than the workplace. That review grouped primary and secondary interventions to reduce the incidence of upper extremity musculoskeletal disorders into three general categories: engineering controls, administrative controls, and modifier interventions.

Engineering Controls

There have been several studies of interventions in circumstances in which the initial physical exposures to the upper extremities are high (e.g., repetition rate, grip force, and posture extremes) that demonstrate the positive impact of reduction in the exposures (Aaräs, 1994; Parenmark, Malmkvist, and Örtengren, 1993). At the time of the Westgaard and Winkel (1997) review, there were few studies evaluating interventions in settings that involved low grip force. A number of recent studies of workers, primarily in settings involving work with computers, now provide supporting evidence that prevalence of upper extremity pain is reduced when sustained awkward postures are mitigated (Nelson and Silverstein, 1998; Aaräs, Ro, and Thoresen, 1999; Tittiranonda, Burastero, and Rempel, 1999; Brisson, Montreuil, and Punnett, 1999). In these studies furniture or hand tools were modified to alter postures while working. For example, in the study by Aaräs et al., use of a different computer mouse that reduced forearm rotation from full pronation to a neutral posture led to a significant reduction in upper extremity pain after six months.

In addition, studies of engineering interventions for computer-related work that reduce static postural loads, sustained posture extremes, and rapid motions have demonstrated decreases in upper extremity pain reports. Further study of these interventions is needed to determine the amount of pain reduction possible, the duration of the salutary effect, and which upper extremity clinical conditions could benefit from these interventions. Some of these studies involved single interventions (e.g., alternative keyboard); however, interventions to control physical exposures must more commonly be studied in the context of multiple interventions.

Administrative Controls

Multidimensional interventions can be classified into two categories. The first, rationalization strategies, includes efforts to improve productivity and musculoskeletal health. Although some studies have successfully demonstrated the accomplishment of these two desirable outcomes, the studies are limited by a lack of specificity. Studies have also demonstrated success in reducing overall absenteeism, turnover, and relevant exposures, but either these studies have included too many variables or the follow-up period has been too short to permit documentation of the simultaneous improvement in productivity and reduction in musculoskeletal disorders (Johansson et al., 1993; Kadefors et al., 1996; Bao, Mathiassen, and Winkel, 1996). The second strategy, modifying organizational culture, places emphasis on participatory team involvement. Several of these studies report success, but they do not clearly distinguish which elements of a complex program are essential, except that the commitment of management, together with the involvement of employees, has been demonstrated to play a major role in successful production system interventions (Geras, Pepper, and Rodgers, 1989; Lockhart, 1986; Narayan and Rudolph, 1993).

Modifier Interventions

These studies are worker-focused and are more often designed like clinical trials. One limitation is that these studies do not isolate the effects of the intervention from those of parallel changes, including psychosocial improvements, such as improved employee/supervisor relationships. Therefore, posited successes may be as much due to a change in the work process as to a change in worker capacity, for example through exercise, education, or training in work technique (Kukkonen, Lammi, and Antti-Poika, 1991; Silverstein et al., 1988; Wigaeus et al., 1992).

Recent Intervention Studies

Several pre-/postintervention studies have been conducted since the review by Westgaard and Winkle. These studies have evaluated various primary and secondary interventions that could affect upper extremity musculoskeletal disorders. The interventions range from the redesign of work to training, across many industries, including, for example, meatpacking (Jones, 1997; Moore and Garg, 1998), health care (Evanoff et al., 1999; Bernacki et al., 1999), computer work (Brisson, Montreuil, and Punnett, 1999; Fernström and Åborg, 1999; Lie and Watten, 1994; Galinsky et al., 2000), and manufacturing (Bonsall et al., 1991; Melhorn et al., 1999; Halpern and Dawson, 1997). In general, these studies report reductions in lost time, rate of musculoskeletal disorders, or turnover and changes in other health endpoints.

A few additional well-controlled intervention studies have also been recently published. Generally, these studies, summarized in Table 8.3, compare one group of workers who receive an intervention to another group who do not, while controlling for covariates. Symptom ratings, such as pain scores, are the primary outcome measure, but a few of the studies also incorporate parallel measures, such as physical examination, sick leave, or turnover rates. All of the studies are of adequate duration (6 to 18 months) to avoid missing an effect. One study (Tittiranonda, Burastero, and Rempel, 1999) found that the benefit of an alternate keyboard intervention was not evident until four months into the study.

Six of the studies in Table 8.3 involve computer users and evaluate interventions aimed at decreasing static muscle loading by providing body support or by reducing sustained posture extremes. For example, in the study by Aarås and colleagues (1999), half of the employees were assigned a new computer mouse that required less pinch force and forearm pronation to use. After six months, this group reported significant reduction in shoulder, forearm, and hand/wrist pain compared with the control group. The authors concluded that the effects of this single intervention may be due to reduced shoulder abduction and an elimination of full forearm pronation.

A similar logic was invoked by Tittranonda and colleagues (1999), who found that an alternative geometry keyboard significantly reduced hand and arm pain after six months when compared with a conventional keyboard. In the study by Brisson and colleagues (1999), subjects receiving six hours of ergonomics training, which focused on decreasing neck twisting and flexion and wrist deviation through use of accessories and adjustment of the workstation, were compared with a reference group. After six months the prevalence of all musculoskeletal disorders was significantly reduced in comparison to the reference group in subjects less than 40 years old. An examination of the body postures while working on the computer revealed that subjects under 40 years of age were more likely to have reduced neck twisting and bending than subjects over 40.

Taken together, these studies provide some limited evidence that reducing sustained awkward postures, a risk factor among computer users identified in the epidemiology chapter (Appendix Table 4.6), can lead to a reduction in pain in the associated region of the upper extremity and neck. The effects of a comprehensive ergonomics program, which included training to reduce shoulder muscle loads, employee participation in the redesign of work methods, changes in production incentives, among other factors, was evaluated by Parenmark and colleagues (1993) in a chain saw assembly plant in comparison to another plant. The ergonomic program led to a 20 percent reduction in sick leave and a 70 percent reduction in turnover rate. The authors attributed these positive outcomes to a number of factors, including an awareness among employees of how to avoid high muscle loads.

There is a paucity of studies on the use of conditioning exercise to prevent injury. Most available studies are of limited scientific rigor or generalizability to the workplace. Seradge, Bear, and Bithell (1993) report the case study of a meatpacking company that achieved a 45 percent

TABLE 8.3 Upper Extremity Musculoskeletal Disorder Intervention Studies (Primary and Secondary) in the Workplace

Reference	Total Initial Participants	Completion Rate	Work	Intervention
Nelson and Silverstein, 1998	632	47%	Office work	New chairs, workstations
Aaräs, Ro, and Thoresen, 1999	181	91%	Computer	Worksurface with forearm support
Rempel et al., 1999	20	100%	Computer	Keyboards
Tittiranonda et al., 1999	80	86%	Computer	Alternative keyboards
Aaräs, Ro, and Thorsen, 1999	67	100%	Computer	Alternative mouse
Parenmark, Malmkvist, and Örtengren., 1993	534	—	Chain saw assembly	Work technique, pace, layout, staffing, wages
Brisson, Montreuil, and Punnett, 1999	627	96%	Computer	Ergonomics training
Kamwendo and Linton, 1991	79	96%	Secretarial	Neck school, exercises
Gerdle et al., 1995	97	81%	Home care	Exercise
Silverstein et al., 1988	178	80%	Assembly	Exercise

[a]Only for participants under 40 years of age.

NOTE: The table includes only studies that were published in a peer-reviewed scientific journal, included a control group, were of longer duration than one month, and measured a health endpoint.

reduction in the incidence of reported carpal tunnel syndrome after 1 year of a program of exercises designed to prevent carpal tunnel syndrome. Silverstein et al. (1988), in a more controlled study of the effects of in-plant exercise on musculoskeletal symptoms, found no statistically significant difference in localized posture discomfort scores between employees who did and did not participate in an on-the-job exercise program aimed at controlling musculoskeletal symptoms of the neck and upper limb.

Duration	Control co-variates	Outcome measures	Positive Effect?
1 year	Yes	Hand/arm symptom	Yes
		Neck/shoulder/back symptoms	Yes
2 year	No	Neck/shoulder pain	Yes
		Forearm/hand pain	No
3 months	Yes	Hand pain	Yes
		Physical examination	Yes
		Nerve conduction	No
6 months	Yes	Hand/arm pain	Yes
		Physical examination	No
6 months	Yes	Shoulder/forearm/wrist pain	Yes
		Sick leave	Yes
18 months	No	Sick leave	Yes
		Turnover	Yes
		Production costs	Yes
6 months	Yes	Neck/upper extremity pain	Yes[a]
		Physical examination	Yes[a]
6 months	Yes	Neck pain	No
		Neck range of motion	No
		Sick leave	No
1 year	Yes	Musculoskeletal complaints	Yes
		Physical examination	Yes
		Lost time	No
1 year	Yes	Neck shoulder discomfort	No

Studies of the effects of stretching exercises provide only suggestive results. Moore and Garg (1998) found, in a pre-/post-test study of 60 workers, that participants in a stretching exercise program achieved, after 36 sessions over 2 months, greater physical flexibility. Conditioning exercise programs may make participants feel better about themselves (Silverstein, 1988; Moore and Garg, 1998) and may encourage workers to attend to physical activity.

Taken together, these studies generally demonstrate a benefit of changes in workstation design, tool design, or training on upper extremity symptoms. The effect on related physical examination findings is less consistent. The value of exercise in reducing musculoskeletal symptoms has found mixed support.

Best Practices

Table 8.4 summarizes the best practices reported by industry representatives at the 1997 conference on effective workplace practices and programs relating to the management and control of upper extremity work-related musculoskeletal disorders. The table reveals a trend similar to that found for the interventions previously described for low back pain. Interventions for upper extremity and neck work-related musculoskeletal disorders involving engineering controls, administrative processes and personal modifiers resulted in positive outcomes for 27 companies. In particular, engineering controls and administrative controls, such as periodic rest breaks and job rotation, were most frequently accompanied by employee involvement, management support, and training. All programs included either engineering or administrative controls in addition to personal modifiers (such as exercise, training, light duty, or medical management). None of the reports demonstrated that personal modifiers were successful by themselves. Companies that instituted exercise or stretching programs also employed engineering or administrative controls. These findings are consistent with the approaches discussed in the high-quality reviews of back interventions in Table 8.1.

CHALLENGES DURING THE PROCESS OF ERGONOMIC INTERVENTION

Those who develop and implement interventions that address the complexity of factors potentially affecting musculoskeletal disorders in the workplace face challenges during the phases of gathering information, applying it to implement interventions and assess their effectiveness, and disseminating both research and practical knowledge. Given the magnitude and the complexity of the problem of musculoskeletal disorders in the workplace, in response to these challenges it would be beneficial to coordinate the efforts of researchers and practitioners in industry, labor, government, and academia.

Collection of Information: Surveillance

Challenges to the collection of information exist in the areas of methods and measures for surveillance. Surveillance of information pertinent to interventions for musculoskeletal disorders in the workplace can be improved by the development of more reliable, valid, sensitive, and specific medical diagnostic tests for relevant musculoskeletal disorders, as well as development of specific criteria that can be used for surveillance for determining cases of musculoskeletal disorders. Criteria should include, separately or in combination as appropriate, systematic methods for the collection of symptom information, minimum physical examination test findings, or physiological measurements. Criteria should also be relevant to specific purposes (for example, surveillance for early identification versus diagnosis for treatment). In addition, effective surveillance would be facilitated by further development of self-report instruments (e.g., by the application of computer technologies).

Collection of Information: Research Pertaining to Developing Interventions

Challenges to the collection of information also exist in the areas of methods and measures for research on ways to improve interventions and more effectively tailor them to the needs of specific workers, jobs, and industries. The development of interventions would benefit from more research to better quantify exposure limits, including cumulative risk for exposure, to apply them to job design to prevent injury, and to use such data as part of the effort to improve biomechanical models for predicting risk of musculoskeletal disorders in designing jobs. Furthermore, useful research would also define the most effective methods for applying multifactorial interventions (e.g., engineering controls, administrative controls, individual modifiers) and for reducing exposure for targeted industries (e.g., better ways of turning and lifting patients, better hand tools that reduce vibration). A continuing program of cooperative research would provide further understanding of the features of specific interventions that best account for their effectiveness (e.g., elucidating the characteristics of relevant work organizational factors, assessing the effect of job rotation as an intervention, and clarifying the mechanisms whereby psychosocial factors, individual worker characteristics, and organizational culture interact with interventions.

Assessing Interventions

The development of the repertoire of effective interventions would be facilitated by an infrastructure that supports standardization of test instruments, standardized reporting, and agreed-on outcome measures that would assist researchers and practitioners to assess the effectiveness of interventions and to define the contexts within which specific interven-

TABLE 8.4 Case Study Best Practices Observations—Upper Extremities and Neck Focus

Environment/Industry	Engineering Controls	Administrative/ Production	Exercise/ Stretching
Large Manufacturing			
3M	✓	✓ Process	
PPG	✓	✓ Process	
Hay & Forge	✓	✓ Process	
Ford	✓	✓ Process	
Samsonite	✓	✓ Process	
Frito-Lay	✓	✓ Process/Rotation	
Construction			
Bechtel		✓ Periodic breaks	✓
TDC	✓		✓
Apparel			
Red Wing Shoe	✓	✓ Rotation	✓
Sequins International	✓		
Fieldcrest-Cannon	✓	✓ Process	
Sara Lee Knit Products	✓	✓ Process	
Small Manufacturing			
Rocco Enterprises	✓	✓ Process/Rotation	✓
Charleston Forge	✓	✓ Process/Rotation	
Lunt Silversmiths	✓		
Perdue, Inc.	✓	✓ Process/Rotation	
Woodpro Cabinetry		✓ Rotation	
Farmland Foods			
Maritime			
Bath Iron Works	✓	✓ Process/Rotation	✓
Newport News Shipbuilding	✓	✓ Process	
Utilities			
PG&E	✓		✓
Montana Power	✓	✓ Rest breaks	✓
Warehousing			
Murphy Warehousing Co.	✓	✓ Process	
Office			
3M		✓ Process	
American Express Financial Advisors	✓	✓ Process	
L.L. Bean	✓	✓ Process	
US West	✓	✓ Process	

Personal Modifier

Light Duty	Multiple Interventions	Employee Involvement	Management Support	Training	Medical Management	Positive Impact Reported
	✓	✓	✓	✓	✓	✓
	✓	✓	✓	✓	✓	✓
	✓	✓	✓	✓		✓
	✓	✓	✓	✓	✓	✓
✓					✓	✓
✓	✓	✓	✓	✓	✓	✓
	✓	✓	✓	✓		✓
				✓		✓
✓	✓	✓	✓		✓	✓
	✓	✓	✓	✓		✓
			✓	✓		✓
		✓	✓			✓
✓	✓			✓		✓
✓		✓		✓	✓	✓
✓	✓	✓		✓	✓	✓
	✓	✓	✓	✓	✓	✓
		✓	✓	✓	✓	✓
	✓	✓	✓	✓	✓	✓
	✓	✓	✓	✓	✓	✓
	✓			✓		✓
	✓			✓		✓
✓	✓		✓	✓		✓
	✓	✓	✓	✓	✓	✓
	✓		✓	✓		✓
	✓		✓	✓		✓
		✓	✓	✓	✓	✓

tions are found to be effective. These methods and measures would also be beneficially applied to assessment of the adjuncts to interventions, including training programs and aids (for workers, managers, researchers, and practitioners), work standards on musculoskeletal disorders and prevention, and manuals for interventions and for ergonomics programs. There is a need, addressed below, for the development of standardized methods for cost-effectiveness analysis of interventions.

Cost-Outcome Effectiveness Analysis

Public and private policy makers, managers, and other leaders and decision makers are faced with the practical challenges of allocating limited resources. They must therefore be informed of the ratio between a program's marginal monetary costs and the marginal effectiveness, expressed both in terms of monetary savings and marginal improvements in health outcomes. Under such rubrics as *prevention effectiveness* (Haddix et al., 1996) and *economic evaluation* (Goossens et al., 1999), a set of analytical techniques is available to address questions of cost outcome. These techniques include: cost-benefit analysis, which expresses both costs and benefits in monetary terms; cost-effectiveness analysis, which expresses outcomes in terms that may not be monetary (e.g., lost work days, reported pain); and cost-utility analysis, which expresses outcome in the common form "quality adjusted life years."

Despite their availability, these techniques have not been widely applied to the study of interventions to relieve or prevent musculoskeletal disorders. Therefore, it is not possible, given existing studies, to provide a systematic summary, or comparison across programs, of the cost-outcome effectiveness of such interventions. Few studies of the effects of interventions for musculoskeletal disorders describe the costs associated with the intervention. Studies of interventions for musculoskeletal disorders employ a wide variety of outcome measures, and methods for determining cost also vary across studies that consider costs. Cost and outcome factors can differ widely, depending on the level of intervention (primary, secondary). In fact, most reports of cost-outcome effectiveness for such interventions provide only anecdotal or case data. Goossens et al. (1999) noted that three recently performed reviews of the economic evaluation of interventions for musculoskeletal pain pointed to the impossibility of reaching confident conclusions, because of the lack of clarity and low quality of the costing methodologies employed.

There are several key methodological issues associated with cost/outcome analysis in this area:

1. Different interventions and the circumstances to which they are applied may result in different time profiles. Some costs may be spread over a long period of time, while others are incurred at the beginning of the intervention; similarly, some outcomes appear quickly, while others require long periods of time.

2. Reduction in cost related to a disorder can be deemed a benefit of the intervention (e.g., when an intervention results in a decrease in the prevalence of a disorder at a workplace). This is sometimes clearly demonstrable with a methodology that controls for the effects of competing—or no—interventions. Moreover, *predicted* reduction in cost is sometimes taken as a benefit (e.g., when an intervention is predicted to prevent cases of a disorder that will not be observed, because they have, by prediction, been prevented). Similarly, assumptions are sometimes made about the interrelationships of benefits to one another (e.g., the assumption that an outcome of improved job satisfaction will imply also an outcome of improved productivity). In all cases, care must be exercised to validate the relationships and predictions.

3. Costs reported under the same label can be determined by different accounting methods (e.g., overhead costs); similarly, outcomes described in similar terms can mask operationally different variables (e.g., job satisfaction, reported pain). The methodology whereby cost and outcome are determined should be precisely explained in any study that assesses cost-outcome effectiveness—a principle violated often in case reports and best practice description.

4. The results of cost-outcome effectiveness studies must be considered only one part of policy and decision analysis, which must also consider such factors as who pays what costs, who reaps what benefits, and what cost/outcome ratio is acceptable. One method of quantifying values is to measure the evaluator's willingness to pay for units of risk reduction.

Despite the current dearth of rigorous, comprehensive cost-outcome effectiveness studies of interventions for musculoskeletal disorders, direction can be found in, for example, Haddix et al. (1996), who provide a general framework applicable to public health prevention initiatives, and Goossens et al. (1999), who propose a framework specific to musculoskeletal disorders. The combined framework (see Box 8.1) is augmented by factors described in existing cost-outcome studies for musculoskeletal disorders; this framework identifies types of costs and benefits that can be considered as part of future efforts toward the development of an accepted methodology that will permit comparison across alternative interventions.

BOX 8.1   Framework for Cost-Outcome Effectiveness Research

Examples of Cost Factors for Intervention/Prevention Programs
Direct Health Care Costs
    Institutional inpatient care
    Institutional outpatient services
    Home health care
    Physician services
    Ancillary services (other professionals and volunteers)
    Overhead (facility, equipment, etc.)
    Medications
    Devices and appliances
    Diagnostic tests
    Rehabilitation
Direct Nonhealth Care Costs
    Program development (analysis, program design)
    Training and education (personnel, materials, facilities)
    Program management
    Transportation
    Modification to workplace (time and cost to design, fabricate/purchase, implement)
Indirect Costs: Wages/Time
    Lost productivity during implementation
    Psychosocial costs (adjustment, stress due to change)

Examples of Beneficial Outcomes of Intervention/Prevention Programs

Number of reported injuries
Number of Workers' Compensation claims
Amount of Workers' Compensation indemnity paid
Reduction in lost days
Reduction in absenteeism
Reduction in recurrences
Reduced number of worker replacements and reduced training of new workers
Improved physical functioning
Motivation
Morale
Job satisfaction
Productivity
Improved perceived quality of life
Reduction in risky behaviors
Reduced fatigue
Improved knowledge of workers about safety

Return to Work

Return to work is one desirable outcome of interventions. Research that elucidates the factors that operate on behalf of return to work would further the understanding of the systematic description of factors presented in Figure 1.2. Such research would usefully address development of prognostic indicators of clinical outcomes; determination of how return to work is affected by functional capacities of the worker and by workplace accommodations; identification of barriers to timely access to health care and to filing workers' compensation claims; and identification of disincentives to compliance with suggested programs.

Dissemination of Information

There is also a challenge of disseminating—to workers, managers, and researchers and practitioners in government, industry, and academia— the surveillance, research, assessment, and effectiveness information discussed above. Features of an improved infrastructure to foster this dissemination would include regular meetings that bring together scientific and best practices experience; an intervention trials network; development and sharing of common tools, training programs, and standards—tailored to users—for implementing ergonomic programs; and mechanisms for disseminating validated best practices.

Particularly helpful would be the expansion of education and training programs to assist workers and employers (especially small employers) in understanding and utilizing the range of possible workplace interventions designed to reduce musculoskeletal disorders. Expanding continuing education for a broad range of professionals concerning risk factors for musculoskeletal disorders—in and out of the workplace—and concerning interventions would also be useful.

SUMMARY

Musculoskeletal injuries in the workplace result from a complex interaction of mechanical stresses, individual host factors, and organizational policy and structure. Furthermore, due to the rapidly changing nature of work and the intense focus on production goals, it is extremely difficult to design and carry out intervention studies in the workplace, particularly those that are prospective, randomized, and controlled. When interpreting the results of existing intervention studies, there are important methodological considerations that must be taken into account to determine the validity of each study.

There is a very large body of published literature about workplace interventions for the primary and secondary prevention of back and upper extremity work-related disorders. Despite the large number of studies published, few meet the strictest criteria for scientific validity. At the same time, there is a another body of information derived from quality improvement studies and best practices that reflect the practical experience within industry. To the degree that there is agreement between the more scientific literature and best practices, this congruence is important in establishing a weight or pattern of evidence. In applying this information, there are several ethical and cost-benefit considerations, as well as practical barriers particularly in optimizing secondary prevention strategies.

The complexity of musculoskeletal disorders in the workplace requires a variety of strategies that may involve the worker, the workforce, and management. The literature shows that no single strategy is or will be effective for all types of industry; interventions are best tailored to the individual situation. Although we have no measure of their relative contributions, there are, however, some program elements that consistently recur within successful programs: management commitment, employee involvement, and directly addressing workplace physical and work organizational factors.

The weight and pattern of the evidence supports the conclusion that primary and secondary prevention interventions to reduce the incidence, severity, and consequences of musculoskeletal injuries in the workplace are effective when properly implemented. The evidence suggests that the most effective strategies involve a combined approach that takes into account the complex interplay between physical stressors and the policies and procedures of industries. When the scientific information is combined with the very practical quality improvement data, the panel is persuaded that continued focus on primary and secondary prevention can reduce the incidence and severity of these widespread musculoskeletal conditions affecting the worker in the workplace. Specifically, the panel concludes that:

1. Interventions must mediate physical stressors, largely through the application of principles of ergonomics.
2. Employee involvement is essential to successful implementation.
3. Employer commitment, demonstrated by an integrated program and supported by best practices review, is important for success.
4. Because of limitations in the scientific literature, a comprehensive and systematic research program, supported by an infrastructure linking industry, labor, government, and academic efforts, is needed to further

clarify and distinguish the features that make interventions effective for specific musculoskeletal disorders.

5. Although generic guidelines have been developed and successfully applied in intervention programs, no single specific design, restriction, or practice for universal application is supported by the existing scientific literature.

6. Study of the relationship between exposure to physical and psychosocial risk factors and musculoskeletal disorders has been constrained by inadequate techniques for quantitative measurement of "dose," analogous to available measures for noise or chemicals. Existing measures are often based on self-report or qualitative metrics. New tools and research instruments are necessary to provide more reliable and valid exposure estimates; these are most important for the study of the effects, if any, at lower-level exposures and for evaluation of the possibility of interaction among different factors when more than one is present. Better measures of exposures and outcomes would permit more effective evaluation of interventions.

9

Work Now and in the Future

Much has been written about the nature of work and how it is influenced by ever advancing technology, shifts in market forces, the demographics of the workforce, and changing occupational structures (National Research Council, 1999a; Howard, 1995). The central theme both now and in the future is diversity in workers, jobs, workplace design, and work location. At the level of industries and occupations, changes have been occurring for a number of years. For example, there has been a shift from blue-collar work to service work, a trend toward teamwork, and an increasing need for all levels of employees to develop new skills for working with technology. Current trends also indicate continuing part-time employment, outsourcing, mobility of workers among jobs both within and between occupations, and an aging workforce with an increasing number of women and minorities. Furthermore , it has been suggested that the current trend in work outside the traditional work setting will continue to expand.

The scholarly treatment of workplace trends has focused almost exclusively on organizational issues and personnel policies rather than on changes in the content of specific jobs and occupations. In this chapter, we attempt to piece together a description of the current and projected content of work and the implications for the occurrence of musculoskeletal disorders. We begin the discussion with an overview of the growth and decline of occupations in the past and the projected trends for the future. This discussion focuses on the types of jobs that have produced the highest percentage of musculoskeletal disorders injury reports in the last decade—those associated with materials handling—and the expected changes anticipated in these jobs in the next decade. The second part of the chapter examines the external variables that influence changes in work, including: (1) workforce demographics, (2) technology, (3) the globalization of markets, and (4) organizational structures, policies, and procedures. The final section presents a summary of the implications of anticipated trends in work on the occurrence of musculoskeletal disorders.

TRENDS IN EMPLOYMENT BY INDUSTRY SECTOR AND OCCUPATION

Distribution of Workers

According to Franklin in the *Monthly Labor Review* (1997), the service-producing industries such as finance, government, health, transportation, communications, wholesale and retail trade, and utilities are the fastest-growing sector in the economy (see Table 9.1). In 1986, these industries represented 66 percent of all jobs; in 1996 they represented 71.2 percent; and by 2006, they are projected to reach 74 percent (almost 112 million jobs). In contrast, goods-producing industries such as mining, construction, and manufacturing declined from 22 percent (23.5 million jobs) in 1986 to 18.5 percent in 1996 and are projected to decline further to 16.2 percent by 2006 (23.4 million jobs). Although this sector is declining in relative terms, the absolute number of people employed is relatively constant due to an increase in total workforce size over the time frame. For our purposes, it is important to note that there are many physical jobs in the service industry (e.g., nursing, parcel delivery, maintenance) and many jobs with no physical demands beyond those traditionally associated with office work in the goods-producing industries (managers, accountants, etc.).

We can relate the sector of employment directly to the task demands through data collected between 1979 and 1993 and analyzed by sector. Landau et al. (1996) used a database of 3,893 jobs from the Arbeitswissenschaftliche Erhebungsverfahren zur Tätikgkeitsanalyse (AET) job analysis system that quantifies many aspects of task demands. Classifying jobs by sector using the Standard Industrial Classification (SIC) code shows which sectors were over- and underrepresented on each dimension of the task. Table 9.2 shows the job sectors that were overrepresented for each type of stressor. Further analysis of these data by gender shows that more men are engaged in heavy dynamic work; in the light active work category, men tended to work with heavier loads. Women's work focuses on more repetitive tasks. With regard to information processing work, men are more likely to hold jobs with high knowledge requirements and qualifications.

Table 9.3 (taken from Silvestri, 1997) shows the percentage of employment by major occupational group for 1986, 1996, and projected for 2006.

TABLE 9.1 Employment by Major Industry Division, 1986, 1996, and Projected 2006 (after Franklin, 1997)

Industry	Thousands of Jobs			Percent Distribution		
	1986	1996	2006	1986	1996	2006
Total[a]	111,374	132,352	150,927	100.0	100.0	100.0
Nonfarm wage and salary[a]	98,727	118,731	136,318	88.6	89.7	90.3
Goods producing	24,538	24,431	24,451	22.0	18.5	16.2
Mining	778	574	443	.7	.4	.3
Construction	4,810	5,400	5,900	3.3	3.1	3.9
Manufacturing	18,951	18,457	18,108	17.0	13.9	12.0
Durable	11,200	10,766	10,514	10.1	8.1	7.0
Nondurable	7,751	7,691	7,593	7.0	5.8	5.0
Service producing	74,189	94,300	111,867	66.6	71.2	73.1
Transportation, communications, utilities	5,247	6,260	7,111	3.7	3.7	3.7
Wholesale trade	5,751	6,483	7,228	5.2	3.9	3.8
Retail trade	17,878	21,625	23,875	16.1	16.3	15.8
Finance, insurance and real estate	6,275	6,899	7,651	5.6	5.2	5.1
Services[b]	22,346	33,586	44,852	20.1	25.4	29.7
Federal government	2,899	2,757	2,670	2.6	2.1	1.8
State and local government	13,794	16,690	18,480	12.4	12.6	12.2
Agriculture[c]	3,327	3,642	3,618	3.0	2.8	2.4
Private household wage and salary	1,235	928	775	1.1	.7	.5
Nonagricultural self-employed and unpaid family workers[d]	8,085	9,051	10,216	7.3	6.8	6.8

[a]Employment data for wage and salary workers are from the BLS Current Employment Statistics (payroll) survey, which counts jobs, whereas self-employed, unpaid family worker, agricultural, and private household data are from the Current Population Survey (household survey), which counts workers.

[b]Excludes SIC 074,5,8 (agricultural services) and 99 (nonclassifiable establishments), and is therefore not directly comparable with data published in *Employment and Earnings*.

[c]Excludes government wage and salary workers, and includes private sector SIC 08.09 (forestry and fisheries).

[d]Excludes SIC 08.09 (forestry and fisheries).

It can be seen that white-collar executive, managerial, and professional jobs are increasing along with technical, marketing, and service work. However, a decline is expected in the number of more physical jobs associated with agriculture, precision production, and operator/fabricator/laborer. Even so, Silvestri (1997) suggests that approximately 26 percent

TABLE 9.2 Sector Analysis of Work Factors (after Landau et al., 1996). Sectors of business were compared for each type of stressor, with significantly overrepresented sectors listed in the table.

Type of Stressor	Overrepresented Sectors
Heavy dynamic work	Building, agriculture, home
Active light work	Manufacturing, home
Static work	Transportation, communications
Proprioceptive input	Building, public sector
Information load	Service, public sector
Mental stress	Service, public sector
Environmental stress	Mining, manufacturing, building

TABLE 9.3 Employment by Major Occupational Group, 1986, 1996, and Projected 2006 (after Silvestri, 1997)

Numbers in Thousands of Jobs

Occupational Group	Employment					
	Number			Percent Distribution		
	1986	1996	2006	1986	1996	2006
Total, all occupations	111,375	132,353	150,927	100.0	100.0	100.0
Executive, administrative, and managerial	10,568	13,542	15,866	9.5	10.2	10.5
Professional specialty	13,589	18,173	22,998	12.2	13.7	15.2
Technicians and related support	3,724	4,618	5,558	3.3	3.5	3.7
Marketing and sales	11,496	14,633	16,897	10.3	11.1	11.2
Administrative support, including clerical	20,871	24,019	25,825	18.7	18.1	17.1
Service	17,427	21,294	25,174	15.6	16.1	16.7
Agriculture, forestry, fishing, and related occupations	3,661	3,785	3,823	3.3	2.9	2.5
Precision production, craft, and repair	13,832	14,446	15,448	12.4	10.9	10.2
Operators, fabricators, and laborers	16,206	17,843	19,365	13.6	13.5	12.8

of workers will fall into the latter three categories in 2007. Among the service occupations, food preparation and service (cooks, bakers, waiters, etc.) are expected to reach 6.3 percent of the workforce, while the health care occupations of nursing, nursing aids, and physical therapy are expected to reach 3.5 percent. In addition, the home health care field is expected to continue its growth, given the trends in medical insurance. Currently, more than 12 million people in the United States are involved in caregiving on either a full-time or part-time basis—some of these are medical professionals, and others are family members and friends. Many of the physical jobs associated with nursing in hospitals and nursing homes that have been linked to musculoskeletal disorders are also present in providing health care in the home.

It is clear from these projections that the future of work will still include a large number of employees performing highly physical jobs involving manual materials handling tasks. This suggests that the workplace of the future will continue to contain risk factors for musculoskeletal disorders.

Musculoskeletal Injuries and Illnesses Reported by Occupation

The percentage of reported injuries or illnesses involving days away from work in 1997 that were attributed to repetitive motion or overexertion from lifting has been tabulated by Ruser (1999). Approximately 43.6 percent of the reports associated with overexertion from lifting and 49.7 percent associated with repetitive motion come from employees working in jobs in the operator/fabricator/laborer category. The next highest categories for lifting were service (18.3 percent) and technical/sales/administrative support (17.7 percent). For repetitive motion, the next highest categories were technical/sales/administrative support (21.6 percent) and precision/production/craft/repair (12.3 percent). It is interesting to note that overall the percentage of injuries or illnesses reported from lifting declined by 25 percent between 1992 and 1997; those attributed to repetitive motion declined by 16 percent. Since jobs in manual materials handling are a major source of reported musculoskeletal injuries and illnesses, we take the analysis another step and examine the types of workers' compensation claims resulting from work in jobs involving manual materials handling. This analysis is supplemented by data collected from a large number of companies on various features of manual materials handling tasks.

Jobs involving such materials handling tasks as construction, meatpacking, parcel package delivery, transportation, and moving were the source of the greatest number of workers' compensation claims filed in the state of Washington between 1990 and 1997 for musculoskeletal disorders of the low back and upper extremities (Silverstein and Kalat, 1999). Another occupation with a significant number of claims was nursing home work that involved lifting and moving patients. According to an analysis performed at the Liberty Mutual Insurance Company

(Dempsey and Hashemi, 1999), 36 percent of these claims, over a 6-year period, were associated with manual materials handling jobs. Of these, approximately 70 percent were for problems with the low back and upper extremities. As for the nature of the injury (as classified by these authors), the highest category was strain (62 percent) followed by fracture (12.8 percent) and laceration (11.6 percent); sprains accounted for 6 percent.

Ciriello and Snook (1999) conducted a study summarizing typical manual materials handling tasks performed at 2,442 locations across the country. They collected and analyzed data on lifting, lowering, pushing, pulling, and carrying activities covering a 13-year period. The results show that lifting tasks were acceptable for 81 percent of the men but for only 10 percent of the women; for lowering tasks, the percentages were 89 and 14; and for carrying tasks, they were 88 and 36 percent, respectively. Moreover, the median weights for the lifting and lowering tasks were significantly higher than the weight limits recommended by the National Institute for Occupational Safety and Health (NIOSH). The authors concluded that additional work was needed to reduce the risks in industry associated with manual lifting tasks. With the growing number of women in the workforce, these data are of particular interest.

The data from Ciriello and Snook (1999) can also be analyzed for time trends to determine whether jobs have become easier or more difficult over the 12 years of data collection. The authors did not conduct a random survey of all jobs, but rather analyzed the jobs that had been submitted to them by insurance agents in their capacity as reducers of potential insurance claims. The authors claim that the jobs are representative of industrial practice, although they acknowledge that sample sizes have decreased over the time period covered. In fact, they probably represent more demanding jobs, as their median weights for lifting and lowering were about 20 kg, well above the 9.1 kg reported by Drury, Law, and Pawenski (1982) in a survey of about 2,000 box-handling jobs in industry. When analyzed for linear time trends, Ciriello and Snook's data show significant changes over 1981 to 1993, with jobs becoming less demanding over time. The changes were quite large in some cases; for example, there was a mean decrease in lifted weight of about 0.5 kg per year and an improvement in both lift distance and height (at the start of the lift) of over 10 mm per year. These trends, coupled with the continued promise of automation of heavy industrial tasks, suggest a decrease in workplace risk factors associated with manual lifting tasks.

EXTERNAL FACTORS INFLUENCING THE NATURE OF WORK

This section provides a general overview of factors that have influenced work in the past and are expected to have a continuing effect in the future. They include workforce demographics, technology, globalization of markets, and internal changes in organizational structures and practices as a result of the other three aspects. The implications of these factors on the nature of work and the occurrence of musculoskeletal disorders is also examined. Some factors may act to increase the risks for musculoskeletal disorders, whereas others may act to decrease the risks.

Workforce Demographics

One major source of change in the workplace is the worker. At the start of the 21st century, it is anticipated that there will be greater participation in the workforce by older workers, ethnic minorities, and women. Between 1990 and 2010, the general population is expected to increase by 25 percent, from 239.3 million to 301.1 million in 2010 (Sternberg and Coleman, 1993). The Bureau of Labor Statistics (1999b) has projected a 12 percent increase in the labor force by 2008. In this time frame, the age distribution in the labor force is projected to shift toward the older ages. The proportion of employees in the United States who are ages 55 to 64 is now growing at a faster pace than any other employee age group. By 2006, the median age of all workers will be 41 years, compared with 38 years in 1996. In 1998, there were over 16 million Americans age 55 or older still working; by 2006, workers 55 years and older will constitute 20 percent of the entire workforce. By 2010, the baby boom generation will start to reach age 65, and between now and then there will be a 16 percent growth in jobs but only a 4 percent growth in population. The baby boom cohort includes about 75 million people. As they start to retire in large numbers, severe labor shortages are predicted to begin as early as 2010 and continue for several decades after that. The problem is not only the shortfall of available employees but also the cost of replacing the more experienced workers with new workers who will require orientation and training. Employers will be looking for incentives to keep the older worker in the labor force. Job satisfaction will be a key consideration.

There is also a trend in the general population and the workforce toward increased ethnic diversity. Sternberg and Coleman (1993) cite Bureau of the Census projections across all ethnic groups: These show a 1.4 percent increase in blacks between 1995 and 2020 (a change from 33.7 to 46.8 million) and a 6.6 percent increase in Hispanics for the same time period (a change from 26.5 to 53.3 million). The percentage of other races is also projected to increase between 1995 and 2020 from 4 to 6.5 percent (a change from 10.7 to 21.2 million). Over the longer term, such demographic changes will continue. For example, by 2050, only about half of the U.S. population (52.8 percent) is projected to be white, compared with almost three quarters (73.6 percent) in 1995 (Day, 1996). Overall, two-thirds of the expected increase in U.S. population by 2050 will have come from net immigration.

Participation rates for women in nearly all age groups are projected to increase. Men's labor force participation rates are expected to remain constant in all five-year age groups; however, their overall rate is expected to decline as the population shifts to the older age groups with lower participation rates. In 1998, 46 percent of the labor force was female; by 2008, women will make up 48 percent of the labor force.

A final demographic consideration is the increased presence of people with disabilities in the workforce. In 1999, the participation rate for persons with disabilities was only 29.7 percent compared with 81.9 percent for people without disabilities (Bureau of the Census, 1999). While projections of these data to future employment are not available, the Department of Labor expects people with disabilities to be one of the populations that will "experience particularly large increases" (U.S. Department of Labor, 1999:13). Some conditions, which may or may not represent legally defined disabilities, arise from illness and injury, such as musculoskeletal disorders. Note that all of these demographic considerations are for *increased* workforce participation. At current historical lows in overall unemployment, more of the population as a whole is now working and thus potentially exposed to musculoskeletal disorder risk factors. Also, because work in the home must still be performed, increase in work participation will increase a potential occupational exposure, augmenting nonoccupational exposure for more Americans.

Another important consideration concerning the future workforce is the significantly increased duration of exposure to keyboards and computer terminals. Although adolescent injury patterns still reflect primarily back injuries, cuts or contusions, and burns (Brooks and Davis, 1996; Parker, 1993), computer use now begins in early childhood when nerve and muscle tissues are developing. Computer games, as well as educational uses, including taking notes in class using a laptop, are common practice among children and adolescents. Harris and Straker (2000) studied the use of laptops in schools and found that a large proportion of users experience discomfort with carrying and using laptop computers. One large study conducted at a major northeastern university found that a significant percentage of the student body is experiencing upper extremity pain associated with keyboard use (Katz et al., 2000). However, associations with well-defined clinical syndromes are not yet known.

Technology

A second major driver of change is technology. Technology not only shapes what people do but how they do it. New occupations are created, and others are eliminated. Skills and knowledge needed to perform some jobs are increased, while the requirements for other jobs are decreased. Although changes in technology leading to the reformatting of work have occurred with some regularity in most work settings, the rate of change has accelerated in recent years. Information technology is becoming a part of *all* jobs as computing power becomes less expensive and more distributed. In industrial and office settings, many information collection, processing, sharing, and dissemination tasks have been transferred to or augmented by computer systems and information networks.

While only a few years ago the National Research Council was investigating the gap between investments in information technology and productivity improvement (National Research Council, 1994), it now appears that the gap has closed and that computing power is having a significant effect on both productivity growth and the nature of work. For example, current work design trends include just-in-time production and lean manufacturing (e.g., Womack and Jones, 1996). Both emphasize reduction of intermediate buffers in processes and the elimination of nonvalue-added work steps. The net effect is more tightly coupled production (and service) systems that have decreased error tolerance and place increased demands on the workforce. Today, there are many physical tasks previously performed by workers that are now being carried out by robots under the remote direction of human operators. A series of workshops organized by the National Institute for Working Life in Sweden as Work Life 2000 has reviewed many of the effects of technological change; for example, microfirms (Summary #20), the information society (Summary #19), information technology (Summary #22), and the welding industry (Summary #12).

From the point of view of musculoskeletal disorders, the rise of technology not only increases the exposure of the workers to computer interfaces (including keyboards and screens), but also it creates more variability in work tasks and more psychosocial demands for quick turnaround performance. Furthermore, work stress may be increased by the fact that computers can monitor the performance of many tasks, thus providing management with keystroke-level information on productivity and errors.

In Industry

In industrial settings, technology has made possible the pursuit of customized product development and just-in-time manufacturing (Wall and Jackson, 1995). As a result, workers are taking on more responsibility for decision making and coordination; they are performing production tasks based on customer demands rather than on a mass production basis.

Under the just-in-time manufacturing scenario, there is pressure for flexibility and responsiveness, products are only manufactured to order, inventories and work in progress are minimized, and workers have to move from one type of task to another in order to respond to the need. In this scenario, workers are assigned several tasks, reducing the opportunity for them to be engaged in repetitive motion for extended periods of time on one task. Workers may also have to work unexpected overtime to provide the rapid response inherent in a just-in-time production system. Again, there is a potential for longer hours of exposure to any workplace risk factors.

At the end of 1998, *Modern Materials Handling* produced a special report outlining the major trends in materials handling technology. One major development is advances in software for warehouse management systems and the development of partnerships between these systems and transportation management systems. These partnerships are a reflection of changes in manufacturing processes (customization, just-in-time production) and the resulting changes in the supply chain. Other developments of note include advances in automating the sorting, storing, and delivery of materials, ranging in size and weight from truck bodies and motor assemblies to small parcels. Modern conveyors are now being equipped with sophisticated sorting and routing systems. Automated storage and retrieval systems are operated from remote workstations. Lift trucks are employed to move pallets from one location to another—an example of the increasing mechanization of materials handling. It is anticipated that these types of advances and others will be encouraged as long as managers believe that improved speed and efficiency in production will more than compensate for the cost of such equipment and that the number of lost hours from disabilities experienced by production line employees will decline.

A prime example of materials handling jobs in the future is the type of work performed in the growing number of distribution centers. To meet the immediate demands of either a final customer or a retail store, the need has shifted to rapid packaging of a variety of components collected from many suppliers. For example, apparel manufacturers have computer systems that store inventory data to pull orders from the distribution center and, ultimately, from the manufacturers. Similarly, Internet booksellers must assemble customer orders from a variety of publishers and rapidly dispatch them.

Distribution centers are characterized by minimal inventory and minimal response time to customer needs. Because of the variety required by customers, distribution centers often feature high-density storage, with storage locations 10 meters above ground level and minimal aisle width for stocking and order picking. Stocking is usually by the pallet-load, while order pickers must manually select from each pallet cases of those items required by each individual customer with customization. This typically requires manual handling in the restricted spaces defined by the pallet and the order-picking vehicle. Much of this work must be carried out at high levels above the ground, further restricting the operator with safety harnesses and more prescribed working methods. There is also a shift from picking entire cases of goods to picking individual pieces to assemble a customized order. Often, this form of order picking is performed along banked storage racks, filled by automated replenishment systems, onto a central conveyor.

Characteristics of such work are the computer-optimized picking schedule (which leaves little room for individual operator skill) and strict production control, often using a financial incentive system to motivate operators to work faster. Under such conditions, the physical handling of items becomes more varied; more manual handling is lateral transfer rather than lifting/lowering. However, the pervasive time stress and the social isolation in these jobs may result in negative psychosocial pressures that can adversely affect worker productivity and job satisfaction. Although there are many shifts away from heavy lifting jobs, there are jobs such as picking and placing that could increase the risk factors for upper-extremity musculoskeletal disorders. Thus work in the future may pose a lower risk for back problems and a higher risk for upper extremity musculoskeletal disorders.

In the Office

In today's office, professional and technical employees, as well as administrative employees, find a large portion of their work is accomplished at a computer keyboard. The technologies that are having the greatest impact on supporting and encouraging this trend include (1) software advances for word processing, spreadsheets, and graphics packages and (2) network services such as electronic mail, distributed collaboration, and the availability of information on the Internet. The keyboard and the mouse, as key interface devices to the computer for information gathering, distributed collaboration, and information provision, have led to a wide debate concerning their role in the development of hand, wrist, arm, and shoulder repetitive stress injuries (e.g., carpal tunnel syndrome, wrist tendinitis, epicondylitis, tension neck syndrome). It is also important to note that screen placement and static loading from poor overall body posture can increase exposure to musculoskeletal disorder risk.

According to Coovert (1995), in the future interfaces with the computer will involve touch screens and voice input. Weiser (1991, 1993) has proposed an intriguing view of the future in which computers will be everywhere but will be invisible. He suggests that three different types of systems will be available in the office of the future: post-it-sized computers called tabs, notepad-sized computers called pads, and wall-sized interactive surfaces called liveboards. Tabs function as an extension of the computer screen—information in a window can be compressed on a tab. A tab can serve as a storage device for a project or it can function as personal identifier for an individual. It would be equipped with a touch-sensitive screen and a series of buttons. A *pad* would be used like a piece of paper, and each office would have several of these. The *liveboard*, which would function like a white board, would support collaborative work and inputs could come from several sources, including pens, scanners, and gestures.

If the interface devices of the future do move away from keyboard and mouse input, many of the physical symptoms currently attributed to computer use will be alleviated. However, the impact of touch screens, voice input, barcode readers, card swipes, and so forth, has yet to be determined. Moreover, their utilization rates are not clear, because no one knows the effectiveness of the new technologies in supporting the work of professionals, newspaper reporters, and scientists, to name a few occupations that might use them. As the office of the future evolves and a greater number of individuals engage in computer-interactive work (from a variety of remote locations, including home offices), there will be a need to carefully examine the implications of new interface devices for musculoskeletal disorder risk factors.

Globalization

Deregulation, inexpensive transportation, and rapid diffusion of distributed computing have driven the globalization of customers, finance, and the production of goods and services (Friedman, 1999). Industry is increasingly spread across more regions of the world. More information is available instantly through Internet technology (Whitman, 1999). Furthermore, the global capital markets are forcing "creative destruction," i.e., the often brutal flow of capital away from enterprises with low shareholder value to enterprises in which the capital will generate the greatest return. Investments are moving rapidly, forcing industries to respond quickly to changing customer demands. We have moved from managerial capitalism of the first part of this century to investor capitalism with more demanding shareholders (e.g., large pension funds). Even national governments are being forced by the instantaneous investment community to reduce their costs and become more open and transparent. Kanter (1995, 1999) characterizes these changes as greater *mobility* (of capital, people, ideas), greater *simultaneity* (of technology or investment information), greater *bypass* (other choices besides large corporations), and greater *pluralism* (with smaller headquarters and decentralized decision making). An important implication of this for the workforce is that workers are increasingly divided into "mobiles" with internationally useful skills and "nonmobiles" who stay in one location and have to accept scarce low-skilled jobs (Kanter, 1999; Porter and Wayland, 1995).

One logical fusion of globalization and technology is electronic commerce, or e-commerce (*Business Week*, 1991). In 1998, e-commerce accounted for approximately $8 billion in retail sales; according to Standard & Poors Industry Surveys (1997), the numbers are projected to increase to $44 billion by 2002. Beyond retail sales, however, is the larger business-to-business commercial sales market that is projected to reach $333 billion on the Internet by 2002. Current users are wealthy and better-educated individuals; however, participation is increasing throughout society. It is anticipated that 40 percent of all businesses will sell their products and services over the Internet in 2000. Using e-commerce, as in traditional forms of direct merchandising, customers can order a wide variety of goods and services directly from producers. The difference now is that a global market structure and the availability of the Internet allow direct customer-producer interactions easily and instantly through a common interface. Some producers sell services, such as travel bookings or information search, for which the delivery process is entirely via the computer. Others sell goods, which eventually must be moved to the location specified by the customer.

In e-commerce, customers have direct interaction with the providers, anywhere in the world and at any time of day. Customers can easily comparison shop, leading producers to make rapid changes of pricing and to develop custom products or packages. The direct voice of the customer pushes producers to be highly competitive, highly responsive, and very open; for example, Internet-based real-time tracking of customer orders. These characteristics have a number of occupational implications. First, round-the-clock operations require round-the-clock support. This implies increased shift work, as well as the stresses and satisfaction that may arise from direct customer interaction. Second, the location of support activities need not be related geographically to the delivery of these services. Thus, airline reservation support can be located in rural America (or indeed anywhere in the world) rather than close to an airline's operational hub. Third, in situations in which physical goods must be delivered, a distribution system is required. This often takes the form of a set of distribution centers, again located for geographic convenience, and whose characteristics were discussed in the previous section. Fourth, there is more product variety, many of the products are lighter and packaged by the piece rather than the case, and the product moves through the system from supplier to customer more rapidly. Finally, the extremely rapid growth, and often equally rapid takeover or demise, of e-commerce companies have implications for the duration of continuous employment and the development of workforce skills.

An important result of globalization from the perspective of musculoskeletal disorders is that global standards are being adopted by multinational businesses as they try to ensure that they are always ready for future changes. Although many companies still use differences in standards between countries to reduce business costs, more progressive companies are using the most stringent world standards as the basis for their global operations (Kanter, 1999). One effect of this is that standards set by a single country may be of little relevance to increasingly global enterprises unless they are the most stringent. An obvious example is the ISO-9000 series of quality standards that have had a great leveling effect across different nations (Kroslid, 1999).

Organizational Structures, Policies, and Procedures

As already noted, technology, the rapid growth of Internet business, and globalization have had a significant impact on how work is organized, managed, and performed. Key organizational changes that can influence the nature of work include downsizing, flatter managerial hierarchies, more teamwork, and greater movement of employees across companies and occupations.

Downsizing

For industrial workers, major overall results are job loss in developed economies, temporary jobs, longer hours of work, more people with two jobs, and subcontract jobs instead of regular employment (Rifkin, 1995). Global competition has forced many companies to downsize their workforce to remain competitive and increase shareholder value. Budros (1999) examines the reasons for downsizing as separate from reorganization. He sees the downsizing trend as being caused by technological innovation, by the existence of highly paid long-term employees, and by the primarily financial orientation of chief executive officers. Possible negative effects of downsizing are increased workloads for those remaining and increased error and injury rates resulting from the removal of company expertise. For example, downsizing combined with just-in-time manufacturing may lead to workers being asked to perform more jobs and a more variable set of tasks over varying amounts of time. All of these factors have the potential of increasing physical and psychosocial stress.

More jobs are being created in small to medium-sized enterprises than in large companies (Budros, 1999), although the major employment sector is still businesses employing over 500 people, accounting for 41 percent of all employment (Rifkin, 1995). The increase of small to medium-sized enterprises can mean more workers who are without the benefit of extensive services, such as onsite medical or ergonomics programs. It also means less unionization, down from 33 percent in 1955 to 16 percent in 1995 (Whitman, 1999). In addition, many operations are being outsourced, leading to reduced levels of job security and more temporary jobs (Whitman, 1999; Budros, 1999). In fact, layoffs in U.S. industry peaked in the period 1992 to 1995, at a time of maximum job growth. The fastest-growing category was in temporary jobs, which rose sixfold between 1972 and 1995 (Whitman, 1999). The total number of temporary jobs is still small; however, it is a major concern of workers (Kanter, 1995, Chapter 6). However, temporary employees may have less access to medical care than is provided by established employers, potentially decreasing early diagnosis and treatment of musculoskeletal disorders.

Length of the Work Week

Some analysts suggest that work hours overall may be increasing in the United States. For example, Schor (1991) analyzed national data on long-term employment hours of work, vacation time, and work in the home, concluding that total hours of work increased by 9 percent between 1969 and 1987. While her data and analyses have been questioned, many people say that they are working harder than they did before, particularly with the advent of telecommuting and the extensive use of computers at home. In a recent study, Jacobs and Greerson (1998) found that men in professional and managerial careers are more likely to work 50 hours or more per week than men in other occupations and women in any occupation. These data are based on self-reports.

Still, the length of the work week has remained constant since 1990, at approximately 34 hours, for nonsupervisory workers in all private-sector jobs (Bureau of Labor Statistics, 2000a). Work hours in the goods producing/manufacturing sectors have also remained constant at approximately 41 hours, with an average overtime between 3.5 and 5 hours. Those workers with the highest number of hours are in the motor vehicle and equipment category and in the primary metals industries category (44 to 46 hours per week). Long working hours, particularly in manual labor jobs, can lead to fatigue and greater exposure to musculoskeletal disorder risk factors.

Rapid Obsolescence of Skills and Knowledge

Increasingly, work at the world-class levels demanded by global competition generates greater worker skill requirements and greater rate of worker knowledge obsolescence. Kanter (1999) shows that even in manufacturing, physical assets represented 63 percent of company capitalization in 1982, but only 38 percent in 1991. The remainder of the assets is largely composed of company knowledge and competence. Indeed, Siemieniuch and Sinclair (1999) show that even if useful industrial knowledge has a half-life as long as 10 years, only 6 percent of the knowledge at the start of a person's working life will be useful at its end 40 years later. When the current workforce retires, it will be producing unknowable offerings (goods and services) for unborn people with uninvented techniques. In turn, this creates a demand for lifelong training. Whitman (1999) notes that companies with a heavy emphasis on training show a 19 percent greater productivity gain over a 3-year interval than other companies. From the viewpoint of musculoskeletal disorders, the implication is that jobs will be more variable over time, thus increasing the variety of any risk exposure.

Sociotechnical Systems and Employee Participation

New forms of organization based on sociotechnical systems concepts are being introduced into many industries, both service and manufacturing (Taylor and Felten, 1993). These involve a more complete systems analysis than is typical in many business change practices, such as business process reengineering (Hammer and Champey, 1993). Note that the same modern business practices appear to be employed by companies of different sizes and in different sectors (Waterson, 1999).

Sociotechnical systems specifically involve the entire workforce in analyzing both the technical system (to find the key variances in the process) and the social system (to find how these variances are controlled). Such reorganizations have been effective in a number of industries and should reduce musculoskeletal risk exposure by the active design of jobs, rather than by assigning to human operators the tasks left over from a mainly automated system (Bainbridge, 1983). Batt (1999) measured the effects of sociotechnical systems as well as total quality management approaches to customer service representatives in a typical service industry and concluded that only the sociotechnical systems redesign had a large and positive effect on both quality and productivity.

The Shift Is from Manufacturing to Service But Manual Labor Jobs Remain

Manual materials handling jobs are moving from manufacturing to service/delivery organizations as more repetitive tasks in production systems are automated. When there is little variability between task cycles, automation can be accomplished relatively easily. For example, moving pallets up to the end of a production line for loading and moving on is relatively straightforward. In such cases, workers will no longer be exposed to the lifting tasks common before the introduction of automation. This can reduce musculoskeletal disorder exposure in manufacturing sectors. However, in the service industry, the tasks are more variable. Maintaining a copier, lifting an elderly patient, restocking supermarket shelves, and order picking in a distribution center all involve humans as the prime agents to move materials, mainly because the item-to-item variability is too high for simple automation. Thus, exposure to musculoskeletal disorder risk may be increasing in service industries even as it declines in manufacturing. The high variability of manual materials handling tasks in the service industry provides some variety in postures and loads from cycle to cycle. This may reduce exposure, but at the same time it reduces the task-specific skills of workers, potentially exposing them to more unexpected loads for which they have not been specifically trained or for which they are not well adapted.

SUMMARY

A central theme for work in the future is the diversity of jobs and workers. As a result, the workplace risk factors associated with the occurrence of musculoskeletal disorders of the upper extremities are expected to increase. In the office, there are many jobs that will require interaction with computers, which can expose a greater fraction of the workforce to keyboards, pointing devices, screen glare, and sedentary work at a variety of workstation configurations. In industry, the quick turnaround demands of e-commerce on distribution centers will involve the rapid movement of a large variety of relatively lightweight products. Workers will be picking pieces and assembling custom combinations rather than handling products by the case load.

Trends suggest that the risk factors associated with heavy manual lifting jobs in manufacturing are projected to decrease, but this may not be true in other sectors of the economy. There are many jobs that will still involve heavy or repetitive work—construction, meatpacking and processing, nursing, parcel handling and delivery, picking and placing of parts, etc. However, whenever possible, the trend is toward automation. In industry, this is resulting in the large-scale automation of storage, retrieval, sorting, and delivery tasks. Such tasks can increase the exposure to high-frequency manual materials handling but with lighter loads.

Continued long working hours and the increasing requirement for shift work (with round-the-clock e-commerce demands), particularly in manual labor jobs, can be expected to increase the opportunities for fatigue and exposure to musculoskeletal disorders risk factors. Also, psychosocial stresses are expected to play a greater role in the workplace of the future. Most workers will be more closely involved with customers, as consumers increasingly demand a combination of high quality, customization, and low price. Exposing the workforce to customers will change the skill requirements. Customer involvement can increase job satisfaction, but also it can increase performance pressure. As jobs become more variable (with repetitive tasks being handled by automation) and are based on new manufacturing paradigms (just-in-time, etc.) there will be a need for flexibility and a pressure to produce on demand. Furthermore, some workers may experience more isolation as support activities are housed in remote locations. More isolation may also occur as computers take over more of the functions that have traditionally relied on human interaction. These trends have implications for an increase in the role of negative psychosocial factors in reports of illness or injury in the workplace. Other factors contributing heavily to the psychosocial environment include reduced job security, more temporary jobs, and outsourcing.

There is a prospect that more workers will lose traditional benefits. More jobs are being created in small- to medium-sized enterprises than in large companies. This shift means more workers will be without extensive medical or ergonomics programs. It also means less unionization.

The changing composition of the workforce will probably require different workplace conditions. As more women enter the workforce (particularly in materials handling jobs) and as the workforce ages, there will be a continuing need to evaluate work tasks—particularly those that involve lifting, lowering, carrying, and repetitive motion.

Finally, with continued globalization comes the increased need for international design standards. A current example is the ISO-9000 series of quality standards, which has had a great leveling effect across nations.

Part III
Implications

10

Patterns of Evidence

M usculoskeletal disorders, especially those associated with low back pain, are very prevalent and a major reason for seeking health care. Overall, in the United States, people make some 69 million clinic visits annually for these disorders. Furthermore, approximately 1 million people take time away from work each year to treat and recover from musculoskeletal pain and loss of function. For workers in their 50s and 60s, musculoskeletal disorders represent the most common cause of disability, and current projections suggest that these figures are on the rise. In sum, data from the general population of workers and nonworkers suggest that the problem of musculoskeletal disorders is a major source of short-term and long-term disability with economic losses in the range of 1 percent of the nation's gross domestic product.

Because most people living in the United States work (more than 80 percent of the adult population), comparisons between the general population and those who work are unreliable. Explicitly, the available data on the general population include work-related as well as nonwork-related musculoskeletal disorders without distinctions. Therefore, rates derived from these general population sources cannot be considered in any sense equivalent to rates for background, reference, or unexposed groups. Nor can they be considered as rates for musculoskeletal disorders associated with any specific work or activity. No comprehensive data are available on occupationally unexposed groups, given the proportion of adults now in the active U.S. workforce; that is, any such nonemployed group would, by definition be unrepresentative of the adult population.

Nevertheless, the magnitude of the problem of work-related musculoskeletal disorders can be gleaned from the Bureau of Labor Statistics data. These data suggest that musculoskeletal disorders are a problem in several industrial sectors and are not limited to the traditional heavy labor environments represented by agriculture, mining, and manufacturing. It was reported, for example, that the service sector accounted for 26 percent of sprains/strains, carpal tunnel syndrome, or tendinitis, while the manufacturing sector accounted for 22 percent. Another database, National Center for Health Statistics, using self-reports provided estimates for back pain among those whose pain occurred at work (approximately 11.7 million) and for those who specifically reported that their pain was work-related (5.6 million). In this survey, the highest-risk occupations among men were construction laborers, carpenters, and industrial truck and tractor equipment operators; among women, the highest-risk occupations were nursing aides/orderlies/attendants, licensed practical nurses, maids, and janitor/cleaners. Other high-risk occupations were hairdressers and automobile mechanics. Many such workers often are employed in small businesses or are self-employed.

The focus of the panel's work has been the review and interpretation of the scientific literature characterizing musculoskeletal disorders of the low back and upper extremities and their relationship to work. Here we provide an integration of the studies that have been reviewed in the chapters on observational epidemiology, biomechanics, basic sciences, and workplace interventions. As noted in the chapter on epidemiology, there are significant data to show that both lower back and upper extremity musculoskeletal disorders can be associated with workplace exposures. Across the epidemiologic studies, the review has shown both strength and consistency of association. Concerns about whether the associations could be spurious have been considered and reviewed. Biological plausibility has been demonstrated in biomechanical and basic science studies, and further evidence to build causal inferences has been demonstrated by intervention studies that demonstrate reduction in the occurrence of musculoskeletal disorders following implementation of interventions.

The purpose of this discussion is to extend beyond the summaries of each of the chapters, and to integrate information among the chapters relevant to the model presented in Figure 10.1 (which reproduces Figure 1.2 for the reader's convenience). Also, with the acknowledgment that each set of studies has inherent limitations that affect the confidence about conclusions, another purpose is to consider the patterns of evidence that emerge across the different types of studies, as noted earlier in the report.

The integration of findings associated with musculoskeletal disorder risk and the workplace can best be addressed by considering the evidence for the presence of linkages representing the various pathways to injury shown in Figure 10.1. There is a large and diverse body of literature addressing the work-relatedness of musculoskeletal disorders, with different aspects of the literature suggesting different mechanisms of injury.

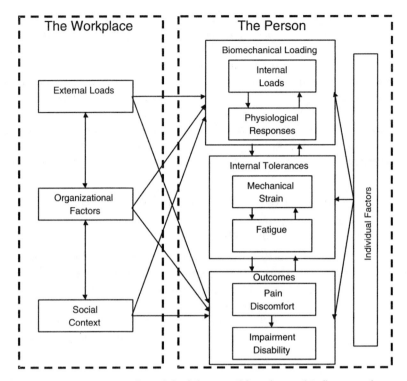

FIGURE 10.1 A conceptual model of the possible roles and influences that various factors may play in the development of musculoskeletal disorders. The dotted box outline on the right indicates the possible pathways and processes that could occur within the person, including the biomechanical load-tolerance relationship and the factors that may mediate the load-tolerance relationship, such as individual factors and adaptation. Outcomes may be a result of this relationship and may be influenced by individual factors, such as conditioning or psychological state. The dotted box on the left indicates the possible influences of the workplace on the sequence of events that can lead to musculoskeletal disorders in the person. Arrows between "the workplace" factors and "the person" box indicate the various research disciplines (epidemiology, biomechanics, physiology, etc.) that have attempted to explain the relationship. For example, epidemiology typically searches for associations between external loading characteristics and reported outcomes, whereas the relationship between external loads and biomechanical loading is usually explored via biomechanical studies (adapted from National Research Council, 1999b).

However, the basic view taken here is that the various methodologies and approaches to exploration are essentially investigating different aspects of the same problem. The figure illustrates the components of the workplace-person interaction that are addressed by these different research approaches. Inherent to this rationale is the idea that there can be many pathways or linkages to injury, and the presence of one pathway does not negate or suggest that there is a lesser association with another potential pathway to injury. The different linkages simply represent different aspects of the same workplace-person *system*. This chapter considers how well these linkages have been established via our review of the literature.

BACK DISORDERS AND THE WORKPLACE

Epidemiologic Evidence

As shown in Figure 10.1, the literature relating to epidemiologic studies of low back disorders has evaluated the linkage between the workplace and low back disorders primarily along two dimensions. First, exposure to external loads in the workplace and its association with low back disorders outcomes has been explored. Second, the association between organizational factors and social context (also called psychosocial factors) has been investigated for their association with low back disorders.

Physical Work Factors

The review of the *observational epidemiology* literature has shown support for the linkage between external load exposure in the workplace and increased low back disorders. Specifically, the review concluded that there is a clear relationship between low back disorders and physical load, frequency of bending and twisting, physically heavy work, and whole-body vibration (with risk ratio estimates up to 9-fold and attributable fractions of between 11 and 66 percent). These findings are reinforced by a review of risk associated with specific industries. For example, industries that tend to impose greater spinal loads on workers, such as patient handling and case distribution in warehouses or distribution centers, present significantly greater risk of low back pain and also greatly benefit from appropriate interventions. When individual physical work risk factors have been identified, and when combinations of these factors (e.g., load location and body postures) have been examined, the relationships between workplace factors and risk become stronger (with risk estimates exceeding 10). Hence, the literature shows that specific components of high-risk jobs (e.g., large load moments) can explain risk in many different types of work environments. These findings further suggest that these are not the only factors that can increase risk, but they must be present at least at some minimal level for risk to increase. Thus, there is a need to quantify the magnitude of risk factors so that the degree of risk can be assessed.

However, while work-related physical load, frequency of bending and twisting, physically heavy work, and whole-body vibration have been implicated in musculoskeletal disorders, evidence for static work postures has been less compelling. Data from different studies did not indicate a relationship between low back disorders and static posture.

Psychosocial Work Factors

The epidemiologic literature that has assessed linkages between psychosocial work factors and low back disorders has also established an association (with risk estimates between 1 and 5). The review of the literature has shown considerable evidence for a relationship between psychological work factors and future back pain. Specifically, evidence has been found for the relationship between low back disorders and job satisfaction, monotonous work, work relations, work demands, stress, and perceived ability to work. While an association between these workplace factors and low back disorder outcomes has been established, these investigations were not designed to delineate an exposure intensity/duration (dose)-response relationship. Still to be explored thoroughly is the interaction between physical and psychosocial work factors in the etiology of low back disorders at work.

Interventions

The intervention literature provides evidence of a different type for the relationship between exposure to work factors and the increased risk of low back disorders. These studies assess the impact of a reduction in physical work factors on reducing low back disorders. The studies reviewed show that a change in the risk of low back disorders was established when changes were made to the physical aspects of work (engineering changes). For example, in manufacturing environments, there is evidence that specific interventions, including lift tables or lift hoists, can be effective in reducing risk. However, the literature also indicates that these interventions will be effective only if they mediate the particular risk factor present in the workplace. With respect to evaluating the mechanisms of effectiveness of these interventions, it has also been shown that the physical changes in the workplace that accompany effective interventions (e.g., lift tables, hoists) can reduce biomechanical loading of the spine in a meaningful way. Thus, appropriate interventions must be sufficiently specific if positive results are to be expected. In addition, the role of psychosocial risk factors was also reinforced, in that changes in the organizational culture (e.g., providing workers with more control over their workplace layout) consistently reduced the rates of low back disorders.

Collectively, these findings establish the linkages represented by arrows going from the "workplace" box to the "outcomes" box in Figure 10.1. Epidemiologic studies, however, do not address the mechanism underlying the workplace-human system response to adverse working conditions. Given that workplace risk factors exist, one would expect that such mechanisms can be explained through other avenues or linkages shown in the figure. Further, relationships among the mechanisms and the role of "dose" must be evaluated through other linkages within this conceptual model.

Biomechanical and Biological Evidence

Our review of the biomechanical and basic biology literature provides a consistent explanation for the linkages established by the epidemiologic literature. Both the physical work factors pathway as well as the psychosocial pathways can be explained by the literature. The biomechanical literature shows that there is abundant evidence for a load-response relationship associated with low back disorders. The biomechanical surveillance literature shows that when workplace exposure is described at a greater level of specificity than is typically available for epidemiologic studies, the findings point consistently to the pathway between work exposure and risk, as well as work exposure and increased loading of the spine. This description includes such factors as precise load location, load moment, spinal load, three-dimensional trunk position, frequency, and kinematics.

Biomechanical modeling efforts over the past two decades have improved significantly to the point at which work exposure can be linked to specific patterns of spine structure loading. The literature also well documents how these loading patterns can cause damage to the pain sensing structures of the spine, including the disc, vertebral body, facet joints, and ligaments. Studies have shown how loading of these structures—at the magnitude associated with some work tasks—can lead to damage of these structures and the perception of pain. For example, spine loading models have been applied to experimental data collected on workers performing tasks that have been shown in epidemiologic studies to be associated with greater risk for low back disorders (for example, patient handling in health care settings, handling cases of material from the floor level). These biomechanical studies indicate that spine loading can exceed the expected spine tolerance during these activities and thus they reinforce the epidemiologic findings. The literature also shows that some level of adaptation occurs in most biological tissue. In sum, infrequent exposure to load increases the risk of low back disorders, moderate exposure reduces risk, and repeated exposure to high loading greatly increases risk of low back disorders. Thus, there appear to be limits of exposure within which risk can be minimized.

Recent biological evidence has also shown that both repeated loading of the spine and higher magnitude of loading can explain deterioration of spinal discs. These findings support the existence of a dose-response relationship of load associated with low back disorders.

Evidence has recently emerged in the scientific literature that points to a mechanism by which psychosocial stress can increase loading of the spine. Increased levels of psychosocial stress appear to act, biomechanically, through increased coactive recruitment of the torso muscles, thereby increasing the loading of the spine. There is also evidence to suggest that exposure to psychosocial stressors may result in greater trunk muscle activity (but not necessarily force) independent of biomechanical load. Psychosocial stressors can also influence pain tolerance and recovery from tissue injury or inflammation. However, further investigations are needed to understand this mechanism of injury more fully.

Individual Factors

Individual factors appear to mediate the biomechanical and biological pathway mechanisms described in Figure 10.1. Some part of the variance in response that has been described in the biomechanical and biological literature appears to be explained by individual host factors that can mediate loading response to external workplace factors as well as mediate tolerances to such loadings. For example, age and gender appear to play a role in determining the magnitude of load tolerance to which the spine may be exposed before damage would be expected. Similarly, differences in spine loading patterns have been documented as a function of gender, experience, and reactions to psychological stress.

Overview

Collectively, these findings have shown that the various linkages in Figure 10.1 between external loads and biomechanical loading of the spine, biomechanical loading and internal tolerances of the spine, and internal tolerances and outcomes (from pain through disability) are well established and provide a plausible pathway between workplace factors and the outcome of low back disorders reported by workers. It is clear that these risk factor pathways are present when the magnitude of the risk factor reaches a specific quantitative level relative to the tissue tolerance level. There is also significant evidence that individual factors such as age, gender, and physical condition play important roles in mediating the response to work factors associated with biomechanical loading and with the tolerance levels for the individual. Thus, the literature also suggests that clear linkages appear in Figure 10.1 between individual factors and biomechanical loading and between individual factors and internal tolerances. Although some literature exists that describes how different individuals respond to pain, the precise mechanisms by which pain is differently experienced among individuals are not well understood.

Collectively, the biomechanical/biological pathway literature agrees well with and independently establishes a causal pathway suggested by the epidemiologic literature. The literature relating to causal factors in work-related low back disorders is coherent and provides ample evidence on how adverse work situations can lead to them.

UPPER EXTREMITY DISORDERS AND THE WORKPLACE

Epidemiologic Evidence

As with low back pain, associations between workplace exposures and upper extremity disorders have considered both physical and psychosocial exposures and evidence provided by intervention studies. The literature on physical exposures documents a strong association between physical factors and upper extremity disorders. The relevant exposures specifically implicated include repetition, force, vibration, and the combinations of repetition and force or repetition and cold. The combination of force and repetition as well as vibration is associated with carpal tunnel syndrome and other disorders of the wrist (relative risk estimates from 2- to 39-fold), and somewhat less strikingly with tendon and muscle-related conditions (relative risk estimates from 3- to 14-fold). The literature on psychosocial factors provides support for an association between high job stress and job demands and upper extremity symptoms. The most dramatic physical exposures occur in manufacturing, food processing, lumber, transportation, and other heavy industries, and these industries have the highest rates of work associated upper extremity disorders (see Chapter 2). However, several epidemiologic studies of physical exposures (force, repetition) and psychosocial exposure (perceived stress, job demands) have documented an elevated risk of upper extremity disorders among computer users. Nonwork-related worry, tension, and psychological distress are also associated with upper extremity symptoms.

Interventions

The epidemiologic findings are complemented by literature on interventions for upper extremity disorders. Several interventions that diminish exposure to force, repetition, and awkward postures have, as hypothesized, reduced upper extremity symptoms. For example, studies have shown that addressing these documented physical risk factors can reduce musculoskeletal symptoms in heavier industries. As discussed in the epidemiologic reviews and the interventions chapter, there is some evidence that using ergonomic principles to modify chairs, workstations, and keyboards can be effective in reducing the prevalence or severity of upper extremity symptoms; in the office setting, results concerning the effects of these interventions on physical findings are mixed. Thus, the exposure-response associations appear to extend robustly across occupation types. Exercise interventions, however, have not been consistently associated with benefit. There is good evidence that interventions are most effective when supported fully by workers and other key stakeholders.

While the epidemiologic literature on psychosocial factors indicates that high levels of job stress and perceived job demands in particular were consistently related to the occurrence of upper extremity symptoms and disorders, few studies have investigated the effects of interventions directed at psychosocial risk factors in workers with these symptoms or disorders. The limited number of worksite studies that have attempted to reduce levels of job stress in workers have reported improvements in a number of nonmusculoskeletal health outcomes. However, the effects of reducing psychosocial job stress on musculoskeletal disorders has not been systematically studied.

Biomechanical and Biological Evidence

The upper extremity biomechanics literature in total reveals a consistent pattern of evidence in support of the pathways illustrated in Figure 10.1. This research supports several components and interactions in the model, including distinct relationships between (1) physical stress factors and external loads in the workplace, (2) external physical loads and internal tissue loads, (3) external physical loads and internal tolerances, and (4) external loads and pain, discomfort, functional limitations, or disability.

Upper extremity exposure to physical stresses (i.e., force, repetition, posture, vibration, and temperature) can be greatly affected by various attributes of work. Force exerted in occupational tasks can be directly affected by the weight of objects handled, frictional characteristics between surfaces grasped and the skin, and the forces required to accomplish tasks. Reductions in the magnitude of the physical attributes of work can produce reductions in exposure to external loads, indicating how physical workplace interventions may directly affect physical stress exposures.

The relationship between external physical loading and internal loads is supported in the literature through biomechanical models that link external forces and postures to tendon loads and the transmission of tendon forces to adjacent anatomical structures. In addition, studies have demonstrated and quantified relationships between exertions and postures and internal loading of the median nerve in the wrist. Additional evidence is provided by electromyographic studies of muscle activity in response to external loads. Several studies have identified an increased risk when the magnitude and duration of two or more physical stresses were considered together.

Evidence for exceeding internal tolerances from loads originated externally comes from physiological studies measuring mechanical strain or fatigue. Further evidence is provided by psychophysical studies of mechanical strain resulting from work in certain postures and exertions. The literature contains numerous studies that have considered multiple properties of forces and posture; however, few studies have dealt with vibration and temperature.

Research reveals short-term effects of pain, discomfort, and limitation of function due to external loads. Although these effects are not necessarily irreversible, the research provides additional support for linkages between external loading and adverse outcomes. Long-term effects of external load are also suggested by cross-sectional studies linking level of external load to upper extremity disorders.

Basic biology studies provide plausible mechanisms for injury to upper extremity tissues (e.g., nerve, tendon, and muscle), and some support for the causality criteria of specificity, temporality, and dose-response. The studies demonstrate damage accumulation in tendon, muscle, and nerve in a dose-response pattern. The endpoints of injury are specific to tissue type and correspond to histological changes observed among patients with related musculoskeletal disorders.

Individual Factors

Individual factors also mediate biological pathways for upper extremity disorders, especially for carpal tunnel syndrome. Nerve function declines with age and other factors (e.g., pregnancy and body mass index). The role of individual factors in mediating the effects of loading on tissues has not been thoroughly investigated.

Overview

The findings of the intervention literature are congruent with those of the basic biology and epidemiology literatures. There is strong support across these bodies of work that high force and repetition are associated with muscloskeletal disorders; in the basic biology data, there is also evidence of alteration of tissue structure. The intervention literature supports the efficacy of tool and workstation design changes, job rotation, and other interventions that directly address these risk factors.

Thus, while the upper extremity literature is less developed than the literature on low back pain, an analogous set of themes emerges, lending further support to the model presented in Figure 10.1. Specifically, external loads and psychosocial factors (components of the "workplace" box) influence outcomes. These exposure-response associations persist when adjusted for individual factors. The basic biology and biomechanics studies provide a plausible basis for the exposure-response relationships. The efficacy of ergonomic interventions further supports the models. The consistent pattern of evidence across these diverse types of studies strengthens the validity of the underlying conceptual model. The pattern of evidence also strengthens the rationale for interventions that ameliorate these exposures.

SUMMARY

By considering collectively the evidence derived from the epidemiology, biomechanics, basic biology, and interventions literatures, we can develop an appreciation for the consistency or pattern of evidence that has emerged from them relating to musculoskeletal disorders in the workplace. Each one of these research approaches has demonstrated relationships between specific components of work exposure and musculoskeletal health. As with all scientific research, however, each approach has limitations. For example, the epidemiologic surveys by work categories or job titles are important because they capture information from large worker populations in actual work settings, but the crudeness of the measure for exposure is not satisfying. Additional epidemiologic studies are available that improve on the measure by asking workers to summarize or average their exposure, but some scientists consider self-reports suspect. Other studies include observations, such as taking an "average" measure of exposure (e.g., researchers observe, in a subsample of workers, the number of lifts and twists per shift and extrapolate to a study population that has the same job category). The biomechanical studies are critical here because both the measure of exposure and the measure of outcome are more closely considered in them. This more refined measure helps to establish confidence in causal inference, but alone, the biomechanical studies do not provide the mechanism.

The basic science studies that document damage and injury mechanisms provide biological plausibility for the associations from the biomechanical studies and epidemiologic studies. The biomechanical studies alone, while elegant, have limitations in that the measurements are more intrusive and obvious than observations in the casual work environment. This intrusiveness limits the generalizability of measures and the implication of findings for the ambient work environment. The epidemiologic findings based on broad population data, however, provide context, indicating that the data from the biomechanics studies are neither isolated nor irrelevant. Although each type of study can be criticized as limited, it is the pattern across the different study designs and types of measures that affects the ability to consider the relationship as causal. Moreover, the strength of the evidence is significantly enhanced by the consistency associated with the pattern of evidence. For example, low back disorder risk has been established through epidemiologic studies for work that involves heavy lifting as well as other risk factors. The relative risks have been derived from a rigorous evaluation of the literature and have been found to be reasonably strong and consistent. Furthermore, the studies control for confounding and indicate a presence of temporal association and dose-response relationships.

The epidemiologic literature that specifically quantifies heavy lifting shows that risk of injury is greatest when loads are lifted from low heights, when the distance of the load from the body is great, and when the torso assumes a flexed, asymmetric posture. Thus, risk estimates significantly increase when work risk factors can be classified with greater precision. These studies typically have relied on more precise endpoints (such as injury logs), but they have limitations to the extent that they have not involved prospective assessments. A number of such studies have the limitation that the results are based on self-reports of injury.

Collectively, a pattern emerges demonstrating that risk is associated with specific characteristics of the workplace. By exploring the biomechanical basis for this risk, the pattern of evidence becomes even stronger. Biomechanical studies have shown that the loading of the spine is increased dramatically when a load is lifted from a low height in an asymmetric posture. According to the basic biology tolerance literature, the spinal load tolerance is also greatly reduced when the torso is positioned in a flexed posture or torsion is applied along the axis of the spine. Basic biological research has also described how spinal loading can lead to cell death within the disc. Furthermore, the basic science literature has described pathways for the perception of pain when specific structures in the spine are loaded under these conditions. Finally, intervention studies have shown how lift tables and lifting hoists are effective in mediating the risk of low back pain in industrial studies. The incorporation of such devices in the workplace permits the load to be raised mechanically, minimizing the load moment and thus reducing the biomechanical loading of the spine. Since risk is lowered when the load is changed from a heavy lift to a light lift, this finding would also be consistent with the rigorous epidemiologic findings. As demonstrated in this example, a pattern of evidence emerges that cuts across independent risk assessment approaches—epidemiologic, biomechanical, basic science, and interventions.

A similar pattern can be described for upper extremity disorders. Biomechanical studies have shown that the extraneural pressure in the carpal tunnel is increased with hand loading and nonneutral wrist postures. Basic science studies demonstrate how extraneural pressures lead to intraneural edema and fibrosis, demyelination, and axon degeneration. These changes in nerve structure cause loss of nerve function. Finally, a recent intervention study has demonstrated that alternative keyboards that reduce nonneutral wrist postures can mediate hand pain in patients with carpal tunnel syndrome.

In conclusion, a clear and strong pattern of evidence emerges after considering the epidemiologic, biomechanical, basic science, and intervention literature collectively. We can conclude with confidence that there is a relationship between exposure to many workplace factors and an increased risk of musculoskeletal disorders.

11

Conclusions and Recommendations

CONCLUSIONS

Based on a comprehensive review and analysis of the evidence, as described above, the panel has reached the following conclusions:

1. Musculoskeletal disorders of the low back and upper extremities are an important national health problem, resulting in approximately 1 million people losing time from work each year. These disorders impose a substantial economic burden in compensation costs, lost wages, and productivity. Conservative cost estimates vary, but a reasonable figure is about $50 billion annually in work-related costs.

2. Estimates of incidence in the general population, as contrasted with the working population, are unreliable because more than 80 percent of the adult population in the United States is in the workforce.

3. Because workplace disorders and individual risk and outcomes are inextricably bound, musculoskeletal disorders should be approached in the context of the whole person rather than focusing on body regions in isolation.

4. The weight of the evidence justifies the identification of certain work-related risk factors for the occurrence of musculoskeletal disorders of the low back and upper extremities.

- The panel concludes that there is a clear relationship between back disorders and physical load; that is, manual material handling, load moment, frequent bending and twisting, heavy physical work, and whole-body vibration. For disorders of the upper extremities, repetition, force, and vibration are particularly important work-related factors.

- Work-related psychosocial factors recognized by the panel to be associated with low back disorders include rapid work pace, monotonous work, low job satisfaction, low decision latitude, and job stress. High job demands and high job stress are work-related psychosocial factors that are associated with the occurrence of upper extremity disorders.

5. A number of characteristics of the individual appear to affect vulnerability to work-related musculoskeletal disorders, including increasing age, gender, body mass index, and a number of individual psychosocial factors. These factors are important as contributing to and modifying influences in the development of pain and disability and in the transition from acute to chronic pain.

6. Modification of the various physical factors and psychosocial factors could reduce substantially the risk of symptoms for low back and upper extremity disorders.

7. The basic biology and biomechanics literatures provide evidence of plausible mechanisms for the association between musculoskeletal disorders and workplace physical exposures.

8. The weight of the evidence justifies the introduction of appropriate and selected interventions to reduce the risk of musculoskeletal disorders of the low back and upper extremities. These include, but are not confined to, the application of ergonomic principles to reduce physical as well as psychosocial stressors. To be effective, intervention programs should include employee involvement, employer commitment, and the development of integrated programs that address equipment design, work procedures, and organizational characteristics.

9. As the nature of work changes in the future, the central thematic alterations will revolve around the diversity of jobs and of workers. Although automation and the introduction of a wide variety of technologies will characterize work in the future, manual labor will remain important. As the workforce ages and as more women enter the workforce, particularly in material handling and computer jobs, evaluation of work tasks, especially lifting, lowering, carrying, prolonged static posture, and repetitive motion, will be required to guide the further design of appropriate interventions.

RECOMMENDATIONS

1. The consequences of musculoskeletal disorders to individuals and society and the evidence that these disorders are to some degree prevent-

able justify a broad, coherent effort to encourage the institution or extension of ergonomic and other preventive strategies. Such strategies should be science based and evaluated in an ongoing manner.

2. To extend the current knowledge base relating both to risk and effective interventions, the Bureau of Labor Statistics should continue to revise its current data collection and reporting system to provide more comprehensive surveillance of work-related musculoskeletal disorders.

- The injury or illness coding system designed by the Bureau of Labor Statistics should be revised to make comparisons possible with health survey data that are based on the widely accepted ICD-9 and ICD-10 coding systems.
- The characterization of exposures associated with musculoskeletal disorders should be refined, including enhanced quantification of risk factors. Currently, exposure is based only on characterization of sources of injury (e.g., tools, instruments, equipment) and type of event (e.g., repetitive use of tools) derived from injury narratives.
- Information collected from each employer should contribute to specificity in denominators for jobs including job-specific demographic features in the workplace, such as age, gender, race, time on the job and occupation.
- Injury and illness information should include, in addition to the foregoing demographic variables, other critical variables, such as event, source, nature, body part involved, time on job, and rotation schedule. Combining these with the foregoing variables would, with appropriate denominator information, allow calculation of rates rather than merely counts or proportions, as is now the case for all lost-workday events.
- Resources should be allocated to include details on non-lost-workday injuries or illnesses (as currently provided on lost-workday injuries) to permit tracking of these events in terms of the variables now collected only for lost-workday injuries (age, gender, race, occupation, event, source, nature, body part, time on job).

3. The National Center for Health Statistics and the National Institute for Occupational Safety and Health should include measures of work exposures and musculoskeletal disorder outcomes in ongoing federal surveys (e.g., the National Health Interview Surveys, the National Health and Nutritional Examinations), and NIOSH should repeat, at least decennially, the National Occupational Exposure Survey.

- To upgrade and improve passive industry surveillance of musculoskeletal disorders and workplace exposures, the National Institute for Occupational Safety and Health should develop adaptable surveillance packages with associated training and disseminate these to interested industries.

- To provide more active surveillance opportunity, the National Institute for Occupational Safety and Health should develop a model surveillance program that provides ongoing and advanced technical assistance with timely, confidential feedback to participating industries.

4. The National Institute for Occupational Safety and Health should take the lead in developing uniform definitions of musculoskeletal disorders for use in clinical diagnosis, epidemiologic research, and data collection for surveillance systems. These definitions should (1) include clear and consistent endpoint measures, (2) agree with consensus codification of clinically relevant classification systems, and (3) have a biological and clinical basis.

5. In addition to these recommendations, the panel recommends a research agenda that includes developing (1) improved tools for exposure assessment, (2) improved measures of outcomes and case definitions for use in epidemiologic and intervention studies, and (3) further quantification of the relationship between exposures and outcomes. Also included are suggestions for studies in each topic area: tissue mechanobiology, biomechanics, psychosocial stressors, epidemiology, and workplace interventions. The research agenda is presented in Chapter 12.

ADDITIONAL CONSIDERATIONS

Because of the importance of continued data collection and research to further elucidate the causes and prevention of musculoskeletal disorders of the low back and upper extremities, the panel believes it would be useful for relevant government agencies, including the National Institute for Occupational Safety and Health, the Occupational Safety and Health Administration, and the National Institute of Arthritis and Musculoskeletal and Skin Diseases to consider the following program initiatives.

1. Expanding research support and mechanisms to study musculoskeletal disorders in terms of risk factors at work, early detection, and effective methods of prevention and their cost effectiveness. Some examples include:

- Developing new mechanisms and linkages among funding agencies (e.g., the National Institute for Occupational Safety and Health, the National Institute of Arthritis and Musculoskeletal and Skin Diseases) to expand ongoing basic research on relevant tissues (e.g., skeletal muscle, tendon, peripheral nerve) to promote study of those parameters that are directly relevant to work-related musculoskeletal disorders.

- Creating mechanisms to stimulate collaboration and cross-training of researchers in the basic and applied sciences directly relevant to work-related musculoskeletal disorders.
- Developing mechanisms to promote research jointly conducted by industry and the relevant academic disciplines on work-related musculoskeletal disorders.

2. Expanding considerably research training relevant to musculoskeletal disorders, particularly with relation to graduate programs in epidemiology, occupational health, occupational psychology, and ergonomics, to produce additional individuals with research training.

3. Expanding education and training programs to assist workers and employers (particularly small employers) in understanding and utilizing the range of possible workplace interventions designed to reduce musculoskeletal disorders. In addition, consideration should be given to expanding continuing education (e.g., NIOSH Education and Research and Training Projects) for a broad range of professionals concerning risk factors that contribute to musculoskeletal disorders inside and outside the workplace.

4. Developing mechanisms for cooperative studies among industry, labor unions, and academia, including:

- Establishing a database of and mechanism for communicating "best practices."
- Providing incentives for industry and union cooperation with due regard for proprietary considerations and administrative barriers.
- Encouraging funding for such studies from industry, labor, academia, and government sources.

5. Revising administrative procedures to promote joint research funding among agencies.

6. Encouraging the exchange of scientific information among researchers interested in intervention research through a variety of mechanisms. Areas that could benefit include the development of (1) research methodologies, especially improved measurement of outcomes and exposures, covariates, and costs and (2) uniform approaches, allowing findings to be compared across studies. In addition, periodic meetings

should be considered to bring together individuals with scientific and "best practices" experience.

In order to implement these suggestions, the scope of research and training activities of the National Institute for Occupational Safety and Health would have to be expanded and funding significantly increased. In addition, other federal agencies (e.g., the National Institute of Arthritis and Musculoskeletal and Skin Diseases, the National Institute of Mental Health) would have to broaden their support of research programs examining musculoskeletal disorders and the workplace. In the panel's view these steps deserve serious consideration.

12

Research Agenda

In the course of its review, the panel identified several important gaps in the science base. The suggestions included in this research agenda are presented in two sections. The first section contains the recommended research for improving methodology—better tools for exposure and outcome assessment as well as further quantification of the relationship between exposures and outcomes. The second section contains research recommendations for specific topic areas, including tissue mechanobiology, biomechanics, psychosocial factors and stress, epidemiology, and workplace interventions.

METHODOLOGICAL RESEARCH

1. Develop improved tools for exposure (dose) assessment.

• Develop practical and consistent methods for objectively measuring physical stress (force, motion, vibration, and temperature) in the workplace and for quantifying occupational exposure (magnitude, repetition, and duration) with precision and accuracy. Use this method to understand the quantitative exposure- or dose-response relationships between (1) exposure to external loads in the workplace and the resultant three-dimensional internal loads and physiological responses and (2) exposure to external loads in the workplace and pain, discomfort, impairment, and disability. Explorations of these relationships must consider interactions and combinations of physical stress factors.

• Develop valid measures of psychosocial exposures that can be used in epidemiologic research and conduct prospective studies on the effects of psychosocial variables on the occurrence, exacerbation, and persistence of musculoskeletal disorders using these well-defined and validated measures of exposure.

2. Develop improved measures of outcomes and case definitions for use in epidemiologic and intervention studies. These should include but not be limited to:

- Develop prognostic tools to identify clinical cases at increased risk for poorer outcomes and to tailor interventions to identified risk factors (e.g., ergonomic stressors, job stress).
- Develop tools and measures that are capable of quantifying the extent of a musculoskeletal disorder with adequate precision so that they can be used as precise dependent measures for prospective epidemiologic studies involving the workplace.
- Further develop and refine standardized survey instruments to identify symptomatic musculoskeletal outcomes with adequate sensitivity and specificity for use in epidemiologic studies in work environments.
- Further develop and refine physical examination and sensory discrimination criteria to identify musculoskeletal outcomes with adequate specificity and sensitivity for use in epidemiologic studies in work environments.
- Develop and refine epidemiologic case definitions of musculoskeletal disorders with adequate sensitivity and specificity for epidemiologic study in work environments. Case definitions that rely solely on self-report information are particularly useful for large survey studies. Case definitions that use both self-report and physical examination data are needed for more detailed studies.
- As these criteria evolve, particular attention needs to be paid to nonspecific pain syndromes that are not congruent with established clinical syndromes. There is a need to develop an appropriate classification of subgroups of nonspecific pain syndromes in order to carry out more effective epidemiologic studies of these syndromes.
- Further develop and refine physiological measures appropriate for use in epidemiologic studies that measure relevant features of the various musculoskeletal disorders, including for example, nerve conduction testing.
- Develop and evaluate definitions of musculoskeletal disorders currently used in epidemiologic studies to identify the best symptom-based and physical exam-based criteria for musculoskeletal disorders that can be recommended as the standards for use in epidemiologic studies of the different syndromes in the work environment.

3. In studies of humans, further quantify the relationships between exposures and outcomes, including:

- Dose-response relationships across the full range of relevant exposures in the context of work.
- Host factors, such as age, sex, previous injury, comorbidity, smoking, and physical condition.
- Interaction of physical and psychosocial factors.

TOPIC AREA RESEARCH

1. Conduct tissue mechanobiology studies directed toward:

- Characterizing ultrastructural and cellular responses to cyclical physical loading exposure for vertebrae/disc, upper extremity tendon and muscle, and peripheral nerve using in vivo (animal) models. This involves:

    —Determining time frame, capacity, and mechanisms of the repair and remodeling responses associated with cyclic loading and injury, including the effect of various patterns of rest and reuse after injury on the mechanisms and time course of recovery.

    —Developing quantitative dose-response models identifying dose-response relationships for injury for tendons, muscles, and nerves.

    —Determining the dose-response relationships between pattern of load (e.g., rate of loading, duty cycle) for repeated loading and functional and structural damage to discs, tendons, muscles, and nerves.

    —Developing an in vivo upper extremity loading model for neuromuscular disorders for the evaluation of mechanisms of injury associated with cyclical loading. Determining the missing steps of the injury pathways associated with repeated loading, especially for muscles, tendons, and nerves. Determining the role of conditioning and health on injury susceptibility.

    —Identifying injury thresholds for sustained and repeated loading (e.g., load duration or load repetition) for disc, tendon, and muscle.

    —Determining thresholds for critical pressure duration for chronic nerve injury.

    —Determining the earliest molecular changes that precede structural damage and inflammatory responses to muscles, tendons, ligaments, bones, and nerves during various types of repetitive loading.

    —Validating noninvasive measures of skeletal muscle functional changes and symptoms associated with repetitive use disorders by establishing their biological basis in controlled scientific studies, with the goal of identifying a noninvasive means of detecting a skeletal muscle damage threshold.

• Determining whether the injury response of muscle, disc, tendon and nerve to repeated loading has more to do with the rate of loading, peak loads, duration, or some other factor. This involves:

—Determining differences among tissues in response to loading.
—Determining the role of conditioning and age in modifying this response.

• Identifying sources and mechanisms of discogenic, muscular, and tendon-related pain, especially as related to the ultrastructural injury and biochemical alterations associated with physical loading.

2. Biomechanical studies directed toward:

• Investigating the role of repetition, change in workshift, and variable repetition patterns (as experienced during work rotation) on changes in loading patterns and tolerance limits for joints and soft tissue.
• Quantifying the relationship between loading of a joint or tendon and the pain process.
• Exploring the influence of psychological stress (including psychosocial) on musculoskeletal response and the mechanical loading of joints.

3. Psychosocial studies directed toward:

• Investigating the mechanisms through which psychosocial stressors contribute to or impact work-related musculoskeletal disorders and the biological basis for such associations.

4. Epidemiologic studies directed toward:

• Taking advantage of existing and newly developed measures of exposure and outcome to undertake longitudinal studies of musculoskeletal disorders directed toward:

—Clarifying the natural history of musculoskeletal disorders resulting from physical and psychosocial work exposures, focusing on both clinical and functional outcomes.
—Examining the separate and interacting influence of physical and psychosocial work stressors in the etiology of musculoskeletal disorders.

—Developing prognostic indicators with the necessary predictive value to guide decisions about return-to-work.

—Determining the length of latency periods between exposures sufficient to permit recovery or repair of tissue or cell damage.

—Defining the effects of various interventions.

—Defining the influence of worker factors, including comorbidity and obesity.

• Investigating the independent and combined contribution of individual psychosocial (e.g., coping styles, stress vulnerability, personal sources of support) and workplace psychosocial (i.e., supervisor support, control, workload, deadlines) variables on symptoms and functional outcomes.

5. Workplace interventions studies directed toward:

• Conducting rigorous evaluations of workplace interventions including but not limited to randomized controlled trials or other scientifically valid approaches.

• Promoting investigation of multifactorial interventions.

• Developing effective methods to measure the efficacy and cost-effectiveness of interventions on the reduction of workplace injuries.

• Coordinating studies of interventions between the research community and industry.

• Validating techniques, standards, and manuals for target industries.

References

Aaräs, A.
   1994   The impact of ergonomics intervention on individual health and corporate prosperity in a telecommunications environment. *Ergonomics* 37:1679-1696.

Aaräs, A., O. Ro, and M. Thoresen
   1999   Can a more neutral position of the forearm when operating a computer mouse reduce the pain level for visual display unit operators? A prospective epidemiological intervention study. (Reprint). *International Journal of Human-Computer Interaction* 11(2):79-94.

Aaräs, A., K.I. Fostervoid, O. Ro, M. Thoresen, and S. Larsen
   1997   Postural load during VDU work: A comparison between various work postures. *Ergonomics* 40(11):1255-1268.

Abrahams, M.
   1967   Mechanical behavior of tendon in vitro: A preliminary report. *Medical and Biological Engineering* 5:433.

Accredited Standards Committee
   2000   ASC Z-365 New Proposed Standard: Control of Cumulative Trauma Disorders. National Safety Council, Secretariat, June 10.

Adams, M., and P. Dolan
   1995   Recent advances in lumbar spinal mechanics and their clinical significance. *Clinical Biomechanics* (Bristol, Avon) 10(1):3-19.

Adams, M.A., and W.C. Hutton
   1985   Gradual disc prolapse. *Spine* 10(6):524-531.
   1982   Prolapsed intervertebral disc. A hyperflexion injury. *Spine* 7(3):184-191.
   1981   The relevance of torsion to the mechanical derangement of the lumbar spine. *Spine* 6(3):241-248.

Adams, M.A., W.C. Hutton, and J.E.E. Scott
   1980   The resistance to flexion of the lumbar intervertebral joint. *Spine* 5:245-253.

Adams, M.A., A.F. Mannion, and P. Dolan
   1999   Personal risk factors for first-time low back pain. *Spine* 24:2497-2505.

Adams, M.A., P. Dolan, et al.
   1987   Diurnal variations in the stresses on the lumbar spine. *Spine* 12:130-137.

Adams, M.A., P. Dolan, et al.
  1988 The lumbar spine in backwards bending. *Spine* 13(9):1019-1026.
Adams, M.A., T.P. Green, et al.
  1994 The strength in anterior bending of lumbar intervertebral discs. *Spine* 19(9):2197-2203.
Ahlberg Hultén, G.K., T. Theorell, and F. Sigala
  1995 Social support, job strain and musculoskeletal pain among female health care personnel. *Scandinavian Journal of Work, Environment, and Health* 21:435-439.
Alcouffe, J., P. Manillier, M. Brehier, C. Fabin, and F. Faupin
  1999 Analysis by sex of low back pain among workers from small companies in the Parisk area: Severity and occupational consequences. *Occupational and Environmental Medicine* 56:696-701.
An, K.N., Y. Ueba, E.Y Chao, W.P. Cooney, and R.L. Linscheid
  1983 Tendon excursion and moment arm of index finger muscles. *Journal of Biomechanics* 16:419-425.
Anderson, C.K., D.B. Chaffin, and G.D. Herrin
  1986 A study of lumbosacral orientation under varied static loads. *Spine* 11(5):456-462.
Anderson, J.A.D.
  1984 Shoulder pain and tension neck and their relation to work. *Scandinavian Journal of Work, Environment, and Health* 19(6):435-442.
Andersson, G.B.
  1997 The epidemiology of spinal disorders. Pp. 93-141 in *The Adult Spine: Principles and Practice*, J.W. Frymoyer, ed. Philadelphia, PA: Lippincott-Raven Publishers.
Andrews, D.M., R.W. Norman, and R.P. Wells
  1996 Accuracy and repeatability of low back pain compression force estimates from self-reports of body posture during load handling. *International Journal of Industrial Ergonomics* 18:251-260.
Antonacchi, M.D., D. Mody, et al.
  1998 Innervation of the human vertebral body: A histologic study. *Journal of Spinal Disorders* 11(6):526-531.
Arad, D., and M.D. Ryan
  1986 The incidence and prevalence in nurses of low back pain. *Australian Nurses Journal* 16:44-48.
Archambault, J.M., J.P. Wiley, and R.C. Bray
  1995 Exercise loading of tendons and the development of overuse injuries. A review of current literature. *Sports Medicine* 20(2):77-89.
Ariens, G.A.M., W. van Mechelen, P.M. Bongers, L.M. Bouter, and G. van der Wal
  2000 Physical risk factors for neck pain. *Scandinavian Journal of Work, Environment, and Health* 26:7-19.
Armstrong, T.J., and D.B. Chaffin
  1978 An investigation of the relationship between displacements of the finger and wrist joints and the extrinsic finger flexor tendons. *Journal of Biomechanics* 11:119-128.
  1979 Some biomechanical aspects of the carpal tunnel. *Journal of Biomechanics* 12:567-569.
Armstrong, R.B., R.W. Ogilvie, and J.A. Schwane
  1983 Eccentric exercise-induced injury to rat skeletal muscle. *Journal of Applied Physiology: Respiratory, Environmental, and Exercuse Physiology* 54:80-93.
Armstrong, T.J., L. Punnett, and P. Ketner
  1989 Subjective worker assessments of hand tools used in automobile assembly. *American Industrial Hygiene Association Journal* 50:639-645.

Armstrong, R.G., G.L. Warren, and J.A. Warren
 1991   Mechanisms of exercise-induced muscle fibre injury. *Sports Medicine* 12:184-207.
Armstrong, T.J., L.J. Fine, R.G. Radwin, and B.S. Silverstein
 1987   Ergonomics and the effects of vibration in hand-intensive work. *Scandinavian Journal of Work, Environment, and Health* 13:286-289.
Armstrong, T.J., J.A. Foulke, B.S. Joseph, and S.A. Goldstein
 1982   Investigation of cumulative trauma disorders in a poultry processing plant. *American Industrial Hygiene Association Journal* 43:103-116.
Armstrong, T.J., R.G. Radwin, D.J. Hansen, and K.W. Kennedy
 1986   Repetitive trauma disorders: Job evaluation and design. *Human Factors* 28(3):325-336.
Armstrong, T.J., R.A. Werner, W.P. Waring, and J.A. Foulke
 1991   Intra-carpal canal pressure in selected hand tasks: A pilot study. Pp. 156-158 in *Designing for Everyone, Proceedings of the Eleventh Congress of the International Ergonomics Association*. London: Taylor & Francis.
Armstrong, T.J., J.A. Foulke, B.J. Martin, J. Gerson, and D.M. Rempel
 1994   Investigation of applied forces in alphanumeric keyboard work. *American Industrial Hygiene Association Journal* 55(1):30-35.
Armstrong T.J., P. Buckle, L. Fine, M. Hagberg, B. Jonsson, A. Kilbom, I.A.A. Kuorinka, B.A. Silverstein, G. Sjøgaard, and E.R.A. Viikari-Juntura
 1993   A conceptual model for work-related neck and upper-limb musculoskeletal disorders. *Scandinavian Journal of Work, Environment, and Health* 19:73-84.
Arndt, R.
 1987   Work pace, stress, and cumulative trauma disorders. *Journal of Hand Surgery* 12:866-869.
Atroshi, I., C. Gummesson, R. Johnsson, E. Ornstein, J. Ranstam, and I. Rosen
 1999   Prevalence of carpal tunnel syndrome in a general population. *Journal of the American Medical Association* 282(2):153-158.
Babenko, V., T. Graven-Nielsen, P. Svensson, A.M. Drewes, T.S. Jensen, and L. Arendt-Nielsen
 1999   Experimental human muscle pain and muscular hyperalgesia induced by combinations of serotonin and bradykinin. *Pain* 82:1-8.
Backman, C., L. Boquist, J. Fridén, R. Lorentzon, and G. Toolanen
 1990   Chronic achilles paratenonitis with tendinosis: An experimental model in the rabbit. *Journal of Orthopaedic Research* 8(4):541-547.
Bai, Y.H., M. Takemitsu, and Y. Takemitsu
 1998   Pathology study of rabbit calf muscles after repeated compression. *Journal of Orthopaedic Science* 3:209-215.
Baidya, K.N., and M.G. Stevenson
 1988   Local muscle fatigue in repetitive work. *Ergonomics* 31:227-239.
Bainbridge, L.
 1983   Ironies of automation. *Automatica* 19(9):775-779.
Baldwin, M.L.
 2000   Musculoskeletal disorders and work disability: The role of socioeconomic factors. Paper prepared for the National Academy of Sciences Panel on Musculoskeletal Disorders and the Workplace.
Balnave, C.D., D.F. Davey, and D.G. Allen
 1997   Distribution of sarcomere length and intracellular calcium in mouse skeletal muscle following stretch-induced injury. *Journal of Physiology* 502:649-659.

Bao, S., S.E. Mathiassen, and J. Winkel
  1996 Ergonomic effects of a management-based rationalization in assembly work—A case study. *Applied Ergonomics* 27:89-99.
Barsky, A.J., and J.F. Borus
  1999 Functional somatic syndromes. *Annals of Internal Medicine* 130:910-921.
  1995 Somatization and medicalization in the era of managed care. *Journal of the American Medical Association* 274:1931-1934.
Bass, E.
  1999 Biaxial Nonlinear Elastic Response of the Human Lumbar Annulus Fibrosus and its Role in the Determination of a Physiologically Relevant Consitutive Relation. Ph.D. thesis, University of California, Berkeley.
Batt, R.
  1999 Work organization, technology, and performance in customer service and sales. *Industrial and Labor Relations* 52.4:532-564.
Battie, M.C., S.J. Bigos, et al.
  1989 Isometric lifting strength as a predictor of industrial back pain reports. *Spine* 14(8):851-856.
Batra, S., L.A. Bronkema, M.J. Wany, and R.R. Bishu
  1994 Glove attributes: Can they predict performance? *International Journal of Industrial Ergonomics* 14:201-209.
Baum, A., and D.M. Posluszny
  1999 Health psychology: Mapping behavioral contributions to health and illness. *Annual Review of Psychology* 50:137-163.
Bean, J.C., D.B. Chaffin, and A.B. Schultz
  1988 Biomechanical model calculation of muscle contraction forces: a double linear programming method. *Journal of Biomechanics* 21(1):59-66.
Belkin, M., W.L. LaMorte, J.G. Wright, and R.W. Hobson, 2nd
  1989 The role of leukocytes in the pathophysiology of skeletal muscle ischemic injury. *Journal of Vascular Surgery* 19(1):14-18.
Bemben, M.G.
  1998 Age-related alterations in musuclar endurance. *Sports Medicine* 25:259-269.
Bendix, A.F., T. Bendix, C. Lund, S. Kirkbak, and S. Ostenfeld
  1997 Comparison of three intensive programs for chronic low back pain patients: A prospective, randomized, observer-blinded study with one-year follow-up. *Scandinavian Journal of Work, Environment, and Health* 29(2):81-89.
Bergenuud, H., and B. Nilsson
  1988 Occupational workload and psychologic factors: An epidemiologic survey. *Spine* 13:58-60.
Bergenuud, H., F. Lindgärde, B. Nilsson, and C.J. Petersson
  1988 Shoulder pain in middle age: A study of prevalence and relation to occupational work load and psychosocial factors. *Clinical Orthop Rel Research* 231:234-238.
Bergqvist, U.
  1995 Visual display terminal work: A perspective on long term changes and discomforts. *International Journal of Industrial Ergonomics* 16:201-209.
Bergqvist, U., E. Wolgast, B. Nilsson, and M. Voss
  1995a The influence of VDT work on musculoskeletal disorders. *Ergonomics* 38(4):754-762.
  1995b Musculoskeletal disorders among visual display terminal workers: Individual, ergonomics, and work organizational factors. *Ergonomics* 38(4):763-776.

Bernacki, E., J. Guidera, J. Schaefer, R. Lavin, and S. Tsai

1999 An ergonomics program designed to reduce the incidence of upper extremity work related musculoskeletal disorders. *Journal of Environmental Medicine* 41(12):1032-1041.

Bernard, B.P.

1997a Work-related musculoskeletal disorders and psychosocial factors. In *Musculoskeletal Disorders and Workplace Factors: A Criticial Review of Epidemiologic Evidence for Work-Related Musculoskeletal Disorders of the Neck, Upper Extremity, and Low Back*, B.P. Bernard, ed. Publication No. 97-141. National Institute for Occupational Safety and Health. Cincinnati, OH: U.S. Department of Health and Human Services.

Bernard, B.P., ed.

1997b *Musculoskeletal Disorders and Workplace Factors: A Criticial Review of Epidemiologic Evidence for Work-Related Musculoskeletal Disorders of the Neck, Upper Extremity, and Low Back.* Publication No. 97-141. National Institute for Occupational Safety and Health. Cincinnati, OH: U.S. Department of Health and Human Services.

Bernard, B., S. Sauter, L. Fine, M. Petersen, and T. Hales

1994 Job task and psychosocial risk factors for work-related musculoskeletal disorders among newspaper employees. *Scandinavian Journal of Work, Environment, and Health* 20:417-426.

Biddle, J., K. Roberts, D.D. Rosenman, and E.M. Welch

1998 What percentage of workers with work-related illnesses receive workers' compensation benefits? *Journal of Occupational and Environmental Medicine* 40(4):325-331.

Biering-Sörensen, F., C.E. Thomsen, and J. Hilden

1989 Risk indicators for low back trouble. *Scandinavian Journal of Rehabilitation Medicine* 21:151-157.

Bigland-Ritchie, B., F. Furbush, and J.J. Woods

1986 Fatigue of intermittent submaximal voluntary contractions: Central and peripheral factors. *Journal of Applied Physiology* 61(2):421-429.

Bigos, S.J., D.M. Spengler, et al.

1986 Back injuries in industry: A retrospective study. II. Injury factors. *Spine* 11(3):246-251.

Bigos, S.J., M.C. Battie, et al.

1992 A longitudinal, prospective study of industrial back injury reporting. *Clinical Orthopaedics* 279:21-34.

Bigos, S.J., M.C. Battie, D.M. Spengler, et al.

1991 A prospective study of work perceptions and psychosocial factors affecting the report of back injury. *Spine* 16:1-6.

Birch, H.L., A.J. Bailey, and A.E. Goodship

1998 Macroscopic "degeneration" of equine superficial digital flexor tendon is accompanied by a change in extracellular matrix composition. *Equine Veterinary Journal* 30(6):534-539.

Birch, H.L., A.M. Wilson, and A.E. Goodship

1997 The effect of exercise-induced localised hypothermia on tendon cell survival. *Journal of Experimental Biology* 200(Part 11):1703-1708.

Blackwell, J.R., K.W. Kornatz, and E.M. Heath

1999 Effect of grip span on maximal force and fatigue of flexor digitorum superficialis. *Applied Ergonomics* 30:401-405.

Boden, L.I., and M. Galizzi

1999 Economic consequences of workplace injuries: Lost earnings and benefit adequacy. *American Journal of Industrial Medicine* 36(5):487-503.

Bogduk, N.
  1995 The anatomical basis for spinal pain syndromes. *Journal of Manipulative Physiological Therapy* 18(9):603-605.
  1991 The lumbar disc and low back pain. *Neurosurgery Clinics of North America* 2(4):791-806.

Bongers, P.M., C.R. de Winter, M.A. Kompier, and V.H. Hildebrandt
  1993 Psychosocial factors at work and musculoskeletal disease. *Scandinavian Journal of Work, Environment, and Health* 19(5):297-312.

Bongers, P.M., C.T.J. Hulshof, L. Dijkstra, H.C. Boshuizen, H.J.M. Groenhout, and E. Valken
  1990 Back pain and exposure to whole body vibration in helicopter pilots. *Ergonomics* 33:1007-1026.

Bongiovanni, L.G., K.E. Hagbarth, and L. Stjernberg
  1990 Prolonged muscle vibration reducing motor output in maximal voluntary contractions in man. *Journal of Physiology* 423:15-26.

Bonsall, J.L., J.E. Squier, C.A. Baron, and G. Parker
  1991 Effect of physiotherapy on sickness absence in industry: A comparative study. *Journal of Social and Occupational Medicine* 41(4):176-180.

Borg, G.A.
  1982 Psychophysical bases of perceived exertion. *Medicine and Science in Sports and Exercise* 14(5):377-381.

Boshuizen, H.C., P.M. Bongers, and C.T.J. Hulshof
  1990 Self-reported back pain in tractor drivers exposed to whole-body vibration. *International Archives of Occupational and Environmental Health* 62:109-115.
  1992 Self-reported back pain in fork-lift truck and freight-container tractor drivers exposed to whole-body vibration. *Spine* 17:59-65.

Bovenzi, M.
  1994 Italian study group on physical hazards in the stone industry. Hand-arm vibration syndrome and dose-response relation for vibration induced white finger among quarry drillers and stonecarvers. *Occupational and Environmental Medicine* 51:603-611.

Bovenzi, M., and A. Betta
  1994 Low-back disorders in agricultural tractor drivers exposed to whole-body vibration and postural stress. *Applied Ergonomics* 25:231-241.

Bovenzi, M., and A. Zadini
  1992 Self-reported low back symptoms in urban bus drivers exposed to whole-body vibration. *Spine* 17:1048-1059.

Bovenzi, M., A. Fiorito, and C. Volpe
  1987 Bone and joint disorders in the upper extremities of chipping and grinding operators. *International Archives of Occupational and Environmental Health* 59:189-198.

Bovenzi, M., A. Franzinelli, and F. Strambi
  1988 Prevalence of vibration-induced white finger and assessment of vibration exposure among travertine workers in Italy. *International Archives of Occupational and Environmental Health* 61:25-34.

Bovenzi, M., L. Petronio, and F. Di Marino
  1980 Epidemiological survey of shipyard workers exposed to hand-arm vibration. *International Archives of Occupational and Environmental Health* 46(3):251-266.

Bovenzi, M., A. Zadini, A. Franzinelli, and F. Borgogni
  1991 Occupational musculoskeletal disorders in the neck and upper limbs of forestry workers exposed to hand-arm vibration. *Ergonomics* 34(5):547-562.

Bovenzi, M., A. Franzinelli, R. Mancini, M.G. Cannavà, M. Maiorano, and F. Ceccarelli
  1995 Dose-response relation for vascular disorders induced by vibration in the fingers of forestry workers. *Occupational and Environmental Medicine* 52:722-730.

Braithwaite, I., J. White, et al.

1998   Vertebral end-plate (Modic) changes on lumbar spine MRI: Correlation with pain reproduction at lumbar discography. *European Spine Journal* 7(5):363-368.

Brantley, P.J., L.S. Dietz, G.T. McKnight, G.N. Jones, and R. Tulley

1988   Convergence between the Daily Stress Inventory and endocrine measures of stress. *Journal of Consulting and Clinical Psychology* 56:549-551.

Brinckmann, P.

1985   Pathology of the vertebral column. *Ergonomics* 28:77-80.

Brinckmann, P., M. Biggemann, and D. Hilweg

1988   Fatigue fracture of human lumbar vertebrae. *Clinical Biomechanics* (Bristol, Avon) 3(Suppl. 1): S1-S23.

Brinckmann, P., M. Biggemann, and D. Hilweg

1989a Prediction of the compressive strength of human lumbar vertebrae. *Clinical Biomechanics 4* (Bristol, Avon)(Suppl. 2):S1-S27.

Brinckmann, P., M. Biggemann, et al.

1989b Prediction of the compressive strength of human lumbar vertebrae. *Spine* 14:606-610.

Brisson, C., S. Montreuil, and L. Punnett

1999   Effects of an ergonomic training program on workers with video display units. *Scandinavian Journal of Work, Environment, and Health* 25:255-263

Brooks, S.V., and J.A. Faulkner

1988   Contractile properties of skeletal muscles from young, adult, and aged mice. *Journal of Physiology* 404:71-82.

1990   Contraction-induced injury: Recovery of skeletal muscles in young and old mice. *American Journal of Physiology* 258:C436-C442.

1994   Skeletal muscle weakness in old age: Underlying mechanisms. *Medicine and Science in Sports and Exercise* 26(4):432-439.

1996   The magnitude of the initial injury induced by stretches of maximally activated muscle fibres of mice and rats increases in old age. *Journal of Physiology* 497:573-580.

Brooks, S.V., E. Zerba, and J.A. Faulkner

1995   Injury to muscle fibres after single stretches of passive and maximally stimulated muscles in mice. *Journal of Physiology* 488:459-469.

Brown, M., and E.M. Hasser

1996   Complexity of age-related change in skeletal muscle. *Journal of Gerontology* Series A, Biological Sciences and Medical Sciences 51:B117-B123.

Brown, M.F., M.V. Hukkanen, et al.

1997   Sensory and sympathetic innervation of the vertebral endplate in patients with degenerative disc disease. *Journal of Bone and Joint Surgery* 79B(1):147-153.

Bru, E., and R.J. Mykletun

1996   Work related stress and musculoskeletal pain among female hospital staff. *Work and Stress* 10(4):309-321.

Brubaker, R.L., C.J.G. Mackenzie, P.R. Eng, and D.V. Bates

1983   Vibration white finger disease among tree fellers in British Columbia. *Journal of Occupational Medicine* 25(5):403-408.

Bruce, S.A., D. Newton, and R.C. Woledge

1989   Effect of age on voluntary force and cross-sectional area of human adductor pollicis muscle. *Quarterly Journal of Experimental Physiology* 74:359-362.

Buchholz, B., V. Paquet, L. Punnett, et al.

1996   PATH: A work sampling-based approach to ergonomic job analysis for construction work. *Applied Ergonomics* 27:177-187.

Buckwalter, J.A.
    1995 Aging and degeneration of the human intervertebral disc. *Spine* 20(11):1307-1314.
Budros, A.
    1999 A conceptual framework for analyzing why organizations downsize. *Organizational Science* 10(1):69-82.
Burdorf, A., and J. Laan
    1991 Comparison of three methods for the assessment of postural load on the back. *Scandinavian Journal of Work, Environment, and Health* 17:425-429.
Burdorf, A., and A. Monster
    1991 Exposure to vibration and self-reported health complaints of riveters in the aircraft industry. *Annals of Occupational Hygiene* 35(3):287-298.
Burdorf, A., G. Govaert, and L. Elders
    1991 Postural load and back pain of workers in the manufacturing of prefabricated concrete elements. *Ergonomics* 34(7):909-918.
Burdorf, A., A. Naaktgeboren, and H.C.W.M. de Groot
    1993 Occupational risk factors for low back pain among sedentary workers. *Journal of Occupational Medicine* 35:1213-1220.
Burdorf, A., M. van Riel, and T. Brand
    1997 Physical load as risk factor for musculoskeletal complaints among tank terminal workers. *American Industrial Hygiene Association Journal* 58:489-497.
Bureau of the Census
    1999 March Current Population Survey. http://www.bls.census.gov/cps/ads1999/sdata.htm
Bureau of Labor Statistics
    1999a Survey of Occupational Injuries and Illnesses. Washington, DC: U.S. Department of Labor.
    1999b Table 5. Civilian labor force 16 years and older by sex, age, race, and Hispanic origin, 1988, 1998, and projected 2008. http://stats.bls.gov/news.release/ecopro.t05.htm.
    2000a Table B-2. Average weekly hours of production or nonsupevisory workers on private nonfarm payrolls by industry. http://stats.bls.gov/news.release/empsit.t12.htm.
    2000b The employment situation: June 2000. *Bureau of Labor Statistics News* July 7.
Burstrom, L.
    1997 The influence of biodynamic factors on the mechanical impedance of the hand and arm. *International Archives of Occupational and Environmental Health* 69(6):437-446.
    1990 Measurements of the impedance of the hand and arm. *International Archives of Occupational and Environmental Health* 62:431-439.
Burstrom, L., and R. Lundstrom
    1988 Mechanical energy absorption in human hand-arm exposed to sinusoidal vibration. *International Archives of Ocupational and Environmental Health* 61:213-216.
Burton, A.K., K.M. Tillotson, C.J. Main, and S. Hollis
    1995 Psychosocial predictors of outcome in acute and subchronic low back trouble. *Spine* 20(6):722-728.
Buseck, M.D., O.D. Schipplein, G.B.J. Andersson, and T.P. Andriacchi
    1988 Influence of dynamic factors and external loads on the moment at the lumbar spine in lifting. *Spine* 13:918-921.
Business Week
    1991 The quality imperative. Special Issue, October 25.

Bystrom, S.E.G., and A. Kilbom
  1990   Physiological response in the forearm during and after isometric intermittent exercise. *European Journal of Applied Physiology* 60:457-466.

Calahan, J., and S.M. McGill
  In   Intervertebral disc herniation. Studies on a porcine model exposed to highly
  press repetitive flexion/extension motion with compressive force. *Journal of Orthopaedic Research.*

Campbell, D.T., and J.C. Stanley
  1966   *Experimental and Quasi-Experimental Designs for Research.* Chicago, IL: Rand McNally.

Cannon, J.G., S.F. Orencole, R.A. Fielding, M. Meydani, S.N. Meydani, M.A. Fiatarone, J.B. Blumberg, and W.J. Evans
  1990   Acute phase response in exercise: Interaction of age and vitamin E on neutrophils and muscle enzyme release. *American Journal of Physiology* 27:R1214-R1219.

Carlson, B.M., and J.A. Faulkner
  1989   Muscle transplantation between young and old rats: Age of host determines recovery. *American Journal of Physiology* 256:C1262-C1266.

Carpenter, J.E., C.L. Flanagan, S. Thomopoulos, E.H. Yian, and L.J. Soslowsky
  1998   The effects of overuse combined with intrinsic or extrinsic alterations in an animal model of rotator cuff tendinosis. *American Journal of Sports Medicine* 26(6):801-817.

Carter, D.R.
  1985   Biomechanics of bone. In *Biomechanics of Trauma,* H.M. Nahum and J. Melvin, eds. Norwalk, CT: Appleton Century Crofts.

Cassidy, J.D., L.J. Carroll, P. Cote, M. Lemstra, A. Berglunc, A. Nygren
  2000   Effect of eliminating compensation for pain and suffering on the outcome of insurance claims for whiplash injury. *New England Journal of Medicine* 342:1179-1186.

Cats-Baril, W.L., and J.W. Frymoyer
  1991   Identifying patients at risk of becoming disabled because of low-back pain: the Vermont Rehabilitation Engineering Center predictive model. *Spine* 16:605-607.

Cavanaugh, J.M.
  1995   Neural mechanisms of lumbar pain. *Spine* 20(16):1804-1809.

Cavanaugh, J.M., S. Kallakuri, and A.C. Ozaktay
  1995   Innervation of the rabbit lumbar intervertebral disc and posterior longitudinal ligament. *Spine* 20(19):2080-2085.

Cavanaugh, J.M., A.C. Ozaktay, et al.
  1997   Mechanisms of low back pain: A neurophysiologic and neuroanatomic study. *Clinical Orthopaedics and Related Research* 335:166-180.

Cavanaugh, J.M., A.C. Özaktay, and S. Vaidyanathan
  1994   Mechano- and chemosensitivity of lumbar dorsal roots and dorsal root ganglia: An in vitro study. *Trans. Orthopaedic Research Society.* New Orleans.

Chaffin, D.B.
  1988   Biomechanical modelling of the low back during load lifting. *Ergonomics* 31(5):685-697.
  1969   A computerized biomechanical model—Development of and use in studying gross body actions. *Journal of Biomechanics* 2:429-441.
  1979   Manual materials handling: The cause of over-exertion injury and illness in industry. *Journal of Environmental and Pathological Toxicology* 2(5):31-66.

Chaffin, D.B., and G.B.J. Andersson
  1991   *Occupational Biomechanics* (Second Edition). New York: John Wiley & Sons.

Chaffin, D.B., and W.H. Baker
   1970   A biomechanical model for analysis of symmetric sagittal plane lifting. *AIIE Transactions* 2(1):16-27.
Chaffin, D.B., and K.S. Park
   1973   A longitudinal study of low-back pain as associated with occupational weight lifting factors. *American Industrial Hygiene Association Journal* 34(12):513-525.
Chaffin, D.B., G.B.J. Andersson, and B.J. Martin
   1999   *Occupational Biomechanics.* Third Edition. New York: John Wiley and Sons, Inc.
Chaffin, D.B., G.D. Herrin, et al.
   1977   A method for evaluating the biomechanical stresses resulting from manual materials handling jobs. *American Industrial Hygiene Association Journal* 38(12):662-675.
Chang, K.Y., S.T. Ho, and H.S. Yu
   1994   Vibration induced neurophysiological and electron microscopical changes in rat peripheral nerves. *Occupational and Environmental Medicine* 51:130-135.
Chard, M.D., T.E. Cawston, G.A. Gresham, and B.L. Hazleman
   1994   Rotator cuff degeneration and lateral epicondylitis: A comparative histologic study. *Annals of Rheumatic Diseases* 53:30-34.
Chase, P.B., and M.J. Kushmerick
   1988   Effects of pH on contraction of rabbit fast and slow skeletal muscle fibres. *Biophysical Journal* 53:935-946.
Chatani, K., M. Kawakami, J.N. Weinstein, S.T. Meller, and G.F. Gebhart
   1995   Characterization of thermal hyperalgesia, c-fos expression, and alterations in neuropeptides after mechanical irritation of the dorsal root ganglion. *Spine* 20(3):277-289.
Chen, C., et al.
   1997   Effects of phospholipase A2 on lumbar nerve root structure and function. *Spine* 22(10):1057-1064.
Cherkin, D.C., R.A. Deyo, J.H. Street, and W. Barlow
   1996a   Predicting poor outcome for back pain seen in primary care using patients' own criteria. *Spine* 21:2900-2907.
Cherkin, D.C., R.A. Deyo, J.H. Street, M. Hunt, and W. Barlow
   1996b   Pitfalls of patient education. Limited success of a program for back pain in primary care. *Spine* 21:345-355.
Chiang, H., S. Chen, H. Yu, and Y. Ko
   1990   The occurrence of carpal tunnel syndrome in frozen food factory employees. *Kao Hsiung Journal of Medical Science* 6:73-80.
Cholewicki, J., and S.M. McGill
   1994   EMG assisted optimization: A hybrid approach for estimating muscle forces in an indeterminate biomechanical model. *Journal of Biomechanics* 27(10):1287-1289.
   1992   Lumbar posterior ligament involvement during extremely heavy lifts estimated from fluoroscopic measurements. *Journal of Biomechanics* 25(1):17-28.
Cholewicki, J., S.M. McGill, and R.W. Norman
   1991   Lumbar spine loads during the lifting of extremely heavy weights. *Medical Science Sports Exercise* 23(10):1179-1186.
Chrousos, G.P., and P.W. Gold
   1992   The concepts of stress and stress system disorders: Overview of physical and behavioral homeostasis. *Journal of the American Medical Association* 267(9):1244-1252.
Ciriello, V.M. and S.H. Snook
   1999   Survey of manual handling tasks. *International Journal of Industrial Ergonomics* 23:149-156.

Clancy, W.G.
  1990   Tendon trauma and overuse inuries. In *Sports-Induced Inflammation: Clinical and Basic Science Concepts*, W.B. Leadbeter, J.A. Bukwalter, and S.L. Gordon, eds. Park Ridge, IL: American Academy of Orthopaedic Surgeons.

Conway, H., and J. Svenson
  1998   Occupational injury and illness rates, 1992-96: Why they fell. *Monthly Labor Review* November:36-58.

Cook, T.D., and D.T. Campbell
  1979   *Quasi-Experimentation: Design and Analysis for Field Settings*. Chicago, IL: Rand McNally.

Cook, C.J., and K. Kothiyal
  1998   Influence of mouse position on muscular activity in the neck, shoulder, and arm in computer users. *Applied Ergonomics* 29:439-443.

Coonrad, R.W., and W.R. Hooper
  1973   Tennis elbow: Its course, natural history, conservative and surgical management. *Journal of Bone and Joint Surgery* 55A:1177-1182.

Cooper, J.E., R.B. Tate, A. Yassi, and J. Khokhar
  1996   Effect of an early intervention program on the relationship between subjective pain and disability measures in nurses with low back injury. *Spine* 21(20):2329-2336.

Coovert, M.D.
  1995   Technological changes in office jobs. Pp. 175-208 in *The Changing Nature of Work*, A. Howard, ed. San Francisco, CA: Jossey-Bass Publishers.

Coppes, M.H., E. Marani, et al.
  1997   Innervation of "painful" lumbar discs. *Spine* 22(20):2342-2349.

Cordray, D.S.
  1986   Quasi experimental analysis: A mixture of methods and judgments. *New Directions in Progam Evaluation* 31:9-28.

Cornefjord, M., K. Sato, K. Olmarker, B. Rydevik, and C. Nordborg
  1997   A model for chronic nerve root compression studies. Presentation of a porcine model for controlled, slow-onset compression with analyses of anatomic aspects, compresssion onset-rate, and morphologic and neurophysiologic effects. *Spine* 22(9):946-957.

Cornefjord, M., K. Olmarker, D. Farley, J. Weinstein, and B. Rydevik
  1995   Neuropeptide changes in compressed spinal nerve roots. *Spine* 20(6):670-673.

Coste, J., G. Delecoeuillerie, A. de Lara Cohen, J.M. Le Parc, and J.B. Paolaggi
  1994   Clinical course and prognostic factors in acute low back pain: An inception cohort study in primary care practice. *British Medical Journal* 308:577-580.

Cowin, S.C., R.T. Hart, et al.
  1985   Functional adaptation in long bones: Establishing in vivo values for surface remodeling rate coefficients. *Journal of Biomechanics* 18:665-684.

Cripton, P., U. Berlemen, et al.
  1985   Response of the lumbar spine due to shear loading. In *Injury Prevention through Biomechanics*. Detroit, MI: Wayne State University.

Croft, P.R., A.C. Papageorgiou, S. Ferry, E. Thomas, M.I. Jayson, and A.J. Silman
  1996   Psychologic distress and low back pain. Evidence from a prospective study in the general population. *Spine* 20:2731-2737.

Dahalan, J.B., B. Jalaluddin, and J.E. Fernandez
  1993   Psychophysical frequency for a gripping task. *International Journal of Industrial Ergonomics* 12:219-230. (Chapter 6)

Daltroy, L.H., M.D. Iversen, M.G. Larson, R. Lew, E. Wright, J. Ryan, C. Zwerling, A.H. Fossel, and M.H.A. Liang
    1997   Controlled trial of an educational program to prevent low back injuries. *New England Journal of Medicine* 337(5):322-328.
Davis, P.J., and J.E. Fernandez
    1994   Maximum acceptable frequencies for females performing a drilling task in different wrist postures. *Journal of Human Ergology* 23:81-92.
Davis, K.G., and C.A. Heaney
    2000   The relationship between psychosocial work characteristics and low back pain: Underlying methodological issues. *Clinical Biomechanics* (Bristol, Avon) 15(6):389-406.
Davis, K.G., W.S. Marras, and T.R. Waters
    1998   Reduction of spinal loading through the use of handles. *Ergonomics* 41(8):1155-1168.
Day, J.C.
    1996   *Day, Population Projections of the United States by Age, Sex, Race, and Hispanic Origin: 1995 to 2050.* U.S. Bureau of the Census, Current Population Reports, P25-1130, February. Washington, DC: U.S. Government Printing Office.
Degens, H., L. Hoofd, and R.A. Binkhorst
    1995   Specific force of the rat plantaris muscle changes with age, but not with overload. *Mechanisms of Ageing and Development* 78:215-219.
Delamarter, R.B., H.H. Bohlman, L.D. Dodge, and C. Biro
    1990   Experimental lumbar spinal stenosis. Analysis of the cortical evoked potentials, microvasculature and histopathology. *Journal of Bone and Joint Surgery* 72-A:110-120.
de Looze, M.P., H.M. Toussaint, J.H. Van Dieen, and H.C.G. Kemper
    1993   Joint moments and muscle activity in the lower extremities and lower back in lifting and lowering tasks. *Journal of Biomechanics* 26:1067-1076.
de Looze, M.P., I. Kingma, W. Thunnissen, M.J. Van Wijk, and H.M. Toussaint
    1994   The evaluation of a practical biomechanical model estimating lumbar moments in occupational activities. *Ergonomics* 37:1495-1502.
Dempsey, P.G., and M.M. Ayoub
    1996   The influence of gender, grasp type, pinch width and wrist position on sustained pinch strength. *International Journal of Industrial Ergonomics* 17:259-273.
Dempsey, P.G., and L. Hashemi
    1999   Analysis of workers' compensation claims associated with manual materials handling. *Ergonomics* 42(1):183-195.
Dennerlein, J.T., E. Dial, C.D. Mote, and D.M. Rempel
    1998   Tensions of the flexor digitorum superficialis are higher than a current model predicts. *Journal of Biomechanics* 31:295-301.
Dennett, X., and H.J. Fry
    1988   Overuse syndrome: A muscle biopsy study. *Lancet* 1(8591):905-908.
Devor, M.
    1995   Pain arising from the nerve root and the dorsal root ganglion. In *Low Back Pain, A Scientific and Clinical Overview*, J.N. Weinstein and S.L. Gordon. Rosemont, IL: American Academy of Orthopaedic Surgeons.
Deyo, R.A., and Y.J. Tsui-Wu
    1987   Descriptive epidemiology of low back pain and its related medical care in the United States. *Spine* 12:264-268.

Dillon, C.F., M. Petersen, and S. Tanaka
No   Self-reported hand and wrist arthritis and occupational data from the 1988 U.S.
date   National Health Interview Survey—Occupational Health Supplement.

Dimberg, L., A. Olafsson, E. Stefansson, H. Aagaard, A. Odén, G.B.J. Andersson, T. Hansson, and C. Hagert
1989   The correlation between work environment and the occurrence of cervicobrachial symptoms. *Journal of Occupational Medicine* 31(5):447-453.

Dionne, C.E., T.D. Koepsell, M. Von Korff, R.A. Deyo, W.E. Barlow, and H. Checkoway
1997   Predicting long-term functional limitations among back pain patients in primary care settings. *Journal of Clinical Epidemiology* 50:31-43.

Dolan, P., M. Earley, and M.A. Adams
1994   Bending and compressive stresses acting on the lumbar spine during lifting activities. *Journal of Biomechanics* 27:1237-1248.

Donaldson, S.K., L. Hermansen, and L. Bolles
1978   Differential, direct effects H+ on Ca2+ -activated force of skinned fibers from the soleus, cardiac, and adductor magnus muscles of rabbits. *Pflugers Archives—European Journal of Physiology* 376:55-65.

Drury, C.G., C.H. Law, and C.S. Pawenski
1982   A survey of industiral box lifing. *Human Factors* 24(5):553-565.

Dubowitz, V.
1985   *Muscle Biopsy: A Practical Approach.* London: Baillière Tindall.

Dwyer, A., C. Aprill, and N. Bogduk
1990   Cervical zygapophyseal joint pain patterns. I: A study in normal volunteers. *Spine* 15(6):453-457.

Dyck, P.J., A.C. Lais, C. Giannini, and J.K. Engelstad
1990   Structural alterations of nerve during cuff compression. *Proceedings of the National Academy of Sciences* 87:9828-9832.

Eisenberg, E., T.L. Hill, and Y. Chen
1980   Cross-bridge model of muscle contraction. Quantitative analysis. *Biophysical Journal* 29:195-227.

Ekberg, K., M. Karlsson, O. Axelson, B. Bjorkqvist, B. Bjerre Kiely, and P. Malm
1995   Cross sectional study of risk factors for symptoms in the neck and shoulder area. *Ergonomics* 38(5):971-980.

Eklund, G., K.E. Hagbarth, and E. Torebjork
1978   Exteroceptive vibration-induced finger flexion reflex in man. *Journal of Neurology and Psychiatry* 41(5):438-443.

Engel, C.C., M. von Korff, and W.J. Katon
1996   Back pain in primary care: predictors of high health-care costs. *Pain* 65:197-204.

Engström, T., J.J. Hanse, and R. Kadefors
1999   Musculoskeletal symptoms due to technical preconditions in long cycle time work in an automobile assembly plant: A study of prevalence and relation to psychosocial factors and physical exposure. *Applied Ergonomics* 30:443-453.

Erdelyi, A., T. Sihvonen, P. Helin, and O. Hanninen
1988   Shoulder strain in keyboard workers and its alleviation by arm supports. *International Archives of Occupational and Environmental Health* 60:119-124.

Estlander, A.M., E.P. Takala, and E. Viikari-Juntura
1998   Do psychological factors predict changes in musculoskeletal pain: A prospective, two-year follow-up study of a working population. *Journal of Occupational and Environmental Medicine* 40:445-453.

Estryn-Behar, M., M. Kaminski, E. Peigne, M.F. Maillard, A. Pelletier, C. Berthier, et al.
    1990   Strenuous working conditions and musculoskeletal disorders among female hos-
            pital workers. *International Archives of Occupational and Environmental Health*
            62:47-57.
Evanoff, B.A., P.C. Bohr, and L.D. Wolf
    1999   Effects of a participatory ergonomics team among hospital orderlies. *American
            Journal of Industrial Medicine* 34(4):358-365.
Farfan, H.F., J.W. Cossette, G.H. Robertson, R.V. Wells, and H. Kraus
    1970   The effects of torsion on the lumbar intervertebral joints: The role of torsion in the
            production of disc degeneration. *Journal of Bone and Joint Surgery, American Vol-
            ume* 52-A(3):468-497.
Färkkilä, M.
    1978   Grip force in vibration disease. *Scandinavian Journal of Work, Environment, and
            Health* 4:159-166.
Färkkilä, S. Aatola, J. Starck, O. Korhonen, and I. Pyykkö
    1986   Hand-grip force in lumberjacks: Two-year follow-up. *International Archives of Oc-
            cupational and Environmental Health* 58:203-208.
Färkkilä, M., I. Pyykkö, O. Korhonen, and J. Starck
    1979   Hand grip forces during chain saw operation and vibration white finger in lum-
            berjacks. *British Journal of Industrial Medicine* 36:336-341.
    1980   Vibration-induced decrease in the muscle force in lumberjacks. *European Journal
            of Applied Physiology and Occupational Physiology* 43:1-9.
Fathallah, F.A., W.S. Marras, and M. Parnianpour
    1998a   An assessment of complex spinal loads during dynamic lifting tasks. *Spine*
            23(6):706-716.
    1998b   The role of complex, simultaneous trunk motions in the risk of occupation-re-
            lated low back disorders. *Spine* 23(9):1035-1042.
Fathallah, F.A., W.S. Marras, and P.L. Wright
    1995   Diurnal variation in trunk kinematics during a typical work shift. *Journal of Spinal
            Disorders* 8(1):20-25.
Faucett, J., and D.M. Rempel
    1996   Musculoskeletal symptoms related to video display terminal use: An analysis of
            objective and subjective exposure estimates. *AAOHN Journal* 44:33-39.
Faulkner, J.A., and S.V. Brooks
    1995   Muscle fatigue in old animals. Unique aspects of fatigue in elderly humans. *Ad-
            vances in Experimental Medicine and Biology* 384:471-480.
Faulkner, J.A., S.V. Brooks, and E. Zerba
    1990   Skeletal muscle weakness and fatigue in old age: Underlying mechanisms. *An-
            nual Review of Gerontology and Geriatrics* 10:147-166.
Faulkner, J.A., D.A. Jones, and J.M. Round
    1989   Injury to skeletal muscles of mice by forced lengthening during contractions.
            Quarterly Journal of Experimental Physiology 74:661-670.
Felton, D.L., and M.E. Maida
    2000   Neuroimmunomodulation. In *Encyclopedia of Stress* (Vol. 3), G. Fink, ed. San Di-
            ego, CA: Academic Press.
Feng, Y., W. Grooten, P. Wretenberg, and U.P. Arborelius
    1999   Effects of arms suspension in simulated assembly line work: Muscular activity
            and posture angles. *Applied Ergonomics* 30:247-253.
Fernström, E.A.C., and C.M. Åborg
    1999   Alterations in shoulder muscle activity due to changes in data entry organisation.
            International Journal of Industrial Ergonomics 23:255-263.

Ferreira, M., M. De Souza Conceição, and P. Hilário Nascimento Salvida
1997 Work organization is significantly associated with upper extremities musculoskeletal disorders among employees engaged in teractive computer telephone task of an international bank subsidiary in São Paulo, Brazil. *American Journal of Medicine* 31:468-473.

Feuerstein, M.
1996 Workstyle: Definition, empirical support, and implications for prevention, evaluation, and rehabilitation of occupational upper-extremity disorders. Pp. 177-206 in *Beyond Biomechanics: Psychosocial Aspects of Musculoskeletal Disorders in Office Work*, S.D. Moon and S.L Sauter. Bristol, PA: Taylor and Francis.

Feuerstein, M., G. Huang, and G. Pransky
1999 Workstyle and work-related upper extremity disorders. Pp. 175-192 in *Psychosocial Factors in Pain*, R.J. Gatchel and D.C. Turk, eds. New York: Guilford.

Feuerstein, M., G.D. Huang, A.J. Haufler, and J.K. Miller
2000 Development of a screen for predicting clinical outcomes in patients with work-related upper extremity disorders. *Journal of Occupational and Environmental Medicine* 42:749-761.

Feuerstein, M., V. Miller, L. Burrel, and R. Berger
1998 Occupational upper extremity disorders in the federal workforce: Prevalence, health care expenditures, and patterns of work disability. *Journal of Occupational and Environmental Medicine* 40:546-555.

Feuerstein, M., A.M. Carosella, L.M. Burrell, L. Marshall, and J. DeCaro
1997 Occupational upper extremity symptoms in sign language interpreters: Prevalence and correlates of pain, function, and work disability. *Journal of Occupational Rehabilitation* 7:187-205.

Feyer, A.M., P. Herbison, A.M. Williamson, et al.
2000 The role of physical and psychological factors in occupational low back pain: A prospective cohort study. *Occupational and Environmental Medicine* 57:116-120.

Fields, H.L., and A.I. Basbaum
1994 Central nervous system mechanisms of pain modulation. In *Textbook of Pain* (3rd edition), P.D. Wall and R. Melzack, eds. New York: Churchill Livingstone.

Fine, Jr., L.J.
1999 Surveillance and occupational health. *International Journal of Occupational and Environmental Health* January-March 5(1):26-9.

Fine L.J., B.A. Silverstein, T.J. Armstrong, C.A. Anderson, and D.S. Sugano
1986 Detection of cumulative trauma disorders of upper extremities in the workplace. *Journal of Occupational Medicine* August 28(8):674-678.

Fishbain, D.A., R.B. Cutler, H.L. Rosomoff, T. Khalil, and R. Steele-Rosomoff
1997 Impact of chronic pain patients' job perception variables on actual return to work. *Spine* 13:197-206.

Fleming, S.L., C.W. Jansen, and S.M. Hasson
1997 Effect of work glove and type of muscle action on grip fatigue. *Ergonomics* 40:601-612.

Flor, H., and D.C. Turk
1989 Psychophysiology of chronic pain: Do chronic pain patients exhibit symptom-specific psychophysiological responses? *Psychological Bulletin* 105(2):215-259.

Floyd, W.F., and P.H. Silver
1955 The function of the erectores spinae muscles in certain movements and postures in man. *Journal of Physiology* 129:184-203.

Frank, L.R., E.C. Wong, L.J. Haseler, and R.B. Buxton
  1999 Dynamic imaging of perfusion in human skeletal muscle during exercise with arterial spin labeling. *Magnetic Resonance in Medicine* 42:258-267.
Frankenhaeuser, M., and B. Gardell
  1976 Underload and overload in working life: Outline of a multidisciplinary approach. *Journal of Human Stress* 2:35-46.
Franklin, J.C.
  1997 Industry output and employment projections to 2006. *Monthly Labor Review* November:39-57.
Franklin, G.M., J. Huag, N. Heyer, H. Checkoway, and N. Peck
  1991 Occupational carpal tunnel syndrome in Washington State, 1984-1988. *American Journal of Public Health* 81(6):741-746.
Frederick, L.J., and T.J. Armstrong
  1995 Effect of friction and load on pinch force in a hand transfer task. *Ergonomics* 38:2447-2454.
Fredriksson, K., L. Alfredsson, M. Köster, C. Bildt Thorbjörnsson, A. Toomingas, M. Torgén, et al.
  1999 Risk factors for neck and upper limb disorders: results from 24 years of follow up. *Occupational and Environmental Medicine* 56:59-66.
Freemont, A.J., T.E. Peacock, et al.
  1997 Nerve ingrowth into diseased intervertebral disc in chronic back pain. *Lancet* 350(9072):178-181.
Freivalds, A., D.B. Chaffin, et al.
  1984 A dynamic biomechanical evaluation of lifting maximum acceptable loads. *Journal of Biomechanics* 17(4):251-262.
Fridén, J., M. Sjøstrom, and B. Ekblom
  1983 Myofibrillar damage following intense eccentric exercise in man. *International Journal of Sports Medicine* 4:170-176.
Friedman, T.L.
  1999 *The Lexus and the Olive Tree: Understanding Globalization.* NY: Farrar, Straus and Giroux.
Fritz, M.
  1991 An improved biomechanical model for simulating the strain of the hand-arm system under vibration stress. *Journal of Biomechanics* 24:1165-1171.
Frymoyer, J.W., M.H. Pope, J.H. Clements, D.G. Wilder, B. McPherson, and T. Ashikaga
  1983 Risk factors in low back pain. An epidemiological survey. *Journal of Bone and Joint Surgery* 65A:213-218.
Fyhrie, D.P., and M.B. Schaffler
  1994 Failure mechanisms in human vertebral cancellous bone. *Bone* 15(1):105-109.
Gagnon, D., and M. Gagnon
  1992 The influence of dynamic factors on triaxial net muscular moments at the L5/S1 joint during asymmetrical lifting and lowering. *Journal of Biomechanics* 25:891-901.
Gagnon, M., A. Plamondon, and D. Gravel
  1993 Pivoting with the load: An alternative for protecting the back in asymmetrical lifting. *Spine* 18:1515-1524.
Galinsky, T.L., N.G. Swanson, S.L. Sauter, J.J. Hurrell, and L.M. Schleifer
  2000 A field study of supplementary rest breaks for data-entry operators. *Ergonomics* 43(5):622-638.
Gallagher, S., C.A. Hamrick, et al.
  1994 Dynamic biomechanical modelling of symmetric and asymmetric lifting tasks in restricted postures. *Ergonomics* 37(8):1289-1310.

Gardner, L.I., D.P. Landsittel, and N.A. Nelson
  1999 Risk factors for back injury in 31,076 retail merchandise store workers. *American Journal of Epidemiology* 150:825-833.
Garg, A., and B. Owen
  1992 Reducing back stress to nursing personnel: an ergonomic intervention in a nursing home. *Ergonomics* 35(11):1353-1375.
Garg, A., D. Sharma, D.B. Chaffin, and J.M. Schmidler
  1983 Biomechanical stresses as related to motion trajectory of lifting. *Human Factors* 25(5):527-539.
Gatchel, R.J., P.B. Polatin, and R.K. Kinney
  1995 Predicting outcome of chronic back pain using clinical predictors of psychopathology: A prospective analysis. *Health Psychology* 14:415-420.
Gatchel, R.J., P.B. Polatin, and T.G. Mayer
  1995 The dominant role of psychosocial risk factors in the development of chronic low back pain disability. *Spine* 20:2702-2709.
Gatchel, R.J., P.B. Polatin, T.B. Mayer, and P.D. Garcy
  1994 Psychopathology and the rehabilitation of patients with chronic low back pain disability. *Archives of Physical Medicine and Rehabilitation* 75:666-670.
Gedalia, U., M. Solomonow, et al.
  1999 Biomechanics of increased exposure to lumbar injury caused by cyclic loading. Part 2. Recovery of reflexive muscular stability with rest. *Spine* 24(23):2461-2467.
Gelberman, R.H., R.M. Szabo, R.V. Williamson, and M.P. Dimick
  1983 Sensibility testing in peripheral-nerve compression syndromes. An experimental study in humans. *American Journal of Bone and Joint Surgery* 65(5):632-638.
Gelberman, R.H., P.T. Hergenroeder, A.R. Hargens, G.N. Lundborg, and W.H. Akeson
  1981 The carpal tunnel syndrome. *Journal of Bone and Joint Surgery* 63A:380-383.
Gemne, G.
  1997 Diagnostics of hand-arm system disorders in workers who use vibrating tools. [Review] [95 refs]. *Occupational and Environmental Medicine* 45(2):90-95.
General Accounting Office
  1997 Worker Protection: Private Sector Ergonomic Programs Yield Positive Results. GAO/HEHS-97-163, August.
Gerard, M.J., and B.J. Martin
  1999 Post-effecs of long-term hand vibration on visuo-manual performance in a tracking task. *Ergonomics* 42:314-326.
Gerard, M.J., T.J. Armstrong, J.A. Foulke, and B.J. Martin
  1996 Effects of key stiffness on force and the development of fatigue while typing. *American Industrial Hygiene Association Journal* 57:849-854.
Gerard, M.J., T.J. Armstrong, A. Franzblau, B.J. Martin, and D.M. Rempel
  1999 The effects of keyswitch stiffness on typing force, finger electromyography, and subjective discomfort. *American Industrial Hygiene Association Journal* 60:762-769.
Geras, D.T., C.D. Pepper, and S.H. Rodgers
  1989 An integrated ergonomics program at the Goodyear Tire & Rubber Company. The forcing strategy. Pp. 21-28 in *Advances in Industrial Ergonomics and Safety* I, A. Mital, ed. London: Taylor & Francis.
Gerdle, B., C. Brulin, J. Elert, P. Eliasson, and B. Granlund
  1995 Effect of a general fitness program on musculoskeletal symptoms, clinical status, physiological capacity, and perceived work environment among home care service personnel. *Journal of Occupational Rehabilitation* 5(1):1-16.

Gjessing, C.G., T.F. Schoenborn, and A. Cohen
1994   Participatory Ergonomic Interventions in Meatpacking Plants National Institute for Occupational Safety and Health. NIOSH Publication No. 94-124. Cincinnati, OH: Department of Health and Human Services.

Gilad, I., and A. Kirschenbaum
1986   About the risks of back pain and work environment. *International Journal of Industrial Ergonomics* 1:65-74.

Glaser, R., and J. Kiecolt-Glaser
1998   Stress-associated immune modulation: Relevance to viral infections and chronic fatigue syndrome. *American Journal of Medicine* 105(3A):35S-42S.

Glasscock, N.F., K.L. Turville, S.B. Joines, and G.A. Mirka
1999   The effect of personality type on muscle coactivation during elbow flexion. *Human Factors* 41(1):51-60.

Goldberger, J., C.H. Waring, and W.F. Tanner
1923   Pellagra prevention by diet among institutional inmates. *Public Health Reports* 38:2361-2368.

Golding, J.S.R.
1952   Electromyography of the erector spinae in low back pain. *Postgrad Medical Journal* 28:401-406.

Goldstein, S.A., T.J. Armstrong, D.B. Chaffin, and L.S. Matthews
1987   Analysis of cumulative strain in tendons and tendon sheaths. *American Industrial Hygiene Association Journal* 20(1):1-6.

Gomer, F., L.D. Silverstein, W.K. Berg, and D.L. Lassiter
1987   Changes in electromyographic activity associated with occupational stress and poor performance in the workplace. *Human Factors* 29(2):131-143.

Goossens, M.E.J.B., S.M.A.A. Evers, J.W.S. Vlaeyen, M. Rutten-van Mölken, and Sj. Vanderlinden
1999   Principles of economic evaluation for interventions of chronic musculoskeletal pain. *European Journal of Pain* 3:343-353.

Gordon, S.J., K.H. Yang, P.J. Mayer, A.H. Mace, V.L. Kish, and E.L. Radin
1991   Mechanism of disc rupture. A preliminary report. *Spine* 16(4):450-456.

Gorsche, R., J.P. Wiley, R. Renger, R. Brant, T.Y. Gemer, and T.M. Sasyniuk
1998   Prevalence and incidence of stenosing flexor tenosynovitis (trigger finger) in a meat-packing plant. *Journal of Occupational and Environmental Medicine* 40(6):556-560.

Granata, K.P., and W.S. Marras
1993   An EMG-assisted model of loads on the lumbar spine during asymmetric trunk extensions. *Journal of Biomechanics* 26(12):1429-1438.

1995a An EMG-assisted model of trunk loading during free-dynamic lifting. *Journal of Biomechanics* 28(11):1309-1317.

1995b The influence of trunk muscle coactivity on dynamic spinal loads. *Spine* 20(8):913-919.

1999   Relation between spinal load factors and the high-risk probability of occupational low-back disorder. *Ergonomics* 42(9):1187-1199.

Granata, K.P., W.S. Marras, and K.G. Davis
1999   Variation in spinal load and trunk dynamics during repeated lifting exertions. *Clinical Biomechanics* (Bristol, Avon) 14(6):367-375.

Granger, D.N.
1988   Role of xanthine oxidase and granulocytes in ischemia-reperfusion injury. *American Journal of Physiology* 255:H1269-H1275.

Grant, K.A., and D.J. Habes
  1997 An electromyographic study of strength and upper extremity muscle activity in simulated meat cutting tasks. *Applied Ergonomics* 28(2):129-137.

Guidotti, T.L.
  1992 Occupational repetitive strain injury. *American Family Physician* 45:585-592.

Gunning, J., and S.M. McGill
  In   Spine posture and prior loading history modulate compressive tolerance and
  press type of failure in the spine. *Spine*.

Guo, H.R., S. Tanaka, W.E. Halperin, and L.L. Cameron
  1999 Back pain prevalence in U.S. industry and estimates of lost workdays. *American Journal of Public Health* 89(7):1029-1035.

Guo, H.R., S. Tanaka, L.L. Cameron, P.J. Seligman, V.J. Behrens, J. Gerr, D.K. Wild, and V. Putz-Anderson
  1995 Back pain among workers in the United States: National estimates and workers at high risk. *American Journal of Industrial Medicine* 28(5):591-602.

Haddix, A.C., S.M. Teutsch, P.A. Shaffer, and D.O. Duñet, eds.
  1996 *Prevention Efectiveness: A Guide to Decision Aalysis and Economic Evaluation.* New York: Oxford University Press.

Hadler, N.M.
  In   Comments on the "Ergonomics Program Standard" proposed by the Occupa-
  press tional Safety and Health Administration. *Journal of Occupational and Environmental Medicine.*

Hagberg, M.
  1981 Work load and fatigue in repetitive arm elevations. *Ergonomics* 24(7):543-555.

Hagberg, M., and D.H. Wegman
  1987 Prevalence rates and odds ratios of shoulder-neck diseases in different occupational groups. *British Journal of Industrial Medicine* 44:602-610.

Hagberg, M., and G. Sundelin
  1986 Discomfort and load on the upper trapezius muscle when operating a word processor. *Ergonomics* 29:1637-1645.

Hagberg, M., G. Michaelson, and A. Ortelius
  1982 Serum creatine kinase as an indicator of local muscular strain in experimental and occupational work. *International Archives of Occupational and Environmental Health* 50(4):377-386.

Hägg, G.M.
  1991 Static work loads and occupational myalgia—A new explanation mode. Pp. 141-144 in *Electropmyographical Kinesiology*, P.A. Anderson, D.J. Hobart, and J.V. Danhoff, eds. Amsterdam: Elsevier Science Publishers.

Hales, T.R., S.L. Sauter, M.R. Peterson, L.J. Fine, V. Putz Anderson, L.R. Schleifer, et al.
  1994 Musculoskeletal disorders among visual display terminal users in a telecommunications company. *Ergonomics* 37(10):1603-1621.

Hallbeck, M.S., and D.L. McMullin
  1993 Maximum power grasp and three-jaw chuck pinch force as a function of wrist position, age, and glove type. *International Journal of Industrial Ergonomics* 11:195-206.

Halpern, C.A., and K.D. Dawson
  1997 Design and implementation of a participatory ergonomics program for machine sewing tasks. *International Journal of Industrial Ergonomics* 20(6):429-440.

Hammer, W., and J. Champey
  1993 *Reengineering the Corporation.* NY: Harper Business.

Handa, T., H. Ishihara, et al.
  1997 Effects of hydrostatic pressure on matrix synthesis and matrix metalloproteinase production in the human lumbar intervertebral disc. *Spine* 22(10):1085-1091.
Hansen, F.R., F. Biering-Sörensen, and M. Schroll
  1995 Minnesota Multiphasic Personality Inventory profiles in persons with or without low back pain. A 20-year follow-up study: See comments. *Spine* 20:2716-2720.
Hansen, N.S.
  1982 Effects on health of monotonous, forced-pace work in slaughterhouses. *Journal of Social and Occupational Medicine* 32;180-184.
Hansson, T.H., T.S. Keller, and D. Spengler
  1987 Mechanical behavior of the human lumbar spine. II. Fatigue strength during dynamic compressive loading. *Journal of Orthopaedic Research* 5(4):479-487.
Hansson, G.-Å., I. Balogh, K. Ohlsson, et al.
  1996 Goniometer measurement and computer analysis of wrist angles and movements applied to occupational repetitive work. *Journal of Electro. Kinesiology* 6:23-25.
Hansson, H.-A., A.M. Engstrom, S. Holm, et al.
  1988 Somatomedin C immunoreactivity in the Achilles tendon varies in a dynamic manner with the mechanical load. *Acta Physiologica Scandinavica* 134:199-208.
Hansson, T., B. Roose, et al.
  1980 The bone mineral content and ultimate compressive strength of lumbar vertebrae. *Spine* 5(1):46-55.
Harber, P., P. Hsu, and L. Pena
  1994 Subject-based rating of hand-wrist stressors. *Journal of Medicine* 36(1):84-89.
Hargens, A.R., D.A. Schmidt, K.L. Evans, M.R. Gonsalves, J.B. Cologne, S.R. Garfin, S.J. Mubarak, P.L. Hagan, and W.H. Akeson
  1981 Quantitation of skeletal-muscle necrosis in a model compartment syndrome. *Journal of Bone and Joint Surgery*—American Volume 63:631-636.
Härkönen, H., H. Riihimäki, S. Tola, T. Mattsson, M. Pekkarinen, A. Zitting, and K. Husman
  1984 Symptoms of vibration syndrome and radiographic findings in the wrists of lumberjacks. *British Journal of Industrial Medicine* 41(1):133-136.
Harris, C., and L. Straker
  2000 Survey of Physical Ergonomics Issues Associated with School Childrens' Use of Laptop Computers. http:..www.curtin.edu.au/curtin/dept/phy...ons/2000laptopfolder/2000IJIElaptop.html
Harvey, R. and E. Peper
  1997 Surface electromyography and mouse use position. *Ergonomics* 40:781-789.
Hasenbring, M., G. Marienfeld, D. Kuhlendahl, and D. Soyka
  1994 Risk factors of chronicity in lumbar disc patients. A prospective investigation of biologic, psychologic, and social predictors of therapy outcome. *Spine* 19:2759-2765.
Haufler, A.J., M. Feuerstein, and G.D. Huang
  2000 Job stress, upper extremity pain and functional limitations in symptomatic computer users. *American Journal of Industrial Medicine* 38:507-515.
Hazard, R.G., L.D. Haugh, S. Reid, J.B. Preble, and L. MacDonald
  1996 Early prediction of chronic disability after occupational low back injury. *Spine* 21:945-951.
Heliövaara, M., M. Mäkelä, P. Knekt, O. Impivaara, and A. Aromaa
  1991 Determinants of sciatica and low-back pain. *Spine* 16:608-614.
Hellsing, A.L., S.J. Linton, and M. Kälvemark
  1994 A prospective study of patients with acute back and neck pain in Sweden. *Physical Therapy* 74:116-124; discussion 25-28.

Hemingway, H., M.J. Shipley, S. Stansfeld, and M. Marmot
  1997 Sickness absence from back pain, psychosocial work characteristics and employment grade among office workers. *Scandinavian Journal of Work, Environment, and Health* 23:121-129.

Hennemen, E., and C.B. Olson
  1965 Relations between structure and function in the design of skeletal muscles. *Journal of Neurophysiology* 28:581-598.

Hennemen, E., G. Somjen, and D.O. Carpenter
  1965a Excitability and inhibitability of motoneurons of different sizes. *Journal of Neurophysiology* 28:599-620.
  1965b Functional significance of cell size in spinal motoneurons. *Journal of Neurophysiology* 28:560-580.

Hennemen, E. H.P. Clamann, J. Gillies, and R. Skinner
  1974 Rank order of motoneurons within a pool, law of combination. *Journal of Neurophysiology* 37:1338-1349.

Herbert, R., K. Janeway, and C. Schecter
  1999 Carpal tunnel syndrome and workers' compensation in New York State. *American Journal of Industrial Medicine* 35(4):335-342.

Hermansen, L.
  1981 Effect of metabolic changes on force generation in skeletal muscle during maximal exercise. *Ciba Foundation Symposium* 82:75-88.

Herrin, G.D., M. Jaraiedi, and C.K. Anderson
  1986 Prediction of overexertion injuries using biomechanical and psychophysical models. *American Industrial Hygiene Association Journal* 47(6):322-330.

Heylings, D.J.
  1978 Supraspinous and interspinous ligaments of the human lumbar spine. *Journal of Anatomy* 125(1):127-131.

Ho, S.T., and H.S. Yu
  1989 Ultrastructural changes of the peripheral nerve induced by vibration: An experimental study. *British Journal of Industrial Medicine* 46:157-164.

Hoekstra, E., J. Hurrell, and N. Swanson
  1995 Evaluation of work related musculoskeletal disorders and job stress among teleservice center representatives. *Applied Occupational and Environmental Hygiene* 10(10):812-817.

Hoekstra, E.J., J. Hurrell, N.G. Swanson, and A. Tepper
  1996 Ergonomic, job task, and psychosocial risk factors for work related musculoskeletal disorders among teleservice center representatives. *International Journal of Human–Computer Interaction* 8(4):421-431.

Holewijn, M., and R. Heus
  1992 Effects of temperature on electromyogram and muscle function. *European Journal of Applied Physiology* 65:541-545.

Holmström, E.B., J. Lindell, and U. Moritz
  1992a Low back and neck/shoulder pain in construction workers: Occupational workload and psychosocial risk factors. *Spine* 17:663-671.
  1992b Low back and neck/shoulder pain in construction workers: Occupational workload and psychosocial risk factors. Part 2: Relationship to neck and shoulder pain. *Spine* 17(6):672-677.

Houtman, I.L.D., P.M. Bongers, P.G.W. Smulders, and M.A.J. Kompier
  1994 Psychosocial stressors at work and musculoskeletal problems. *Scandinavian Journal of Work, Environment, and Health* 20:139-145.

Howard, A., ed.
  1995 *The Changing Nature of Work.* San Francisco, CA: Jossey-Bass Publishers.
Howe, J.F., J.D. Loeser, and W.H. Calvin
  1977 Mechanosensitivity of dorsal root ganglia and chronically injured axons: A physiological basis for the radicular pain of nerve root compression. *Pain* 3:25-41.
Hsiang, S.M., G.E. Brogmus, and T.K. Courtney
  1997 Low back pain (LBP) and lifting technique: A review. *International Journal of Industrial Ergonomics* 19:59-74.
Hubbard, R.P., and K.J. Chun
  1988 Mechanical responses of tendons to repeated extensions and wait periods. *Journal of Biomechanical Engineering* 110(1):11-19.
Hughes, R.E., and D.B. Chaffin
  1995 The effect of strict muscle stress limits on abdominal muscle force predictions for combined torsion and extension loadings. *Journal of Biomechanics* 28(5):527-533.
Hunt, H.A., and R.V. Habeck
  1993 *The Michigan Disability Prevention Study: Research Highlights.* Kalamazoo, MI: Uphohn Institute for Employment Research.
Hunter, K.D., and J.A. Faulkner
  1997 Pliometric contraction-induced injury of mouse skeletal muscle: Effect of initial length. *Journal of Applied Physiology* 82:278-283.
Hurrell, J.J., Jr.
  1987 An overview of organizational stress and health. Pp. 31-45 in *Stress Management in Work Settings*, L.R. Murphy, and T.F. Schoenborn, eds. NIOSH Publication No. 87-111. Washington, DC: U.S. Department of Health and Human Services.
Hurri, H.
  1989 The Swedish back school in chronic low back pain II. Factors predicting the outcome. *Scandinavian Journal of Rehabilitation Medicine* 21:41-44.
Hutton, W., and M. Adams
  1982 Can the lumbar spine be crushed in heavy lifting? *Spine* 7(6):586-590.
Hutton, W.C., Y. Toribatake, et al.
  1998 The effect of compressive force applied to the intervertebral disc in vivo. A study of proteoglycans and collagen. *Spine* 23:2524-2537.
Imrhan, S.N.
  1991 The influence of wrist position on different types of pinch strength. *Applied Ergonomics* 22:379-384.
Institute of Medicine
  1997 *Enabling America: Assessing the Role of Rehabilitation Science and Engineering.* E.N. Brandt, Jr., and A.M. Pope, eds. Committee on Assessing Rehabilitation Science and Engineering. Division of Health Sciences Policy. Washington, DC: National Academy Press.
Ishihara, H., and J.P.G. Urban
  1999 Effects of low oxygen concentration and metabolic inhibitors on proteoglycan and protein synthesis rates in the intervertebral disc. *Journal of Orthopaedic Research* 17(6):829-835.
Ishihara, H., D.S. McNally, et al.
  1996 Effects of hydrostatic pressure on matrix synthesis in different regions of the intervertebral disc. *Journal of Applied Physiology* 80(3):839-846.
Iwata, H., S. Makimo, and K. Miyashita
  1987 Prevalence of Raynaud's phenomenon in individuals not using vibrating tools. *Japanese Journal of Industrial Health* 29:500-503.

Jacobs, J.A., and K. Gerson
  1998 Who are the overworked Americans? *Review of Social Economy* 56(4):442-459.
Jager, M., A. Luttmann, and W. Laurig
  1991 Lumbar load during one-hand bricklaying. *International Journal of Industrial Ergonomics* 8:261-277.
Jarvholm, U., J. Styf, M. Suurkula, and P. Herberts
  1988a Intramuscular pressure and muscle blood flow in supraspinatus. *European Journal of Applied Physiology and Occupational Physiology* 58(3):219-224.
Jarvholm, U., G. Palmerud, J. Styf, P. Herberts, and R. Kadefors
  1988b Intramuscular pressure in the supraspinatus muscle. *Journal of Orthopaedic Research* 6(2):230-238.
Jeng, O.J., R.G. Radwin, and A.A. Rodriquez
  1994 Functional psychomotor deficits associated with carpal tunnel syndrome. *Ergonomics* 37(6):1055-1069.
Jensen, B.R., K. Jorgensen, and G. Sjøgaard
  1994 The effect of prolonged isometric contractions on muscle fluid balance. *European Journal of Applied Physiology and Occupational Physiology* 69:439-444.
Jensen, B.R., M. Pilegaard, and G. Sjøgaard
  2000 Motor unit recruitment and rate coding in response to fatiguing shoulder abductions and subsequent recovery. *European Journal of Applied Physiology* 83:190-199.
Jensen, M.C., and M.N. Brant-Zawadzki, et al.
  1994 Magnetic resonance imaging of the lumbar spine in people without back pain. *The New England Journal of Medicine* 331(2):69-73.
Jensen, R.C.
  1987 Disabling back injuries among nursing personnel: Research needs and justification. *Research in Nursing and Health* 10(1):29-38.
Jerome, S.N., L. Kong, and R.J. Korthuis
  1994 Microvascular dysfunction in postischemic skeletal muscle. *Journal of Investigative Surgery* 7:3-16.
Johansson, J.A., R. Kadefors, S. Rubenowitz, U. Klingenstierna, I. Lindstrom, T. Engstrom, and M. Johansson
  1993 Musculoskeletal symptoms, ergonomics aspects, and psychosocial factors in two different truck assembly concepts. *International Journal of Industrial Ergonomics* 12:35-48.
Johansson, J.A., and S. Rubenowitz
  1994 Risk indicators in the psychosocial and physical work enviroment for work related neck, shoulder and low back symptoms: a study among blue and white collar workers in eight companies. *Scandinavian Journal of Rehabilitation Medicine* 26:131-142.
Johnson, E.O., T.C. Kamilaris, G.P. Chrousos, and P.W. Gold
  1992 Mechanisms of stress: A dynamic overview of hormonal and behavioral homeostasis. *Neuroscience and Biobehavioral Reviews* 16:115-130.
Johnson, W.G., M.L. Baldwin, and R.J. Butler
  1998 Back pain and work disability: The need for a new paradigm. *Industrial Relations* 37:9-34.
Jones, D.A., D.J. Newham, J.M. Round, and S.E. Tolfree
  1986 Experimental human muscle damage: Morphological changes in relation to other indices of damage. *Journal of Physiology* 375:435-448.
Jones, R.J.
  1997 Corporate ergonomics program of a large poultry processor. *American Industrial Hygiene Association Journal* 58:132-137.

Joseph, B.
  2000 Process and Outcome Measurements of an Ergonomics Program. Briefing for the
        Panel on Musculoskeletal Disorders and the Workplace, Washington, D.C., Sep-
        tember.
Josephson, M., and E. Vingard
  1998 Workplace factors and care seeking for low-back pain among female nursing
        personnel. *Scandinavian Journal of Work, Environment, and Health* 24:465-472.
Jubrias, S.A., I.R. Odderson, P.C. Esselman, and K.E. Conley
  1997 Delcine in isokinetic force with age: Muscle cross-sectional area and specific force.
        Pflugers Archives—European Journal of Physiology 434:246-253.
Junge, A, J. Dvorak, and S. Ahern
  1995 Predictors of bad and good outcomes of lumbar disc surgery: A prospective clini-
        cal study with recommendations for screening to avoid bad outcomes. *Spine*
        20:460-468.
Kadefors, R., T. Engstrom, J. Petzell, and L. Sundstrom
  1996 Ergonomics in parallelized car assembly: A case study with reference also to
        productivity aspects. *Applied Ergonomics* 27:101-110.
Kadhiresan, V.A., C.A. Hassert, and J.A. Faulkner
  1996 Properties of single motor units in medial gastrocnemius muscles of adult and
        old rats. *Journal of Physiology (London)* 493(Part2):543-552.
Kahn, A.A., A. Khan, and K. Kroenke
  2000 Symptoms in primary care: Etiology and outcome. *Journal of General Internal Medi-
        cine* 15(Supplement 1):76-77 (abstract).
Kaji, H., KH. Honma., M. Usui, Y. Yasuno, and K. Saito
  1993 Hypothenar hammer syndrome in workers occupationally exposed to vibrating
        tools. *Journal of Hand Surgery—British.* 18B(6):761-766.
Kaldor, G., and W.J. DiBattista
  1978 *Aging, Volume 6: Aging in Muscle.* New York: Raven Press Books, Ltd.
Kallakuri, S., J.M. Cavanaugh, and D.C. Blagoev
  1998 An immunohistochemical study of innervation of lumbar spinal dura and longi-
        tudinal ligaments. *Spine* 23(4):403-411.
Kamwendo, K., and S.J. Linton
  1991 A controlled study of the effect of neck school in medical secretaries. *Scandinavian
        Journal of Rehabilitation Medicine* 23:143-152.
Kamwendo, K., S.J. Linton, and U. Moritz
  1991a Neck and shoulder disorders in medical secretaries: Part I. Pain prevalence and
        risk factors. *Scandinavian Journal of Rehabilitation Medicine* 23:127-133.
  1991b Neck and shoulder disorders in medical secretaries. Part II. Ergonomical work
        environment and symptom profile. *Scandinavian Journal of Rehabilitation Medicine*
        23(3):135-142.
Kanter, E.M.
  1995 *World Class: Thriving Locally in the Global Economy.* NY: Simon & Schuster.
  1999 Challenges in the global economy. *The Washington Quarterly* 22(2):39-58.
Kaplansky, B.D., F.Y. Wei, and M.V. Reecers
  1998 Prevention strategies for occupational low back pain. *Occupational Medicine* 13:33-
        45.
Karasek, R.A.
  1985 *Job Content Questionnaire and User's Guide.* JCQ Users Center, University of
        Massachusetts, Lowell.

Karasek, R.A., and T. Theorell

1990   *Healthy Work. Stress, Productivity and the Reconstruction of Working Life*. New York NY: Basic Books.

Karhu, O., P. Hansi, and I. Kuorinka

1977   Correcting working postures in industry: A practical method for analysis. *Applied Ergonomics* 8:199-201.

Katz, J.N., B.C. Amick, B.B. Carroll, C. Hollis, A.H. Fossel, and C.M. Coley

2000   Prevalence of upper extremity musculoskeletal disorders in college students. *American Journal of Medicine* 109:586-588.

Kawakami, M., J.N. Weinstein, K.F. Spratt, K. Chatani, R. Traub, S.T. Meller, and G.F. Gebhart

1994a Experimental lumbar radiculopathy. Immunohistochemical and quantitative demonstrations of pain induced by lumbar nerve root irritation of the rat. *Spine* 19(16):178-1794.

Kawakami, M., J.N. Weinstein, K. Chatani, K.F. Spratt, S.T. Meller, and G.F. Gebhart

1994b Experimental lumbar radiculopathy. Behavioral and histologic changes in a model of radicular pain after spinal nerve root irritation with chromic gut ligatures in the rat. *Spine* 19(16):1795-1802.

Kawakami, M., T. Tamaki, et al.

1997   The role of phospholipase A2 and nitric oxide in pain-related behavior produced by an allograft of intervertebral disc material to the sciatic nerve of the rat. *Spine* 22(10):1074-1079.

Kawakami, M., T. Tamaki, et al.

1996   Pathomechanism of pain-related behavior produced by allografts of intervertebral disc in the rat. *Spine* 21(18):2101-2107.

Kawakami, N., and Y. Fujigaki

1996   Reliability and validity of the Japanese version of Job Content Questionnaire: Replication and extension in computer company employees. *Industrial Health* 34:295-306.

Kawakami, N., F. Kobayashi, S. Araki, et al.

1995   Assessment of job stress dimensions based on the job demands-control model of employees of telecommunication and electric power companies in Japan: Reliability and validity of the Japanese version of the Job Content Questionnaire. *International Journal of Behavior and Medicine* 2:358-375.

Kayama, S., K. Olmarker, et al.

1998   Cultured, autologous nucleus pulposus cells induce functional changes in spinal nerve roots. *Spine* 23(20):155-158.

Keir, P.J., J.M. Bach, and D.M. Rempel

1998   Effects of finger posture on carpal tunnel pressure during wrist motion. *Journal of Hand Surgery* 23A:628-634.

Keir, P.J., R.P. Wells, D.A. Ranney, and W. Lavery

1997   The effects of tendon load and posture on carpal tunnel pressure. *Journal of Hand Surgery* 22A:628-634.

Kelsey, J.L., A.L. Golden, and D.J. Mundt

1990   Low back pain/prolapsed lumbar intervertebral disc. *Rheumatologic Diseases Clinics of North America* 163:699-715.

Kelsey, J.L., P.B. Githens, et al.

1984   An epidemiologic study of lifting and twisting on the job and risk for acute prolapsed lumbar intervetebral disc. *Journal of Orthopaedic Research* 2(1):61-66.

Keyserling, W.M.
  1986 Postural analysis of the trunk and shoulders in simulated real time. *Ergonomics* 29:569-583.
Keyserling, W.M., D.S. Stetson, B.A. Silverstein, et al.
  1993 A checklist for evaluating ergonomic risk factors associated with upper extremity cumulative trauma disorders. *Ergonomics* 36:807-831.
Kiecolt-Glaser, J.K., P.T. Marucha, W.B. Malarkey, A.M. Mercado, and R. Glaser
  1995 Slowing of wound healing by psychological stress. *Lancet* 347:1194-1196.
Kilbom, Å.
  1994 Assessment of physical exposure in relation to work-related musculoskeletal disorders—What information can be obtained from systematic observations? *Scandinavian Journal of Work, Environment, and Health* 20:30-45.
Kim, C.-H., and J.E. Fernandez
  1993 Psychophysical frequency for a drilling task. *International Journal of Industrial Ergonomics* 12:209-218.
Kippers, V., and A.W. Parker
  1984 Posture related tomyoelectric silence of erectores spinae during trunk flexion. *Spine* 9:740-745.
Kirkaldy-Willis, W.H.
  1998 The three phases of the spectrum of degenerative diseases. In *Managing Low Back Pain*, W.H. Kirkaldy-Willis, ed. NewYork: Churchill-Livingston.
Kirkendall, D.T., and W.E. Garrett, Jr.
  1998 The effects of aging and training on skeletal muscle. *American Journal of Sports Medicine* 26:598-602.
Kirschbaum, C., and D.H. Hellhammer
  1989 Salivary cortisol in psychobiological research: An overview. *Neuropsychobiology* 22:150-169.
Kivekäs, J., H. Riihimäki, K. Husman, K. Hänninen, H. Härkönen, T. Kuusela, M. Pekkarinen, S. Tola, and A.J. Zitting
  1994 Seven-year follow-up of white-finger symptoms and radiographic wrist findings in lumberjacks and referents. *Scandinavian Journal of Work and Environmental Health* 20:101-106.
Klein, M.G., and J.E. Fernandez
  1997 The effects of posture, duration, and force on pinching frequency. *International Journal of Industrial Ergonomics* 20:267-275.
Klenerman, L., P.D. Slade, I.M. Stanley, et al.
  1995 The prediction of chronicity in patients with an acute attack of low back pain in a general practice setting. *Spine* 20:478-484.
Knibbe, J.J., and N.E. Knibbe
  1996 Back pain. How nurses can identify and prevent the problem. *Review of Enferm* 19(210):57-64.
Knowlton, R.G., and J.C. Gilbert
  1983 Ulnar deviation and short-term strength reductions as affected by a cuve-handled ripping hammer and a conventional claw hammer. *Ergonomics* 26:173-179.
Kokot, K., R.M. Schaefer, M. Teschner, U. Gilge, R. Plass, A. Heidlund
  1988 Activation of leukocytes during prolonged physical exercise. *Advances in Experimental Medicine and Biology* 240:57-63.
Kornberg, M.
  1988 MRI diagnosis of traumatic Schmorl's node. A case report. *Spine* 13(8):934-935.

Korthuis, R.J., D.N. Granger, M.I. Townsley, and A.E. Taylor
1985 The role of oxygen-derived free radicals in ischemia-induced increases in canine skeletal muscle vascular permeability. *Circulation Research* 57:599-609.

Koskimies, K., I. Pyykkö, J. Starck, and R. Inaba
1992 Vibration syndrome among Finnish forest workers between 1972 and 1990. *International Archives of Occupational and Environmental Health* 64:251-256.

Krause, N., L.K. Dasinger, and F. Neuhauser
1998 Modified work and return to work: A review of the literature. *Journal of Occupational Rehabilitation* 8(2):113-139.

Kraus, J.F., K.B. Schaffer, D.L. McArthur, and C. Peek-Asa
1997 Epidemiology of acute low back injury in employees of a large home improvement retail company. *American Journal of Epidemiology* 146:637-645.

Kraushaar, B.S., and R.P. Nirschl
1999 Tendinosis of the elbow (tennis elbow). Clinical features and findings of histological, immunohistochemical, and electron microscopy studies. *Journal of Bone and Joint Surgery* (American) 81(2):259-278.

Kristensen, T.S.
1996 Job stress and cardiovascular disease: A theoretical critical review. *Journal of Occupational Health and Psychology* 1:246-260.

Kroenke, K.
1997 Symptoms and science: The frontiers of primary care research. *Journal of General Internal Medicine* 12:509-510.

Kroenke, K., and A.D. Mangelsdorff
1989 Common symptoms in ambulatory care: Incidence, evaluation, therapy, and outcome. *American Journal of Medicine* 86:262-266.

Kroenke, K., and R.K. Price
1993 Symptoms in the community: Prevalence, classification, and psychiatric comorbity. *Archives of Internal Medicine* 153:2474-2480.

Kroenke, K., and R. Swindle
2000 Cognitive-behavioral therapy for somatization and symptom syndromes: A critical review of controlled clinical trials. *Psychotherapy and Psychosomatics* 69:205-215.

Kroenke, K., R.L. Spitzer, J.B.W. Williams, M. Linzer, S.R. Hahn, F.V. deGruy, et al.
1994 Physical symptoms in primary care: Predictors of psychiatric disorders and functional impairment. *Archives of Family Medicine* 3:774-779.

Kromodihardjo, S., and A. Mital
1987 Biomechanical analysis of manual lifting tasks. *Transactions of the ASME* 109:132-138.

Kroslid, D.
1999 In Search of Quality Management—Rethinking and Reinterpreting. Unpublished Ph.D. Dissertation, Linkoping Institute of Technology, Sweden.

Kukkonen, R., S. Lammi, and M. Antti-Poika
1991 Effects of dynamic muscular exercise and working habits on neck/shoulder pain among hospital workers. Pp. 135-137 in *Designing for Everyone: Proceedings of the 11th Congress of the International Ergonomics Association Vol. 1*, Y. Queinnec and F. Daniellou, eds. London: Taylor & Francis.

Kurppa, K., E. Viikari-Juntura, E. Kuosma, M. Muuskonen, and P. Kivi
1991 Incidence of tenosynovitis or peritendinitis and epicondylitis in a meat-processing factory. *Scandinavian Journal of Work, Environment, and Health* 17(1):32-37.

Lagerström, M., M. Wenemark, M. Hagberg, and E. Wigaeushelm
  1995   Occupational and individual factors related to musculoskeletal symptoms in five
         body regions among Swedish nursing personnel. *International Archives of Occupa-
         tional and Environmental Health* 68:27-35.
Lancourt, J., and M. Kettelhut
  1992   Predicting return to work for lower back pain patients receiving worker's com-
         pensation. *Spine* 17:629-640.
Landau, K., et al.
  1996   On the analysis of sector-related and gender-related stresses at the workplace: An
         analysis of the AET data bank. *International Journal of Industrial Engineering* 17:175-
         186.
Langberg, H., D. Skovgaard, M. Karamouzis, J. Bulow, and M. Kjaer
  1999   Metabolism and inflammatory mediators in the peritendinous space measured
         by microdialysis during intermittent isometric exercise in humans. *Journal of
         Physiology* 515(Pt. 3):919-927.
Larsson, R., P.A. Oberg, and S.E. Larsson
  1999   Changes of trapezius muscle blood flow and electromyography in chronic neck
         pain due to trapezius myalgia. *Pain* 79:45-50.
Larsson, S.E., L. Bodegard, K.G. Henriksson, and P.A. Oberg
  1990   Chronic trapezius myalgia. Morphology and blood flow studied in 17 patients.
         Acta Orthopaedica Scandinavica 61:394-398.
Larsson, S.E., G. Bengtsson, L. Bodegard, K.G. Henriksson, and J. Larsson
  1988   Muscle changes in work-related chronic myalgia. *Acta Orthopaedica Scandinavica*
         9:552-556.
Last, J.M.
  1988   *A Dictionary of Epidemiology*, Second Edition. New York: Oxford University Press.
Latko, W.A., T.J. Armstrong, J.A. Foulke, et al.
  1997   Development and evaluation of an observational method for assessing repetition
         in hand tasks. *American Industrial Hygiene Association Journal* 58:278-285.
Latko, W.A., T.J. Armstrong, A. Franzblau, S.S. Ulin, R.A. Werner, and J.W. Albers
  1999   A cross-sectional study of the relationship between repetitive work and the preva-
         lence of upper limb musculoskeletal disorders. *American Journal of Industrial Medi-
         cine* 36:248-259.
Lau, E.M., P. Egger, D. Coggon, C. Cooper, L. Valenti, and D. O'Connell
  1995   Low back pain in Hong Kong: Prevalence and characteristics compared with
         Britain. *Journal of Epidemiology and Community Health* 49:492-494.
Laughlin, M.H., and R.B. Armstrong
  1982   Muscular blood flow distribution patterns as a function of running speed in rats.
         American Journal of Physiology 244:H296-H306.
Laughlin, M.H., S.J. Mohrman, and R.B. Armstrong
  1984   Muscular blood flow distribution patterns in the hindlimb of swimming rats.
         American Journal of Physiology 246:H398-H403.
Lavender, S.A., Y.C. Li, G.B.J. Andersson, and R.N. Natarajan
  1999   The effects of lifting speed on the peak external forward bending, lateral bending,
         and twisting spine moments. *Ergonomics* 42(1):111-125.
Lawrence, R.C., CG. Helmick, F.C. Arnett, R.A. Deyo, D.T. Felson, E.H. Giannini, S.P. Heyse,
R. Hirsch, M.C. Hochberg, G.G. Hunder, M.H. Liang, S.R. Pillemer, V.D. Steen, and F. Wolfe
  1998   Estimates of the prevalence of arthritis and selected musculoskeletal disorders in
         the United States. *Arthritis and Rheumatism* 41(5):778-799.

Lazarus, R.S.
  1974   Psychological stress and coping in adaptation and illness. *International Journal of Psychiatry in Medicine* 5:321-333.
LeBlanc, A.D., H.J. Evans, V.S. Schneider, R.E. Wendt, and T.D. Hedreck
  1994   Changes in intervertebral disc cross-sectional area with bed rest and space flight. *Spine* 19(7):812-817.
Leclerc, A., M.F. Cristofari, B. Delemoere, P. Mereau, C. Teyssier Cotte, and A. Tourancher
  1998   Carpal tunnel syndrome and work organisation in repetitive work: A cross sectional study in France. *Occupational and Environmental Medicine* 55:180-187.
Lehmann, T.R., K.F. Spratt, and K.K. Lehmann
  1993   Predicting long-term disability in low back injured workers presenting to a spine consultant. *Spine* 18:1103-1112.
Leigh, J.P., and R.M. Sheetz
  1989   Prevalence of back pain among fulltime United States workers. *British Journal of Industrial Medicine* 46:651-657.
Leino, P.I., and V. Hänninen
  1995   Psychosocial factors at work in relation to back and limb disorders. *Scandinavian Journal of Work, Environment, and Health* 21:134-142.
Leino, P., and G. Magni
  1993   Depressive and distress symptoms as predictors of low back pain, neck-shoulder pain, and other musculoskeletal morbidity: A 10 year follow-up of metal industry employees. *Pain* 53:89-94.
Lemasters, G.K., M.R. Attenbury, A.D. Booth Jones, O. Bhattacharya, N. Ollila Glenn, C. Forrester, et al.
  1998   Prevalence of work-related musculoskeletal disorders in active union carpenters. *Occupational and Environmental Medicine* 55:421-427.
Leskinen, T.P., H.R. Stalhammar, et al.
  1983   A dynamic analysis of spinal compression with different lifting techniques. *Ergonomics* 26(6):595-604.
Letz, R., M.G. Cherniack, F. Gerr, D. Hershman, and P. Pace
  1992   A cross sectional epidemiological survey of shipyard workers exposed to hand-arm vibration. *British Journal of Industrial Medicine* 49(1):53-62.
Levi, L.
  1972   Introduction: Psychosocial stimuli, psychophysiological reactions, and disease. In *Stress and Distress in Response to Psychosocial Stimuli*, L. Levi, ed. Oxford: Pergamon Press.
Lie, I., and R.G. Watten
  1994   VDT work, oculomotor strain, and subjective complaints: An experimental and clinical study. *Ergonomics* 37(8)1419-1433.
Lieber, R.L., and J. Fridén
  1988   Selective damage of fast glycolytic muscle fibres with eccentric contraction of the rabbit tibialis anterior. *Acta Physiologica Scandinavica* 133:587-588.
Lieber, R.L, and J. Fridén
  1993   Muscle damage is not a function of muscle force but active muscle strain. *Journal of Applied Physiology* 74:520-526.
Lieber, R.L., T.M. Woodburn, and J. Fridén
  1991   Muscle damage induced by eccentric contractions of 25% strain. *Journal of Applied Physiology* 70:2498-2507.
Liira, J.P., H.S. Shannon, L.W. Chambers, and T.A. Haines
  1996   Long-term back problems and physical work exposures in the 1990 Ontario Health Survey. *American Journal of Public Health* 86:382-387.

Lilienfeld, A., and D. Lilienfeld
  1980 *Foundations of Epidemiology*. New York: Oxford University Press.
Liles, D.H., S. Deivanayagam, et al.
  1984 A job severity index for the evaluation and control of lifting injury. *Human Factors* 26(6):683-693.
Lin, M.L., and R.G. Radwin
  1998 Agreement between a frequency-weighted filter for continuous biomechanical measurements of repetitive wrist flexion against a load and published psychophysical data. *Ergonomics* 41(4):459-475.
Lin, M.L., R.G. Radwin, and S.H. Snook
  1997 A single metric for quantifying biomechanical stress in repetitive motions and exertions. *Ergonomics* 40:543-558.
Lind, A.R., C. Williams, J.S. Petrofsky, R.M. Glaser, and C.A. Phillips
  1982 Evaluation of the amplitude and frequency components of the surface EMG as an index of fatigue. *Ergonomics* 25:213-223.
Lindman, R. M. Hagberg, K.A. Angqvist, K. Soderlund, E. Hultman, and L.E. Thornell
  1991 Changes in muscle morphology in chronic trapezius myalgia. *Scandinavian Journal of Work, environment, and Health* 17:347-355.
Lindström, I., C. Ohlund, and A. Nachemson
  1994 Validity of patient reporting and predictive value of industrial physical work demands. *Spine* 19:888-893.
Linqvist, B.
  1993 Torque reaction in angled nutrunner. *Applied Ergonomics* 24(3)174-180.
Linton, S.
  1990 Risk factors for neck and back pain in a working population in Sweden. *Work and Stress* 4:41-49.
Linton, S.J., and K. Halldén
  1998 Can we screen for problematic back pain? A screening questionnaire for predicting outcome in acute and subacute back pain. *Clinical Journal of Pain* 14:209-215.
Linton, S.J., N. Buer, J. Vlaeyen, and A.L. Hellsing
  1999 Are fear-avoidance beliefs related to a new episode of back pain? A prospective study. *Psychology and Health* 14:1051-1059.
Lockhart, R.W.
  1986 Effective back injury prevention at an electrical utility. Pp. 173-175 in *Proceedings of the 19th Annual Conference of the Human Factors Association of Canada*. Richmond (Vancouver): Human Factors Association of Canada.
Loeser, J.D., S.E. Henderlite, and D.A. Conrad
  1995 Incentive effects of workers' compensation benefits: A literature synthesis. *Medical Care Research and Review* 52(1):34-59.
Loisel, P., L. Abenhaim, P. Durand, J.M. Esdaile, S. Suissa, L. Gosselin, R. Simard, J. Turcotte, and J. Lemaire
  1997 A population-based, randomized clinical trial on back pain management. *Spine* 22(24):2911-2918.
Lonn, J.H., B. Glomsrod, M.G. Soukup, K. Bo, and S. Larsen
  1999 Active back school: Prophylactic management for low back pain. A randomized, controlled, 1-year follow-up study. *Spine* 24(9):865-871.
Lotz, J.C., and J.R. Chin
  2000 Intervertebral disc cell death is dependent on the magnitude and duration of spinal loading, spine. *Spine* 25(12):1477-1483.

Lotz, J.C., O.K. Colliou, J.R. Chin, N.A. Duncan, and E. Liebenberg
  1998   Compression-induced degeneration of the intervertebral disc: An in vivo mouse model and finite-element study. *Spine* 23(23):2493-2506.
Low, P.A., and P.J., Dyck
  1977   Increased endoneurial fluid pressure in experimental lead neuropathy. *Nature* 269:427-428.
Low, P.A, P.J. Dyck, and J.D. Schmelzer
  1982   Chronic elevation of endoneurial fluid pressure is associated with low-grade fiber pathology. *Muscle Nerve* 5:162-165.
Low, P.A., H. Nukada, J.D. Schmelzer, R.R. Tuck, and P.J. Dyck
  1985   Endoneurial oxygen tension and radial topography in nerve edema. *Brain Research* 341:147-154.
Luecken, L.J., E.C. Suarez, C.M. Kuhn, J.C. Barefoot, J.A. Blumenthal, I.C. Siegler, and R.B. Williams
  1997   Stress in employed women: Impact of marital status and children at home on neurohormone output and home strain. *Psychosomatic Medicine* 59:352-359.
Lundberg, U., and M. Frankenhaeuser
  1999   Stress and workload of men and women in high-ranking positions. *Journal of Occupational Health Psychology* 4:142-151.
Lundberg, U., and G. Johansson
  In   Stress and health risks in repetitive work and supervisory monitoring work. In
  press   *Engineering Psychophysiology: Issues and Applications,* R. Backs and W. Boucsein, eds. New Jersey: Lawrence Erlbaum Associates.
Lundberg, U., B. Melin, G.W. Evans, and L. Homberg
  1993   Physiological deactivation after two contrasting tasks at a video display terminal: Learning vs. repetitive data entry. *Ergonomics* 36(6):601-611.
Lundberg, U., R. Kadefors, B. Melin, G. Palmerud, P. Hassmen, M. Engstrom, and I.E. Dohns
  1994   Psychological stress and EMG activity of the trapezius muscle. *International Journal of Behavioral Medicine* 1(4):354-370.
Lundberg, U., B. Melin, M. Ekström, I. Elfsberg Dohns, L. Sandsjö, G. Palmerud, et al.
  1999   Psychophysiological stress responses, muscle tension, and neck and shoulder pain among supermarket cashiers. *Journal of Occupational Health Psychology* 4(3):245-255.
Lundborg, G.
  1988   *Nerve Injury and Repair.* Edinburgh: Churchill Livingstone.
Lundborg, G., and L.B. Dahlin
  1996   Anatomy, function, and pathophysiology of peripheral nerves and nerve compression. *Hand Clinics* 12(2):185-193.
Lundborg, G., R. Myers, and H. Powell
  1983   Nerve compression injury and increased endoneurial fluid pressure: A "miniature compartment syndrome." *Journal of Neurology, Neurosurgery, and Psychiatry* 46:1119-1124.
Lundborg, G., L.B. Dahlin, H.W.A. Hansson, M. Kanje, and L.E. Necking
  1990   Vibration exposure and peripheral nerve fiber damage. *Journal of Hand Surgery (American)* 15:346-351.
Lundborg, G., L.B. Dahlin, N. Danielsen, H.A. Hansson, L.E. Necking, and I. Pyykko
  1987   Intraneural edema following exposure to vibration. *Scandinavian Journal of Work, Environment, and Health* 13:326-329.

Lundström, R., T. Nilsson, L. Burström, and M. Hagberg
1999 Exposure-response relationship between hand-arm vibration and vibrotactile perception sensitivity. *American Journal of Industrial Medicine* 35:456-464.

Luo, H.P., H.C. Hsu, J.J. Grabowski, B.F. Morrey, and K.N. An
1998 Mechanical environment associated with rotator cuff tears. *Journal of Shoulder and Elbow Surgery* 7(6):616-620.

Luoma, K, H. Riihimäki, et al.
2000 Low back pain in relation to lumbar disc degeneration. *Spine* 25(4):487-492.

Luopajärvi, T., I. Kuroinka, M. Virolainen, and M. Holmberg
1979 Prevalence of tenosynovitis and other injuries of the upper extremities in repetitive work. *Scandinavian Journal of Work, Environment, and Health* 5(Suppl 3):48-55.

Lynch, G.S., and J.A. Faulkner
1998 Contraction-induced injury to single muscle fibers: Velocity of stretch does not influence the force deficit. *American Journal of Physiology* 275:C1548-C1554.

Macfarlane, G.J., I.M. Hunt, and A.J. Silman
2000 Role of mechanical and psychosocial factors in the onset of forearm pain: Prospective population based study. *British Medical Journal* 321:1-5.

Mackinnon, S.E., A.L. Dellon, A.R. Hudson, and D.A. Hunter
1994 Chronic nerve compression—An experimental model in the rat. *Ann Plastic Surgery* 13(2):112-120.

Macpherson, P.C., R.G. Dennis, and J.A. Faulkner
1997 Sarcomere dynamics and contraction-induced injury to maximally activated single muscle fibres from soleus muscles of rats. *Journal of Physiology* 500:523-533.

Magnavita, N., L. Bevilacqua, P. Mirk, A. Fileni, and N. Castellino
1999 Work-related musculoskeletal complaints in sonologists. *Journal of Occupational and Environmental Medicine* 41(11):981-988.

Magni, G., C. Moreschi, S. Rigatti-Luchini, and H. Merskey
1994 Prospective study on the relationship between depressive symptoms and chronic musculoskeletal pain. *Pain* 56:289-297.

Magni, G., M. Mofitti, C. Moreschi, H. Merskey, and S.R. Luchini
1993 Chronic musculoskeletal pain and depressive symptoms in the National Health and Nutrition Examination I. Epidemiological follow-up study. *Pain* 53:161-168.

Magnusson, M.L., M.H. Pope, D.G. Wilder, and B. Areskoug
1996 Are occupational drivers at an increased risk for developing muscuskeletal disorders? *Spine* 21:710-717.

Main, C.J., P.L.R. Wood, S. Hollis, C.C. Spanswick, and G. Waddell
1992 The distress and risk assessment method: a simple patient classification to identify distress and evaluate the risk of poor outcome. *Spine* 17:42-52.

Malaviya, P., D.L. Butler, G.P. Boivin, F.N. Smith, F.P. Barry, J.M. Murphy, and K.G. Vogel
2000 An in vivo model for load-modulated remodeling in the rabbit flexor tendon. *Journal of Orthopaedic Research* 18(1):116-125.

Malchaire, J., A. Piette, and L.S. Rodriguez-Diaz
1998 Temporary threshold shift of the vibration perception threshold following a short duration exposure to vibration. *Ann Occupational Hygiene* 42:121-127.

Mannion, A.F., P. Dolan, and M.A. Adams
1996 Psychological questionnaires: Do "abnormal" scores precede or follow first-time low back pain? *Spine* 21:2603-2611.

Marcus, M., and F. Gerr
1996 Upper extremity musculoskeletal symptoms among female office workers: Associations with video display terminal use and occupational psychosocial stressors. *American Journal of Industrial Medicine* 29:161-170.

Marley, R.J., and J.E. Fernandez
  1995 Psychophysical frequency and sustained exertion at varying wrist postures for a drilling task. *Ergonomics* 38:303-325.

Maroudas, A.
  1988 Nutrition and metabolism of the intervertebral disc. Pp. II:1-37 *The Biology of the Intervertebral Disc*, P. Ghosh, ed. Boca Raton, FL: CRC Press.

Marple, R.L., K. Kroenke, C.R. Lucey, J. Wilder, and C.A. Lucas
  1997 Concerns and expectations in patients presenting with physical complaints: Frequency, physician perceptions and actions, and 2-week outcome. *Archives of Internal Medicine* 157:1482-1488.

Marras, W.
  1992a Toward an understanding of dynamic variables in ergonomics. *Occupational Medicine: State of the Art Review* 7: 655-677.

Marras, W.S., and K.G. Davis
  1998 Spine loading during asymmetric lifting using one versus two hands. *Ergonomics* 41(6):817-834.

Marras, W.S., and K.P. Granata
  1995 A biomechanical assessment and model of axial twisting in the thoracolumbar spine. *Spine* 20(13):1440-1451.
  1997a Changes in trunk dynamics and spine loading during repeated trunk exertions. *Spine* 22(21):2564-2570.
  1997b Spine loading during trunk lateral bending motions. *Journal of Biomechanics* 30(7):697-703.

Marras, W.S., and C.M. Sommerich
  1991a A three-dimensional motion model of loads on the lumbar spine: I. Model structure. *Human Factors* 33(2):123-137.
  1991b A three-dimensional motion model of loads on the lumbar spine: II. Model validation. *Human Factors* 33(2):139-149.

Marras, W.S., K.P. Granata, and K.G. Davis
  1999 Variability in spine loading model performance. *Clinical Biomechanics* (Bristol, Avon) 14(8):505-514.

Marras, W.S., A.I. King, and R.L. Joynt
  1984 Measurement of loads on the lumbar spine under isometric and isokinetic conditions. *Spine* 9(2):176-187.

Marras, W.S., K.G. Davis, et al.
  1999a A comprehensive analysis of low-back disorder risk and spinal loading during the transferring and repositioning of patients using different techniques. *Ergonomics* 42(7)904-926.
  1999b Spine loading and trunk kinematics during team lifting. *Ergonomics* 42(10):1258-1273.

Marras, W.S., K.G. Davis, C.A. Heaney, A.B. Maronitis, and W.G. Allread
  2000 The influence of psychosocial stress, gender, and personality on mechanical loading of the lumbar spine. *Spine* 25:3045-3054.

Marras, W.S., K.P. Granata, et al.
  1999 Effects of box features on spine loading during warehouse order selecting. *Ergonomics* 42(7):980-996.

Marras, W.S., S.A. Lavender, et al.
  1995 Biomechanical risk factors for occupationally related low back disorders. *Ergonomics* 38(2):377-410.

Marras, W.S., S.A. Lavender, et al.
　1993　The role of dynamic three-dimensional trunk motion in occupationally related low back disorders. The effects of workplace factors, trunk position, and trunk motion characteristics on risk of injury. *Spine* 18(5):617-628.
Marras, W., F. Fathallah, R. Miller, et al.
　1992b　Accuracy of a three-dimensional lumbar motion monitor for recording dynamic trunk motion characteristics. *International Journal of Industrial Ergonomics* 9:75-87.
Marras, W.S., W.G. Allread, D.L. Burr, and F.A. Fathallah
　2000a　Prospective validation of a low-back disorder risk model and assessment of ergonomic interventions associated with manual materials handling tasks. *Ergonomics* 43(11):1866-1886.
Marras, W.S., K.G. Davis, C.A. Heaney, A. Maronitis, and W.G. Allread
　2000b　Biomechanical responses to psychosocial stress. *Spine* 25:3045-3054.
Marras, W.S., K.G. Davis, C.A. Heaney, A.B. Maronitis, and W.G. Allread
　In　The influence of psychosocial stress, gender, and personality on mechanical
　press　loading of the lumbar spine. *Spine*.
Marshall, M.M., J.R. Mozrall, and J.E. Shealy
　1999　The effects of complex wrist and forearm posture on wrist range of motion. *Human Factors* 41:205-213.
Martin, B.J., and H.S. Park
　1997　Analysis of the tonic vibration reflex: Influence of vibration variables on motor unit synchronization and fatigue. *European Journal of Applied Physiology and Occupational Physiology* 75(6):504-511.
Martin, B.J., J.P. Roll, and M. Hugon
　1990　Modulation of cutaneous flexor responses induced in man by vibration-elicited proprioceptive or exteroceptive inputs. *Aviation, Space, and Environmental Medicine* 61:921-928.
Martin, R., D.B. Burr, et al.
　1998　*Skeletal Tissue Mechanics.* New York: Springer.
Martina, B., B. Bucheli, M. Stotz, E. Battegay, and N. Byr
　1997　First clinical judgment by primary care physicians distinguishes well between nonorganic and organic causes of abdominal or chest pain. 1997. 12:459-465.
Marucha, P.T., J.K. Kiecolt-Glaser, and M. Favagehi
　1998　Mucosal wound healing is impaired by examination stress. *Psychosomatic Medicine* 60(3):362-365.
McCarron, R.F., M.W. Wimpee, et al.
　1987　The inflammatory effect of nucleus pulposus. A possible element in the pathogenesis of low-back pain. *Spine* 12(8):760-764.
McComas, A.
　1996　*Skeletal Muscle Form and Function.* Champaign, IL: Human Kinetics.
McCully, K.K., and J.A. Faulkner
　1985　Injury to skeletal muscle fibres of mice following lengthening contractions. *Journal of Applied Physiology* 59:119-126.
　1986　Characteristics of lengthening contractions associated with injury to skeletal muscle fibers. *Journal of Applied Physiology* 61:293-299.
McGill, S.M.
　1997　The biomechanics of low back injury: Implications on current practice in industry and the clinic. *Journal of Biomechanics* 30(5):465-475.
　1991　Electromyographic activity of the abdominal and low back musculature during the generation of isometric and dynamic axial trunk torque: implications for lumbar mechanics. *Journal of Orthopaedic Research* 9(1):91-103.

McGill, S.M., and V. Kippers
  1994 Transfer of loads between lumbar tissues during the flexion-relaxation phenomenon [see comments]. *Spine* 19(19):2190-2196.
McGill, S.M., and R.W. Norman
  1985 Dynamically and statically determined low back moments during lifting. *Journal of Biomechanics* 18(12):877-885.
  1987 Effects of an anatomically detailed erector spinae model on L4/L5 disc compression and shear. *Journal of Biomechanics* 20(6):591-600.
  1986 Partitioning of the L4-L5 dynamic moment into disc, ligamentous, and muscular components during lifting [see comments]. *Spine* 11(7):666-678.
McGill, S.M., R.W. Norman, and J. Cholewicki
  1996 A simple polynomial that predicts low-back compression during complex 3-D tasks. *Ergonomics* 39:1107-1118.
McKenna, K.M., S. McGrann, A.D. Blann, and J.A. Allen
  1993 An investigation into the acute vascular effects of riveting. *British Journal of Industrial Medicine* 50;160-166.
Melhorn, J., L. Wilkinson, P. Gardner, W. Horst, and B. Silkey
  1999 An outcomes study of an occupational medicine intervention program for the reduction of musculoskeletal disorders and cumulative trauma disorders in the workplace. *Journal of Enviornmental Medicine* 41(10):833-845.
Melin, B., and U. Lundberg
  1997 A biopsychosocial approach to work-stress and musculoskeletal disorders. *Journal of Psychophysiology* 11:238-247.
Melin, B., U. Lundberg, J. Soderlund, and M. Granqvist
  1999 Psychological and physiological stress reactions of male and female assembly workers: A comparison between two different forms of work organization. *Journal of Organizational Behavior* 20:47-61.
Melzack, R.
  1999 Pain and stress: A new perspective. In *Psychosocial Factors in Pain*, R.J. Gatchel and D.C. Turk, eds. New York: The Guilford Press.
Messmer, K., F.U. Sack, M.D. Menger, R. Bartlett, J.H. Barker, and F. Hammerson
  1988 White cell-endothelium interaction during postischemic reperfusion of skin and skeletal muscle. *Advances in Experimental Medicine and Biology* 242:95-98.
Miller, J.A., A.B. Schultz, D.N. Warwick, and D.L Spencer
  1986 Mechanical properties of lumbar spine motion segments under large loads. *Journal of Biomechanics* 19(1):79-84.
Mital, A., T. Kuo, and H.F. Faard
  1994 A quantitative evaluation of gloves used with non-powered hand tools in routine maintenance tasks. *Ergonomics* 37:333-343.
Miyashita, K., S. Shiomi, N. Itoh, T. Kasamatsu, and H. Iwata
  1983 Epidemiological study of vibration syndrome in response to total hand-tool operating time. *British Journal of Industrial Medicine* 40:92-98.
Modern Materials Handling
  1998 Top trends and developments of 1998. December:42-48.
Moffett, J.K., D. Torgerson, S. Bell-Syer, D. Jackson, H. Llewlyn-Phillips, A. Farrin, and J. Barber
  1999 Randomised controlled trial of exercise for low back pain: Clinical outcomes, costs, and preferences. *British Medical Journal* 319(7205):279-283.
Moore, A., R. Wells, and D. Ranney
  1991 Quantifying exposure in occupational manual tasks with cumulative trauma disorder potential. *Ergonomics* 34:1433-1453.

Moore, J.S., and A. Garg
  1998   The effectiveness of participatory ergonomics in the red meat packing industry: Evaluation of a corporation. *International Journal of Industrial Ergonomics* 21(1):47-58.
  1995   The strain index: A proposed method to analyze jobs for risk of distal upper extremity disorders. *American Industrial Hygiene Association Journal* 56:443-458.
  1994   Upper extremity disorders in a pork processing plant: relationships between job risk factors and morbidity. *American Industrial Hygiene Association Journal* 55(8):703-715.
Moore, R.J.
  2000   The vertebral end-plate: What do we know? *European Spine Journal* 9:92-96.
Morris, J.M., D.B. Lucas, and B. Bresler
  1961   Role of the trunk in stability of the spine. *Journal of Bone and Joint Surgery* 43-A:327-351.
Morse, T., C. Dillon, N. Warren, C. Levenstein, and A. Warren
  1998   The economic and social consequences of work-related musculoskeletal disorders: The Connecticut Upper-Extremity Surveillance Project (CUSP). *International Journal of Occupational and Environmental Health* 4:209-216.
Mosekilde, L., and L. Mosekilde
  1986   Normal vertebral body size and compressive strength: Relations to age and to vertebral and iliac trabecular bone compressive strength. *Bone* 7:207-212.
Mosconi, T., and L. Kruger
  1996   Fixed-diameter polyethylene cuffs applied to the rat sciatic nerve induce a painful neuropathy: Ultrastructural morphometric analysis of axonal alterations. *Pain* 64:37-57.
Murata, K., S. Araki, F. Okajima, and Y. Saito
  1996   Subclinical impairment in the median nerve across the carpal tunnel among female VDT operators. *International Archives of Occupational and Environmental Health* 68:75-79.
Murthy, G., N.J. Kahan, A.R. Hargens, and D.M. Rempel
  1997   Forearm muscle oxygenation decreases with low levels of voluntary contraction. *Journal of Orthopaedic Research* 15:507-511.
Myers, R.R., A.P. Mizisin, H.C. Powell, and P.W. Lampert
  1982   Reduced nerve blood flow in hexachlorophene neuropathy. Relationship to elevated endoneurial fluid pressure. *Journal of Neuropathology and Experimental Neurology* 41:391-339.
Nachemson, A.L., and J.M. Morris
  1964   Lumbar intradiscal pressure. *Acta Orthopaedica Scandinavica Supplementum* 43:1077-1092.
Nagata, C., H. Yoshida, S.M. Mirbod, Y. Komura, S. Fujita, R. Inaba, H. Iwata, M. Maeda, Y. Shikano, Y. Ichiki, and S. Mori
  1993   Cutaneous signs (Raynaud's pnenomenon, sclerodactylia, and edema of the hands) and hand-arm vibration exposure. *International Archives of Occupational and Environmental Health* 64:587-591.
Nagi, S.Z., L.E. Riley, and L.G. Newby
  1973   A social epidemiology of back pain in a general population. *Journal of Chronic Disability* 26:769-779.
Narayan, M., and L. Rudolph
  1993   Ergonomic improvements in a medical device assembly plant: A field study. Pp. 812-816 in *Proceedings of the Human Factors and Ergonomics Society 37th Annual Meeting*. Seattle, WA: Human Factors and Ergonomics Society.

Nathan, P.A., R.C. Keniston, L.D. Myers, and K.D. Meadows
  1992   Longituninal study of median nerve sensory conduction in industry: Relation-ship to age, gender, hand dominance, occupational hand use, and clinical diagnosis. *Journal of Hand Surgery* 17A:850-857.
National Academy of Social Insurance
  2000   *Workers' Compenations: Benefits, Coverage and Costs, 1997-1998.* Washington, DC: National Academy of Social Insurance.
National Committee for Injury Prevention and Control
  1989   Injury prevention: Meeting the challenge. *American Journal of Preventative Medicine* 5(3 Suppl.):1-103.
National Research Council
  1994   *Organizational Linkages: Understanding the Productivity Paradox,* D.H. Harris, ed. Panel on Organizational Linkages, Committee on Human Factors. Commission on Behavioral and Social Sciences and Education. Washington, DC: National Academy Press.
  1995   *Preventing HIV Transmission: The Role of Sterile Needles and Bleach.* J. Normand, D. Vlahov, and L. Moses, eds. Panel on Needle Exchange and Bleach Distribution Programs. Commission on Behavioral and Social Sciences and Education. National Research Council: Washington, DC.
  1999a *The Changing Nature of Work: Implications for Occupational Analysis.* Committee on Techniques for the Enhancement of Human Performance: Occupational Analysis. Commission on Behavioral and Social Sciences and Education. Washington, DC: National Academy Press.
  1999b *Work-Related Musculoskeletal Disorders: Report, Workshop Summary, and Workshop Papers.* Steering Committee for the Workshop on Work-Related Musculoskeletal Injuries: The Research Base. Washington, DC: National Academy Press.
Necking, L.E., L.B. Dahlin, J. Fridén, G. Lundborg, R. Lundstrom, and L.E. Thornell
  1992   Vibration-induced muscle injury. An experimental model and preliminary findings. *Journal of Hand Surgery—British Volume* 17:270-274.
Necking, L.E., R. Lundstrom, LB. Dahlin, G. Lundborg, L.E. Thornell, and J. Fridén
  1996a Tissue displacement is a causative factor in vibration-induced muscle injury. *Journal of Hand Surgery—British Volume* 21:753-757.
Necking, L.E., R. Lundstrom, G. Lundborg, LE. Thornell, and J. Fridén
  1996b Skeletal muscle changes after short term vibration. *Scandinavian Journal of Plastic and Reconstructive Surgery and Hand Surgery* 30:99-103.
Nelson, N.A., and B.A. Silverstein
  1998   Workplace changes associated with a reduction in musculoskeletal symptoms in office workers. *Human Factors* 40(2):337-350.
Newham, D.J., D.A. Jones, and R.H. Edwards
  1986   Plasma creatine kinase changes after eccentric and concentric contractions. *Muscle and Nerve* 9:59-63.
Newham, D.J., K.R. Mills, B.M. Quigley, and R.H. Edwards
  1983   Pain and fatigue after concentric and eccentric muscle contractions. *Clinical Science* 64:55-62.
Nielsen, H.M., M. Shalicky, and A. Viidik
  1998   Influence of physical exercise on aging rats. II. Life-long exercise modifies the aging changes of the mechanical properties of limb muscle tendons. *Mechanisms of Aging and Development* 100(3):243-260.
Nikolaou, P.K., B.L. Macdonald, R.R. Glisson, A.V. Seaber, and W.E. Garrett, Jr.
  1987   Biomechanical and histological evaluation of muscle after controlled strain injury. *American Journal of Sports Medicine* 15:9-14.

Nilsson, T., L. Burström, and M. Hagberg
    1989   Risk assessment of vibration exposure and white fingers among platers. *International Archives of Occupational and Environmental Health* 61:473-481.
Noonan, T.J, T.M. Best, A.V. Seaber, and W.E. Garrett, Jr.
    1994   Identification of a threshold for skeletal muscle injury. *American Journal of Sports Medicine* 22:257-261.
Nordstrom, D.L., F. DeStafano, R.A. Vierkant, and P.M. Layde
    1998   Incidence of diagnosed carpal tunnel syndrome in a general population. *Epidemiology* 9(3):342-345.
Nordstrom, D.L., R.A. Vierkant, F. DeStefano, and P.M. Layde
    1997   Risk factors for carpal tunnel syndrome in a general population. *Occupational and Environmental Medicine* 54(10):734-740.
Norman, R., R. Wells, et al.
    1998   A comparison of peak vs. cumulative physical work exposure risk factors for the reporting of low back pain in the automotive industry. *Clinical Biomechanics* 13:561-573.
Novak, G.J., O.D. Schipplein, J.H. Trafimow, and G.B.J. Andersson
    1993   Influence of erector spinae muscle fatigue on the lumbo-sacral moment during lifting. *European Journal of Experimental Musculoskeletal Research* 2(1):39-44.
Noyes, F.R., J.L. De Lucas, and P.J. Torvik
    1994   Biomechanics of ligament failure: An analysis of strain-rate sensitivity and mechanisms of failure in primates. *Journal of Bone and Joint Surgery* 56A:236-253.
Nuwayhid, I.A., W. Stewart, and J.V. Johnson
    1993   Work activities and the onset of first-time low back pain among New York City fire fighters. *American Journal of Epidemiology* 137:539-548.
Oberg, T., L. Sandsjo, and R. Kadefors
    1994   Subjective and objective evaluation of shoulder muscle fatigue. *Ergonomics* 37(8):1323-1333.
Oblieniene, D., H. Schrader, G. Bovim, I. Miseviciene, and T. Pain
    1999   Pain after whiplash: A prospective controlled inception cohort study. *Journal of Neurology, Neurosurgery, and Psychiatry* 66:279-283.
Ochsner, M., M. Love, R. Lynch, L. DeJohn, and S. Huie
    1998   What is happening to injured computer users? A study of CWA District 1 members. *New Solutions* 8(3):309-328.
O'Driscoll, S.W., E. Horii, R. Ness, T.D. Cahalan, R.R. Richards, and K.N. An
    1992   The relationship between wrist position, grasp size, and grip strength. *Journal of Hand Surgery* 17A:169-177.
Ogilvie, R.W., R.B. Armstrong, K.E. Baird, and C.L. Bottoms
    1988   Lesions in the rat soleus muscle following eccentrically biased exercise. *American Journal of Anatomy* 182(4):335-346.
Oh, S.A., and R.G. Radwin
    1997   The effects of power hand tool dynamics and workstation design of handle kinematics and muscle activity. *International Journal of Industrial Ergonomics* 20:59-74.
    1998   The influence of target torque and torque build-up time on physical stress in right angle nutrunner operation. *Ergonomics* 41(2):188-206.
Ohlsson, K., R.G. Attewell, B. Paisson, B. Karlsson, I. Balogh, B. Johnsson, A. Ahlm, and S. Skerfving
    1995   Repetitive industrial work and neck and upper limb disorders in females. *American Journal of Industrial Medicine* 27:731-747.

Öhlund, C., C. Eek, S. Palmbald, B. Areskoug, and A. Nachemson
    1996   Quantified pain drawing in subacute low back pain. Validation in a nonselected outpatient industrial sample. *Spine* 21:1021-1030; discussion 31.
Ohshima, H., H. Tsuji, et al.
    1989   Water diffusion pathway, swelling pressure, and biomechanical properties of the intervertebral disc during compression load. *Spine* 14(11):1234-1244.
Ohshima, H., J. Urban, et al.
    1995   Effect of static load on matrix synthesis rates in the intervertebral disc measured in vitro by a new perfusion technique. *Journal of Orthopaedic Research* 13:2-29.
Ohshima, H., and J.P.G. Urban
    1992   The effect of lactate and pH on proteoglycan and protein synthesis rates in the intervertebral disc. *Spine* 17(9):1079-1082.
Ojima, H., S. Miyake, M. Kumashiro, et al.
    1991   Dynamic analysis of wrist circumduction: A new application of the biaxial flexible electrogoniometer. *Clinical Biomechanics* 16:221-229.
Okada, A.
    1986   Physiological response of the rat to different vibration frequencies. *Scandinavian Journal of Work, Environment, and Health* 12:362-364.
Olmarker, K., and K. Larsson
    1998   TNF-alpha and nucleus pulposus-induced nerve root injury. *Spine* 23(23):2538-2544.
Olmarker, K., and R.R. Myers
    1998   Pathogenesis of sciatic pain: Role of herniated nucleus pulposus and deformation of spinal nerve root and DRG. *Pain* 7:9-105.
Olmarker, K., B. Rydevik, and B. Holm
    1989   Edema formation in spinal nerve roots induced by experimental, graded compression. An experimental study on the pig cauda equina with special reference to differences in effects between rapid and slow onset of ecompression. *Spine* 14:579-563.
Olmarker, K., M. Iwabuchi, K. Larsson, and B. Rydevik
    1998   Walking analysis of rats subjected to experimental disc herniation. *European Spine Journal* 7(5):394-399.
Olsen, T.L., R.L. Anderson, S.R. Dearwater, A.M. Kriska, J.A. Cauley, D.J. Aaron, et al.
    1992   The epidemiology of low back pain in an adolescent population. *American Journal of Public Health* 82:606-608.
O'Malley, P.G., J.L. Jackson, G. Tomkins, J. Santoro, E. Balden, and K. Kroenke
    1999   Antidepressant therapy for unexplained symptoms and symptom syndromes: A critical review. *Journal of Family Practice* 48:980-993.
Ory, F.G., F.U. Rahman, V. Katagade, A. Shukla, and A. Burdorf
    1997   Respiratory disorders, skin complaints, and low-back trouble among tannery workers in Kanpur, India. *American Industrial Hygiene Association Journal* 58:740-746.
Ozaktay, A.C., S. Kallakuri, and J.M. Cavanaugh
    1998   Phospholipase A2 sensitivity of the dorsal root and dorsal root ganglion. *Spine* 23(12):1297-1306.
Ozaktay, A.C., et al.
    1995   Phospholipase A2-induced electrophysiologic and histologic changes in rabbit dorsal lumbar spine tissues. *Spine* 20(24):2659-2668.
Palmer, K., G. Crane, and H. Inskip
    1998   Symptoms of hand-arm vibration syndrome in gas distribution operatives. *Occupational and Environmental Medicine* 55(10):716-721.

Palmgren, T., M. Gronblad, et al.
  1999 An immunohistochemical study of nerve structures in the anulus fibrosus of human normal lumbar intervertebral discs. *Spine* 24(20):2075-2079.
Papageorgiou, A.C., G.J. Macfarlane, E. Thomas, P.R. Croft, M.I.V. Jayson, and A.J. Silman
  1997 Psychosocial factors in the workplace: Do they predict new episodes of low back pain? *Spine* 22:1137-1142.
Parenmark, G., A.-K. Malmkvist, and R. Örtengren
  1993 Ergonomic moves in an engineering industry: Effects on sick leave frequency, labor turnover, and productivity. *International Journal of Industrial Ergonomics* 11:291-300.
Park, H.S., and B.J. Martin
  1993 Contribution of the tonic vibration reflex to muscle stress and muscle fatigue. *Scandinavian Journal of Work, Environment, and Health* 19:35-42.
Park, R.M., N.A. Nelson, M.A. Silverstein, and F.E. Mirer
  1992 Use of medical insurance claims for surveillance of occupational disease: An analysis of cumulative trauma in the auto industry. *Journal of Occupational Medicine* 34:731-737.
Parker, J.F.
  1993 A human factors guide for aviation maintenance. Pp. 1:30-33 in *Proceedings of the Human Factors and Ergonomics Society 37th Annual Meeting*, Seattle.
Parnianpour, M., M. Nordin, N. Kahanovitz, and V. Frankel
  1988 The triaxial coupling of torque generation of trunk muscles during isometric exertions and the effect of fatiguing isoinertial movements on the motor output and movement patterns. *Spine* 13:982-992.
Partheni, M., G. Miliaras, C. Constantoyannis, and N. Papadakis
  1999 Whiplash injury—Letter to the editor. *Journal of Rheumatology* 26:1207-1208.
Patterson-Kane, J.C., E.C. Firth, D.A. Parry, A.M. Wilson, and A.E. Goodship
  1998a Effects of training on collagen fibril populations in the suspensory ligament and deep digital flexor tendon of young thoroughbreds. *American Journal of Veterinary Research* 59(1):64-68.
Patterson-Kane, J.C., A.M. Wilson, E.C. Firth, D.A. Parry, and A.E. Goodship
  1998b Exercise-related alterations in crimp morphology in the central regions of superficial digital flexor tendons from young thoroughbreds: A controlled study. *Equine Veterinary Journal* 30(1):61-64.
  1997 Comparison of collagen fibril populations in the superficial digital flexor tendons of exercised and nonexercised thoroughbreds. *Equine Veterinary Journal* 29(2):121-125. [Published erratum appears in *Equine Veterinary Journal*, 1998, 30(2):176.]
Pearce, R.H., B.J. Rimmer, et al.
  1987 Degeneration and the chemical composition of the human lumbar intervertebral disc. *Journal of Orthopaedic Research* 5(2):198-205.
Pedowitz, R.A., A.R. Hargens, S.J., Mubarak, and D.H. Gershuni
  1990 Modified criteria for the objective diagnosis of chronic compartment syndrome of the leg. *American Journal of Sports Medicine* 18:35-40.
Pedowitz, R.A., S.R., Garfin, A.R. Hargens, M.R. Swenson, R.R. Myers, J.B. Massie, and B.L. Rydevik
  1992 Effects of magnitude and duration of compression on spinal nerve root conduction. *Spine* 17:194-199.

Pelmear, P.L., and W. Taylor
  1992 Clinical picture (vascular, neurological, and musculoskeletal). Pp. 26-40 in *Hand-Arm Vibration: A Comprehensive Guide for Occupational Health Professionals*, P.L. Pelmear, W. Taylor, and D.E. Wasserman, eds. New York: Van Nostrand Reinhold.

Perez-Castro, A.V., and K.G. Vogel
  1999 In situ expression of collagen and proteoglycan genes during development of fibrocartilage in bovine deep flexor tendon. *Journal of Orthopaedic Research* 17:139-148.

Petrofsky, J.S., R.M. Glaser, C.A. Phillips, A.R. Lind, and C. Williams
  1982 Evaluation of the amplitude and frequency components of the surface EMG as an index of fatigue. *Ergonomics* 25:213-223.

Philips, H.C., and L. Grant
  1991 The evolution of chronic back pain problems. *Archives of Behavior Research and Therapy* 29:435-441.

Phillips, S.K., S.A. Bruce, D. Newton, and R.C. Woledge
  1992 The weakness of old age is not due to failure of muscle activation. *Journal of Gerontology* 47:M45-M49.

Pickett, C.W.L., and R.E.M. Lees
  1991 A cross sectional study of health complaints among 79 data entry operators using video display terminals. *Journal of Social and Occupational Medicine* 41:113-116.

Pietri, F., A. Leclerc, L. Boitel, J.F. Chastang, J.F. Morcet, and M. Blondet
  1992 Low-back pain in commercial travelers. *Scandinavian Journal of Work, Environment, and Health* 18:52-58.

Pietri-Taleb, F., H. Riihimäki, E. Viikari-Juntura, and K. Lindström
  1994 Longitudinal study on the role of personality characteristics and psychological distress in neck trouble among working men. *Pain* 58:261-267.

Pocekay, D., S.A. Mccurdy, S.J. Samuales, K. Hammond, and M.B. Schenker
  1995 A cross sectional study of musculoskeletal symptoms and risk factors in semiconductor workers. *American Journal of Industrial Medicine* 28:861-871.

Porter, M.E., and R.E. Wayland
  1995 Global competition and the localization of competitive advantage. *Advances in Strategic Management* 11A:63-105.

Porter, R.W., M.A. Adams, and W.C. Hutton
  1989 Physical activity and the strength of the lumbar spine. *Spine* 14(2):201-203.

Potter, R.G., and J.M. Jones
  1992 The evolution of chronic pain among patients with musculoskeletal problems: A pilot study in primary care. *British Journal of General Practice* 42:462-464.

Potvin, J.R., S.M. McGill, and R.W. Norman
  1991 Trunk muscle and lumbar ligament contributions to dynamic lifts with varying degrees of trunk flexion [see comments]. *Spine* 16(9):1099-1107.

Potvin, J.R., R.W. Norman, and S.M. McGill
  1991 Reduction in anterior shear forces on the L4/L5 disc by the lumbar musculature. *Clinical Biomechanics* 6:88-96.

Powell, M., M. Wilson, et al.
  1986 Prevalence of lumbar disc degeneration observed by magnetic resonance in symptomless women. *Lancet* Dec. 13:1366-1367.

Praemer, A., S. Furner, and D. P. Rice
  1999 *Musculoskeletal Conditions in the United States*. Rosemont, IL: American Academy of Orthopaedic Surgeons.

Pransky, G., T. Snyder, D.E. Dembe, and J.E. Himmelstein
    1999   Under-reporting of work-related disorders in the workplace: A case study and review of the literature. *Ergonomics* 42(1):171-182.
Pring, D.J., A.A. Amis, and R.R. Coombs
    1985   The mechanical properties of human flexor tendons in relation to artificial tendons. *Journal of Hand Surgery—British Volume* 10(3):331-336.
Pryce, J.
    1980   The wrist position between neutral and ulnar deviation that facilitates the maximum power grip strength. *Journal of Biomechanics* 13:505-511.
Punnett, L., and W. M. Keyserling
    1987   Exposure to ergonomic stressors in the garment industry: Application and critique of job-site work analysis methods. *Ergonomics* 30:1099-1116.
Punnett, L., L.J. Fine, W.M. Keyserling, G.D. Herrin, and D.B. Chaffin
    1991   Back disorders and nonneutral trunk postures of automobile assembly workers. *Scandinavian Journal of Work, Environment, and Health* 17(5):337-346.
Putz-Anderson, V., and T.L. Galinsky
    1993   Psychophysically determined work durations for limiting shoulder girdle fatigue from elevated manual work. *International Journal of Industrial Ergonomics* 11:19-28.
Pyykko, I., O. Korhonen, M. Farkkila, J. Starck, S. Aatola, and V. Jantti
    1986   Vibration syndrome among Finnish forest workers, and follow-up from 1972 to 1983. *Scandinavian Journal of Work, Environment, and Health* 12:307-312.
Radanov, P., M. Sturzenegger, and G. Di Stefano
    1994   Prediction of recovery from dislocation of the cervical vertebrae (whiplash injury of the cervical vertebrae) with initial assessment of psychosocial variables. *Orthopaedics* 23:282-286.
Radwin, R.G., and O. Jeng
    1997   Activation force and travel effects on overexertion in repetitive key tapping. *Human Factors* 39:130-140.
Radwin, R.G., and S. Oh
    1992   External finger forces in submaximal five-finger pinch prehension. *Ergonomics* 35:275-288.
Radwin, R.G., and B.A. Rufalo
    1999   Computer key switch force-displacement characteristics and short-term effects on localized fatigue. *Ergonomics* 41(1):160-170.
Radwin, R.G., T.J. Armstrong, and D.B. Chaffin
    1987   Power hand tool vibration effects on grip exertions. *Ergonomics* 30:833-855.
Radwin, R.G., S. Oh, T.R. Jensen, and J.G. Webster
    1992   External finger forces in submaximal static prehension. *Ergonomics* 35(3):275-288.
Rais, O.
    1961   Heparin treatment of peritenomyosis (peritendinitis) crepitans acuta. *Acta Chirurgica Scandinavica* Supplement 268.
Ranney, D., R. Wells, and A. Moore
    1995   Upper limb musculoskeletal disorders in highly repetitive industries: Precise anatomical physical findings. *Ergonomics* 38:1408-1423.
Ready, A.E., S.L. Boreskie, S.A. Law, and R. Russell
    1993   Fitness and lifestyle parameters fail to predict back injuries in nurses. *Canadian Journal of Applied Physiology* 18:80-90.
Reisbord, L.S. and S. Greenland
    1985   Factors associated with self-reported back pain prevalence: A population-based study. *Journal of Chronic Diseases* 38:691-702.

Rempel, D.
1995   Musculoskeletal loading and carpal tunnel presure. Pp. 123-132 in *Repetitive Motion Disorders of the Upper Extremity*. Rosemont, IL: American Academy of Orthopedic Surgeons.

Rempel, D., R. Manojlovic, D.G. Levinsohn, T. Bloom, and L. Gordon
1994   Dexterity performance and reduced ambient temperature. *Journal of Hand Surgery* 19A:106-110.

Rempel, D., P.J. Keir, W.P. Smutz, and A. Hargens
1997a   Effects of static fingertip loading on carpal tunnel pressure. *Journal of Orthopaedic Research* 15:422-426.

Rempel, D., P. Tittiranonda, S. Burastero, M. Hudes, and Y. So
1999   Effect of keyboard keyswitch design on hand pain. *Journal of Environmental Medicine* 41(2):111-119.

Rempel, D., E. Serina, E. Klinenberg, B. Martin, T. Armstrong, J. Foulke, and S. Natajarian
1997b   The effect of keyboard keyswitch make force on applied force and finger flexor activity. *Ergonomics* 40:800-808.

Rifkin, J.
1995   *The End of Work*. NY: Putnam.

Riihimäki, H., S. Tola, T. Videman, and K. Hänninen
1989a   Low-back pain and occupation: A cross-sectional questionnaire study of men in machine operating, dynamic physical work, and sedentary work. *Spine* 14(2):204-209.

Riihimäki, H., G. Wickström, K. Hänninen, and T. Luopajärvi
1989b   Predictors of sciatic pain among concrete reinforecment workers and house painters: A five year follow-up. *Scandinavian Journal of Work and Environmental Health* 15:415-423.

Riihimäki, H., E. Viikari-Juntura, G. Moneta, J. Kiuha, T. Videman, and S. Tola
1994   Incidence of sciatic pain among men in machine operating, dynamic physical work, and sedentary work. A three-year follow-up. *Spine* 19(2):138-142.

Riley, M.W., and D.J. Cochran
1984   Dexterity performance and reduced ambient temperature. *Human Factors* 26:207-214.

Roberts, N., C. Gratin, et al.
1997   MRI analysis of lumbar intervertebral disc height in young and older populations. *Journal of Magnetic Resonance Imaging* 7(5):880-886.

Rodgers, S.H.
1988   A job analysis in worker fitness determination. *Occupational Medicine State of the Art Reviews* 3:219-239.
1992   A functional job analysis technique. *Occupational Medicine State of the Art Reviews* 7:679-711.

Roquelaure, Y., S. Mechail, C. Dano, S. Fanello, F. Benetti, D. Bureau, J. Mariel, Y.H. Martin, F. Derriennic, and D. Penneau-Fontbonne
1997   Occupational and personal risk factors for carpal tunnel syndrome in industrial workers. *Scandinavian Journal of Work, Environment, and Health* 23:364-369.

Rossignol, M., and J. Baetz
1987   Task-related risk factors for spinal injury: Validation of a self-administered questionnaire on hospital employees. *Ergonomics* 30:1531-1540.

Rossignol, M., M. Lortie, and E. Ledoux
    1993   Comparison of spinal health indicators in predicting spinal status in a 1-year longitudinal study. *Spine* 18:54-60.
Rotham, K.J., and S. Greenland
    1998a Measures of effect and measures of association (Chapter 4). Pp. 53-55 in *Modern Epidemiology* (Second Edition). Philadelphia: Lippincott Raven.
    1998b Applications of stratified analysis methods (Chapter 16). P. 296 in *Modern Epidemiology* (Second Edition). Philadelphia: Lippincott Raven.
Roto, P., and P. Kivi
    1984   Prevalence of epicondylitis and tenosynovitis among meatcutters. *Scandinavian Journal of Work, Environment, and Health* 10(3):203-205.
Rubin, B.B., A. Smith, S. Liauw, D. Isenman, A.D. Romaschin, and P.M. Walker
    1990   Complement activation and white cell sequestration in postischemic skeletal muscle. *American Journal of Physiology* 259:H525-H531.
Rufai, A., M. Benjamin, et al.
    1995   The development of fibrocartilage in the rat intervertebral disc. *Anat Embryol* 192:53-62.
Ruser, J.W.
    1998   Denominator choice in the calculation of workplace fatality rates. *American Journal of Industrial Medicine* 33:151-156.
    1999   The changing composition of lost-workday injuries. *Monthly Labor Review* June:11-17.
Rydevik, B., and G. Lundborg
    1977   Permeability of intraneural microvessels and perineurium following acute, graded nerve compression. *Scandinavian Journal of Plastic and Reconstructive Surgery* 11:179-187.
Rydevik, B., G. Lundborg, and C. Nordborg
    1976   Intraneural tissue reactions induced by internal neurolysis. *Scandinavian Journal of Plastic and Reconstructive Surgery* 10:3-8.
Rydevik, B., R.R. Myers, and H.C. Powell
    1989   Pressure increase in the dorsal root ganglion following mechanical compression. Closed compartment syndrome in nerve roots. *Spine* 14:574-576.
Rydevik, B.L., R.A. Pedowitz, A.R. Hargens, M.R. Swenson, R.R. Myers, and S.R. Garfin
    1991   Effects of acute graded compression on spinal nerve root function and structure: An experimental study on the pig cauda eqiuna. *Spine* 16:487-493.
Sackett, D.L.
    1979   Bias in analytic research. *Journal of Chronic Diseases* 32:51-68.
Sadamoto, T., F. Bonde-Petersen, and Y. Suzuki
    1983   Skeletal muscle tension, flow, pressure, and EMG during sustained isometric contractions in humans. *European Journal of Applied Physiology and Occupational Physiology* 51:395-408.
Sadock, B.J., and V.A. Sadock, eds.
    1999   *Kaplan and Sadock's Comprehensive Textbook of Psychiatry, Volume II.* New York: Lippincott Williams & Wilkins.
Saltin, B., G. Sjøgaard, F.A. Gaffney, and L.B. Rowell
    1981   Potassium, lactate, and water fluxes in human quadriceps muscle during static contractions. *Circulation Research* 48:118-124.
Sampson, S.P., M.A. Dadalamente, L.C. Hurst, and J. Seidman
    1991   Pathobiology of the human A1 pulley in trigger finger. *Journal of Hand Surgery* 16A:714-721.

Saraste, H., and G. Hultman

1987 Life conditions of persons with and without low-back pain. *Scandinavian Journal of Rehabilitative Medicine* 19:109-113.

Sauter, S.L., and N.G. Swanson

1996 An ecological model of musculoskeletal disorders in office work. In *Beyond Biomechanics: Psychosocial Aspects of Musculoskeletal Disorders in Office Work*, S.D. Moon and S.L. Sauter. London: Taylor and Francis.

Sauter, S.L., L.M. Schleiffer, and S.J. Knutson

1991 Work posture, workstation design, and musculskeletal discomfort in a VDT data entry task. *Human Factors* 33(2):151-167.

Schacter, S.L., and J.E. Singer

1962 Cognitive, social, and physiological determinants of emotional state. *Psychological Review* 69:379-399.

Schechtman, H., and D.L. Bader

1997 In vitro fatigue of human tendons. *Journal of Biomechanics* 30(8):829-835.

Scheer, S.J., T.K. Watanabe, and K.L. Radack

1997 Randomized controlled trials in industrial low back pain. Part 3. Subacute/ chronic pain interventions. *Archives of Physical Medicine and Rehabilitation* 78:414-423.

Scheffer, M., and H. Dupuis

1989 Effects of hand-arm vibration and cold on skin temperature. *Int Arc Occupational and Environmental Health* 61:375-378.

Schiefer, R.E., R. Kok, M.I. Lewis, and G.B. Meese

1984 Finger skin temperature and manual dexterity—some intergroup differences. *Applied Ergonomics* 15:135-141.

Schierhout, G.H., J.E.Meyers, and R.S. Bridger

1995 Work related musculoskeletal disorders and ergonomic stressors in the South Africa workforce. *Occupational and Environmental Medicine* 52:46-50.

Schipplein, O.D., T.E. Reinsel, G.B.J. Andersson, and S.A. Lavender

1995 The influence of initial horizontal weight placement on the loads at the lumbar spine while lifting. *Spine* 20:1895-1898.

Schoenmarklin, R.W., and W.S. Marras

1989a Effects of handle angle and work orientiation: I. Wrist motion and hammering performance. *Human Factors* 31(4):397-411.

1989b Effects of handle angle and work orientation on hammering: II. Muscle fatigue and subjective ratings of discomfort. *Human Factors* 31(4):413-420.

1993 Dynamic capabilities of the wrist joint in industrial workers. *International Journal of Industrial Ergonomics* 11:207-224.

Schor, J.B.

1991 *The Overworked American.* NY: Basic Books.

Schultz, A.B., and G.B. Andersson

1981 Analysis of loads on the lumbar spine. *Spine* 6(1):76-82.

Schultz, A., G. Andersson, K. Haderspeck, and A. Nachemson

1982a Loads on the lumbar spine: Validation of a biomechanical analysis by measurements of intradiscal pressures and myoelectric signals. *Journal of Bone and Joint Surgery* 64-A:713.720.

Schultz, A., G.B. Andersson, R. Ortengren, R. Bjork, and M. Nordin

1982b Analysis and quantitative myoelectric measurements of loads on the lumbar spine when holding weights in standing postures. *Spine* 7(4):390-397.

Schultz, A., R. Cromwell, et al.
   1987   Lumbar trunk muscle use in standing isometric heavy exertions. *Journal of Ortho-paedic Research* 5(3):320-329.
Schwartz, J.E., T.G. Pickering, and P.A. Landsbergis
   1996   Work-related stress and blood pressure: Current theoretical models and consid-erations from a behavioral medicine perspective. *Journal of Occupational Health and Psychology* 1:287-310.
Schwarzer, A.C., C.N. Aprill, and N. Bogduk
   1995   The sacroiliac joint in chronic low back pain. *Spine* 20(1):31-37.
Sejersted, O.M., and A.R. Hargens
   1985   Internal pressure and nutrition of skeletal muscle. Pp. 263-283 in *Tissue Nutrition and Viability*, A.R. Hargens, ed. New York: Springer-Verlag.
Sejersted, O.M., A.R. Hargens, K.R. Kardel, P. Blom, O. Jensen, and L. Hermansen
   1984   Intramuscular fluid pressure during isometric contraction of human skeletal muscle. *Journal of Applied Physiology: Respiratory, Environmental, and Exercise Physi-ology* 56:287-295.
Selye, H.
   1956   *The Stress of Life*. New York: McGraw-Hill.
Seradge, H., C. Bear, and D. Bithell
   1993   Preventing carpal tunnel syndrome and cumulative trauma disorder: Effect of carpal tunnel decompression exercises: An Oklahoma experience. *Journal of the Oklahoma State Medical Association 2000* April(4):150-153.
Seradge, H., et al.
   1995   In vivo measurement of carpal tunel pressure in the functioning hand. *Journal of Hand Surgery* 20A:855-859.
Sexton, W.L., and D.C. Poole
   1995   Costal diaphragm blood flow heterogeneity at rest and during exercise. *Respira-tion Physiology* 101:171-182.
Seyama, A.
   1993   The role of oxygen-derived free radicals and the effect of free radical scavengers on skeletal muscle ischemia/reperfusion injury. *Surgery Today* 23:1060-1067.
Shannon, H.S., V. Walters, W. Lewchuk, J. Richardson, L.A. Moran, T. Haines, and D. Verma
   1996   Workplace organizational correlates of lost-time accident rates in manufacturing. *American Journal of Industrial Medicine* 29:258-268.
Sharp, M.A., V.J. Rice, et al.
   1997   Effects of team size on the maximum weight bar lifting strength of military per-sonnel. *Human Factors* 39(3):481-488.
Shephard, R.J.
   1999   Age and physical work capacity. *Experimental Aging Research* 25:331-343.
Shepherd, J.T., C.G. Bolmqvist, A.R. Lind, J.H. Mitchell, and B. Saltin
   1981   Static (isometric) exercise. Retrospection and introspection. *Circulation Research* 48:I179-I188.
Siddall, P.J., and M.J. Cousins
   1997a   Neurobiology of pain. *International Anesthesiology Clinics* 35(2):1-26.
   1997b   Spinal pain mechanisms. *Spine* 22(1):98-104.
Siemieniuch, C.E., and M.A. Sinclair
   1999   Knowledge lifecycle management in manufacturing organisations. Pp. 322-332 in *Contemporary Ergonomics*, M.A. Hanson, E.J. Lovesey, and S.A. Robertson, eds. London: Taylor & Francis.

Silverstein, B., and J. Kalat
  1999   *Work-Related Disorders of the Back and Upper Extremity in Washington State,
         1990-1987.* Technical Report # 40-2-1999, March. Olympia, WA: Safety and Health
         Assessment and Research for Prevention Program.
Silverstein, B.A., L.J. Fine, and T.J. Armstrong
  1986   Hand wrist cumulative disorders in industry. *British Journal of Industrial Medicine*
         43(11):779-784.
  1987   Occupational factors and carpal tunnel syndrome. *American Journal of Industrial
         Medicine* 11:343-358.
Silverstein, B.A., T.J. Armstrong, A. Longmate, and D. Woody
  1988   Can in-plant exercise control musculoskeletal symptoms? *Journal of Occupational
         Medicine* 30(12):922-927.
Silverstein, B.A., D.S. Stetson, W.M. Keyserling, and L.J. Fine
  1997   Work-related musculoskeletal disorders: Comparison of data sources for surveil-
         lance. *American Journal of Industrial Medicine* 31(5):600-608.
Silvestri, G.T.
  1997   Occupational employment projections to 2006. *Monthly Labor Review.* Novem-
         ber:58-83.
Simon, G., R. Gaer, S. Kisely, and M. Piccinelli
  1996   Somatic symptoms of distress: An international primary care study. *Psychoso-
         matic Medicine* 58:481-488.
Simonsen, E.B., H. Klitgaard, and F. Bojsen-Moller
  1995   The influence of strength training, swim trainin and aging on the Achilles tendon
         and m. soleus of the rat. *Journal of Sports Medicine* 13(4):291-295.
Simmonds, M.J., S. Kumar, and E. Lechelt
  1996   Psychosocial factors in disabling low back pain: Causes or consequences? *Disabil-
         ity and Rehabilitation: An International Multidisciplinary Journal* 18:161-168.
Sjøgaard, G.
  1990   Exercise-induced muscle fatigue: The significance of potassium. *Acta Physiologica
         Scandinavica Supplementum* 593:1-63.
  1996   The significance of sustained muscle loading versus dynamic muscle loading at
         low forces in workplace design. P. 19 in *Marconi Computer Input Device Research
         Conference Proceedings,* D. Rempel and T. Armstrong, eds. Berkeley, CA: Univer-
         sity of California.
  1986   Water and electrolyte fluxes during exercise and their relation to muscle fatigue.
         Acta Physiologica Scandinavica Supplementum 556:129-136.
Sjøgaard, G., and B.R. Jensen
  1997   Muscle pathology with overuse. Pp. 17-40 in *Chronic Musculoskeletal Injuries in the
         Workplace,* D. Ranney, ed. Philadelphia, PA: W.B. Saunders Company.
Sjøgaard, G., and A.J. McComas
  1995   Role of interstitial potassium. *Advances in Experimental Medicine and Biology* 384:69-
         80.
Sjøgaard, G., and K. Sjøgaard
  1998   Muscle injury in repetitive motion disorders. *Clinical Orthopaedics and Related Re-
         search* 21-31.
Sjøgaard, G., U. Lundberg, and R. Kadefors
  2000   The role of muscle activity and mental load in the development of pain and
         degenerative processes on the muscle cellular level during computer work. *Euro-
         pean Journal of Applied Physiology* 83(2/3):99-105.

Sjøgaard, G., G. Savard, and C. Juel
    1988 Muscle blood flow during isometric acivity and its relation to muscle fatigue. *European Journal of Applied Physiology and Occupational Physiology* 57:327-335.
Sjøgaard, G., B. Kiens, K. Jorgensen, and B. Saltin
    1986 Intramuscular pressure, EMG and blood flow during low-level prolonged static contraction in man. *Acta Physiologica Scandinavica* 128:475-484.
Skie, M., J. Zeiss, N.A. Ebraheim, and W.T. Jackson
    1990 Carpal tunnel changes and median nerve compression during wrist flexion and extension seen by magnetic resonance imaging. *Journal of Hand Surgery* 15A:934-939.
Skjeldal, S., A. Torvik, B. Grogaard, L. Nordsletten, and T. Lyberg
    1993 Histological studies on postischemic rat skeletal muscles. With emphasis on the time of leukocyte invasion. *European Surgical Research* 25:348-357.
Smedley, J., P. Egger, C. Cooper, and D. Coggon
    1995 Manual handling activities and risk of low back pain in nurses. *Occupational and Environmental Medicine* 52:160-163.
    1997 Prospective cohort study of predictors of incident low back pain in nurses. *BMJ* 314:1225-1228.
Smith, E.M., D.A. Sonstegard, and W.H. Anderson
    1977 Carpal tunnel syndrome: Contribution of flexor tendons. *Archives of Physical Medicine and Rehabilitation* 58:379-385.
Smith., J.K., M.B. Grisham, D.N. Granger, and R.J. Korthuis
    1989 Free radical defense mechanisms and neutrophil infiltration in postischemic skeletal muscle. *American Journal of Physiology* 256:H789-H793.
Smith, M.J., and P. Carayon-Sainfort
    1989 A balance theory of job design for stress reduction. *International Journal of Industrial Ergonomics* 4:67-79.
Smith, M.J., and P. Carayon
    1996 Work organization, stress, and cumulative trauma disorders. In *Beyond Biomechanics: Psychosocial Aspects of Musculoskeletal Disorders in Office Work*, S.L. Moon and S.D. Sauter, eds. New York: Taylor and Francis.
Smutz, P., E. Serina, and D.M. Rempel
    1994 A system for evaluating the effect of keyboard design on force, posture, comfort and productivity. *Ergonomics* 37:1649-1660.
Smyth, J., M.C. Ockenfels, L. Porter, C. Kirschbaum, D.H. Hellhammer, and A.A. Stone
    1998 Stressors and mood measured on a momentary basis are associated with salivary cortisol secretion. *Psychoneuroendocrinology* 23(4):353-370.
Snook, S.H., D.R. Vaillancourt, V.M. Ciriello, and B.S. Webster
    1995 Psychophysical studies of repetitive wrist flexion and extension. *Ergonomics* 38(7):1488-1507.
Snook, S.H., D.R. Vaillancourt, V.M. Ciriello, and B.S.Webster
    1997 Maximum acceptable forces for repetitive ulnar deviation of the wrist. *American Industrial Hygiene Association Journal* 58:509-517.
Snook, S.H., B.S. Webster, et al.
    1998 The reduction of chronic nonspecific low back pain through the control of early morning lumbar flexion. A randomized controlled trial. *Spine* 23(23):2601-2607.
Snook, S.H., V.M. Ciriello, and B.S.Webster
    1999 Maximum acceptable forces for repetitive wrist extension with a pinch grip. *International Journal of Industrial Ergonomics* 24:579-559.

Snow, J.
   1936   On the mode of communication of cholera. In *Snow on Cholera*. New York: The Commonwealth Fund.

Solomonow, M., He Zhou, et al.
   2000   Biexponential recovery model of lumbar viscoelastic laxity and reflexive muscular activity after prolonged cyclic loading. *Clinical Biomechanics* (Bristol, Avon) 15(3):167-175.

Solomonow, M., B.H. Zhou, et al.
   1998   The ligamento-muscular stabilizing system of the spine. *Spine* 23(23):2552-2562.

Sommer, C., J.A. Gailbraith, H.M. Heckman, and R.R. Myers
   1993   Pathology of experimental compression neuropathy producing hyperesthesia. *Journal of Neuropathology and Experimental Neurology* 52(3):223-233.

Sommerich, C.M., J.D. McGlothlin, and W.S. Marras
   1993   Occupational risk factors associated with soft tissue disorders of the shoulder: A review of recent investigations in the literature. *Ergonomics* 36(6):697-717.

Speiler, E.A.
   1994   Perpetuating risk? Workers' compensation and the persistence of occupational injuries. *Houston Law Review* 31(1):119-264.

Spengler, D.M., S.J. Bigos, et al.
   1986   Back injuries in industry: A retrospective study. I. Overview and cost analysis. *Spine* 11(3):241-245.

Standard & Poors
   1997   Industry Surveys. http://www.dri.standardpoors.com/services/industry/index.html

Stenlund, B.
   1993   Shoulder tendinitis and osteoarthritis of the acromioclavicular joint and their relation to sports. *British Journal of Sports Medicine* 27(2):125-130.

Stenlund, B., I. Goldie, M. Hagberg, C. Hogstedt, and O. Marions
   1992   Radiographic osterarthrosis in the acromioclavicular joint resulting from manual work or exposure to vibration. *British Journal of Industrial Medicine* 49:588-593.

Sternbach, R.A.
   1986   Survey of pain in the United States: The Nuprin pain report. *Clinical Journal of Pain* 2:49-53.

Sternberg III, C.W., and W.G. Coleman
   1993   *America's Future Work Force: A Health and Education Policy Issues Handbook*. Westport, CT: Greenwood Press.

Stetson, D.S., W.M. Keyserling, B.A. Silverstein, and J.A. Leonard
   1991   Observational analysis of the hand and wrist: A pilot study. *Applied Occupational and Environmental Hygiene* 6:927-937.

Stetson, D.S., B.A. Silverstein, W.M. Keyserling, R.A. Wolfe, and J.W. Albers
   1993   Median sensory distal amplitude and latency: Comparisons between nonexposed managerial/professional employees and industrial workers. *American Journal of Industrial Medicine* 24:175-189.

Stobbe, T.J., R.W. Plummer, R.C. Jensen, and M.D. Attfield
   1988   Incidence of low back injuries among nursing personnel as a function of patient lifting frequency. *Journal of Safety Science* 19:21-28.

Stratakis, C.A., P.W. Gold, and G.P. Chrousos
   1995   Neuroendocrinology of stress: Implications for growth and development. *Hormone Research* 43:162-167.

Strömberg, T., L.B. Dahlin, A. Brun, and G. Lundborg
    1997   Structural nerve changes at wrist level in workers exposed to vibration. *Occupa-
           tional and Environmental Medicine* 54:307-311.
Strömberg, T., G. Lundborg, B. Holmquist, and L.B. Dahlin
    1996   Impaired regeneration in rat sciatic nerves exposed to short term vibration. *Jour-
           nal of Hand Surgery (British)* 21:746-749.
Strunin, L., and L.I. Boden
    2000   Paths of reentry: Employment experiences of injured workers. *American Journal
           of Industrial Medicine* 38:373-384.
Stubbs, M., M. Harris, et al.
    1998   Ligamento-muscular protective reflex in the lumbar spine of the feline. *Journal of
           Electromyography and Kinesiology* 8(4):197-204.
Suadicani, P., K. Hansen, A.M. Fenger, F. Gyntelberg
    1994   Low back pain in steelplant workers. *Occupational Medicine* 44:217-221.
Sum, J.
    1996   Navigating the California Workers' Compensation System: The Injured Worker's
           Experience. California Commission on Health and Safety and Workers' Compen-
           sation. http://www.dir.ca.gov/CHSWC/navigate/navigate.html.
Sunderland, S.
    1978   *Nerve and Nerve Injuries.* Edinburgh: Churchill-Livingstone.
Susser, M.
    1973   *Causal Thinking in the Health Sciencies: Concepts and Strategies in Epidemiology.* New
           York: Oxford University Press.
Svensson, H.-O., and G.B.J. Andersson
    1983   Low-back pain in 40- to 47-year-old men: work history and work environment
           factors. *Spine* 8:272-276.
    1989   The relationship of low-back pain, work history, work environment, and stress.
           Spine 14:517-522.
Szabo, R.M, and L.K. Chidgey
    1989   Stress carpal tunnel pressures in patients with carpal tunnel syndrome and nor-
           mal patients. *Journal of Hand Surgery* 14A:624-627.
Szabo, R.M., and N.A. Sharkey
    1993   Response of peripheral nerve to cyclic compression in a laboratory rat model.
           Journal of Orthopaedic Research 11:828-833.
Takeuchi, T., M. Futatsuka, H. Imanishi, and S. Yamada
    1986   Pathological changes observed in the finger biopsies of patients with vibration-
           induced white finger. *Scandinavian Journal of Work, Environment, and Health* 12:280-
           283.
Tanaka, S., M. Petersen, and L. Cameron.
    In   Prevalence and risk factors of tendinitis and related disorder of the distal upper
  press   extremity among U.S. workers: Comparisons to carpal tunnel syndrome. *Ameri-
           can Journal of Internal Medicine.*
Tanaka, S. D.K. Wild, L.L. Cameron, and E. Freund
    1997   Association of occupational and non-occupational risk factors with the preva-
           lence of self-reported carpal tunnel syndrome in a national survey of the working
           population. *American Journal of Industrial Medicine* 32(5):550-556.

Tanaka, S., D.K. Wild, P.J. Seligman, W.E. Haperin, V.J Behrens, and V. Putz-Anderson
  1994   Prevalence and work-relatedness of self-reported carpal tunnel syndrom among U.S. workers' analysis of the Occupational Health Supplement data of the 1988 National Health Interview Survey. *American Journal of Industrial Medicine* 27(40):451-470.

Tanzer, R.C.
  1959   The carpal tunnel syndrome: A clinical and anatomical study. *Journal of Bone and Joint Surgery* 41-A(4):626-634.

Taylor, H., and N.M. Curran
  1985   *The Nuprin Report.* New York: Louis Haris and Associates.

Taylor, J.C., and D.F. Felten
  1993   *Performance by Design: Sociotechnical Systems in North America.* Englewood Cliffs, NJ: Prentice Hall.

Taylor, W., D. Wasserman, V. Behrens, D. Reynolds, and S. Samueloff
  1984   Effect of the air hammer on the hands of stonecutters. The limestone quarries of Bedford, Indiana, revisited. *British Journal of Industrial Medicine* 41:289-295.

Theorell, T., and R.A. Karasek
  1996   Current issues relating to psychosocial job strain and cardiovascular disease research. *Journal of Occupational Health and Psychology* 1:9-26.

Tittiranonda, P, S. Burastero, and D. Rempel
  1999   Risk factors for musculoskeletal disorders among computer users. *Occupational Medicine STAR* 14:17-38.

Toomingas, A., L. Alfredsson, and Å. Kilbom
  1997a Possible bias from rating behavior when subjects rate both exposure and outcome. *Scandinavian Journal of Work, Environment, and Health* 23:370-377.

Toomingas, A., T. Theorell, H. Michélsen, and R. Nordemar
  1997b Associations between self related psychosocial work conditions and musculoskeletal symptoms and signs. *Scandinavian Journal of Work, Environment, and Health* 23:130-139.

Torgén, M., J. Winkel, L. Alfredsson, et al.
  1999   Evaluation of questionnaire-based information on previous physical loads. *Scandinavian Journal of Work, Environment, and Health* 25:246-254.

Toussaint, H.M., A.F. De Winter, Y.H.M.P. de Looze, J.H. Van Dieen, and I. Kingma
  1995   Flexion relaxation during lifting: Implications for torque production by muscle activity and tissue strain at the lumbo-sacral joint. *Journal of Biomechanics* 28:199-210.

Trafimow, J.H., O.D. Schipplein, G.J. Novak, and G.B.J. Andersson
  1993   The effects of quadriceps fatigue on the technique of lifting. *Spine* 18:364-367.

Tsuang, Y.H., O.D. Schipplein, J.H. Trophema, and G.B.J. Andersson
  1992   Influence of body segment dynamics on loads at the lumbar spine during lifting. *Ergonomics* 35:437-444.

Turk, D.C., and H. Flor
  1999   Chronic pain: A biobehavioral perspective. In *Psychosocial Factors in Pain: Critical Perspectives*, R.J. Gatchel and D.C. Turk, eds. New York: Guilford Press.

Tyrell, A.R., T. Reilly, et al.
  1985   Circadian variation in stature and the effects of spinal loading. *Spine* 10:161-164.

Uchiyama, S., P.C. Amadio, H. Coert, L.J. Berglund, and K.N. An
  1997   Gliding resistance of extrasynovial and intrasynovial tendons through the A2 pulley. *Journal of Bone and Joint Surgery* 79A:219-224.

Ulin, S.S., CM. Ways, T.J. Armstrong, and S.H. Snook
    1990   Perceived exertion and discomfort versus work height with a pistol-shaped screw-driver. *American Industrial Hygiene Association Journal* 51(11):588-594.
Ulin, S.S., S.H. Snook, T.J. Armstrong, and G.D. Herrrin
    1992   Preferred tool shapes for various horizontal and vertical work locations. *Applied Occupational and Environmental Hygiene* 7(5):327-337.
Ulin, S.S., T.J. Armstrong, S.H. Snook, and A. Franzblau
    1993a   Effect of tool shape and work location on perceived exertion for work on horizontal surfaces. *American Industrial Hygiene Association Journal* 54:383-391.
Ulin, S.S., T.A. Armstrong, S.H. Snook, and W.M. Keyserling
    1993b   Perceived exertion and discomfort associated with driving screws at various work locations and at different work frequencies. *Ergonomics* 36:833-846.
Urban, J.P.G., and J.F. McMullin
    1985   Swelling pressure of the intervertebral disc: Influence of proteoglycan and collagen contents. *Biorheology* 22:145-157.
U.S. Army Missile Research and Development Command
    No   *Human engineering requirements for military systems, equipment, and facilities (MIL-H*
    date   *46855)*. U.S. Army Missile Research and Development Command, Redstone Arsenal, Alabama.
U.S. Department of Labor
    1999   *Futurework: Trends and Challenges for Work in the 21st Century*. Washington, DC: U.S. Department of Labor.
van der Weide, W.E., J.H.A.M. Verbeek, H.J.A. Sallé, and F.J.H. van Dijk
    1999   Prognostic factors for chronic disability from acute low-back pain in occupational health care. *Scandinavian Journal of Work, Environment, and Health* 25:50-56.
Van Eck, M., H. Berkhof, N. Nicolson, and J. Sulon
    1996   The effects of perceived stress, traits, mood states, and stressful daily events on salivary cortisol. *Psychosomatic Medicine* 58:447-458.
van Poppel, M.N., B.W. Koes, T. Smid, and L.M. Bouter
    1997   A systematic review of controlled clinical trials on the prevention of back pain in industry. *Occupational and Environmental Medicine* 54(12):841-847.
van Poppel, M.N.M, B.W. Koes, W. Devillé, T. Smid, and L.M. Bouter
    1998   Risk factors for back pain incidence in industry: A prospective study. *Pain* 77:81-86.
van Tulder, M.W., W.J.U. Assendelft, B.W. Koes, and L.M. Bouter
    1997   Methodologic guidelines for systematic reviews in the Cochrane Collaboration Back Review Group for spinal disorders. *Spine* 22:2323-2330.
Venning, P.J., S.D. Walter, and L.W. Stitt
    1987   Personal and job-related factors as determinants of incidence of back injuries among nursing personnel. *Journal of Occupational Medicine* 29:820-825.
Vernon-Roberts, B.
    1988.   Disc pathology and disease states. Pp. 73-119 in *The Biology of the Intervertebral Disc*, P. Ghosh, ed. Boca Raton, FL: CRC Press.
Vernon-Roberts, B., and C.J. Pirie
    1973   Healing trabecular microfractures in the bodies of lumbar vertebrae. *Annals of Rheumatic Disease* 32(5):406-412.
Videman, T., M. Nurminen, and J.D. Troup
    1990   1990 Volvo Award in clinical sciences. Lumbar spinal pathology in cadaveric material in relation to history of back pain, occupation, and physical loading. *Spine* 15(8):728-740.

Videman, T., T. Nurminen, et al.
1984   Low-back pain in nurses and some loading factors of work. *Spine* 9(4):400-404.
Viikari-Juntura, E.
1996   Second International Scientific Conference on the Prevention of Work-Related Musculoskeletal Disorders, PREMUS 95, September 24-28, Montréal, Canada. *Scandinavian Journal of Environmental Health* 22(1):68-70.
1984   Tenosynovitis, peritendinitis and the tennis elbow syndrome. *Scandinavian Journal of Work, Environment and Health* 10:443-449.
Viikari-Juntura, E.J., J. Vuori, B.A. Silverstein, R. Kalimo, E. Juosma, and T. Videman
1991   A life-long prospective study on the role of psychosocial factors in neck-shoulder and low back pain. *Spine* 16(9):1056-1061.
Virokannas, H.
1995   Dose-response relation between exposure to two types of hand-arm vibration and sensorineural perception of vibration. *Occupational and Environmental Medicine* 52:332-336.
Volinn, E.
1999   Do workplace interventions prevent low-back disorders? If so, why? A methodologic commentary. *Ergonomics* 42:258-272.
1997   The epidemiology of low back pain in the rest of the world. A review of surveys in low- and middle-income countries. *Spine* 22:1747-1754.
von Korff, M., L. LeResche, and S.F. Dworkin
1993   First onset of common pain syndromes: A prospective study of depression as a risk factor. *Pain* 55:251-258.
Waersted, M., R.A. Bjorklund, and R.H. Westgaard
1991   Shoulder muscle tension induced by two VDU-based tasks of different complexity. *Ergonomics* 34(2):137-150.
Wall, T.D., and P.R. Jackson
1995   New manufacturing initiatives and shopfloor job design. Pp. 139-174 in *The Changing Nature of Work*, A. Howard, ed. San Francisco, CA: Jossey-Bass Publishers.
Walker, P.M., T. F. Lindsay, R. Labbe, D.A. Mickle, and A.D. Romaschin
1987   Salvage of skeletal muscle with freee radical scavengers. *Journal of Vascular Surgery* 5:68-75.
Walsh, A., O. Colliou, et al.
2000   *An In Vivo Model of Dynamic Loading Induced Intervertebral Disc Degeneration.* Adelaide, Australia: International Society for the Study of the Lumbar Spine.
Wang, J.L., M. Parnianpour, et al.
2000   Viscoelastic finite-element analysis of a lumbar motion segment in combined compression and sagittal flexion. Effect of loading rate. *Spine* 25(3):310-318.
Warren, G.L., D.A. Hayes, D.A. Lowe, B.M. Prior, and R.B. Armstrong
1993   Materials fatigue initiates eccentric contraction-induced injury in rat soleus muscle. *Journal of Physiology* 464:477-489.
Warwick, R., and P.L. Williams, eds.
1973   *Gray's Anatomy, 35th British Edition.* Philadelphia: W.B. Saunders Company.
Wasson, J.H., H.C. Sox, and C.H. Sox.
1981   The diagnosis of abdominal pain in ambulatory male patients. *Medical Decision Making* 1:215-224.
Waters, T.R., V. Putz-Anderson, and S. Baron
1998   Methods for assessing the physical demands of manual lifting: A review and case study from warehousing. *American Industrial Hygiene Association Journal* 59(12):871-881.

Waters T.R., V. Putz-Anderson, A. Garg, and L.J. Fine
 1993 Revised NIOSH equation for the design and evaluation of manual lifting tasks. *Ergonomics* 36:749-776.
Waters, T.R., S.L. Baron, L.A. Piacitelli, V.P. Anderson, T. Skov, M. Haring-Sweeney, D.K. Wall, and L.J. Fine
 1999 Evaluation of the revised NIOSH lifting equation. A cross-sectional epidemiologic study. *Spine* 24(4):386-394, discussion 395.
Waterson, P.E.
 1999 The use and effectiveness of modern manufacturing practices: A survey of UK industry. *International Journal of Psychosocial Rehabilitation* 37(10):2271-2292.
Watkins, L.R., S. F. Maier, and L.E. Goehler
 1995 Cytokine-to-brain communication: A review and analysis of alternative mechanisms. *Life Science* 57(11):1011-1026.
Wegman, D.H., and L.J. Fine
 1990 Occupational health in the 1990s. *Annual Review of Public Health* 11:89-103.
Weinstein, J.
 1986 Mechanism of spinal pain: The dorsal root ganglion and its role as a mediator of low back pain. *Spine* 11:999-1001.
Weinstein, J.N., M. Pope, R. Schmidt, et al.
 1987 The effects of low frequency vibration on dorsal root ganglion substance P. *Neuroorthopaedics* 4:24-30.
Weiser, M.
 1991 The computer for the 21st century. *Scientific American* 265:94-103.
 1993 Some computer science issues in ubiquitous computing. *Communications of the ACM* 36:74-83.
Weiss, N.D., L. Gordon, T. Bloom, Y. So, and D.M. Rempel
 1995 Position of the wrist associated with the lowest carpal-tunnel pressure: Implications for splint design. *Journal of Bone and Joint Surgery* 77A(11):1695-1699.
Wells, J., J.F. Zipp, P.T. Schuette, and J. McEleney
 1983 Musculoskeletal disorders among letter carriers. A comparison of wieght carrying, walking, and sedentary occupations. *Journal of Occupational Medicine* 25(11):814-820.
Wells, R.P., A. Moore, J. Potvin, et al.
 1994 Assessment of risk factors for development of work-related musculoskeletal disorders (RSI). *Applied Ergonomics* 25:157-164.
Werneke, M.W., D.E. Harris, and R.L. Lichter
 1993 Clinical effectiveness of behavioral signs for screening chronic low-back pain patients in a work-oriented physical rehabilitation program. *Spine* 18:2412-2418.
Werner, R.A., C. Bir, and T.J. Armstrong
 1994 Reverse Phalen's maneuver as an aid in diagnosing carpal tunnel syndrome. *Archives of Physical Medicine and Rehabilitation* 75:783-786.
Werner, R., T.J. Armstrong, C. Bir, M.K. Aylard
 1997 Intracarpal canal pressures: The role of finger, hand, wrist, and forearm position. *Clinical Biomechanics* 12(1):44-51.
Westgaard, R.H., and A. Aarås
 1985 The effect of improved workplace design on the development of musculoskeletal illnesses. *Applied Ergonomics* 16:91-97.
Westgaard, R.H., and R. Bjorklund
 1987 Generation of muscle tension additional to postural muscle load. *Ergonomics* 30(6):911-923.

Westgaard, R.H., and C.J. de Luca
  1999 Motor unit substitution in long-duration contractions of the human trapezius muscle. *Journal of Neurophysiology* 82(1):501-504.
Westgaard, R.H., and T. Jansen
  1992a Individual and work related factors associated with symptoms of musculoskeletal complaints. I. A quantitative registration system. *British Journal of Industrial Medicine* 49:147-153.
  1992b Individual and work related factors associated with symptoms of musculoskeletal complaints. II. Different risk factors among sewing machine operators. *British Journal of Industrial Medicine* 49:154-162.
Westgaard, R.H., and J. Winkel
  1997 Ergonomic intervention research for improved musculoskeletal health: A critical review. *International Journal of Industrial Ergonomics* 20:463-500.
Westgaard, R.H., C. Jensen, and K. Hansen
  1993 Individual and work related risk factors associated with symptoms of musculoskeletal complaints. *International Archives of Occupational and Environmental Health* 64:405-413.
White, A.A., and M.M. Panjabi
  1990 *Clinical Biomechanics of the Spine* (Second Edition). Philadelphia: J.B. Lippincott Company.
Whitman, M. N.
  1999 Global competition and the changing role of the American corporation. *The Washington Quarterly* 22(2):59-82.
Wiesel, S.W., N. Tsourmas, et al.
  1984 Study of computer-assisted tomography: I. The incidence of positive CAT scans in an asymptomatic group of patients. *Spine* 9(6):549-556.
Wieslander, G., D. Norbäck, C.J. Göthe, and L. Juhlin
  1989 Carpal tunnel syndrome (CTS) and exposure to vibration, repetitive wrist movements, and heavy manual work: a case-referent study. *British Journal of Industrial Medicine* 46:43-47.
Wigaeus H.E., M. Hagberg, and S. Hellstrom
  1992 Prevention of musculoskeletal disorders in nursing aides by physical training. Pp. 364-366 in *Occupational Health for Health Care Workers*. Ecomed, Germany: UPP-Study Group.
Wiktorin, C., L. Karlqvist, J. Winkel, et al.
  1993 Validity of self-reported exposures to work postures and manual material handling. *Scandinavian Journal of Work, Environment, and Health* 19:208-214.
Wilkie, D.R.
  1986 Muscular fatigue: Effects of hydrogen ions and inorganic phosphate. *Federation Proceedings* 45:2921-2923.
Williams, D.A., M. Feuerstein, D. Durbin, and J. Pezzulo
  1998 Healthcare and indemnity costs across the natural history of disability in occupational low back pain. *Spine* 23(21):2329-2336.
Winkel, J., and S.E. Mathiassen
  1994 Assessment of physical work load in epidemiologic studies: concepts, issues and operational considerations. *Ergonomics* 37:979-988.
Womack, J., and D. Jones
  1996 *Lean Thinking*. NY: Simon and Schuster.

Woo, S.L.-Y., M.A. Gomez, and W.H. Akeson
1985 Mechanical behaviors of soft tissues: Measurements, modifications, injuries, and treatment. Pp. 109-133 in *Biomechanics of Trauma*, H.M. Nahum and J. Melvin, eds. Norwalk, CT: Appleton Century Crofts.

Woo, S.L., M.A. Ritter, D. Amiel, T.M. Sanders, M.A. Gomez, S.C. Kuei, S.R. Garfin, and W.H. Akeson
1980 The biomechanical and biochemical properties of swine tendons—long term effects of exercise on the digital extensors. *Connective Tissue Research* 7(3):177-183.

World Health Organization
1985 Identification and Control of Work-Related Diseases. Technical Report No. 174. Geneva: World Health Organization.

Xu, Y., E. Bach, and E. Orhede
1997 Work environment and low back pain: the influence of occupational activities. *Occupational and Environmental Medicine* 54:741-745.

Yamashita, T., Y. Minaki, et al.
1993 Mechanosensitive afferent units in the lumbar intervertebral disc and adjacent muscle. *Spine* 18(15):2252-2256.

Yamashita, T., Y. Minaki, et al.
1996 A morphological study of the fibrous capsule of the human lumbar facet joint. *Spine* 21(5):538-543.

Yasuma, T.
1990. Histological changes in aging lumbar intervertebral discs. Their role in protrusions and prolapses. *Journal of Bone and Joint Surgery* A-72(2):220-229.

Yelin, E.H.
1997 The earnings, income, and assets of persons aged 51 to 61 with and without musculoskeletal conditions. *Journal of Rheumatology* 24:2024-2030.

Yelin, E.H., L.S. Trupin, and D.S. Sebesta
1999 Transitions in employment, morbidity, and disability among persons aged 51 to 61 with musculoskeletal and non-musculoskeletal conditions in the U.S., 1992-1994. *Arthritis and Rheumatism* 42:769-779.

Yingling, V.R., and S.M. McGill
In Anterior shear of spinal motion segments: kinematics, kinetics and resulting
press injuries. *Spine.*

Yoshizawa, H., J. O'Brien, et al.
1980 The neuropathology of intervertebral discs removed for low back pain. *Journal of Pathology* 132:95-104.

Zerba, E., T.E. Komorowski, and J.A. Faulkner
1990 Free radical injury to skeletal muscles of young, adult, and old mice. *American Journal of Physiology* 258:C429-C435.

Zetterberg, C., G.B. Andersson, and A.B. Schultz
1987 The activity of individual trunk muscles during heavy physical loading. *Spine* 12(10):1035-1040.

Zetterberg, C., A. Forsberg, E. Hansson, H. Johansson, P. Nielsen, B. Danielsson, et al.
1997 Neck and upper extremity problems in car assembly workers: A comparison of subjective complaints, work satisfaction, physical examination and gender. *International Journal of Industrial Ergonomics* 19:227-289.

APPENDIX A

Answers to Questions Posed by Congress

The questions below provided the impetus for the study. The charge to the panel, prepared by the NRC and the IOM, was to conduct a comprehensive review of the science base and to address the issues outlined in the questions. The panel's responses to the questions follow.

1. What are the conditions affecting humans that are considered to be work-related musculoskeletal disorders?

The disorders of particular interest to the panel, in light of its charge, focus on the low back and upper extremities. With regard to the upper extremities, these include rotator cuff injuries (lateral and medial), epicondylitis, carpal tunnel syndrome, tendinitis, tenosynovitis of the hand and wrist (including DeQuervains' stenosing tenosynovitis, trigger finger, and others) and a variety of nonspecific wrist complaints, syndromes, and regional discomforts lacking clinical specificity. With regard to the low back, there are many disabling syndromes that occur in the absence of defined radiographic abnormalities or commonly occur in the presence of unrelated radiographic abnormalities. Thus, the most common syndrome is nonspecific backache. Other disorders of interest include back pain and sciatica due to displacement and degeneration of lumbar intervertebral discs with radiculopathy, spondylolysis, and spondylolisthesis, and spinal stenosis (ICD 9 categories 353-357, 722-724, and 726-729).

2. What is the status of medical science with respect to the diagnosis and classification of such conditions?

Diagnostic criteria for some of the musculoskeletal disorders considered to be work-related and considered in this report are clear-cut, especially those that can be supported by objective ancillary diagnostic tests, such as carpal tunnel syndrome. Others, such as work-related low back pain, are in some instances supported by objective change, which must be considered in concert with the history and physical findings. In the case of radicular syndromes associated with lumbar intervertebral disc herniation, for example, clinical and X-ray findings tend to support each other. In other instances, in the absence of objective support for a specific clinical entity, diagnostic certainty varies but may nevertheless be substantial. The clinical picture of low back strain, for example, while varying to some degree, is reasonably characteristic.

Epidemiologic definitions for musculoskeletal disorders, as for infectious and other reportable diseases, are based on simple, unambiguous criteria. While these are suitable for data collection and analysis of disease occurrence and patterns, they are not appropriate for clinical decisions, which must also take into account personal, patient-specific information, which is not routinely available in epidemiologic databases.

3. What is the state of scientific knowledge, characterized by the degree of certainty or lack thereof, with regard to occupational and non-occupational activities causing such conditions?

The panel has considered the contributions of occupational and non-occupational activities to the development of musculoskeletal disorders via independent literature reviews based in observational epidemiology, biomechanics, and basic science. As noted in the chapter on epidemiology, when studies meeting stringent quality criteria are used, there are significant data to show that both low back and upper extremity musculoskeletal disorders can be attributed to workplace exposures. Across the epidemiologic studies, the review has shown both consistency and strength of association. Concerns about whether the associations might be spurious have been considered and reviewed. Biological plausibility for the work-relatedness of these disorders has been demonstrated in biomechanical and basic science studies, and further evidence to build causal inferences has been demonstrated in intervention studies that show reduction in occurrence of musculoskeletal disorders following implementation of interventions. The findings suggest strongly that there is an occupational component to musculoskeletal disorders. Each set of studies has inherent strengths and limitations that affect confidence in the conclusions; as discussed in Chapter 3 (methodology), when the pattern of evidence is considered across the various types of studies, complementary strengths are demonstrated. These findings were considered collectively through integration of the information across the relevant bodies of scientific evidence. Based on this approach, the panel concludes, with a high degree of confidence, that there is a strong relationship between certain work tasks and the risk of musculoskeletal disorders.

4. What is the relative contribution of any causal factors identified in the literature to the development of such conditions in (a) the general population, (b) specific industries, and (c) specific occupational groups?

A. Individual Risk Factors

Because 80 percent of the American adult population works, it is difficult to define a "general population" that is different from the working population as a whole. The known risk factors for musculoskeletal disorders include the following:

Age—Advancing age is associated with more spinal complaints, hand pain, and other upper extremity pain, e.g., shoulder pain. Beyond the age of 60, these complaints increase more rapidly in women than men. The explanation for spinal pain is probably the greater frequency of osteoporosis in women than in men. The explanation for hand pain is probably the greater prevalence of osteoarthritis affecting women. However, other specific musculoskeletal syndromes do not show this trend. For example, the mean age for symptomatic presentation of lumbar disc herniation is 42 years; thereafter, there is a fairly rapid decline in symptoms of that disorder.

Gender—As noted above, there are gender differences in some musculoskeletal disorders, most particularly spinal pain due to osteoporosis, which is more commonly found in women than in men, and hand pain due to osteoarthritis, for which there appears to be a genetic determinant with increased incidence in daughters of affected mothers.

Healthy lifestyles—There is a general belief that the physically fit are at lower risk for musculoskeletal disorders; there are few studies, however, that have shown a scientific basis for that assertion. There is evidence that reduced aerobic capacity is associated with some musculoskeletal disorders, specifically low back pain and, possibly, lumbar disc herniations are more common in cigarette smokers. Obesity, defined as the top fifth quintile of weight, is also associated with a greater risk of back pain. There currently is little evidence that reduction of smoking or weight reduction reduces the risk.

Other exposures—Whole-body vibration from motor vehicles has been associated with an increase in risk for low back pain and lumbar disc herniation. There is also evidence that suboptimal body posture in the seated position can increase back pain. Some evidence suggests that altering vibrational exposure through seating and improved seating designs to optimize body posture (i.e., reduce intradiscal pressure) can be beneficial.

Other diseases—There is a variety of specific diseases found in the population that predispose to certain musculoskeletal disorders. Among the more common are diabetes and hypothyroidism, both associated with carpal tunnel syndrome.

B. Work-Related Risk Factors

Chapter 4 of this report explores the enormous body of peer-reviewed data on epidemiologic studies relevant to this question. Detailed reviews were conducted of those studies judged to be of the highest quality based on the panel's screening criteria (presented in the introduction and in Chapter 4). The vast majority of these studies have been performed on populations of workers in particular industries in which workers exposed to various biomechanical factors were compared with those not exposed for evidence of symptoms, signs, laboratory abnormalities, or clinical diagnoses of musculoskeletal disorders. A small number of studies have been performed in sample groups in the general population, comparing individuals who report various exposures with those who do not.

The principal findings with regard to the roles of work and physical risk factors are:

• Lifting, bending, and twisting and whole-body vibration have been consistently associated with excess risk for low back disorders, with relative risks of 1.2 to 9.0 compared with workers in the same industries without these factors.

• Awkward static postures and frequent repetitive movements have been less consistently associated with excess risk. For disorders of the upper extremity, vibration, force, and repetition have been most strongly and consistently associated with relative risks ranging from 2.3 to 84.5.

The principal findings with regard to the roles of work and psychosocial risk factors are:

• High job demand, low job satisfaction, monotony, low social support, and high perceived stress are important predictors of low back musculoskeletal disorders.

- High job demand and low decision latitude are the most consistent of these factors associated with increased risk for musculoskeletal disorders of the upper extremities.
- In addition, in well-studied workforces, there is evidence that individual psychological factors may also predispose to risk, including anxiety and depression, psychological distress, and certain coping styles. Relative risks for these factors have been generally less than 2.0.

5. What is the incidence of such conditions in (a) the general population, (b) specific industries, and (c) specific occupational groups?

There are no comprehensive national data sources capturing medically defined musculoskeletal disorders, and data available regarding them are based on individual self-reports in surveys. Explicitly, these reports include work as well as nonwork-related musculoskeletal disorders without distinction; therefore, rates derived from these general population sources cannot be considered in any sense equivalent to rates for background, reference, or unexposed groups, nor conversely, as rates for musculoskeletal disorders associated with any specific work or activity. There are *no* comprehensive data available on occupationally unexposed groups and, given the proportion of adults now in the active U.S. workforce, any such nonemployed group would be unrepresentative of the general adult population. According the 1997 report from the National Arthritis Data Workgroup (Lawrence, 1998), a working group of the National Institute of Arthritis and Musculoskeletal and Skin Diseases, 37.9 million Americans, or 15 percent of the entire U.S. population, suffered from one or more chronic musculoskeletal disorders in 1990 (these data cover all musculoskeletal disorders). Moreover, given the increase in disease rates and the projected demographic shifts, they estimate a rate of 18.4 percent or 59.4 million by the year 2020. In summary, data from the general population of workers and nonworkers together suggest that the musculoskeletal disorders problem is a major source of short- and long-term disability, with economic losses in the range of 1 percent of gross domestic product. A substantial portion of these are disorders of the low back and upper extremities.

The Bureau of Labor Statistics (BLS) data, while suffering a number of limitations, are sufficient to confirm that the magnitude of work-related musculoskeletal disorders is very large and that rates differ substantially among industries and occupations, consistent with the assumption that work-related risks are important predictors of musculoskeletal disorders. BLS recently estimated 846,000 lost-workday cases of musculoskeletal disorders in private industry. Manufacturing was responsible for 22 percent of sprains/strains, carpal tunnel syndrome, or tendinitis, while the service industry accounted for 26 percent. Examining carpal tunnel syndrome alone, manufacturing, transportation, and finance all exceeded the national average, while for the most common but less specific sprains and strains, the transportation sector was highest, with construction, mining, agriculture, and wholesale trade all higher than average. These data suggest that musculoskeletal disorders are a problem in several industrial sectors, that is, the problems are not limited to the traditional heavy labor environments represented by agriculture, mining, and manufacturing.

The National Center for Health Statistics (NCHS) survey data provide added information on self-reported health conditions of the back and the hand. This survey presents estimates for back pain among those whose pain occurred at work (approximately 11.7 million) and for those who specifically reported that their pain was work-related back pain (5.6 million).

The highest-risk *occupations* among men were construction laborers, carpenters, and industrial truck and tractor equipment operators, and among women the highest-risk occupations were nursing aides/orderlies/attendants, licensed practical nurses, maids, and janitor/cleaners. Other high-risk occupations were hairdressers and automobile mechanics, often employed in small businesses or self-employed.

Among men, the highest-risk *industries* were lumber and building material retailing, crude petroleum and natural gas extraction, and sawmills/planing mills/millwork. Among women, the highest-risk industries were nursing and personal care facilities, beauty shops, and motor vehicle equipment manufacturing.

Questions from the NCHS survey on upper-extremity discomfort elicited information about carpal tunnel syndrome, tendinitis and related syndromes, and arthritis. Carpal tunnel syndrome was reported by 1.87 million people; over one-third of these were diagnosed as carpal tunnel syndrome by a health care provider and half were believed to be work-related. Tendinitis was reported by 588,00 people, and 28 percent of these were determined to be work-related by a health care provider. Over 2 million active or recent workers were estimated to have hand/wrist arthritis. The survey did not report these conditions by either occupation or industry.

6. *Does the literature reveal any specific guidance to prevent the development of such conditions in (a) the general population, (b) specific industries, and (c) specific occupational groups?*

A. Development and Prevention in Working Populations

Because the majority of the U.S. population works, the data for the population as a whole apply to the 80 percent who are working. There is substantial evidence that psychosocial factors, in addition to the physical factors cited above (see response to Question 4), are significant contributors to musculoskeletal disorders. Relevant factors are repetitive, boring jobs, a high degree of perceived psychosocial stress, and suboptimal relationships between worker and supervisor.

The weight and pattern of both the scientific evidence and the very practical quality improvement data support the conclusion that primary and secondary prevention interventions to reduce the incidence, severity, and consequences of musculoskeletal injuries in the workplace are effective when properly implemented. The evidence suggests that the most effective strategies involve a combined approach that takes into account the complex interplay between physical stressors and the policies and procedures of industries.

The complexity of musculoskeletal disorders in the workplace requires a variety of strategies that may involve the worker, the workforce, and management. These strategies fall within the categories of engineering controls, administrative controls, and worker-focused modifiers. The literature shows that no single strategy is or will be effective for all types of industry; interventions are best tailored to the individual situation. However, there are some program elements that consistently recur in successful programs:

1. Interventions must mediate physical stressors, largely through the application of ergonomic principles.
2. Employee involvement is essential to successful implementation.
3. Employer commitment, demonstrated by an integrated program and supported by best practices review, is important for success.

Although generic guidelines have been developed and successfully applied in intervention programs, no single specific design, restriction, or practice for universal application is supported by the existing scientific literature. Because of limitations in the scientific literature, a comprehensive and systematic research program is needed to further clarify and distinguish the features that make interventions effective for specific musculoskeletal disorders.

B. Development and Prevention in Specific Occupations

Occupations that involve repetitive lifting, e.g., warehouse work, construction, and pipe fitting, particularly when that activity involves twisting postures, are associated with an increased risk for the complaint of low back pain and, in a few studies, an increased risk for lumbar disc herniation.

The prevalence of osteoarthritic changes in the lumbar spine (disc space narrowing and spinal osteophytes) is significantly greater in those whose occupations require heavy and repetitive lifting compared with age-matched controls whose occupations are more sedentary. Despite these radiographical differences, most of the studies show little or no difference in the prevalence of low back pain or sciatica between those with radiological changes of osteoarthritis and those with no radiological changes. Based on the current evidence, modification of the lifting can reduce symptoms and complaints. Specific successful strategies, which include ergonomic interventions (such as the use of lift tables and other devices and matching the worker's capacity to the lifting tasks), administrative controls (such as job rotation), and team lifting, appear successful. Despite enthusiasm for their use, there is marginal or conflicting evidence about lifting belts and educational programs in reducing low back pain in the population with heavy lifting requirements. Some examples of positive interventions include:

Truck drivers—Vibration exposure is thought to be the dominant cause for the increased risk for low back pain and lumbar disc herniation. There are some data to support the efficacy of vibrational dampening seating devices.

Hand-held tool operators—Occupations that involve the use of hand-held tools, particularly those with vibration, are associated with the general complaints of hand pain, a greater risk of carpal tunnel syndrome, and some tenosynovitis. Redesign of tools is associated with reduced risks.

Food processing—Food processing, e.g., meat cutting, is associated with a greater risk of shoulder and elbow complaints. Job redesign appears to reduce this risk, but this information is largely based on best practices and case reports.

7. What scientific questions remain unanswered, and may require further research, to determine which occupational activities in which specific industries cause or contribute to work-related musculoskeletal disorders?

The panel's recommended research agenda is provided in Chapter 12 of the report.

APPENDIX B

Dissent

Robert M. Szabo

The report of the Panel on Musculoskeletal Disorders and the Workplace of the National Research Council (NRC) and the Institute of Medicine (IOM) has used significant interpretations of the scientific literature that I consider inaccurate and misrepresentations, particularly with issues in the upper extremity. It also does not reflect the scientific evidence regarding the usefulness or urgency of interventions. I am also troubled by some of the methodological issues employed. For instance, in the epidemiology chapter, the panel set selection criteria for accepting which articles to review. Despite voicing my concerns at our panel meetings, numerous epidemiological articles that did not meet the selection criteria were used to support the biomechanics chapter. The panel agreed and we wrote, "Few high-quality intervention studies related to the primary and secondary prevention of low back pain are available in the literature." No high-quality intervention studies related to the primary and secondary prevention of upper extremity disorders in general and carpal tunnel syndrome in particular are available in the literature. To circumvent the issue of not having reasonable scientific intervention studies available, the panel took a "best practices" approach, which I think is not very scientific. Prospective studies are of the greatest value; however, none is available at the present time. *What needs to be emphasized is that no study has demonstrated that any intervention affects the short- or long-term outcome of developing an impairment, a disease, or a disorder with a positive physical examination correlate.* In other words, symptoms of pain may have been reduced. For example, one study (Tittranonda et al., 1999)[67] cited in the report on more than one occasion is particularly misleading. The authors of this small study explored the use of an alternative keyboard design on hand pain in patients *already diagnosed* with carpal tunnel syn-

439

drome and measured symptoms of pain. The participants abandoned the use of these alternative keyboards despite a "positive" effect. One might be led to believe by the NRC-IOM report that this study prevented carpal tunnel syndrome or provided evidence of a worthwhile intervention. I don't think so. Another study was misrepresented as demonstrating an association between computer keyboard use and slowed median nerve velocity. Not mentioned in discussing that study was that there were no *abnormal* median nerve velocities and there were *no clinical carpal tunnel syndromes*. Carpal tunnel syndrome is wrongly presented as being associated with computer keyboard use. Despite the panel's recognition of the lack of scientific evidence to link carpal tunnel syndrome to keyboard use, the report does not acknowledge this fact.

In order to determine the association between risk factors (exposures) and a disease (outcome variable), both the risk factors and the disease should be well defined. When a fall on the outstretched hand results in a fracture at the wrist, the relationship between the trauma and the injury is clear. This is often not the case for work-related musculoskeletal disorders. Some conditions, like carpal tunnel syndrome, have a pathogenesis that can be defined and measured objectively with electrodiagnostic studies. The majority of work-related musculoskeletal disorders of the upper extremity fall into a more amorphous category, such as hand pain when there is no objective way to define the condition or measure its severity and there is no clear anatomical basis for the symptoms.

Carpal tunnel's clinical picture of pain and paresthesias on the palmar-radial aspect of the hand, often worse at night, is readily recognized. Carpal tunnel syndrome is a condition of middle-aged people and is more common in females. In the first population-based study, the mean age at diagnosis was 50 years for men and 51 years for women; women accounted for 78.5 percent of the cases.[62] Most middle-aged people work, so more often than not, carpal tunnel syndrome occurs in working people. The role that work-related activities play in its pathogenesis is controversial. On the basis of six cases, no controls, and a definition of occupation that included housewives, Brain in 1947 was the first to implicate occupation as a causal factor in the disorder.[11] A high prevalence of work-related musculoskeletal disorders, including carpal tunnel syndrome, has been reported in professions requiring high-force wrist motions, such as assembly line workers, meatpackers, and material handlers. Much of the recent focus, however, has been on keyboard operators, whose activities, while extremely repetitive, do not require high force. It is not universally accepted that job-related factors are important determinants for predicting the appearance of carpal tunnel syndrome.[25,68] In the general population, its prevalence is the same whether people perform repetitive activities or not.[6] A recent study reported that its prevalence for repetitive hand or wrist motion was 2.4 percent compared with 2.7 percent for nonrepetitive motion (95 percent CI for the difference, –2 percent, –1.5 percent; P = .69).[6] Reports from workers and survey data tend to overestimate the prevalence of a disorder because social, cultural, and medicolegal factors have a major influence. In 1988 the National Health Interview Survey showed that 1.4 percent (1.87 million) of working adults in the United States reported that they had a "condition affecting the wrist and hand called carpal tunnel syndrome." Only 675,000 indicated that a *health care provider* had made this diagnosis.[66] Carpal tunnel syndrome must be distinguished from the vast array of upper extremity musculoskeletal complaints collectively called repetitive motion disorders. Many of these conditions are the product of somatization, the reporting of somatic symptoms that have no pathophysiological explanation, amplified by medicalization, whereby uncomfortable bodily states and isolated symptoms are reclassified as diseases for which medical treatment is sought.[8,9]

The association of carpal tunnel syndrome with work-related risk factors is a recurring theme of causation among workers, ergonomists, lawyers, and physicians. The majority of the literature that tries to establish this as a causal association fails to meet the appropriate standards of epidemiological validity.[63,68] To conclude that carpal tunnel syndrome is a repetitive motion disorder, one must ask the question, "How significant a risk factor is repetition for the development of carpal tunnel syndrome?" To answer this question, one must consider the interaction of job exposures (extrinsic risk factors) with various innate anatomic, physiological, or behavioral characteristics of the worker (intrinsic risk factors) that render him or her more likely to develop the disorder. Occupational risk factors alone do not explain its occurrence; rather, it is the culmination of many distinct converging causal links. The majority of cases are likely due to intrinsic risk factors. One investigation concluding that carpal tunnel syndrome is closely correlated with health habits and life-style[49] is supported by an analysis showing that 81.52 percent of the explainable variation in electrophysiologically defined carpal tunnel syndrome was due to body mass index, age, and wrist depth/width ratio, whereas only 8.29 percent was due to job-related factors.[24] There may be important interactions between extrinsic and intrinsic risk factors that are yet to be understood. While there is a biologically plausible mechanism to relate forceful grip to compression of the median nerve,[64,65] there is no such correlate to postulate biological plausibility with regard to repetition.

In reviewing the published literature on work-related repetitive hand injuries, Hagberg et al. estimated the attributable fraction by (OR – 1)/OR (where OR was the estimated odds ratio) and concluded that exposure to physical workload factors, such as repetitive and forceful gripping, is probably a major risk factor for at least 50 percent, and as much as 90 percent, of all of the carpal tunnel syndrome cases in several types of worker populations.[27] Greenland has pointed out that attributable fractions are dependent on the prevalence of cofactors of exposure (factors that enhance exposure effects on risk and causal mechanisms that do not involve exposure).[26] Because the cofactors are inadequately accounted for in the investigations considered, the estimations offered by Hagberg, as well as the ones used in the NRC-IOM report, must be interpreted with caution.

Many factors have been identified in the pathogenesis of carpal tunnel syndrome but are rarely considered as possible confounders or effect modifiers in epidemiological studies of occupationally related disorders. Nathan and colleagues studied the relationship of tobacco, caffeine, and alcohol to the prevalence of carpal tunnel syndrome in 1,464 workers confirmed by nerve conduction examinations.[46] They found when comparing workers with carpal tunnel syndrome to those without it that there was a 19 percent greater lifetime use of tobacco, a 75 percent greater history of alcohol abuse, and a 5 percent greater use of caffeine. In female workers, current tobacco, caffeine, and alcohol consumption independently predicted 5 percent of the explainable risk for definite carpal tunnel syndrome.

In a case-control study of 600 patients presenting for an independent medical exam, Stallings and colleagues found that obesity was associated with positive findings on nerve conduction exams for median neuropathy with an odds ratio of 3.92 (95 percent confidence interval = 2.65 to 5.79).[59] In a study analyzing the computer records of all personnel on active naval duty in all Navy medical facilities from 1980 to 1988, Garland and colleagues found first hospitalization rates (those patients undergoing surgery) for carpal tunnel syndrome were strongly related to age, sex, and race.[22] The occupations with high risk were boatswain's mates and enginemen, an occupation similar in description to civilian industrial painters and maintenance workers. The standardized incidence ratio for male boatswain's mates was 1.7, whereas for women in the same occupation it was 9.8. Female ocean systems technicians had a standardized incidence ratio of 5.6, whereas men in the same occupation had a standardized incidence ratio below 1.0. Gender was therefore a far more predictive risk factor for carpal tunnel syndrome than job exposure. The higher incidence rates for women could not be accounted for by the differential selection of high-risk occupations by women. Low-risk jobs included occupations analogous to secretarial work, including clerical duties and data entry using typewriters and computers.[22]

Silverstein and colleagues, in what has been regarded as a classic study, determined the prevalence of carpal tunnel syndrome among 652 active workers (in 39 jobs from 7 different industrial sites). Specific hand force and repetitiveness characteristics were then estimated for different jobs. An equal number of men and women was identified. The prevalence of carpal tunnel syndrome ranged from 0.6 percent among workers in low-force, low-repetition jobs to 5.6 percent among workers in high-force, high-repetition jobs. Silverstein's data shows work to be a risk factor only when both high force and high repetition are present, but the precision of her estimated odds ratio of 15.5 (95 percent confidence interval = 1.7 – 141.5) suffers from an extremely small sample size. High repetitiveness appeared to be a greater risk factor than high force, but neither was statistically significant alone.[58] Of particular concern, however, is that there were only 14 cases of carpal tunnel syndrome identified, which were associated with 11 jobs. Stetson et al. carried out a study of 240 industrial workers from the automotive industry. Electrodiagnostic studies were done on all subjects to assess median nerve conduction. Hand-intensive tasks correlated with decreased nerve conduction, but there were no significant differences in the measurement means for repetitiveness and pinch between the nonexposed and exposed groups.[61]

DeKrom et al. analyzed a population of primarily hospital patients to estimate the etiological relationship between workload and carpal tunnel syndrome.[16] The diagnosis was based on clinical history as well as neurophysiological testing. Activities with the flexed wrist, such as grasping or the packing of products, resulted in an increased risk positively correlated with the duration of these activities, such that the odds ratio was as high as 8.7 for maximum exposure. Similarly, activities with the wrist extended, such as scrubbing or ironing, were associated with an increased risk of carpal tunnel syndrome, which was correlated with the duration of exposure with the odds ratio as high as 5.4. Obesity was also found to be a risk factor. Exposures were estimated, but the methodology was not discussed regarding the classification criteria.

The scientific evidence fails to be definitive in connecting occupational hand use and proven carpal tunnel syndrome. In 1991, Stock identified 54 potentially relevant studies on upper extremity cumulative trauma disorders and was able to retrieve 49. Of these 49, only 3 met her inclusion criteria emphasizing adequate definitions of populations, exposures, and outcomes. All three studies were cross-sectional in design. She concluded that when the results of these studies were compared, they provided strong evidence of a causal relationship between repetitive, forceful work and the development of musculoskeletal disorders of the tendons and tendon sheaths in the hands and wrists and nerve entrapment of the median nerve at the carpal tunnel.[63] Only two of the studies, however, specifically examined carpal tunnel syndrome; one was the Silverstein study mentioned above. The authors of the other study in her review had opposite findings based on objective electrodiagnostic criteria.[50] Several concerns limit the use of existing data to resolve the relationship between job-related risk factors and carpal tunnel syndrome.

Carpal tunnel syndrome is a combination of signs and symptoms, and no single test absolutely confirms its diagnosis. The validity and reliability of many of the diagnostic tests used are not fully established. Since electrodiagnosis is considered the "gold standard," all predictors of carpal tunnel syndrome are judged against it.[36] Carpal tunnel syndrome verified by strict electrodiagnostic criteria is not common among workers. At first it would seem that the critical issue is whether only studies that use electrodiagnosis should be considered in attempts at resolving the role of job-related risk factors. Comparison of several different median nerve conduction study techniques, however, demonstrates a variety of sensitivities.[35] The problem is that no single technique can identify all carpal tunnel syndrome patients without misclassifying an unacceptable number of normals. One must consider the specific techniques that investigators employ in their study. Using three separate electrodiagnostic criteria examining a normal population, one study showed that 23 of 50 (46 percent) had at least one false-positive test for carpal tunnel syndrome.[53] The disorder is progressive and can present with symptoms before physical findings are present. Some of these symptoms, however, are nondiagnostic of carpal tunnel syndrome and can be present in other disorders. Therefore, studies that measure only symptoms may overestimate the problem. Besides nerve conduction studies, the diagnosis of carpal tunnel syndrome is based on history and physical examination. The history and the physical examination, including a variety of sensory tests, rely on a person's verbal reports of sensation or pain. In a motivated and honest patient, a combination of these tests may suffice to demonstrate the nerve deficit. However, if issues of secondary gain cloud the case, the patient's reports may be unreliable. The patient may have a very low threshold for perceiving discomfort, and suggestible individuals that are warned about the disorder from coworkers or trade publications may subconsciously amplify minor discomforts until they are perceived as significant symptoms. Electrophysiological studies measuring median nerve function are the only objective way to demonstrate the nerve deficit. When properly used, these tests have sensitivity and specificity near 90 percent.[35,41] Unfortunately, the majority of epidemiological studies of carpal tunnel syndrome have not used these studies in their diagnoses, and it is therefore uncertain whether all reported cases in these studies were indeed carpal tunnel syndrome. The accuracy one requires in the diagnosis depends on its purpose. In surveillance of incidence of the disorder in an industry for monitoring purposes, case definition should maximize sensitivity at the expense of specificity.[37] For epidemiological studies concerned with causation, specificity of case diagnosis should also take precedence over sensitivity for the sake of validity.[12] Of the nonelectro-diagnostic tests for carpal tunnel syndrome, sensory testing with Semmes Weinstein monofilaments or the Durkan pressure test seems to be best for this role, but neither has been used in epidemiological studies,[17,23,42] nor has a hand symptom diagram, which may be an acceptable compromise.[39] Accepting less specific diagnostic criteria when trying to establish causal relationships has led to many of the controversies surrounding work-related carpal tunnel syndrome.

Definition of the disorder based on clinical tests is liable to mis-classification, because no clinical test has been proven valid. The National Institute for Occupational Safety and Health (NIOSH) proposed a surveil-lance case definition for work-related carpal tunnel syndrome: the pres-ence of median nerve symptoms; one or more occupational risk factors; and objective evidence by physical examination findings, including the Tinel or Phalen signs or decreased pinprick sensation, or positive diag-nostic nerve conduction studies. Using the NIOSH surveillance case definition, if a worker develops classical symptoms and has abnormal electrodiagnostic studies of the median nerve in the face of a work task that is highly forceful and repetitive, then the presumption is that the symptom complex is work related.[43] The work by Silverstein and her colleagues[58] formed the basis for this case definition; however, the diag-nosis in their study was based on reported symptoms not confirmed with electrodiagnosis. When applying this case definition without using elec-trodiagnostic studies to a sample of symptomatic workers, Katz et al. found that 38 percent of subjects were misclassified; 50 percent of workers satisfying the case definition did not have carpal tunnel syndrome, while 25 percent not satisfying the case definition did have it.[37] Misclassification if nondifferential would dilute any association if present; however, mis-classification is likely to be differential in these studies due to detection bias: workers in at-risk jobs are more likely to get medical attention, be identified as subjects in a study, and be overdiagnosed because of work-ers' compensation and the current climate of medicolegal issues. Using Katz's data, this misclassification error could overestimate any associa-tion by 62 percent if differential.[37] In a population of workers with a 10 percent prevalence of carpal tunnel syndrome, when the NIOSH case definition is applied to the entire population, 85 percent of the workers who meet the criteria for the NIOSH definition of the disorder will not have it.[37] As pointed out by Wolens, Silverstein's study suggests only that individuals exposed to high rates of force and repetition more frequently meet the NIOSH definition of work-related carpal tunnel syndrome.[72] Of remarkable interest concerning this study is the finding that so few work-ers even meet this case definition. Considering the poor positive predic-tive value of this definition for diagnosis of the disorder, there are even far fewer industrial workers with true carpal tunnel syndrome. Since true carpal tunnel syndrome is an uncommon work-related disease, it is universally unacceptable to attribute a case of carpal tunnel syndrome to a person's work-related activities without evaluating all other avocational stresses and life-style risk factors. From my own experience, carpal tunnel syndrome is a frequent disorder in patients who are not employed.

"The definitive cause (or even strong association) of work-related musculoskeletal disease has yet to be established."[29] To infer that a statistical association between job-related exposure factors and carpal tunnel syndrome is evidence of etiology, it should be demonstrated that the job exposure occurred before the disorder emerged. The temporal relationship between physical load factors and the onset of carpal tunnel syndrome has not been demonstrated in either cross-sectional or case-control studies examining prevalence. Armstrong and Chaffin noted that carpal tunnel syndrome subjects used a wrist position that deviated from the straight position more frequently and exerted greater hand forces in all wrist positions than nondiseased subjects; however, they could not establish whether the differences in work methods was a cause or an effect of the disorder.[5] The majority of studies to date are prevalence studies in which exposures were measured at the same time that disease status was established. Only Nathan's study followed up a cohort of original participants (five years later); this study found no association between job and electrophysiological evidence of carpal tunnel syndrome.[48] Other strong evidence of a causal relationship could be made if workplace modifications were shown to reduce the incidence of carpal tunnel syndrome; no study has demonstrated this.

Many epidemiological studies apply a single general class descriptor to different worker groups and then measure prevalence of carpal tunnel syndrome across groups. More precise measurement of exposure variables, such as position (of wrists, fingers, elbows, and neck), static loading, temperature, and vibration are necessary. These can be obtained with careful biomechanical characterizations of specific job tasks. Precise ergonomic measures, however, are of little value if ultimately subjects are grouped into broad categories based on what can be observed without such measurements.[47] Harber et al. attempted to determine individual rather than average group exposures in a cross-sectional study of 50 supermarket checkers. With this approach, they failed to detect any association between wrist flexion/extension and symptoms. Instead they demonstrated an association between wrist pronation and symptoms and lumbar flexion (posture) and symptoms.[29] Some studies perform a somewhat detailed biomechanical evaluation of the job classifications and then generalize the findings to all workers in that job category.[5,14] Classification of exposure by industry is imprecise and may lead to erroneous associations between exposure and outcome. Random exposure misclassification based on the subject's self-reports of occupational hand use could be responsible for biasing any association between hand use and electrophysiological evidence of median neuropathy at the wrist toward the null in the studies of Nathan et al. and Schottland et al.[48-50,57] However, prevalence of exposure may generate a spurious trend associated with a third variable, such as age,[19] as found in all of the studies of Nathan et al. and in the study of Schottland et al. In these studies, age may be increasing as the prevalence of exposure is increasing. If the true relative risk associated with exposure is the same in each age group, and the electrophysiological test has the same misclassification probabilities in each age group, then the apparent relative risk of carpal tunnel syndrome associated with the exposure will change systematically as age increases, producing a spurious trend with age.[19] Furthermore, variation in prevalence exposure could mask a real trend in relative risk associated with some unidentified third variable. Weislander et al. found an exposure response trend for self-reported years of exposure to vibrating hand tool use and repetitive wrist motion.[71] Since referents were less likely to be sensitive to occupational stresses, they would be less likely to recall and report symptoms of carpal tunnel syndrome. The evaluation of job exposure status was also not blinded as to the subjects' health status. Both of these factors could lead to information bias that is differential and that would overestimate the difference between the case and control exposures.

Generally there has also been a failure to measure background exposure. A full-time worker spends approximately 20 percent of the hours in a year doing his or her job; exposures to risk factors during the remaining 80 percent of the time have not been measured. Hales and Bernard concluded that 16 of 22 studies reported a positive association between occupational factors (repetition being only one) and carpal tunnel syndrome, but not a single one of these studies had quantified both exposure and disease ascertainment.[28]

Confounding can result in incorrectly attributing the etiology of carpal tunnel syndrome to the wrong risk factor. Obesity is identified in several studies as a significant risk factor,[15,16,49,70,71] yet it is not controlled for in the majority of the studies as a potential confounder. With the exception of gender and age, very few other associations were even considered in the design or analysis phase of published studies. Cannon et al. performed a case-control study of the personal and environmental factors associated with carpal tunnel syndrome in workers at an aircraft engine manufacturing company.[13] A total of 30 patients with carpal tunnel syndrome (3 men and 27 women) and 90 matched controls (9 men and 81 women) were compared. Information on age, sex, race, weight, occupation, number of years employed, worker's compensation status, history of diabetes mellitus, presence of hypertension, history of arthritis or hyperthyroidism, use of oral contraceptives or postmenopausal estrogens, and history of gynecological surgery was collected. The use of vibratory hand tools and a history of gynecological surgery, specifically hysterectomy and oophorectomy, were most strongly associated with the onset of carpal tunnel syndrome. Obesity, nonwhite race, and employment in jobs requiring repetitive motion tasks involving the wrist were more prevalent among subjects than controls but did not achieve statistical significance. The gender difference in this study highlights the problem of differences in the types of jobs assigned to women; they may have been assigned a disproportionate amount of the most highly repetitive work, and therefore the association between repetition and carpal tunnel syndrome may even be weaker than reported.

To test the hypothesis that carpal tunnel syndrome is associated with occupational risk factors, a study incorporating electrophysiological tests, physical examinations, and questionnaires was performed at a ski assembly plant where jobs were classified as repetitive and nonrepetitive.[7] Repetitive jobs were defined as activities that required repetitive or sustained flexion, extension, or ulnar deviation of the wrist or use of a pinch-type grip. The conclusion drawn, based on a crude prevalence ratio of 4.92 (95 percent confidence interval = 1.17 - 20.7), was that carpal tunnel syndrome was associated with jobs requiring frequent and sustained hand work. This study, however, had several limitations. Diabetes mellitus, a known intrinsic risk factor, was present more commonly among those diagnosed with carpal tunnel syndrome and was not controlled for in the analysis. As people with diabetes mellitus are known to be more susceptible to nerve compressive lesions, that condition should be treated as a potential confounder or effect modifier and its association with exposure analyzed.

Nathan et al. conducted a longitudinal cross-sectional study of the cause of carpal tunnel syndrome in industry, by evaluating sensory conduction of the median nerve in relation to age, gender, hand dominance, occupational hand use, and clinical diagnosis.[48] In this study, the only one that addresses the issue of temporality, investigators reexamined 630 hands of 316 (67 percent) of the same workers from a five-year previous study group, which consisted of 942 hands of 471 industrial workers. The palmar segmental stimulation technique was employed, and slowing was defined as a maximum latency difference (MLD) of 0.4 msec or more after adjustment for temperature variation. No significant change in the prevalence of slowing between 1984 and 1989 (23 percent in 1984, 22 percent in 1989) was found, and slowing strongly correlated with increased age even in apparently healthy, symptom-free subjects, but not with gender. Although slowing continued to be more prevalent in the dominant hand, there was no increase in the difference in prevalence of slowing between the dominant and nondominant hands between 1984 and 1989, suggesting that the role of industrial hand use in median nerve slowing is minimal. Slowing was no longer correlated in any fashion with occupational hand use. In particular, no correlation existed between rate of repetition and prevalence of slowing. The prevalence of probable carpal tunnel syndrome (symptoms and physical exam consistent with the disorder) was still strongly correlated with the degree of slowing. Nathan concluded that age and hand dominance were more important than any job-related factor in the prediction of slowing after five years. In a case-control study, Schottland et al. replicated Nathan's results and found that exposure to the repetitive tasks in a poultry plant was not associated with electrophysiological changes in median nerve function. A power analysis of their data suggests that if an association was present, it would have been observed with their sample population.[57]

Social determinants of carpal tunnel syndrome may confound the interpretation of many studies. Few studies address social determinants involved in predicting the disorder; only one specifically substantiated cultural differences as a possible predictive risk factor for the reporting of carpal tunnel symptoms.[51] Since so much of the diagnosis of carpal tunnel syndrome relies on subjective data, it is a critical omission of most studies not to have considered psychosocial, legal, and cultural factors as confounders of exposure effects. "Teaching 25 years ago regarded carpal tunnel syndrome as a problem that would resolve following surgery when it was indicated."[43] When patients with carpal tunnel syndrome appear to have some relationship between their symptoms and their work, the problem is different. In one study of workers' compensation patients, individuals with less abnormal nerve conduction velocities were more likely to have persistent symptoms and more often changed jobs based on those symptoms than those with more prominent nerve conduction abnormalities.[31] Higgs found that those workers undergoing carpal tunnel release in his study who had legal representation were twice as likely to have poor outcomes. He concluded that "for the average employee, the enticement of substantial financial gain, coupled with the legal premise that a more-disabled person may receive even greater rewards, provides ample incentive to prolong recovery."[30] There is no doubt that psychosocial issues prolong disability.[10] The population of workers' compensation recipients experience worse outcomes following medical, surgical, and rehabilitative interventions,[30,31] yet when Katz and colleagues studied the perceived improvement in quality of life and the perceived improvement in symptoms in a group of workers' compensation recipients and nonrecipients after surgery for carpal tunnel syndrome, they found no difference.[38] Subjects in this study, however, understood they were participating in a research project that would have no impact on their compensation benefits. Adams et al., in a retrospective cohort study on outcome of carpal tunnel surgery in workers' compensation patients, found no association between the biological severity of the disorder and the postoperative duration of disability.[2] And 67 percent of the cases returned to the same job. The authors concluded that disability following carpal tunnel syndrome surgery may be related to other medical, psychosocial, administrative, legal, or work-related factors. Franklin similarly concluded that a number of factors need to be considered when interpreting outcome studies in workers' compensation patients: factors that predict good or poor outcome may not be the same as in the general population; comparable procedures have worse outcomes in the workers' compensation patients; outcomes after surgery are strongly correlated with the duration of preoperative disability but not the biological severity of the initial injury.[21]

Both people involved with repetitive activities and those who are not develop carpal tunnel syndrome. In order to deliver rational preventive measures for workers with the disorder, valid and scientifically sound information about the true association between repetitive exposures and median neuropathy must be established. Without incidence data, we cannot estimate the excess fraction that is the relevant attributable risk parameter to measure in planning and policy questions.[26] Knowledge of the true associations has direct implications for the primary, secondary, and tertiary prevention. Primary prevention is aimed at reducing or controlling the workplace risk factors. Does job modification work? Would alternating between high-risk and low-risk jobs decrease the incidence of carpal tunnel syndrome in the workplace? Is there a critical exposure duration (threshold) that, once reached, should lead to retirement or change to a low-risk job? Although keyboarding appears to have a protective effect from developing symptoms of median nerve compression,[16,51] a tremendous amount of money is being spent on the design, promotion, and use of new keyboards. Many of these ergonomic designs, which claim to reduce symptoms, are based on changing the forearm rotation to less pronation. One study suggests that 45 degrees of pronation is the ideal position to reduce carpal tunnel pressures.[54] The usual shoulder position of 20-30 degrees abduction when seated in front of a computer terminal rotates the forearm to that optimal position with the common keyboard design. Some physical conditions tend to precipitate symptoms of the forearm, wrist, or hand when using a computer. Anatomical abnormalities, such as limitation of pronation of the forearm, may result in significant abduction of the shoulder and elbow in order to place the hand in a neutral position. For these few people, alternative keyboard designs may prove useful. Wrist splints have long been used in the treatment of carpal tunnel syndrome but are now marketed as protection for people in high-risk occupations. Since wrist flexion/extension increases carpal tunnel pressure, which in turn inhibits median nerve function, it seems reasonable to use a splint that maintains the wrist in neutral position; however, one study demonstrated that carpal tunnel pressures were higher with splint use at baseline and during repetitive hand activity, perhaps suggesting some external compression.[55]

Epidemiological studies of occupational carpal tunnel syndrome have usually not isolated the issue of wrist or finger position from grip force and repetition. Motion analysis studies of sign language interpreters for the deaf and grocery checkers[18,29] have shown that workers with symptomatic hands had more frequent and more extensive flexion and extension than nonsymptomatic workers, suggesting that extreme flexion or extension may be an extrinsic risk factor. However, the chain of causality can also be read in the opposite direction; that is, median nerve impairment may interfere with proprioception, resulting in exaggerated motions. One case-control study demonstrated increased risk factors related to activities associated with either wrist flexion or wrist extension but not to activities associated with both wrist flexion and extension.[16] This demonstrates lack of consistency that needs to be explained by future studies.

A major criticism of the term "repetitive stress" is that it implies that the etiology is due to repetition. The word "injury" implies damage to tissues. "Repetition and stress" imply that repetitive mechanical forces applied to tissues cause the injury, yet no information exists regarding the frequency, magnitude, duration, or rate that renders these forces harmful. We know that forces exceeding the mechanical limits of tissue lead to irreversible damage, yet physiological forces allow for normal maintenance and enhanced wound healing.[3] The relationship between physical loads and musculoskeletal disease has still not been quantified, and contradictory evidence persists due to poor measurement of exposures and lack of specific diagnoses. Arguably, symptoms of aches and pains that precede the status of disease or injury are important to recognize, as many patients present themselves with such symptoms. Progression to disease, however, is the exception rather than the rule, or one would expect a greater prevalence in reports of disease states. The relative contribution of occupational and nonoccupational physical loads to causing symptoms has not been addressed sufficiently in epidemiological studies. Nevertheless, ergonomists promote the concept that from the perspective of prevention and treatment, all work-related factors that can be modified should be.[69]

There has been an increased advocacy of ergonomics as a solution to the incidence of repetitive motion injury in the workplace. This has resulted in a proliferation of ergonomic literature in which conclusions are based on associations and suggestions.[56,67] Ergonomics is defined as the study of how human beings use machines;[4] however, it often refers to the craft of designing workplace equipment, including computers, to minimize health problems or injuries.[1] Despite the widespread use of ergonomic methods in industry, there is controversy over their effect. Some have asserted that there is little substantive evidence that these methods are either valid or reliable.[60] Others have found that ergonomics have resulted in substantial improvements in the workplace.[52] There is little doubt that most ergonomic interventions increase comfort in the work environment, which is of great benefit to the worker. While ergonomists may create a more comfortable environment, they have not lowered the incidence of well-documented medical conditions, such as carpal tunnel syndrome. In fact, one study from Australia reported an increase in the incidence of "repetitive stress injuries" even after ergonomic redesign of the workstation and instituting rest periods from keyboarding every hour.[32]

On one final note, I think it important to look at the historical perspective with regard to what we've learned about work-related musculoskeletal injuries over time. Both the scientific community and nonmedical journalists are reporting an epidemic of disability from work-related musculoskeletal injuries. In order to understand why more people are becoming work-disabled, one must examine overall societal trends in disability. Since the middle of the 20th century, consecutive generations in the United States have become more disabled as assessed from self-reports, and it is unclear whether this is due to improved survival of the chronically ill, to lowered cultural thresholds for defining disability, or to real increases in disability incidence.[20]

The United States is not the first country to experience an epidemic of so-called work-related musculoskeletal problems. Between 1960 and 1980, Japan experienced an epidemic of cervicobrachial disorders.[45] The epidemic became so widespread that in 1964 (even before the widespread introduction of personal computers) the Japanese Ministry of Labor set ergonomic standards for keyboard operators. These standards ultimately failed, however, to decrease the number of new reported cases.

In Australia at a telecommunications company, Telecom Australia, which had 90,000 workers, the rate of "repetitive stress injuries" began to rise in late 1983, peaked in late 1984 (30 times higher than the 1982 rate), and declined in 1985, reaching 1983 levels in 1987. The patients were most often keyboard operators who complained of pain that was neither consistent from patient to patient nor did it conform to any known neurological pathway, anatomical structure, or physiological pattern. There were no objective clinical findings other than random tenderness; clinical investigations were negative, and symptoms failed to respond to any form of physical treatment.[34]

In Australia, there was little evidence of a dose-response relationship of repetitive stress injury to keystroke rate, age, or job duration.[32] Neither ergonomics, new technology, nor psychosocial theory explained the Australian epidemic. Miller and Topliss studied 229 consecutive patients referred with a label of repetitive stress injury.[44] Of these patients, 29 fulfilled the usual criteria for a specific disorder, such as deQuervain's tenosynovitis or rheumatoid arthritis. Evaluation of the remaining 200 workers showed that 100 percent had anxiety, irritability, and/or lowering of mood; 91 percent had sleep disturbances; 84 percent had chronic fatigue; 61 percent had frequent tension headaches; and 78 percent had decreased sensation involving both hands in a nondermatomal distribution. Ergonomic measures that the investigators instituted for all office workers, including cessation of keyboard use, writing, or other activities that aggravated arm pain, failed to relieve symptoms in 78 percent of patients. Medications were used in all cases, and physiotherapy was used in 94 percent. All the patients reported that the treatment had little effect on their long-term progress.

Ultimately the incidence of repetition strain injury in Australia fell just as precipitously as it increased. What caused the Australian epidemic? In a time of relative prosperity, with technological changes and computerization of clerical tasks that threatened those less adaptable to change, and in a country with as many physicians and pharmacists per capita as any industrialized nation, the inability to work because of a physical ailment became more socially acceptable.[33,34] Kiesler and Finholt concluded that the repetitive stress injury epidemic in Australia was more indicative of social problems than of workplace factors, and dissatisfaction was a major contributor, as was social legitimization of complaints related to repetitive stress injury.[40] Political and social factors can act in both directions. The single factor that had the greatest influence on the decline of repetitive stress injury in Australia was a judicial decision in the case *Cooper v. the Commonwealth* (1987). The Supreme Court found that the employer was not guilty of negligence and the plaintiff had not suffered an injury. All costs were awarded against the plaintiff, and soon thereafter the Australian repetitive stress injury epidemic disappeared.[34]

REFERENCES

1. Review & outlook: ergo, lawsuits. In The Wall Street Journal. Edited, New York, 1999.
2. Adams, M. L.; Franklin, G. M.; and Barnhart, S.: Outcome of carpal tunnel surgery in Washington State workers' compensation. Am J Ind Med, 25(4): 527-36, 1994.

3. Amiel, D.; Constance, C.; and Lee, J.: Effect of loading on metabolism and repair of tendons and ligaments. In Repetitive motion disorders of the upper extremity, pp. 217-230. Edited by Gordon, S. L.; Blair, S. J.; and Fine, L. J., 217-230, Rosemont, Illinois, American Academy of Orthopaedic Surgeons, 1994.

4. Armstrong, T.: Ergonomics and cumulative trauma disorders. Hand Clinics, 2(3): 553-565, 1986.

5. Armstrong, T. J., and Chaffin, D. B.: Carpal tunnel syndrome and selected personal attributes. J Occup Med, 21(7): 481-6, 1979.

6. Atroshi, I.; Gummesson, C.; Johnsson, R.; E., O.; Ranstam, J.; and Rosén, I.: Prevalence of carpal tunnel syndrome in a general population. JAMA, 282(2): 153-158, 1999.

7. Barnhart, S.; Demers, P. A.; Miller, M.; Longstreth, W., Jr.; and Rosenstock, L.: Carpal tunnel syndrome among ski manufacturing workers. Scand J Work Environ Health, 17(1): 46-52, 1991.

8. Barsky, A. J., and Borus, J. F.: Functional somatic syndromes. Ann Intern Med, 130: 910-921, 1999.

9. Barsky, A. J., and Borus, J. F.: Somatization and medicalization in the era of managed care. JAMA, 274: 1931-1934, 1995.

10. Bonzani, P. J.; Millender, L.; Keelan, B.; and Mangieri, M. G.: Factors prolonging disability in work-related cumulative trama disorders. J Hand Surgery, 22A(1): 30-34, 1997.

11. Brain, W. R.; Wright, A. D.; and Wilkinson, M.: Spontaneous compression of both median nerves in the carpal tunnel. Lancet, 1: 277-282, 1947.

12. Brenner, H., and Savitz, D.: The effects of sensitivity and specificity of case selection on validity, sample size, precision, and power in hospital-based case-control studies. Am J Epidemiol, 132: 181-192, 1990.

13. Cannon, L. J.; Bernacki, E. J.; and Walter, S. D.: Personal and occupational factors associated with carpal tunnel syndrome. J Occup Med, 23(4): 255-8, 1981.

14. Chiang, H. C.; Ko, Y. C.; Chen, S. S.; Yu, H. S.; Wu, T. N.; and Chang, P. Y.: Prevalence of shoulder and upper-limb disorders among workers in the fish-processing industry. Scand J Work Environ Health, 19(2): 126-31, 1993.

15. Chong, I.: Solving 'white collar' pain problems. Occup Health Saf, 62(9): 116-20, 1993.

16. DeKrom, M. C. T. F. M.; Kester, A. D. M.; Knipschild, P. G.; and Spaans, F.: Risk factors for carpal tunnel syndrome. Am J Epidemiol, 132(6): 1102-1110, 1990.

17. Durkan, J. A.: The carpal-compression test. An instrumented device for diagnosing carpal tunnel syndrome. Orthop Rev, 23(6): 522-5, 1994.

18. Feurstein, M., and Fitzgerald, T. E.: Biomechanical factors affecting upper extremity cumulative trauma disorders in sign language interpreters. J. Occup Med, 34: 257-264, 1992.

19. Flegal, K. M.; Brownie, C.; and Haas, J. D.: The effects of exposure misclassification on estimates of relative risks. Am J Epidemiol, 123: 736-751, 1986.

20. Frank, J. W.; Pulcins, I. R.; Kerr, M. S.; Shannon, H. S.; and Stansfeld, S. A.: Occupational back pain - an unhelpful polemic. Scan J Work Environ Health, 21(3): 3-14, 1996.

21. Franklin, G. M.: Outcomes research in Washington state workers' compensation. Am J Ind Med, 29: 642-648, 1996.

22. Garland, F. C.; Garland, C. F.; Doyle, E. J.; Balazs, L. L.; Levine, R.; Pugh, W. M.; and Gorham, E. D.: Carpal tunnel syndrome and occupation in U.S. Navy enlisted personnel. Arch Environ Health, 51(5): 395-407, 1996.

23. Gellman, H.; Gelberman, R. H.; Tan, A. M.; and Botte, M. J.: Carpal tunnel syndrome. An evaluation of the provocative diagnostic tests. J Bone Joint Surg [Am], 68(5): 735-7, 1986.

24. Gerr, F., and Letz, R.: Risk factors for carpal tunnel syndrome in industry: blaming the victim? J Occup Med, 34(11): 1117-9, 1992.

25. Gerr, F.; Letz, R.; and Landrigan, P. J.: Upper-extremity musculoskeletal disorders of occupational origin. Annu Rev Public Health, 12: 543-66, 1991.

26. Greenland, S., and Robins, J. M.: Conceptual problems in the definition and interpretation of attributable fractions. Am J Epidemiol, 128(6): 1185-1197, 1988.

27. Hagberg, M.; Morgenstern, H.; and Kelsh, M.: Impact of occupations and job tasks on the prevalence of carpal tunnel syndrome. Scand J Work Environ Health, 18(6): 337-45, 1992.

28. Hales, T., and Bernard, B. P.: Epidemiology of work-related musculoskeletal disorders. Orthop Clin North Am, 27(4): 679-709, 1996.

29. Harber, P.; Bloswick, D.; Beck, J.; Pena, L.; Baker, D.; and Lee, J.: Supermarket checker motions and cumulative trauma risk. J Occup Med, 35(8): 805-11, 1993.

30. Higgs, P. E.; Edwards, D.; Martin, D. S.; and Weeks, P. M.: Carpal tunnel surgery outcomes in workers: effect of workers' compensation status. J Hand Surg, 20A: 354-360, 1995.

31. Higgs, P. E.; Edwards, D. F.; Martin, D. S.; and Weeks, P. M.: Relation of preoperative nerve-conduction values to outcome in workers with surgically treated carpal tunnel syndrome. J Hand Surg, 22A(2): 216-221, 1997.

32. Hocking, B.: Epidemiological aspects of repetition strain injury in Telecom, Australia. Med J Aust, 147: 218-222, 1987.

33. Ireland, D. C. R.: The Australian experience with cumulative trauma disorders. In Occupational Disorders of the Upper Extremity, pp. 79-66. Edited by Millender, L. H.; Louis, D. S.; and Simmons, B. P., 79-66, New York, Churchill Livingstone, 1992.

34. Ireland, D. C. R.: Repetition strain injury: the Australian Experience - 1992 update. J Hand Surg, 20A(3): 553-556, 1995.

35. Jablecki, C. K.; Andary, M. T.; So, Y. T.; Wilkins, D. E.; and Williams, F. H.: Literature review of the usefulness of nerve conduction studies and electromyography for the evaluation of patients with carpal tunnel syndrome. AAEM Quality Assurance Committee. Muscle Nerve, 16(12): 1392-1414, 1993.

36. Johnson, E. W.: Diagnosis of carpal tunnel syndrome. The gold standard [editorial]. Am J Phys Med Rehabil, 72(1): 1, 1993.

37. Katz, J. N.; Larson, M. G.; Fossel, A. H.; and Liang, M. H.: Validation of a surveillance case definition of carpal tunnel syndrome. Am J Public Health, 81(2): 189-93, 1991.

38. Katz, J. N.; Punnett, L.; Simmons, B. P.; Fossel, A. H.; Mooney, N.; and Keller, R. B.: Workers' compensation recipients with carpal tunnel syndrome: the validity of self-reported health measures. Am J Public Health, 86(1): 52-56, 1996.

39. Katz, J. N., and Stirrat, C. R.: A self-administered hand diagram for the diagnosis of carpal tunnel syndrome. J Hand Surg [Am], 15(2): 360-3, 1990.

40. Kiesler, S., and Finholt, T.: The mystery of RSI. Am Psychol, 43: 1004-1015, 1988.

41. Kimura, J.: The carpal tunnel syndrome: localization of conduction abnormalities within the distal segment of the median nerve. Brain, 102(3): 619-35, 1979.

42. Koris, M.; Gelberman, R. H.; Duncan, K.; Boublick, M.; and Smith, B.: Carpal tunnel syndrome. Evaluation of a quantitative provocational diagnostic test. Clin Orthop, (251): 157-61, 1990.

43. Louis, D. S.; Calkins, E. R.; and Harris, P. G.: Carpal tunnel syndrome in the work place. Hand Clinics, 12(2): 305-308, 1996.

44. Miller, M. H., and Topliss, D. J.: Chronic upper limb pain syndrome (repetitive strain injury) in the Australian workforce: a systematic cross sectional rheumatological study of 229 patients. J Rheumatol, 15: 1705-1712, 1988.

45. Nakaseko, M.; Tokunage, R.; and Hosokawa, M.: History of occupational cervicobrachial disorders in Japan and remaining problems. J Hum Ergol, 11: 7-16, 1982.

46. Nathan, P. A.: Intrinsic causes of keyboard injuries [letter]. J Occup Med, 35(11): 1084-6, 1993.

47. Nathan, P. A.; Keniston, R. C.; Meadows, K. D.; and Lockwood, R. S.: Validation of occupational hand use categories. J Occup Med, 35(10): 1034-42, 1993.

48. Nathan, P. A.; Keniston, R. C.; Myers, L. D.; and Meadows, K. D.: Longitudinal study of median nerve sensory conduction in industry: relationship to age, gender, hand dominance, occupational hand use, and clinical diagnosis. J Hand Surg [Am], 17(5): 850-7, 1992.

49. Nathan, P. A.; Keniston, R. C.; Myers, L. D.; and Meadows, K. D.: Obesity as a risk factor for slowing of sensory conduction of the median nerve in industry. A crosssectional and longitudinal study involving 429 workers. J Occup Med, 34(4): 379-83, 1992.

50. Nathan, P. A.; Meadows, K. D.; and Doyle, L. S.: Occupation as a risk factor for impaired sensory conduction of the median nerve at the carpal tunnel. The Journal of Hand Surgery, 13B: 167-170, 1988.

51. Nathan, P. A.; Takigawa, K.; Keniston, R. C.; Meadows, K. D.; and Lockwood, R. S.: Slowing of sensory conduction of the median nerve and carpal tunnel syndrome in Japanese and American industrial workers. J Hand Surg, 19B(1): 30-4, 1994.

52. Nelson, N., and Silverstein, B.: Workplace changes associated with a reduction in musculoskeletal symptoms in office workers. Human Factors, 40(2): 337-350, 1998.

53. Redmond, M. D., and Rivner, M. H.: False positive electrodiagnostic tests in carpal tunnel syndrome. Muscle Nerve, 11(5): 511-8, 1988.

54. Rempel, D.; Bach, J. M.; Gordon, L.; and So, Y.: Effects of forearm pronation/supination on carpal tunnel pressure. J Hand Surg, 23A: 38-42, 1998.

55. Rempel, D.; Manojlovic, R.; Levinsohn, D. G.; Bloom, T.; and Gordon, L.: The effects of wearing a flexible wrist splint on carpal tunnel pressure during repetitive hand activity. J Hand Surg, 19A: 106-110, 1994.

56. Rempel, D.; Tittiranonda, P.; Burastero, S.; Hudes, M.; and So, Y.: Effect of keyboard design on hand pain. JOEM, 41: 11-119, 1999.

57. Schottland, J. R.; Kirschberg, G. J.; Fillingim, R.; Davis, V. P.; and Hogg, F.: Median nerve latencies in poultry processing workers: an approach to resolving the role of industrial "cumulative trauma" in the development of carpal tunnel syndrome. J Occup Med, 33(5): 627-31, 1991.

58. Silverstein, B. A.; Fine, L. J.; and Armstrong, T. J.: Occupational factors and carpal tunnel syndrome. Am J Ind Med, 11(3): 343-58, 1987.

59. Stallings, S. P.; Kasdan, M. L.; Soergel, T. M.; and Corwin, H. M.: A case-control study of obesity as a risk factor for carpal tunnel syndrome in a population of 600 patients presenting for independent medical examination. J Hand Surgery, 22A(2): 211-215, 1997.

60. Stanton, N. A., and Young, M. S.: What price ergonomics? Nature, 399(May 20): 197-198, 1999.

61. Stetson, D. S.; Silverstein, B. A.; Keyserling, W. M.; Wolfe, R. A.; and Albers, J. W.: Median sensory distal amplitude and latency: comparisons between nonexposed managerial/professional employees and industrial workers. American Journal of Industrial Medicine, 24:175-189: 175-189, 1993.

62. Stevens, J. C.; Sun, S.; Beard, C. M.; O'Fallon, W. M.; and Kurland, L. T.: Carpal tunnel syndrome in Rochester, Minnesota, 1961 to 1980. Neurology, 38: 134-138, 1988.

63. Stock, S. R.: Workplace ergonomic factors and the development of musculoskeletal disorders of the neck and upper limbs: a meta-analysis. Am J Ind Med, 19(1): 87-107, 1991.

64. Szabo, R. M., and Chidgey, L. K.: Stress carpal tunnel pressures in carpal tunnel patients and normal patients. J Hand Surg, 14A(4): 624-627, 1989.

65. Szabo, R. M.; Gelberman, R. H.; Williamson, R. V.; and Hargens, A. R.: Effects of increased systemic blood pressure on the tissue fluid pressure threshold of peripheral nerve. J Orthop Res, 1: 172, 1983.

66. Tanaka, S.; Wild, D. K.; Seligman, P. J.; Behrens, V.; Cameron, L.; and Putz-Anderson, V.: The US prevalence of self-reported carpal tunnel syndrome: 1988 national health survey data. Am J Public Health, 84: 1846-1848, 1994.

67. Tittiranonda, P.; Rempel, D.; Armstrong, T.; and Burastero, S.: Effect of four computer keyboards on computer users with upper extremity musculoskeletal disorders. Am. J. Ind. Med., 35: 647-661, 1999.

68. Vender, M. I.; Kasdan, M. L.; and Truppa, K. L.: Upper extremity disorders: a literature review to determine work-relatedness. J Hand Surg, 20A: 543-541, 1995.

69. Viikari-Juntura, E.: Risk factors for upper limb disorders. Implications for prevention and treatment. Clin Orthop, 351: 39-43, 1998.

70. Werner, R. A.; Albers, J. W.; Franzblau, A.; and Armstrong, T. J.: The relationship between body mass index and the diagnosis of carpal tunnel syndrome. Muscle Nerve, 17(6): 632-6, 1994.

71. Wieslander, G.; Norback, D.; Gothe, C. J.; and Juhlin, L.: Carpal tunnel syndrome (carpal tunnel syndrome) and exposure to vibration, repetitive wrist movements, and heavy manual work: a case-referent study. Br J Ind Med, 46(1): 43-7, 1989.

72. Wolens, D.: Invited epidemiologic comment. Hand Clinics, 12(2): 308-311, 1996.

Appendix C

Panel Response to the Dissent

D r. Szabo's dissent focuses on whether the panel was consistent in evaluating the literature relevant to this report. His dissent deals almost exclusively with only one of the musculoskeletal disorders considered in the report; specifically he ascribes to the panel overstatements about the research findings relating carpal tunnel syndrome to work exposures of a variety of types.

Dr. Szabo states correctly that criteria for the inclusion of studies in the report differed for the analysis of biomechanical exposures and for the analysis of epidemiologic associations. The four bodies of literature reviewed—tissue mechanobiology, biomechanics, epidemiology, and workplace interventions—have differing study designs, measurement techniques, and outcome variables. The selection criteria used in determining the quality of particular studies necessarily varied among these literatures (see Chapter 1, pp. 22). These criteria were set early in the panel's deliberations. Specifically, the biomechanics papers required detailed measures of biomechanical exposure, while the epidemiologic studies did not require that same kind of detail. Similarly, the epidemiologic papers had to meet criteria for epidemiologic inference that were not required of the biomechanics papers. The panel discussed the distinction carefully before agreeing to adopt it. The distinction would be problematic only if the panel made epidemiologic inferences from studies included in the biomechanics section that failed to meet criteria for epidemiologic studies. We did not do that.

Dr. Szabo contends that the panel concluded that interventions examined in this study prevented carpal tunnel syndrome; this misstates our report, which clearly states otherwise (see Chapter 8, pp. 313). The report states that interventions influenced pain reports and not the occurrence of specifically defined disorders of the upper extremities. The studies are summarized in Table 8.3. The report does not state that interventions prevent carpal tunnel syndrome or, indeed, any other upper-extremity disorder. The emphasis, rather, is on amelioration of symptoms, which is the end point in the relevant literature. Furthermore, the comments on upper extremity interventions carefully state that interventions influence symptoms, not the incidence of specific disorders (Chapter 8, p. 313):

> Studies of engineering interventions for computer-related work that reduce static postural loads, sustained posture extremes, and rapid motions have demonstrated decreases in upper extremity pain reports. Further study of these interventions is needed to determine the amount of pain reduction possible, the duration of salutary effect, and which upper extremity clinical conditions could benefit from these interventions.

Dr. Szabo uses the case of carpal tunnel syndrome with regard to low-force, high-repetition exposures (primarily the use of computer keyboards) as the causal factor to suggest that the relationship of musculoskeletal disorders to work exposure may not be sound. The panel has recognized that the evidence for low-force, high-repetition exposures is weaker than for other relationships among risk factors and musculoskeletal outcomes; however, strong evidence for causal relationships between physical work and musculoskeletal disorders is provided throughout the report.

The epidemiology section as it relates to the upper extremity was carefully written. We discuss the cross-sectional designs of most studies and possible implications for causal inference, including the potential for the "healthy worker" effect. In 9 studies, carpal tunnel syndrome was defined by a combination of a history of symptoms and physical examination or nerve conduction testing. In these studies there were 18 estimates of risk based on various specificities of carpal tunnel syndrome diagnosis and varying degrees of work exposure. Of these, 12 showed significant odds ratios greater than 2.0 (range 2.3 to 39.8), 4 showed nonsignificant odds ratios of greater than 2.0, and 2 showed nonsignificant odds ratios of between 1.7 and 2.0. The epidemiology section, however, does not draw specific conclusions regarding carpal tunnel syndrome. The report points out that just three articles dealt with keyboard work; indeed, keyboard work is not a major consideration or focus in the report.

Dr. Szabo's dissent provides an incomplete view of a study published in the *Journal of the American Medical Association* (Atroshi, 1999). He states: "In the general population the prevalence of Carpal Tunnel Syndrome is the same whether people perform repetitive activities or not." In the panel's view, the nature of the design in that study and its survey instruments were such that the power to demonstrate this association was not high. The study, however, did show a significant risk for carpal tunnel syndrome for blue-collar work, use of excessive force of the hands, working with excessively flexed or extended wrist, or the use of hand-held vibratory tools; these findings are not mentioned by Dr. Szabo.

Dr. Szabo cites the paper of Greenland and Robins (1988) to suggest that without knowledge of cofactors that contribute to carpal tunnel syndrome, "estimates offered by Hagberg as well as the ones used in the NAS report must be interpreted with caution." In fact, the thrust of the Greenland and Robins argument is that such attributable risk calculations may severely underestimate (not overestimate, as implied by Dr. Szabo) the proportion of cases in which the etiologic factor is important because of possible interactions between that factor and the cofactors. Greenland and Robins cite numerous examples in which a small excess risk masks a much larger effect of a primary study factor.

Several articles cited by Dr. Szabo in his discussion of the epidemiology literature on carpal tunnel syndrome did not meet the quality criteria (insufficient participation and inadequate exposure measures were common problems) used by the panel in selecting articles for the epidemiology review and so are not included in the report.

In his dissent, Dr. Szabo states, "More importantly, reliance on ergonomics to the exclusion of medical and health risk factors can have adverse consequences for the patient." Nowhere in its report does the panel suggest the exclusive use of ergonomic interventions.

It is important to reemphasize the fact that we made a major effort to base our conclusions on literature that met accepted scientific criteria and that the report represents consensus of all of the panel members except for Dr. Szabo. At the same time, the report makes plain the panel's view that the literature about musculoskeletal disorders is incomplete, as all clinical and scientific literatures are, and also emphasizes the importance of continuing research on a variety of fronts. There is, however, sufficient basis in the research to date to support our conclusions and recommendations.

Jeremiah A. Barondess, *Chair*	Jeffrey N. Katz
Mark R. Cullen	Kurt Kroenke
Barbara de Lateur	Jeffrey C. Lotz
Richard A. Deyo	Susan E. Mackinnon
Sue K. Donaldson	William S. Marras
Colin G. Drury	Robert G. Radwin
Michael Feuerstein	David Rempel
Baruch Fischhoff	David Vlahov
John W. Frymoyer	David H. Wegman

APPENDIX D

Contributors to the Report

Authors of Commissioned Papers and Titles of Papers

Kai-Nan An, Mayo Clinic and Mayo Foundation, Rochester, Minnesota
   Paper: Relationship of Repetitive Loading to Tendon Injury
Michael Adams, University of Bristol, United Kingdom
   Paper: Mechanical Damage to Intervertebral Discs in the Workplace
Marjorie Baldwin, East Carolina University, Greenville, North Carolina
   Paper: Musculoskeletal Disorders and Work Disability: The Role of
   Socioeconomic Factors
Paulien Bongers, TNO Arbeid, Hoofddorp, Netherlands
   Paper: Are Psychosocial Factors at Work or in the Private Life and
   Psychological Problems, Risk Factors for Symptoms and Signs of
   the Upper Limbs (Shoulder, Elbow, Hand/Wrist or Arm)
   (coauthored with Anja Kremer and Jolanda ter Laak)
Helena Brisby, Göteborg University, Gothenburg, Sweden
   Paper: Mechanical Deformation of Spinal Nerve Roots: A Literature
   Review Regarding Musculoskeletal Disorders and the Workplace
   (coauthored with Kjell Olmarker and Björn Rydevik)
Alexander Burdorf, Erasmus University, Rotterdam, Netherlands
   Paper: Scientific Evidence on Physical Load and Back Disorders in
   Occupational Groups
Alfred Franzblau, University of Michigan, Ann Arbor
   Paper: Review of the Epidemiological Literature Pertaining to
   Upper Extremity Musculoskeletal Disorders (UEMSDs) Among
   Workers
Tony Keaveny, University of California, Berkeley
   Paper: Effect of Damage Accumulation in Bone Tissue (coauthored
   with Michael Liebschner)

W. Monroe Keyserling, University of Michigan, Ann Arbor
  Paper: Selection of Scientific Papers for Upper Extremity
  Biomechanics
Anja Kremer, TNO Arbeid, Hoofddorp, Netherlands
  Paper: Are Psychosocial Factors at Work or in the Private Life and
  Psychological Problems, Risk Factors for Symptoms and Signs of
  the Upper Limbs (Shoulder, Elbow, Hand/Wrist or Arm)
  (coauthored with Paulien Bongers and Jolanda ter Laak)
William Kuzon, Jr., University of Michigan, Ann Arbor
  Paper: Does Skeletal Muscle Injury Contribute to Repetitive Use
  Disorder? (coauthored with Nicholas Watson)
Michael Liebschner, University of California, Berkeley
  Paper: Effect of Damage Accumulation in Bone Tissue (coauthored
  with Tony Keaveny)
Steven Linton, Örebro Medical Center, Sweden
  Paper: Workplace and Individual Psychological Risk Factors for
  Back Pain
Stuart McGill, University of Waterloo, Ontario, Canada
  Paper: Physical Job Demands and the Risk of Low Back Injury:
  Issues and Evidence from Epidemiological, Biomechanical
  Modelling and In Vitro Specimen Approaches
Kjell Olmarker, Göteborg University, Gothenburg, Sweden
  Paper: Mechanical Deformation of Spinal Nerve Roots: A Literature
  Review Regarding Musculoskeletal Disorders and the Workplace
  (coauthored with Helena Brisby and Björn Rydevik)
Raymond Robin, Foresite Design, Inc., Hollywood, Florida (Internet
  form design)
Björn Rydevik, Göteborg University, Gothenburg, Sweden
  Paper: Mechanical Deformation of Spinal Nerve Roots: A Literature
  Review Regarding Musculoskeletal Disorders and the Workplace
  (coauthored with Helena Brisby and Kjell Olmarker)
Jolanda ter Laak, TNO Arbeid, Hoofddorp, Netherlands
  Paper: Are Psychosocial Factors at Work or in the Private Life and
  Psychological Problems, Risk Factors for Symptoms and Signs of
  the Upper Limbs (Shoulder, Elbow, Hand/Wrist or Arm)
  (coauthored with Paulien Bongers and Anja Kremer)
Nicholas Watson, University of Michigan, Ann Arbor
  Paper: Does Skeletal Muscle Injury Contribute to Repetitive Use
  Disorder? (coauthored with William Kuzon, Jr.)

Presenters

Frazier Anderson, Livonia Transmission Plant, Michigan
Stephen Burastero, Lawrence Livermore National Laboratories,
　　Livermore, California
John Caiza, Livonia Transmission Plant, Michigan
John Clinton, Michigan Truck Plant, Wayne
Chuck Columbus, Livonia Transmission Plant, Michigan
John Fischer, Livonia Transmission Plant, Michigan
John Frank, University of California, Berkeley
Rochelle Habeck, Michigan State University, East Lansing
Chris Henderson, The Turkey Store Company, Barron, Wisconsin
Jim Hubbs, Livonia Transmission Plant, Michigan
Brad Joseph, Ford Motor Company, Dearborn, Michigan
Barbara Judy, West Virginia University, Morgantown
William Koch, Livonia Transmission Plant, Michigan
Thomas Koczara, Michigan Truck Plant, Wayne
Ed Lloyd, Michigan Truck Plant, Wayne
Angie Litteral, Michigan Truck Plant, Wayne
Andrea Maurer, Livonia Transmission Plant, Michigan
Gary Miller, Livonia Transmission Plant, Michigan
Doug Milligan, Livonia Transmission Plant, Michigan
Franklin Mirer, United Auto Workers, Detroit, Michigan
Genie O'Shesky, Michigan Truck Plant, Wayne
Paul Prindville, Livonia Transmission Plant, Michigan
Gordon Reeve, Ford Motor Company, Detroit, Michigan
Glenn Robitaille, Livonia Transmission Plant, Michigan
John Ruser, Bureau of Labor Statistics, Washington, DC
Richard Sabol, AMETEK, Kent, Ohio
Rodger Wantin, Livonia Transmission Plant, Michigan
Gloria White, Michigan Truck Plant, Wayne
Jeff Wood, Michigan Truck Plant, Wayne

GENERAL PUBLIC CONTRIBUTORS: RESPONSES TO BROADCAST PANEL REQUESTS DURING THE INFORMATION-GATHERING PROCESS

The Presenters at Public Forum, July 17, 2000

Edward Bernacki, American College of Occupational and
　　Environmental Medicine
Steven Conway, American Chiropractic Association
Tee Guidotti, American College of Preventive Medicine

Mark Heidebrecht, Occupational Injury Prevention Rehabilitation
    Society
William Kojola, AFL-CIO Department of Occupational Safety and
    Health
Peter Mandell, American Association of Orthopaedic Surgeons
Eilenn Meier, National Association of Orthopaedic Nurses
Roger Merrill, Perdue Farms Incorporated
Timothy Pinsky, American Osteopathic Association

Organization/Individual Statements Submitted for the Record
July 17, 2000, Public Forum

American Society of Safety Engineers
BODYMIND Counseling/Consulting
Nortin Hadler, University of North Carolina
International Association for the Study of Pain
CSERIAC/Human Systems Information Analysis Center
Julio Taleisnik, The Hand Care Center

Organization and Individual Response to
General Mailing Regarding Interventions

Allied Health of Wisconsin, S.C.
American Psychological Association
American Red Cross
T. John Baumeister, Stevens Health Center
BODYMIND Counseling/Consulting
Richard Butler, University of Minnesota
CSERIAC/Human Systems Information Analysis Center
Bayco Packaging Systems, Inc.
Nortin Hadler, University of North Carolina
Kurt Hegmann, The University of Utah
Human Factors and Ergonomics Society
Morton Kasdan, Louisville, Kentucky
Jerome Kynion, Health and Safety Communications
Dean Louis, The University of Michigan
Occupational Injury Prevention Rehabilitation Society
Julio Taleisnik, The Hand Care Center
United Food and Commercial Workers International Union, AFL-CIO
    and CLC

Appendix E

Biographical Sketches of Panel Members and Staff

Jeremiah A. Barondess (*Chair*) is president of the New York Academy of Medicine. He is a member of the Institute of Medicine (IOM) and has been involved in a number of National Academies activities, including the IOM Council (1978-1981) (member), the IOM Committee on Changing Health Care Systems and Rheumatic Disease (chair), the Council on Health Care Technology (vice chair), and the Committee to Plan a Private/Public Sector Entity for Technology Assessment in Medical Care (chair). He has training as a generalist in internal medicine, measurement of quality in clinical care, and health policy, as well as in medical institute administration.

Mark R. Cullen is a professor of medicine and public health in the occupational and environmental medicine program at the Yale University School of Medicine. He is a member of the Institute of Medicine and has been involved in many National Academies activities, including his recent membership on the NRC Steering Committee for the Workshop on Work-Related Musculoskeletal Injuries: The Research Base. He served on the Board on Health Sciences Policy and was vice chair of the Roundtable on Environmental Health Sciences, Research, and Medicine. His areas of expertise are in environmental medicine/health and occupational medicine, and his interests include clinical aspects of occupational and environmental disease.

Barbara de Lateur is professor, director, and Lawrence Cardinal Shehan chair in the Department of Physical Medicine and Rehabilitation at Johns Hopkins University. She is a member of the Institute of Medicine, and she is an expert in physical medicine and rehabilitation. Her clinical interests include therapeutic exercise and the management of pain, and her research interests include the effects of exercise training on gait, balance, and fall risk in the elderly.

Richard A. Deyo is a professor of medicine and professor of health services who is the section head of General Internal Medicine at the University of Washington Medical Center in Seattle. His research is in the area of low back pain, including the psychosocial predictors of disability. He is currently co-director of the Robert Wood Johnson Clinical Scholars Program at the University of Washington and principal investigator for the Back Pain Outcome Assessment Team, a multiyear project funded by the Agency for Health Care Policy and Research. He has a long-standing research interest in the measurement of patient functional status and in the management of low back problems.

Sue K. Donaldson is a professor of physiology and professor and dean of nursing in the School of Nursing at Johns Hopkins University. She is a member of the Institute of Medicine and has been involved in many National Academies activities. She was a member of the IOM Committee on the NIH Research Priority-Setting Process, the Committee on Assessing Rehabilitation Science and Engineering, and the Committee on Enhancing Environmental Health Content in Nursing. Her areas of expertise are physiology and nursing, with interests in academic administration, biophysics, physiology, nursing, and aging.

Colin G. Drury is professor of industrial engineering at the University at Buffalo and the founding executive director of the Center for Industrial Effectiveness. His work concentrates on the application of human factors to error and injury reduction in industrial process control, quality control, maintenance, and safety. Currently, he is principal investigator for studies of human reliability in aircraft inspection and maintenance. He is a member of the Committee on Human Factors, and also served as cochair of the NRC Steering Committee for the Workshop on Work-Related Musculoskeletal Injuries: The Research Base.

Michael Feuerstein is a professor of Medical/Clinical Psychology and Preventive Medicine/Biometrics at the Uniformed Services University in Bethesda, Maryland. He is also a clinical professor of psychiatry in the Division of Behavioral Medicine at Georgetown University Medical Center. His clinical, research, and consultative activities are directed at the explication of the multidimensional nature of occupational musculoskeletal disorders and disability (with a focus on ergonomic and psychosocial factors) and the development and evaluation of integrated prevention and management strategies.

Baruch Fischhoff is university professor of social and decision sciences and of engineering and public policy in the Department of Social and Decision Sciences at Carnegie Mellon University. His expertise is in the areas of social sciences and psychology, and his research is in judgment and decision making, risk perception, risk management, risk communication, informed consent, science policy, and decision procedures and theory. He is a member of the Institute of Medicine and was a member of the NRC's Commission on Behavioral and Social Sciences and Education. He was a member of the NRC Steering Committee for the Workshop on Work-Related Musculoskeletal Injuries: The Research Base.

John W. Frymoyer is the dean (retired) of the College of Medicine, emeritus professor in the Department of Orthopaedics and Rehabilitation, and former director of the McClure Musculoskeletal Research Center at the University of Vermont. The McClure Center performs research in the areas of low back pain, sports medicine, scoliosis, and joint replacement. He is the editor of the two-volume *The Adult Spine* and founding editor of the *Journal of the American Academy of Orothopaedic Surgeons*.

Jeffrey N. Katz is associate professor of Medicine at Harvard Medical School and a practicing rheumatologist and co-director of the Spine Center at Brigham and Women's Hospital in Boston. He has performed research on clinical, epidemiologic, and health services delivery aspects of carpal tunnel syndrome and other upper extremity disorders, lumbar spinal stenosis and other spinal conditions, and total joint arthroplasty.

Kurt Kroenke is a medical doctor at Regenstrief Institute for Health Care in Indianapolis and a professor of medicine at the Indiana University School of Medicine. His clinical research has focused on the optimal evaluation and management of common symptoms, such as fatigue, dizziness, and other physical complaints. He conducts research on depression and other mental disorders in primary care.

Jeffrey C. Lotz is the director of the University of California at San Francisco Orthopaedic Bioengineering Laboratory. The laboratory is within the Department of Orthopaedic Surgery and devoted to conducting basic research in several areas of orthopaedics, including the biomechanics of the spine, intervertebral disc, and the hand. He is an expert in medical engineering and has received awards in the areas of low back pain research and spinal research.

Susan E. Mackinnon is chief, Division of Plastic and Reconstructive Surgery, and Shoenberg professor of plastic and reconstructive surgery at the

Washington University School of Medicine in St. Louis. Her research interests and expertise are in carpal tunnel syndrome, brachial plexus, cumulative trauma disorder, facial palsy, hand and upper extremity disorders and injury, peripheral nerve, and thoracic outlet syndrome. She has focused on peripheral nerve regeneration, and she performed the world's first successful nerve allograft transplantation.

Frederick J. Manning is a senior program officer in the Institute of Medicine's Division of Health Sciences Policy Division and study director. In six years at the Institute of Medicine (IOM), he has served as study director for projects addressing a variety of topics, including medical isotopes, potential hepatitis drugs, blood safety and availability, rheumatic disease, resource sharing in biomedical research, and chemical and biological terrorism. Before joining the IOM, he spent 25 years in the U.S. Army Medical Research and Development Command, serving in positions that included director of neuropsychiatry at the Walter Reed Army Institute of Research and chief research psychologist for the Army Medical Department.

William S. Marras is a professor of industrial and systems engineering at the Ohio State University. He is the director of the university's Biodynamics Laboratory and co-director of the Institute for Ergonomics. He also is the recipient of the Honda Endowed Chair in Transportation Research. He holds academic appointment in the Department of Industrial, Welding, and Systems Engineering, the Department of Physical Medicine, and the Biomedical Engineering Center. His research involves industrial biomechanics issues, laboratory biomechanics studies, mathematical modeling, and clinical studies of the back and wrist. He was a member of the NRC Steering Committee for the Workshop on Work-Related Musculoskeletal Injuries: The Research Base and is currently a member of the Committee on Human Factors.

Anne S. Mavor is the study director for the Panel on Musculoskeletal Disorders and the Workplace. She is also currently the staff director for the Committee on Human Factors and the Committee on the Youth Population and Military Recruitment. Her previous work as an NRC senior staff officer has included studies on occupational analysis and the enhancement of human performance, modeling human behavior and command decision making, human factors in air traffic control automation, human factors considerations in tactical display for soldiers, scientific and technological challenges of virtual reality, emerging needs and opportunities for human factors research, and modeling cost and performance for purposes of military enlistment. For the past 25 years, her work has concentrated on human factors, cognitive psychology, and information system design.

James P. McGee is the senior research associate for the Panel on Musculoskeletal Disorders in the Workplace. He also supports NRC panels and committees in the areas of applied psychology (e.g., the ongoing panel on soldier systems; and prior committees on air traffic control automation and on the changing nature of work) and education (e.g., the committee on educational interventions for children with autism). Prior to joining the NRC, he held scientific, technical, and management positions in human factors psychology at IBM, RCA, General Electric, General Dynamics, and United Technologies corporations.

Andrew M. Pope is director of the Division of Health Sciences Policy at the Institute of Medicine and served as study director for the Organ Procurement and Transplantation Policy study. With expertise in physiology, toxicology, and epidemiology, his primary interests focus on environmental and occupational influences on human health. Dr. Pope's previous research activities focused on the biochemical, neuroendocrine, and reproductive effects of various environmental substances on food-producing animals. During his tenure at the National Academy of Sciences and since 1989 at the Institute of Medicine, Dr. Pope has directed and edited numerous reports on environmental and occupational issues; topics include injury control, disability prevention, biological markers, neurotoxicology, indoor allergens, and the inclusion of environmental and occupational health content in medical and nursing school curricula. Most recently, Dr. Pope directed the fast-track study on NIH priority-setting processes, and a review of fluid resuscitation practices in combat casualties.

Robert G. Radwin is a professor and chair of the Department of Biomedical Engineering at the University of Wisconsin-Madison. His fields of interest include analytical methods for measuring and assessing exposure to physical stress in the workplace; ergonomics aspects of manually operated equipment and human-computer input devices; causes and prevention of work-related cumulative trauma disorders and peripheral neuropathies; occupational biomechanics; and rehabilitation engineering and was just appointed a member of the Committee on Human Factors.

David Rempel is a professor of medicine in the Division of Occupational and Environmental Medicine at the University of California, San Francisco, and holds joint appointments in the Departments of Mechanical Engineering and Bioengineering at the University of California at Berkeley. He is director of the ergonomics program at Berkeley. He is board certified in internal medicine, preventive medicine (occupational medicine), and ergonomics. His research interests include understanding mechanisms of upper extremity tendon, nerve, and muscle injury and repair associated with repeated loading, occupational biomechanics, musculoskeletal disorder epidemiology, and hand tool design.

Robert M. Szabo is chief, Hand and Microvascular Service, Department of Orthopaedics; professor, Department of Orthopaedic Surgery; and professor, Department of Surgery, Division of Plastic Surgery, at the University of California at Davis. His current research interests include nerve compression lesions, nerve repair and regeneration biology, tendon healing and adhesion formation, and the epidemiology of repetitive trauma and injury prevention. He specializes in complex hand, upper extremity, and shoulder reconstructions after tumor resections, as well as soft tissue and bone transfers to the lower extremities.

David Vlahov is director of the Center for Urban Epidemiologic Studies at the New York Academy of Medicine. He is on a leave of absence from Johns Hopkins University, where he is professor and deputy chairman in the Department of Epidemiology. He has coordinated several large clinical epidemiologic studies of HIV infection among drug users (e.g., the ALIVE study) and is the principal evaluator of the Washington, D.C., and Baltimore needle exchange programs. He has a particular interest in research methods in field settings. He was a member of the NRC Steering Committee for the Workshop on Work-Related Musculoskeletal Injuries: The Research Base.

David H. Wegman is the founding chair of the Department of Work Environment in the Engineering College at the University of Massachusetts, Lowell, now one of the leading preventive medicine (occupational medicine) research centers. His research has focused on epidemiologic studies of occupational respiratory disease, musculoskeletal disorders, and cancer. A continuing research interest has been in developing methods to study subjective outcomes, such as musculoskeletal and respiratory or irritant symptoms reports.

Alexandra K. Wigdor is deputy director of the Commission on Behavioral and Social Sciences and Education (CBASSE) and formerly director of the Division on Education, Labor, and Human Performance. A member of the National Research Council research staff since 1978, she has been instrumental in developing the education and behavioral science program in CBASSE.

Index

A

Absenteeism, 1, 11, 17, 30, 47-52 (passim),
58. 153, 157, 351, 364
  age factors, 51
  back disorders, 53-54, 97, 123, 143,
    147, 153, 154, 157
  Bureau of Labor Statistics, 50, 51, 52
  epidemiologic studies, 97, 98, 435
  preventive interventions, 305-306, 316-
    317, 319, 326, 327
  surveillance, 305-306
  upper extremity disorders, 98, 110,
    183, 315-317
  workers' compensation and, 28-29, 58
Adenosine triphosphate, 202
Administrative controls, 8, 304, 307, 368,
  437
  see also Ergonomic interventions
  back disorders, 8, 309, 311, 312, 313
  rest breaks, 111-112, 160, 161, 162, 174,
    181, 183, 263, 274, 320
  upper extremity disorders, 183, 315-
    316, 322
African Americans, *see* Race/ethnicity
Age factors, 2, 4, 6, 9, 11, 10, 32, 89, 90,
    330, 336, 347, 365, 373, 433
  see also Elderly persons
  absenteeism, 51
  back disorders, 7, 39, 40, 43, 44, 51, 55,
    151

carpal tunnel syndrome, 51, 56, 286,
  360, 442, 447-448
databases, 39, 40, 43, 44, 46-47, 48, 366
  ergonomic interventions, 304
  gender and, 39, 42, 51, 337
  hand disorders, 54-55
  muscle contraction, 203
  peripheral nerve, 217-218
  psychosocial factors, 141, 151
  skeletal muscle, 209, 210, 217-218
  tendinitis, 51
  tendons, other, 198-199
  upper extremity disorders, 7, 51, 55,
    56, 183, 286, 360, 433
  vertebral bone and disc, 188, 189-190,
    193-194, 217-218, 433
Agricultural workers, *see* Farm workers
Alcohol consumption, 75-76, 442
Allodynia, 186-187
American Academy of Orthopaedic
  Surgeons, 57
American National Standards Institute,
  307
Animal models, 5, 22, 65, 66, 67, 184, 216
  peripheral nerve, 213, 216
  skeletal muscle, 207-208, 216
  spinal discs, 193, 194, 216
  tendons, 197-199, 216-217
Annual Survey of Occupational Injuries
  and Illnesses, 44-45, 49, 60-61